GALILEO
AT WORK

Galileo at age sixty, drawn by Ottavio Leoni at Rome in May 1624 and engraved by him the following year. (From an original print in the author's collection. Photo by University of Toronto Photographic Services.)

GALILEO
AT WORK
HIS SCIENTIFIC
BIOGRAPHY

Stillman Drake

DOVER PUBLICATIONS, INC.
NEW YORK

Published in Canada by General Publishing Company, Ltd., 30 Lesmill Road, Don Mills, Toronto, Ontario.
Published in the United Kingdom by Constable and Company, Ltd., 3 The Lanchesters, 162–164 Fulham Palace Road, London W6 9ER.

Bibliographical Note

This Dover edition, first published in 1995, is an unabridged and unaltered republication of the work first published by The University of Chicago Press in 1978.

Library of Congress Cataloging-in-Publication Data

Drake, Stillman.
    Gallileo at work : his scientific biography / Stillman Drake.
        p.   cm.
    Includes index.
    ISBN 0-486-28631-2 (pbk.)
    1. Galilei, Galileo, 1564–1642. 2. Astronomers—Italy—Biography. I. Title.
QB36.G62D69   1995
520'.92—dc20
[B]   95-4646
                                     CIP

Manufactured in the United States of America
Dover Publications, Inc., 31 East 2nd Street, Mineola, N.Y. 11501

*With ambiguity but without
equivocation, this book is
dedicated to
Florence*

CONTENTS

Contents

Contents

Contents

Contents

PREFACE

Once some fathers came to see him, and he was working
in his garden and observing how the buds came out. He said,
"I am ashamed that you see me in this clown's habit; I'll
go and dress myself as a philosopher."
"Why don't you have this work done by someone else?"
"No, no; I should lose the pleasure. If I thought it as much
fun to have things done as it is to do them, I'd be glad to."

This anecdote about Galileo in his old age at Arcetri was told
to Robert Southwell, later president of the Royal Society, when
as a young man he visited Vincenzio Viviani, Galileo's last pupil
and first biographer. We are now so accustomed to seeing Galileo
dressed up as a philosopher that though the story has a delightful homey ring of authenticity, it is likely to sound made up.
Yet it is not the kind of story that would be made up in 1661,
especially not by an Italian talking to an English visitor. We
may take it as a fact that Galileo enjoyed doing things for himself and profited from the opportunities thus afforded him for
making observations, recognizing all the while that such activities were considered unsuitable to a philosopher.

There is no shortage of biographies of Galileo portraying him
as a profound scholar, holding a lofty place in the succession
of scientific pioneers from Aristotle through Ptolemy and Copernicus to Descartes and Newton. It is my purpose neither to contradict such accounts nor to add to their number, but rather to
show you Galileo in his working clothes, tending his scientific
garden and watching buds develop while his university colleagues

were determining the necessary structure and ultimate purpose of the entire universe. Galileo's fellow-gardeners are for the most part unknown to fame, though they were closely linked to Galileo's attitudes and his methods of investigation. Two of the most acute were clerics; none were philosophers. Better than the professors, intelligent laymen caught the significance to their own epoch of Galileo's labors. Finding those to their liking, they gave him what encouragement he received during his lifetime, furnishing also grist to his mill from their own observations and reflections. You will meet these supporters of Galileo as well as scholars and theologians who vigorously opposed him.

Galileo was at once a lively participant in late Renaissance Italian culture and an anachronism in its halls of academic learning. If it was the fault of his nineteenth-century biographers to overemphasize the anachronism, it is perhaps a fault of his modern biographers to overemphasize cultural traditions that surrounded him. Those have great statistical value, but they tell us nothing about a particular individual human being. Just as there might be no man of exactly average height, so there may have been no exactly typical scientist in Galileo's time. From the thoughts of all his predecessors and contemporaries we cannot confidently describe exactly his own thought; for that, we need to know just how he spent his time.

Tedious indeed it must seem to plod year by year through the life of a scientist. That is nevertheless the only sure way to find out what things actually shaped his thought, as distinguished from those that ought to have shaped it as determined by probable reasoning. In the case of Galileo, documents are plentiful—well over two thousand letters written by, to, or about him; thousands of pages of manuscript notes and treatises; notarial records, court proceedings, and account books. Together with his printed works and some by adversaries or friends, these fill twenty large volumes in the National Edition of Galileo's works. This great mass of first-hand evidence affords a solid base for such conjectures as must be made concerning motives, methods of work, interests, and the like beyond those explicitly set forth by Galileo himself or by men who knew him personally.

To the best of my knowledge, such a project has not been previously undertaken. This one began as an attempt to put in chronological order all of Galileo's scientific work, from his student days to the end of his life. Except for letters and published books, most of the material we have from Galileo's own hand is undated. To put it all in serial order, and to date as nearly as possible all documents relevant to his scientific career, has been the guiding objective in my selection of things to be included here. Until that has been done once, however tentatively in some respects, it is hardly possible to speak with confidence about Galileo's own main interests, and hence about the probable sources and motivations of his contributions to science.

It has been easy enough in the past to single out dramatic aspects of Galileo's life and relate those, not to his less celebrated activities, but to the works of others before and after him and to the society in which he lived. His studies of motion, his telescopic discoveries, and his clash with the church have been repeatedly so treated with little attention to the relations between those justly esteemed accomplishments and Galileo's own work in areas less dramatic—in the behavior of fluids, for instance, or in the nature of continuous magnitude, in strength of materials, in the force of percussion, and the like. Yet even to name these suggests that their mutual relations had a certain bearing on Galileo's conception of science. Even less attention has ordinarily been given to Galileo's musical background, his respect for common sense, his mistrust of logical virtuosity, and other matters which at first glance might seem insignificant or tangential to his science. The possibility remains that a better understanding of Galileo's scientific development will emerge from noticing recurrent themes within his own varied activities than by studying either the long-range emergence of a Scientific Revolution out of ancient mathematics and medieval philosophical speculation, or the temporary societal shock occasioned by Galileo's main achievements that have up to now received so much attention. The only way to determine whether that is so is to put his varied activities in chronological order to see whether one led to another, and if not, what led to each.

Some of those activities are already so well known that in order to make room for others less familiar, they will here receive little more than bare mention. Some, especially among Galileo's early unpublished writings, are so little known as to need, in my opinion, fairly full description. Thus the contents of Galileo's most famed books, easily accessible in English and presumably already read by most persons interested in his scientific biography, will not be outlined herein; rather, so far as possible, dates will be identified at which various parts of those books originated in Galileo's mind. This policy permits inclusion of translations of substantial parts of letters and treatises not previously seen in English.

The result is—I hope necessarily from the nature of my main objective—an uneven narrative; episodes of great interest are separated by periods of arduous labor or scientific idleness, at least in appearance, though to omit either would render later episodes less understandable. Even Galileo's difficulties in having certain books published are not irrelevant. My intention is to give a fair overall view of Galileo's scientific career, which of course contains interludes of distraction from science by its philosophical and religious adversaries. How the resulting picture can be reconciled with others currently accepted is a question I have preferred not to discuss. Modern portrayals appear to me to employ certain selections of evidence from Galileo's writings mingled with thoughts of men before and after him in order to show a smooth transition from ancient to modern science. In this book I am concerned rather with the transition between science as it was taught *to* Galileo and science as it was later taught *by* him. Hence my scant references to other biographies of Galileo does not mean that I have neglected to read them; rather, for the purpose of chronologically ordering Galileo's scientific work, it has been necessary to go back always to original sources and it seemed best to cite those directly.

The basic source of documentation is the National Edition of Galileo's works directed and edited by Antonio Favaro: *Le Opere di Galileo Galilei* (20 volumes, Florence, 1890–1909, reprinted with additions in the 1930s and 1960s). References to this work are given in the notes by volume and page number alone without repetition of its title; when line numbers are required, they follow the page number in parentheses. Since the Galilean correspondence is arranged chronologically in volumes 10 to 18, with few exceptions, letters will be usually identified only by year and month. English translations are cited in the notes by shortened titles that are identified in the first appearance of each.

Opinions expressed and conclusions drawn in this book are grounded to the best of my ability on careful weighing of all the available original documentary evidence. That does not mean that all documents agree, for obviously some were of a partisan character, some represented recollections of varying reliability, and some were written by persons not fully informed. Fortunately a good deal is known about many of the writers which is of assistance in assessing conflicts of evidence. Wrong judgments can be minimized only by considering all available original documents, while relatively few can be presented for reasons of space. My opinions and conclusions have no other claim to consideration than that they have been formed from all the documents. Where they may conflict with the opinions or conclusions of others, I hope that further research will be stimulated rather than that they will be rejected either as outmoded or as bizarre. Views of early historians and biographers who lacked information now available to us were not always thereby rendered untenable, as some more recent writers have tended to suppose. Neither is it likely that a completely correct historical appraisal of Galileo's scientific work has yet been reached. Hence I have not shrunk from supporting either seemingly outmoded or previously unventured opinions when the evidence for them seemed strong to me. Documents here translated into English for the first time present such evidence, perhaps overlooked in the past.

Readers may wish to consider other accounts of Galileo's life and work in which sharply contrasting overall views have been set forth. Since the literature is vast and multilingual, it may be useful to select a few items from it, mainly in English and of relatively recent date, that may profitably be consulted as a sampling, with brief identifying remarks on each. An extensive bibliography of books and articles since 1940 will be found in the work edited by Ernan McMullin. Items listed here are arranged in order of their original publication.

Alexandre Koyré: *Études Galiléennes* (Paris, 1939; repr. 1966).
This work set a new pattern for examination of Galileo's science, presenting it as inspired by abstract thought rather than induction from experience, contrary to all past opinion. Platonism and medieval philosophy were emphasized, and Galileo's name was in effect hyphenated with that of Descartes. Further essays written by Koyré in 1943–53 were collected after his death in *Metaphysics and Measurement* (London and Cambridge, Mass., 1968).

Giorgio de Santillana: *The Crime of Galileo* (Chicago, 1955). A biography centering on Galileo's conflict with the church.

Santillana's replies to my reading of the trial documents will be found in an appendix to the book next listed.

Ludovico Geymonat: *Galileo Galilei* (Torino, 1957; S. Drake, tr., New York, 1965).

A biography stressing Galileo's philosophy of science, critical of Koyré's Platonist appraisal and sympathetic to the view that Galileo took the instrumentalist position with respect to mathematics.

Arthur Koestler: *The Sleepwalkers* (London and New York, 1959). In a long section of this book strongly opposing the interpretation by Santillana, this author portrays Galileo's work as an incorrect and irresponsible attack against the social order, without any proper scientific foundation, which brought about his downfall and discredited science in the process.

Thomas B. Settle: "An Experiment in the History of Science," *Science* 133 (1961): 19–23.

Corroboration of an experimental claim made by Galileo which had been ridiculed in 1953 by Koyré on logical and historical grounds; for his arguments, see *Metaphysics and Measurement*, listed above.

Pio Paschini: *Vita e Opere di Galileo Galilei* (Rome, 1964; repr. 1965).

The most detailed modern biography, published by the Pontifical Academy of Sciences after the author's death in 1962. The work had been completed in 1944, and though some additions and corrections were made, much subsequent research was left out of account.

Ernan McMullin (ed.): *Galileo Man of Science* (New York, 1967). A collection of studies by specialists in various disciplines written from different standpoints and reflecting a wide range of opinions. Of special value is the editor's introductory essay which presents a balanced view of Galileo's work in the light of research up to a decade ago.

Maurice Clavelin: *The Natural Philosophy of Galileo*, first published as *La Philosophie Naturelle de Galilée* (Paris, 1968). English translation by A. J. Pomerans (Cambridge, Mass., 1974).

The most comprehensive study to date of Galileo's philosophy and science, with the author's views of their probable sources. Critical of Koyré's thesis in some important respects, the book suffers somewhat from neglect of work published abroad but presents an original position based on careful study of Galileo's own principal works.

William R. Shea: *Galileo's Intellectual Revolution* (New York and London, 1972).

Contains papers dealing with Galileo's writings from 1610 to 1632, in which the role of experiment is regarded as subsidiary and the Archimedean model of nonempirical mathematical physics is stressed. Scant attention is paid to the role of arguments *ad hominem* in Galileo's books of the period studied, so that a dogmatic rather than a scientific attitude is frequently attributed to him by the author.

James MacLachlan: "A Test of an 'Imaginary' Experiment of Galileo's," *Isis* 64 (1973): 374–79.

Experimental confirmation of a phenomenon described by Galileo which had been ridiculed by Koyré in 1960.

Winifred L. Wisan: "The New Science of Motion: A Study of Galileo's *De motu locali*," *Archive for History of Exact Sciences* 13 (1974): 103–306.

The most detailed study of Galileo's work on motion yet published, emphasizing possible sources for it and proposing interpretations and datings for many of his working papers at variance with those which seem to me most probable.

R. H. Naylor: "Galileo and the Problem of Fall," *British Journal for History of Science* 7 (1974): 105–34. One of several articles by this writer opposing my interpretations of Galileo's working papers on motion.

Dudley Shapere: *Galileo, A Philosophical Study* (Chicago, 1974).

A modern philosopher's analysis of Galileo's contributions, stressing the derivative character and general inadequacy of both his science and his philosophy.

Basic differences of opinion among modern historians of science exist concerning (1) the sources employed by Galileo in his investigations, and (2) the relations of Galileo's science to philosophy and religion at his time. As to (1), I take it as evident that Galileo had read Aristotle, Euclid, Archimedes, Ptolemy, and Copernicus, as well as that he made observations and measurements of his own. Those sources would suffice to account for what he did in science, and he named them all many times. Other historians seek in addition to establish a continuity between medieval and Galilean science. Yet characteristic enterprises of the late Italian Renaissance attempted to break from the Middle Ages, and neither Galileo, nor his adversaries, nor his supporters appealed to medieval writings in support of their positions. Since medieval physics and astronomy do not suffice to account for Galileo's contributions and are unnecessary in explaining them, I consider the supposed continuity to be a still unverified hypothesis except in the trivial sense that medieval concepts entered into Galileo's university education and were reflected in his unpublished early writings at Pisa.

The relation of Galileo's science to philosophy and religion emerges from contemporary records; philosophers and theologians opposed him, the former unanimously and the latter not without a certain division of opinion at even the highest levels. Whether or not physical science as conceived by the mature Galileo was a threat to philosophy or religion is hard to say. Galileo believed that it was not. When the representative of philosophy in his *Dialogue* feared its subversion by new sciences, Galileo's spokesman replied:

Philosophy itself cannot but benefit from our disputes, for if our conceptions prove true, new achievements will be made; if false, their rebuttal will further confirm the original doctrines. No, save your concern for certain philosophers; come to their aid and defend them. As to science itself, it can only improve.

As to religion, Galileo wrote in his *Letter to Christina:*

Copernicus never discusses matters of religion or faith, nor does he use any arguments that depend in any way upon the authority of sacred writings which he might have interpreted erroneously. . . . He did not ignore the Bible, but he knew very well that if his doctrine were proved, then it could not contradict the Scriptures when they were rightly understood. . . .
In discussions of physical problems we ought to begin not from the authority of scriptural passages, but from sense experiences and necessary demonstrations; for the holy Bible and the phenomena of nature proceed alike from the divine Word, the former as the dictate of the Holy Ghost and the latter as the observant executrix of God's commands.

These and similar passages strongly suggest that Galileo meant to restrict his science to the narrow domain within which no appeal need be made beyond sense experiences and necessary demonstrations. Such a domain, though very small, would be exempt from the jurisdiction of philosophers and theologians. Even had Galileo not regarded that domain as ample for his purposes and as meriting investigation for its own sake, his experiences with philosophers and theologians had convinced him that to remain within it was the only way he might hope for freedom of inquiry.

Now it is true that very few, if any, scientists between the time of Galileo and the nineteenth century were willing to pay such a price for freedom, and most (if not all) of them loved to play the philosopher and to pronounce also on religious issues. That does not constitute evidence, however, that Galileo himself wanted science to decide philosophical and theological questions. Nor is it apparent to me, after a quarter-century of reading what he wrote in letters, books, and notes, that Galileo's science owed anything whatever to the philosophers. No precepts of Aristotle, Plato, the atomists, or the Stoics sufficed to lead him to the law of free fall or to his telescopic discoveries in the sky; nor, so far as I see, were such precepts necessary for those achievements. The same is true for Galileo's science of strength of materials, his hydraulics, his investigations of pendulums, and everything else that he regarded as scientific. Hence I consider past studies of Galileo's philosophy, without disrespect to those who have industriously pursued them, as neither necessary nor sufficient to convey a basic understanding of his scientific career. Science, he said, enabled one to philosophize better, not the other way round.

It is not unreasonable to believe that the vast literature concerning Galileo will be able to absorb without serious damage one book in which his scientific work is considered without also entering into possible philosophic implications. Yet since others have read this book in typescript, I know I may be alone in that opinion, for none of them have failed to warn me against neglecting higher and more profound issues than, say, Eudoxian proportion theory and mathematical paradoxes of the infinite. Still, since that is as high as my own studies reach, and since others do so well at extending the domain of Galileo's science for him and then demolishing it with deeper philosophical insight, it seems to me that we should divide the labor according to our respective tastes and interests. I am certain that in the many translations which here will occupy space that might have been given to conjecturing about Galileo's philosophical opinions and beliefs, they will find at least some things which will more amply confirm their own conjectures, or which may incline them to agree with colleagues who have guessed differently about such matters. For my own part, I respect them all equally as students of problems on which I hold no opinion.

I sincerely hope that readers will enjoy a glimpse of Galileo tending his scientific garden in shabby clothes, and not dressed up like a philosopher. That garden was not without weeds, some of which he may have cultivated in ignorance of their noxious influence on the surrounding flowers, or simply because he liked to watch buds come out and did not have the heart to destroy them, weeds or not. As he was to make Sagredo say concerning his own "soupdish" paradox in *Two New Sciences*:

The speculation appears to me so delicate and wonderful that I should not oppose it even if I could. To me it would be a sort of sacrilege to mar so fine a structure, trampling on it with some pedantic attack.

I share that sentiment when I consider Galileo's theory of the tides, supposed by some to be an embarrassment to us who admire the Florentine pioneer of mechanical explanation. I feel similarly about his "Platonic cosmogony" and other Galilean suggestions that were later expelled from science by the superior accomplishments of Sir Isaac Newton.

An appendix includes brief biographies of men, obscure or famous, with whom Galileo corresponded. These could not have been written without the aid of Antonio Favaro's concluding volume of Galileo's *Opere*. To the John Simon Guggenheim Memorial Foundation I am again obliged for a fellowship in 1976–77 that enabled me to complete this project of many years. Miss Beverly Jahnke has earned my gratitude by preparing typescript from very messy draft chapters. My wife, Florence Selvin Drake, has not only patiently borne with me during the long evolution of this scientific biography, but has wrenched me from the National Central Library at Florence when Galileo's manuscripts were keeping me too long from the galleries and the lovely countryside of that marvelous city.

Preface

After this book was written I had the pleasure of reading *Il Mondo di Carta*, by Professor Enrico Bellone of the University of Genoa, published in October 1976. Its title is taken from Galileo's *Dialogue*, where it was said that his subject was the sensible world and not a world on paper. Professor Bellone deals with what he calls "the second scientific revolution" of the late eighteenth and early nineteenth centuries, a revolt by scientists against the patronage of philosophers who had always assumed the right to explain to them what they were doing and instruct them as to how they could legitimately do it. In that respect it seems to me, though the matter was not discussed by Professor Bellone, that the second revolution was a realization of objectives proposed by Galileo in what I have long called his abortive scientific revolution; that is, the attempt to restrict science to investigations in which no appeal need be made beyond sensate experience and necessary demonstrations, leaving all else to philosophy as the price of escaping from its jurisdiction. Cartesians and Newtonians were unwilling to pay that price and enjoyed philosophical speculations. The nineteenth-century reaction was so strong that editors of scientific journals tended to reject speculative papers, and it is said that even Einstein's 1905 paper on relativity nearly fell under the ban.

If Professor Bellone is correct, as I believe he is, it is no wonder that interest in Galileo rather suddenly reawakened among physicists in the nineteenth century and that early historians of science recognized in his writings the marks of science as they knew it. Things have greatly changed since then, both in science and in history of science, which like political history is periodically rewritten to the taste of new generations of historians. Professor Herbert Butterfield coined the term *Whig history* to designate accounts in which past events are selected and evaluated to fit current conceptions of progress. That epithet is now often applied by historians of science to nineteenth-century accounts of Galileo and his work. During the present century, when charmed quarks have come to be esteemed good science and paper worlds have regained the popularity they enjoyed in the Middle Ages, Galileo's thought has been linked to the occult qualities and substantial forms of medieval science. Though that appears to me to be equally Whiggish in Professor Butterfield's sense, the fact remains that whatever happens to be the current fancy about the nature and goal of science, Galileo is agreed to hold a prominent place in its history.

ONE

1564-89

I

THE FLORENTINE FAMILY from which Galileo descended was originally named Bonaiuti. During the fifteenth century a doctor named Galileo Bonaiuti brought great distinction to it by eminence both as a physician and in public affairs, as a result of which one branch of the family took the name of Galilei in his honor.[1]

Vincenzio Galilei, the father of Galileo, was born at Florence in 1520. As a talented lutenist and teacher of music he attracted the attention of Giovanni Bardi, patron of the Florentine Camerata, an association of cultured men with a particular interest in developments in late Renaissance music. Under Bardi's patronage Vincenzio went to Venice to study music theory with Gioseffo Zarlino, the last great exponent of a classical tradition that ascribed all consonance of sounds to the governance of numerical ratios. Vincenzio became one of the principal rebels against such theories and an advocate of new musical practices.

In 1563 Vincenzio married Giulia Ammannati of Pescia and settled in the countryside near Pisa, where Galileo was born on 15 February 1564.[2] His mother was an educated woman but willful and difficult; little affection for her is evinced in the letters of either Galileo or his younger brother, Michelangelo. Muzio Tedaldi, a relative of hers by marriage, was a customs official and businessman with whom Vincenzio participated in transactions in wool while at Pisa. In 1572 he returned to Florence with his wife and his other children, leaving Galileo to dwell for a time with Tedaldi.

1

Galileo joined his family at Florence in 1574 and was tutored at first by Jacopo Borghini, after which he was sent to the Camaldolese monastery at Vallombroso to study grammar, logic, and rhetoric.[3] Attracted by the quiet and studious life of the monks, Galileo joined the order as a novice. Vincenzio, however, had different plans for his son. Under the pretext that the boy's eyes needed medical care, he removed Galileo to Florence to resume his studies with Vallombrosan monks at their monastery there but no longer as a prospective member of the order. Vincenzio, who wished him to become a physician in the tradition that had brought the family distinction, made arrangements with Tedaldi for Galileo to again live with him in Pisa, where he was enrolled at the University as a medical student in the autumn of 1581.

The medical curriculum was based on the works of Galen and Aristotle's books on natural science. Galileo soon became impatient with these and among his professors gained the reputation of being the very spirit of contradiction. Long afterward, in the margin of an opponent's book, Galileo recorded an example of his youthful objections to Aristotle. Early in his studies, he said, he questioned the Aristotelian rule that the speed of a falling body was proportional to its size; having seen large hailstones striking the ground together with small ones, he could not believe that they had originated farther up or had begun their descents later than the others.[4]

Early in 1583, during his second year at the University of Pisa, an event occurred that was to be decisive in Galileo's scientific career. There are two accounts of this, written only after his death and from recollections recounted by Galileo in his old age to his first biographers.[5] They are not in exact agreement, but from them the probable events can be reconstructed consistently with what is known about Galileo, his father, and Ostilio Ricci, who was then attached to the Tuscan court. At the time of his death in 1603, Ricci held the title of mathematician to the grand duke of Tuscany, a position that was later to be acquired by Galileo. Ricci's duties in 1583 included instruction in mathematics of the court attendants.

It was the custom of the Tuscan court to move from Florence and reside at Pisa each year from Christmas to Easter, and during that period in 1582–83 Galileo met Ricci. One day he went to pay a visit to his new acquaintance, found him lecturing on

Euclid to the court pages, and remained to listen. Fascinated by this first taste of genuine mathematics, as Galileo later remembered the event, he returned to hear further lectures—though since those were officially open only to members of the court he did not make his presence known to Ricci.

Galileo then began to study Euclid on his own and soon had some questions which he took to Ricci. His native talent for mathematics was promptly recognized by Ricci, who asked him who his teacher was. Galileo confessed that he had heard only Ricci's own lectures, whereupon he was encouraged to pursue his studies and was offered any assistance he might need. During the summer of 1583 at Florence, Galileo sought Ricci out and brought him to his father's house where the two older men became friends. Galileo pretended to be studying Galen at home that summer, when in reality he was reading Euclid. Ricci told Vincenzio that his son preferred mathematics to medicine and asked permission to instruct him. Vincenzio, however, wished him first to complete his medical course; accordingly he thought it best that any assistance from Ricci should appear to be surreptitious and against his wishes, in order that Galileo would be afraid to neglect his study of Galen.

Vincenzio's books show him to have been a good mathematician; reasons for his opposition at this time will become clear presently. In order to understand the role played by mathematics in Galileo's later science, a short digression is appropriate here with regard to the text of Euclid Galileo had in hand. In all probability it was the Italian translation published by Niccolò Tartaglia in 1543, reprinted cheaply in 1565. In the universities only Latin texts were used, but Ricci taught in Italian and is said to have been a pupil of Tartaglia's. Although two Latin Euclids existed in the sixteenth century, it was only in Tartaglia's Italian commentary that a crucial difference between them had been fully and clearly explained. One Latin text was a medieval version based on an Arabic Euclid, in which the Eudoxian theory of proportion set forth in Book Five had been vitiated by a spurious definition put in place of Euclid's.[6] The other Latin version was first published from a Greek manuscript in 1505, and though it contained the correct definition it did not clarify the difference between Eudoxian theory and the medieval arithmetical theory of proportion based mainly on Book Seven, which latter was still taught in the universities despite Tartaglia's clarifications, for in universities no use was made of the vernacular translation.

The importance of Eudoxian proportion theory to Galileo's science cannot be exaggerated. Until the application of algebra to the general solution of geometrical (as well as arithmetical) problems, not achieved until after Galileo's work was completed,[7] rigorous connection of mathematics with physical events was possible only through some theory of proportionality. Physical concepts were therefore much affected by the proportion theory employed. Arithmetical theories, basic to medieval developments in physics, were not easily reconcilable with mathematically continuous change, especially change of speed; for speed seemed to exist only in connection with motion and not instantaneously. Now, continuous change of speed was a necessary assumption in the study of actual falling bodies, and as a result of this the Eudoxian theory establishing proportionality between continuous magnitudes was essential to any great advance over medieval physics. An analogous impasse existed in music theory, and underlay a part of Vincenzio's quarrel with Zarlino in 1588–89. Since Galileo was at that time in Florence, his father's activities may have had an important bearing on his own subsequent studies of motion in a way to be mentioned at the appropriate place.

Ricci also introduced Galileo to the study of Archimedes, undoubtedly by way of a selection of texts published by Tartaglia in 1543.[8] Tartaglia's book included both the Archimedean works that were related to physics, *On Plane Equilibrium* and *On Bodies in Water*. The latter work had been omitted from the more nearly complete (and much more expensive) collection of Archimedean works published at Basel in 1544.[9] Since centers of gravity and floating bodies were precisely the problems of mathematical physics to which Galileo first directed his attention, it can hardly be questioned that he began his study of Archimedes with Tartaglia's edition.

II

When Galileo returned to Pisa in the autumn of 1583, he devoted his time to mathematics and philosophy and absented himself frequently from required medical lectures. Early in 1584 word reached Vincenzio at Florence that his son was in danger of failing in medicine. Accordingly Vincenzio visited Tedaldi at Pisa, supposing that Galileo was neglecting all his studies, but there he learned that on the contrary Galileo was reading incessantly. It cannot have been hard for the father to guess the truth of the matter. Confrontation followed with Galileo, who frankly confessed his lack of interest in medicine and his preference for mathematics and philosophy. According to his first biographer, Vincenzio Viviani, Galileo had then just finished studying Euclid, Book Five.

Knowing the limited job opportunities for mathematicians and their penchant for idle theorizing, Vincenzio threatened to withdraw his financial support unless Galileo promised to drop these studies and complete the medical course. Galileo refused to do that but asked his father's patience, saying that if permitted one more year at the university he would thereafter take care of himself. Vincenzio sought a ducal scholarship for him for the year 1584–85; when it was refused, being a not unreasonable man, he continued Galileo's support for that year.[10]

This makes understandable Galileo's composition during the summer of 1584 of a set of lecture notes on natural philosophy in the Aristotelian tradition, and another on scientific method as taught in Aristotle's *Posterior Analytics*. His promise to his father made it incumbent on him to prepare to provide for himself. In order to obtain a teaching position it would be necessary to prepare lectures—not on Euclid, for he could count on Ricci's recommendation in mathematics—but on Aristotelian science. A teaching post in natural philosophy was more probable than a chair in mathematics, the former being taught in every school while the latter existed only in large universities. Galileo's reputation among the Pisan professors, however, made it unlikely he would get their endorsement to teach natural philosophy, so he needed concrete evidence of preparation.

Galileo's proposed lectures on Aristotelian science survive to a considerable extent and were published in his collected works under the title *Juvenilia*.[11] Their date is indicated by a passage in which the fall of Jerusalem is said to have occurred 1,510 years before and is implied to have taken place in the year 74 A.D.[12] The shorter work based on Aristotle's *Posterior Analytics* is not dated, though watermarks in the paper show it to have been probably composed at Pisa, either before 1586 or around 1589.

The contents of Galileo's *Juvenilia* need not detain us here, as they reveal a conception of science taught to him rather than that which he later adopted. Father William A. Wallace is now publishing an English translation and commentary in which the sources and style of the work will be analyzed, together with its relation to late sixteenth-century Aristotelian traditions.[13] He has identified passages taken by Galileo from a celebrated work by Christopher Clavius, Jesuit professor of mathematics at the Collegio Romano, and from another widely used text by the Jesuit Benedict Pereira, which were recast by Galileo for easier understanding by students when delivered orally.[14] It was formerly questioned whether the *Juvenilia* truly represented Galileo's own writing or was but his copy of lectures by Pisan professors. Father Wallace has convinced me that it is genuinely a work of Galileo's and is therefore of importance to Galileo's philosophical biography, though its relevance to his later advances in science remains dubious to me in view of the attacks he made soon afterward against Aristotle's physics in *De motu*. As to the shorter work based on the *Posterior Analytics*, that seems to me not to touch on the principal Aristotelian ideas with which Galileo's later conception of science did indeed have much in common.[15]

III

After leaving the University of Pisa without a degree in the spring of 1585, Galileo taught mathematics privately at Florence and Siena, holding also some public teaching position at Siena during the academic year 1585–86. His first scientific treatise was written in Italian in 1586. Called *La Bilancetta*[16] (The Little Balance), it described the construction and use of a device similar to the Westphal balance still in use today for determination of specific gravities. Galileo did not claim its invention, and indeed such instruments must have been in use by jewelers and gold merchants long before. What he did introduce was a practical way to determine with great precision the position of the counterweight. A fine wire was tightly wound along the arm of the balance so that the number of windings from center to suspension point could be counted with the thumbnail. Galileo used the same technique later to improve precision measurement in astronomy.

The treatise opened with a little critical essay in the history of ancient science. The celebrated story that Archimedes, while bathing, had hit upon the solution of a problem given to him by the king of Syracuse and had run naked through the streets shouting "Eureka!" had long been accompanied by two rival conjectures about his solution.[17] Both seemed to Galileo clumsy procedures unworthy of the fine mind of Archimedes. Accordingly he supplied a solution based only on propositions taken from Archimedes' own book on floating bodies, under which the necessary operations were quite simple and straightforward.

Late in 1586 Galileo began to compose a Latin dialogue on certain problems of motion; he left this unfinished, rewriting it later in lecture or chapter form.[18] The dialogue style was then very popular in books explaining scientific matters; Galileo used it in his first published booklet (1605) and again in his two last and most famous books. The unfinished dialogue of 1586–87 deserves attention as showing Galileo's early challenge to Aristotelian authority, his Archimedean application of mathematics to physics, and his interest in scientific questions raised by practical men. An outline of its contents here will provide an opportune place for introducing some of the ancient and medieval scientific ideas that Galileo was later to confront many times in defending his own positions.

Six specific questions were proposed, though only two were fully discussed. Answers given to the others in the later version called *De motu*[19] probably indicate what Galileo had in mind. Most of the problems now seem trivial, but they were not necessarily so in the physics of that time. Thus the first question was whether a body reversing its direction of motion must come to rest at the point of return, as Aristotle had asserted. Galileo denied that a stone thrown up, for example, must be at rest before it can start back down. To understand Aristotle's position we must recall that, by his definition, any motion whatever must occupy time; it made no sense to speak of motion or rest at a mathematical instant, as it now does. Having the proper mathematics (calculus) for dealing with continuous change, we can speak of the speed and direction of motion at any given mathematical instant; without that mathematics, such concepts merely led to Zeno's paradoxes. Likewise, we can identify the last instant of rest with the first instant of motion, whereas for Aristotle, as for philosophers contemporary with Galileo, it would be a contradiction to conceive the same body to be in motion and at rest at the same instant. The difference between Galileo and his predecessors (and most of his contemporaries) on this matter will become apparent in various forms as we proceed.

The second question also sounds odd, though in a different way—why an iron ball begins falling more slowly than a wooden one, but then soon passes it by. We might expect Galileo to have replied "It doesn't"; but on the contrary he thought this a fact that required explanation. He was not satisfied with the explanation given by one of his professors at Pisa,[20] based on mixtures of the Aristotelian "elements" of air and earth, though he accepted the professor's assertion of the fact. If you place a croquet ball and a large ball bearing on an inclined plane, you will see the effect very strikingly.[21] What happens in free fall is too swift for observation; hence false analogies of this kind often escaped detection.

The third question was why natural motion is swifter at the end than in the beginning, while forced motion is swiftest at the beginning. Here it is appropriate to clarify the meaning of "natural" and "forced" motion, a distinction we no longer make. Aristotle had coined the term "physics" from the Greek word *physis*, or nature, to designate the study of nature. The conspicuous fact about nature is change, of which motion is the special case of change of place with respect to time. Indeed, Aristotle had declared that "to be ignorant of motion is to be ignorant of nature," so closely is all physics linked to the study of motion. Aristotle's physics was accordingly the science of *natural* motion, that is, of motion undertaken spontaneously by a body released from all constraint. Heavy bodies had natural motion downward, light bodies natural motion upward. *Forced* motions had no vital place in physics as the science of *nature*. Aristotle paid little attention to them, since they could take place in any number of inconsistent ways and could not therefore, in his system, be the subject of any proper science.

Galileo continued to use the rather handy distinction between natural and forced motions in this sense. We have eliminated it by reducing "natural motion" to "the force of gravity." Far from doing that, Galileo later added a third class of motions, "neutral" motions, as we shall see. Later still he noticed that in some cases a natural motion might become a forced motion simply by reason of our viewpoint, as when a body should pass the center of the earth through an imaginary tunnel.

The fourth question was why some bodies will fall faster through air than through water, while others may fall through air but not through water. This was the principal question discussed in the 1586–87 dialogue, an answer being regarded by Galileo as a necessary preliminary to his treatment of the others. His analysis depended on the principle of Archimedes concerning loss of weight by immersion in a medium, and this led in turn to the rule that regardless of their weights, all bodies of the same material should fall with the same speed through the same medium. That conclusion had been reached much earlier by Giovanni Battista Benedetti, a pupil of Tartaglia's, who published it in 1553[22] and in 1554[23] replied to various attacks against it. Benedetti further refined the argument in 1585,[24] and possibly Galileo had seen that book before he composed his dialogue on motion. On the other hand he did not even mention, let alone adopt, Benedetti's explanation of acceleration in fall, which was much superior to Galileo's own first idea on the subject. Benedetti's explanation was medieval in origin; its importance justifies another digression.

Because Aristotle's physics was little concerned with forced motions, it gave no plausible explanation for the continued motion of an object thrown after it leaves the hand. Since Aristotle had postulated physical contact with some mover to account for any motion that was not natural, he suggested that what moved a thrown object was its contact with the surrounding air, to which the hand was supposed to impart some of its moving power. By the sixth century (and probably much earlier) it had been suggested alternatively that some kind of force is impressed in the object thrown. In the fourteenth century Jean Buridan gave the name *impetus* to this supposed impressed force and explored many of its implications. Among these was the idea that impetus may not only be impressed by an external force, but also accompanies any speed acquired naturally in free descent. A body commencing to fall gains a certain speed in its "first" motion when only heaviness, and not impetus, is acting; in the "next" motion, that acquired speed adds impetus to the body's natural motion, and so on again and again. This theory could not serve for mathematically continuous change of speed, in which there is no "first" motion different from all the rest.[25] Galileo's first explanation will be outlined below, and he did not abandon it until 1604.

Aristotle had also taught that the speed of a heavy body in falling was proportional to its size or weight and inversely proportional to the resistance of the medium.[26] Here "resistance" is

not quite the right word, which would be more like "corporeal-
ity" or "bodily quality." This did not mean density of the medium, in the sense of specific weight as taken up by Galileo.
Neither was Aristotle's idea that of viscosity, or of friction with
the medium. Rather, the resistance was attributed to the fluid's
having more or less "body," rather as when we say a wine has
"body," a term hard to define but easy to understand. Ancient
physics had many undefined qualitative terms; not even "speed"
was defined, but only "equal speed" and "greater speed."[27] How
Galileo dealt in 1586–87 with the role of the medium in fall will
be discussed after the final two questions posed in his dialogue
have been stated.

The fifth question, credited to a military friend of Galileo's
who died in 1590, was why a cannonball moves straight for a
longer stretch when shot more nearly vertically upward. Galileo's
answer was not set forth until 1591.

The final question was why heavier balls travel faster and
farther than light ones when fired with the same charge, and
was likewise answered only in 1591 by the medieval impetus
notion of greater receptiveness to impressed force on the part
of denser bodies.

Next came an argument that action of the air could not account for observed motions of thrown bodies, and that rotation
of a heavy sphere must be regarded as a mixed motion, partly
natural and partly forced. Only in the case of the heavenly
spheres could rotation be considered entirely natural, their
centers being at the center of the universe, which Galileo at first
assumed, with Aristotle, to be the earth. A marble sphere so
situated might move with only natural motion, once started,
but the earth itself (he said) should be considered at rest because of its very nature. And since action of the medium failed
to explain projectiles and rotations of heavy bodies, Galileo concluded that when a body has other than natural motion it is
moved by a force impressed in it by the mover. This was again
in accordance with medieval impetus theory, and Galileo introduced it by saying that it had many learned adherents.

The discussion next turned to the arrangement of the universe
in such a way that denser matter was situated nearer the center
not by necessity, but as a matter of fact, such an arrangement
being reasonable because spaces near the center are more constricted. The dialogue then clarified the terms *heavy* and *light*
by showing them to be always relative only. Galileo rejected

Aristotle's view that the element earth is absolutely heavy and the element fire absolutely light; all that could be said was that in the nature of things some substance must be the heaviest known and some other the lightest. Next came definitions of *equally heavy* and *heavier* in terms of volume and weight in a given medium. Natural motion in a medium was explained in terms of relative heaviness or lightness with respect to that medium. Here the spokesman for Galileo alluded to his recent analysis of Archimedes' procedure for determining alloys (that is, *La Bilancetta*) and set forth some theorems depending on the principle of Archimedes. A discussion of why we do not feel the weight of air ended with the remark that water, though heavy, does not sink in water because it cannot *exert* its weight there.

These preliminaries concluded, the dialogue took up the first question—no rest in reversed straight motion—with a proof that the force impressed in a projectile hurled upward must be always decreasing. Galileo's approach was different from that of medieval impetus theory, though his conclusion was the same. Medieval writers held that impetus decreased in heavy bodies because it conflicted with either or both of two things: (1) external resistance, and (2) inherent tendency to motion in a contrary direction. Galileo argued mathematically that no two points can be assigned in the line of forced motion at which the force remains the same, or the body would move farther than any previously assigned terminus. By like reasoning, no interval of rest can occur at the turning point.

After rejecting Aristotle's opinion that motion in a void would have to be instantaneous, Galileo discussed speeds of fall. Condemning the two rules attributed to Aristotle, he asserted that speed in any medium depends on the relative weights of body and medium so that bodies of the same kind, regardless of weight, move naturally with the same speed in a given medium.

Next the second question was taken up, beginning with a discussion of the residual impressed force in the projectile when it begins to fall back. A similar force was shown to be present in a body supported on high. Hence in fall the speed will increase only as long as the body is losing this contrary impressed force. In the relatively short falls we can observe, the constant speed natural to the body may not be reached; moreover, optical problems make it difficult to know whether or not a uniform terminal speed is operating. Here the dialogue on motion broke off, uncompleted.

IV

It was probably for the purposes of his private teaching in 1586–87 that Galileo originally composed a manuscript "Treatise on the Sphere, or Cosmography" that survives only in five copies made in the years 1602–6.[28] As we have it, the treatise begins with a short statement about the subject matter and method of cosmography which appears to have been added to it at that later time and will be discussed in chapter 4. The body of the work, probably belonging mainly to 1586–87, is a conventional discussion of climatic geography and spherical astronomy following the thirteenth-century *Sphere* of Sacrobosco which had been a standard university textbook for over three centuries. It contained no discussion of planetary astronomy, which was ordinarily reserved for a separate course, but it did present standard arguments taken from Ptolemy to show that the earth was at rest in the center of the universe. Galileo remarked that though there had been great mathematicians and astronomers who had assigned motion to the earth, he would follow the customary opinion. The fact that his treatise was written in Italian rather than in Latin indicates that it was intended for private rather than for university lectures, though it is probable that once having composed it, Galileo adopted it as the basis for his first-year lectures on astronomy during his professorships at both Pisa and Padua. Except for the opening statement about method it is of little interest, closely resembling scores of similar treatises that survive from the sixteenth and seventeenth centuries designed to give students a working knowledge of the terminology and principles of geography and astronomy without a discussion of actual calculations or the use of astronomical tables.

In 1587 Galileo learned that a chair of mathematics was open at the University of Bologna and he obtained some recommendations in support of his candidacy for it. One of these mentioned his teaching at Siena and certified his competence in philosophy and the humanities, but said nothing of any original theorems that would show his mathematical ability. Now, from letters early in 1588 it is known that Galileo had visited the Jesuit mathematician Christopher Clavius at Rome some time before, leaving with him some theorems on the centers of gravity of parabolic solids of revolution. This visit to Rome must have taken place in 1587, probably in the autumn of that year. A

12

letter to Bologna written in Galileo's behalf at Rome in February 1588 by Enrico Cardinal Caetano suggests that the purpose of Galileo's visit to that city had been to seek support for his application for the vacant chair of mathematics.

Galileo had worked on centers of gravity of parabolic solids[29] during 1587, inspired by the Archimedean treatise *On Plane Equilibrium* and a book by Federico Commandino (published in 1565) in which the subject was extended to solids. An original and ingenious device hit upon by Galileo for his analysis gained attention from eminent mathematicians both in Italy and abroad. It also won for him the friendship of Marquis Guidobaldo del Monte, a former pupil of Commandino and author of the most important book on mechanics published in the sixteenth century.

Galileo's new contribution to the analysis of centers of gravity was founded on a theorem that if weights in arithmetical progression are equally spaced along the arm of a balance, their center of gravity divides the balance arm in the ratio 2:1. In order to prove this he appealed simply to two different ways of looking at the same set of suspended weights. When weights are taken in arithmetical progression, the heaviest weight can be divided into as many units as there are different weights, the next heaviest weight into one less of the same units, and so on. The center of gravity of the original weights along the whole balance arm can thus be seen to fall at the same point as the center of gravity of a similar arithmetical progression of weights suspended in reversed order at half-distances along the half-arm on the side of the larger original weights. The theorem then follows from a simple proportionality relationship previously established as a lemma.

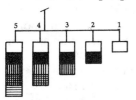

This formed the basis for a powerful method of attack on interesting special problems in which the arithmetical progression enters, so to speak, only at one remove; thus the differences of successive square numbers are in an arithmetical progression, a fact that Galileo used in some quite advanced theorems about centers of gravity of parabolic solids. When he sent this work to Guidobaldo for comment in 1588, however, he received in reply the same objection that Clavius had already raised. Both critics believed that Galileo's identification of the two centers of gravity begged the question. Galileo answered

Guidobaldo by simply redrawing the above diagram so that all the columns of weights were shown as contiguous.

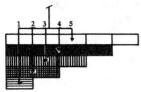

Guidobaldo promptly and graciously acknowledged that Galileo had indeed been right; whether Clavius was similarly convinced is not known.

The little work on centers of gravity was endorsed not only by Guidobaldo but also by Giuseppe Moletti, professor of mathematics at Padua, before his death in March 1588. Nevertheless, the chair at Bologna was given to G. A. Magini, a Paduan astronomer who already had several published books to his credit.[30] An eminent Belgian mathematician, Michael Coignet,[31] received a copy of Galileo's theorems from the geographer Abraham Ortelius, who was at Rome, and wrote to Galileo in praise of his extension of the work of Archimedes, remarking especially on its practical value. This constituted Galileo's first recognition abroad.

V

Despite Galileo's failure to obtain the chair at Bologna, the year 1588 saw an unusual distinction conferred on him that shows the high esteem in which his literary as well as his mathematical talents were held. Baccio Valori, then Consul of the celebrated Florentine Academy, invited Galileo to deliver to its members two lectures on the location, arrangement, and dimensions of the places described in Dante's *Inferno*.[32] The lectures were intended to settle a dispute between partisans of two rival views held by sixteenth-century commentators on Dante. Though of interest more from a literary than a scientific standpoint, they suggest early 1589 as the date of an intermediate version of Galileo's unpublished treatise on motion. Evidence for this dating lies in the nature of the opening theme of this ten-chapter version, very different from anything in the others. Here Galileo expounded God's reasons for having placed the elemental region (bounded by the moon's orbit) at the center of the universe— namely, to have it as far as possible from the sight of the blessed residents of Heaven lest they be offended by its grossness. Galileo's lectures on the geography of Hell late in 1588 probably inspired this theological gambit, abandoned in the final version that is traditionally called *De motu*.

The ten-chapter version, also left unfinished,[33] contained the first proof framed by Galileo on the basis of Euclid Book Five, Definition Five, which he applied to show that bodies of given specific weight have heavinesses directly proportional to their volumes. Here it is appropriate to mention an aspect of Galileo's scientific work that became very prominent somewhat later. This is the importance of precise measurement, already evident in *La Bilancetta*. It was probably in 1588–89 that Galileo began to reflect on the nature of measurement and its vital role in science. Now, it is one thing to prove a proportionality mathematically—as that bodies of the same specific weight have their weights proportional to their volumes—and it is another thing to verify this in fact. Demonstration unsupported by experience belongs to what Galileo called "a world on paper," while actual measurements belong to what he (but not Plato) called "the real world." Generally speaking, actual measurements are never precisely in agreement with the proposition proved, though in the case just mentioned no serious problem arises; weights and volumes can be measured with great precision, in a different sense from "mathematical precision." We always need some *unit* of measurement, and there is a practical limit to the subdivision of such units. That fact became a part of the dispute between Vincenzio Galilei and Zarlino when the latter published his *Musical Supplements* in 1588,[34] for Zarlino claimed that the semitone *cannot* be divided into two equal parts, against Vincenzio's contention that modern musical practice made such division necessary. The basis of this argument (which was only a part of the whole disagreement) is so important not just to music but to physical science that a digression on it is justified here.

To say that the semitone, represented by the ratio 9:8, cannot be divided equally, which in a musical context meant finding its square root, amounted to saying that there is no such thing as the square root of 9/8. There is none in numbers, as Euclid defined "number," that is, in positive integers. Traditional musical theory, grounded in the ratios of small numbers and supported by purely arithmetical proportion theory, accordingly denied the existence or possibility of the division in question. Vincenzio, following the ancient example of Aristoxenus, asserted nevertheless that the trained ear of a musician suffices to effect this division, whatever theorists might say about its harmonic value.

The question thus became whether the kind of mathematical precision demanded by theory is of any practical musical significance. On that, Vincenzio was right; not only did it have no practical significance, but whole areas of harmony that were demanding exploration by skilled musicians were closed off by the ancient theory for which Zarlino was spokesman, no matter how much he was willing to modify it. The test of musical consonance is in the trained ear, not in the number system. Vincenzio was spokesman for a system of musical temperament that would enable instruments of different families to be played pleasantly together, whether or not it conformed to numerical ratio rules. His younger contemporary, Simon Stevin, was to declare that integers had nothing to do with the case and that not the unit but the irrational twelfth root of two was the key to harmonic modulation; in theory, that is how pianos are now tuned.[35] Bach's "Well-Tempered Clavichord" would never have been written had Zarlino won the argument against Galileo's father.

Vincenzio's exasperation against mathematical dogma in music may well have had much to do with his earlier discouragement of Galileo's first enthusiasm for mathematics, quite apart from his natural desire to see his son in a useful, well-paid, and honored profession such as medicine. Vincenzio was himself a very capable mathematician, but he had good reason to know how perverse and crippling the demand for mathematical rigor can be. Intermediate between mathematics and the real world were (1) the senses, to which Vincenzio appealed, and (2) measurement, to which Galileo was going to appeal, recognizing as he did that "certainty" does not mean the same kind of thing in mathematical reasoning and in actual measurement of physical things.

When Zarlino published arguments against Vincenzio in 1588, the latter carried out some actual experiments to destroy the ancient idea that "sonorous numbers" rule musical consonance. The simplest case was the ratio 3:2, which was supposed to govern the perfect fifth, as indeed it does for like strings under equal tension, for which lengths in the ratio 3:2 sound the interval of the fifth. Sixteenth-century books on music theory, however, showed this ratio as also governing relative tensions, relative weights of hammers (which ring after striking an anvil), and relative volumes of organ pipes. Vincenzio found by experiment that in fact equal strings sound the perfect fifth under tensions related as 4:9, not as 3:2. He published this result in 1589, in reply to Zarlino.[36]

That Galileo took part in Vincenzio's experiments at Florence in 1588–89 is likely for a number of reasons. A note he made in connection with the revision of his dialogue into chapter form, late in 1588 or early in 1589, mentioned the phenomenon of the pendulum for the first time.[37] It is hard not to notice pendulum effects when experimenting with string tensions, since to do that one must hang weights on strings and then sound the strings. This necessarily results in swinging weights. Again, Galileo's later notes on motion (1603–4) include an experiment, or rather a precise measurement, in which time had to be equally divided into eight parts, which is easy to do musically but was virtually impossible otherwise at that time.[38] That the idea occurred to him at all suggests his earlier acquaintance with musical experiments.

During the summer of 1589 Galileo traveled with a young Florentine nobleman and some companions, perhaps aimlessly but more likely in search of employment. Then, in July 1589, Filippo Fantoni, who had long held the chair of mathematics at Pisa, vacated it. Galileo was appointed in his place, probably largely as a result of his lectures to the Florentine Academy and of his patronage by Guidobaldo del Monte. This appointment marked the end of Galileo's years of preparation and the beginning of his formal scientific career.

TWO

1589-92

GALILEO BEGAN HIS lectures as professor of mathematics at the University of Pisa in November 1589. His salary was 60 florins per year, just half the amount to which his predecessor had risen, which in turn had been less than was paid to most of the other professors. Galileo's financial needs were probably not great until 1591, when the death of his father left him with the responsibilities of head of the family. Nevertheless, his patrons Guidobaldo del Monte and Baccio Valori were soon quietly pressing for his appointment to the chair at Padua vacated by the death of Moletti. The more prestigious position at Padua could hardly be hoped for by a young man without experience in another university.

Coinciding in time with Galileo's appointment at Pisa was that of Jacopo Mazzoni, a philosopher and man of letters who had published a learned work on Dante.[1] Despite differences of opinion on natural philosophy, Galileo and Mazzoni held many animated and friendly discussions in which they were frequently joined by Girolamo Mercuriale, an elderly professor of medicine still remembered for his pioneer book on physical exercise and health.[2] It was at Pisa that the Roman mathematician Luca Valerio met Galileo, in conversations he recalled years later when they began to correspond about mathematics and motion. Valerio's most important work was on centers of gravity, and since it is known that Galileo renewed his studies in that field in 1590, that was probably also the year of his meeting with Valerio.

Late in life Galileo recalled that it was about this time that he had first investigated the curve called the cycloid, traced out by a point on the rim of a wheel rolling along a flat surface. He sought to relate the area of one arch of this curve to the area of the rolling circle.[3] The ratio of those areas is in fact 3:1, but Galileo was unable to prove this; by cutting out paper models which he weighed with care, he decided that some slightly different ratio, not exactly numerical, must hold.

During his term at Pisa Galileo revised and completed his treatise *De motu*, using material from the earlier dialogue on motion and the intermediate version. Many additions were made, and a commentary by Galileo on Ptolemy's *Almagest* (of which no other trace has been found) was mentioned as being nearly ready to be published.[4] This was probably not written before 1591, since it is safe to assume that Galileo's first-year lectures on astronomy were based on his *Treatise on the Sphere*, planetary theory being first taken up in 1590–91. It is therefore probable that *De motu* was completed in Galileo's last year at Pisa, 1591–92, and discussion of it will accordingly be deferred to the end of this chapter.

Perhaps the best-known story about Galileo relates to the Leaning Tower of Pisa. Since the story is now treated by historians of science as legendary, we should begin by considering the exact words of its first appearance (1657), in which Viviani was repeating his recollection of what Galileo himself had told him during his final years of blindness at Arcetri:

At this time, it appearing to him that for the investigation of natural effects there was necessarily required a true knowledge of the nature of motion, there being a philosophical and popular axiom that "Ignorance of motion is ignorance of nature," he quite gave himself over to its study; and then, to the great discomfort of all the philosophers, through experiences and sound demonstrations and arguments, a great many conclusions of Aristotle himself on the subject of motion were shown by him to be false which up to that time had been held as most clear and indubitable, as (among others) that speeds of unequal weights of the same material, moving through the same medium, did not at all preserve the ratio of their heavinesses assigned to them by Aristotle, but rather, these all moved with equal speeds, he showing this by repeated experiments [*esperienze*] made from the height of the Leaning

Tower of Pisa in the presence of other professors and all the students.[5]

That such an event actually occurred has been hotly contested on grounds supported not by Viviani's account but rather by various later paraphrases of it which, with assorted embellishments, have introduced improbabilities not germane to the historical issue. Thus some have asserted that Galileo claimed an impossible exact coincidence for the arrival on the ground of a cannonball and a musket ball; others have told the story as if an iron ball and a wooden ball had been used; still others ridicule the claim, never made by Galileo or Viviani, that he had been the first to perform such an experiment. Whether or not anyone had tried it from so great a height is not known, but Simon Stevin had tried it from a height of thirty feet and had published his findings in 1586.[6]

In fact what Viviani described was not an experiment at all; it was a demonstration. Galileo already knew what would happen and used the Leaning Tower to demonstrate this to others. That would have been in keeping with what is known about his flair for the dramatic. Viviani's words "all the students" have been taken by some to mean an assembly of the entire Pisan student body, saying then that although such an event must have left some record at the university, none is found. But Viviani's words more probably meant "all his students," some of whom had presumably argued with Galileo by citing their professors of philosophy, and it would then be natural for him to invite those professors to witness a test. Finally, Viviani stated clearly that the weights were of the same material and of different weights; examination of *De motu* shows that in 1591 Galileo's conclusion was indeed limited to bodies of the same kind falling through the same medium.

The credibility of this hotly debated event will be discussed again in the final chapter. It has suffered not only from such unhistorical embellishments as mentioned, but also from the fact that Viviani was responsible for several palpable errors in chronology about other events relating to Galileo. Thus he placed Galileo's discovery of isochronism of the pendulum in 1583 and even implied that this led him to the *pulsilogium*, a device for timing the pulse, while still a student at Pisa.[7] The very considerable evidence against that dating for either event, however, does not weigh against the separate matter of the Leaning Tower demonstration. Neither does Viviani's statement that Galileo first noticed isochronism of pendulums by watching the swings of a lamp in the cathedral at Pisa necessarily suffer from the fact that what is now called by guides "Galileo's lamp" was not installed until late in 1587. "As if there had been no [cathedral] lamp before this one," remarked Antonio Favaro, "or as if it had swung to a different law of physics."[8] More probably Galileo noticed isochronism of pendulums in connection with his father's musical experiments in 1588, entered his first note concerning pendulums at that time, and subsequently recalled that he had seen cathedral lamps swinging without ever considering their law of motion, as Galileo had Sagredo say in *Two New Sciences*.[9] But it was not until 1602 that Galileo made careful observations of long pendulums, as we shall see, and the *pulsilogium* followed in 1603 as the invention of a Venetian doctor of his acquaintance who made many valuable applications of physics to medicine.[10]

II

Galileo's scientific work up to the end of his professorship at Pisa is reflected in *De motu*. This affords a mine of information about the development of his analysis of motion, both from its many additions to the earlier versions and from the rewriting and rearrangement of material in them. A summary of its contents is therefore in order, both to show Galileo's concept of physics about the time of his move to Padua and to set a background for his later resumption there of studies of motion conducted in a very different way.

The first eight chapters of *De motu*, except for one, consist mainly of material taken from the earlier versions in which natural motion was dealt with by using the hydrostatic principle of Archimedes. The exception is chapter 6, "In which is explained the analogy between bodies moving naturally and weights on a balance." In chapter 9 the same analogy was taken up again to become the key to a series of attacks against Aristotle. Chapter 9 began,

When a person has discovered the truth about something and has established it with great effort, then, on viewing his discoveries more carefully, he often realizes that what he has taken such pains to find might have been perceived with the greatest ease. For truth has the property that it is not so deeply concealed as many have thought; indeed, its traces shine brightly in various places and there are many paths by which it is approached. Yet it often happens that we do not see what is quite near at hand and clear. And we have a clear example of this right before us. For everything that was demonstrated and explained above so laboriously, is shown to us by Nature so openly and clearly that nothing could be plainer or more obvious.

This passage is evidently autobiographical; when Galileo wrote it, he had just recently perceived the true power of what he had already put into chapter 6 without fanfare. There the analogy of the balance had been introduced primarily to establish the proposition that "the heavier cannot be raised by the less heavy." On this assumption it is easy to understand why solids lighter than water are not completely submerged. In illustrating this, Galileo noted that "In the case of bodies moving naturally, as in weights on a balance, the cause of all motions—up as well as down—can be referred to weight alone." Next came an open challenge to Aristotle: "What moves moves, as it were, by force and by the extruding action of the medium." Aristotle, in his *De caelo*, had rejected any notion "that an external agent is the cause of the elements moving up or down, or that they are moved by force, the 'extrusion' that some allege,"[11] meaning the atomists, opposed by Aristotle on everything.

Galileo did not abandon the concept of natural motion, though he did go so far as to say here, "In the same way, the stone is thrust from its position and impelled downward by the medium because it is heavier than the medium. It is therefore clear that even this kind of motion may be called 'forced,' though it is commonly . . . called natural." To regard all motions as forced might have led Galileo to a physics like ours, but in chapter 7 he again spoke of natural motions as caused by heaviness and lightness, accounting thus for their speed or slowness. Galileo's early theory of acceleration in fall required his conception of an artificial lightness as imparted to a stone thrown upward, and he could not very well have artificial lightness without its natural counterpart.

A criterion adopted by Galileo at this point for distinguishing forced motion was absence of contact with the moving agent.

Upward motion of a piece of wood released at the bottom of a tank of water could then be regarded as natural, like the rise of the lighter pan of a balance, while continued rise of the wood beyond the surface of the water could only be forced motion. Continued motion after loss of contact with the mover required a force, for which at this period Galileo accepted the impressed force called impetus in the medieval tradition. All discussion of projectile motions in *De motu* was carried out along this line, and (as others have remarked) one may, in reading parts of *De motu*, fancy oneself listening to Jean Buridan's lectures at Paris in the mid-fourteenth century.[12]

With this simplified "balance" approach in hand, Galileo proceeded to demolish several Aristotelian positions previously attacked in earlier versions but in more detail. Then, in chapter 14, he took up the question of speeds along inclined planes, laying the basis for most of his important work on motion when he resumed those studies at Padua a decade later.

Galileo remarked that others had not previously discussed this question, a claim that has been criticized. The critics have confused his investigation of *speeds* along inclined planes with that of *forces* required to move bodies up inclined planes, which had indeed been undertaken by Pappus of Alexandria in the third century, or with the correct rule for *equilibrium* of weights supported on different inclined planes given by Jordanus Nemorarius in the thirteenth century.

Galileo reduced equilibrium on planes to the lever law, beginning by considering the nature of the effective weights of the same body on two different inclined planes. To determine this he considered a simple balance situated above two planes having different slopes but both tilted downward in the same direction. Taking the balance arm as his horizontal diameter, he drew a circle with two planes as tangents, and its radii to the points of tangency, at which he considered to be situated weights counterbalanced by a weight at the other extremity of the balance. The descent of the body along either tangent, he asserted, would be as that of a body supported on the circle at the respective points of tangency; in such descent, the actual weight effective in either case would be as the weight holding the balance in equilibrium at the point vertically above it. Only along the vertical tangent would the weight exert its full effect downward. Hence the "same heavy body will descend vertically with greater force than on an inclined plane in proportion as the length of the descent on the incline is greater than the vertical fall." He then remarked:

> But this proof must be understood on the assumption that there is no accidental resistance occasioned by roughness of the moving body or of the inclined plane, or by the shape of the body. We must assume that the plane is, so to speak, incorporeal, or at least that it is very carefully smoothed and perfectly hard, so that as the body exerts pressure on the plane it may not cause a bending and somehow be at rest on it as in a trap. And the moving body must be perfectly smooth and of a shape that does not resist motion, e.g., perfectly spherical and of the hardest material, or else a fluid like water. If all is arranged thus, then any body on a plane parallel to the horizon will be moved by the very smallest force; indeed, by a force less than any given force.

There followed two demonstrations of the above proposition, and this cautionary remark:

> Our demonstrations, as we also said above, must be understood of bodies free from all external resistance. But since it is perhaps impossible to find such bodies in the realm of matter, one who performs an experiment on this subject should not be surprised if the experiment fails; that is, when a large sphere, even though it is on a horizontal plane, cannot be moved with a minimal force. For in addition to the causes already mentioned, there is also this one—that a plane cannot actually be parallel to the horizon, since the surface of the earth is spherical and a plane cannot be parallel to such a surface. Hence, since the plane touches the sphere in only one point, if we move away from that point we shall be moving upward.

These early qualifications give us a clue to Galileo's thought at this stage on the roles of mathematical reasoning and experimental tests. The validity of mathematical proofs is unaffected by the physical assumptions chosen in applying them, but confidence in those assumptions may be affected by experimental test of any implied conclusions. Whether the test induces us to abandon, modify, or accept the assumptions usually depends on the magnitude of the disparities found.

Except for its treatment of speeds on inclined planes, chapter 14 was sound and had an important bearing on Galileo's later studies. But having started with the idea that equilibrium conditions and effective weights on different planes should govern speeds along them, Galileo deduced speed ratios that were easily tested and failed completely. At this stage Galileo tried to dismiss great disparities by the same considerations that he later adduced only for small ones:

Just as was said before of vertical motions, so also in the case of the motions on planes it happens that the ratios we have set down are not observed. This happens not only for the reasons just now given, but also—and this is accidental— because a lighter body descends more quickly than a heavier one at the beginning of its motion. How this comes about we shall make clear at the proper place, for this question depends on the question why natural motion is accelerated.

A marginal note added to chapter 14 was of profound significance to the restricted inertial concept that later appeared in Galileo's physics, reserved as that was to motions of heavy bodies near the earth's surface and accessible to precise measurement. In order to introduce this note it is necessary to speak first of chapter 16, "On the question whether circular motion is natural or forced," because the idea first occurred to him while writing that. By "circular motion" was meant rotation of a round body about an axis internal to it, not motion in a circular path around some exterior point. Much confusion about early physics has arisen from neglect of this.[13] Until Galileo's time the traditional view of the heavens saw stars and planets not as free bodies, but as lights fixed in crystalline spheres and their motions as occasioned by rotations around axes passing through the earth. When medieval writers suggested that an initial impetus conferred by the Creator would suffice to keep the stars in perpetual uniform rotation, the analogy was to the spinning of a grindstone and not to a hurled object. Experience showed that impetus could be conferred in two ways, by throwing or by spinning, the continuation of motion being straight or circular according to the motion imparted. No physicist, least of all Galileo, supposed that a thing could be moved so as to continue in a circular *path* when set free.

Galileo's intention in chapter 16 was to show that a body might be moving, and yet its motion might be neither natural nor forced, contrary to Aristotle's classification. Thus a marble sphere situated at the center of the universe and rotating about it would not be moving naturally, since it would not be approaching the center of the universe, nor would it be moving forcibly, since neither would it be receding from the center of the universe. Various other cases were also considered, according to whether the sphere were of uniform material or not and whether its center were at the center of the universe or not. Having classified some such motions as "neither natural nor forced" and others as "alternately forced and natural," Galileo went back to chapter 14 and added this note:

From this it follows that mixed motion (except circular) does not exist. For since the forced motion of heavy bodies is away from the center, and their natural motion is toward the center, a motion cannot be compounded from these two which is partly upward and partly downward—unless perhaps we should say that such a mixed motion is that which takes place along the circumference of a circle around the center of the universe.

Galileo then canceled the parenthetical words "except circular," above, and continued:

But such motion will be better described as "neutral" than as "mixed." For "mixed" partakes of both; "neutral," of neither.

The place at which this was added in chapter 14 was at the end of a mathematical proof that "A body subject to no external resistance can be moved on a plane which slopes neither up nor down, by a force smaller than any given force whatever." It is evident that the previous words "on the circumference of a circle around the center of the universe" referred to motions *supported* on such a surface and free from friction or other resistance. These alone would be motions in which there was neither approach toward nor departure from the common center of heavy things, except for the rotations of homogenous spheres discussed in chapter 16. Unsupported motions were obviously excluded, because unsupported heavy bodies *do* approach the common center.

Many years passed before Galileo studied the actual behavior of bodies projected horizontally, considered as things that very nearly met the conditions described above. His concept of neutral motions, neither natural (because they were not undertaken spontaneously on release from constraint), nor forced (because they could be started by a force smaller than any assigned force), had nevertheless been formed while he was still at Pisa.

In chapter 15 Galileo rejected Aristotle's assertion that no ratio can exist between straight and circular motions—or indeed curved and straight lines. In reply Galileo appealed to the Eudoxian definition (Euclid Book Five, Definition Four) that had been absent from the standard Euclid of the Middle Ages. The same chapter also appealed to Archimedes *On Spiral Lines*, a work of special importance to the mathematical analysis of motion.

The significance of chapter 16 to the origin of Galileo's restricted inertial principle has already been mentioned, but two other matters in that chapter deserve attention. The first is that in speaking here of the diurnal rotation of the stars, Galileo gave not even a passing remark to the Copernican view that it is the earth, and not the starry sphere, that rotates. Though in chapter 20 he alluded to the *De revolutionibus* of Copernicus on a mathematical issue, throughout *De motu* he dealt with the earth as center of the universe. From this it would appear that he had read *De revolutionibus* but remained unconvinced of Copernican astronomy. The second is that in chapter 16 rotations of nonhomogeneous spheres around centers other than the center of the universe were classified as "sometimes natural and sometimes forced," according to the position of the heavier hemisphere in different parts of such rotations.

Chapter 17 exhibited Galileo's familiarity with and endorsement of impetus theory, though in it he offered an explanation of acceleration in free fall different from that of medieval writers. The interesting thing is that even after his introduction of "neutral motions," Galileo did not at once see their bearing on projectile motions but long remained satisfied to invoke "impressed force" to account for motions continued after loss of contact with a mover. It was in chapter 17 that he introduced "artificial lightness," mentioned above in connection with chapters 6 and 7:

I say that that is naturally light which moves upward naturally. And I say that that is light preternaturally, or accidentally, or by force, whose upward motion is contrary to nature, is accidental, and is by force; and such is the stone which is set in motion by force. And in the case of this stone its natural and intrinsic weight is lost in the same way as when it is placed in a medium heavier than itself. For a stone which floats in mercury, and does not sink, loses all its weight; indeed it loses weight and assumes lightness to such an extent that it promptly resists even a great deal of weight brought externally if one tries to press it down.

For his impending treatment of projectile motion Galileo needed the concept of natural upward motion (as that of a block of wood released under water) and of forced upward motion (as that of a hurled stone), together with the related notions of natural lightness and artificial or "accidental" lightness. Later on he modified those concepts, removed altogether the concept of force, and considered that motion alone should be considered as imparted to the hurled object, and not also a force or any other quality, temporary or permanent.[14] After *De motu*, little that Galileo wrote justifies his usual characterization as "father of dynamics." In his later writings force appeared almost always as an effect rather than as a cause of motion.

In chapter 19 Galileo rejected Aristotle's idea that the weight of a body becomes greater, or more effective, as the body nears its proper place, once popular in explaining accelerated falling motion. Galileo's explanation, adumbrated in the dialogue version of 1587, appealed to residual contrary force that became dissipated during the early stages of fall. In *De motu* he said:

After I had thought this out, and happened to be reading a couple of months later what Alexander [of Aphrodisias] says on the subject, I learned from him that this had also been the view of the very able philosopher Hipparchus. . . . I should say, though, that Hipparchus was not entirely above criticism, for he left unexplained a difficulty of great importance.

This remark is of autobiographical importance. Galileo had been, and was still, misinformed about the comprehensiveness of the theory attributed to Hipparchus, and also about what Alexander of Aphrodisias had said on the subject as reported by Simplicius in his commentary on *De caelo*. Galileo's misinformation came from Benedict Pereira's book mentioned above in connection with the sources of Galileo's *Juvenilia*.[15] A new edition of Pereira's book was printed at Venice in 1586, after Galileo left Pisa. In the memoranda Galileo wrote after compos-

ing his unfinished dialogue on motion there is a specific reference to Pereira's book, following a memorandum about Hipparchus and Alexander. From these things there is little doubt
that Galileo had covered the case supposedly neglected in antiquity (that of bodies beginning fall from a support on high)
before he reread Pereira's book. It is of interest that two or
three years later, when writing *De motu*, he acknowledged the
theory as originating with Hipparchus but still relied on Pereira
and did not take the trouble to consult Simplicius directly. Had
he done so, he would probably have corrected the lingering error
rather than invite criticism from philosophers; for, as he noted
in another memorandum,

There will be many who, when they read my writings, will
turn their minds not to reflecting on whether what I have
written is true, but solely to seeking how they may, justly or
unjustly, undermine my arguments.[16]

Galileo's explanation of the matter he thought Hipparchus
had neglected to cover is illuminating with regard to his thought
as a physicist. That enough impressed upward force remained
in a stone at its highest point to slow its subsequent fall tem-
porarily is plausible, but how does one account for the initial
slowing of descent from rest when a stone is merely dropped?
Galileo replied that any body detained on high, as by resting on
a board, will possess just as much upward impressed force as
would equal its natural tendency downward due to its weight,
for if it did not, it would not remain there at rest. In chapter 22
Galileo showed, by a diagram identical with those used in modern elementary textbooks, that bodies of different weight resting
on the same table must be receiving different upward "pushes"
from the table—a conception even now disturbing to many beginning students of physics.

Chapter 20 gave Galileo's demonstration that no rest occurs
at the turning point in reversed straight motion, which had been
the first question proposed in the early dialogue version. A long
deleted passage shows how Galileo moved in *De motu* from
purely philosophical and classificatory arguments, traditional
at the time in physics, to mathematical treatment in terms of
what amounts to moving the frame of reference, a device later
used with great effect by Christiaan Huygens in developing the
concept of relativity of motion after Galileo publicized that in

his *Dialogue* of 1632. In the same chapter there was a brief comment on the problem of impact between bodies moving horizontally, a topic rarely mentioned by Galileo. His early concern with continuity in change, in cases where common sense as well as Aristotle seemed against him, was evidenced thus:

> Do not be confused by the argument that if the weight and the [upward] projecting force are equal *at* some time, then the body must be at rest *for* some time. For it is one thing to say that the weight of the body at some time comes to be equal to the projecting force, and it is another thing to assert that it remains in this state of equality during an interval of time.

Chapter 21 demonstrated, against Aristotle, that unbounded natural motion need not imply infinite speed. In the discussion Galileo stated clearly his belief that natural acceleration does not continue indefinitely but that a fixed terminal speed is reached. His principal argument was drawn from experience, which shows that initial impetus is gradually lost. Though his examples were of motion through a medium, Galileo related the reaching of a fixed terminal speed not to effects of the medium (as he was to do later), but rather to his theory of heaviness and lightness. He then went on to show mathematically how a law of acceleration might lead to speeds approaching some maximum that was never reached, citing Apollonius and Eutocius. He again alluded to the failure of experimental tests to vindicate the ratios of speeds he had deduced from his theory and related those failures to the existence of acceleration. A decade was to elapse before he gave serious attention to the analysis of actual accelerations of bodies falling freely, descending along inclined planes, or swinging in circular arcs.

Chapter 23, which concluded *De motu*, concerned the question that had been ascribed in the dialogue version to a friend, Dionysius Font: why projection in a straight line is longer as the angle of projection becomes steeper. The same question had been implicitly answered by Tartaglia in 1537.[17] Galileo's discussion appears in the main to follow that of Tartaglia except for its phrasing in terms of impetus, a concept that was not utilized by Tartaglia. Here Galileo recognized that composition of motions took place, though as yet he did not discuss the shape of the trajectory—something that later became of great importance in his work on motion. Indeed, when in 1632 Galileo wrote to Cesare Marsili that his interest in the shape of projectile paths dated back more than forty years, he probably had in mind this last chapter of *De motu*, tending to confirm 1592 as the latest probable date of that treatise in its final form.[18]

III

To summarize Galileo's scientific career as professor at the University of Pisa, in physical science he had progressed about as far as he could under the traditional preoccupation with the search for causes as such. His *De motu* was a creditable improvement over contemporary academic discussions of motion by philosophers, as in books published by his former professors Girolamo Borri and Francesco Buonamici. On the other hand it was not a sufficiently convincing analysis to Galileo for him to publish it. Actual tests of the ratios of speeds he had deduced for bodies on inclined planes did not bear them out, just as the fall of bodies from the Leaning Tower had not borne out Aristotle's deduced rules for freely falling bodies. The use of more mathematical arguments than then customary in dealing with motion had enabled Galileo to refute many received opinions but had not led him to conclusions fully borne out by experience. As he was later to remark, it is much easier to detect error than to reach truth.[19]

There is little doubt that Galileo had offended professors of philosophy at Pisa by contradicting Aristotle. There is also a story that he had offended a highly placed personage by giving an unfavorable opinion on a scheme for dredging the port of Livorno. It was not expected that his contract would be renewed on its expiration in 1592, and his father's death in 1591 had made it necessary for him to obtain a better salary.

As early as the spring of 1590 Galileo's friends and patrons had been exploring the possibility of his getting the chair of mathematics at the University of Padua. That had been left vacant since 1588, the Venetian officials who governed the university being very jealous of its reputation and in no hurry to appoint anyone until certain that a worthy successor to Moletti (and some even more distinguished predecessors at Padua) had been found. One of the rival candidates was G. A. Magini, who coveted the chair in his native city but had taken the post at Bologna to which Galileo had unsuccessfully aspired. That Galileo had established a good reputation as a mathematician during his term at Pisa, whatever was thought of him by philosophers, is shown by his receiving the appointment at Padua in 1592. In this he had had strong support not only from Guidobaldo and Valori, but also from G. V. Pinelli, a Genoese who had long resided in Padua and whose cultural attainments and friendship with eminent scholars and churchmen throughout Italy gave unusual weight to his recommendation. In the summer of 1592 Galileo obtained permission from the grand duke to leave Tuscany and take the chair of mathematics at Padua.

THREE

1592-99

GALILEO'S INAUGURAL LECTURE at the University of Padua was delivered on 7 December 1592 in the Great Hall, to a large audience and in splendid style. His salary was now 180 florins, three times what he had earned at Pisa. Situated only twenty-five miles from the busy seaport of Venice, Padua had a great many foreign students and a stream of distinguished visitors entering or leaving Italy. Interchange of information in every field was active, scholarly standards were high, and the atmosphere of liberty in the Venetian republic afforded the young professor greater scope for his ideas and activities.

As early as March 1593 Galileo was consulted by a Venetian official on a practical matter, the placement of oars in naval galleys. He replied with an analysis of the oar as a lever in which the fulcrum is the sea, and not the oarlock, receiving in return information about shipbuilding practices and reasons for them. Galileo's visits to the Venetian arsenal, which had recently been expanded and was active in shipbuilding, probably began at this time. All the documents from his early years at Padua indicate his interest in technological rather than philosophical questions.

The discussion of oars and ships may have been the immediate motivation for composition of a brief treatise on mechanics in 1593, of which a copy survives; there is also a copy of the slightly expanded 1594 version and another of about that time.[1] It was greatly extended around 1601–2, and perhaps again at Florence. The early versions are brief and omit detailed proofs, emphasis being placed on the practical understanding of the five simple machines. Examples of compound machines with cranks and gears were included in the oldest version but omitted from the others. A brief terminal discussion of the force of percussion evinces Galileo's familiarity with the ancient pseudo-Aristotelian *Questions of Mechanics*, which probably inspired his later work on the strength of materials, on composition of speeds, and on the structure of the continuum.

In the 1593 version there were no prefatory remarks. The 1594 revision began with this short introduction, likewise reminiscent of the ancient *Questions of Mechanics*:

The science of mechanics is that faculty which teaches the reasons and gives us the causes of marvelous effects that we see made by various instruments, moving and raising very great weights with little strength [*forza*; for an idea similar to our "force," Galileo usually used *virtù*]. And wishing here to discourse of this matter, we shall begin by theorizing on the nature of the primary and simplest instruments, to which others may be reduced or from which they are compounded. There are five of the said primary instruments; that is, lever, capstan, pulley, screw, and wedge (or force of percussion), which are in a way all reducible to one only, that is, to the balance or *libra*; hence it is necessary to understand and thoroughly grasp the nature of the balance, which we shall now undertake to explain.[2]

Until about 1600, then, Galileo regarded reasons and causes as essential to mechanics, which was the traditional view. He was soon to shift his emphasis, however, to the utility of mechanical devices. To say that great weights may be lifted with the application of little force was a commonplace at the time, as it had been since the ancient *Questions of Mechanics*. In 1602 Galileo was not only to remove this notion from his preface, but even to make it a chief target of criticism in his exposure of delusions that had misled mechanics in the past, had contaminated the science, and was still the basis of many fraudulent claims and illusory schemes.

Galileo's *Mechanics* was originally composed as the syllabus for a course of private instruction paid for by interested students. It was written in Italian, which was not then used at Padua in formal university lectures. Another such private course offered by Galileo from his earliest years at Padua dealt with military architecture and fortification. Yet another, added in

1598, concerned a calculating instrument of Galileo's devising. Students in these private courses were mainly young foreign noblemen, especially Germans and Poles. The extent of Galileo's private tutoring after 1600 will be summarized in the next chapter from his account books, which before that year are inadequate to provide a reliable picture.

The first modern treatise on mechanics had been published in Latin by Guidobaldo del Monte in 1577 and translated into Italian in 1581.[3] There are interesting differences between that book and Galileo's *Mechanics*. Galileo did not stress, as had Guidobaldo, disparities between theoretical conclusions and actual practice. Guidobaldo had dwelt on errors of his predecessors Jordanus Nemorarius and Tartaglia, while Galileo confined himself to presenting the subject matter clearly and briefly. Guidobaldo saw an unbridgeable gap between statics and dynamics, while Galileo remarked as early as 1593 that since any small force will disturb equilibrium, no distinction need be made between the power required to sustain a weight and that needed to move it.[4] Accordingly he formulated as a general rule something that his patron had expressly denied—proportionality between forces, weights, speeds, distances, and times such that whatever might be gained in one must be lost in another.

II

In September 1593 Guidobaldo wrote an invitation to Galileo to visit him at Monte Baroccio, near Urbino, as Galileo probably did in the summer of 1594. His patron wanted to show him a book on perspective he had written but not yet published, which is of interest not only for its treatment of optics but also for discussion of theater design.[5] Galileo left no writings on optics, though he taught it privately in 1601 and perhaps other years. Guidobaldo was also writing a book on the Archimedean screw;[6] this was probably related to a patent Galileo obtained in September 1594 on a device for raising water by horse power.[7] Since Giuseppe Ceredi had obtained a Venetian patent in 1567 for use of an Archimedean screw to raise water, Galileo's machine must have introduced some novel feature in order to be granted a separate patent.

Galileo's official lectures dealt with Euclid in every year, and in alternate years with spherical and planetary astronomy.[8] The latter were given mainly for medical students, who had to be able to cast horoscopes; speculative astronomy was taught by professors of philosophy who lectured on Aristotle's *De caelo*.

It is uncertain when Galileo first became converted to Copernican astronomy. An important clue may be found in a story told in his famous *Dialogue* of 1632,[9] where it was placed in the mouth of Giovanfrancesco Sagredo, a Venetian who studied with Galileo about 1597 and became one of his closest friends. According to this story a foreigner visiting Padua gave lectures on Copernican astronomy that Sagredo, considering the whole matter a majestic folly, did not hear. Speaking later with others who had attended, however, he came to realize that there might be something to it, especially because those who jeered were not really familiar with the Copernican arguments. One man in particular, said Sagredo, "told me that the matter was not entirely foolish. Since I considered this man intelligent and rather conservative, I was sorry I had not gone," and eventually Sagredo came round to the new system.

Now, it may be that the conservative listener was Galileo, a possibility that has been neglected because of doubt cast on the whole episode by identification of the lecturer as "a certain foreigner from Rostock,[10] whose name I believe was Christian Wursteisen, a supporter of the Copernican opinion." A Christian Wursteisen had in fact existed, but he was of Basel, died in 1588, never visited Padua, and did not support Copernicus but simply mentioned him casually at the end of his published commentary on the *Sphere* of Sacrobosco, of which several editions were printed. But on 5 November 1595, a *Christopher* Wursteisen was enrolled in the school of law at the University of Padua,[11] and he may have arrived in Padua some time before that date. Quite possibly he went there from the University of Rostock to complete a course in law and gave lectures that were heard by Galileo. Rostock was the first university in Europe at which Copernican astronomy is known to have been taught. Galileo, writing the *Dialogue* several decades after the event, might easily have confused the given name of the lecturer with that of the Swiss commentator on Sacrobosco. In any event Galileo's first serious interest in Copernican astronomy is more likely to date from 1595 than from any other year, in view of the following facts.

It was in 1595 that Fra Paolo Sarpi, a friend of Galileo's at Venice, entered in his notebooks a succinct summary of a novel tidal theory[12] that was later developed and strongly supported by Galileo as one of his own most highly prized discoveries. His earliest known written account of the theory dates from 1616, but a letter he wrote to Johann Kepler in 1597 implies that Galileo had adopted it some years earlier. There is nothing in Sarpi's extensive notebooks to indicate that he himself held Copernican views, nor was his summary of the tidal theory there preceded by any reflections that could have naturally led him to it. Sarpi's biographer, Fulgenzio Micanzio, was highly critical of men who had claimed discoveries which he thought rightly belonged to Sarpi, including Galileo himself in the matter of the telescope.[13] Nevertheless, when Micanzio mentioned Sarpi's own tidal theory as having been set forth in a letter to one Marioti, he did not link it in any way with Galileo's theory based on the Copernican motions of the earth which had become widely known through the 1632 *Dialogue*, which was published long before Micanzio wrote his biography of Sarpi. Indeed, Micanzio had meanwhile carried out at Venice tidal observations on behalf of Galileo. Accordingly it is probable that the 1595 entries in Sarpi's notebooks summarized not his own theory, but one explained to him by Galileo during a visit to Venice in that year. Certain internal evidence in the entries tends to bear out this suggestion.

In Galileo's account of the tides a key analogy used was the disturbance of water being carried in a barge from the mainland to Venice, whenever the speed of the barge was changed. Thus if the barge struck an obstacle, the water contained in it ran back and forth for some time, rising and falling at the ends. Galileo's theory probably occurred to him while watching this effect during a trip to Venice, by analogy between this water and that of the sea beneath. If a sea-basin were moving irregularly, its waters should be set in oscillation and tides would result. Assuming that the earth had the two Copernican motions, one around its axis and the other around the sun, their speeds would be additive during half the day, while one would be subtracted from the other during the other half. A sea large enough to have water near one coast moving appreciably faster than that near the other should then exhibit tidal oscillations whose period would depend on length and depth, east-west orientation, period of return, and other factors in fluid motion, every such sea eventually settling into its own characteristic cycle of ebb and flow. Implications and further developments of this theory will be touched on later in connection with Kepler's thoughts on tides in 1597–98; Galileo's own mature account occupies the Fourth Day of his 1632 *Dialogue*.

III

It was in 1596 that Galileo composed a treatise on the measuring of heights and distances by sighting and triangulation[14] which survives as the appendix to a more important book he published ten years later. In 1595 or 1596 Galileo had devised an instrument for gunners that served all the purposes of two separate instruments introduced by Tartaglia in 1537, and some others as well. One of Tartaglia's instruments was an elevation gauge for cannons, consisting of a sort of carpenter's square with one arm longer than the other, a fixed quadrant arc divided into twelve equal arcs, and a plumb line hung from the vertex. The longer arm was placed in the mouth of the cannon, touching the bottom of the barrel, and the elevation was read in "points" of 7.5° each where the plumb line cut the quadrant. (That is how *point-blank* came to mean "dead level.") That this instrument was clumsy to carry around was of no concern to artillerymen.

In the same book Tartaglia described another instrument, the *squadra*, for estimating the distance and height of a target. It consisted of a rigid square with equal arms, having a smaller square fixed in it, facing the other direction and graduated into two "shadows" (*ombre*, a word borrowed from the sundial), one along either arm. Sights were provided along one arm, and a plumb line from the vertex crossed either the "right shadow" or the "versed shadow" according as the angle of sighting was less or greater than 45°. This instrument was also awkward to carry but could be used for topographical surveying, estimation of river widths, and various other practical problems.

In connection with his teaching of military architecture, in which the elevation gauge was in fact mentioned,[15] Galileo added some useful scales to its quadrant. Galileo's more elaborate quadrant was divided also into degrees, making it useful for astronomical observations during long marches; a clinometer scale was added for measuring the slope of a rampart,[16] and a double scale graduated from zero at the center to 100 at either end was provided. This last scale not only served all the purposes of the "shadows" on Tartaglia's other instrument, but also greatly simplified calculations by introducing a kind of decimal units. Need for two separate instruments was eliminated by measuring the elevation of a cannon in a different way, described below. The single combined instrument was made with equal arms and removable quadrant, hinged so that it could be conveniently carried in the field. For this instrument Galileo wrote his treatise on sighting and triangulation in 1596, not just for gunners but for surveyors as well.

In determining the elevation of a cannon, Galileo remarked, it was not without peril to stand in front of the gun exposed to enemy fire. It would be better to remain near the breech, where a gunner normally stood. The feet of the instrument were then placed on the gun's barrel and the elevation was read from the center of the quadrant rather than from one end. But because the metal of a cannon barrel thickens from mouth to breech, a "movable foot" was provided which slid along the forward arm and was fixed by a setscrew wherever required for a given gun.

Galileo's hinged *squadra* with its quadrant removed happened to be shaped like a drafting instrument, invented not long before by Guidobaldo, which was marked with a pair of scales on either face.[17] One scale was used for constructing regular polygons of a given number of sides in a circle whose diameter equaled the separation of the arms; the other gave equal divisions of a line into a given number of parts. Galileo engraved these scales, both being useful to military architects, on his instrument.

In 1597 new scales were added which transformed the device into a calculating instrument. First added were pairs of lines graduated according to the relative densities of various metals and stones, and according to the cube-root relation of diameter to volume. With these two scales, knowing the proper charge for a cannon of any bore and a ball of any material, gunners could quickly obtain the equivalent charge for any other bore and material of ball. Galileo called this the "problem of caliber," solved up to this time only approximately by referring to empirical tables with considerable risk of burst guns and wasted trial shots.

Galileo's density lines also bore markings for precious metals, useful to artisans and craftsmen in a variety of problems. By analogy to the cube-root lines, Galileo next added square-root lines useful in dealing with area problems. Scales for construction of a regular polygon on a line of given length, and others for equating the areas of different regular polygons, or circles and squares, completed the 1597 instrument. Galileo called it the "geometric and military compass" and composed a manual of instructions explaining its uses.[18] To this manual, his 1596 treatise on sighting and triangulation was added as an appendix.

In this form the calculating sector could be used to solve quickly any area problem of figures bounded by straight lines, but Galileo was not satisfied until it could deal with figures bounded by straight lines and circular arcs in any combination. He achieved this in 1598, and at that time made further changes that produced the first modern calculating instrument applicable to practical mathematical problems of every kind.

IV

Meanwhile Galileo's former colleague at Pisa, Jacopo Mazzoni, had published a book comparing Aristotelian and Platonic philosophies[19] which included a mistaken argument against Copernicus; he thought the increase in our visual horizon on ascending a mountain implied that changes should occur in our stellar horizon if the earth did not remain at the center, in contradiction of observation. In May 1597 Galileo wrote at length to explain why the reasoning had no weight against Copernican astronomy. The letter constitutes the first documentary evidence of Galileo's interest in Copernican astronomy. After remarking that his friend seemed to be coming round to some of Galileo's positions on other matters, he wrote:

But to tell the truth, however bravely I rested in those other positions, I was at first much confused and shaken to see your Excellency so resolute and outright in impugning the opinions of the Pythagoreans and Copernicans about the motion and place of the earth, which, being [now] held by me to be much more probable than that other view of Aristotle and Ptolemy, made me attend to your argument, as something on which (and on other things depending on it) I have some feelings. Therefore, trusting that your infinite friendship permits me without wounding you to say in defense of my idea what has occurred to me, I mention this to you so that either you may make known my error and correct me, or else, if your Excellency's reason is satisfied, the opinion of those great men and my own belief may not remain desolated.[20]

Galileo's parenthetical remark concerning things dependent on the Copernican astronomy alluded to his tidal theory. About this time Johann Kepler published his first book (*Prodromus . . . continens mysterium cosmographicum . . .*) and gave two copies to Paul Hamberger to be left with astronomers in Italy. Both were given to Galileo, who on 4 August 1597 wrote to thank Kepler in haste, explaining that he had had the book only a matter of hours without time to study it, though the return of Hamberger to Germany made it imperative for him to write at once. He rejoiced to see that Kepler supported Copernicus, whose view Galileo said he had now held for some years:

. . . as from that position I have discovered the causes of many physical effects which are perhaps inexplicable on the common hypothesis. I have written many reasons and refutations of contrary arguments which up to now I have preferred not to publish, intimidated by the fortune of our teacher Copernicus, who though he will be of immortal fame to some, is yet by an infinite number (for such is the multitude of fools) laughed at and rejected.[21]

Kepler's reply did not ask Galileo what physical effects Galileo thought were explained by the earth's motion, though he guessed correctly that these must be principally the tides. At the time he merely asked Galileo to undertake some careful astronomical observations, if he had suitable instruments, in the hope of detecting annual parallax in a fixed star. This effect is in fact so tiny that it was not definitely established until the nineteenth century, and Galileo did not even attempt to comply with Kepler's request. Writing to another friend a few months later, Kepler mentioned Galileo's letter and expressed his own view that no explanation of the tides could be correct which did not involve the moon, adding that anything caused by motion of the earth in the seas would be a forced motion, whereas the tides must be the result of natural motion. These events are of interest in showing how very different were Kepler's and Galileo's conceptions of scientific explanation. They also provide an opportunity here to clarify some common misunderstandings of Galileo's tidal theory by bringing in some further events of later years.

In 1609 Kepler offered his own tidal theory in the introduction to his most important astronomical book, the *Astronomia Nova*. There he stated that if our seas were not held back by their heaviness, they would be drawn to the moon, which attracted them as it rose above the horizon and passed overhead, creating a sort of tidal bulge. This sounds very much like the later explanation of tides given by Isaac Newton, especially in connection with some other remarks by Kepler in the same place. In fact, however, it would leave unexplained the occurrence of two high tides each lunar day and would not account for the absence of tides on islands, which would seem to be as much affected by a tidal bulge as the shores of seas. Kepler's suggestion also lacked any clue to the monthly changes from spring to neap tides and back, other than the vague and ancient notion of lunar dominion over the seas. Galileo, who in due course fitted all these phenomena (and in addition an annual change in size of tides) into his own mechanical tidal theory,[22] accordingly came to regard Kepler's theory as no better than the ancient ad hoc coupling of moon with tides and as giving not a scientific but an occult-property explanation. For saying so in his *Dialogue*, Galileo has been criticized on grounds that miss the point of his own tidal theory, and his conception of scientific explanation along with it.

Fundamental to Galileo's approach was the idea that any motion should be explained in terms of other motions, if possible, rather than by appeal to hidden causes. Lunar influence, like all the other celestial influences favored by astrologers, could be nothing more than such a hidden cause. Accordingly he began his explanation of the tides by considering the earth as having two independent motions, each circular, around two different centers, the sun and the earth's axis. With respect to the sun or to any other fixed star, widely separated points on the earth's surface must in general have different speeds, and any given point must have continually varying speeds throughout the day. So far as the rigid parts of the earth are concerned, differences in absolute speed (as Galileo called this) between separated points could have no effect, all the solid parts moving together. Water, however, does not immediately or uniformly receive changing speeds from its container, and it moreover tends to retain whatever speed it has; hence parts of water in a large sea-basin would be moved with respect to each other and with respect to the shores. Lakes, small seas, and seas extending no great distance from east to west even though large, would be affected little or not at all. Since water speedily flattens out when free to run, midsea islands experience no rise and fall of water, but where a long north-south coast impedes free flow, water will rise against it or flow back from it periodically as a result of this "primary cause of the tides," in Galileo's phrase.

In recent years it has become customary to say that Galileo's tidal theory could account for but one high tide per day, around noon, and one low tide around midnight. What might be said with some propriety, with proper qualifications for position of shore and for islands, would be that the primary cause alone would account for but one daily shift from high to low tide—a fact never denied by Galileo, though he did not connect either state with any particular time of day. Galileo's theory, however, invoked this primary cause not alone, but always in conjunction with a secondary cause which must *overpower* the primary cause immediately after high tide. This secondary cause was the weight of water which did not permit it to remain out of level, and which not only brought the water back to level but, as with a pendulum, went on to depress it nearly as much by reason of its tendency to retain speed as already mentioned. The period of oscillation from high to low tide was thus independent, or nearly so, from the period of cyclical disturbance of water by the primary cause, and the oscillations observed were connected in Galileo's theory with the east-west length of the sea and with its depth, being of greater period for wider and for shallower seas. Observation showed that for the Mediterranean this period was about six hours from high to low.

We may now return to the moon's association with the daily periods, asking why Galileo thought it unnecessary to account for that, or rather, seeing how he did account for it. His very interesting attitude toward this question has been overlooked by all critics, I believe, though nothing could be more significant with respect to Galileo's concept of scientific explanation. The only tides that had been observed over many centuries, he said, were those of the Mediterranean, which happen to be about six hours. Lunar influence was therefore not the cause of the tides, but the contrary; the tides were the cause of lunar influence theories, in his view. If the period were six hours and twelve minutes, it would be necessary that the tides at any port should recur in twenty-four hours forty-eight minutes, which is the period of the moon's return to a given position with respect to the meridian at any port; hence lunar theories would be bound to have arisen in lieu of proper scientific explanation. They therefore had no more value in Galileo's eyes than any other popular superstition.

Whatever one may think of Galileo's tidal theory, it should be noted that, taken as a whole, it accounted coherently for the phenomena known to him about tides around the Mediterranean, his description of which in the *Dialogue* is fairly detailed and accurate. Although Kepler's theory appears closer to that which is now accepted, it was in many ways less so, principally by reason of its omission of various considerations included by Galileo in his list of further factors, over and above those mentioned here.

Kepler lived all his life in southern Germany, Austria, and Bohemia, where he had no opportunity to observe tides and had to depend on indirect information. Doubtless this included the fact that for any particular place, the moon's position is closely linked to the state of the tide. It probably did not include the fact that for various places reasonably close to the same longitude, the widest differences in time of high tide may occur. Thus at Dover and Dieppe it was known to sixteenth-century sailors that high tide differed by an hour and a half, more than would be expected under the tidal-bulge theory if they were a thousand miles apart in longitude, so great are the local differences in those tides by reason of shape of basin, orientation of coast, position with respect to the English Channel currents, and so on. But some similar facts were known to Galileo; for example, he remarked that tides at Venice were reciprocal to those on the Syrian coast, though the latter should reciprocate at Gibraltar, while Venice was midway. He saw this to be a result of the length and orientation of the Adriatic, which transmitted the Mediterranean tide rather than having a tide of its own. Thus many seeming anomalies did not conflict with his tidal theory, as they did with the simple lunar attraction theory of Kepler.

V

Revision of Galileo's "military compass" and the manual of instructions for its use occupied much of his time during 1598. The problem of dealing with any area whatever bounded by straight lines and circular arcs in any combination came down to the devising of a scale for approximating the area of any segment of a circle. This Galileo succeeded in doing, but the "adjoined lines" (as he called them) required a double graduation, one for the half-chord and one for the altitude. Accordingly it had to be placed near the outer edge of each arm, where he had previously placed the scale for constructing a regular polygon on a given line. This was duly transferred to the place of Guidobaldo's polygonal line, which was eliminated because the more useful scale could also serve its purpose. Likewise, Guidobaldo's scale for division of lines into integral parts was replaced by a simple scale of equal fine graduations; this could be used for the same purpose with only a little more trouble, while it made possible also the solution of all rule-of-three problems, the most frequently occurring practical problems of all.

The "geometric and military compass" or sector of Galileo as made for him at Padua by Marcantonio Mazzoleni. This example, without clinometer scale, is owned by the Civic Collection of Applied Art and Engravings, Castello Sforzesco, Milan. Galileo's own instrument, preserved at the Museum of History of Science at Florence, is illustrated full size, showing both faces, in *Opere di Galileo*, 2:341.

With these alterations Galileo's sector became a calculating instrument capable of solving quickly and easily every practical mathematical problem that was likely to arise at the time. By March 1599 Galileo had greatly expanded his manual of instructions for the finished sector, following the order of the manual for the earlier design and adding to the appendix on triangulation a number of passages showing how to obviate tedious numerical calculations by utilizing the rule-of-three scale.

In July 1599 Galileo had Marcantonio Mazzoleni move into his house as his instrument maker, bringing his family and receiving rooms, meals, and a small annual stipend. Galileo furnished the brass blanks and other materials, paying Mazzoleni twenty-five lire for each finished instrument and selling these for thirty-five lire. Considering the cost of materials and of support for Mazzoleni, this cannot have been a very profitable operation, though it is often said that Galileo made his sector chiefly to augment his income. In a sense that is true, but the profit was not from manufacture and sale of his sector; it came from tuition fees (usually 120 lire) charged to students who wished to learn its uses. In 1600 Galileo entirely rewrote his manual of instruction for buyers of the instrument, now no longer primarily a military one. The "problem of caliber" was moved from the first to the twentieth chapter, the new manual opening with many uses of the rule-of-three lines including such ordinary problems as monetary exchange and compound interest.

In July 1599 Kepler wrote to Edmund Bruce, a Scot then residing at Padua who was deeply interested in astronomy. Kepler expressed surprise at having heard nothing further from Galileo. In fact Galileo had not made the observations Kepler had requested, having neither good astronomical instruments nor any interest in searching for parallax that had escaped the most diligent and well-equipped astronomers. Galileo's earliest known celestial observations came five years later and had, at the outset, no Copernican objective.[23] Kepler had meanwhile become interested in magnetism and believed that compass observations might give a clue to the original position of the earth's poles. He wanted information about magnetic dip at Padua, having secured such data from other cities. Bruce passed this letter on to Galileo, with whom he was anything but friendly.

In October Galileo was reappointed to his chair for four years at a salary of 320 florins, renewable two more years by mutual agreement. His financial situation became difficult soon afterward because of the marriage of his sister Livia, for whom he undertook to provide a large dowry jointly with his brother, a professional musician who was living in Germany. Galileo never married, but about this time he had entered into a liaison with a Venetian woman named Marina Gamba who was to bear him three children.[24] There is a story that an enemy of Galileo's tried to use the fact that he had taken a mistress to prevent his reappointment in 1599. The governors of the university are said to have reacted instead by saying that to keep a mistress Galileo would certainly need more money. The story is probably apocryphal, but its existence serves to illustrate the reputation for humane and liberal government enjoyed by the University of Padua.

VI

Galileo's early years at Padua were spent mainly in activities having a practical bearing, to judge from surviving documents alone. Yet there must have been lively discussions of which no record remains, which continued to affect Galileo's convictions and acquainted him with counterarguments he would later have to meet in defending them.

The home of G. V. Pinelli was, until his death in 1601, a mecca for intellectuals at Padua and for traveling scholars. At the disposal of his friends was an enormous library of books and manuscripts, literary, philosophical, and scientific. Pinelli greatly admired Fra Paolo Sarpi for the breadth and accuracy of his knowledge, and it was probably at his house that Galileo, who had briefly resided there, first met Sarpi. Paolo Gualdo, Lorenzo Pignoria, and Antonio Querengo (who replaced Pinelli as Padua's leading intellectual host after 1601) were among the distinguished men of letters outside the university who became friends of Galileo at Pinelli's home. There Galileo met cardinals Robert Bellarmine and Cesare Baronius, as well as G. B. della Porta and Marino Ghetaldi when they visited Padua.

At the University of Padua the faculties of medicine and of philosophy were especially famous. At the time of Galileo's arrival the first chair of philosophy was held by Francesco Piccolomini and the second chair by Cesare Cremonini. It had long been the custom that those chairs should hold the best available champions of opposing schools of thought. In 1601 Cremonini moved to the first chair. He had originally been appointed to replace Giacomo Zabarella, whose writings on logic, natural philosophy, and proper methods in science represented the apex of enlightened Aristotelianism after a century of vigorous debate at Padua. By the traditional alternation of chairs, Cremonini's ranking position from 1601 on meant that Zabarella's championship of logic against mathematics in science was again dominant at Padua. It can hardly be doubted that much thoughtful debate between the best mathematician and the ablest philosopher in Italy before 1604 preceded the spirited confrontation between Galileo and Cremonini destined to occur in that year.

Glimpses are also caught of another group at Padua, partly inside and partly outside the university, of men who had a taste for alchemy, astrology, and arcane speculation. Angelo Ingegneri, friend of Torquato Tasso, knew and liked these men but felt with Galileo that their pursuits were at best vain and at worst pernicious.[25] Active opposition to Galileo existed almost from his first days at Padua which, in his opinion, was ultimately traceable to one archenemy who "was always studying diabolical books";[26] the reference appears to be to alchemy, which Galileo derided in his *Dialogue*.[27] A leader in this group was Giacomo Antonio Gromo, an elderly former soldier who settled in Padua to pursue studies of alchemy and medicine until his death in 1603. Others hostile to Galileo in this faction were Edmund Bruce, Baldessar Capra, his father Aurelio, and his tutor Simon Mayr.

Thus the most advanced Aristotelian philosophy of science, much intelligent interest in science by literary and religious leaders, and the active pursuit of science from a mystical viewpoint were all well represented around Galileo during his early years at Padua. Toward the mystics he remained cool if not contemptuous. Progressive Aristotelianism attracted him, but he disliked the commitment of its advocates to defend every saying of Aristotle against contradiction. Best of all he liked the tolerant though critical spirit of the literary circle, in which restless curiosity and concern for common sense, good manners, and style prevented any system from becoming the sole arbiter of all knowledge. With that circle Galileo shared delight in the dialect of the Paduan countryside which had become a vogue in the sixteenth century through plays and dialogues written by Angelo Beolco under the pseudonym Ruzzante. Since this was to become important in Galileo's first known public dispute, a word about it here is in order.

Sophisticated poets early in the sixteenth century produced a literature (called Arcadian) in which the supposedly simple, honest life of the peasant shamed courtiers and city dwellers. This absurdly idealistic notion of bucolic bliss was ridiculed by Ruzzante, who knew at first hand the hard realities of peasant life and delighted in their wit and vulgarity about it. In his writings he presented country people in ordinary pursuits, speaking rudely and to the point. Intellectuals who disliked polite pretense and affectation were captivated, and the rustic dialect became popular among them. Ruzzante's homely characters knew that reasoning is the property of every man, that sharpers use it to impose on the simple, and that brute facts are not made pleasant by talking around them. Such views were not unrelated to the development of Galileo's concept of physical science,[28] while their academically disreputable source assured its immediate unpopularity with the official custodians of philosophical propriety.

FOUR

1600-1602

I

THE *Seicento* OPENED for Galileo rather appropriately with a new theme when his collaboration was sought by a distinguished foreigner in a field he had neglected. On 3 January 1600 the astronomer Tycho Brahe wrote to G. V. Pinelli asking him to induce Galileo to correspond with him. There was an ulterior motive. Tycho told Pinelli he was sending a young assistant, Francis Tengnagel, to Italy, but did not tell him that his purpose was to find some scientist abroad who would write a laudatory biography with which the Danish astronomer wished to impress the Holy Roman Emperor. This project had later repercussions at Rome and Bologna, but here we are concerned only with its relation to Galileo.[1]

Upon Tengnagel's return home he was able to report that Galileo had read Tycho's *Astronomical Letters*, which suggests that he had conversed with Galileo and had mentioned the prospective biography. On 4 May Tycho wrote directly to Galileo, describing his astronomical system as superior to those of Aristotle or Copernicus and inviting correspondence. Galileo did not reply, probably knowing what lay behind the flattering invitation. Antipathy toward Tycho in Galileo's later writings may have had its basis in this incident. Sagredo was briefly involved in negotiations between Tycho and Magini at Tengnagel's request, but later Tengnagel wrote very disparagingly of Sagredo and Galileo to Magini.[2]

Serious financial problems began in 1601 for Galileo when his sister Livia married Taddeo Galletti. Galileo undertook to pay

50

a dowry of 1,800 ducats, 800 payable immediately and the balance of 1,000 at 200 per year for five years. His salary was still only 320 ducats, but he understood that his brother Michelangelo would share the burden. Galileo had to borrow 600 ducats at once; he wrote to his brother (then in Poland) for his share and legal acknowledgment of further obligation. Michelangelo, however, resented the generous dowry Galileo had decided on, and by May 1602 Galileo had to apply for a two-year advance against his salary, receiving half that amount.

It was probably financial pressure that induced Galileo to expand greatly his private tutoring at this time. His account books for 1601–7[3] give a picture of those activities and suggest a probable pattern for earlier and later years, for which the records are sketchy. In each year tabulated he had about twenty students, mainly in four private courses.

Course	Times Given 1601–7	No. of Students Total	No. of Students Average	Nationality of Students German	Polish	French	Italian	?
Fortification	6	25	4	17	3	4		1
Use of sector	7	42	6	18	6	4	1	13
Cosmography	3	13	4	3	9			1
Euclid	3	14	5	4		6	1	3

Other private courses given during the same period included Arithmetic, two students (1601); Optics, five students (1601); Mechanics, four students (1602); Surveying, one student (1602). Use of the sector had also been taught in 1598, 1599, and 1600, and was again given in 1608 and 1609.

The course in cosmography was first mentioned in Galileo's account books at Padua in June 1602, and though it may have been offered by him earlier it is probable that the interesting short preface on method was first added about that time to the much older text mentioned in chapter 1. As will be seen from the opening sentence, this addition appears to have been written by Galileo as a memorandum to himself in connection with an intended revision which was not carried out, the memorandum being simply copied by the scribe as the opening part of the syllabus sold to Galileo's students:

In the Treatise on the Sphere (which we shall more appropriately call Cosmography), as in other sciences, the subject should be [first] pointed out, and then we should touch on the order and method to be followed in this [science].

Accordingly, we say that the subject of Cosmography is the world, or we mean the universe, as indicated by the word [cosmography] itself, which only means "description of the world." But of everything that might be considered about the world, only a part belongs to the Cosmographer, which is to reflect on the number and order of the parts of this world and the shape, size, and distance of [each of] these, and especially about their motions, leaving to the Natural Philosophers consideration of the qualities of the said parts of the world.

As to the method, the Cosmographer customarily proceeds in his reflections in four ways, the first of which embraces the appearances, or phenomena, and these are nothing but sensate observations we see every day, as for example the rising and setting of stars; the darkening now of the sun and again of the moon; the latter's showing herself now crescent, now at quarter, now full, and again completely dark; the moving of the planets with very different motions; and many other such appearances. In the second place there are hypotheses, and these are nothing but some suppositions relating to the structure of the celestial orbs such as correspond with the appearances, as it would be when, guided by what appears to us, we should assume the heavens to be spherical and to be moved circularly, sharing diverse motions, [and] the earth to be stable, situated at the center. Third there follow geometrical demonstrations with which, by means of some properties of circles and straight lines, the particular events that follow from the hypotheses are demonstrated. And finally, what has been demonstrated by lines being [then] calculated by arithmetical operations, [this] is reduced to tables from which without trouble we may later at our pleasure find the arrangement of the celestial bodies at any moment of time.[4]

On the face of it there is nothing at all remarkable today about this description of the method of the cosmographer; it is simply a statement of scientific method as generally understood in the nineteenth century and as taught to me from a book printed in 1925. In Galileo's day, however, the prevailing notion of scientific method was quite different, at least as taught in the universities from Aristotle's *Posterior Analytics* and as debated by philosophers. In the above statement the phrase "as in the other sciences" suggests that Galileo viewed the method of the cosmographer as applicable quite generally; yet nothing was included concerning principles or causes, the starting point and goal of all sciences as viewed by philosophers.

The direct source of Galileo's statement was, as might be expected, the introductory chapter of Ptolemy's *Almagest*. Ptolemy was in fact the first great scientific cosmographer, writing on both geography and astronomy. He began the *Almagest* by remarking that Aristotle had divided theoretics into three classes: physical, mathematical, and theological (or metaphysical). No agreement was to be hoped for among philosophers, he said, in the first and third of these, for the ultimate nature of matter is hidden from us and metaphysics is amenable only to thought or conjecture. In the mathematical theory of the heavens, on the other hand, agreement can be reached by proceeding from appearances to hypotheses and thence to geometric and arithmetic demonstrations based thereon. But Ptolemy did not extend these remarks beyond the realm of astronomy, and if others had done so for physics, or even for the specific science of motion (as Galileo was destined to do), I have not run across an example. In any event the most probable direct source of Galileo's conception was Ptolemy's *Almagest*.

The Alexandrian school of which Ptolemy was a late representative originated about 300 B.C. The home of the Aristotelian school remained at Athens for some time thereafter, Theophrastus succeeding Aristotle as head of the Lyceum and being in turn followed by Strato of Lampsacus, who for a time had lived at Alexandria as tutor to Ptolemy II. I consider it very dubious to look upon Ptolemy's astronomy as Platonist in spirit (as many do) simply because it emphasized mathematics. It was Aristotle, not Plato, whom Ptolemy explicitly cited, and Ptolemy was concerned above all with the fitting of mathematical demonstrations to actual appearances in the world of sense, a world which Plato considered essentially illusory. The distinctively quantitative aspect of Alexandrian science (as distinguished from Athenian science) had made its appearance around 250 B.C. with Eratosthenes and his friend Archimedes. Though at first, with Archimedes, empirical data played no evident role, observation and measurement soon became of prime importance, and the separation of quantitative astronomy from causal physics had already been recommended by Geminus two centuries before

Ptolemy,[5] perhaps to obviate interference by philosophers in much the way Galileo was to attempt later.

There was a good reason for Galileo to add his remarks on method in 1602 to his earlier syllabus on cosmography, for meanwhile he had come to prefer the Copernican astronomy and could not in good conscience teach as a fact that the earth was motionless and at the center of the universe, something he had been able to do until 1595. Without revising his old treatise, however, he could teach those things as hypotheses based on appearances, and it is worthy of note that he specifically included them as examples of just that in the introduction translated above. Coming to the motion of the earth in his treatise, he then said:

> The present question is worthy of consideration inasmuch as there have not been lacking very great philosophers and mathematicians who, deeming the earth to be a star, have made it movable. Nevertheless, following the opinion of Aristotle and Ptolemy, we shall adduce those reasons for which it may be believed entirely stable.[6]

The earth cannot have a straight motion, Galileo went on to argue, remarking that in any event no one had ever denied this:

> But that it may be moved circularly is more probable, and has therefore been believed by some, moved principally by their opinion that it is an almost impossible thing that the whole universe except the earth should make a revolution from east to west and back to east again in twenty-four hours; whence they have believed rather that the earth in that time makes one revolution from west to east. Ptolemy, considering this opinion, argues as follows to destroy it.

Without committing himself, Galileo went on to outline Ptolemy's arguments, interestingly including one from centrifugal force mistakenly attributed to Ptolemy by Copernicus. Nothing was said about the Copernican annual motion of the earth, which was irrelevant in any case to the principal matters dealt with in cosmography. These concerned definitions and explanations of horizon, meridian circle, equator, zodiac, colures, tropics, and polar circles; right and oblique ascensions of stars, the seasons, life in various climatic zones, latitude and longitude, eclipses, and lunar phases. A final section dealt with the phenomenon of precession of the equinoxes and the introduction after Ptolemy of two additional spheres to account for the supposed motion of trepidation.

Planetary motions were not discussed by Sacrobosco, though in the final chapter of his *Sphere* he defined the terms *eccentric*, *epicycle*, and *equant*. Galileo omitted those definitions from his *Cosmography*, since planetary theory was taught as a separate study and they belonged properly to that course. It had long been the practice in universities to separate planetary theory from spherical astronomy, so that the charge frequently made by historians that Galileo hypocritically concealed his Copernican preference in his *Cosmography* is entirely unfounded.

II

In volume 81 of the Galilean manuscripts there are many horoscopes and related calculations by Galileo belonging probably to the years 1601–2 for the most part. The horoscopes relate to members of his own family, friends, students, and some unidentified persons. Sagredo was the subject of particularly detailed astrological calculations. Among these papers (f. 32) there is also a drawing related to the "wheel of Aristotle," suggesting that Galileo's analysis of that paradox began very early and perhaps put him on to the consideration of continuous magnitude on which he wrote a treatise, now lost, while at Padua. The paradox originated in the ancient *Questions of Mechanics*,[7] as had the 1594 preface to Galileo's syllabus on mechanics which was substantially altered and expanded about this time.

Galileo's course on mechanics given in 1602 was probably based on expansion of his earlier brief syllabus into a substantial treatise of which several contemporary manuscript copies exist. This important treatise is difficult to date with certainty, but since it contains no mention of the law of falling bodies, which was known to Galileo in 1604, it was probably written before that year. Galileo was seriously ill in 1603, and in that year his attention seems to have been turned to investigations of motion as such, starting from the concept of *moment* introduced in the expanded treatise on mechanics. Various bits of evidence make the period 1601–2 the most probable time of composition of Galileo's *Mechanics* into essentially final form. Early in 1602 Sagredo sent Galileo two screw-cutting machines for adjustment and mentioned a perpetual screw of the kind Galileo had discussed at the end of his previous syllabus. In April 1602 Galileo wrote to Baccio Valori to say that he would bring a model of his water-raising machine to Florence that summer. These and other evidences of Galileo's special interest in mechanical problems during this period justify the assumption that his *Mechanics* as we have it was mainly completed at Padua by 1602. How different it was in approach from the Pisan *De motu* will become apparent in the ensuing summary of its contents.

The prefatory section of the revised *Mechanics*[8] was entitled "On the utilities that are derived from mechanical science and its instruments." No longer was there any promise to reveal causes as in the 1594 preface. Now it was declared that people were mistaken in believing that they could "raise very great weights with a small force, as if with their machines they could cheat nature, whose instinct—nay, whose most firm constitution —is that no resistance can be overcome by a force that is not more powerful than it. How false such a belief is I hope to make most evident with true and rigorous demonstrations that we shall have as we go along."

Galileo proceeded to explain that given any weight and any distance, it is obviously possible to move the weight through the distance with any arbitrary force, however small, simply by dividing the weight into suitable small pieces. This operation is conducted not by a force smaller than the weight, but by a force that acts many times through the distance that the whole weight traverses only once. The speed of the operation is reduced by the extra time necessarily consumed; one could say that nature had been cheated only if the same speed were maintained by the small force as by a great one, which Galileo said was simply impossible. He then remarked that one great advantage of using a machine is that a great weight can be moved all at once without division into pieces, which is often desired, but that the price paid is a loss in speed equivalent to the gain in power. Another advantage of machines is the convenience of applying force in certain ways when direct application would be awkward. Finally, machines permit the use of inanimate forces, or the strength of animals, in place of more valuable manpower.

The text proper began with three definitions in the spirit of Euclid and Archimedes. First, "heaviness" (*gravità*) was defined as the tendency to move naturally downward; in solid bodies this is greater or less according to the amount of matter present. Next, "moment" was defined as the tendency to move downward caused not just by the weight, but also by the arrangement of heavy bodies, as when we place a given weight far from the center along the arm of a balance. In this way a small weight may balance a larger one. Later in the text Galileo named speed as a factor in moment. "Center of gravity" was defined as that point in a body around which parts of equal moments are arranged, a definition previously given by Commandino.

To the definitions there were adjoined three suppositions or postulates: (1) A heavy body will move down along the line joining its center of gravity to the general center of all heavy things. (2) Heavy bodies receive every impetus or heaviness in their centers of gravity as the seat of every moment. (3) The center of gravity of two equal weights is in the middle of the straight line joining their centers of gravity. Galileo was then prepared to give a quite remarkable proof of the lever law, much easier to follow than the classic proof by Archimedes and differing from it in a very interesting way. In the classic proof, which may have been taken by Archimedes from a still earlier source,[9] the law is first proved for cases in which the distances of the weights from the point of balance are commensurable, and is then extended to incommensurable distances. In effect the proof proceeds by breaking up the weights into unit pieces equally spaced along the lever arm and then considering the centers of gravity of two groupings. In Galileo's proof, the original case is that of a homogeneous rod or bar, which is subsequently divided at any arbitrary point. The distinction of commensurable-incommensurable is thus eliminated, appeal being made to the Eudoxian theory of proportionality.

Therefore imagine the heavy solid *CFDE*, of uniform density and of uniform size throughout, such as a cylinder or similar figure. Let this be suspended by its endpoints *C* and *D*, from the line *AB*, equal in length to the solid. Now dividing this line *AB* equally at the point *G*, and suspending it from this point,

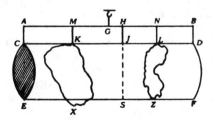

there can be no doubt that it will balance in this point *G*, because the line drawn from the point straight to the center of the earth would pass through the center of gravity of the solid *CF*. And of the latter, parts of equal *moments* would exist around such a line; and it would be the same if from the points *A* and *B* there were suspended the two halves of the heavy body *CF*. Next suppose the said heavy body to be cut into two unequal parts along the line *JS*; it is obvious that the part *CS* (as also the other part *SD*) would no longer remain in position, having no other supports than the two strings *AC* and *BD*. Therefore, coming to the point *J*, suppose a new string to be added, tied at the point *H* perpendicularly above the cut *JS*; this then sustains jointly both parts of the solid in their pristine state. Hence it follows that no change being made either of weight or of position in the parts of the solid with respect to the line *AB*, the same point *G* remains the center of equilibrium as it has been from the first. Moreover, since the part *CS* of the solid is connected to the balance through the two strings *CA* and *JH*, there can be no doubt that if we cut these two strings and add a single other at *MK*, equidistant from these two, then since the center of gravity of the solid *CS* lies directly beneath this, the solid will not change or move its place, but will keep the same position with respect to the line *AH*. And doing the same with the other part, *JF* (that is, cutting the strings *HJ* and *BD*, and adding in the center the sole suspension *NL*), it is likewise apparent that this will not vary its site or relation with respect to the balance *AB*. Hence the parts of the whole solid *CF* being the same with respect to the balance *AB* as they have been all along, *CS* hanging from the point *M* and *SD* from the point *N*, there is no doubt that equilibrium will still exist at the same point *G*. Now here it begins to become apparent that the two weights *CS* (the greater) and *SD* (the lesser), hanging from the ends of the line *MN*, must be of equal *moment* and give rise to equilibrium in the point *G*, the distance *GN* being greater than *GM*.

   To carry out our full intent it now remains only for us to demonstrate that the ratio which exists between the weights *CS* and *SD* exists also between the distances *NG* and *GM*; and this will not be difficult to prove. For the line *MH* being one-half the line *HA*, and *NH* being half of *HB*, all *MN* will be one-half the whole line *AB*, of which *BG* is also one-half. Hence *MN* and *GB* will be equal to one another; and from these taking away the common part *GN*, the remainder *MG* will be equal to the remainder *NB*, to which *NH* is likewise equal; whence *MG* is equal to *NH*; and adding the part *GH* to both, *MH* will equal *GN*. Now, having already demonstrated that *MG* equals *HN*, that ratio which line *MH* has to *HN*, distance *NG* will have to distance *GM*; but the ratio of *MH* to *HN* is that of *KJ* to *JL*, and of its double *CJ* to the double *JD*—and in a word, of the solid *CS* to the solid *SD*, of which solids the line *CJ* and *JD* are the lengths. Hence it is concluded that the ratio of distance *NG* to distance *GM* is the same as that of the size of the solid *CS* to the size of the solid *SD*; which, manifestly, is the same as the ratio of the weights [*gravità*] of those same solids.

And from what has been said it seems to me clearly understood not only how the two unequal heavy bodies *CS* and *SD* weigh equally when hanging from distances inversely proportional [to their weights], but moreover how, in the nature of things, this is the same effect as if equal weights were suspended at equal distances, since in a certain sense the heaviness of the weight *CS* virtually spreads out beyond the support at *G*, and that of the weight *SD* shrinks back from it, as any speculative mind can understand by examining closely what has been said about the present diagram. And, the same heaviness of the weights and the same boundaries of the suspensions being maintained, even though the shapes are varied by reduction to spherical or some other shapes such as *X* and *Z*, it will not be doubted that the same equilibrium will follow, shape being a qualitative circumstance and powerless to alter weight, which derives rather from quantity. Hence we conclude in general that it is true that unequal weights weigh equally when suspended from unequal distances having inversely the same ratio as the weights.

Having established the lever law, Galileo proceeded to apply it to the capstan or winch and to the pulley; pulley systems of any complexity were analyzed in the manner that had been devised by Guidobaldo. Then, to introduce the screw, Galileo discussed the inclined plane. His derivation of equilibrium conditions followed that in *De motu* but eliminated the concept of speeds in favor of that of moments.[10] As preface to this discussion Galileo asserted that on a perfectly horizontal plane

a spherical body would remain still, though with a disposition to be moved by an extremely small force. For we have understood that if such a plane tilted by only a hair, the said ball would move spontaneously toward the lower side and would on the other hand have resistance toward the higher side, nor could it be moved in that direction without force. Hence it is clear that on an exactly level surface the ball would remain at rest, so that any the least force would be sufficient to move it, just as on the other hand any little resistance, such as that merely of the surrounding air, would be capable of holding it still. From this we may take it as an indubitable axiom that heavy bodies, all external and adventitious impediments being removed, can be moved in the horizontal plane by any minimal force.

A discussion based on examples of motion over a mirror or a frozen lake now replaced Galileo's two formal mathematical demonstrations of the same proposition in *De motu*. This does not mean that he had turned away from Archimedean procedures, but rather that in writing physics from a practical standpoint he preferred to emphasize actual observation interspersed with mathematical proofs, as he was to do again in his book on bodies in water. In the present instance this approach meant that he did not need to include his former specification in *De motu* that the surface of the earth is not level, but spherical, so that a body moving literally horizontally would necessarily be rising as it departed from the single point of tangency with the earth. That fact, unimportant in practical applications, constituted merely one of the adventitious impediments listed in *De motu* so far as the *Mechanics* was concerned. In *De motu*, where the approach was purely theoretical, the fact that the earth's surface is not literally horizontal demanded notice; in the *Mechanics* it was an accidental circumstance. Thus for the purposes of practical mechanics Galileo regarded inertial motions as horizontal, whereas for the purposes of theoretical analysis any inertial motion was necessarily maintained equidistant at all times from the center toward which the unsupported body would naturally move. This continued to be his practice later on, giving rise to modern debates over the illusory question which treatment Galileo himself regarded as correct for every possible purpose. Either the treatment in *De motu* or that in the *Mechanics* was legitimate, since Galileo did not rest the two on the same assumptions or demonstrations, and it is necessary in reading his works on physics to notice the context, theoretical or practical, of each particular discussion by Galileo.

The derivation of equilibrium conditions on inclined planes in the *Mechanics* was that of *De motu* but with some refinements, apart from the elimination of speeds in favor of moments. It began this time with a remark about the error of Pappus in presuming that some arbitrary force is needed to move any body along the horizontal plane. "It will be better," Galileo said, "given the force that would move the object vertically upward (which will equal the weight of the object), to seek the force that will move it on the horizontal plane. This we shall attempt to do, with an attack different from that of Pappus." Galileo then noted that it is only at the beginning of motion—the point of tangency with the vertical circle in his diagram taken from *De motu*—that the tendency to move downward is the same along the inclined plane and along the arc of the circle. That noted, a relationship was established between motions beginning along an inclined plane, along the arc of a circle supporting the body, or along the same arc when supported from the center of the circle as in the case of the pendulum. This opened a new field for investigations that were soon to follow. Next, Galileo turned to consider the screw as an inclined plane wrapped around a cylinder, which had been his main purpose in introducing the inclined plane in this work. The chapter ended by explaining why the different distances moved by two bodies connected over a pulley by a rope, one moving along an incline and the other vertically, did not invalidate Galileo's general conclusion that any gain in power is offset by loss in speed:

since heavy bodies do not have any resistance to transverse motions except in proportion to their removal from the center of the earth. . . . Therefore it is very important to consider along what lines the motions are made, and especially by inanimate heavy bodies, whose moments have their whole power and their entire resistance in the line perpendicular to the horizon; for in other lines, transversely rising or falling, they have only a power, impetus, or resistance that is greater or less according as the inclinations approach more or less to the vertical.

This laid the basis for relating all static forces to simple weights, taking account of directions.

The penultimate chapter explained the Archimedean water-screw, much as in the earlier texts of 1593–94. As in those versions, the treatise ended with a supplementary essay on the force of percussion, brushing aside the pseudo-Aristotelian discussion in the *Questions of Mechanics* and considering simple falling weights or bodies driven horizontally by impact. In this section Galileo adopted the idea that the product of speed and weight ought to be constant for a given force:

And in brief, it is seen in all other instruments that any great resistance may be moved by any given little force, provided that the space through which this force is moved shall have to the space through which the resistant shall be moved that ratio which exists between this large resistant and the small force; and this is by the necessary constitution of nature.[11]

The discussion remained unsatisfactory, but a related remark about connected systems in Galileo's previous discussion of the lever law made it natural for him to integrate effects of speed with his concept of moment. Speaking of unequal bodies placed in equilibrium on a lever, he wrote:

The heavy body *A* being placed at the point *D*, and the other [*B*] at the point *E*, it will not be unreasonable that the former, falling slowly to *A*, raises the latter swiftly to *B*, restoring with its heaviness that which comes to be lost by its slowness of motion. And from this reasoning we may arrive at the knowledge that speed of motion is capable of increasing moment in the moveable body in the same ratio as that in which this speed of motion is increased.[12]

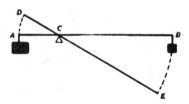

III

A letter from Sagredo to Galileo on 8 August 1602 shows that Galileo had been making experiments with samples of lodestone, fitting them with armatures (steel casings) to increase their efficiency. This work had doubtless been stimulated by William Gilbert's book on the magnet, published in 1600, of which Galileo was given a copy by a philosopher (probably Cremonini) who, he said, seemed afraid to keep it on his shelves lest it infect his other books.[13] Very likely these experiments recalled to Galileo's mind Kepler's letter to Bruce three years before, in which a theory of magnetic clues to the original position of the earth's axis had been mentioned and experimental determinations of magnetic dip at Padua had been requested. Either in that connection, or because he recalled Kepler's supposed rule relating planetary speeds to their distances from the sun, Galileo soon began to expound something to his friends that induced Edmund Bruce to write to Kepler, on 15 August 1602, that Galileo was advancing to his students and others certain of Kepler's ideas as his own. Bruce added that he had done and was doing all he could to have the honor redound to Kepler's credit and not Galileo's. As it happened, Kepler had moved to Prague and Bruce's letter was returned undelivered. For a time he thought Kepler dead, and then wrote again a year later to repeat the same charge in 1603. A page of calculations found among Galileo's notes on motion may throw light on what he had said in 1602 that caused Bruce to attribute his ideas to Kepler.[14]

Kepler's *Prodromus* had been occupied mainly with accounting for the number of planets and the sizes of their orbits, relating the construction of the universe to the five Platonic solids by means of nested spheres inscribed in and circumscribed around those geometrical figures. Galileo never commented on that speculation, unless it was when he said later that Kepler's manner of philosophizing was very bold, perhaps too bold, and quite different from his own.[15] In chapter 20, however, Kepler tried to relate the speeds of the planets to their distances from the sun. (When he reprinted the book a quarter-century later, having meanwhile found the true relationship, Kepler added notes chiding himself for an error he had made in his original attempt.) This had led in 1596 to a seemingly remarkable agreement of observations with a specious rule relating planetary speeds and mean solar distances. Kepler's original tabulation must have been very striking to Galileo, however little he was willing to accept Kepler's rationalization of the figures he had obtained.

The calculations I assign to 1602 are on f. 146,[16] where there is but a single abbreviated word, *mom*[*ent*], which nevertheless identifies the nature of the calculations. Galileo took from Kepler's book certain numbers to use for the relative distances of the outer planets from the sun. As a matter of fact the figures in question were not distances at all, but times; they were the numbers of days calculated by Kepler for a complete revolution of Saturn in its orbit, and for a complete revolution about the sun in each other orbit if the planet there moved not with its own speed but with Saturn's. The ratios of those artificial periods were therefore the same as the ratios of the orbital circumferences, and hence as the orbital radii, so that for Galileo's purposes they would serve, he being concerned only with ratios and not with individual distances.

Having noted in his *Mechanics* that the moment of a heavy body remained the same if reduction of its weight were offset by a corresponding increase in its speed, Galileo wondered whether something analogous would account for the greater speeds of planets the nearer they were to the sun. One could think of each planet as on the arm of a lever with the sun at the fulcrum; its *moment* would then be the product of its distance from the sun and its weight, if it had weight. Weight had no meaning for planets,[17] but speed did; and if speed and weight could exactly offset one another, why could not weight vanish and be replaced by speed alone? This idea started Galileo calculating, but he quickly found that the moments implied for Saturn and Jupiter were the wrong way around, and Saturn should outrun Jupiter instead of the reverse. Hence Galileo sought a place beyond Saturn from which to measure distances, instead of from the sun, while preserving the observed speed ratios and equalizing the moments. He then used the same point to get a distance for Mars, and using the relative speeds of Saturn and Mars he computed their "moments"; but these did not balance, and with that failure the f. 146 computations ended.

Many years later (in his *Dialogue*) Galileo asserted that a place could be found beyond Saturn from which all the planets could have been dropped in uniformly accelerated motion toward the sun, each reaching its observed orbital speed at its present distance from the sun.[18] The statement is incorrect, but in a curious way; it is wrong by a factor of two, so to speak, and is not simply unrelated to facts. Newton later showed that the sun's gravitational force would have to be doubled at the instant each planet was turned into its orbit, if they attained their speeds as in Galileo's hypothesis.[19] Since Galileo did not even know the law of free fall in 1602, and never suggested the existence of universal gravitation, his idea could not have originated from any calculations like those of Newton. Hence it seems odd that his suggestion was related in any simple way to them.

Now, by following Galileo's own procedure on f. 146 and extending this to comparisons of the distance and speed of Saturn with those of each other planet in the same manner employed by him for Jupiter, certain ratios may be obtained which are very different from those that Kepler had published in 1596. These are shown in the following tabulation, expressed (anachronistically) in decimal fractions for ease of comparison. It is not unreasonable to suppose that Galileo himself computed similar ratios, on a sheet no longer extant, and in that way perceived in 1602 a relation from which he later derived the erroneous conjecture that he included in the *Dialogue*.

	Distance Ratio of Saturn to Planet	*Speed Ratio of Planet to Saturn*	*Square Root of Distance Ratio*
Saturn	1.00	1.00	1.00
Jupiter	1.75	1.42	1.32
Mars	6.03	2.60	2.46
Earth	9.17	3.17	3.03
Venus	12.75	3.71	3.57
Mercury	24.79	5.06	4.98

The similarity of ratios in the last two columns is of course no accident; it is now expressed by saying that the squares of planetary orbital speeds are proportional to the reciprocals of their distances from the sun. Hence it is little wonder that the conjecture Galileo later based on this, though mistaken, was systematically related to Newton's correct analysis. Galileo would have regarded it as a relation of each planet to Saturn, not as a relation between every pair of planets, and he would have expressed it in the language of proportionality familiar to him by saying that the speed of any planet was to Saturn's speed as the distance of Saturn is to the mean proportional between that distance and the distance of the planet. That was not at all what Kepler had published in 1596, but to Bruce it may well have seemed that anything Galileo was saying about planetary distances and speeds must have been taken from Kepler without acknowledgment.

Later on, after Galileo had discovered the law of free fall, he was apparently deceived by a superficial resemblance between the statement above and a consequence of that law, formulating the conjecture that he published in the *Dialogue* as a result. This will be discussed in chapter 8, § IV.

IV

The watermark on f. 146, discussed above, is an imperial eagle. Only one other sheet among Galileo's notes on motion, f. 173, bears the same watermark. This sheet contains nothing but some diagrams and a brief notation concerning the *moments* of balls beginning their descents from the same point and moving down different inclined planes to the horizontal. One of the diagrams on f. 173 probably led Galileo to his first correct result about motions along inclined planes, found on f. 180r. This result was used by Galileo early in the 1632 *Dialogue* for the purpose of explaining a certain fact about accelerated motions to the general reader,[20] but it was not included as a theorem in *Two New Sciences*. Its place was there taken by a more general proposition[21] which Galileo derived in 1604, after he had recast the result recorded on f. 180r to express it in terms of impetus rather than in terms of *moment*.[22]

The interesting result obtained on f. 180r was that in the time that a body starting from rest will reach a given point along an incline, it would in vertical descent reach the point of intersection with the vertical by a perpendicular to the incline drawn from the point reached in the incline.

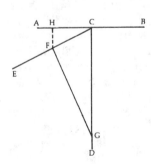

If a circle is drawn through points *C*, *F*, and *G*, a simple and effective proof of equal times along *CF* and *CG* follows from what I shall call "Galileo's theorem" in the next section, where it is discussed. The absence of such a circle in the above diagram, together with the unconvincing proof on f. 180r which Galileo based at this time on an unsupported assertion relating *moments* to times, makes it highly probable that when he announced this proposition he had not yet discovered the important rule of equality of times for descents along chords of vertical circles, sent to Guidobaldo late in 1602.

In the same handwriting as that of f. 180r Galileo wrote out on another sheet two propositions relating to the *moment of heaviness* of a body falling vertically or descending along an inclined plane.[23] No folio number can now be assigned to that sheet, the two propositions mentioned having later been cut from it by Galileo to paste over an abandoned proof on f. 179, probably in 1606. Likewise, f. 180 is now a cut sheet from which a memorandum was removed that now survives only in a copy made in 1618 at Florence. The earliest proof of Galileo's theorem, to be discussed below, is on another cut sheet, f. 160,[24] in handwriting very similar to that of the propositions just mentioned. These probably all belong to 1602, when it appears that Galileo, having revised and expanded his *Mechanics*, decided to write a new treatise on motion. Several propositions for this were neatly written out before he fully realized the importance of acceleration, and the sheets bearing these were mutilated in the course of subsequent revisions of the projected treatise.

From August to October 1602 Galileo was in correspondence with Paolo Sarpi and Sagredo concerning magnetic experiments. Among Galileo's notes on motion there is a sheet (f. 121) bearing a very elaborate drawing based on a diagram in William Gilbert's book on the magnet and therefore dating after 1600. A part of this diagram was then used for a speculation about descent along a circular arc, a topic which Galileo had been considering when he wrote to Guidobaldo in October 1602. On f. 121v there are two diagrams, one probably related to pendulums and the other to descents along planes of equal height intersecting a vertical circle through the highest point. This latter was the source of Galileo's theorem—that the time of descent along any chord of a vertical circle to its lowest point remains the same, regardless of the length and slope of the

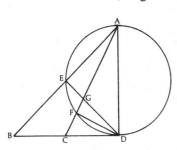

plane. Given Galileo's two erroneous conclusions in *De motu*, that acceleration may be neglected and that the "speeds" of descent (regarded as constant) along two different planes of equal height are inverse to the lengths of the planes, any Euclidean geometer could easily reach Galileo's theorem by inspection of this diagram. It was left unlettered by Galileo, who however flagged it with a numbered tab for future reference. Lettering has been added here for our convenience in following the Euclidean reasoning.

It it assumed that two different speeds along *AB* and *AC*, each being regarded as uniform and dependent only on slope, have the ratio of distances *AC* and *AB*, respectively; it is to be shown that the times along *AE* and *AF* are identical. Since *AD* is the mean proportional between *AE* and *AB*, as also between *AF* and *AC*, we have *AE:AD::AD:AB* and *AF:AD::AD:AC*. By division, *AE:AF::AC:AB*. Now, *AC:AB* was taken as the ratio of speed along *AB* to speed along *AC*, and is seen to equal *AE:AF*. But when speeds are proportional to distances traversed, the times are necessarily equal;[25] hence *AE* and *AF* are traversed in the same time.

The same reasoning applies to descents along chords to the lowest point of a vertical circle as to descents along chords through the highest point. The truth of the result is easily confirmed by placing two boards of different lengths against the sides of a large vertical hoop, with their lower ends at the bottom, and releasing balls along both simultaneously. Since Galileo believed at that time, as in *De motu*, that speeds along differently inclined planes were inverse to "moments of heaviness" on such planes, he wrote out a proof based on that concept in which he appealed to "the elements of mechanics." This proof is found on f. 160*r* and was reproduced almost verbatim as the first alternative proof of Proposition Six on accelerated motion in *Two New Sciences* many years later.[26]

It will be remembered that in establishing equilibrium conditions for weights on inclined planes, Galileo had identified downward tendency at any point along the lower quadrant of a vertical circle with that along the tangent inclined plane at that point. He now conjectured that descents along arcs of the lower quadrant should be completed in the same time regardless of length of arc, as was true for chords and seemed to be true of pendulums. He communicated this opinion to Guidobaldo and received in reply certain objections; Guidobaldo's letter is lost, but Galileo's reply (translated below) preserves two of these. Guidobaldo could not believe that one body might go many miles while another body moved only an inch; and second, Guidobaldo's own experiments (rolling balls in the rim of a vertical hoop) had not confirmed Galileo's opinion.

Galileo's reply to Guidobaldo described the use of long pendulums in improving certain experiments, which makes it highly probable that he had begun making studies of the pendulum earlier in 1602. The *pulsilogium* described in 1603 by Santorre Santorio,[27] then a doctor in Venice and later professor of medicine at Padua, was probably inspired by discussions of such experiments with his friend Galileo. It is doubtful that they had begun much earlier than 1602, since it is evident that Galileo had not previously mentioned them to Guidobaldo in connection with the matter they were discussing. It was on 29 November 1602 that Galileo replied to Guidobaldo as follows:

You must excuse my importunity if I persist in trying to persuade you of the truth of the proposition that motions within the same quarter-circle are made in equal times. For this having always appeared to me remarkable, it now seems even more remarkable that you have come to regard it as false. Hence I should deem it a great error and fault in myself if I should permit this to be repudiated by your theory as something false; for it does not deserve this censure, nor yet to be banished from your mind—which better than any other will be able to keep it more readily from exile by the minds of others. And since the experience by which the truth has been made clear to me is so certain, however confusedly it may have been explained in my other [letter], I shall repeat this more clearly so that you, too, by making this [experiment], may be assured of this truth.

Therefore take two slender threads of equal length, each being two or three braccia long [four to six feet]; let these be *AB* and *EF*. Hang *A* and *E* from two nails, and at the other

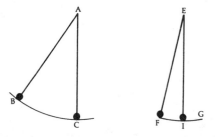

ends tie two equal lead balls (though it makes no difference if they are unequal). Then removing both threads from the vertical, one of them very much as through the arc *CB*, and the other very little as through the arc *IF*, set them free at the same moment of time. One will begin to describe large arcs like *BCD* while the other describes small ones like *FIG*. Yet in this way the moveable [that is, movable body] *B* will not consume more time in passing the whole arc *BCD* than that used up by the other moveable *F* in passing the arc *FIG*. I am made quite certain of this as follows.

The moveable *B* passes through the large arc *BCD* and returns by the same *DCB* and then goes back toward *D*, and it goes 500 or 1,000 times repeating its oscillations. The other goes likewise from *F* to *G* and then returns to *F*, and will similarly make many oscillations; and in the time that I count, say, the first 100 large oscillations *BCD*, *DCB*, and so on, another observer counts 100 of the other oscillations through *FIG*, very small, and he does not count even one more—a most evident sign that one of these large arcs *BCD* consumes as much time as each of the small ones *FIG*. Now, if all *BCD* is passed in as much time [as that] in which *FIG* [is passed], though [*FIG* is] but one-half thereof, these being descents through unequal arcs of the same quadrant, they will be made in equal times. But even without troubling to count many, you will see that moveable *F* will not make its small oscillations more frequently than *B* makes its larger ones; they will always go together.

The experiment you tell me you made in the [rim of a vertical] sieve may be very inconclusive, perhaps by reason of the surface not being perfectly circular, and again because in a single passage one cannot well observe the precise beginning of motion. But if you will take the same concave surface and let ball *B* [in a diagram now missing, presumed to be as below] go freely from a great distance, as at point *B*, it will go through

 a large distance at the beginning of its oscillations and a small one at the end of these, yet it will not on that account make the latter more frequently than the former. Then as to its appearing unreasonable that given a quadrant 100 miles long, one of two equal moveables might traverse the whole and [in the same time] another but a single span, I say that it is true that this contains something of the wonderful, but our wonder will cease if we consider that there could be a plane as little tilted as that of the surface of a slowly running river, so that on this [plane] a moveable will not have moved naturally more than a span in the time that on another plane, steeply tilted (or given great impetus even on a gentle incline), it will have moved 100 miles. Perhaps the proposition has inherently no greater improbability than that triangles between the same

parallels and on equal bases are always equal [in area], though one may be quite short and the other 1,000 miles long. But keeping to our subject, I believe I have demonstrated that the one conclusion is no less thinkable than the other. Let *BA* be

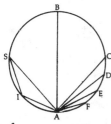

the diameter of circle *BDA* erect to the horizontal, and from point *A* out to the circumference draw any lines *AF*, *AE*, *AD*, and *AC*. I show that equal moveables fall in equal times, whether through the vertical *BA* or through the inclined planes along lines *CA*, *DA*, *EA*, and *FA*. Thus leaving at the same moment from points *B*, *C*, *D*, *E*, and *F*, they arrive at the same moment at terminus *A*; and line *FA* may be as small as you wish.

And perhaps even more surprising will this, also demonstrated by me, appear: That line *SA* being not greater than the chord of a quadrant, and lines *SI* and *IA* being any whatever, the same moveable leaving from *S* will make its journey *SIA* more swiftly than just the trip *IA*, starting from *I*. This much has been demonstrated by me without transgressing the bounds of mechanics. But I cannot manage to demonstrate that arcs *SIA* and *IA* are passed in equal times, which is what I am seeking.[28]

Do me the favor of conveying my greetings to Sig. Francesco and tell him that when I have a little leisure I shall write to him of an experiment that has come to my mind for measuring the force of percussion. And as to his question, I think that what you say about it is well put, and that when we commence to deal with matter, then by reason of its accidental properties the propositions abstractly considered in geometry commence to be altered, from which, thus perturbed, no certain science can be assigned—though the mathematician is so absolute about them in theory. I have been too long and tedious with you; pardon me, and love me as your most devoted servitor.

It is evident that Galileo had as yet obtained no very precise data from experiments of rolling balls on inclined planes and even despaired of finding them in close agreement with mathematical deductions. Since acceleration was not mentioned, it is unlikely that he had begun to study it closely, as he was soon to do. On the other hand he was already devising experiments designed to yield measurements of physical phenomena. Concerning the force of percussion two different experimental approaches by Galileo are known, one of which may safely be ascribed to the year 1608. The other was described by Evangelista Torricelli after the death of Galileo, who had told him of it in his last days; it may well be that which first occurred to him in 1602:

> The experiments favoring [an infinite percussive force], inventions of that famous old man [Galileo], were these. When he was living at Padua he had many bows made, all of different strengths. Then he took the weakest of all, and from the middle of its bowstring he suspended a lead ball of about two ounces, attaching it by a thread of say one braccio. The bow being held [horizontally] in a vise, he raised this ball and let it drop; by means of a [movable] gong placed underneath, he observed through how great a distance the impetus of the ball curved the bowstring and drew it down; let us suppose this to be about four inches. Then, to the string of the same bow, there was attached a resting weight sufficiently large to curve the bowstring and draw it down through that same distance of four inches, and this weight was noted to be about ten pounds.
>
> This done, he took another bow, stronger than the first, and to its string he attached the same lead ball [of two ounces] by the same thread; letting this drop from the same height, he noted the [smaller] distance through which it pulled the bowstring. Next he attached resting lead that had this same effect, finding that the ten pounds which were enough the first time no longer sufficed, more than twenty being required. And taking bows gradually stronger, he found that to equal the force of that same lead ball through that same fall there was always required more and more weight, according as the experiment was made with stronger and stronger bows.
>
> "Therefore," he said, "if I were to take a very strong bow, the lead ball of no more than two ounces will have an effect equivalent to a thousand pounds of lead; and taking a bow a thousand times stronger than that one, [already] very strong, that same little ball will have the effect of one million pounds of lead—a most evident sign that the force of [percussion of] that little weight [dropped] at that [distance of] one braccio is infinite."[29]

Concerning the pendulum experiments made by Galileo in 1602, it is evident from his letter to Guidobaldo that he had ascertained that only the length, and not the weight of bob, affected the period of swing. This probably suggested to him a linkage with free fall, since in *De motu* he had argued that speed was independent of weight. With a friend he had counted the swings of equal long pendulums starting through different arcs and had noted the interesting fact that the difference in counts did not become greater than one. The reason for this is that through very small arcs each swing takes the same time, and unless a pendulum is very heavily weighted it will quickly be reduced to swinging through a small arc and will then beat in exact time with the one started through a small arc. Galileo knew that there was some difference in time for a large and a small arc, for otherwise the two counters would remain exactly together, but he regarded the difference as negligible and so described it on the two occasions when he mentioned pendulums in his later *Dialogue*.

FIVE

1603-4

THREE LETTERS WRITTEN by Galileo and a dozen written to him are extant from 1602, almost exactly the same count as in 1604. From 1603, in marked contrast, there are only two known letters, one in January from Sagredo concerning a debt of Galileo's to him and another Venetian, and the other written by Galileo in February requesting a year's advance in salary. Probably the reason for this meager correspondence in 1603 was a serious illness, harbinger of many others of the same kind, described by his son after Galileo's death as having afflicted him "from about the fortieth year of his life to its end" with severe rheumatic or arthritic pain in various parts of his body.[1] Illnesses confining him to bed were frequently mentioned in Galileo's letters from March 1605 on.

Galileo was in the fortieth year of his life in 1603. But when Viviani reported the origin of Galileo's bodily afflictions, though he had before him the account mentioned above, he implied a date ten years earlier, probably as the result of a miscalculation; for Viviani wrote:

He was troubled for more than forty-eight years of his age, up to the end of his life, by very severe pains and twinges that molested him bitterly at changes of weather, in various parts of his body. These originated in him by his having been, in the company of two noble friends of his, in the burning heat of one summer at a villa in the countryside of Padua, where they went to rest in a very cold room to escape the most uncomfortable hours of the day. When all were asleep, a

74

servant thoughtlessly opened a vent through which, for pleasure, there used to be released a perpetual artificial wind generated by the motions and the fall of water which ran nearby. This wind, being excessively cold and damp, meeting with their very lightly clothed bodies during a time of two hours while they were reposing there, gradually introduced into them so bad a quality in their limbs that upon their awakening, one had torpor and chills, another intense headache and various disorders; all fell into grave illness of which one of them died in a few days, the second lost his hearing and did not survive a great time, and Galileo got the aforesaid indisposition, from which he could never free himself.[2]

It is probable that Viviani's figure should have been thirty-eight years, not forty-eight; Galileo's death having come at the end of 1641, this would agree with 1603 as the year of the incident indicated by his son and suggested also by a document cited below. The place was identified by Antonio Favaro as Costozzo, near Padua, where in 1883 there were still standing at least two sixteenth-century villas having special rooms originally ventilated by underground conduits connected with nearby mountain caves. Severe chills could indeed have been suffered by persons falling asleep in those rooms, in addition to which noxious gases are said to have mingled sometimes with the cavern air, for which reason the ancient ventilating ducts were long ago blocked off.[3]

That the summer of 1603 was the time of Galileo's initial serious illness receives further support from an event related in his *Defense* concerning the "military compass," published in 1607:

A certain Johann Eutel Zieckmesser, five years after I had invented and begun to publish my instrument, when more than forty of these were around in various countries, arrived in Padua; and having an instrument to which had been transferred certain lines taken from mine (others being left off and in their place still others added), he, perhaps not knowing that the first and true inventor of such an instrument was in Padua, met with a pupil of mine, Michael Wustrou of Brunswick,[4] who had already learned the use of my compass from me, and by telling him that he had a marvelous invention, put him in great desire to see it. Finally he showed that instrument to him, which was immediately recognized by the said gentleman, who then told me of it when I was ill in bed, and a few days later he left Padua. As soon as I recovered my health, hearing that my rivals and especially my ancient adversary . . . were spreading word that the invention of that instrument might not be mine, contrary to what I had always said, I was compelled (though not without difficulty) to have the said Fleming confront me so that at a meeting it could be made clear to any who cared which one of us was the legitimate inventor of the instrument.[5]

Galileo's account books show that by mid-1603 at least twenty of his calculating sectors were in the hands of foreigners, making the above figure of forty manufactured in all up to that time quite plausible.

The onset of recurrent rheumatic seizures in 1603 would account for the great variability in handwriting characteristic of Galileo's notes on motion during his years at Padua. Few of those notes were written before 1603. Some later notes were written in a small, cramped hand, and of those some are written slantingly on the page, as often happens when one attempts to write in bed. Galileo's recurrent illnesses can occasionally be dated from letters, suggesting probable dates for groupings of notes in the cramped hand. Notes in handwriting of a particular type, whether this or another, are often found to be related in other ways also, as by topic, logical connections, or similarity of paper used.

II

Since no account of Galileo's discoveries about free fall and descent along inclined planes can be trusted unless it is consistent with some specific chronological ordering of all his surviving notes on motion, it is advisable before we proceed further to consider what any such ordering involves. In all, nearly 200 pages of these notes exist. Some pages have multiple entries, some have only diagrams or calculations, and a number (about thirty pages) are not in Galileo's hand but are copies, for which most of the originals in his own hand are also preserved in the same volume. No page or entry is specifically dated, though one (f. 128) can be positively identified as belonging to October 1604.[6] To put all these in any one logically and psychologically consistent order is an arduous task, especially because on some pages Galileo made notes at various widely separated times. Yet since all the notes were the work of one man, they must have had a single chronological sequence. To make sure that any ordering is free of serious implausibilities requires attention to handwriting, vocabulary, watermarks in paper, color and condition of ink, and in addition to the implications in that ordering of what was known to Galileo at every stage, and what remained to be discovered.

Watermarks have turned out to be of special value in determining which notes were written at Padua and which at Florence, this division coming in mid-1610. Dated correspondence shows that Paduan paper was not used by Galileo after that time, except of course when he added a note to some page already started at Padua. All the notes copied by others were from Paduan originals and are on paper bearing a single Florentine watermark,[7] even though two different copyists were concerned. The purpose of these copies is clear; in 1618 Galileo decided to organize everything of value from his Paduan notes on motion and incorporate this into the treatise on which at least two earlier starts had been made. Since it would be convenient to have the propositions separated, in order that other material could be suitably inserted, Galileo had two pupil-assistants (Mario Guiducci and Niccolò Arrighetti) copy selected Paduan propositions one to a sheet, using one side only when possible. The unique watermark shows that all copies were made over a relatively short time and from the same supply of paper, that is, at Galileo's house and under his direction.[8]

All copies are faithful to the originals when those also survive, and each original on watermarked paper shows a Paduan watermark and handwriting compatible with Galileo's prior to 1610. Those facts strongly support the assumption that copies no longer accompanied by originals were also made from documents written before 1610 and now lost. Galileo's attention was diverted from motion to telescopic researches in 1610, and by the time he resumed work on motion his handwriting had altered quite noticeably. Moreover the ink used while he was at the University of Padua was noncorrosive and remains black or blue, whereas that which he used at Florence was frequently corrosive and is now often brown. Thus it is possible to sort out with confidence the notes made at Padua, and when these are arranged it appears that Galileo's basic work on motion was essentially complete before the advent of the telescope.

Most of the notes on motion were transcribed and published by Antonio Favaro; the exceptions are mainly sheets with only diagrams and calculations, a few of which have turned out to be very important in the reconstruction of Galileo's year-to-year work. Entries are identified here by folio number and position on the page, numbering from top to bottom recto and then continuing on the verso. Since some pages are now bound in reverse order to that of composition, the numbering on a page may not be chronological; thus 164–4 was written before 164–1, for example. Published notes, which constitute the great majority, will be further identified in notes by reference to line and page numbers in the eighth volume of Favaro's edition of the works of Galileo.

It is certainly not claimed that the ordering I have adopted is correct and final, but only that, in addition to meeting the criteria already described, it minimizes the number and seriousness of logical and psychological puzzles I have encountered in innumerable orderings I have considered. By a logical puzzle I mean a case in which it seems that Galileo was ignorant of something already known to him if the ordering is correct, or that he took for granted something he did not yet know. By a psychological puzzle I mean a case in which it seems that Galileo wasted effort on a clumsy proof after having already found a neat one, or attacked problems that could not assist the work in hand at the time. In minimizing such puzzles, *all* the extant notes must be taken into account, and even seemingly extraneous markings on the paper (called "doodlings" by Americans), since any number of appealing arrangements can be made of selected documents by excluding others from consideration.

III

The vast majority of Galileo's notes relating to descent on inclined planes involve use of the law of free fall, which states that distances from rest are proportional to the squares of elapsed times from rest. Galileo's theorem can be rigorously and easily proved from that law, as was done in later *Two New Sciences*.[9] It would be a psychological puzzle if Galileo, having once used the law of fall to prove that theorem, should have later devised the weak proof found on f. 160*r*, ignoring acceleration and appealing to "moments of weight" and "the elements of mechanics." The latter phrase makes it highly probable that he had f. 160r in hand when writing to Guidobaldo in October 1602. The other proof he mentioned in that letter—that descent along conjugate chords to the lowest point takes less time than along the single chord connecting their endpoints—is not found among his surviving notes but can be reconstructed by using the same two false assumptions originally used to prove Galileo's theorem.[10]

Two other theorems follow immediately from Galileo's theorem without considering acceleration at all. One of these is written on f. 140r in a firm, clear hand;[11] the other is on f. 127v in a somewhat irregular hand,[12] for which reason I think that Galileo's illness in the summer of 1603 came between them. Accompanying the former are several unlettered diagrams whose purpose is fairly evident: Galileo was considering the nature of a certain path of least time. He was not concerned with what we now call the brachistochrone, that is, the path traversed between two points in the shortest possible time by a body descending under no constraint except that of the supporting surface which prevents straight fall. Galileo reserved his consideration to straight paths of descent from rest along inclined planes. Such a path of least time cannot be the shortest distance to the vertical line through the point to be reached, since that would be a horizontal line and the body would not move naturally along it at all. Neither can it be the line of swiftest motion, since that would be the vertical through the initial point and the body would never reach the other vertical. Yet somewhere between the horizontal and the vertical through the initial point there must be a straight line along which descent will be completed more quickly than along any other. Galileo's simple and elegant solution depended only on the chord rule I call by his name, and of course on the notion that a body has a certain "speed" along any incline depending only on the slope, which speed may be treated as constant along that slope.

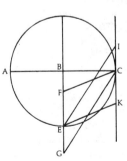

By Galileo's theorem, travel along *CE* takes the same time as along that part of *EI* that lies within the circle, and along *CG* (equal and parallel to *EI*) the time is the same as along *EI*, hence from *C* the body will reach *E* before it would reach *G*.

Likewise *CE* takes the same time as the part of *EK* lying inside the circle, while all *EK* takes the same time as all *CF*; hence from *C* the body will reach *E* sooner than it will reach *F*. In *Two New Sciences* this became Proposition Thirty on accelerated motion, after Galileo's theorem had there been proved from the law of free fall.

On f. 164 Galileo wrote a note similar to his later Proposition Eight; this sheet is now bound in reverse, so that his first note on it will be called 164-4[13] in accordance with the procedure described above. No further entries were made on f. 164 for a long time, as shown by handwriting and content; this was one of several sheets on which, having written a proposition useful to his projected treatise, Galileo kept the paper clear for further such entries. Another such sheet, f. 172, is of special interest because it was started shortly before Galileo became concerned with acceleration as such. The first entry on it, 172-3, is significant as containing reasoning by one-to-one correspondence, though not yet applied to infinite sets. Its intention was to explain the conclusion of Galileo's theorem in terms of constant but differing speed along each slope; an explanation of certain changes subsequently made by Galileo is given later.

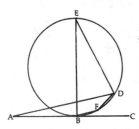

(172-3) Let there be a horizontal plane along line *ABC* and two planes inclined to it along lines *DB* and *DA*; I say that the same moveable will move more slowly through *DA* than through *DB* in the ratio of length *DA* to length *DB*.

Indeed, erect *BE* from *B* vertical to the horizontal, and from *D* draw *DE* perpendicular to *BD*, meeting *BE* at *E*. Around triangle *BDE* describe a circle tangent to *AC* at point *B*; from this, draw *BF* parallel to *AD*, and connect *FD*. It is clear that the tardity through *FB* will be similar to the tardity through *DA*. But since [by Galileo's theorem] the moveable moves in the same time through *DB* and *FB*, clearly the speeds [at first, speed] through *DB* to the speeds [at first, speed] through *FB* are as *DB* to *FB*, so that two moveables coming from points *D* and *F* by lines *DB* and *FB* always travel through proportional parts of the entire lines *DB* and *FB* in the same times [from rest]. But since angle *BFD* in the segment is equal to angle *DBA* with the tangent, while angle *DBF* is alternate to *BDA*, triangles *BFD* and *ABD* are similar, and as *BD* is to *BF*, so *AD* is to *BD*. Therefore as *AD* is to *BD*, so the speed through *DB* is to the speed through *DA*, and conversely, the tardity along *DA* is [in the same ratio] to the tardity through *DB*.[14]——If this [next postulate] is assumed, the rest can be demonstrated: therefore it is to be postulated [:] Increases or diminutions in speed of motion are in the ratio in which moments of heaviness are increased or diminished; and since it is clear that for the same moveable, the moments of heaviness over plane *DB* are to the moments of heaviness over plane *DA* as length *DA* is to DB, for that reason the speed through *DB* is to the speed through *DA* as *DA* is to *DB*.[15]

As indicated by two bracketed insertions in the fourth sentence above, Galileo first wrote this entire proposition in terms of overall speeds, ignoring acceleration (as he had done in *De motu*). It was probably while experimenting with long pendulums, as recommended to Guidobaldo, that acceleration began to concern him. A question now arose in Galileo's mind about the proposition of f. 180*r*, in which two motions began from the same point along different slopes, and he wrote on f. 180*v* the following memorandum, subsequently cut off:

I deem this proposition necessary to the preceding.
The speeds of moveables that begin motion with unequal moments [as on f. 180*r*] are always to each other in the same ratio as if they progressed with uniform motion; as for example, a moveable through *AC* begins motion with a moment [that is] to the moment through *AD* as *DA* is to *AC*. If progress were in equable motion, the time through *AC* would be to the time through *AD* as *AC* is to *AD*, which in accelerated [motion] I doubt; therefore demonstra——[16]

Galileo also drew on f. 180*v* a right triangle with **several** parallels to its base; since he left it unlettered, it is probable that he did not write out any proposition connected with it at this time, but merely speculated on change of speed as being represented by the changing lengths of those parallels. In the course of such reflections an important idea occurred to him which he did write out neatly on f. 163, another of the sheets thereafter kept clear for a long time:

(163–3) Let there be naturally accelerated motion from *A* to *B*; I say that if the speeds at all points were the same as that found at point *B*, the space *AB* would be run through twice as quickly, since all the speeds at single points of line *AB* would have, to as many [speeds] of which each was equal to speed *BC*, the same ratio as [that of] triangle *ABC* to rectangle *ABCD*. It follows from this that if there is an elevated plane *BA* to the horizontal CD such that *BC* is double *BA*, a moveable from *A* to *B* and then from *B* to *C* will run through these in equal times; for after it is at *B* it is moved in the same uniform speed that it had at terminus *B* after fall *AB*. It is further clear that the whole time through *ABE* [*AB* = *BE*] is three-halves that through *AB*.[17]

In *De motu* Galileo had proved mathematically that any force, however small, should in principle move a body along the horizontal plane. In revising the *Mechanics* he had repeated this, adding that a frictionless body on a horizontal plane was indifferent to motion or rest. Hence the idea of uniform continuance along the horizontal after descent along an incline was already a natural one to him. The watermark on the paper and an otherwise puzzling notation on f. 187 (described below) convince me that Galileo arrived at this proposition before he had the law of free fall.[18]

To judge by handwriting, Galileo's next notes on motion were made while his hand was affected by illness in 1603. On f. 127*v* the reasoning of f. 140*r* was extended to the straight path of least time from a point to a slanted line. From this his attention turned to a purely mathematical investigation on f. 130*v*, without mention of times or speeds, in connection with an elaborate diagram as originally drawn, to which he later added points and calculations related to the law of fall.[19] Having solved two least-time problems, he appears to have sought late in 1603 for some mathematical minimum property related to his diagrams for them. What he found was the rectangle of minimum area of those made up from an incline to the horizontal and its part to the 45° intercept. The diagram shows him to have been thinking about fall along equal conjugate chords in the lower quadrant of circles of different radii.

In the same hand, on f. 187*r*, an attempt was made to deduce the relation of times along two conjugate chords by reasoning from the double-speed rule of 163–3.[20] It would be a psychological puzzle if Galileo had approached that problem in this way after he knew the law of free fall, and in fact it was quickly solved by him following his discovery of that law. Above this unsuccessful attempt Galileo drew a new diagram in an attempt to determine a rule for times to places along a line inclined at 22.5°, the angle corresponding to the minimum rectangle derived on f. 130v. It is accordingly safe to suppose him still ignorant of the law of fall at this stage, near the end of 1603 or early in 1604.

IV

During the winter of 1603–4 Galileo discussed with Vincenzo Gonzaga, duke of Mantua, the possibility of his employment at that court. He was offered 300 ducats and living expenses for himself and a servant. This was less attractive to him than the 320 ducats paid by the university, where private tutoring and the sale of mathematical instruments paid for the services of Mazzoleni and augmented his net income. He countered with a request for 500 ducats and expenses for himself and two servants, made not directly to the duke but to a secretary during a visit to Mantua early in 1604. No agreement was reached. Galileo also asked Sagredo to assist him in efforts to obtain a better salary at Padua, but was told in April 1604 that there was little prospect of success.

About this time Gonzaga wrote to Galileo asking about a man named Capra at Padua, who was supposed to know a secret of medicine he wanted. Galileo replied that this was Aurelio Capra, a Milanese who had brought his son Baldessar to Padua to study medicine. Aurelio, who gave private fencing lessons, was interested in the alchemical pursuits of the group gathered around Gromo. He was also close to Simon Mayr, Baldessar's German mathematical tutor, who among other things professed to know the secret of a pill that could keep a man well and strong forty days without eating. Baldessar was reported to be attempting to combine empirical and theoretical medicine and was cultivating astronomy and astrology. In the same letter Galileo mentioned the friendship of Aurelio Capra with Giacomo Alvise Cornaro, who was later to play an important role in Galileo's relations with the Capras.

In May 1604 Costanzo da Cascio wrote from Naples to ask Galileo for the demonstration that two bodies of the same material and shape had the same speed, regardless of weight, through a given medium. He had heard the proof from Galileo at Padua but had forgotten it, and now wished to answer objections to the proposition by opponents at Naples. One adversary was probably Giovanni Camillo Glorioso, who wrote a few days later from Naples to introduce himself to Galileo, whose chair at Padua he was eventually to obtain.

Another activity of Galileo's in the spring of 1604 is suggested by a letter from Antonio de' Medici later that year asking about a ball that could be made to float "between two waters." This device was later described by Galileo in a letter to Nicole Fabri de Peiresc, as well as in *Two New Sciences*.[21] It was used to fool some friends who were trying to obtain exact equilibrium in water of a wax ball by weighting it with iron filings. Galileo placed salt water in a bowl and then laid fresh water on it, which is easily done by using a sheet of paper that is then gently removed. A wax ball slightly heavier than water will then descend slowly to the salt water and come to rest on top of it; since diffusion of the salt is quite slow, the ball may remain suspended thus for many hours. It is evident that much of Galileo's book on floating bodies published in 1612 was based on earlier experiments, some of which appear to belong to 1604.

Still another event of importance to Galileo's studies of motion took place at Venice, probably no later than this time. A Greek Jesuit named Eudaemon-Ioannes later told a colleague at Rome that when he was at Padua Galileo had assured him that a ball dropped from the mast of a ship fell to its foot whether the ship was at rest or in motion. Galileo asserted in 1624 that he had made that experiment[22] and in 1632 declared that he had already known the result in advance.[23] Venice is the most probable place for Galileo to have made the test, suggested by reasoning in *De motu* and the *Mechanics* concerning the indifference of a body to rest or motion and applied on f. 163 to motion continued horizontally.

V

Meanwhile Galileo had not neglected the problems of motion along inclined planes. The old question of proving that bodies moving under natural acceleration along different planes from the same point could nevertheless maintain relative positions similar to those under uniform speeds at different rates, raised on f. 180*v* before Galileo's illness in 1603, remained unanswered, and the attempt to discover some rule for times or speeds along a 22.5° plane by using the diagram on f. 187*v* had yielded no result. It was probably in the spring of 1604 that Galileo realized the necessity of having some actual measure of speeds in naturally accelerated motion, leading to results of great consequence that must have surprised him as much as they delighted him, though they in turn gave rise to a new and perplexing problem.

It will be remembered that at the end of his letter to Guidobaldo late in 1602, Galileo had remarked on the disparity between the absolute conclusions of mathematicians and the results of tests with actual material bodies. That was an echo of his earlier remark in *De motu* that tests did not bear out his first (and quite erroneous) deductions about ratios of speeds on different inclined planes. Static propositions, like the law of the lever or the proportionality of weights to volumes for uniform materials, could indeed be very precisely confirmed by actual measurements, but it seemed that no such thing was to be hoped from experiments with moving bodies. It is probable that Galileo had made some inclined plane experiments in 1602, before writing to Guidobaldo, but of a kind that only revived his despair of useful results. He certainly made some experiments with long pendulums at that time, and in *Two New Sciences*, speaking of the fall of bodies of different weights, he wrote a passage that may give us a clue to his thoughts in 1602:

> In a small height it may be doubtful whether there is really no difference [in speeds], or whether there is a difference but it is unobservable. So I fell to thinking how one might many times repeat descents from small heights and accumulate many of those minimal differences of time that might intervene between the arrival of the heavy body at the terminus and that of the light one, so that added together in this way they would make up a time not only observable but easily observable.
>
> In order to make use of motions as slow as possible . . . I also thought of making moveables descend along an inclined plane not much raised above the horizontal. On this, no less than in the vertical, one may observe what is done by bodies differing in weight. Going further, I wanted to be free of any hindrance that might arise from contact of these moveables with the said tilted plane.[24]

Galileo then went on to describe the use of pendulums, as he had recommended to Guidobaldo in late 1602. But let us stop here to consider the implications of the above remarks, assuming that Galileo was describing his earliest steps along this line. The problem concerned descent of bodies of different weights. Now, among all the surviving notes, only f. 160r spoke of "moments of weight" (*momenta ponderis*) rather than "moments of heaviness" (*momenta gravitatis*), found often both before and after f. 160r. All of Galileo's theoretical conclusions indicated that weight as such should not matter, whereas any actual test by rolling balls of different weight on inclined planes "not much raised above the horizontal" would show that in practice, especially on wooden planes, it does matter. This may well have been one of the things Galileo had in mind when he wrote the final paragraph of his letter to Guidobaldo. Also, a diagram on f. 173 explicitly shows two balls descending along different slopes. Hence there is some reason to believe that by the time Galileo wrote to Guidobaldo late in 1602 he had already prepared a grooved inclined plane and had had some experience in observing phenomena of balls rolling down it, though thus far with no specific results useful to him for his projected treatise on motion. On the contrary, from the last paragraph of his 1602 letter it appears that he was discouraged about finding any close agreement between mathematical conclusions about motion and tests with material objects.

The document we are about to consider bears out these indications that Galileo had previously used equipment of the kind just described but was still ignorant of the law of descent. The same equipment became invaluable when now he sought a measure of actual speeds, with results on f. 107v that may be as startling to the modern reader as they must have been to Galileo.[25]

The source of the numbers tabulated in the third column at top left is revealed by the calculations to their right. In each of these some integer is multiplied by sixty and then a number less than sixty is added to the product, the total thus obtained being entered in the third column. That these were measures of distances is certain; except for weight and amounts of money, nothing else could then be measured with an accuracy of three significant places. Moreover, precise measurement of distances is conducted just as indicated by the calculations mentioned. Take a short ruler divided accurately into sixty equal parts as small as you can conveniently see; mark a long rod at intervals equal to the length of your ruler, and you can quickly measure with great accuracy any distance not longer than the rod, to

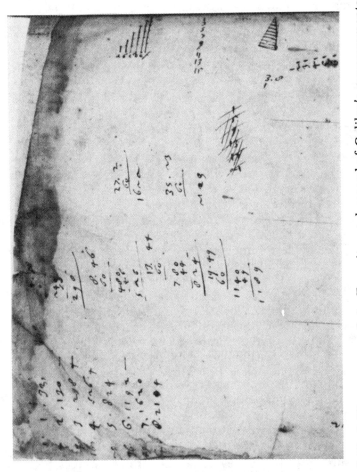

Folio 107*v*, vol. 72, Galilean manuscripts. Experimental record of Galileo's measurements of distances traversed along an inclined plane during eight equal times from rest. (Reproduced with permission of Biblioteca Nazionale Centrale, Florence. Photo by University of Toronto Photographic Services.)

those finest units. The number of units is an integer times sixty plus a number less than sixty.

Now, the numbers in the third column are very nearly, but not quite exactly, the successive distances that a freely falling body would traverse in eight successive equal times from rest. Galileo was obviously not measuring such distances, which cannot be done even today without very elaborate equipment because a body falling freely goes much too fast. But a ball on any gentle slope follows the same law of motion, and that is what Galileo's equipment permitted him to deal with. His work can be reconstructed because there are limits to the slope that can be used successfully for eight equal times and a manageable length of plane.

As to Galileo's units of distance, other notes reveal that they were what he called *punti*; by measuring some of his diagrams the unit turns out to have been about 29/30 mm, which is also extremely close to the unit along the rule-of-three scale on his own sector, preserved at the Science Museum in Florence. The principal line on f. 130v is 180 *punti*, as is that on f. 166, where the unit is named; and on f. 174 Galileo used 60 *punti* as a base. All those (and other like) drawings were made at this period, 1603–5. Since the last number in the third column is about 2,000 *punti*, it is reasonable to assume that his plane was tilted 60 *punti* in 2,000, or 1.7°, and that it was about two meters long, at least as to the part used. We can then calculate from Galileo's data the units of time, which turns out to imply 0.55 seconds each, a very probable duration for reasons soon to be mentioned.[26] Taking everything into account—including a change Galileo made in the last number and a peculiarity of the second number—it is found that a tilt of over 2° or of less than 1.5° would lie outside the limits of slope that could have been used successfully for Galileo's measurements.

For a long time it was agreed by all historians that Galileo was unable to experiment accurately concerning accelerated motion because there were then lacking any accurate watches or other instruments for measuring short times. That is true if by "measuring short times" we mean expressing them in astronomical seconds or any other arbitrary unit. But in this experiment Galileo was not interested in measuring individual times; he was only concerned to equalize them in order to get at an exact, though indirect, measure of *speeds*. It is very easy to equalize short times, particularly times of about half a second, because that is what we do whenever we dance or sing. At a half-second beat, an error of $\frac{1}{64}$ second is detectable by most people, and an error of $\frac{1}{32}$ by anyone. Galileo was the son of one musician and the brother of another, while he himself was a competent performer on the lute. And indeed, when we compute the deviations of Galileo's data from the theoretical distances, only one figure—the last—falls outside the range of accuracy within $\frac{1}{64}$ second. That is the one figure that Galileo changed at the end, bringing it to almost exact accuracy. Here are the calculations:[27]

TIME	TIME²	DISTANCE (CENTIMETERS)	DISTANCE (POINTS)	FIGURES IN f.107v	DIFFERENCE (POINTS)	DISTANCE IN 1/64 SECOND (POINTS)
.55	.30	3.176	32.9	33	+ .1	1.8
1.10	1.21	12.705	131.4	130	− 1.4	3.7
1.65	2.72	28.59	295.7	298	+ 2.3	5.6
2.20	4.84	50.82	525.7	526	+ .3	7.4
2.75	7.56	79.41	821.5	824	+ 2.5	9.3
3.30	10.89	114.3	1,182.4	1,192	+ 9.6	11.2
3.85	14.82	155.6	1,609.8	1,620	+10.2	13.1
4.40	19.36	203.3	2,103.1	2,123 [2,104]	+20.1 [+ .9]	14.9

Galileo's procedure, as I reconstruct it, was this. He tied gut frets around his grooved plane, as frets are tied on the neck of a lute, so that they are snug but can be moved as needed; to set their initial positions it sufficed to sing a march tune, release the ball on one beat, and mark its approximate positions at following beats.[28] With the frets roughly in place, the ball made a sound on striking the plane after passing over each one; they were then adjusted until each of those sounds was judged to be exactly on a beat. It remained only to measure their distances from the point at which the resting ball touched the plane. In practice, unless the ball is very massive, it will be slightly delayed by the first fret, when it is not up to any great speed, so that the second fret will be a little closer to the first than it should be by theory. That is exactly what is seen in the above tabulation; Galileo's figure 130 should be 132 in theory. By the time the ball reaches the last fret it is going pretty fast—nearly 1,000 *punti* per second—making it hard to be sure just where that fret should be. Galileo initially had it 2,123 *punti* from rest, over which he later wrote 2,104. That had been the only interval greater than can be accounted for by tolerance of $\frac{1}{64}$-second deviation from perfect timing. When Galileo made this correction, he also marked some of the other original measurements + or − to indicate intervals at which the sound was in his judgment a little early or late on subsequent trials, though not enough to require his adjusting the frets.

The arrangement of work on f. 107v and noticeable differences in ink and in the writing of numerals indicate that Galileo did not immediately perceive the law of free fall from the data he had obtained. Also evident is the fact that he had no inkling of that law before he made the experiment. In that case he would have tied frets at their exact theoretical positions to begin with, and a single run of the ball would have shown the correctness of the rule. The + and − signs and change of the last figure show that on the contrary, he remained uncertain of any rule at the outset and was merely seeking measures of speeds in successive equal times. The canceled numbers 1–5–9–13–17–21 are best explained as a first guess at some regularity, which turned out to be 1–4–9–16 and so on. Arithmetical progression belonged not to cumulative but to successive distances, as noted in a much smaller hand in the margin, later and with the paper turned sideways.

It is important to note that the very way in which Galileo approached determination of an actual measure of speeds in descent predisposed him to assume that speeds are related to distances traversed. The numbers he entered as data were measures of distances, useful as measures of speeds only because the times were equal—since for equal times the overall speeds are as distances traversed. The notion that speeds must somehow be related directly to distances was thus fixed in Galileo's mind as he began these investigations, and continued for a time to dominate his attempts to find, and then to rationalize, a rule of acceleration.

SIX

1604-6

IT WAS PROBABLY early in 1604, while considering the data obtained on f. 107*v*, that Galileo wrote the numbers 1 to 8 beside them as ordinal designations of the speeds they represented, and shortly afterward he added in the extreme left-hand margin the squares of those numbers, which are seen to differ in ink and style of "6." It was evident then that the data obtained were almost exactly the products of the first datum, 33, by the successive square numbers from 1 to 64. The distances he had measured were accordingly nearly as the squares of the designated speeds. The way in which distances in natural descent accumulated was therefore different from the way in which individual speeds accumulated, the former following the square numbers while the latter followed the natural numbers. Taking a new sheet, f. 152*r*, Galileo made an entry at the top that again shows he had not yet hit on the law of free fall:

> 4 miles with 10 of speed in 4 hours
> 9 miles with 15 of speed in hours[1]

The source of the numbers 10 and 15 was simply the sums $1 + 2 + 3 + 4$ and $1 + 2 + 3 + 4 + 5$, Galileo's first hypothesis being that speeds accumulated as the natural numbers while distances accumulated as their squares.[2] The accumulation in the first line being allowed four units of time, the question was whether an additional unit of time would produce the second line. To reduce both lines to a common speed, Galileo wrote a 6 above the 4 for time in the first line; if 4 miles at 15 of speed

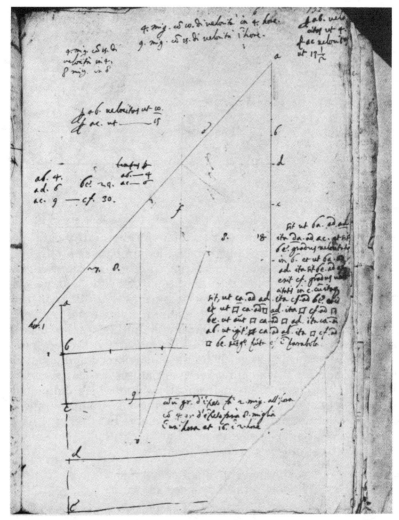

Folio 152*r*, vol. 72, Galilean manuscripts. Galileo's preliminary attempt to find consistent ratios for distances, speeds, and times in free fall assuming accumulated impetus (in Italian), and his later conclusion (in Latin) that speeds plotted against distances fall along a parabola. (Reproduced with permission of Biblioteca Nazionale Centrale, Florence. Photo by University of Toronto Photographic Services.)

took 4 hours, then 4 miles at 10 of speed would take 6 hours. Having thus given a meaning to "15 of speed,"[3] he wrote the implication that 8 miles at 15 of speed should take 8 hours, incompatible with the hypothesis that the second line represented the next step after the first line, with one more unit of speed and of time. It had been only a coincidence that the square of the ratio 10:15 was the ratio 4:9; the accumulation of speeds and of distances was still unexplained.

At the bottom of f. 152r Galileo drew a new diagram and made a new entry in Italian:

with one degree of impetus it makes 2 miles to the hour; with 4 degrees of impetus it will make 8 miles in one hour and 16 in two hours

In the "first" motion from rest, *AB*, only the natural tendency downward acted, here assigned by Galileo one degree of speed or one mile to the hour. At *B*, one degree of impetus was added by virtue of that speed. From *B* to *C* the body accordingly moved with two degrees of speed, and at *C* two degrees of impetus were added. Thus the body arrived at *D* with four degrees of speed, to which four degrees of impetus were then added, so that it would travel eight miles in one hour. This appeared to vindicate both the old triangle of speeds on f. 180r and the double-speed rule of 163–4. The question remained, however, why square numbers had appeared for the measured distances; to get the square number, 16, it seemed necessary to double the time, for no evident reason, and in any case that did not alter the supposed speed. Galileo put f. 152r aside for a while, puzzled but certain he was on the right track.

Satisfied with the notion of impetus as a means of rationalizing both the fact of acceleration and the use of his double-distance rule, Galileo next recast the proposition of f. 180r in terms of impetus rather than moment of heaviness. This he did on f. 147v,[4] another sheet that appears to be bound in reverse order since on this side it bears the mark of a pasted tab for future reference (as do ff. 121, 127, and 140). He then generalized it somewhat in the manner of Proposition Nine of *Two New Sciences*, though by purely geometrical reasoning and another appeal to impetus. Also on f. 147v (which had previously been used for a large diagram similar to one first sketched on f. 173v,

only partly lettered and then abandoned) there is a little notation of the accumulation of successive speeds under the impetus
concept of small discrete increments.

On the other side of this page, f. 147*r*, Galileo started out to
determine the ratio of times along the vertical and along a given
incline starting from the same point and reaching a given horizontal; this should yield the demonstration called for in Galileo's
memorandum of f. 180*v* but not previously found. It is evident
that f. 180 was again under his eyes, since he had just revised
f. 180*r* in terms of impetus. Some tentative notes show that he
began by supposing the desired ratio to be known for a higher
horizontal line, and he had hardly started on his inquiry when
he noticed that the simplest thing to do would be to assume that
the times to the upper horizontal line were as the vertical line
AE and the incline *AB*. That assumption, which corrected the
error made in *De motu* of supposing the speeds to be inversely
proportional to those same lines,[5] led at once to a reconciliation
of all his previous results and a demonstration of the law of
free fall. It was therefore written as a sort of organizational
memorandum:

(f. 147–2) After it has been demonstrated that the times
through *AB* and *AC* are equal [Galileo's theorem], it must be
shown that the time through *AD* is to the time through *AE* as
DA is to the mean proportional between *DA* and *AE*. For the
time through *DA* is to the time through *AC* as line *DA* is to *AC*;
but the time through *AC* (which is that through *AB*) is to
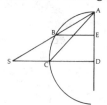
the time *AE* as line *BA* is to *AE*, which is
as *SA* is to *AD*. Therefore, by equidistance
of ratios in perturbed proportionality [cf.
Euclid Book Five, Definition Eighteen],
the time through *AD* is to the time
through *AE* as line *SA* is to line *AC*. And
since *AC*, as has been demonstrated
[f. 58*r*] is the mean proportional between
SA and *SB*, while as *SA* is to *AB*, so *DA* is to *AE*, therefore
the time through *AD* is to the time through *AE* as *DA* is to the
mean proportional between *DA* and *AE*, which was to be proved.

This conclusion gave the law of free fall in its mean-proportional form of expression, used by Galileo thenceforth in relating times and distances in descent.[6] Times and distances were

both mathematically continuous magnitudes and had been recognized as such by Aristotle himself; there was therefore no reason why they should not change continuously for the falling body. Speeds, however, seemed incapable of existing instantaneously. Hence Galileo was very slow to accept physical change of speed as literally mathematically continuous and to link it directly to time, which would mean literal acceptance of the concept of instantaneous speed in the modern sense.

After writing 147–2, Galileo added at the top of the page (written around the diagram and therefore afterward) an attempt to explain why weight as such should not enter into motions along inclined planes, speeds of bodies along them being determined by slope of plane alone. This unsuccessful gambit, based on an argument in *De motu*, confirms the early date of f. 147.

(147–1) It is to be considered that just as all heavy things rest in the horizontal [plane], the greater [weight] as well as the smaller, so they should move with the same speed [whether heavy or light] along inclined planes just as [they do] in the vertical itself. It would be good to demonstrate this, saying that if the heavier were faster, it would follow [*ad absurdum*] that the heavier would be slower, unequal things being joined, etc. [as had been done in *De motu* for free fall].

Moreover not only homogeneous heavy bodies would move at the same speed, but also heterogeneous ones such as a body of wood and lead. For since it was shown before [in *De motu*]

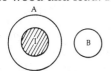 that large and small homogeneous things must move equally, you argue: Let *B* be a wooden sphere and *A* a lead one of such size as to have at its center a hollow for *B*, and let this [hollow lead sphere] also be heavier than a solid wooden sphere equal [in volume] to *A*, so that for the adversary it should move faster than *B*. Then if *B* were placed in *I*, the hollow, *A* [thus filled] would move more slowly than when it was lighter [and empty], which is absurd.[7]

Beneath this argument appears the word *Paralogism* written by Galileo in a different hand, probably in 1607. It was true that weight did not enter into the law of acceleration, as the equal speed of fall of bodies differing in weight plainly showed. The argument already given in *De motu* sufficed to establish this. The same argument, however, could not be extended to descent along inclined planes as in the above attempt to do that. In free fall the heavier body could not weigh down on the lighter when both were of the same material and moving through the same medium. On inclined planes, however, the fact of support from below deprived the analogous argument of cogency, as Galileo recognized in due course.

It was probably at this time that Galileo entered in the right-hand margin of f. 107v an Archimedean diagram of speeds growing in arithmetical progression, the column of successive odd numbers that represent the differences between successive square numbers, and the little triangle of speeds similar to that of f. 180r. If successive speeds grew as the odd numbers, then cumulative speeds from rest would necessarily be as the square numbers. On f. 152r he made, in Latin, a little table of distances and their corresponding times, showing times of 4 and 6 for distances of 4 and 9. The speeds previously shown as 10 and 15 were now made 20 and 30, holding the same ratio but reflecting the double-distance rule. A further notation on 147–2, in a smaller hand, suggests that f. 174r[8] was next written, recording the implications of making times along planes of the same height proportional to their lengths. Still in this very small hand, Galileo drew a more elaborate diagram based on a line 60 *punti* long, carefully measuring the other lines to confirm the relations he had established and verifying by subtraction the times and distances along a broken line. Using the newfound law of free fall, calculations were also made in this small hand on blank parts of ff. 130 and 187.

At this time Galileo's handwriting degenerated for a period, probably by a severe rheumatic attack. He corrected an earlier result obtained on f. 189v, concerning pendulums, and on f. 189r he calculated a verification of the second proposition communicated earlier to Guidobaldo, that descent takes less time along two conjugate chords in a vertical circle than along the single chord joining their endpoints,[9] thus extending the work previously done on f. 174r. (See p. 101 for work on f. 189r.)

On an unused part of f. 189v Galileo guessed at a general rule for times along two planes unequal in both slope and length.[10] By trying a numerical example he saw that his conjecture was wrong; he then found by trial the compound ratio which yielded the correct general rule and canceled his original guess.

In the autumn of 1604 Galileo wrote out a purported proof of his old chord law, needed in accordance with his organizational memorandum on 147–2. This was written out on the unused side of f. 172,[11] one of several sheets begun about 1602 and then saved for further theorems useful to his projected treatise. The proof was invalid by circularity of argument, mentioning "as demonstrated" the proposition that times of fall along planes of equal height are proportional to their lengths. Immediately below this, he wrote out a proof of the rule found on f. 189*v* for descents along planes unequal in both slope and length.[12] Proportionality of times to lengths of plane in descent from the same height, however, had not been demonstrated; it had merely been established (on ff. 174*r* and 189*r*) as consistent with Galileo's other findings. Noticing this defect in the proof Galileo drew an ink line through it, but not through the proof beneath, which would be valid whenever Galileo's theorem was properly proved.

Galileo next attempted to derive the law of free fall directly from his old triangle of speeds, in which velocities acquired in fall were represented as proportional to distances from rest. The derivation survives only in a copy made later at Florence by Mario Guiducci; this is found on f. 85*v*, where it was later canceled by Galileo, who used f. 85*r* to write out a new (and unrelated) theorem.

In order to understand this attempted demonstration, as well as another similar one soon afterward, it is essential to keep in mind the distinction between instantaneous velocity, referred to in Latin on f. 85*v* as *velocitas*, and overall speed through a distance from rest, which was not explicitly named in this attempted demonstration but was only implied in its conclusion.[13] To distinguish the two concepts I shall use the Italian word *velocità* to signify instantaneous velocity and employ the ordinary English word *speed* to mean overall speed through a distance. The same convention will be adopted in later instances in which Galileo used the same word for either meaning and failed to clarify this, as by saying "at *A*" or "through *AB*," or by some other device.

The purpose of f. 85*v* was to justify the mean-proportional rule (of 147–2) applied to distances from rest as a measure of the times of descent. For this it was necessary to introduce a relationship of square roots, which Galileo attempted to do by first establishing a ratio of squares, using a diagram that he had drawn, unlettered, on f. 180*v* under his old query concerning the maintenance in accelerated motion of a ratio expected between uniform motions. This showed a right triangle in which speeds acquired were represented by parallels to the base, as in the margin of f. 107*v*.

Taking up again a line of reasoning similar to that of 172–3, Galileo considered that for very small distances near any of these parallels, the speed must be very nearly the same as that represented by the given parallel, which in turn was simply proportional in length to the distance along the vertical from the point of rest. It accordingly seemed reasonable to consider the overall speed from rest as made up of the sum of a very large number of speeds through very small distances of this kind and hence as represented by the area of the triangle down to a given parallel. The areas, as a ratio of squares, thus represented a ratio of overall speeds from rest, while the corresponding lengths of vertical lines represented a ratio of velocitá, or speeds acquired at the given points. It was not until about a year later, when writing f. 179, that Galileo was confronted with evidence that something was wrong with this kind of argument.

Having created a relationship between distances of fall and overall speeds through those distances, which utilized lines and areas (corresponding to numbers and their squares), Galileo thought he saw his way clear to reverse the reasoning to obtain the relationship of distances to times, a relationship he already knew to be in accord with experimental measurement through f. 107*v*. As in the case of Galileo's theorem in 1602, arrival at a correct result (verified by actual test) merely rendered him uncritical for a time of the assumptions he had adopted to arrive at the result.

(f. 85*v*) I assume the acceleration of bodies falling along line *AL* to be such that velocità grow in the ratio of the spaces traversed, so that the velocità at *C* is to the velocità at *B* as space *CA* is to space *BA*, etc.

Matters standing thus, assume *AX* making some angle with *AL*, and take equal parts *AB*, *BC*, *CD*, *DE*, etc., drawing *BM*, *CN*, *DO*, *EP*, etc. Thus the velocità at *B*, *C*, *D*, and *E* of the body falling through *AL* are to one another as the distances *AB*, *AC*, *AD*, *AE*, etc. and are therefore to one another as lines *BM*, *CN*, *DO*, and *EP*.

But since velocità are increased successively at *all* points of line *AE*, and not just at those designated, therefore all these velocità [taken together] are related, one [case] to

98

another, as all the lines [together] drawn from all points of line
AE parallel to the said *BM, CN,* and *DO.* But these [parallels]
are infinitely many, and they constitute the triangle *AEP;*
therefore the velocità at all points of line *AB* are, to the velocità
at all points in line *AC,* as is triangle *ABM* to triangle *ACN,*
and so on for the others; that is, these [overall speeds through
AB and *AC*] are in the squared ratio of lines *AB* and *AC.*

But since, in the ratio of increases of [speed in] acceleration,
the times in which such motions are made must be diminished,
therefore the time in which the moveable goes through *AB* will
be to the time in which it goes through *AC* as line *AB* is to that
[line] which is the mean proportional between *AB* and *AC.*[14]

This vindicated the rule Galileo had been successfully using to
determine *times* in descent. The effective *speeds* through *AB* and
AC were as the squares of the distances from rest to *B* and *C* in
his diagram. But looking back at f. 152*r*, Galileo saw that he
had there assigned numbers for speeds through two distances
that were as the square roots, not the squares, of those distances.
If every individual degree of velocità followed that rule, the consequence would be what he next wrote out on f. 152*r*:

As *BA* to *AD,* let *DA* be to *AC,* and let *BE* be the
degree of velocità at *B*; and as *BA* to *AD,* let *BE* be
to *CF; CF* will be the degree of velocità at *C.* And since
as *CA* is to *AD* so *CF* is to *BE,* then as the square of
AC to the square of *AD,* so will be the square of *CF* to the
square of *BE*; further, since as the square of *CA* to the square
of *AD,* so *CA* is to *AB,* the square of *CF* will be to the square of
BE as *CA* is to *AB*; therefore points *E* and *F* are on a parabola.[15]

Which was the correct way to represent velocità, that is, individual speeds during motion accelerated from rest? Galileo
had no way, of course, to measure such changing individual
speeds; he had only been able to measure certain overall speeds
from rest. Or rather, not even that; what he had found, by measuring distances covered in a series of equal time intervals from
rest, were certain ratios existing between overall speeds during
such intervals of time. Where measurable distances were concerned, he had experimental evidence that speeds in acceleration
did grow in an arithmetical progression, that of the odd numbers
from unity when the time intervals were equal. Hence Galileo
would naturally prefer to keep the triangular representation of

f. 85*v*, which provided a plausible basis for the appearance of square numbers and thereby for the odd-number rule, though only the parabolic representation of f. 152*r* seemed appropriate for individual velocità.

Around the end of September 1604 Galileo had an opportunity to discuss various problems of motion with Paolo Sarpi, who wrote to him soon afterward with further questions. On 16 October Galileo replied that in rethinking the whole matter he had found a proof for the square law, the odd-number rule, and other things he had long been asserting, if granted the assumption that velocità are proportional to distances from rest. His demonstration was written out in Italian on f. 128 (which bears the same watermark as the cover sheet of the letter to Sarpi) and differs from that of f. 85*v* principally in naming an actual physical phenomenon which implies the definition of *velocità* to be discussed next.[16] A clue to Galileo's rethinking of the problem may be found on f. 189*r*, where he sketched the triangle of speeds again but with a semiparabola included and with the parallels that, one way or the other, must represent velocità. His reflections, to judge from the language he used on f. 128, probably went along these lines:

"The question is whether velocità at points along the line of fall should be represented by parallels to the base of a parabola passing through the point of rest, or by such parallels going on out to the hypotenuse of a right triangle. In the latter case, the individual velocità reached by a body at any two points would be directly proportional to the distances of those two points from rest; the other way, they would be as the square roots of those distances. Is there any way to tell what particular velocità a body actually has reached at different points in fall? . . . Yes, there is; experiments with horizontal bows show that when the same weight falls twice as far, it stretches the bowstring twice as much, and pile drivers show that the weight strikes twice as hard from a doubled height. Since in those actions the weight stays the same and only the velocità is increased, that *must* be proportional to distance fallen from rest. So the lines ending at the parabola here on f. 189*r*, related as the square roots of velocità, are really something quite different—as it were, they are the very contraries of the speeds which on f. 85*v* were shown to be related as the squares of the individual velocità. But the

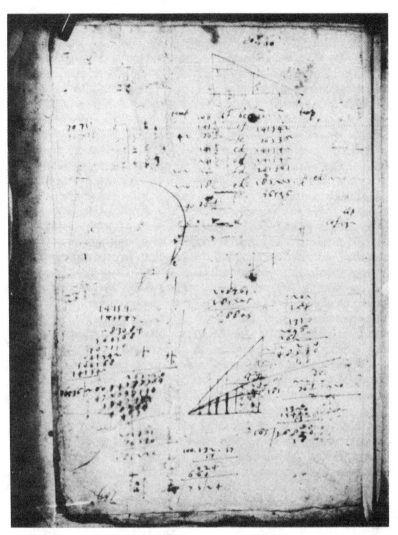

Folio 189r, vol. 72, Galilean manuscripts. Calculations verifying that descent takes less time along two conjugate chords to bottom of a vertical circle than along single chord connecting their extremities. At lower right (turned 90°), parabola of speeds (f. 152r) in triangle of speeds (ff. 85v, 107v, 180v). Line appearing to extend triangle belongs to earlier calculations, over which sketch was done. (Reproduced with permission of Biblioteca Nazionale Centrale, Florence. Photo by University of Toronto Photographic Services.)

contraries of speeds are *times*—and indeed I do get the times by taking the square roots of distances from rest, the same distances whose squares are as the speeds from rest. So I need not worry any longer about this parabola, since I already have the rule for comparing times."

Later on, as will be seen, Galileo decided to identify velocità with times, but not until he had got over the ancient prejudice against the notion of truly instantaneous speeds. It was more natural at first to think of speeds and times as contraries and to relate each separately to distances which he could measure. At this stage, he had simply defined the word *velocità* to mean "whatever it is in fact that increases proportionally to distance from rest in fall, as seen in the effects of a striking weight." This transformed *velocità* into what we call v^2 and consider to be a derived rather than a basic physical entity.[17] But obviously if we did consider it an independent entity basic to the analysis of falling bodies, we would take it as proportional to distance fallen just as Galileo did.

Galileo proceeded to demonstrate the times-squared law in such a way, and he adhered to this strange terminology for nearly five years before he shifted to our present way of speaking about velocity as proportional to time in free fall. Meanwhile he went on developing theorems relating times to distances in free descent, perfectly correctly. Despite common statements that Galileo began by assuming velocities (in our present, and his later sense) to be proportional to distances from rest, rather than to times, there is no evidence in his notes on motion that he ever made that assumption. It became ascribed to him only because of his choice of words in 1604 and by disregard of his specification of "machines that act by striking" in the ensuing demonstration.

Beside the old unlettered triangle on f. 180*v*, Galileo now drew freehand an open-ended triangle, also unlettered but otherwise exactly like the diagram he proceeded to draw on each page of the demonstration written out for Paolo Sarpi:[18]

(f. 128) I suppose (and perhaps I shall be able to demonstrate this) that the naturally falling body goes continually increasing its velocità according as the distance increases from the point from which it parted, as for example the heavy body departing from the point *A* and falling through the line *AB*, I suppose that the degree of velocità at point *D* is as much greater than

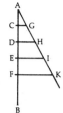

the degree of velocità at *C* as the distance *DA* is greater than *CA*, and so the degree of velocità at *E* is to the degree of velocità at *D* as *CA* to *DA*, and so at every point of the line *AB* it is found with degrees of velocità proportional to the distances from the terminus *A*. This principle appears to me very natural [that is, physical], and one that corresponds to all the experiences we seen in instruments and machines that work by striking, where the percussent works so much the greater effect, the greater the height from which it falls. And this principle assumed, I shall demonstrate the rest.

Draw line *AK* at any angle with *AF*, and through points *C, D, E,* and *F* draw the parallels *CG, DH, EI,* and *EK*. Since lines *FK, EI, DH,* and *CD* are to one another as *FA, EA, DA,* and *CA*, therefore the velocità at points *F, E, D,* and *C* are as lines *FK, EI, DH,* and *CG*. So the degrees of velocità go continually increasing at all points of line *AF* according to the increase of parallels drawn from those same points. Moreover, since the speed with which the body has come from *A* to *D* is compounded from all the degrees of velocità it had at all the points of line *AD*, and the speed with which it has passed through line *AC* is compounded from all the degrees of velocità that it has had at all points of line *AC*, therefore the speed with which it has passed line *AD* has that ratio to the speed with which it has passed line *AC* which all the parallel lines drawn from all points of line *AD* over to [line] *AH* have to all the parallels drawn from all points of line *AC* over to [line] *AG*; that is, the [ratio of the] square of *AD* to the square of *AC*. Therefore the speed with which it has passed line *AD* has to the speed with which it has passed line *AC* the square of the ratio that *DA* has to *AC*.

And since speed has to speed the contrary proportionality of that which time has to time—because it is the same to increase speed as to diminish time—therefore the time of motion through *AD* has to the time of motion through *AC* that ratio which is the square root of the ratio which distance *AD* has to distance *AC*. The distances, then, from the beginning of motion are as the squares of the times; and dividing [into equal times], the spaces passed in [successive] equal times are as the odd numbers from unity—which corresponds to what I have said all along and have observed by experiments. And thus all truths agree with one another. . . .[19]

At precisely this time Galileo's studies of motion were suddenly interrupted by an astronomical event of profound significance to his scientific career, and though he did a few additional things related to motion during 1605 it will be best to postpone discussion of them until that other event has been dealt with.

II

Astronomical tables in general use predicted a conjunction of Jupiter and Mars in Saggitarius for 8 October 1604. Because such events were astrologically important, a great many astronomers throughout Europe were observing the skies that night. Nothing unusual was seen, and in fact the predicted conjunction did not occur until late afternoon on 9 October. That night many astronomers were again making observations, and some noticed a new star near the place of the conjunction. Later on there were various claims that it had been observed earlier, some placing it late in September, but it is clear that those assertions resulted from the difference in calendars used in Catholic and Protestant lands. The new star was very bright, more so than Jupiter and approaching the brightness of Venus, but because of the season it was visible only for a short time after sunset.

At Padua the new star was first seen on the night of 10 October by Baldessar Capra, Simon Mayr (his German mathematical tutor), and a friend of theirs. The skies were cloudy for a few nights thereafter, so they were unable to confirm the observation until the evening of 15 October. It was on 16 October that Galileo wrote to Sarpi concerning his proof of the law of free fall; since his letter mentioned nothing about the new star it is evident that he had not yet heard about it. He himself had shown very little interest in astronomy up to this time, though he was obliged to teach it, and there is no record of his having made astronomical observations before 1604. He first heard of the new star from an elderly man of very distinguished family, Giacomo Alvise Cornaro, a good friend of his, mentioned earlier as also closely associated with the Capras, Gromo, and the alchemical group at Padua. It was through Cornaro that the Paduan observers sent word of their discovery to Galileo, if not immediately after its confirmation at least very soon afterward.

Galileo was at once interested in the phenomenon, which according to the Aristotelian philosophers could not be truly a celestial event at all, but must be located in the elemental sphere beneath the moon. No change in the heavens was possible according to Aristotelian dogma, since the substance of which they were made was perfect and inalterable. A famous supernova had previously appeared in 1572, the first to be very carefully observed and studied. Visible for more than a year, it is called Tycho's star because the famed Danish astronomer not only observed it himself with great care, but collected from astronomers all over Europe their observations and demonstrated from its total absence of parallax that it must be situated among the fixed stars. Galileo recalled having been shown that star as a child. A supposed new star had been detected in 1600 or 1601, in the Swan, but since it was not conspicuous it had not been the occasion of much discussion.

Tycho's star gave rise to a host of pamphlets, mainly of astrological character, but it does not appear that Aristotelian philosophers paid much attention to the opinions of astronomers, the best of whom agreed with Tycho's findings which truly offered a threat to Peripatetic prestige. The nova of 1604, however, was destined to become a storm center, especially at Padua, with Galileo as leader in the battle against the Aristotelians.

Except for a fascinating unfinished draft letter written about the end of January 1605,[20] none of Galileo's letters about the nova survive; yet he must have written a good many, since he preserved the answers he received to some. His first move was to write to other cities, especially Verona, to obtain data on observations elsewhere in order to determine whether they revealed any parallax or evidence of motion on the part of the new star. His own earliest recorded observation was made on 28 October. Information supplied by Ilario Altobelli at Verona from careful observations there made it evident that no parallax could be detected, so that the star must be far beyond the moon. Altobelli's letters show that he had no regard for the opinions of the Aristotelians, whom he called "semiphilosophers," urging Galileo to explain to them patiently the nature of parallax by starting from terrestrial illustrations and showing how it conclusively established the location of the nova.

The brightness of the star excited much curiosity, so Galileo delivered three public lectures on it to very large audiences. These were probably given in November, when the star was still visible after sunset, and they were heard by more than a thousand persons. From late November until Christmas the nova was too close to the sun to be seen, after which it reappeared in the early morning sky. Galileo was the first to observe it at Padua when it again became visible. It had declined noticeably in brightness but remained in exactly the same place with respect to the fixed stars.

Galileo's lectures on the new star have not survived except for the first page and a fragment near the end,[21] but their content can be fairly well determined by his own description of them in the unfinished letter mentioned above and from some books published early in 1605 by others at Padua and by Galileo under a pseudonym.[22] His two chief purposes in the November lectures were to explain the nature and application of parallactic reasoning to measurement of distances and to refute the Aristotelian theory that new stars and comets were sublunar phenomena in the supposed region of fire above the air and below the moon. At this stage of the affair there was no mention of the Copernican system. One fixed star more or less has no bearing on the planetary motions, and for Galileo to have attempted to relate the two would only have weakened his attack on the Aristotelians in the minds of a general audience.

The public lectures were promptly challenged in debates on the university campus by Cesare Cremonini, Galileo's personal friend and scientific adversary from at least this time on. It is my opinion that the controversy over the location of the nova of 1604 marked a crucial turning point in Galileo's conception of scientific investigation. His piecemeal approach to physical science through mathematics, taking this or that application as it happened to be discovered, threatened the entire body of Aristotelian science, which could not tolerate gaps or inconsistencies among its parts. Both men understood this; their differences arose because Galileo felt no obligation to protect Aristotelianism from harm, while Cremonini did. The aftermath of this debate is easy to follow in Galileo's subsequent clashes with philosophers, and ultimately with the theologians who came to their support. There is no better glimpse of its beginnings than this statement, published by Antonio Lorenzini but almost certainly written by Cremonini:

But the Mathematicians are not satisfied, and they adduce the expressed view that it is bad judgment to abandon the senses and go searching for reason. But O, Gentle Spirits who come contradicting not out of obstinacy but from love of Truth, boast not that you have an opinion that is [sensibly] manifest in this matter. For if we were close to the Star there would be

106

no difficulty, but since opinion is uncertain in distant things, know that you do not start from the senses any more than we do. Our argument is drawn from the principles of physical things known by the senses when located at a suitable distance, and is confirmed by Philosophical induction. Your argument is likewise derived from the senses, but is asserted of things unbelievably distant. And just as ours is Physical, so yours is Astronomical, and partly of that Science called Optics, which is delightful not only for its certainty (which it draws from its father, the geometer) but also for the marvels it promises. For it is indeed a remarkable thing and a stupendous prerogative to know sizes and distances from afar, and that very delight, through hope of its extension by the certainty of your [mathematical] principles, is the cause of your deception (be this said in peace) in the application of your principles, because you depart too far from mother Physics, the origin of Astronomy.[23]

No mathematician, let alone mathematicians in general, had previously said that it is bad judgment to abandon the senses and go searching for reason. The view of mathematicians, especially those who were Platonists, had always been just the opposite. In the present controversy, however, Galileo had expressed precisely this opinion. His idea was simple and direct: whenever it is possible to find a mathematical rule which is exemplified by things accessible to sensory verification and which is not contradicted by further experience, we may be certain that that rule holds wherever applied. Parallactic displacement is such a rule, used in surveying fields and in judging the distances and heights of remote objects. Therefore parallax is equally reliable in celestial observations, Galileo maintained, and it was bad judgment to refute any of the conclusions thus established by appealing to reasons of a quite different kind, that is, by invoking the unchangeability of the heavens or any supposed qualitative differences between terrestrial and celestial objects.

It was this position to which Cremonini would never assent. The "principles of physical things known by the senses when located at a suitable distance" on which he depended had nothing to do with measurements of any kind. Measurements as such could never be physical principles, which comprised certain qualities and properties capable of determining the behavior of the things. One might as well confuse the weight of a thing, which was a mere measure, with its heaviness, which was the property that determined its motion. The concept of a science in which measurements, rather than qualities or essences, would govern physical conclusions was unacceptable to the philosophical mind. Such a science strongly appealed to Galileo, who conceived it not as a substitute for or a rival of philosophy, but as a basis of establishing at least some reliable knowledge that would not have to be continually revised. There would always be other knowledge that science could not touch, and he was content to leave that to philosophers. That attitude is so conspicuous in all Galileo's later books that to confuse his science with any particular philosophy based on a set of principles in the traditional sense is indefensible. Whether Galileo's attitude was a threat to any philosophy is quite another question. Galileo did not think it was; as he said later, "Philosophy itself cannot but benefit from our disputes, for if our conceptions prove true, new achievements will be made; if false, their refutation will further confirm the original doctrines."[24] Philosophers took the opposite view and attacked Galileo throughout his life on nearly everything he published.

Galileo replied to Cremonini, though ostensibly to Lorenzini, with the *Dialogue of Cecco di Ronchitti*[25] in rustic dialect, filled with scorn for philosophical astronomy and insisting on measurement as the only secure criterion. His peasant spokesman scoffed at the idea that the substance of the new star had any relevance to its location; for all mathematicians cared, it might be made of polenta. Philosophy had nothing to do with measurement, on which any land surveyor spoke with more knowledge than the professors.

The uses of parallax, obfuscated in Lorenzini's book, were made clear at some length by homely illustrations. At the instruction of Matteo, who spoke for Galileo, Natale moved right and left, backward and forward, observing from the ground and from high in a tree and describing the changing apparent positions of other trees with respect to one another, their apparent heights, and the like. The seemingly unnecessarily elaborate discussion had its roots in Galileo's reflections early in 1605, after he had delivered the public lectures and when he had decided that he should publish a treatise based on them, of which only meager traces survive.

From an unfinished draft letter probably written late in January 1605 for his old friend Girolamo Mercuriale at Pisa, who had applied for a copy of Galileo's lectures on the new star, the course of his reflections on it can be outlined. The star had diminished in brightness from the start, suggesting to Galileo that it might be moving away from the earth. The effect was not decisive before the nova had been lost to view because of the increasing proximity of the sun, so he had to await its reappearance after Christmas to make sure whether it had continued to decrease in apparent size and to know whether it had moved at all with respect to the fixed stars. Then, when its continual shrinkage and lack of parallactic displacement were confirmed, Galileo solicited the opinions of others about its origin and its place. Several replies from Verona showed a consensus that the origin of the nova had something to do with the conjunction of Jupiter with Mars and that its place in the sky, if not among the fixed stars themselves, was at least as distant as the outer planets.

It then occurred to Galileo that if the diminution in apparent size were in fact occasioned by increasing distance from the earth, some parallactic displacement ought eventually to be observable. For example, when the star had diminished to one-half its original size, it would necessarily have moved to at least double its original distance from the earth; and being assumed to have started no closer than Jupiter, it would have been seen at places widely separated along its line of motion. Unless that line happened to pass through the earth, some shift of its position among the fixed stars would eventually be observable. Furthermore, if the earth itself moved, as Copernicus believed, an additional and different parallactic shift might be found. Hence it appeared to Galileo that the momentous Copernican question was on the verge of being definitively answered. Accordingly he included in the Cecco *Dialogue* a discussion of parallax in three different planes, though when that book went to the printer in mid-February there had been no observable shift. Since he was preparing others for an expected discovery, Galileo included in his book two oblique references to the Copernicans, both favorable.

When the Cecco *Dialogue* was reprinted at Verona, probably about June 1605, hardly any changes were made in it except that the two favorable references to Copernicans in the Padua edition had both been made unfavorable. There is some evidence that Galileo was himself responsible for the changes made, which also included rewriting of a terminal poem in Italian and deletion of marginal references to Lorenzini found in the Padua edition. While it is possible that some editor at Verona made the significant changes relating to Copernicans, that is not very likely, since all at Verona who had corresponded with Galileo probably believed him to have been the true author, were friendly to him, and had said nothing against Copernicus in their letters. It therefore appears likely that Galileo, confronted with failure of the first possible confirmation of Copernicanism by direct observation, lost faith in it from 1605 until 1610.[26]

III

Galileo spent the summer of 1605 at Florence as special tutor to the young prince Cosimo de' Medici. There he presented him with one of his sectors, instruction in the use of which was a good course in practical mathematics, and he promised to dedicate to Cosimo a published book on the instrument. Before he left Padua (probably during March when Galileo was again ill in bed), he wrote out a draft proof that less time is taken along two conjugate chords than along the single quadrant chord.[27] The complete proof was not put together until later, and was rather complicated because of the necessity of correlating two different sets of proportionalities. (Galileo's claim to Guidobaldo in 1602 that he had a proof from mechanics was based on his mistaken belief then that acceleration could be ignored.)

After his return from Florence Galileo prepared a very elaborate drawing of a quadrant chord, two equal conjugate chords to it, a path made up of four equal chords, and part of an eight-chord path.[28] He computed in detailed tables the times along each of these from the highest point and along parts of them beginning from lower points, carried out to six places. In the course of this work he discovered how to reduce the times to a common standard, whatever path was chosen. An additional or an ulterior purpose in this work is discoverable in some notations Galileo wrote across the face of the diagram, in which he raised the question of the ultimate circular fall corresponding to infinitesimal successive chords and made some conjectures about possible general rules for circular descent related to straight fall. These attempts remained idle, and no theorems concerning circular fall as such are found among Galileo's notes at this or any other period.

Galileo now attempted to found his long-projected treatise on strong logical grounds, starting from Euclid Book Five, Definition Five. The two pages used were ff. 138 and 179, the former bearing a watermark found only in 1605 among Galileo's dated letters. On f. 138*r* is a theorem taken from Archimedes' *On Spiral Lines* demonstrating the proportionality of times and distances in uniform motion which appears as the first proposition in the third day of *Two New Sciences*.[29]

The theorem on f. 138*v* was new; Galileo wrote it for a special purpose which ended in failure. Its purpose was to prepare for f. 179–1, the proposition needed to break the circular argument of f. 173–1 and permit rigorous derivation of the law of free fall from Galileo's theorem. As first written, 138–2 had a diagram of complete generality, over which was then pasted one in which the spacing grows from left to right in roughly the order 1–3–5 and so on, for a reason that is reflected in two additions, here placed in square brackets, made to this proposition and its proof.

(138–2) If there are any number of spaces, and others of matching multitude thereto, which when taken in pairs have the same ratio; and if two moveables move through these so that in any pair of corresponding spaces the [speeds of the] motions are [equal and] equable, then as all spaces in the antecedent motion are to all spaces in the consequent motion, so will be the time for all motion in the first to the time of motion in all space of the second.

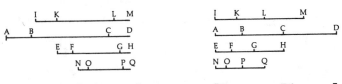

[Original Diagram]   [Pasteover Diagram]

Since indeed the [speeds of the] motions through the two spaces *AB* and *EF* are [equal and] equable, then by the preceding [138–1] as the space *AB* is to *EF*, so will be the time *IK* to *NO*; and it is likewise demonstrated that as *BC* to *FG*, so *KL* to *OP*, and as *CD* to *GH*, so *LM* to *PQ*; and since *AB* is to

EF as *BC* is to *FG*, and *CD* to *GH*, then as *IK* to *NO*, so will *KL* be to *OP* and *LM* to *PQ*. Moreover, since as *AB* is to *EF*, *BC* is to *FG*, and *CD* is to *GH*, then as *AB* alone is to *EF* alone, so all *AD* is to all *EH*; and it is similarly concluded that as *IK* singly is to *NO* singly, so all *IM* is to all *NQ*. But as *AB* alone is to *EF* alone, so *IK* is to *NO*; therefore as the whole space *AD* is to the whole space *EH*, so time *IM* is to time *NQ*, which was to be shown.[30]

The interest of this theorem lies in its explicit attempt to reason about proportionality in terms of one-to-one correspondence. The feebleness of 172–3 as a means of justifying ratios in accelerated motion taken as if it were uniform motion was apparent to Galileo; he knew what the facts were, but he was hard put to justify logically the use of such ratios. A valid and useful procedure would be to limit their use to different linear descents through the same vertical height along different slopes. Without that limitation he was obliged to add the words *equal and*, belied by the diagram and producing only a self-evident truth. Those additions were probably made after the collapse of the sequence of arguments on f. 179, below. They served only the purpose of showing Galileo why he had come to grief, and account for his abandonment of this theorem in further attacks on the basic problem. What he needed to be able to say was not "equal and," but "in the same arithmetical progression with regard to their successors and," or something of the kind, which probably accounts for the pasteover diagram; but since he could not see how to make the desired result follow from that, even apart from the awkwardness of any such specification, he was unable to draw any fruit from the application of one-to-one correspondence to finite segments. To apply f. 138–2 to the proposition he wished to prove, he would have had to assume infinitely many "segments"—not points—in a finite line. It was a problem that had been created earlier, in the margin of f. 107*v*, when the Archimedean representation of an arithmetical progression had been enclosed in a triangle, ignoring the fact that the former always contains a *first* line, whereas the latter comes to a point.

Before Galileo became aware of the difficulty and vitiated the usefulness of 138–2 by adding "equal and," he wrote out 179–1, for which 138–2 had been written. The two documents are in very similar handwriting, and 179–1 refers to 138–2 as "the preceding." Galileo's purpose on 179–1 was to prove the propor-

tionality of times to distances from rest for planes of the same
height; this had been assumed on 147-2 and confirmed by measurements on f. 174, as indeed by all Galileo's calculations for
the elaborate diagram on f. 166. But he still lacked a proof, and
this was the one proposition which, combined with Galileo's
theorem, would rigorously prove the law of free fall.

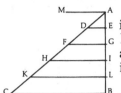

(179–1) If the same moveable is carried
in the vertical and in an inclined plane
having the same height, the times of motion
are to one another as the lengths of the
inclined plane and of the vertical.

To the horizontal *CB* let there be the
vertical *AB* and the inclined plane *AC*, of
which the height is the same, that is, the vertical *AB*. Along
these let the same moveable descend; I say that the time of
motion along *AB* is to the time of motion along *AC* as length
AB is to length *AC*.

Indeed, since it is assumed that in natural descent the
moments of velocità grow continually according to the ratio
of departure in the vertical from the horizontal in which motion
began, it is clear that producing the horizontal line *AM* parallel
to *BC*, and taking in the vertical any number of points *E*, *G*, *I*,
and *L*, through which are drawn the parallels to the horizontal
ED, *GF*, *IH*, and *LK*, then the moment or degree of velocità
of the moveable at point *E* will be the same with the degree of
speed of motion through *AC* at point *D*, since points *E* and *D*
have the same vertical distance from the horizontal *AM*; and
it is likewise concluded that the moment of velocità at points *F*
and *G* is the same, and furthermore [those] at points *H* and *I*,
K and *L*, *C* and *B*. And since velocità is always intensified in
the ratio of [vertical] departure from the terminus [above],
it follows that in motion *AB* there are as many different degrees
or moments of velocità as there are points in line *AB* farther
and farther from terminus *A*, to which there correspond as
many in line *AC*, and these [correspondences] are determined
by the parallel lines in which the same degrees of velocità exist.

Therefore it is as if in line *AB* there are innumerable spacelets,
so to speak, and others [in *AC*] equal in a certain sense to that
multitude [added later: taken in pairs] according to the same
rule of correspondence and marked along *AC* by innumerable
parallel lines extended from points of line *AB* to line *AC* [added
later: the intercepted spaces *AD*, *DF*, *FH*, etc. corresponding
one by one to spaces *AE*, *EG*, *GI*, etc., according to the ratio

of *AD* to *AB*]; and these [spacelets] exist in single pairs corresponding in the same degree of speed.

Therefore from the preceding [138–2], all the times of the movements from *AB* have, to the times of movements likewise taken [conjointly] through *AC*, the same ratio as that of all the spaces of line *AB* to all the spaces of line *AC*. Moreover this is the same as [saying that] the time of fall through *AB* is to the time of fall through *AC* as line *AB* is to line *AC*, which was to be demonstrated.[31]

The close relationship of this argument to those of f. 85*v* and the demonstration for Sarpi is evident. The phrase "degree of velocità" used in them is again found in 179–1, for the last time, where "moment of velocità" is first introduced as synonymous with it. The argument begins by associating the infinitude of velocità in the vertical with that along the incline, one to each point, but then the reasoning switches to tiny intervals of distance rather than mathematical points, so that the same phrase must be translated as "degree of speed." It was only by speaking of *finite* intervals, however small, that Galileo was able to utilize f. 138*v* to arrive at a conclusion concerning times along the vertical and the incline. The validity of 179–1 was therefore restricted to quantum-changes in speed along the two lines, "innumerable so to speak," as Galileo put it, but nevertheless countable and not mathematically continuous.

Before proceeding to the other propositions on f. 179 it may be mentioned that the assumption which began the argument was correct in saying that moments of velocità grow with the *vertical* departure from rest alone, regardless of slope, but was not correct in inserting "continually according to the ratio of departure," at least in the sense that velocità at any two points are in the ratio of the distances of those points from rest. Galileo made no use in his argument of that ratio (as he had done in the proof for Sarpi for a different purpose), so that the proof above did not suffer from its unnecessary inclusion.

As was the case with his first proof of Galileo's theorem and the proof for Sarpi, the correctness of the conclusion of 179–1, known to Galileo on other evidence, tended to support his faith in the unnecessary additional assumption. What followed as 179–2 was a simple corollary relating directly the times along any two slopes.[32] It was only in attempting to prove 179–3 that he came to realize that something was wrong. That proposition he abandoned when he had hardly begun the proof, and either then or later he pasted over it two slips of paper altering the basis of analysis from "moments of velocità" to "moments of heaviness."[33] I believe those slips to have been cut from a page written in 1603, at the time of writing f. 180r, and to have been pasted over 179–3 early in 1606. They indicated Galileo's decision to abandon the kinematic for the earlier dynamic approach to accelerated motion, but this was not followed up. For a considerable time, Galileo abandoned his work on motion again in favor of other pressing matters that will be described in chapter 7.

The proposition of 179–3 was in accordance with a part of the proof of the law of free fall written for Sarpi. When Galileo wrote it, he had no doubt that it was correct, and it is of some interest that the same mistake was made many years later by G. W. Leibniz in his *Essay on Dynamics*, in a passage he did not go back to correct when he wrote the correct statement a few pages later.[34]

(179–3) If in the line of descent two unequal distances be taken from the beginning of motion, the moments of speed with which the moveable goes through those distances are to one another in the squared ratio of such descents.

Let the line of natural descent be *AB*, in which, from the beginning of motion, let two distances *AC* and *AD* be taken. I say that the moments of speed with which the moveable goes through *AD* are to the moments of speed with which it goes through *AC* in the squared ratio of distances *AD* and *AC*.

Assume line *AE*, making an angle with *AB*——[35]

Since here the phrase *momenta velocitatis* was applied to motions *through* two distances, it must be read as "moments of speed," though in 179–1 and 179–2 the same phrase had been applied to velocità *at* two points in the line of fall and retained the sense of "moments of velocità" under the convention adopted in this book. The difficulty that necessarily arose from identifying the two conceptions first struck Galileo as he began the proof, perhaps in the course of lettering his diagram. Evidently he first drew the two lines as in the proof for Sarpi except that this time they represented different *motions*, one vertical and one along a slope. The points *A* and *B* were lettered, and then *C* and *D* were placed between them, *E* being added to indicate indefinite continuation of motion along the slope (as *B* indicated this along the vertical). No trouble arose in drawing lines *CK* and

DL for speeds acquired at *C* and *D*, equal to those acquired at *K* and *L* (by 179–1). But the speeds *FG* and *HI*, I believe, called Galileo's attention to a seeming anomaly. Thinking of *AC* as a unit distance and *CK* as a unit speed, the speeds through descents greater than *AC* ought, by the rule of squaring, to become very much greater than the parallels representing speeds at *H*, *D*, and so on, whereas the speed through *AF*, by the same rule of squaring, ought to diminish much more rapidly than parallels such as *FG*, above *AC*, since squaring a fraction diminishes it while squaring a number increases it.[36] Hence it had been an illusion to suppose that the parabola of f. 152*r* could be ignored, and the whole logical basis of the law of free fall was again up in the air.

Galileo's reason for abandoning 179–3 may have differed from this, which is offered only as one of various plausible explanations. At this point Galileo knew that the times-squared law was correct, and that the conclusion of 179–1 was also correct, but that the manner in which squaring entered into the acquired and the overall speeds could not be that expressed in 179–3 and used in f. 85*v* and the proof for Sarpi. He did not abandon 179–1 even in 1618, when it was copied by Niccolò Arrighetti and criticized by him. At that time Galileo merely added a further clarification to it; ultimately the part of the assumption used in deriving it which was both necessary and sufficient became Galileo's one postulate on natural acceleration in *Two New Sciences*, where 179–1 became Proposition Three and was proved by appeal to that postulate.[37]

In preparation for the events which followed when Galileo returned to his studies of motion in 1607, it should be mentioned once more that the concept of "speed at a point" long appeared to Galileo as a mere fiction, if not a contradiction in terms. Speed required motion, which could not take place at a point. Very small distances and very small times sufficed for his purposes. He did not mind using the mean-proportional rule to determine times from distances, because times and distances were universally granted to be continuous magnitudes. Speed as such was not, and Galileo was slow to follow in this regard the direction in which his mathematics pointed. It is a mistake to think that he assumed from the outset that mathematics governed nature and physics must conform to it; rather, mathematics gradually forced his hand in this thorny question of literally continuous change.

SEVEN

1606-8

I

By The End of 1605 the new star had become very dim and was no longer seen after Christmas, when it had again passed the sun. How much Galileo had done in developing his original lectures into a discourse concerning the origin of the phenomenon and its diminution and disappearance is not known. Thus far he had left Capra's remarks unanswered, and since he had reason to suspect that unprecedented opposition to his reappointment as professor was connected with the arguments over the new star, it is likely that early in 1606 he intended to publish his own views more conventionally than he had done in the Cecco dialogue. At any rate there is a letter of his dated 2 February 1606, to Guidobaldo del Monte, in which he said he was transmitting "my Book of Astronomical Considerations."[1] No book by that title was published by Galileo, and since Capra's book had been called *Astronomical Consideration about the New Star of 1604*, what Galileo sent to Guidobaldo was probably the manuscript of his intended reply. Among his notes on motion there is one sheet of calculations (f. 134*v*) possibly related to the new star and having one of the watermarks associated with 1605.

Late that same year Ludovico delle Colombe obtained a license to publish a book on the nova of 1604 that was probably printed in January 1606 and would have reached Galileo in February.[2] Colombe's opinion was that the 1604 star was not new, but had always been in the heavens, a theory he promised on his title page to reconcile with all true astronomy, philosophy, and theology. A devastating answer to it was published at Florence in June 1606, entitled *Considerations of Alimberto Mauri on some*

117

Passages in the Discourse *of Lodovico* [sic] *delle Colombe.*[3] After a year of inquiries Colombe, still unable to find any flesh-and-blood Alimberto Mauri, suspected that the attack had really been written by Galileo. I believe he was right, since much in the book that would hardly have been written by any other professor of astronomy at the time fits Galileo's style and outlook. Certainly Galileo had a large part in the book, if it was not entirely his. I shall refer to its author as "Mauri," and it is my opinion that parts of it were taken from the "Astronomical Considerations" Galileo had sent to Guidobaldo, hastily rearranged and supplemented to attack a new opponent rather than belatedly reply to an old one.

Colombe's theory was that beyond the stars we ordinarily see there are other stars too remote for unaided vision, one or another of which is sometimes magnified by a lenticular portion of the Crystalline Sphere as it slowly rotates between them and the fixed stars. In this way he was able to account for the absence of parallax shown by the new star while at the same time saving the Aristotelian heavens from any change. This was precisely the kind of ad hoc philosophical astronomy that Galileo liked least of all. The reply by "Mauri" cited some of the arguments of Cecco against the supposed incorruptibility of the heavens and the notion of an element of fire, it ridiculed Lorenzini, and went on to discuss some misapprehensions about optics which Colombe had accepted from standard authors of the time. (Neither Cecco nor Lorenzini had been explicitly mentioned by Colombe.) "Mauri" calculated mathematically the minimum duration of visibility of a star on Colombe's hypothesis, showing this to be not one year but some forty years. He showed a very keen understanding of the history of astronomy, necessary for interpreting ideas about the starry sphere, the crystalline sphere, and spheres added by Arab astronomers for motions unknown in Aristotle's time, remarking that observation alone (and not philosophy) could improve astronomy. Most striking of all is this passage from "Mauri" in reply to Colombe's repudiation of epicycles:

This is great. Philosophers want uniformity [of motion] in the stars, and not imaginary or feigned uniformity, but true and real. And since the motion of the sun, for example, appears sometimes slower and again faster, while Saturn is now retrograde and again stationary, this uniformity is clearly repugnant to sense. So they run to the Astronomers for help (since the

Philosophers cannot manage this matter for themselves), in order that they may bring forward the reason for such appearances and thus maintain in men's minds as truths these ideas of Philosophers about uniform and regular skies. So the Astronomers, as faithful friends of theirs, have thought day and night about epicycles, eccentrics, and equants, and have given them those frameworks, so that if they wish they can easily triumph in contests against the most ferocious opponent.

But now behold how those instruments, formerly not in their possession, are by Philosophers harmfully vilified out of contempt for the donors, or else are abused through ignorance in such matters, and how in place of victory these make them lose the battle. Take our modern Peripatetic here, for example, who for some reason does not perceive that by his declaring epicycles imaginary, he likewise affirms thereby his axioms and regularities to be imaginary. For if it is true (as it is most true) that effects follow from their causes, how can they ever deem the celestial movements really regular when the epicycles, eccentrics, and equants, by means of which alone they can save (or rather, cause) uniformity of motions, are held fabulous and fictitious?[4]

"Mauri" concluded that Colombe had better stick to his philosophical astronomy and leave mathematical astronomy out of it, since it was hopeless to make them agree in principle. The implication was that if the philosophers had not long ago run into trouble and appealed for help to mathematicians, the latter would never have bothered with epicycles, eccentrics, and equants for the planets. There is a good deal of historical truth to this. Traditionally it was Plato who first asked mathematicians to rationalize all observed heavenly motions in terms of uniform revolutions in perfect circles. The task was carried out by Eudoxus, and again centuries later, in a different way, by Hipparchus and Ptolemy, who introduced the mathematical devices named. These had been used for nearly 1,500 years without challenge.

"Mauri" remarked in several places that astronomy could be improved only by attention to observations, not by new hypotheses, and that in fact there already existed sufficient accurate observations for the task. This also was historically correct. Recent precise observations made by Tycho Brahe provided the raw data, and Johann Kepler was engaged at this very time in the task of utilizing them in a proper planetary theory, published in 1609, after which epicycles and equants were no longer needed.

In 1606, however, they still provided the only planetary theory consistent with observations. "Mauri" had much else to say about Colombe's scorn for them, and in particular when Colombe said that they were fictions invented by astronomers only because they could not otherwise explain planetary stations and retrogradations, "Mauri" replied:

Epicycles were invented to save any appearance that could not be correspondingly well satisfied by other means; indeed, I say further, to save appearances for which Astronomers had rendered sufficient causes also in other ways, as by eccentrics. So I do not know why you want to restrict the use and jurisdiction of those poor epicycles. I believe this is only because it is their destiny always to be beaten down and put upon by your Peripatetics. Yet, in their favor, they have like valorous knights continually risked life with all its possessions, maintaining with lance on thigh the conformity and uniformity of celestial movements which, without their aid, would long ago have been smashed by experience itself.[5]

The movements meant were of course the philosophical uniform circular motions that the Peripatetics themselves insisted on. Nothing in mathematics demanded such motions for planets.

In my opinion Galileo composed the "Mauri" book in March/April 1606, using to some extent material already drafted during 1605 but directing his new attack against philosophical astronomy as such. Late in April 1606 Galileo went to Venice, determined to stay until the question of his reappointment (and salary) was settled. It happened that he arrived just as the quarrel between the Venetian government and Pope Paul V came to a head, and he was obliged to remain until mid-May before he could get a hearing. In this famous dispute Cardinal Bellarmine, as theologian to the pope, caused Venice to be placed under the interdict, and Paolo Sarpi as theologian to the Venetian government advised its defiance. This was the first successful instance of the kind, during which Galileo was present at the expulsion of the Jesuits from Venetian territory. When he was finally able to get a hearing on his own problem, he was assured of reappointment although the salary question remained unsettled.

II

Galileo's long delay in printing his book on the "military compass" and dedicating it to Cosimo de' Medici is best explained by supposing him to have held this back as bait for employment at the Tuscan court. Not much effort had to be expended in preparing the book for printing, as it differs little from the manuscript copies circulated from 1601 to 1605. During June the printer did his work at Galileo's own house; only sixty copies were printed, some dated June and others July 1606.[6] The reason for private printing was to maintain Galileo's virtual monopoly on the instrument; no illustration of his sector or instructions for calculating its scales was included, and copies went only to owners and buyers of Galileo's sector. Despite these precautions, however, the work was plagiarized in a doubly offensive manner, as will be seen.

Toward the beginning of July Galileo heard from Vincenzio Giugni that the Grand Duchess Christina had expressed her wish that he visit Florence again this summer, as the year before. During July the printer finished his work on the *Military Compass*, dedicated to Cosimo de' Medici. Early in August the Tuscan ambassador at Venice advised the court that Galileo had received the terms he wanted in his reappointment, and about the end of that month Galileo arrived again in Florence to express his gratitude. He returned to Padua in mid-October, only to be taken ill by "a serious and dangerous malady that took away all my force."

It was probably late in 1606 or early in 1607 that Galileo devised the thermoscope as a means of noting changes in temperature. This consisted of a glass bulb with a long narrow neck attached; when heated and then placed with the end of the neck in a glass of water, it became a kind of reversed thermometer. As the bulb cooled, water rose in the neck, and thereafter with changes in temperature of the surrounding air the level of the water also altered. Several indications exist for the dating of this device. Writing in 1638, Benedetto Castelli described it and said Galileo had shown it to him over thirty-five years before, or around 1602. That was probably the time that Castelli went to Padua, but the only years he is known to have studied with Galileo there are 1604–6, being transferred to La Cava before April 1607. It will be seen in chapter 16 that in connection with a device shown at Bologna in 1626, Galileo recalled his having shown a similar one at Padua twenty years before, or in 1606. In December 1606 Galileo paid for a *foglietta da bere*, a kind of glass drinking-straw having a flat mouthpiece perforated with small holes.[7] Such a device, if clogged, would exhibit the effect used in the thermoscope, which may owe its invention to that observation. The thermoscope was adapted to medical use by Santorre Santorio; in 1612 Sagredo heard of it from a friend at Venice and wrote to Galileo, who replied that it had been his invention. Sagredo was absent from Venice and Padua in 1605–7 (and again 1608–11), so if Galileo's invention occurred at this time he would not have known of it until later. His correspondence about it with Galileo will be described in due course.

Early in April 1607 Baldessar Capra published a Latin plagiarism of Galileo's book on the sector, including instructions for constructing it and a claim of his own originality and priority of invention.[8] This book doubly offended Galileo by ending his monopoly and by suggesting that he had dedicated to Prince Cosimo something not really his own.

A copy of this book was given by Aurelio Capra to Giacomo Alvise Cornaro in April 1607. On the next day Cornaro returned it with a letter protesting that the invention was Galileo's, who had been given no credit and was even treated as a thief. Cornaro soon afterward provided Galileo with an affidavit attesting to the following events. About five years earlier[9] Capra and his father had induced Cornaro to persuade Galileo to teach them the uses of his compass, which was in fact done at Cornaro's own house. Early in 1605 the same two men borrowed from Cornaro a compass that Galileo had made for him, saying that Baldessar wished to make one for himself. Later on Cornaro's compass had been returned to him by them.

Because Baldessar was but seventeen years old when Galileo made his first sector, and began the study of mathematics only in 1602 after the arrival of Simon Mayr at Padua, his claim to invention of the instrument was patently false. Galileo secured affidavits from several persons who had received his sector long before and proceeded to bring charges against Capra. Under direct examination by` Galileo before the governors of the university, Capra could not explain many things found in the book published over his own name, making it probable that much of it had been written by Mayr before his departure in 1605. Substantial parts of the book were in fact taken from manuscript copies of Galileo's instructions circulated before 1605. Capra was expelled from the university and unsold copies of his book were confiscated.

Because some thirty copies had already passed beyond the boundaries of Venetian jurisdiction, Galileo published an account of the proceedings in his *Defense Against the Calumnies and Impostures of Baldessar Capra*, written in May and June of 1607, sending copies to Cosimo de' Medici and to foreign mathematicians to clear his name.[10]

III

During the summer of 1607 it appears that Galileo turned his attention to problems of hydrostatics and the strength of materials. The latter was to form an important part of *Two New Sciences*, especially in the Second Day, parts of which were not written until 1633–36. Eliminating those parts (identifiable from correspondence in those years) and another part belonging to 1608, Galileo's work in 1607 consisted mainly of the first six propositions later published, and a part of the tenth.[11]

Galileo began by considering the example of a beam projecting from a solid wall. If sufficient weight were added at the end, the beam must eventually break, and fracture took place at the entrance of the beam into the wall. Galileo considered the beam as one arm of a lever, the other arm being the cross section of the beam. Whatever held the beam together was assumed to be uniformly distributed over the cross section, and the load which would just break the beam was taken as balanced by a vertical lever arm whose length was half the thickness of the beam. Proceeding from these assumptions, Galileo worked out the relations of breaking strengths for beams of the same material but differing proportions of length, breadth, and thickness. In this he made use only of ratios and compound ratios, so that his neglect of strain and compression did not invalidate his theorems. It is only when those are anachronistically rewritten as algebraic equations that they are defective.

It is known from Galileo's later correspondence with Antonio de' Medici that he had composed a treatise on hydrostatics before the summer of 1608, which he left at Florence in the summer of that year. His interest in the subject had begun as early as 1586, but if (as is probable) he had a folder of notes on it, that, like the folder he certainly had on strength of materials, is no longer extant. All that can be said is that by 1608, and probably in 1607, he had put his ideas together in treatise form. His many later writings on hydrostatics, published and unpublished, provide clues to the manner in which he began his investigations so that he might progress beyond the work done by Archimedes. His basic conception was that moment, as the combined effect of weight and speed, could be extended to problems of fluid mechanics. Such a conception had its roots, as Galileo remarked in 1612, in the pseudo-Aristotelian *Questions of Mechanics*. It had already led Galileo to speculate about the speeds and distances of the planets and to refine his first derivation of equilibrium conditions on inclined planes so that his *Mechanics* included the notion of virtual velocities at the point of tangency between a vertical circle and an inclined plane.

This approach to hydrostatics, which Galileo called "more physical" than that of Archimedes, afforded a basis on which those conclusions reached by Archimedes that were of particular interest to Galileo could be independently established, while phenomena became capable of analysis that had remained inaccessible from the Archimedean principle alone. But, as with Galileo's early work on strength of materials, we have no manuscripts from this period relating to hydrostatics, those having perhaps been discarded when Galileo composed a book on the subject in 1611–12.

Toward the end of 1607 Galileo returned once again to his projected treatise on motion. It was about this time that he completed a proof of his old theorem that motion to the bottom of a vertical circle takes less time along two conjugate chords than the single chord joining their extremities, making a final notation on f. 148, put aside in 1605. He now wrote out the demonstration, with all its lemmas, on unused parts of ff. 172 and 163, started in 1603.[12] Neat copies of theorems previously proved were made on ff. 127[13] and 164,[14] while f. 168[15] was newly composed in the same hand, giving new derivative theorems on accelerated motion.

Two memoranda added to f. 164 late in 1607 are of special interest. The first of these set forth an apparent paradox that Galileo later exploited near the beginning of his *Dialogue* to show his readers the need of caution in applying the word *swifter* to accelerated motions. The second, in flat contradiction of the abandoned 179–3, asserted briefly and clearly the correct rule for speeds in uniform acceleration. Both are in the same hand as the neat copies and new theorems just mentioned, and these two memoranda show that Galileo had reached complete clarity on puzzles of accelerated motion that had long plagued him:

> A 164–5. Remarkable! Now, is motion through the vertical *AD* swifter than that through the incline *AB*? It seems so, since equal spaces are traversed more quickly along *AD* than along *AB*. But also it seems not, because drawing the horizontal *BC*, the time through *AB* is to the time through *AC* as *AB* is to *AC*, whence the same moments of velocità [exist in motion] through *AB* and [through] *AC*; and indeed that speed is one and the same with which in equal times unequal spaces are passed which have the same ratio as the times.[16]

On f. 179 the phrase *momenta velocitatis* had been introduced as synonymous with *gradus velocitatis*, used previously on ff. 85*v*, 152*r*, and in the proof for Sarpi. In the canceled 179–3, however, the new phrase had been used only in the sense of "moments of speed" through some distance, however small. In the above statement of the old paradox, first noted on f. 180 at the time of writing 172–3, however, it must be translated "moments of velocità," for here Galileo was speaking not of a single "moment" through *AB* and another through *AC*, but of all the truly instantaneous velocità existing in each. The bold identification of an overall speed with the totality or aggregate of an infinitude of separate "degrees" or "moments" was not an entirely new idea to Galileo, being implied on f. 163–3 in deriving the double-distance rule, as well as in f. 85*v* and the proof for Sarpi. What was new was his decision to deal with speeds in acceleration as not separate and additive, but as literally continuously changing:

164–6. The moments of velocità of things falling from a height are to one another as the square roots of the distances traversed.[17]

With this decision the paradox vanished, being clearly seen to have arisen from ambiguity in applying the term "swifter motion" in comparing overall speeds under different accelerations, or in uniform and in accelerated motions, as Galileo explained to his readers later in the *Dialogue*.

The inherent difficulty in reaching the decision to treat speeds in natural acceleration as truly mathematically continuously changing is hard for us to appreciate. Fundamentally the difficulty arose from the concept of cause, which had to be abandoned for continuous change of speed. Newton himself was unable to find a cause behind his law of gravitation, and that distressed him. Medieval thinkers had accounted for changing speed in fall by assigning heaviness as the cause of the "first" motion from rest, and increments of impetus as the causes of successive changes in speed of motion while the original cause continued to act uniformly. But if nothing new were added to the original cause of downward motion, there appeared to be no cause for changes in speed that were actually observed to take place in fall. For such reasons Galileo had repeatedly tried to ground the law he knew to be true on some kind of addition of separate speeds, always unsuccessfully in terms of mathematically rigorous derivation. The decision represented by 164–6 put an end to such efforts and made possible a rigorous mathematics of accelerated motion by a fundamental redefinition of velocità which permitted speed, like space and time, to undergo truly continuous change.

As will soon be seen, this step put into Galileo's hands a means of determining the relative speeds of a body at any two points in its line of natural motion, and thereby enabled him to test the conservation of uniform horizontal motion in which he had long believed but for which he had had only rough observations as evidence in support of his arguments in *De motu*. In testing this he was led directly to a new and important discovery. First, however, he appears to have turned to a different matter, one that had occupied him on earlier occasions, though other circumstances delayed for a time his pursuit of the consequences of mathematically continuous acceleration.

Probably it was Galileo's review of his earlier theorems on motion late in 1607, including the demonstration written for Sarpi in 1604, that once more directed his attention to percussion. In any case there is reason to assign to early 1608 a very interesting experiment described by Galileo in his last essay on the force of percussion.[18] A heavy beam balance was fitted at one end with a pair of buckets, the lower one being hung by ropes from the handles of the upper one. The upper bucket was filled with water and was provided with a hole in its bottom, an inch or two in diameter, that could be suddenly opened. These buckets were counterbalanced by a weight at the other end of the balance beam, to which more weight could be conveniently added.

With the system in balance, the hole in the upper bucket was opened and it was expected that the impact of the jet of water striking the lower bucket would add to the effective weight on that side, raising the counterweight. Addition of weight to bring the beam back to a level position would then give a measure in dead weight of the force of this jet. But in fact when the valve was opened, the balance arm on the bucket side *rose* at first, and then very gradually returned of its own accord to the level position.

This unexpected event and its consequences were discussed much later by Galileo in a dialogue intended for inclusion in *Two New Sciences* but withheld as unsatisfactory. Paolo Aproino, a student of Galileo's who received his degree and left Padua in mid-1608, was made Galileo's spokesman in that dialogue, as one who had been present at the experiment together with Daniello Antonini.

Another experimental activity of Galileo's at this time was the armaturing of a powerful piece of lodestone owned by Sagredo, the purchase of which by the grand duke of Tuscany was negotiated by Galileo. With Galileo's armature the stone which weighed 56 ounces could lift 132 ounces of iron.

During March and April of 1608 Galileo was again ill, and a letter he wrote on 3 May shows the small cramped hand associated with his rheumatic seizures. It was probably in May or June that he performed a new experiment on motion that was to be of far-reaching importance. He was compelled, however, against his wishes, to journey to Florence in July at the insistence of the Grand Duchess Christina. Galileo's unusual reluctance to visit Florence may have been inspired largely by the experiment the results of which were recorded on f. 116v, in a tiny but neat hand such as frequently followed these illnesses.[19]

Previously Galileo had studied only motions supported along inclined planes or in circular arcs, as with the pendulum. The key to his new venture into unsupported motion lay in the above 164–6: "The moments of velocità of things falling from a height are to one another as the square roots of the distances traversed." When Galileo wrote that, late in 1607 or early in 1608, he was thinking only of free vertical fall from rest. Probably when he lay ill in March/April 1608 it occurred to him that this rule of changing speeds in fall offered him a means of testing his long-standing belief that horizontal motion without friction or resistance should be uniform in speed, at least for small distances near the earth's surface.

Galileo's restricted inertial concept had its roots in *De motu*, though it had not been stated there in 1591. Rather, Galileo at first had demonstrated only that a body supported on a horizontal plane could in principle be set in motion by any force however small.[20] Even a decade later, in his revised *Mechanics* of 1601–2, he had not declared that motion once imparted would remain uniform in speed. That was first implied in the double-distance rule for bodies moving horizontally after initial acceleration, probably written in 1603 and then made more general on f. 163–4 in 1607.[21] In actual practice the rolling of a ball along a smooth level surface is not uniform, since it is slowed by various forms of resistance. Friction and kindred resistances would, however, virtually disappear if the ball were allowed to roll off the end of a table, so that its horizontal motion during fall ought to remain very nearly uniform. Now, if there were a way to determine the ratio of two speeds with which the same ball left the end of the same table, it should be found that the ratio of its horizontal advances during fall to the floor is the same as that ratio of speeds. Such a train of thought probably led Galileo to the experiment recorded on f. 116*v*, next to be discussed, for the key to the needed ratio lay in the statement of 164–6.

Alternatively, Galileo may have wished to verify the independent composition of two different motions, a purpose for which the experiment in question would have served equally well. Medieval impetus theory, like Aristotelian physics, supposed that when two different tendencies to motion were present in the same body, only the stronger would determine its actual motion. When the stronger tendency was violently imparted, as in a ball thrown horizontally, it was assumed that conflict between this and the natural tendency to fall weakened the horizontal motion until the constant vertical tendency became stronger and brought the ball to earth. Yet the ancient *Questions of Mechanics* had discussed independent composition of motions, which turned out to be a key to the inertial concept.[22]

Whichever was Galileo's purpose in carrying out the experiment of f. 116*v*, its result opened up to him the analysis of projectile trajectories and led quickly to resolution of his old problems in dealing with speeds in acceleration. In writing about projectiles in *Two New Sciences* long afterward, he introduced the example of a body moving uniformly along a horizontal surface, passing over its edge, and then entering into a motion that was compounded from uniform horizontal and uniformly accelerated vertical motions.[23] He proceeded to derive mathematically the shape of the resultant path, though there was nothing to suggest that historically he had first derived the parabolic shape of the path and then tested it experimentally. His notes on motion indicate the contrary—that discovery of the parabolic trajectory was a by-product of the experiment recorded on f. 116v, which promptly opened up for him a large new field of investigation.

The drawing on f. 116v shows a table of height 828 *punti*, or about 78 cm; above its surface Galileo marked the vertical distances 300, 600, 800, and 1,000 *punti*. Through these distances a ball was allowed to descend to the table, where it was deflected horizontally; the distances to the places where it struck the floor were then noted along the lower horizontal line. Finally a fifth test was made in which the ball descended 828 *punti* to the table, for which there is squeezed in a related calculation. The purpose of this extra test, not originally contemplated, will be discussed presently.

For each of the horizontal distances marked along the floor there is another distance that Galileo marked *doveria*, that is, "it should be." The *doveria* figures were calculated, but were in no sense predicted values. Knowing the acceleration due to gravity and its modification by an inclined plane, we would proceed nowadays by computing in advance where the ball should land each time, and then test this. Galileo had no way of doing that.[24] But given the actual horizontal advance that corresponded to any one vertical drop before deflection, he could calculate what the other horizontal advances should be for other initial vertical drops, using the ratios of speeds implied by 164–6. That is how he obtained the *doveria* figures. The vertical drop he took as a basis was 300 *punti*, for which the actual horizontal advance was 800 *punti*; this is clear from the way he made the calculations, and from the fact that only the 800 mark lacks a *doveria* figure. All the *doveria* figures were obtained by applying the rule of 164–6 to this shortest drop and its corresponding advance.

It may seem remarkable that round numbers—300 and 800—served as Galileo's base data, but that was no chance event.

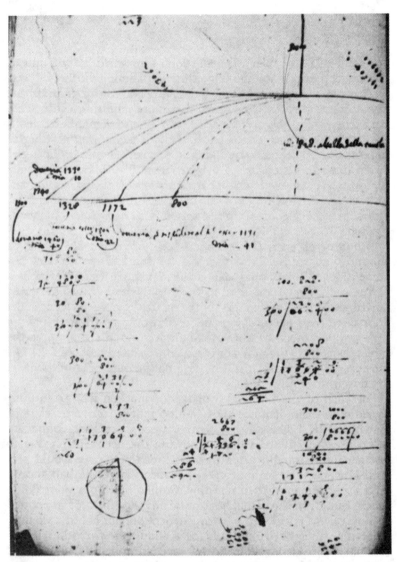

Folio 116*v*, vol. 72, Galilean manuscripts. Record of measurements of distances traversed by a ball after leaving an inclined plane at speeds having known ratios and falling through the same vertical height, with Galileo's calculations of distances expected assuming horizontal inertial motion. This experiment also disclosed the parabolic trajectory of projectiles. (Reproduced with permission of Biblioteca Nazionale Centrale, Florence. Photo by University of Toronto Photographic Services.)

Knowing that he would have to use two figures in all his calculations, he took the precaution of making them round figures for convenience. That is why the height of the table was not a round figure, but was 828 *punti*, not an easy number to compute with. His first step in this experiment, I believe, was to adjust the height of his table until the drop through 300 *punti* corresponded to an advance through a round number of units, which turned out to be 800 *punti*. To that we doubtless owe his having written down the exact height of the table, something that was essential in reconstructing and verifying his actual experiment. The results are tabulated, together with data from another of his experiments, below.

Although f. 116*v* shows only the vertical heights of descent to the table, it is virtually certain that Galileo used an inclined plane along which he had marked those heights, probably the same grooved plane he had used for the experiment on f. 107*v*, but tilted at 30°.[25] Using a similar apparatus, with a curved deflector at its end to smooth the transition to horizontal motion, very good approximations to Galileo's data have been obtained. The seemingly strange fact that his *doveria* figures were all larger than his recorded data illustrates the difference between predictions from theory, such as we would now use, in which case actual figures are expected to be generally smaller than predicted, and Galileo's calculated comparisons based on the first pair of experimental data, which happened to reflect a slightly less efficient roll and advance than the rest.

It remains to explain the extra test in which descent to the table was from a vertical height of 828 *punti*, the same as the distance from table to floor. The purpose of this trial was to test the double-distance rule, according to which a body should move, in a second time equal to that under which it was accelerated uniformly from rest, double the distance previously moved, advancing in uniform motion at the last and highest speed reached. In fact Galileo's ball advanced horizontally 1,340 *punti* when dropped 828 *punti*, in good agreement with his other experimental data and with the *doveria* figure calculated as the others had been, but this was much less than the 1,656 *punti* that seemed to be implied by the double-distance rule. In fact, a frictionless sliding object such as a cake of ice descending on heated tracks would advance that greater distance, whereas a rolling ball absorbs about 28% of the energy from gravitation in accelerating its rotation. Galileo never realized this difference between sliding and rolling, and never having attempted to measure accurately the times in free vertical fall, he supposed them to be directly comparable to the times in rolling-ball experiments.[26]

It is probable that the discrepancy between this added test and the double-distance rule was attributed by Galileo to a change in speed occasioned by deflection; at any rate, that would explain another related experiment for which data are found on f. 114, performed a little later, in which no horizontal deflection was made. Repetition of both experiments by my colleague James H. MacLachlan at the University of Toronto, using a plane inclined at 30°, closely corroborated Galileo's results. The data and calculations for both experiments are combined in the following tabulation.[27]

LENGTH OF ROLL ON PLANE (PUNTI)	VERTICAL HEIGHT (PUNTI)	TIME (SECONDS)	TERMINAL SPEED (PUNTI PER SECOND)	HORIZONTAL DISTANCE TRAVELED IN AIR (PUNTI) THEORY f.116	GALILEO	PERCENT DIFFERENCE FROM THEORY	HORIZONTAL DISTANCE TRAVELED IN AIR (PUNTI) THEORY f.114	GALILEO	PERCENT DIFFERENCE FROM THEORY
200	100	.343	1,168				261	253	-3.2
400	200	.484	1,651				344	337	-1.9
600	300	.593	2,022	805	800	-.7	398	395	-.8
900	450	.727	2,477				456	451	-1.2
1,200	600	.839	2,860	1,139	1,172	+2.8	499	495	-.8
1,600	800	.969	3,303	1,315	1,328	+1.0	542	534	-1.4
1,656	828	.986	3,360	1,338	1,340	+.2			
2,000	1,000	1.083	3,692	1,470	1,500	+2.0	574	573	~0

Since the highest point of release Galileo used was about six feet above the floor, he was able to observe the approximate shapes of the paths of the ball in the air each time, which he also sketched on f. 116v. Seeing these to be approximately parabolic, and having since his earliest days devoted much attention to parabolas and their properties, Galileo next proceeded (on f. 117r), to make proper drawings of parabolas in conformity with his odd-number rule of successive vertical distances and assumed uniform horizontal motions. On the same worksheet he drew a parabola of projection, with its tangent of elevation, beginning its analysis on f. 117v. He was now in a position to proceed with a thorough analysis of projectile trajectories, but the necessity of going to Florence forced him to postpone this until the autumn.

One scientific matter that came up during Galileo's summer at Florence in 1608 was recorded in an essay he wrote late in 1611:

I know that your Highness [Cosimo II de' Medici] well recalls how a few years ago I happened in your presence to contradict some engineers, otherwise excellent in their profession, who were devising a method of weaving together a very broad esplanade of timbers. . . . These men made a great point of the increase in support from the broadness of surface spread over a large body of water, expecting that this would necessarily make it capable of bearing two or three times as much weight as could be computed exactly for the [separate] planks and beams. Concerning that belief I said that no faith should be placed in that framework, however broad, for support beyond that which its separate and disunited parts [would bear].[28]

This incident was probably the source of later friction between Galileo and Giovanni de' Medici, a military engineer, during the dispute over floating and sinking of bodies in water waged at Florence in 1611–12. The marriage of Cosimo in the summer of 1608 was a principal reason for the Grand Duchess Christina's insistence that Galileo come to Florence. For the celebrations, construction of an esplanade on the river Arno was undertaken, and apparently Galileo was present at the engineering discussions. His treatise on hydrostatics, previously mentioned, was left with Antonio de' Medici at this time.

EIGHT

1609-10

UPON HIS RETURN from Florence to Padua in October 1608
Galileo entered into one of his richest and most varied periods
of discovery. It opened with further work in hydrostatics,
strength of materials, and the paths of projectiles, as is evident
from a letter written to Antonio de' Medici in February 1609 to
outline Galileo's activities since the preceding summer. The
"great new thing" about the nature of fluids that he mentioned
can be identified from later correspondence between Galileo
and Daniello Antonini, who had left Padua in 1609. Galileo appears to have challenged him to discover "a balance of equal
arms in which an ounce of water on one side may easily raise
a hundred pounds of weight on the other, by means of that force
by which a boat can float in a few gallons of water." Not knowing that Galileo had meanwhile departed for Florence, Antonini
sent his answer to Padua, and it is only from subsequent letters
that the nature of the missing correspondence can be deduced.
Galileo's idea is found among later notes: At one end of a balance hang the 100-pound weight; at the other, affix an upright
cylinder containing a small amount of water. From a beam
suspend another 100-pound weight, formed as a piston capable
of just entering the cylinder and pressing the water up around
itself. In that position the balance will be in equilibrium, though
at one end it bears a heavy weight and at the other end but a
few ounces.[1]

The nature of Galileo's work on strength of materials late in
1608 was disclosed in the same letter to Antonio de' Medici. He

had, he said, solved the problem of finding a beam so shaped that it would be equally resistant to breakage (that is, would bear exactly the same maximum loading) at any point. To solve this problem he required a lemma concerning a property of parabolas, and though all his other papers on strength of materials are lost, this one sheet survives among Galileo's notes on motion, to which it was evidently transferred when he was working on the parabolic trajectory.[2] The sheet on which it was written (f. 102) bears a "rhinoceros" watermark, found also on dated letters of Galileo's written at this period as well as on virtually every page of his Paduan work on parabolic trajectories. Moreover, these are mainly written in a small and rather cramped hand. The fact that Galileo was again ill upon his return to Padua in October 1608 lends further support to the dating of this material in late 1608 and early 1609.

It was also probably at this time that Galileo recorded the data from the experiment on f. 114 previously mentioned, in which were measured the distances of horizontal travel of a ball leaving an inclined plane without horizontal deflection. Galileo was unable to calculate *doveria* figures in this case (or at any rate none are found), which was complicated by the necessity of considering oblique "impetus."

Galileo's analysis of parabolic trajectories in early 1609 began with definitions of *amplitude* of a semiparabola as its horizontal base and *altitude* as its vertical height. To these he added the concept of *impetus*, first as a measure of impact on the particular horizontal studied, and then in general for any point along the parabola. The reappearance of the word *impetus* after its brief use and abandonment in 1604 is not surprising, for the key lies again in f. 164–6, which inspired the experiment recorded on f. 116*v* and Galileo's discovery of the parabolic trajectory. Impetus now involved the vertical component of natural descent, equivalent to downward velocity at any point and therefore proportional to time from rest. For any given parabola, the horizontal component had also to be taken into account, so that impetus was measured by the hypotenuse of a right triangle; the rule for it was one of what we call vector addition and Galileo (following Euclid, Book Ten) called "equality in the square."

Galileo now began to deal unabashedly with instantaneous velocities, treating them no longer as related to mean proportionals of distances of fall but as simply proportional to *times* from rest. In almost precisely the words used for the second and third propositions of the Fourth Day in *Two New Sciences* nearly thirty years later, Galileo wrote this out on f. 91v,[3] in a cramped hand on paper with the rhinoceros watermark.

The derivation on f. 91v comprised a combination of the mean-proportional rule and the double-distance rule. Both had been in Galileo's possession since 1604, but he was able to combine and reconcile them logically only after many studies of motions on inclined planes and several fruitless attempts to find rigorous logical foundations for accelerated motion. When he later wrote that nature had led him by the hand to definition of uniform acceleration as that in which equal increments of speed are added in equal times, he did not mean that nature had *immediately* shown him this, as some have supposed him to have mis-leadingly claimed, but rather that step by step, over years of study, he had been *inexorably* led to it by the observed phenomena of nature.

Some other Paduan notes are on paper with a very large cross-bow watermark, written in a bold large hand. These relate to supported motions on inclined planes and to problems rather than theorems. They belong, in my opinion, to the period from March to May 1609, after Galileo's recovery, at least for the most part. Some of the problems attacked were quite difficult, and two were left unfinished for a great many years, Galileo's work on motion having been suddenly interrupted by the telescope, as discussed below. Several of his propositions on the parabolic trajectory, and all the calculations for gunnery tables, were like-wise the work of much later years, but the essential theorems were laid down by mid-1609.

Early in 1609 Galileo sent his demonstration that a parabolic line through the corners of a rectangle divided its area in the ratio of one-third to two-thirds to a friend in Rome for delivery to Luca Valerio, whose book on centers of gravity and quadra-ture of the parabola (published in 1604) he greatly admired. Galileo had forgotten his meeting with Valerio at Pisa nearly twenty years before, of which the Roman mathematician re-minded him in reply, praising Galileo's demonstration. The cor-respondence thus opened resulted in Galileo's sending to Valerio for criticism two principles on which he intended to establish his treatise on motion, now greatly expanded, in June 1609.

Galileo's letter is lost, but from Valerio's reply the second of Galileo's two principles can be identified as the assumption used for 179–1, later the sole postulate on accelerated motion in *Two New Sciences*. The first principle was clearly misunderstood by Valerio, whatever it was; I believe it was equivalent to Proposition Seven in *Two New Sciences*[4]—that descents along different planes take equal times when the vertical heights are in "duplicate ratio" of their lengths. The Euclidean term *duplicate ratio* meant "squared ratio," but could also mean simply the ratio 2:1, which is how Valerio seems to have taken it. He approved both principles on metaphysical and causal grounds, also praising an accompanying theorem as "worthy of Archimedes"; this was probably 179–1. Valerio's reply was delayed and did not reach Galileo until mid-July, by which time he had been caught up in energetic activities of a very different kind that caused him to put aside his projected treatise on motion for nearly a decade.

II

In June 1609 Galileo was again bedridden at Padua, where he was visited by an influential Venetian, Piero Duodo. Once more concerned about the inadequacy of his salary to meet his obligations, Galileo asked Duodo to inquire whether it might be increased. Duodo wrote from Venice on 29 June that the prospects were very poor. Galileo was detained in Padua that summer because a student who had boarded with him for four years was completing his doctorate. About 19 July,[5] however, Galileo went to Venice, where in conversations with friends he learned for the first time of an invention that might be of use to him in improving his financial situation. Many years later he published his recollection of the events:

In Venice, where I happened to be at the time, news arrived that a Fleming had presented to Count Maurice [of Nassau] a glass by means of which distant objects could be seen as distinctly as if they were nearby. That was all. Upon hearing this news I returned to Padua, where I then resided, and set myself to thinking about the problem. The first night after my return I solved it, and on the following day I constructed the instrument and sent word of this to these same friends at Venice with whom I had discussed the matter the day before. Immediately afterward I applied myself to the construction of another and better one, which six days later I took to Venice, where it was seen with great admiration by nearly all the principal gentlemen of that Republic for more than a month on end, to my considerable fatigue.[6]

Though Galileo first heard of the Dutch telescope while visiting Venice in July 1609, news of it was already widespread throughout Europe. A patent on it had been applied for early in October 1608 by a spectacle-maker of Middleburg named Hans Lipperhey. No patent was granted, but Lipperhey was given a monetary grant to make three more such instruments for the government, on condition that he would not disclose his method to others. It happened that an embassy from the king of Siam was visiting the Hague at this time, and also a Spanish general to whom the new spyglass was shown, so a printed newsletter concerning those events carried a description of the new invention which circulated widely.[7] Rival claimants soon appeared, notably Zacharias Jansen and Adrien Metius, though from an early account it appears that only Lipperhey's instrument was of real value at the beginning, the others being little more than toys.

A copy of the newsletter was already in the hands of Paolo Sarpi in November 1608, and he commenced directing inquiries to various correspondents concerning the authenticity of the claims made for the new device. To Jacques Badovere, who had resided and studied with Galileo at Padua in 1597, Sarpi wrote in a second letter on 30 March 1609:

I have given you my opinion of the Holland spectacles. There may be something further; if you know more about this I should like to learn what is thought there. I have practically abandoned thinking about physical and mathematical matters, and to tell you the truth my mind has become, either through age or habits, a bit dense for such speculations. You would hardly believe how much I have lost both in health and composure through attention to politics.[8]

Sarpi's duties after his appointment in 1606 as official theologian and adviser to the Venetian Republic and his wounding in an assassination attempt account for the lapse of his correspondence with Galileo. Sarpi's opinion of his decline in intellectual powers, however, was not shared by others. The Venetians continued to have the highest regard for his practical advice, both political and scientific, and this turned out to be a great advantage to Galileo in mid-1609.

Details of Galileo's first acquaintance with the telescope were printed in his *Starry Messenger* early in 1610:

About ten months ago a report reached my ears that a certain Fleming had constructed a spyglass by means of which visible objects, though very distant from the eye of the observer, were distinctly seen as if nearby. Of this truly remarkable effect several experiences were related, to which some persons gave credence while others denied them. A few days later the report was confirmed to me in a letter from a noble Frenchman at Paris, Jacques Badovere, which caused me to apply myself wholeheartedly to inquire into the means by which I might arrive at the invention of a similar instrument. This I did shortly afterwards, my basis being the theory of refraction. First I prepared a tube of lead, at the ends of which I fitted two glass lenses, both plane on one side while on the other side one was spherically concave and the other convex. Then, placing my eye near the concave lens, I perceived objects satisfactorily large and near, for they appeared three times closer and nine times larger than when seen with the naked eye alone. Next I constructed another one, more perfect, which represented objects as enlarged more than sixty times.[9]

It is probable that as soon as Galileo heard the rumors at Venice he visited Sarpi to learn his opinion and was shown Badovere's lost reply to the letter previously cited. Since there is no surviving direct correspondence between Badovere and Galileo, Galileo's statement that a letter of Badovere's promptly confirmed the existence of the instrument suggests that he saw that letter when at Venice toward the end of July. About the same time a stranger arrived in Padua en route to Venice with one of the foreign instruments. This was seen by friends of Galileo, one of whom wrote to Rome about it on 1 August 1609. Probably Galileo heard at Venice (only twenty-five miles away) that an example was then in Padua; in any event he returned there on 3 August, only to learn that the foreigner had gone on to Venice where he hoped to sell his instrument for a high price.

Galileo had no time to lose. His first move was later described by him thus:

My reasoning was this. The device needs . . . more than one glass. . . . The shape would have to be convex, . . . concave, . . . or bounded by parallel surfaces. But the last-named does not alter visible objects in any way; . . . the concave diminishes them, and the convex, though it enlarges them, shows them indistinct and confused. . . . I was confined to considering what would be done by a combination of the convex and the concave. You see how this gave me what I sought.[10]

Though logicians and some historians have derided this statement, because in fact a telescope with two convex lenses can be made to exceed in both power and breadth of field the type used by Galileo, there is no reason to doubt that he did in fact approach the problem as he said. The historical question of discovery (or in this case, rediscovery) relates to results, not to rigorous logic. We have already seen other instances in which Galileo made important discoveries by good reasoning from unsound assumptions; indeed, it is likely that most scientific discoveries involve an element of that kind.[11] If Galileo was the "Alimberto Mauri" of 1606, he had already given attention to the role of shape and curvature in optical magnification. In any case a test of the combination he described, using spectacle lenses, showed that the effect could be obtained. Galileo wrote to Venice to announce this, and there can be little doubt that it was to Sarpi that he addressed his communication early in August 1609.

Meanwhile it was Sarpi to whom the Venetian government had assigned the task of investigating and advising them as to purchase of the foreigner's instrument. A price of one thousand ducats had been asked, and the owner forbade any examination of the instrument except by looking through it. Sarpi advised against its purchase, doubtless confident that Galileo could at least equal it, and the foreigner departed. Meanwhile Galileo was grinding lenses that should give greater magnification. There was at the time no "theory of refraction" in the modern sense; all that Galileo meant by that phrase was consideration of the focal lengths of the two lenses, that is, the radii of their sperical surfaces. The power of a simple telescope is essentially a matter of the ratio of the two focal lengths, a fact that would not have taken Galileo long to discover once he had confirmed the effect. The principal technical problem was to grind a deeper concave eyepiece than customarily used for spectacles to correct myopia; for this, a small ball could serve as a grinding tool.

It was on 21 August that Galileo returned to Venice with his eight-power telescope. Its capabilities were demonstrated from the campanile in St. Mark's square, and by 26 August he was richly rewarded by the Venetian government for it. As he related the events to his brother-in-law Benedetto Landucci at Florence, they were as follows:

. . . all my hope of returning home is taken away, but by a useful and honorable event. It is nearly two months since news spread here that in Flanders there had been presented to Count Maurice a spyglass . . . by which a man two miles away can be distinctly seen. . . . As it appeared to me that it must be founded on the science of optics, I began to think about its construction, which I finally found, and so perfectly that one which I made far surpassed the reputation of the Flemish one. And word having reached Venice that I had made one, it is six days since I was called by the Signoria, to which I had to show it together with the entire Senate, to the infinite amazement of all; and there have been numerous gentlemen and senators who, though old, have more than once climbed the stairs of the highest campaniles in Venice to observe at sea sails and vessels so far away that, coming under full sail to port, two hours and more were required before they could be seen without my spyglass. For in fact the effect of this instrument is to represent an object that is for example fifty miles away as large and near as if it were but five.

Now having known how useful this would be for maritime as well as land affairs, and seeing it desired by the Venetian government, I resolved on the 25th of this month to appear in the College and make a free gift of it to his Lordship [the Doge]. And having been ordered to wait in the room of the Pregadi, there appeared presently the Procurator Priuli, who is one of the governors of the University. Coming out of the College, he took my hand and told me how that body . . . would at once order the honorable governors that, if I were content, they should renew my appointment for life and with a salary of one thousand florins per year . . . to run immediately. . . . Thus I find myself here, held for life, and shall have to be satisfied to enjoy my native land sometimes during the summer months.[12]

Galileo had understood the offer to mean an immediate increase from 520 to 1,000 florins per year, but when the official document was written it assigned him that salary only after expiration of his existing contract a year later, for life and without possibility of future increase. Whether he had misunderstood Priuli, or Priuli had misunderstood the instructions, does not matter. Galileo, who felt that he was not bound by the promise to stay for life so long as he had not collected any of the promised benefits, reopened his negotiations for employment at the Tuscan court. His former pupil Cosimo de' Medici, who had become grand duke on the death of Ferdinando I in February 1609, quickly made known to Galileo (through Enea Piccolomini) his desire for one of the new instruments. This afforded Galileo a double opportunity; first to renew his campaign for employment, and second, to attempt to make a still more powerful telescope without permitting rivals at Padua and Venice a chance to guess how this might be done. To that end he asked Piccolomini to send him glass blanks from Florence made to specifications provided by Galileo, which were duly sent to him about the middle of September.[13]

III

There are clues in two letters of this period which suggest that in October Galileo made a hasty visit to Florence to repair any damage to his standing there which might have resulted from his presenting so valuable a device to a foreign government. Thus, writing to Belisario Vinta, secretary to the recently crowned Grand Duke Cosimo, on 30 October, Galileo opened with the words: "Immediately on my return to Padua," rather as if they had recently conversed at Florence. Of much greater interest and possible significance is a remark in a letter dated 30 January 1610 to the same dignitary: "That the moon is a body very similar to the earth [was] already partly shown by me to our Serene Lord [Cosimo], though imperfectly, I not having had yet an instrument of the excellence that I now have." This seems to imply also that Galileo had already used his original telescope of about eight-power to view the moon, confirming its mountainous character (already affirmed by "Mauri" in 1606 on the basis of reasoning from naked-eye illumination effects) in the presence of the grand duke. The only time Galileo could have been in Florence between August 1609 and January 1610 was during the month of October, just before the new academic year began at Padua. It is also worth noting that on 4 November Galileo complained to the governors of the University of Padua of an intrusion on his customary hours of lecturing, much as if he were laying a basis for dissatisfaction that would give him a pretext for leaving Padua.

It was probably toward the end of November 1609 that Galileo succeeded in making a new telescope of about twenty-power. As will be seen, his first carefully recorded lunar observation with this instrument was made on 1 December 1609, and on 4 December, replying to an inquiry from Florence when he expected to be there next, he said he would arrive by the first of July 1610 and remain through September, adding: "I shall have with me a certain improvement in the telescope, and perhaps some other *invenzione*." The last word can mean "discovery," and may relate to Galileo's early progress in observations recorded in a letter dated 7 January 1610,[14] a memorable night in the history of astronomy.

This important letter survives in two copies, a complete one made in the seventeenth century and another, lacking the final page, copied in the eighteenth century from a copy made earlier by Vincenzio Viviani from the original owned by Galileo's son after his father's death. Viviani described it in an annotation, duly copied by the later scribe: "From Sig. Vincenzio Galilei. Copied by me [Viviani] from an original draft, incomplete, on one rectangular sheet." What this means is that Viviani had before him a single folded folio sheet, that is, four normal pages of letter size, in Galileo's own handwriting but with neither salutation nor conclusion, the text ending abruptly. The continuation is found in the seventeenth-century copy now in the Vatican library, but without indication of the name of the person to whom Galileo intended to send the letter he had so carefully drafted. In all probability this letter was never actually sent; as with the unfinished draft letter on the new star of 1604, intended for Girolamo Mercuriale, Galileo again thought better of disclosing what he had discovered in the heavens.

The Vatican copy includes relevant drawings, mentioned in the text of the letter, rather crudely copied but sufficing to show that Galileo had already observed the moon through a full lunation. They illustrate various conclusions by events occurring between new moon and first quarter. It is probable that the original drawings were made in December 1609 and that Galileo had not observed the moon through the telescope much, if any, before that month.

I long questioned the authenticity, not so much of the contents of this letter (as Galileo's), but of its dating as shown only in the Vatican copy. I am now satisfied that Galileo composed it about the beginning of January 1610 from notes and drawings he had made during December 1609, intending to send it to a friend at

Florence, probably Enea Piccolomini, who had supplied the glass blanks and by whom it would immediately be shown to the Grand Duke Cosimo. Favaro dubitatively mentioned Antonio de' Medici as intended recipient, but the style of address (*V.S. Ill.*ᵐᵃ) precludes that. The letter began: "To satisfy you I shall briefly recount . . ." and toward the end said, "It now remains to me, to satisfy entirely your command . . ."; hence the addressee had presumably asked Galileo for an account of his recent telescopic observations and for instructions in the best use of the instrument. In August, Piccolomini had intimated that he might visit Galileo during the winter. Galileo's letter said toward the end that "we may believe that we have been the first in the world [*i primi al mondo*] to have seen anything in the celestial bodies from so near." The plural pronoun might mean only the writer himself, but Galileo seldom used *we* in that way in his private letters, and the plural form of *first* seems to mean that the intended recipient had already participated in some observations of the kind.

The authenticity of this letter has further support from astronomical researches conducted by Professor Guglielmo Righini,[15] as well as from a manuscript record of Galileo's early notes on the satellites of Jupiter now preserved in the Department of Rare Books and Special Collections at the University of Michigan, which I call the Ann Arbor document (p. 149). Professor Righini's conclusions in turn receive support from other documentary evidence not used by him in establishing them. His two main conclusions, based on Galileo's drawings as published in the *Starry Messenger*, are as follows:

First, Galileo's drawing of the moon as thinly crescent right after new moon permitted Professor Righini to identify a sufficient number of actual features to conclude that Galileo depicted the moon at an age of four days fifteen hours, plus or minus two hours. Because of the hours of sunset at Padua, he could have done this only on 2 October 1609 or 29 January 1610 during the months preceding publication of his book and after construction of the telescope he used. Professor Righini, considering only the events up to December, concluded that the observation represented in Galileo's book was that of 2 October 1609. So early a use of the twenty-power telescope is incompatible with other evidence; hence I believe that what Galileo drew for the *Starry Messenger* was a new observation, made carefully on 29 January 1610, replacing the first rough sketch he had included in the draft letter. That sketch I suppose to have been made from an observation on 1 December 1609, when the moon was slightly older than five days on its first appearance after sunset.

Second, Galileo's two drawings of the moon at first and last quarter in the *Starry Messenger* show a libration of nearly 9° vertically, measured by a particular crater selected by Galileo to illustrate an illumination phenomenon described in his text. Professor Righini noted that so large a libration occurred only between 3 December and 18 December 1609, and not between any other similar phases during the months in question. For reasons evident to common sense, Galileo greatly exaggerated the diameter of the selected crater in his printed illustrations, which were rather small. Probably he alluded to the crater Albategnius, shown in a modern photograph here alongside one of Galileo's pictures and answering entirely to the description he gave of it. In order to show the contrasting illumination of the rim at first and last quarter he was obliged to depict it in his small engraving as relatively larger than any crater could be and still display sharply the illumination effects described.

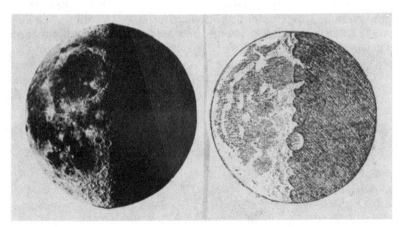

Moon at last quarter, (*left*) as seen through a high-power telescope (Lick Observatory Photographs) and (*right*) as drawn by Galileo (from his *Starry Messenger*). (Photo by University of Toronto Photographic Services.)

It is therefore highly probable that Galileo observed the moon nightly during December 1609, except when cloudy skies prevented this, and compiled the unsent letter from his notes early in January 1610. Nearly all the salient points about the moon's illumination later described in his book were noted in the letter, though with less detail. Nothing, however, had been said about stars up to the point at which the Viviani copy ended, the continuation on another sheet having been separated from the letter even before that passed to Galileo's son.

It is also probable that having composed this much of his draft letter, Galileo put it aside for a few days before writing the usual concluding paragraph, date, and signature. These were added on the night of 7 January 1610, in a form not entirely appropriate to the rest of the letter but recording a momentous observation made that very night—though Galileo had as yet no inkling how important it would turn out to have been. This concluding passage is rather abruptly begun and then followed by remarks that would more normally follow the comment on priority. It reads as follows:

And besides my observations of the moon, I have observed the following in other stars. First, that many fixed stars are seen with the telescope that are not [otherwise] discerned; and only this evening I have seen Jupiter accompanied by three fixed stars, totally invisible by their smallness, and the configuration was in this form

nor did they occupy more than about one degree of longitude.

The planets are seen very rotund, like little full moons, and of a roundness bounded and without rays. But the fixed stars do not appear so; rather they are seen fulgorous and trembling much more with the telescope than without, and so irradiated that what shape they possess is not revealed.

It now remains for me, to satisfy entirely your command, to tell you what should be done in using the telescope, which in brief is that the instrument must be held firm, and hence it is good, to escape the shaking of the hand that arises from motion of the arteries and from breathing, to fix the tube in some stable place. The glasses should be kept clean and polished by a cloth, or else cloud is generated there by the breath, humid or foggy air, or vapor which evaporates from the eye itself, especially when warm. It is best that the tube be capable of being lengthened a bit, say about three or four inches, because I find that to see distinctly nearby objects the tube should be longer, and shorter for those more distant. It is good that the convex glass, which is the one far from the eye, should be partly covered and that the opening left should be oval in shape, since thus are objects seen much more distinctly.

And so much I can tell you at present, with all my heart saluting you and wishing you well.

From my house, 7 January 1610
Your affectionate servant
Galileo Galilei[16]

Just before these additions Galileo had remarked that he was about to complete a telescope which would bring him even closer to the moon, as near as two terrestrial radii. (Though he said "diameters," it is evident that he expected the new instrument to be about thirty-power.) But it is very doubtful that he had actually finished the stronger instrument when he wrote the above additions, since it would have been natural to say so if he had.

Galileo had undoubtedly noticed some things about the stars during a month of lunar observations, but there is a plausible reason for his having said nothing about them. Although for lunar observations the spherical and chromatic aberrations of his telescope would not be particularly troublesome, the difference in appearance between stars and planets would be imperceptible and there would be nothing to say except that more stars were seen through the telescope than with the naked eye.

There is nothing remarkable about such stars, and while Galileo was occupied with the moon he would have had no reason to pay attention to them. The general fuzziness, and colored haloes around bright stars, would detract from their interest. Now, it happens that Galileo had had some trouble with his eyes from early youth which from time to time caused him to see bright lights as irradiated and with colored rings.[17] People so afflicted for any reason quickly learn that their vision is improved by peering through the clenched fist or between the fingers, or through any very small aperture. Hence it is likely that Galileo hit on the idea of stopping down the objective lens, in the manner recommended at the end of his letter, not through any process of reasoning but simply by analogy with his own experience. To grind a wide lens and then use only its center goes against common sense. Nevertheless it works quite remarkably with any spherical lenses, especially those not perfectly ground. The stars first became sharp and distinct, and distinguishable from planets, when Galileo applied to his objective lens a cardboard stop of medium aperture, probably on 7 January 1610.

In short, I believe that Galileo made many observations of the moon before he discovered anything worth mentioning about other heavenly bodies. The wording in the *Starry Messenger* made it appear that a new instrument was responsible, so I formerly supposed that on that night he had just finished the thirty-power telescope mentioned. But I find no reference anywhere in which Galileo positively claims to have used a thirty-power telescope astronomically; even two years later his notes show that he employed telescopes of eighteen- and twenty-power for further observations of the satellites of Jupiter. Hence I now take his words "I had prepared an excellent instrument for myself" on the night of 7 January to mean not that he had completed a new telescope, but that he had modified the same twenty-power instrument he had used in December. *Prepared* does not necessarily mean "constructed." Masking the objective lens opened a new world for him. The most unusual conformation of new stars that he saw was a triplet of starlets in a short straight line close to Jupiter, so that was chosen for the letter. It did not occur to Galileo at this time that there was anything else unusual about those starlets.

On some page now missing, probably at the end of the draft letter itself, Galileo made entries of further observations of the same stars on the nights through 11 January, some of which he

Galileo's earliest surviving record of satellite observations, noted at the bottom of a draft letter of presentation of his telescope to the Doge of Venice four months earlier. (Courtesy of the University of Michigan Library, Rare Books and Special Collections, Ann Arbor.)

subsequently copied into the Ann Arbor document. All of them were ultimately entered in a journal of observations[18] opened by Galileo on the night of 15 January 1610, from which I reconstruct the originals as follows:

On the 8th day, Jupiter was seen thus and was therefore direct and not retrograde.
The 9th day was cloudy.
On the 10th day it was seen thus , that is, conjoined with the most westerly [star] so that it hid this, from what one may believe.
On the 11th day it was in this guise and the star nearer Jupiter was half the size of the other and very close to the other, whereas the other evenings all three of the said stars appeared of equal size and equally far apart.

When Galileo transferred the entries from the missing page to his journal, he moved back to the 11th an additional reflection inappropriate there, which probably originally appeared at the end of the following entry:[19]

On the 12th day it was seen in this arrangement
The westerly star was a little smaller than the easterly, and Jupiter was in the middle, distant from either star about as much as its own diameter; and perhaps there was a third [star], very small and very close to Jupiter—or rather, there really was, I having observed with great diligence and the night being darker [whence it appears that around Jupiter there are three moving stars invisible to everyone up to this time].

The resolving power of Galileo's telescope was about 1.25 minutes of arc, so that the third satellite would have been seen by him first about two hours later at night, just as Galileo said. These entries presumably filled up the paper he was using, and he began to make notes on the Ann Arbor document, to which he first transferred those previous observations which included three satellites. Those alone were of use to him for his next purpose, which was to discover how these three stars moved.

As I interpret the Ann Arbor document,[20] it throws an interesting light on Galileo's actual process of reaching the conclusion that he was seeing bodies which literally circulated around Jupiter. It was probably not until the night of the 12th that Galileo decided there were definitely three stars, all moving, though in his journal and in his book he moved that conclusion back to the 11th. Nor do I think he realized on the 11th that

First page of Galileo's journal of observations of Jupiter's satellites, with notes in Italian to 15 January 1610; this was continued in Latin from that night to 17 March. (*Opere di Galileo*, 3 [pt. 2]: 427. Photo by University of Toronto Photographic Services.)

there was an actual circulation of these stars in orbits around Jupiter, a conclusion he probably first reached after his first observation on the night of the 15th. It was only then that he opened his journal, copying into it his previous notes (with the transposition mentioned). Later the same night he entered a second observation, after which time his new notes of original entry were put into the journal, in Latin, for his projected book.

Three little diagrams in the lower right-hand corner of the Ann Arbor manuscript show that Galileo did not at once jump to the conclusion that the stars were literally orbiting around Jupiter. The minimum assumption was that they moved with respect to Jupiter, and in appearance they moved back and forth along a straight line in some way. At first there was no way of identifying a particular satellite among the three originally discerned. When four appeared, on 13 January, a problem arose how one star might pass another, if that was what they did. When Galileo drew the diagrams mentioned, his arrows indicated a theory irreconcilable with true orbiting around Jupiter. This again is an indication that he was wedded neither to the Copernican system nor to the philosophical idea that all heavenly motions must necessarily be circular in form. When the latter became the simplest hypothesis for explaining what was actually seen, on the night of 15 January 1610, Galileo adopted it. This in turn explains something that has troubled some historians and philosophers of science in recent times—why was Galileo adamant against explanations of celestial phenomena other than his own, though logically they may seem to have been every bit as justifiable as his at the time? The answer is that when one has *not* simply jumped to a conclusion, but has been forced to it by systematic attempts to account for actual observations, one is likely to be impatient with ideas already known to be incorrect through one's own successive efforts.

Some years ago the astronomer Jean Meeus wondered why it had taken Galileo so long—a whole week—to discover that there are four large satellites of Jupiter, and not just three.[21] The probability that an entire week should pass without all four being visible at once is vanishingly small, even allowing for a cloudy night that intervened. Meeus therefore computed the positions of the satellites at the hours given by Galileo for his observations and compared the results with Galileo's published diagrams. He found that Galileo had been astonishingly accurate, considering all the circumstances. On 7 January four satellites had indeed been visible, but one was so far from the others that the field of view of Galileo's instrument (about twelve minutes of arc) could not have included all four. During the next few days only two or three were visible, or were sufficiently far from one another and from Jupiter for Galileo's telescope to discern them separately.

GALILEO		CALCULATION	
Or. *Occ.* Jan. 7 · ·④ ·		*East* IV ii i ●	*West* III 16ʰ30ᵐ
Jan. 8 ④ · · ·		IV ● i ii iii	17ʰ00ᵐ
Jan. 10 · · ④		IV III ii ● i	17ʰ00ᵐ
Jan. 11 · · ④		iii iv ●· i	17ʰ00ᵐ
Jan. 12 *hora noctis tertia* · ·④ ·		III i iv● ii iii i iv● ii	17ʰ00ᵐ 20ʰ00ᵐ
Jan. 13 · ④ · · ·		ii ● iii iv	17ʰ00ᵐ
Jan. 15 *hora noctis tertia* ④ · · · ·		● i ii iii iv	19ʰ00ᵐ

Galileo's first observations of Jupiter's satellites (*left*) and their actual positions at the indicated times (*right*) as computed by Jean Meeus. Galileo's narrow telescopic field made him miss IV initially, and low resolving power caused him to see two satellites as one on two nights. (After *Sky and Telescope* for February 1964, by permission of the publishers.)

It was in fact quite a long time before Galileo's observations were confirmed by other astronomers. At first there were no telescopes other than his which were powerful enough to detect the satellites of Jupiter. Experienced astronomers at Bologna were unable to see them even through Galileo's telescope despite the fact that Galileo was present and tried to explain to others how to look through the instrument. There is indeed a claim, made four years later by Simon Mayr, that he had observed the satellites before Galileo. Apart from the fact that Mayr did not describe any observation earlier than that made by Galileo on 8 January 1610 (which Mayr dated as 29 December 1609, using the Julian calendar), there is another great improbability in Mayr's claim. He said that it was not until the end of February 1610 that he could be sure there were four satellites, and not just three. Considering that a modern astronomer wondered why it took Galileo a whole week to make this determination, it would be rash to credit a man who said this discovery took more than two months. Mayr did not supply a single drawing or indication of any satellite position observed by him in 1609 or 1610, beyond one verbal description applicable to Galileo's second observation on 8 January 1610.

The accuracy of Galileo's diagrams of Jupiter's satellites from the very beginning was established several years ago. More recently the accuracy of Galileo's drawings of the moon with respect to features he observed and wished to emphasize in his text has been vindicated by Professor Righini. Only the exaggerated size of one crater,[22] necessary to show the illumination features for which Galileo depicted it, can justify statements that Galileo's lunar diagrams were inaccurate. They were certainly very incomplete, being in no sense maps of the moon, nor did Galileo represent them as such. The first known attempt to map the moon was made by Thomas Harriot in mid-1609, before Galileo had conceived of any astronomical use for his instrument. Galileo's diagrams were intended only as illustrations of certain specific phenomena of lunar illumination and were designed principally to demonstrate that the surface of the moon was not perfectly smooth and spherical as claimed by philosophers.

IV

It was probably during this winter, after Galileo's interest in astronomy had been revived by the lunar observations but before his startling new discoveries in the stars distracted him from other researches for a considerable time, that he formulated in his mind the "Platonic cosmogony" mentioned earlier in connection with f. 146. It will be recalled that in 1602, shortly before his resumption of work on motion, Galileo attempted to relate speeds of planetary motions to their distances from the

sun, using data from Kepler's first book. At that time he had
no idea of explaining how the planets had originally arrived at
their speeds, nor did he have any inkling of the law of free fall.
If, as I believe, he did arrive at a rule relating planetary speeds
inversely to the square roots of their distances from the sun, on
a now lost sheet continuing the calculations of f. 146, his work
at the time stopped there.

Late in 1604 Galileo became interested in the new star, and
on f. 134r (bearing a crossbow watermark of dimensions found
also on his notes on motion belonging to 1605) there is a drawing of concentric circles related to some astronomical calculations on the reverse of that sheet. The circles certainly represent
orbits, probably of earth, Mars, and Saturn to judge from the
calculations. Now, at the top of the largest circle there is an
added diagram quite unrelated to the calculations, showing the
same lines as those used early in 1609 on f. 91v to establish the
impetus or "moment of swiftness" acquired at either of two
points in vertical fall; this diagram and discussion will be found
in Theorem Three in the Fourth Day of *Two New Sciences*. The
rule is that the ratio of impetuses is as the distance from rest to
the first point is to the mean proportional of the two distances.
Clearly this additional diagram on f. 134r was drawn after 164–6,
and almost certainly after f. 91v, relating a conclusion about
free fall to some astronomical speculation.

It will be recalled that Galileo's calculations on f. 146 had required him to utilize a point beyond Saturn's orbit in order to
invert a ratio of distances from the sun. Such a point can be
found for any pair of planets, but it will not be the same point
for every pair of planets. In the *Dialogue* Galileo mistakenly
asserted that a single point existed from which, if all the planets
had moved in uniform acceleration toward the sun until they
reached their present distances, they would have reached their
present speeds as calculated on data from the best astronomers,
being then turned by the will of God into perpetual circular
motion at those speeds. This idea probably occurred to him late
in 1609 as the result of an analogy between the statements
(1) that planetary speeds are inversely as the square roots of
their distances from the sun and (2) that speeds in fall are as
the square roots of their distances from rest, together with the
fact that distance ratios have their inverted counterparts from
a suitably chosen point in the same line. Having already made

the calculations for statement (1), if I am correct about Galileo's procedure in 1602, he did not trouble to verify his "Platonic cosmogony" by making direct free-fall computations; otherwise he would have discovered that no single point could serve for all planet-pairs. As it was, relying on his memory two decades later, he wrote in the *Dialogue*:

Suppose all the said globes to have been created in the same place and there assigned tendencies to motion, descending toward the center until they had acquired those degrees of speed which originally seemed good to the Divine mind. Those speeds being acquired, we suppose that the globes were set in rotation, each retaining in its orbit its predetermined speed. . . .To investigate this, we must take from the most skilled astronomers the sizes of the orbits in which the planets revolve, and likewise the times of their revolutions. From these we determine how much faster Jupiter moves than Saturn. . . . From the ratios of the speeds of Jupiter and Saturn and from the distance between their orbits, and from the ratio of acceleration of natural motion, one may determine at what height and distance from the center of their revolutions must have been the place from which they originally departed. . . . It is [then] asked whether Mars, descending from there to its orbit, is found to agree in size of orbit and speed of motion with what is found by calculation, and the same is done for Venus and Mercury, the size of whose orbits and speeds of motions agree so closely with those given by the computations that the matter is truly wonderful.[23]

NINE

1610-11

THE *Starry Messenger* was written in January and February of 1610; the latest observation added was for 2 March, and on 12 March the book was already printed at Venice. It was dedicated to Cosimo de' Medici, after whom Galileo christened the satellites of Jupiter "the Medicean stars." Among things contained in the book were the measurement of a lunar peak (calculated to be four miles), evidence that the Milky Way and nebulas are composed of myriads of tiny stars not separately discernible, and charts of previously unseen stars in some conspicuous constellations. Incorrect explanations were offered for the coppery color of the moon in eclipse and for certain puzzling appearances of the satellites of Jupiter, based on the idea of lunar and Jovial atmospheres. Galileo later withdrew his hypothesis of a lunar atmosphere, while the appearances of the satellites long remained hard to explain except on the ad hoc assumption of surface features that would affect reflection of light, impossible to confirm directly even with modern telescopes.

Galileo's first telescopic observations helped to support the Copernican system, largely because the circulation of four stars around Jupiter showed that heavenly bodies could indeed revolve around centers other than the earth. He did not, however, declare in the *Starry Messenger* that the earth was a planet. What he said in his dedication to Cosimo de' Medici was that the stars Galileo had named after him went around Jupiter just "as all planets go around the sun"—a statement as compatible with the Tychonic as with the Copernican astronomy. Visual

evidence decisive to Galileo in favor of Copernicus was not discovered until the end of 1610, because Venus remained too close
to the sun to observe early in that year. Even the phases of Venus
were not decisive to those who clung to the dynamically absurd
Tychonic system and would not apply the rule of parsimony in
hypotheses.

Galileo was in Venice when his book was published there on
12 March 1610, and the next day he wrote to Belisario Vinta saying that he would send a specially bound dedication copy to
Cosimo, together with his own excellent telescope so that the
grand duke might see with his own eyes the new stars named in
his honor. But since it was not easy for unpracticed observers
to see these, he himself would come to Pisa for the Holy Week
vacation if Vinta thought that desirable. It would not do to put
this visit off until summer, since then Jupiter would be too close
to the sun for the observations to be made. Writing again on 19
March to say that the book and the original telescope were on
their way, Galileo mentioned that he wished to send copies and
examples to other princes in honor of the grand duke, but that
only ten telescopes he had made, of more than a hundred tried,
would serve to reveal the new satellites. That as many as ten
such instruments had been made successfully between the beginning of December and the middle of March is truly remarkable. Meanwhile Galileo had determined that the outer satellite
orbited in about fifteen days (actually 16¾), the first step necessary in identifying all four orbits, which he hoped soon to do.
The 550 copies of his book, issued only a week before, were
already sold, Galileo having received only six copies instead of
the thirty agreed upon. He planned a second edition, much expanded, in Italian, as requested by many and preferred by himself; this was to include diagrams of an entire lunation. But
though the *Starry Messenger* was reprinted later in 1610 at
Frankfort, no new edition was ever published along the lines
indicated by Galileo.

On the same day, 19 March, Vinta wrote from Pisa (where
the Tuscan court resided at this time of year) to acknowledge
receipt of his advance copy of the book; he had shown this to
the grand duke, who was anxious to see the new stars and who
wished Galileo to come there during the Easter vacation. A week
later the Tuscan ambassador at Venice, Giovanni Bartoli, warned
Vinta that Galileo was laughed at for having claimed new dis-

coveries in the heavens and for having duped the government with a so-called invention that could be bought anywhere for a few lire, said to be of the same quality as his. In fact there were at that time none in Italy of that quality except Galileo's, and it was many months before even the Jesuit astronomers at Rome were able to obtain an instrument sufficiently powerful to confirm the discoveries Galileo had already claimed.

On 3 April Galileo's good friend Martin Hasdale dined in Prague with the Spanish ambassador to the Holy Roman Emperor and with Mark Welser of Augsburg, banker to the Jesuits, who brought with him a copy of Galileo's book and said that the opinion of Kepler as imperial astronomer should be sought. On 15 April Hasdale struck up a friendship with Kepler, whom he met at a luncheon with the Saxon ambassador. Kepler expressed great admiration for Galileo, saying he had corresponded with him years before, and approved his book though he regretted its failure to mention Copernicus, Giordano Bruno, and "various Germans who had anticipated such discoveries."

The Tuscan ambassador, Giuliano de' Medici, to whom Galileo had sent a copy of his book, asked Kepler to give his opinion in writing, not as a friend of Galileo's but with utter frankness. Kepler wrote to the imperial ambassador at Venice, Georg Fugger, asking whether a copy had been sent to the emperor. Fugger replied that Galileo was deemed by those versed in mathematics to have written a dry discourse remote from philosophical foundations, and was a man given to stealing the inventions of others, in this case having easily improved the invention of a certain Belgian. Hence Fugger had not bothered to inform the emperor.

On 19 April Kepler forwarded to Galileo, through the Tuscan ambassador, a very long commentary that was published soon afterward as Kepler's *Conversation with the Starry Messenger*.[1] It supported Galileo's findings, though Kepler had not yet been able to make observations for himself for want of a suitable telescope. His support was of great value to Galileo in the face of rising opposition from various quarters. On his way to Pisa Galileo stopped over in Bologna on 24–25 April to show Magini and other astronomers Jupiter's satellites. Martin Horky, a new protegé of Magini's, gleefully reported to Kepler in a letter dated 27 April that though Galileo's instrument was admirable for terrestrial observations, it had completely failed to show others what he claimed in the heavens.[2] He prefaced this with a nasty description of Galileo's person and reputation, and finished it by saying that before Galileo departed on the 26th, sad and miserable, Horky had secretly taken wax impressions of his lenses from which he would make a better telescope than Galileo's. About this time Hasdale saw at Prague a letter from Magini saying that Galileo's instrument was a deception; since colored glasses showed three suns in an eclipse, doubtless Galileo's glasses had similarly deceived him. Professor Flaminio Papazzoni, professor of philosophy at Bologna, planned to refute Galileo's whole book publicly after Easter.[3] In Magini's opinion the four new planets assumed by Galileo were simply ridiculous; though Magini wrote this before Galileo's visit to Bologna on 24–25 April, nothing known to have happened then is likely to have changed Magini's view.

On 7 May Galileo wrote again to Vinta, saying that he had delivered three public lectures about the new satellites and his other observations. The whole university was present, he said, and all were so satisfied that those who at first opposed his book there had given up. Moreover he had had a very long letter, almost a book, from the imperial mathematician (Kepler) approving his findings;[4] hence the grand duke need no longer worry about the attacks. Pursuant to his recent conversations at Pisa, Galileo now formally applied for employment, requesting 1,000 florins salary and sufficient free time to bring to completion certain works described as:

. . . two books on the system and constitution of the universe— an immense conception full of philosophy, astronomy, and geometry;[5] three books on local motion,[6] an entirely new science, no one else, ancient or modern, having discovered some of the very many admirable properties that I demonstrate to exist in natural and forced motions, whence I may reasonably call this a new science discovered by me from its first principles; three books on mechanics, two pertaining to the principles and foundations[7] and one on its problems[8]—and though others have written on this same material, what has been written to date is not one-quarter of what I write, either in bulk or otherwise. I have also various little works on physical subjects such as *On sound and voice, On vision and colors, On the tides, On the composition of the continuum, On the motions of animals,*[9] and still more.

Galileo wished also to write on military matters, to reprint his *Compass*, and to complete his investigations of the new satellites.

Finally, as to the title and the scope of my duties, I wish in addition to the name of Mathematician that his Highness adjoin that of Philosopher. . . . Whether I can and should have this title I shall be able to show their Highnesses whenever it is their pleasure to give me a chance to deal with this in their presence with the most esteemed men of that profession.[10]

On 22 May Vinta replied that the grand duke would be pleased to accept his services, with ample time to write and publish for the public benefit under his auspices, having also resolved to give him an honorable title and relieve him of obligation to teach at teach at Pisa. Galileo accepted on 28 May; on 5 June Vinta gave the title as "Chief Mathematician of the University of Pisa and Philosopher to the Grand Duke," to which Galileo wished "Mathematician" also added to "Philosopher." Finally he asked that the grand duke absolve him of any further obligation to his two brothers-in-law arising from default on dowry payments by his brother Michelangelo, Galileo himself having more than paid his share. His new service was to begin in October 1610 and to be for life.

II

Within three months of publication of the *Starry Messenger*, the opposition began to make itself heard. Horky went to Modena to publish a book against Galileo and his friend and supporter at Bologna, G. A. Roffeni. When Magini was told of this he ordered Horky to leave, whereupon Horky went to Milan and visited with Galileo's disgraced plagiarist, Baldessar Capra. A copy of his book, called *Excursion against the Starry Messenger*,[11] was sent to Francesco Sizzi at Florence, who was also writing a book in opposition to Galileo's astronomical discoveries of which more will be said presently.

Galileo's formal appointment by the grand duke, dated 10 July 1610, conformed in every respect to Galileo's wishes. On 25 July Galileo, writing to Vinta about some other matters, mentioned his discovery that the body of Saturn was seen through his telescope as if it were made of three stars (a large disk, touched on either side by a smaller disk). Apart from some further observations of the Medicean stars sent to Kepler on 28 June, this is the only record of further scientific work done by Galileo during this tumultuous period of correspondence and preparation for the move to Florence.

Early in August Francesco Sizzi obtained a license to publish his *Dianoia*, the first attack against Galileo's book to introduce theological issues into the debate over the reality of Galileo's newly discovered "planets."[12] Sizzi dedicated his book to Giovanni de' Medici, the member of that family least favorable to Galileo.

On 9 August Kepler again wrote to Galileo at length. Telescopes at Prague, he said, generally magnified no more than ten times; most of them only tripled the diameter, and the only one which achieved twenty-power was very poor in illumination. This shows how difficult it was, even with the resources of an imperial office, to obtain instruments that could show the satellites of Jupiter when several months had elapsed after their discovery by Galileo.[13] Kepler had also received Horky's book, which he deplored as adolescent and petulant. Wishing to be better able to answer the many who now opposed his support of Galileo, Kepler hinted his wish to have a proper telescope, or at least to know of other witnesses to the discoveries than Galileo himself. Galileo replied on 19 August that good telescopes were troublesome to make, though he had now designed machinery to assist in the manufacture. The grand duke himself was a further witness, for they had observed the satellites together often at Pisa, and many others had seen them in other cities in Italy. That certain Venetians scorned him did not bother Galileo; the satellites would continue to stay with Jupiter. The chief philosopher at Padua (Cremonini) had always refused to look, though Galileo had repeatedly offered to show him the new discoveries. The chief philosopher at Pisa (Giulio Libri) tried to argue the satellites out of the sky; these men seemed to think that philosophy was to be found in books, not in nature.

Galileo left Padua early in September, planning to visit Magini again in Bologna en route to Florence and to discuss with him the many things being written all over Europe about the Medicean stars. Just at this time Kepler was able for the first time to confirm the new discoveries, using a telescope made by

Galileo for the Elector of Cologne—one of the ten he had mentioned in March, of which Galileo sent one to the Elector, one
to Maximilian of Bavaria, and one to Francesco Cardinal del
Monte, brother of the late Guidobaldo. From Florence on 17
September Galileo wrote to Clavius at Rome, having learned
that the Jesuit astronomers could not confirm the new satellites
with any telescope at Rome; Galileo had meanwhile perfected
his own instrument so that he could see Jupiter even in daylight.
News that Kepler had finally observed the satellites arrived at
the beginning of October, and Galileo forwarded to him new
information and an anagram concealing news of the strange
apparent shape of Saturn. Anagrams were then frequently used
as means of establishing priority of discovery without revealing
what had been found, giving the writer time to publish at his
leisure.

Mark Welser of Augsburg[14] introduced himself to Galileo by
letter toward the end of October, enclosing a little treatise dis-
puting Galileo's measurement of a lunar mountain written by
J. G. Brengger. Galileo wrote at once to thank Welser, and a
little later sent him a long and detailed reply to the points raised
by Brengger. The same question of the existence of lunar mountains was also raised soon afterward in a public debate at
Mantua, attracting wide attention when the arguments of Galileo's adversary were circulated in manuscript.

Before Galileo explained his anagram to Kepler in mid-
November, Kepler had published it (without solving the riddle)
in a booklet describing his own confirmation of the satellites
around Jupiter.[15] About this time John Wedderburn, who had
been Galileo's pupil, published a reply to Horky's diatribe against
the new discoveries. Wedderburn recounted how Galileo, while
still at Padua, had used his telescope at close range to magnify
the parts of insects, communicating his observations to Cremonini.[16]

Benedetto Castelli, Galileo's former pupil, wrote to him in
December 1610 that if the Copernican system were true it should
be possible to observe phases of Venus like those of the moon.
Castelli had no telescope, and Venus had not been visible in
1610 until October, at which time Galileo said he had begun to
observe it, describing to Castelli the appearances he had expected. On 11 December Galileo sent a new anagram about this

to Prague, for Kepler, who tried in vain to unscramble it. Clavius now advised Galileo that the Jesuits had seen the satellites at Rome.

Observation of the phases of Venus late in 1610 was the crucial event that finally confirmed for Galileo the correctness of the Copernican astronomy. Neither the Aristotelian nor the Ptolemaic system could account for this phenomenon, and though the Tychonic system could explain it as well as the Copernican, Galileo rejected that system not because of astronomy but because of physics. To suppose the earth unmoving while attributing to the sun a power to carry along with it all the planets, despite the much greater size of some planets than that of the earth, was possible only for those who could regard heavenly bodies as made of some different substance and regulated by different laws than those on earth. That view of the nature of stars and planets had long been popular among philosophers; Aristotelians, in particular, based physical science on the principle that celestial bodies were devoid of any kind of matter that could be found on earth. Galileo, on the other hand, contended that the only sound way to reason about heavenly bodies was by analogy with terrestrial experience.

On New Year's Day 1611 Galileo sent to the Tuscan ambassador at Prague the solution to his Venus anagram, explaining how the phases of that planet showed that it must orbit

. . . around the sun, as do also Mercury and all the other
planets—something indeed believed by the Pythagoreans,
Copernicus, Kepler, and myself, but not sensibly proved as it
now is by Venus and Mercury. Hence Kepler and other Copernicans may glory in having believed and philosophized well,
though this is but a prelude, and will continue a prelude,
to our being reputed by the generality of bookish philosophers
as men of little understanding and practically as fools.[17]

The year 1611 was destined to evidence a polarization of the bookish philosophers and the scientists into two opposed camps, through a variety of controversies. Early in January Welser acknowledged Galileo's reply to Brengger. He expressed satisfaction with Galileo's arguments for the rough surface of the moon, but noted that a further suggestion had been made by Brengger—that philosophers could still say the moon was smooth by maintaining that any seeming irregularities were encased in smooth crystal. Ludovico delle Colombe was to advocate the same notion in Italy, perhaps independently.

At Pisa the principal chair of philosophy was left vacant late in 1610 by the death of Giulio Libri, another philosopher who, like Cremonini, had refused to look at the sky through the telescope. Galileo remarked sardonically that since he would not look at the new discoveries while on earth, he would perhaps see them on his way to heaven. One of the persons considered for Libri's chair was Flaminio Papazzoni of Bologna, who not long before had undertaken publicly to refute everything in the *Starry Messenger*. Though another candidate had been recommended to him by friends at Padua, when Galileo was consulted about the appointment he endorsed Papazzoni, whom he had met when he visited Magini at Bologna and who was supported by Galileo's good friend there, G. A. Roffeni.

Galileo, in poor health in 1611, blamed the air of Florence and went to stay at the Villa delle Selve of his friend Filippo Salviati, a few miles west of the city. As soon as he was well he wished to visit Rome to exhibit the new discoveries and explain their "great consequences," doubtless a reference to the Copernican implications he saw in the phases of Venus. The grand duke not only acceded to his wish but provided him with transportation and with lodging at the Trinità del Monte, then the Tuscan embassy at Rome. Galileo left Florence on 23 March, recording nightly observations of the satellites of Jupiter along his route (San Casciano, Siena, San Quirico, Acquapendente, Viterbo, Alonterosi)[18] and arriving at Rome on the 29th.

Among the first persons he visited was Christoper Clavius, still professor at the Roman College of the Jesuits though now very old.[19] Cardinal Bellarmine, always cautious, requested from the four mathematicians there (Clavius, Odo Maelcote, Christopher Grienberger, and G. P. Lembo) a formal report on Galileo's claimed celestial discoveries. All four signed a statement confirming Galileo's findings, though Clavius held that as to the surface of the moon this was not rough, but merely unevenly dense and rare, making it appear rough to our eyes. During Galileo's stay at Rome the Jesuits of the Collegio Romano paid him the unusual honor of a meeting at which Father Maelcote delivered an oration praising the *Starry Messenger*. Galileo also talked with Bellarmine about the Copernican astronomy, as is known from a later remark of Bellarmine's.[20] Welser wrote to a friend that he had long resisted Galileo's announcements, in agreement with the chief mathematicians of his acquaintance, but that all were now converted, in particular Father Clavius, who had so assured Welser of their truth that he no longer had any doubts.

Even while at Rome, however, Galileo received news of a growing opposition. At Perugia, for instance, the telescope was derided as putting into the sky things that were not really there. Galileo answered this in a letter to Piero Dini, his good friend at Rome, saying that he would pay 10,000 *scudi* to anyone who made a telescope that would create satellites around one planet and not around others. Sizzi's *Dianoia* reached Rome, where the Jesuits joked at its childish arguments. Others urged Galileo to reply to it, but instead he went so far as to apologize for Sizzi and said he had rather have his friendship than triumph in a quarrel with him. Kepler called the book a puerile Peripatetic speculation about "a world on paper," the same phrase Galileo later used to characterize the kind of philosophical science he scorned.[21] In his letter to Dini, Galileo improved his estimate of the period of Jupiter's outermost satellite from fifteen days to more than sixteen days, and gave his first estimate for the innermost satellite as less than two days. He had promised the grand duke to continue in Rome his investigations of the periods of all the satellites, the first step in predicting their positions.

One event at Rome was of great importance to Galileo's scientific career and was symptomatic of the polarization between university science, which was primarily philosophical, and the new pursuit of factual knowledge in a way that appealed to laymen. Federico Cesi, a young nobleman who divided his time between Acquasparta and Rome, had in 1603 founded with three friends the Academy of the Lincei, to be devoted to the study of natural phenomena and to eschew rhetorical displays common to most Italian academies of the period. Only one new member had been subsequently added; this was Giovanni Battista della Porta of Naples.[22] Cesi gave a banquet for Galileo on 14 April, all Linceans then in Rome being present, together with a number of guests. Galileo was made a member while still at Rome, as were five other persons present that night, shortly afterward. The only two professors there, Francesco Pifferi of Siena and J. C. Lagalla of the Sapienza at Rome, were not made

members. The facts that the Academy doubled in size in 1611
and that university professors remained outside are significant,
and Cesi's discussions with Galileo may have had a bearing on
both.[23] Galileo's departure from university circles had left him
without the continual flow of intellectual news he had enjoyed
at Padua; this was effectively remedied by correspondence with
Cesi and the growing membership of the Lincean Academy,
which soon spread beyond Italy.

While at Rome Galileo exhibited the phenomenon of sunspots,
though at the time he considered them mere curiosities and
made no study or even mention of them in letters. Later in the
year he realized their importance, as will be seen.

Galileo returned to Florence on 3 June, where a number of
letters awaited him. In one of these Daniello Antonini recalled
a proposition of Galileo's, probably from the time of his studies
of motion at Padua around 1609; this was that a body acquiring
speeds in proportion to its distances from rest must be moved
instantaneously. Though cited in Latin, in Antonini's Italian
letter, that proposition is not found among Galileo's notes; he
offered a proof of it only in his last book.[24] Antonini believed
he had discovered a counterexample, or at least a kind of motion
that approximated closely such a growth in speeds. Another
letter of Antonini's a month later recalled Galileo's opinion that
bodies contain very small void spaces, which tends to confirm
that his early work on strength of materials belonged to 1608 or
thereabouts, when Antonini and his friend Aproino studied with
him at Padua.

There was also a long letter from Brengger replying to Galileo's defense of the lunar mountains. The disputation on this
topic which had taken place at Mantua and circulated in manuscript with some passages offensive to Galileo was generally
attributed to the Jesuit Giuseppe Biancani (Blancanus), who
however denied that he had done more than advise its author
against such passages. Since the scientific point at issue had
been adequately explained in the *Starry Messenger*, the pro-
tracted and notorious controversy need not detain us here.

On 24 June Antonini wrote to congratulate Galileo on his
having determined the periods of the satellites of Jupiter. For
reasons that will appear later, it is probable that Galileo had
already reached figures near those that he published in his next

book early in 1612. Though Galileo continued to refine them, these earliest results were not very different from findings three centuries later:

Galileo (1611) 1 day 18.50 hours; 3 days 13.3 hours; 7 days 4 hours; 16 days 18− hours
Encyclopedia Britannica (1910) 1 day 18.48 hours; 3 days 13.5 hours; 7 days 4 hours; 16 days 18+ hours

Antonini had not been able to find Sizzi's *Dianoia*, but his guess about it recalls the Paduan dispute over the new star; he said it must be a "Cremoninata": "Is it possible that there are such oafish men in the world, and what is worse, that they are deemed the wise ones? What can be done to make everyone confess the truth if it does not suffice to see with one's own eyes? On the one hand I laugh at this; on the other, I become angry." He suggested at this time that a parabolic lens ought to serve as a telescope by bringing all parallel rays to a single focus; it is of interest that Galileo opined in his (lost) reply that the lens should rather be hyperbolic. Antonini answered that he still preferred his idea, which he planned to test by using a good parabolic burning mirror as a mold in which molten glass could be poured to obtain a convex parabolic lens.

About the time Galileo left Rome Ludovico delle Colombe wrote to Clavius approving his denial of the mountainous surface of the moon.[25] Like Brengger, Colombe proposed that perfect sphericity of the moon could be maintained by holding that it was encased in smooth transparent crystal, beneath which Galileo saw his mountains and craters. At the end of June Gallanzone Gallanzoni, secretary to Cardinal Joyeuse, sent Galileo a copy of Colombe's letter with a request for his comments, desired by the cardinal. Galileo's reply, directed against all philosophical hypotheses created solely to support Aristotle and Ptolemy, included this passage:

Getting back to our main purpose, if we still want to let anyone imagine whatever he pleases, and if someone says that the moon is spherically surrounded by transparent invisible crystal, then I shall willingly grant this—provided that with equal courtesy it is permitted me to say that this crystal has on its outer surface a great number of enormous mountains, thirty times as high as terrestrial ones, which, being of diaphanous substance, cannot be seen by us; and thus I can picture to myself another moon ten times as mountainous as [I said] in the first place. . . . The hypothesis is pretty; its only fault is that is neither demonstrated nor demonstrable. Who does not see that this is a purely arbitrary fiction that puts nothingness as existing and proposes nothing more than simple noncontradiction?

One might, Galileo said, equally well define *earth* to include the atmosphere out to the top of the highest mountain and then say "the earth is perfectly spherical."

Meanwhile Cesi wrote that Lagalla was printing a book against Galileo's lunar discoveries and defending the Peripatetic position, ignoring some changes suggested by Cesi.[26] There is also a very interesting letter at this time (July 1611) written by Kepler to Nicholas Wickens; Kepler had been talking with Simon Mayr, who congratulated himself on his having already discovered the periods of two of Jupiter's satellites. The bearing of this will become evident in chapter 13.

III

About the first week in August a memorable dispute arose between Galileo and some philosophers over the conditions governing the floating and sinking of bodies in water. Letters of the period, especially between Galileo and Ludovico Cigoli at Rome, together with later manuscripts and books, permit reconstruction of the events as follows.

Galileo, his friend Filippo Salviati, and two professors of the University of Pisa were discussing condensation when one of the professors, Vincenzio di Grazia, brought up the example of ice, which he considered to be simply condensed water. Galileo replied that ice should rather be regarded as rarefied water, since ice floats and must therefore be less dense than water. The professors contended that ice floated because of its broad flat shape, which made it impossible for the ice to cleave downward through the water. Galileo pointed out that ice held forcibly under water and then released seemed to manage to cleave through it upward, even though then its own weight ought to help hold it down. When it was argued that a sword struck flat on water resists, while edgewise it cuts easily through water, Galileo explained the irrelevance of this observation. He granted that the *speed* of motion through water was indeed affected by shape, as Aristotle himself had said, but not the simple *fact* of rising or sinking through water, which was the point at issue. Water offered resistance not to division, but to speed of division, while spontaneous rising or sinking of solids in water was governed only by the Archimedean principle. This discussion did not convince the professors.

Three days later, Di Grazia told Galileo that he had met someone who said he could show Galileo by experiments that shape did play a role in floating and sinking in water; this was Colombe, who had not been present at the initial conversation. Galileo wrote out the conditions of the contest: Colombe was to show by experiment that a sphere of some material that sank in water would not sink if the same material were given some other shape. Canon Francesco Nori was to referee the experiments presented by both sides. Colombe added the stipulation that he would decide on the material and shapes to be used, the material to be of nearly the same density as water itself, and Filippo Arrighetti was made cojudge with Nori.

During the next few days Colombe exhibited to many people his experiments, made with lamina, spheres, and cylinders of ebony. Galileo perceived that the contest was going to become a verbal one in this way; the real issue concerned the rising or sinking of bodies placed *in* water, not the behavior of bodies placed on its surface and incompletely wetted. Presumably he had the support of the referees on this, because when the meeting at Nori's house was scheduled, Colombe failed to appear (a fact already known to Cigoli at Rome on 23 August). Galileo then sent to Colombe a newly worded challenge, specifying that all the materials used were to be placed entirely in the water before each experiment with them. A date was set for the meeting, this time at Salviati's house in Florence (not at his villa, several miles distant from the city).

By this time gossip about the contest came to the attention of Cosimo de' Medici, who told Galileo not to engage in public disputes but rather to write out his arguments in a dignified form worthy of a court representative. When the scheduled meeting took place Galileo accordingly refused to enter into oral dispute with Colombe, saying that he would instead write out his position along with his arguments for it. This he did during September in a manuscript which includes his account of the entire affair up to this point. Addressed to Cosimo, it was apologetic in tone; it did not purport to be a complete treatise on hydrostatics, but was confined to the specific points at issue in the previous oral disputes.

The beginning and ending of this essay were as follows:

Many are the reasons, most serene Lord, for which I have set myself to the writing out at length of the controversy which in past days has led to so much debate by others. The first and most cogent of these was your hint, and your praise of the pen as the unique remedy for purging and separating clear and sequential reasoning from confused and intermittent alter- cations in which they especially who defend the side of error on one occasion noisily deny that which they had previously affirmed, and on the next, pressed by the force of reason, attempt with inappropriate distinctions and classifications, cavils, and strained interpretations of words to slip through one's fingers and escape by their subtleties and twistings about, not hesitating to produce a thousand chimeras and fantastic caprices little understood by themselves and not at all by their listeners. By these the mind is bewildered and confusedly bandied about from one phantasm to another, just as, in a dream, one passes from a palace to a ship and thence to a grotto or beach, and finally, when one awakes and the dream vanishes (and for the most part all memory of it also), one finds that one has been idly sleeping and has passed the hours without profit of any sort.

The second reason is that I desire that your Highness should become fully and frankly informed of what has taken place in this affair; for the nature of contests being what it is, those who through carelessness are induced to support error will shout loudest and make themselves more heard in public places than those through whom speaks truth, which unmasks itself tranquilly and quietly, though slowly. Hence I can well believe that just as in the squares and temples and other public places, the voices of those who dissent from what I assert have been far more often heard than those of others who agree with me, so likewise at court they have tried to advance their opinion by forestalling me there with their sophisms and cavils; these I hope to disperse and send up in smoke, even though they may have gained the ear and assent of some men prior to a careful reading of this essay of mine.

In the third place, I have deemed it good not to leave this matter unresolved, for just as at the outset the erroneous side had for nearly everyone the face and appearance of truth, so it might continue to deceive many persons with that same appearance, causing them on some momentous occasions to fall into serious error by taking false axioms for true principles.

Finally, having been chosen by your Highness as your personal mathematician and philosopher, I cannot permit the malignity, envy, or ignorance (and perhaps all three) of anyone to bear stupidly against your prudence; for that would be to abuse your incomparable benignity. On the contrary, I shall always put down (and with very little trouble) their every impudence, and this I do with the invincible shield of truth, demonstrating that what I have have asserted in the past was and is absolutely true, and that to the extent that I have departed from the commonly accepted Peripatetic opinions, this has come about not from my not having read Aristotle or not having understood as well as they his reasoning, but because I possess stronger demonstrations and more evident experiments than theirs. And in the present dispute, in addition to showing the approach I take to the study of Aristotle, I shall reveal whether I have well understood his meaning in two or three readings only, compared with them, to some of whom the reading of Aristotle fifty times may seem a small matter; and then I shall show whether I have perhaps better investigated the causes of the matters which constitute the subject of the present contest than did Aristotle. . . .[27]

Here I expect a terrible rebuke from one of my adversaries, and I can almost hear him shouting in my ears that it is one thing to deal with matters physically, and quite another to do so mathematically, and that geometers should stick to their fantasies and not get entangled in philosophical matters— as if truth could ever be more than one; as if geometry up to our time had prejudiced the acquisition of true philosophy; as if it were impossible to be a geometer as well as a philosopher —and we must infer as a necessary consequence that anyone who knows geometry cannot know physics, and cannot reason about and deal with physical matters physically! Consequences no less foolish than that of a certain physician who, moved by a fit of spleen, said that the great doctor [Girolamo Fabricio of] Acquapendente, being a famed anatomist and surgeon, should content himself to remain among his scalpels and ointments without trying to effect cures by medicine—as if knowledge of surgery destroyed and opposed a knowledge of medicine. I replied to him that having many times recovered my health through the supreme excellence of Signor Acquapendente, I could depose and certify that he had never given me to drink any compound of cerates, caustics, threads, bandages, probes, and razors, nor had he ever, instead of feeling my pulse, cauterized me or pulled a tooth from my mouth. Rather, as an excellent physician, he purged me with manna, cassia, or rhubarb, and used other remedies suitable to my ailments. Let my adversaries see whether I treat the material in the same terms as Aristotle, and whether he himself does not, where necessary, introduce geometrical demonstrations. And then let them have the kindness to desist from their bitter enmity toward geometry—to my astonishment indeed, since I had not thought anyone could be enemy to a total stranger.

Finally, Aristotle says at the end of his text that one must compare the heaviness of a body with the resistance to division of the medium, because if the power of the heaviness exceeds the resistance of the medium, the body will descend, and if not, it will float. I need not trouble to reply beyond that which has already been said: that it is not resistance to division (which does not exist in air or in water), but rather it is the heaviness of the medium which must be compared with the heaviness of the body; and if the heaviness be greater in the medium, the body will not descend therein, nor can it be entirely submerged, but a part only, because in the space which it occupies in the water there cannot exist a body which weighs less than an equal quantity of water. But if the body be heavier than the water it will descend to the bottom, where it is more natural for it to rest than a less heavy body. And this is the true, unique, proper, and absolute cause of floating or sinking.

As for your chip, gentle adversaries, it will float when it is coupled with so much air as to form with that a composite body less heavy than as much water as would fill the space which the said composite occupies in the water; but if you put simple ebony into the water, in accordance with our agreements, it will go to the bottom though you make it thinner than paper.

Most serene Lord, I have taken the trouble (as your Lordship has seen) to keep alive my true proposition, and along with it many others that follow therefrom, preserving it from the voracity of the falsehood overthrown and slain by me. I know not whether the adversaries will give me credit for the work thus accomplished, or whether they, finding themselves under a strict oath obliged to sustain religiously every decree of Aristotle (perhaps fearing that if disdained he might invoke to their destruction a great company of his most invincible heroes), have resolved to choke me off and exterminate me as a profaner of his sacred laws. In this they would imitate the inhabitants of the Isle of Pianto when, angered against Orlando, in recompense for his having liberated so many innocent virgins from the horrible holocaust of the monster, they moved against him, lamenting their strange religion and vainly fearing the wrath of Proteus, terrified of submersion in the vast ocean.[28] And indeed they would have succeeded had not he, impenetrable though naked to their arrows, behaved as does the bear toward small dogs that deafen him with vain and noisy barking. Now I, who am no Orlando, possess nothing impenetrable but the shield of truth; for the rest, naked and unarmed, I take refuge in the protection of your Highness, at whose mere glance must fall any madman who imperiously attempts to mount irrational assaults.[29]

IV

About the middle of September Flaminio Papazzoni, who had been appointed professor of philosophy at Pisa on Galileo's recommendation, was asked to come to Florence for some specific purpose which he was rather reluctant to carry out. Galileo had earlier promised the grand duke that if given the title of philosopher he would show his right to it by confronting the most esteemed members of the profession, and he appears to have decided that this would be an excellent way to start. Papazzoni was not happy about being asked to defend the prevailing views against his own benefactor before even having assumed the new chair, but it was a command performance. Galileo easily won the debate in the presence of members of the ruling family and other court attendants.

On 30 September Maffeo Cardinal Barberini, with whom Galileo had conversed at Rome earlier in the year, visited Florence for a few days on his way to Bologna. Cardinal Gonzaga happened also to be in Florence, and the grand duke invited Galileo and Papazzoni to repeat their arguments in the presence of the two cardinals at a court dinner on 2 October. Barberini took Galileo's side as the argument progressed, while Gonzaga supported Papazzoni. The Grand Duchess Christina was particularly interested in Galileo's idea that water offered no resistance to division as such, exemplified by its behavior in contrast with that of even the finest powders, such as flour. Others brought up the phenomenon of floating needles, for which Galileo had an ingenious explanation that was, however, misunderstood by "a great personage"[30] in such a way as to have later repercussions which will be recounted in chapter 11. The whole event was a triumph for Galileo, though he fell seriously ill immediately after it.

Galileo's victorious debate at the beginning of October resulted in his putting aside the essay and composing an entirely different kind of treatise on hydrostatics generally, including phenomena involving the hydrostatic paradox and some effects of surface tension. During the latter part of 1611, however, illness prevented his answering many letters. On 19 December he described the symptoms that had oppressed him while making notes for his next book: "These things disturbed my mind and made me melancholy, which in turn augmented them; yet I have done something, haltingly, and in a few days I will send you a *Discourse* on a certain dispute with some Peripatetics. That sent, I want to spend a few days replying to letters, meanwhile not neglecting celestial observations, with some exquisite addition thereto."

The new observations concerned sunspots and will be discussed in the following chapter. The first letter to Galileo on this subject had arrived from Rome in September 1611, and his reply to it showed that he had by then reached a conclusion concerning the sun's rotation on its axis. There is abundant evidence that Galileo exhibited sunspots to others during his visit to Rome in April 1611; thus G. B. Agucchi wrote on 16 June 1612, "It is already more than a year since you told me orally of the solar spots and their motion around the body of the sun." Galileo had met Agucchi at the Trinità del Monte in Rome during April 1611. On 11 December 1612 Odo Maelcote of the Jesuit Roman College wrote to Kepler that Galileo had shown him sunspots "while at Rome last year." Years later the Jesuit mathematician Paul Guldin recalled that Galileo had shown him sunspots at that same time and that he had communicated this to Christopher Scheiner at Ingolstadt—a statement of great interest in the light of later events. Hence it is probable that Galileo first interested himself in sunspots shortly before his journey to Rome in 1611; in letters he wrote in 1612, the earliest date implied by his own words was January 1611.

As early as June 1611 Galileo had already found fairly accurate periods for all four satellites, having previously given approximate periods for the innermost and outermost satellites to Piero Dini while he was still at Rome in April. Agucchi, to whom

Galileo had been introduced there by Luca Valerio, wrote on 9 September to ask for numerical data regarding each orbit and period on behalf of himself and some gentleman at Rome who was preparing a lecture. Galileo's reply has not survived, but its contents are evident from the next letter of Agucchi, dated 14 October, saying that by acting on Galileo's suggestions as to method, and using the diagrams published in the *Starry Messenger*, he had arrived at certain results and wanted to know if they were approximately right. Clearly Galileo preferred not to disclose his latest findings before he had satisfied himself as to their accuracy, intending then to publish them; in particular, he did not want them made public in a lecture by someone unknown to him. Agucchi understood this and promised not to pass information received from Galileo on to the other gentleman, who in any event had decided meanwhile to change the subject of his oration. Agucchi's results were in fact quite close to Galileo's as to the periods:[31]

Agucchi 1 day 18.33 hours; 3 days 15 hours; 7 days 4 hours;
16 days 20 hours
Galileo 1 day 18.5— hours; 3 days 13.3 hours; 7 days 4 hours;
16 days 18— hours

In sending his results Agucchi asked in a postscript for the magnitudes of the satellites, either as compared with stars of the sixth magnitude or in terms of their visual diameters in seconds of arc. Galileo replied, approving Agucchi's periods except that the longest was excessive by about two hours. Agucchi's inquiry about visual diameters probably led Galileo to estimate the diameter of Jupiter at fifty seconds of arc in a note belonging to 1611,[32] which was followed by more precise determinations in January and June 1612.[33]

TEN

1612

I

GALILEO's *Discourse on Bodies on or in Water*, begun during his illness at Florence late in 1611, was completed at Salviati's villa in the spring of 1612.[1] It opened with data on the periods of Jupiter's satellites and some remarks about sunspots. Galileo then outlined the 1611 dispute over floating bodies and said that this had given rise to further questions, to be solved by a procedure different from that of Archimedes but confirming his conclusions as well. Aristotle's doctrines were unsatisfactory in this matter; bare authority was to be replaced by reason, and results valuable to engineers were promised. First the principle of Archimedes was set forth, in language much like that of *De motu*, and then Galileo offered to show how a small amount of water, with its little weight, could raise and sustain a much heavier solid body. That was the phenomenon that had attracted his attention in 1608, though his first notes on it have not survived.

For his purposes Galileo needed to define *specific weight*, essentially similar to what is called "specific gravity" now, in contrast with ordinary weight which takes no account of the surrounding medium. That concept had long been familiar to specialists; Galileo's task was to make it clear to ordinary readers. Similarly the word *moment*, which had for years been Galileo's key to both statics and his studies of motion, was presented to the public; Galileo here introduced it not by means of a formal definition, but by first remarking that equal weights moving with equal speed were of the same force or *moment*. Following this were illustrations (expanded in the second edition, which appeared the same year) in which moment was simply the power or effectiveness of a motion or a resistance. Galileo stated that speed can increase moment in such a way that unequal weights become balanced and of the same moment when the weights are inversely proportional to the speeds of their motions. By this concept, worked out earlier for ordinary mechanics, Galileo proposed to show that a body heavier than water may be lifted by a much smaller weight of water than its own when the water must be moved more swiftly than the solid by reason of its being constrained within a containing vessel.[2]

Galileo proceeded to develop mathematically the basic propositions of hydrostatics for water in finite containers, concluding this first section with the remark that if it had not been necessary to explain the seeming paradox of a heavy beam lifted by a small quantity of water, he would have contented himself only with what Archimedes had demonstrated about floating bodies. He then examined some criticisms of Archimedes published in 1591 by an Aristotelian professor at Pisa, Francesco Buonamici, who had assigned the cause of floating or sinking to difficulty or ease of dividing the medium. There was no reason, Galileo said, to prefer one authority to another in matters concerning which nature speaks to us. The authority of Archimedes was worth no more than that of Aristotle; the position of Archimedes was right because it agreed with experiments. Galileo held that neither air nor water presents resistance to division as such, "but all are divided and penetrated by any minimal force, as I shall demonstrate."

Tiny particles of mud, he said, could never make their way to the bottom of a vessel if water had any resistance to cleavage at all. The surface of water, where it is in contact with air, exhibits that kind of resistance, but water alone does not. In principle a massive ship might be moved through still water by pulling it with a slender thread. "I cannot see what minute power or force we can possibly find or imagine, than which the resistance of water to division and penetration is not still weaker, from which we must necessarily conclude that it is nothing."

If the shape of an object could prevent its sinking, Galileo argued, a sharp point should assist sinking and a blunt surface should assist floating. But a wax cone placed in water, point down, will float, while it will sink if placed in water with its blunt base downward.[3]

Bodies in Water was Galileo's first published work on a physical topic. It could hardly be expected to enjoy the wide appeal of the *Starry Messenger*; yet it did excite great interest because of the many things contained in it which at first sight appeared incredible or paradoxical, but which could be verified by simple experiments requiring no special equipment. Probably the only things in it that were new to Galileo at the time of its composition were the sections relating to phenomena which we now ascribe to surface tension (the name for which was not coined until the mid-eighteenth century). The concept that a force smaller than any previously assigned force should suffice to move any large body along a frictionless horizontal surface had already appeared in *De motu*, but its connection with the idea that fluids have no resistance to horizontal division as such may not have occurred to Galileo before 1611.

II

Galileo's principal scientific work in 1612 related to sunspots. In mid-September 1611 Ludovico Cigoli at Rome had written to Galileo about observations made by the painter known as Passignano, Domenico Crespi, who believed the spots to originate near the center of the sun and to make their way to its surface along spiral lines, so that they appeared sometimes to be moving toward the edge of the sun and sometimes away from it. Replying on 1 October, Galileo had said:

I am glad to hear that Sig. Passignano is observing the sun and its revolutions, but you must tell him to note that the part of the sun we see below at its rising is above at its setting, whence it may appear to him that on that account the sun might have some other revolution of its own than that which I truly believe it does have, and that I think is observed in the changes of its spots. I shall be glad to see this gentleman's observations [which had been offered] to compare them with mine.

The mistake Passignano had made is evident from two rough sketches drawn in Cigoli's first letter. It was a mistake easy to make, since until the detection and study of sunspots, which was just commencing, there had been no way to know that the sun shows us very nearly the same face all day long. Galileo had already reached that conclusion, though he still attached no special importance to sunspots.

Paolo Gualdo wrote late in 1611 to say that Lorenzo Pignoria had heard from Mark Welser that in Germany, too, observations of sunspots had begun, after which two of Gualdo's friends at Padua had seen spots near the sun's center resembling eyes and a nose. On 18 November Welser notified Johann Faber, a Lincean at Rome, that friends of his (Christopher Scheiner and Adam Tanner, as it turned out) had seen apparent spots on the sun and believed they must be stars coming into the line of sight. This was communicated to Galileo by Cesi on 3 December.

Mentioning Passignano's promise to write to Galileo and send him sunspot observations, Cigoli told Galileo that certain men ill-disposed toward him had met in Florence at the house of Archbishop Alessandro Marzimedici to discuss how best to attack those who believed the earth to move. One, probably Colombe, asked that a priest denounce Galileo's extravagant opinions from the pulpit. Cigoli's information was from a friendly priest, probably Luigi Maraffi, who perceived in this request personal malice against Galileo and rebuked the offender.

Thus, just when Galileo moved from Florence to Le Selve where for a time he was out of touch with Florentine intrigues, a league including religious elements as well as his philosophical opponents was being formed against him, though not without resistance among the former. The move to Le Selve not only reduced Galileo's ability to defend himself against them, but also resulted in long delays in his receipt of letters addressed to him at Florence, which affected some events in the ensuing sunspot controversy.

On 6 January 1612 Mark Welser addressed a letter to Galileo transmitting a pseudonymous booklet about sunspots[4] and asked for Galileo's comments. Because Galileo had moved to Le Selve these did not come into his hands until late March, after he had heard of the existence of this book from others. Only one letter of Galileo's during January 1612 is extant, addressed to Margarita Sarocchi, a friend of Luca Valerio's at Rome. She was revising an epic poem she had published in 1603 and Valerio had asked Galileo to make criticisms and suggestions to her. At this time, Galileo wrote, he could not do more than acknowledge receipt of the book, being so troubled with pain in the chest and kidneys, insomnia, and loss of blood that neither his hand nor his brain was capable of labor.

The book sent by Welser had been printed at his own expense and contained three letters on sunspots addressed to him by "Apelles." He remarked that he did not suppose sunspots would be anything new to Galileo, whose comments he wished, though at least the book would show him that Germans also were following the trail Galileo had blazed by his new observations in the heavens.

Early in February Cesi wrote that printed letters on sunspots had been sent to Clavius, though Cesi had not yet seen them. A month later he advised Galileo that "Apelles" thought the apparent spots to be really moving stars. In mid-March Cesi received a letter from Galileo, now lost, in which sunspots were evidently not mentioned, so that it is safe to say he had not yet seen Welser's letter and the accompanying book. Galileo's letter criticized Lagalla's *On the Phenomena in the Orb of the Moon*, declaring it unsuited to have been published by a Lincean. Cesi assured Galileo that Lagalla (whom he had met at Cesi's banquet in Rome) was not a member of their Academy and that no Lincean would have written so offensively against Galileo's conclusions in the *Starry Messenger*. He classed Lagalla's book with Sizzi's as an imbecility. A week later he wrote again to say that it had awakened many dormant defenders of Galileo, and that while Lagalla was supported by all scholastics and Peripatetics, genuine philosophers did not doubt the moon's rough surface and wished only that Galileo would follow up his earlier discoveries himself.

On 23 March Welser wrote to express surprise that he had had no reply to his letter of 6 January, "a most unusual thing in view of your usual friendly courtesy; hence I question whether this is because of your poor health, or whether my request—or your response—may have gone astray." Now, on 2 April Salviati addressed a letter from Le Selve to Galileo at Florence, showing that Galileo had left the villa before the end of March and intended to remain in Florence for some time. The purpose of Galileo's journey was to put his completed *Bodies in Water* into the hands of a printer, and while at Florence he visited with Benedetto Castelli, asking him to oversee the printing. There he found Welser's waiting letter and book, on reading which he resolved to reply at length on the basis of new and carefully made sunspot observations. Probably before returning to Le Selve he asked Castelli also to start making such observations at Florence.

"Apelles" declared that he had first seen apparent spots on the sun about May 1611, a date in accord with Paul Guldin's recollection that he had sent word of sunspots to Scheiner from Rome during Galileo's visit there. Not until October, however, after Galileo had already replied to Cigoli's inquiry on behalf of Passignano, did "Apelles" commence his serious observations. He then reasoned that if located on the sun's surface, the apparent spots must either remain at the same places or, if the sun rotated, return after a time. He had seen neither thing happen, from which he concluded that these were not literally spots on the sun, but stars of some kind which revolved either around the earth or around the sun, passing from time to time between us and its shining body.

Because a conjunction of Venus with the sun (transit of Venus) had been forecast for 11 December 1611, "Apelles" had looked for a large apparent spot on 12 December. Finding none, he concluded that either Venus was too bright with light of its own to be seen against the sun, or that it had passed not in front of the sun but behind it. In the latter case Venus must revolve around the sun, not around the earth, as some ancients had supposed and as fitted the Tychonic system, which conclusion he adopted.

To all this and some other poorly reasoned conclusions Galileo replied at length to Welser, composing a short treatise in letter form on his return to Le Selve. Dated 4 May 1612, this was to become the first of Galileo's three *Sunspot Letters* published in 1613 under the auspices of the Lincean Academy at Rome.[5] Its tone, though perhaps somewhat patronizing, was not unfriendly to "Apelles," but Galileo rejected his conclusions on nearly every point.

On 8 May Castelli wrote, evidently in reply to a letter from Galileo after seeing proofs of early pages of *Bodies in Water*, that the printer was very diligent but inept at reading type before pulling pages, so that there would be many errors which he would correct before any copies were sold. With this letter Castelli sent diagrams of sunspot observations recorded by first drawing a perfect circle on paper and then fitting the sun's telescopic image exactly to it, insuring exact placement of spots traced on the paper. The method was described and duly credited to Castelli in Galileo's second sunspot letter, in order that "Apelles" might obtain accurate recordings in place of the very poor illustrations in this book. But Castelli had gone further; perhaps at Galileo's suggestion (who at first estimated the period of rotation to be about fifteen days), he had divided the sun's hemisphere into fifteen equal parts and found that the daily progress of a spot followed the versine relationship. Galileo was thus in a position to demonstrate mathematically that the spots must be on the very surface of the sun, or very little distant from it, as he was to do in his second letter to Welser.

On 12 May Galileo sent to Cesi a copy of his long letter to Welser with a covering letter which said:

I have finally concluded, and believe I can demonstrate necessarily, that they are contiguous to the surface of the solar body, where they are continually generated and dissolved, just like clouds around the earth, and are carried around by the sun itself, which turns on itself in a lunar month with a revolution similar [in direction] to those others of the planets, that is, from west to east[6] around the poles of the ecliptic; which news I think will be the funeral, or rather the extremity and Last Judgment of pseudophilosophy, of which [event] signs were already seen in the stars, in the moon, and in the sun. I wait to hear spoutings of great things from the Peripetate to maintain the immutability of the skies, which I don't know how can be saved and covered up, since the sun itself indicates [mutations] to us with most manifest sensible experiences. Hence I expect that the mountains of the moon will be converted into a joke and a pleasantry in comparison with the whips of these clouds, vapors, and smokings that are being continually produced, moved, and dissolved on the face of the sun. I have written this [to Welser] in a letter [enclosed] of six folios [twenty-four pages] that will be good for the volume.

Some explanation of Galileo's comment that sunspots would make a joke of the previous controversies over lunar mountains may be useful. Those had created more furor than is generally recognized. There had been many attacks on the existence of Jupiter's satellites, based on the idea that those were illusions created by telescope lenses; yet it was the existence of lunar mountains that astronomers and philosophers alike found hardest to accept. Clavius, for instance, had made that his one reservation about Galileo's announced discoveries. Lagalla's hostile book had centered on the same issue. So had Brengger's critical essay, which first induced Welser to write to Galileo, as also the unpleasant incident at Mantua in which Biancani was involved. Any challenge to perfect sphericity of the perfect heavenly bodies constituted the worst threat of all in the eyes of philosophers, whose reasons in support of this dogma (despite contrary telescopic evidence) outnumbered their arguments against any other revelation made in the *Starry Messenger*. Galileo now expected that the sunspots would cause philosophers so much trouble that their earlier worries about lunar mountains would pale into insignificance.

On 8 June Paolo Gualdo wrote from Padua to say that Sagredo had sent him Galileo's letter on sunspots, which he had shown to many of his friends. "Meanwhile I tell you that by this writing of yours you have excited great arguments in bookstores among these philosophers. One who saw it told Sig. Cremonini that I wanted also to show it to him; he replied, 'I do not wish to see it. Indeed, I question whether you should trouble your head [about it] and thus be compelled not to put full faith in your philosophy as you have done in the past.' His book *On the Heavens* has not yet gone to the printers; as soon as it is published I shall see that you are the first to have it, if indeed it deserves to be honored [by a place] among your things, as he honors yours among his."

III

It was not until 14 August that Galileo sent off his second sunspot letter to Welser; this was dated from Florence, where Galileo had remained since about mid-May 1612. On 9 June, Cesi had offered to publish "your two letters to Sig. Welser, alone or with others," alluding to the letter in reply to Brengger's objections against lunar mountains and the first sunspot letter. This original plan of Cesi's was changed; ultimately the Lincean Academy, under Cesi's direction, published Galileo's correspondence with Welser on sunspots only, together with Welser's replies.[7] The second sunspot letter, containing important comments on Galileo's view of the relation of science to philosophy, will be considered before we return to other events of mid-1612.

Galileo's first sunspot letter had been appropriately confined to discussion of views that had been published by "Apelles," Welser having asked for such comments together with some reasons for Galileo's differing views. In the second letter he now added specific data taken from his continuing observations, on the basis of which he could demonstrate mathematically that the spots were situated on the sun's surface or extremely close to it. The new data showed their daily progress to be proportional to the versines of equal arcs, confirmed by Castelli shortly after Galileo sent his first letter off to Welser. Without the aid of diagrams drawn by Castelli's method it had not been possible to measure sunspot motions accurately enough to be sure of this.

This was not Galileo's only mathematical argument in favor of placing the spots on the sun itself. He demonstrated that bodies moving in different orbits, even if removed only short distances from the sun's surface, could not reasonably account for the observed changes in separation between identifiable spots as they moved across the sun's face from day to day. Then, allowing that the spots might be moved either by actual contact with a rotating sun or by some medium rotating around it, he began to apply terrestrial physics to the heavens:

It could happen either way. Yet to me it seems much more probable that the movement is of the solar globe rather than its surroundings. I am led to believe this because first, I think the circumambient substance to be very fluid and yielding—a proposition that appears quite novel in the ordinary philosophy. . . . Now, an orderly movement such as the universal motion of all the spots seems incapable of having its root and basis in a fluid substance whose parts do not cohere. . . . But orderly motion would occur in a solid and consistent body, where the motion of the whole and of the parts is necessarily one, as may be believed of the solar body in contrast with its ambient. Such motion then, communicated to the ambient by contact [with the sun], and to the spots by the ambient, or else conferred directly [by the sun] on the spots, could carry them around. And if anyone should wish to have the rotation of the spots around the sun proceed from motion that resides in the ambient and not in the sun, I think it would be necessary in any case for the ambient to communicate this movement to the solar globe as well. For I seem to have observed that physical bodies have physical inclination to some motion (as heavy bodies downward), which motion is exercised by them through an intrinsic property and without need of a particular external mover, whenever they are not impeded by some obstacle. And to another motion they have a repugnance (as the same heavy bodies do to motion upward), and therefore they never move in that manner unless thrown violently by an external mover.

Finally, to some movements they are indifferent, as are these same heavy bodies to horizontal motion, to which they have neither inclination (since it is not toward the center of the earth) nor repugnance (since it does not carry them away from that center). And therefore, all external impediments removed, a heavy body on a spherical surface concentric with the earth will be indifferent to rest and to movements toward any part of the horizon. And it will maintain itself in that state in which it has once been placed; that is, if placed in a state of rest, it will conserve that; and if placed in movement toward the west (for example), it will maintain itself in that movement. Thus a ship, for instance, having once received some impetus through the tranquil sea, would move continually around our globe without ever stopping; and placed at rest it would perpetually remain at rest, if in the first case all extrinsic impediments could be removed, and in the second case no external cause of motion were added.

Now if this is true (as indeed it is), what would a body of ambiguous nature do if continually surrounded by an ambient that moved with a motion to which it [the body] was indifferent? I do not see how one can doubt that it would move with the motion of the ambient. And the sun, a body of spherical shape suspended and balanced upon its own center, cannot fail to follow the motion of its ambient, having no intrinsic repugnance or extrinsic impediment to rotation. It cannot have an internal repugnance, because by such a rotation it is neither removed from its place, nor are its parts permuted among themselves. Their natural arrangement is not changed in any way, so that as far as the constitution of its parts is concerned, such movement is as if it did not exist. As to external impediments, it does not seem that any obstacle can impede without contact, except perhaps by magnetic power; and in this case all that is in contact with the sun is its ambient, which not only does not impede the movement which we seek to attribute to it, but itself has this movement. This may be further confirmed, as it does not appear that any movable body can have a repugnance to a movement without having a natural propensity to the opposite motion, for in indifference no repugnance exists; hence anyone who wants to give the sun a resistance to the circular motion of its ambient would be putting in it a natural propensity for circular motion opposite to that. But this cannot appeal to any balanced mind.[8]

Soon after hearing from Welser that "Apelles" was at a disadvantage in reading the sunspot letters because they were written in Italian, Galileo asked Paolo Gualdo and Martino Sandelli at Padua to make a Latin translation of the book with a view to its publication by Cesi, saying:

> I wrote it in the common language because I need to have everyone able to read it, and for that same reason I wrote my last little treatise [*Bodies in Water*] in the same language; and the reason that moves me is my seeing how young men are sent to the university indiscriminately to make themselves into doctors, philosophers, and the like, so that many who apply themselves to those professions are most inept for them, just as others who would be apt are occupied by family cares or in other occupations remote from literature, who then, though as Ruzzante says they have good horse sense, persuade themselves that those miserable pamphlets that contain great new things of logic and philosophy remain way over their heads; and I want them to see that just as Nature has given them, as well as philosophers, eyes to see her works, so she has given them brains capable of perceiving and understanding these.[9]

IV

Bodies in Water had meanwhile been sent to many persons and replies now began to come back. Sagredo was delighted by it, being (as he said) neither a Peripatetic nor crazy; by including the arguments of his opponents Galileo had thrown doubt on "patent and demonstrated truths" asserted in philosophy that gave reputation to foolishness. Gualdo wrote that *Bodies in Water* was in the hands of the Paduan philosophers, who would not get down to practical tests of what Galileo had subtly reasoned about, and would concede nothing without proof: "In fact you have administered certain syrups that give them bad cramps." Agucchi told how a number of his friends who at first upheld the objections Galileo himself had recounted, in the end gave up because of his mathematical proofs and the experiments he offered. Cardinals Capponi and Del Monte were particularly enthusiastic, while Bellarmine, Deti, and Gonzaga were merely polite in acknowledging Galileo's book.

The reaction of Lagalla to Galileo's book was of a kind that Galileo lampooned in his famous *Dialogue*. At first Lagalla was going to write a book in reply to *Bodies in Water*, but then on reflection he decided that Galileo spoke truly in saying that only specific weight mattered in floating and sinking because that was implied by Aristotle himself in *De caelo* when writing of mixtures of air and earth. Likewise shape was irrelevant, as Galileo had said, because Lagalla found this to be Aristotle's true opinion though he had seemed to say the contrary.[10]

Welser found *Bodies in Water* a book that was curious and useful, one "that will again floor philosophers of the ordinary school." Cigoli reported that a friend believed philosophers would find it not to their taste; he himself recalled that Michelangelo, when he first commenced designing buildings, was attacked for having ruined architecture by departing from Vitruvius.

The first book to be published in reply to Galileo was called *Considerations of the Unknown Academician* and appeared in August 1612.[11] Its author is usually said to have been Arturo d'Elci, treasurer of the University of Pisa, whose name indeed appears in the dedicatory material but who there declared himself not the author but the translator of the contents (from Latin into Italian). In my opinion it was composed by Flaminio Papazzoni, whose situation in the entire dispute had been rather uncomfortable. Galileo's book was aimed against the position Papazzoni had been obliged to defend at the court of the grand duke as the official spokesman for the University of Pisa; yet he owed his appointment to Galileo and it would have been ungracious to attack his book openly. Papazzoni dissociated himself from the faction at Pisa hostile to Galileo, as did also the author of the *Considerations*. He had told Giovanni Ciampoli in the summer of 1612 that he "blushed to write against Galileo."

The *Considerations* gave a reasonable and nonpartisan exposition of the Aristotelian position, unlike the three other books subsequently published against *Bodies in Water*. Galileo seems to have regarded Papazzoni as the author, sending him a copy of the expanded second edition to which he had added some material related to the *Considerations*, with a letter challenging him to reply to that. Papazzoni replied with dignity that he wrote only in defense of Aristotle.

In mid-1612 Galileo received a number of letters of scientific interest. Cesi inquired concerning the Copernican astronomy, thinking it would be improved if one could do away with eccentrics and epicycles. Mentioning Tycho's abandonment of solid celestial spheres and Kepler's agreement, Cesi asked Galileo which of two epicyclic arrangements Copernicus had used to account for differing distances of the moon. Galileo commended Cesi's interest in Copernicus, saying that we should not desire

Nature to accommodate herself to what seems to us most orderly and best arranged but should accommodate our intellects to what Nature has done, knowing that to be best; and since Nature is pleased to have wandering stars go around different centers (as do the planets, the moon, and Jupiter's satellites), we may be sure that that is most perfect and admirable. "And though Sig. Lagalla calls those philosophers fools who hold as really true the eccentrics and epicycles, I am nevertheless content to remain among their number, having sensible experience and Nature on my side, rather than deny what is palpable and be followed by infinitely many gentlemen." The moon circles the earth, while the planets do not; who would deny the revolutions of the Medicean stars around Jupiter, or of Mercury and Venus around the sun? In that sense epicycles are far from imaginary; there are *only* such motions and no star at all moves concentrically to the earth. But to believe that in order to execute such motions Nature has any need of solid epicyclic orbs is an idle fancy and an unnecessary chimera. Finally, Galileo said, Copernicus made use now of one and now the other of the two arrangements concerning which Cesi had inquired.

Sagredo, who as already mentioned had left Venice in 1608 on a diplomatic mission and never saw Galileo again, had returned and was in frequent correspondence with him. In July 1612 he wrote to say that their friend Agostino da Mula had told him of a device that was being used by Santorre Santorio, now a professor at the University of Padua, for the measurement of heat. Much interested in this, Sagredo had begun experimenting with the thermoscope and sent some drawings of it to Galileo, who replied that the device was an invention of his. By 1615 Sagredo had brought the instrument to such perfection that it was able to detect differences in temperature caused by the proximity of a person's body, or by its being placed near a light.

Meanwhile Galileo had asked Carlo Cardinal Conti about the theological admissibility of changes in the heavens. The cardinal replied that not only did the Bible fail to support Aristotle on inalterability of the heavens, but if anything it implied the contrary. Nevertheless he advised Galileo not to commit himself to any explanation of sunspots without careful thought; the circular motions of the earth described by Copernicus could be reconciled with the Bible only by saying it spoke the language of the common people. Conti further informed Galileo that Diego de

Zuñiga, in a commentary on Job,[12] had asserted Copernican astronomy to agree better with the Bible than did the ordinary views. It will be seen that Galileo guided himself by the cardinal's letter when he later argued for freedom of scientific inquiry.

Cesi, replying to Galileo's remarks on epicycles, mentioned Kepler's announcement of elliptical planetary orbits. Thus whether or not Galileo had yet seen the *Astronomia Nova* of 1609, he was already aware of this important development, the cornerstone of modern astronomy. He never discussed elliptical orbits, but not because he thought that planets moved in perfect circles. That was a philosophical, not a scientific requirement, as "Mauri" had noted, and in a note written in Lagalla's book about this time Galileo declared concentric planetary orbits false and impossible.[13] Small deviations, however, did not interest Galileo, as shown by his treatments of equal speed of fall and of the Archimedean postulate that balance--pans hang parallel. Planetary orbits are very nearly circular; their ellipticity could not be detected by inspection of even the largest-scale map of the solar system. Hence despite the importance to theoretical astronomy of Kepler's discovery, Galileo never pursued it.

Two letters written to Galileo in August indicate the mounting dislike of his friends for philosophical science. Sagredo had begun the study of optics under G. C. Glorioso, who was destined soon to gain Galileo's former chair at Padua. "You may see whether I have lost the love of mathematics," wrote Sagredo, "when at may age I have come back as a pupil. And although in the letters I wrote to you I did distinguish philosophers from mathematicians (at which you show yourself to have been a bit scandalized), I want you to know that I used those two names in accordance with the ordinary popular meaning that calls philosophers those who understand nothing about physical things— or rather who, being utterly incapable of understanding these, make profession of being Nature's own secretaries, and having gained that reputation would dull men's senses and deprive them also of the use of reason." Luca Valerio, commenting on *Bodies in Water* as having raised serious doubts against the Peripatetics, added: "But whatever the truth of the matter, I myself am pleased to philosophize freely and not by the rules of a certain philosophical grammar, or grammatical philosophy—if indeed that deserves to be called *philosophy* which is in use for the most part today, [suitable only] when one is bored with chewing one's nails—when I reflect with genuine desire to know the truth, and not to acquire by glibness the appearance of learning."

V

During August Galileo sent to the printer some additions to be made in a second edition of *Bodies in Water*, the original edition having been quickly sold out and the book being still in demand. Three of the additions are of particular interest and will be described below. Also included was some material written in reply to the *Considerations of the Unknown Academician* which had just appeared. (Both Agucchi and Cesi, to whom Galileo had forwarded a copy, ascribed probable authorship of this to Papazzoni.)

The second edition opened by saying that Galileo was now assured by continued observations that the spots were contiguous to the sun, had various durations, and sometimes reappeared with revolution of the sun on its axis with a period of about a lunar month.

The Unknown Academician had challenged use of the word *moment* because it was not a recognized philosophical term; Galileo amplified his earlier definition in these words:

The efficacy [of motion or resistance to motion] depends not only on simple heaviness, but on speed of motion, and on the different slopes of the lines along which motion is made; for a descending weight makes greater impetus in a steep line than in one less steep. And in sum, whatever is the occasion of such efficacy, it always keeps the name of *moment*, nor in my opinion is this sense new in our language, since if I am not mistaken we say often "This is a weighty business, but that other is of small moment," or "Let us consider lighter matters and leave out those of moment"—metaphors that are, I think, taken from mechanics.[14]

Galileo also added a prefatory theorem relating to the ratio of the weights of a floating solid and of the water displaced by it in a finite container, placing this before his previous initial comparison of volumes. But the most interesting addition made was an illustration of the hydrostatic paradox in a form that enabled Galileo to exemplify vividly both his concept of *moment* and the use of virtual velocities in his approach, already described as "different from that of Archimedes":

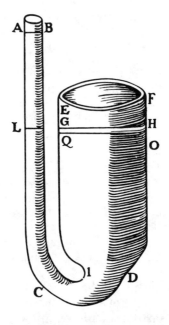

Consider the above figure (which, if I am not mistaken, may serve to reveal the errors of some practical mechanicians who on false premises sometimes attempt impossible tasks) in which, to the large vessel *EIDF*, the narrow pipe *ICAB* is connected, and suppose water in them to the level *LGH*, which water will rest in that position. This astonishes some people, who cannot conceive how it is that the heavy weight of water *GD*, pressing downwards, does not lift and push away the small quantity contained in the pipe *CL* which nevertheless resists and hinders it. But the wonder will cease if we suppose that the water *GD* goes down only to *QD* and ask what the water *CL* has done. It, to make room for the other descending from *GH* to *QO*, would have in the same time to ascend to the level *AB*. And the rise *LB* will be greater in proportion to the descent *GD* as the width of the vessel *GD* is to that of the pipe *IC*, or as the water *GD* is to the water *CL*. But since the moment of the speed of motion in one vessel compensates that of the weight in the other, what is the wonder if the swift rise of the lesser water *CL* shall resist the slow descent of the greater amount *GD*?[15]

A still longer addition dealt with the matter of the resistance to division supposed by Galileo's adversaries (and probably most readers) to inhere in water and other fluids. Galileo pointed out that the parts of a fluid are not themselves divided by a sinking body; they are merely elbowed aside, so to speak. It was his view that fluids are already divided into their indivisible constituent parts, which like all other bodies offer no resistance to purely horizontal motion. At the end of this discussion he noted that a certain small resistance to sinking can be observed, but that it operates only at the commencement of sinking, on the surface of the water, and not during descent after submersion. The effects of surface resistance are seen in small objects which can be gently floated but which proceed to the bottom once wetted.

While writing these additions, Galileo made further notes in his copy of the *Considerations of the Unknown Academician*. One is of scientific interest and was further developed in a letter that will be cited in chapter 11, § II, though it was probably conceived about August 1612.

VI

On 7 September 1612 Galileo formally proposed a method of using observations of the satellites of Jupiter to determine longitudes on earth, especially by ships at sea. This set in train a long series of negotiations over many years which began with transmission of Galileo's proposal by the Tuscan secretary of state to the ambassador at Madrid for attention by the king of Spain. Basically the idea was to regard Jupiter as a clock in the sky whose "hands" were the four satellites. Knowing the time at which any given arrangement would be seen at a fixed place, such as Florence, an observer of that arrangement elsewhere would know the difference in his local time from that at Florence, and since that is what is meant by difference in longitude, the problem could in principle be solved by tables of positions, occultations, and eclipses of Jupiter's satellites. Galileo had already calculated tables of fair accuracy for such a purpose, and he continued to refine and correct them for many years. The practical difficulties of applying this procedure on ships were considerable, and Galileo had suggestions also regarding those, though he was never able to convince the admirals.

The first stimulus to Galileo for this proposal was apparently his recognition of eclipses of the satellites, though he did not give particular stress to this in his proposal. In fact such events, though far more frequent than lunar or solar eclipses, are nevertheless occasional; positions of the satellites, on the other hand, can be observed on any clear night except for a month or so each year. As a result, tables of satellite positions would be of more use at sea though less precise than eclipse tables. Positions could give longitude within about three degrees, whereas an eclipse observation determined it so exactly that later in the seventeenth century the first really accurate map of France was made by that technique.[16]

Now, as Galileo pointed out during his negotiations with Spain, lunar eclipses had historically provided one of the only two reliable means of determining longitudes. Very likely his discovery of satellite eclipses had served, by association of ideas, to suggest their use for determination of longitude, and that in turn led him to think of using the more practical though less accurate method of satellite positions.

At first Galileo had been merely puzzled by some of his observations in which satellite eclipses played a role, but by the end of 1612 he was able to predict them quite closely for months ahead. Because this required consideration of the earth's motion around the sun,[17] it doubtless served to clinch even further his Copernican convictions, though to explain this whole matter to persons not versed in astronomy would have cost him more trouble than it would have been worth.

ELEVEN

1612-13

GALILEO'S SECOND LETTER to Welser on sunspots reached Cesi early in September, and he again expressed his wish to print the letters. Soon afterward, in a debate at the Roman College, a Dominican father (perhaps Maraffi) upheld the Copernican system, adducing among other things the revolutions of sunspots. The Jesuits maintained sunspots to be small stars, following "Apelles." Cesi reported this to Galileo, foreseeing that the Peripatetics would sooner allow a fluid sky than changes in the heavens. Cesi agreed with Valerio that Galileo should include something about this in his letters, to be used as the opening section of the projected volume of Lincean correspondence.

Welser, who had not yet received Galileo's second letter, advised Faber that three further letters of "Apelles"[1] were being printed. In order to provide background for interim correspondence, an outline of their contents will be given here though they were not seen in Italy until somewhat later. The first new letter of "Apelles," dated 6 January 1612 (shortly after printing of his original book), consisted mainly of further incorrect reasons for his belief that Venus should have appeared as a large spot on the sun on 12 December 1611. He now mentioned the phases of Venus, saying that when Galileo was first observing that phenomenon others at Rome were doing the same. That is quite possible, and indeed probable, but since no one else had announced or drawn any conclusions from this before Galileo, it was inappropriate to detract by innuendo from Galileo's discovery and explanation of the facts. Indeed, it is hard to understand

195

why this adversary should now bring up the phases of Venus after ignoring them in his previous letters, unless it was to belittle Galileo; they had nothing whatever to do with sunspots. A fallacious mathematical proof was also offered to show that one particular spot could not have been located on the sun.

The second new letter, dated 14 April, was quite brief. It announced the purported discovery by "Apelles" of a fifth satellite of Jupiter, not in line with the others but south of the ecliptic. He found it difficult to account for its origin but expressed delight that his previous prediction was coming true that sunspots resembled Jupiter's satellites. This supposed satellite declined markedly in brightness for ten days and then vanished. Possibly he had seen a telescopic nova, but ten days should have sufficed for him to determine that it remained fixed and could not be a satellite. Even brief confusion of a fixed star with the satellites on the part of an astronomer is strange; to publish this error months later indicates the author's anxiety to discredit Galileo's celestial discoveries.

In his third letter, dated 25 July, "Apelles" introduced the word *helioscope* to name the instrument he had now devised for sunspot observations, of which the principal feature was the holding of paper at right angles to the telescope as done by Castelli in April. Galileo's diagrams of sunspots sent to Welser were said to agree exactly with his own for April, "Apelles" probably intending readers to suppose that Galileo had borrowed his methods of drawing diagrams from him. He asserted that Tycho's opinion that Venus revolved around the sun had been first confirmed in hir ̣evious book, then by Roman astronomers, and by Galileo— though it is clear from his own letter of January 1612 that he knew the phases of Venus to have been discovered a year earlier. Without replying to Galileo's arguments, he repeated that sunspots were not on the sun and should be considered as a kind of stars similar to Jupiter's satellites.

Meanwhile Cesi had composed a little work he called *Celiscopio*, devoted principally to refutation of the supposed solid orbs in the heavens. It was written in the form of a letter to Porta, and Cesi was thinking of including it together with Porta's reply in his proposed volume of Lincean correspondence. Giovanni Demisiani, who had coined the word *telescope* in 1611, proposed the title *Helioscopia* for that volume, but this suggestion was discarded when the new "Apelles" letters arrived at Rome in October, the name *helioscope* having already been invented by the German. On 13 October Cesi asked Galileo to reply to the new "Apelles" letters by writing again to Welser. This was to be Galileo's third sunspot letter; an engraver was at work on diagrams for the second, and it was planned to reprint both publications of "Apelles" together with Galileo's replies. It was now generally believed in Rome that the antagonist was a Jesuit.

A second attack against *Bodies in Water* now appeared, written by Giorgio Coresio, a Greek professor at Pisa.[2] Castelli began to list its errors, having already received Galileo's notes on the *Considerations of the Unknown Academician*. Galileo had decided that any reply to his adversaries on floating bodies should appear as a defense by a friend; the only exception was an intelligent critique sent in September by Tolomeo Nozzolini to Archbishop Marzimedici and forwarded by him to Galileo. Galileo's reply to this will be mentioned later.

On 5 November 1612 Father Niccolò Lorini, an elderly Dominican at Florence much liked by the ruling family, replied to an inquiry from Galileo concerning an alleged attack launched by him against his views. Probably word had been sent to Galileo at Le Selve, where he was again residing with Salviati, about some conversation at Florence on All Saints' Day that had been critical of the Copernicans. Lorini denied that he had "commenced to speak against anyone in matters of philosophy, either with [Benedetto] Pandolfini or anyone else." According to Lorini, others had begun the conversation into which he entered "only to show I was still alive," saying merely that "that opinion of Ipernicus, or whatever his name is, appears to be against Holy Scripture." The incident was the first in a series of theological oppositions to Galileo that was to be followed up a year later and to become public and serious a year after that. Lorini's initial participation seems to have been more incidental than malevolent. He had evidently seen the name of Copernicus only in writing,[3] knew nothing of astronomy, and simply was against unorthodoxy of any kind.

Cesi had begun to encounter resistance to the *Sunspot Letters* from church censors, but did not believe they would insist on the Aristotelian incorruptibility of the heavens. He had previously discussed that question with Cardinal Bellarmine, as Galileo had independently raised it with Cardinal Conti, and Cesi's opinion was that the only trouble would be with "the Peripatetics and Thomists," not with the church officially. Nevertheless he cautioned Galileo in writing his third sunspot letter to confine himself to reasoned arguments and not to treat his (Jesuit) opponent with sharpness.

Cesi did not receive the third sunspot letter until the end of November. Because a license to print the proposed book had already been obtained on 2 November, further approval from the censors was necessary and entailed delays in the printing. Just as Galileo was completing this letter he had happened to look again at Saturn and found to his surprise that its "companions" had vanished. He mentioned this fact at the end of the final letter to Welser and had already formed some hypothesis to explain the event, as he went on to predict their reappearance at the middle of 1613.[4] This first hypothesis of his seems to have invoked some notion of solar illumination related to the positions of Saturn and the observer in latitude with respect to the ecliptic. Since my previous abridged translation was mistaken, the passage is here given in full:

The two small Saturnian stars, which at present are hidden, will perhaps be revealed a little for two months around the summer solstice of the next year 1613 and then will be hidden, remaining so [until] around the winter solstice of the year 1614, [22 December 1613] around which time it may happen that they will again make some show of themselves for some months, again hiding themselves until the next following winter [1614], at which time I believe more firmly that they will appear again and will not be hidden further—except that at the following summer solstice, of the year 1615, they will seem to try to hide but I believe will not be entirely concealed, but indeed will shortly afterward return to being seen and we shall see them distinctly and larger and brighter than ever; and I daresay that we shall see them for many years without any interruption whatever. But if I do not yet doubt their return, I have reservations about the other particular events, now merely based on probable conjecture; yet whether things fall out just this way or some other, I tell you that this planet also, perhaps no less than horned Venus, agrees admirably with the great Copernican system on which propitious winds now universally are seen to blow to direct us with so bright a guide that little [reason] remains to fear shadows or crosswinds.[5]

This was Galileo's first unequivocal published support of Copernicus. Earlier in the same letter he had set forth his conception of the proper scope of scientific inquiry:

In my opinion we need not entirely give up contemplating things just because they are very remote from us, unless we have indeed determined that it is best to defer every act of reflection in favor of other occupations. For in our speculating we either seek to penetrate the true and internal essence of natural substances or content ourselves with a knowledge of some of their properties. The former I hold to be as impossible an undertaking with regard to the closest elemental substances as with more remote celestial things. The substances composing the earth and the moon seem to me to be equally unknown, as do those of our elemental clouds and of sunspots. I do not see that in comprehending substances near at hand we have any advantage except copious detail; all the things among which men wander remain equally unknown, and we pass by things both near and far with very little or no real acquisition of knowledge. When I ask what the substance of clouds may be and am told that it is a moist vapor, I shall wish to know in turn what vapor is. Peradventure I shall be told that it is water, which when attenuated by heat is resolved into vapor. Equally curious about what water is, I shall then seek to find that out, ultimately learning that it is this fluid body which runs in our rivers and which we constantly handle. But this final information about water is no more intimate than what I knew about clouds in the first place; it is merely closer at hand and dependent upon more of the senses. In the same way I know no more about the true essences of earth or fire than about those of the moon or sun, for that knowledge is withheld from us and is not to be understood until we reach the state of blessedness.

But if what we wish to fix in our minds is the apprehension of some properties of things, then it seems to me that we need not despair of our ability to acquire this respecting distant bodies just as well as those close at hand—and perhaps in some cases even more precisely in the former than in the latter. Who does not understand the periods and movements of the planets better than those of the waters of our various oceans? Was not the spherical shape of the moon discovered long before that of the earth, and much more easily? Is it not still argued whether the earth rests motionless or goes wandering, whereas we know positively the movements of many stars? Hence I should infer that although it may be vain to seek to determine the true substance of the sunspots, still it does not follow that we cannot know some properties of them, such as their location, motion, shape, size, opacity, mutability, generation, and dissolution. These in turn may become the means by which we shall be able to philosophize better about other and more controversial qualities of natural substances. And finally, by elevating us to the ultimate end of our labors, which is the love of the divine Artificer, this will keep us steadfast in the hope that we shall learn every other truth in Him, the source of all light and verity. . . .[6]

Your Excellency remarks that at your first reading of my tract on floating bodies it appeared paradoxical to you, but that in the end the conclusions were seen to be true and clearly demonstrated. You will be pleased to learn that the same has happened here with many persons who have the reputation of good judgment and sound reasoning. There remain in opposition to my work some stern defenders of every minute point of the Peripatetics. So far as I can see, their education consisted in being nourished from infancy on the opinion that philosophizing is and can be nothing but to make a comprehensive survey of the texts of Aristotle so that from divers passages they may quickly collect and throw together a great number of solutions to any proposed problem. They wish never to raise their eyes from those pages—as if this great book of the universe had been written to be read by nobody but Aristotle, and his eyes had been destined to see all for posterity. These fellows who subject themselves to such strict laws put me in mind of certain capricious painters who occasionally constrain themselves, for sport, to represent a human face or something else by throwing together now some agricultural implements, again some fruits, or perhaps the flowers of this or that season. Such bizarre actions, so long as they are proposed in jest, are both pretty and pleasant, and reveal greater resourcefulness in some artists than in others according as they have been able the more cleverly to select and apply this or that material to the form depicted. But if anyone were to pursue all his studies in such a school of painting and should then conclude in general that every other manner of representation was blameworthy and imperfect, it is certain that Cigoli and other illustrious painters would laugh him to scorn.[7]

After point-by-point replies to "Apelles," Galileo identified the origin of all such speculations offered in lieu of truly scientific investigation:

200

I believe that there are not a few Peripatetics on this side
of the Alps who go about philosophizing without any desire to
learn the truth and the causes of things, for they deny these
new discoveries or jest about them, saying that they are illusions. It is about time for us to jest right back at them and
say that these men likewise have become invisible and inaudible.
They go about defending the inalterability of the sky, a view
which perhaps Aristotle himself would abandon in our age.
Their view of sunspots resembles that of Apelles, save that where
he puts a single star for each spot, these fellows make each
spot a congeries of many minute stars which gather together
in greater or smaller numbers to form spots of irregular and
varying shapes. Now though it is true in general that when many
objects unite, each in itself being too small or too distant to
be visible, they may form an aggregate which becomes perceptible to our sight; still one may not conclude as these men do
from such a generalization; one must come down to the particular things observed in stars and in spots. A captain who has
but a small number of soldiers to defend a fortress must not
dash with his whole force to some point under attack, leaving all
other positions open and undefended. When trying to defend
the inalterability of the heavens, one must not forget the perils
to which other positions just as essential to the Peripatetic
philosophy may be exposed. To maintain the integrity and
solidity of that philosophy, its other propositions must be supported by saying that some stars are fixed and others wandering;
those are called "fixed" which are all in one single sphere and
which move with its motion while remaining fixed with respect
to each other, and "wandering" stars are those of which each
has its own special motion. These propositions being true,
the "solar stars" cannot be said to be fixed, for if they did not
change with respect to one another it would be impossible
to see the continual mutations that are observed in the spots,
and the same patterns would always return. . . . Hence anyone
who wished to maintain that the spots were a congeries of
minute stars would have to introduce into the sky innumerable
movements, tumultuous, uneven, and without any regularity.
But this does not harmonize with any plausible philosophy.
And to what purpose would it be done? To keep the heavens free
from even the tiniest alteration of material. Well, if alteration
were annihilation, the Peripatetics would have some reason for
concern; but since it is nothing but mutation, there is no reason
for such bitter hostility to it. It seems to me unreasonable to
call "corruption" in an egg that which produces a chicken.

Besides, if "corruption" and "generation" are discovered in the moon, why deny them to the sky? If the earth's small mutations do not threaten its existence (if, indeed, they are ornaments rather than imperfections in it), why deprive the other planets of them? Why fear so much for the dissolution of the sky as a result of alterations no more inimical than these?[8]

II

In December 1612, having completed his *Sunspot Letters*, Galileo considered having the Linceans print his work on centers of gravity of paraboloids,[9] probably in the form of a letter to Luca Valerio. Ensuing correspondence shows that he sent this to Cesi, who in discussing the matter with Valerio found that he was then revising his own book on a similar subject, published in 1603–4. Galileo accordingly gracefully withdrew his work from publication at this time, for which Valerio expressed his gratitude. In fact Valerio did not reprint his book, and Galileo eventually placed his investigations of centers of gravity in an appendix to his own last book in 1638.

Also in December a third book against *Bodies in Water* was printed at Florence, by Colombe.[10] As with the other two, Galileo wrote extensive notes in reply to this and turned them over to Castelli for editing. He appears also to have solicited comments from others. Sagredo replied that he would have no remarks to offer about attacks against Galileo's book because it would be a waste of time even to read them. He mentioned at this time that though there was no shortage of candidates for Galileo's old chair at Padua, it was still vacant, and word had gone round that because of his illnesses and dissatisfactions in Florence Galileo might return. He said that in his opinion nothing better could happen, but that animosity there against Galileo's sudden departure in 1610 was very great. Sagredo, who had been studying optics under Glorioso's tutelage, sent a copy of Kepler's *Dioptrics*[11] to Galileo.

Galileo's one direct reply to a critic of *Bodies in Water*, as mentioned earlier, was addressed to Tolomeo Nozzolini. Although Favaro opined this to have been written in 1613, I believe it to belong to the end of 1612 when Galileo had returned to Florence from Le Selve for a short time. Two matters in his reply are of particular interest, the first of which explained a misunderstood reference in his book to a kind of "magnetic attraction" between air and dry surfaces.

To begin with, you name as something introduced by me a certain magnetic force with which I would have the air, adhering to an ebony chip, sustain it without letting it submerge in the water. Now, on this it is good that you should know that this term "magnetic force" is not mine, but that of a principal gentleman,[12] disagreeing with my opinion and adhering to my adversaries, who was present on a certain occasion when it pleased their Highnesses to see some experiments on this matter, where there were also some other adversaries of mine. When I was showing how a thin leaf of silver floated between little ridges of water, I attributed the cause of the effect to the air contained within these ridges and touching the leaf, inasmuch as [the entirety of] what lay beneath the water level was a volume no heavier than a like volume of water. The said gentleman, I believe not understanding very well what I meant by saying that this air was the cause, interrupted me to say in the presence of their Highnesses and other persons: "Then you mean to give the air a magnetic force, so that it can by simply touching govern the bodies contiguous to it?" Hence, coming in my treatise to an occasion for mentioning the way in which the air causes rest in chips heavier than water I said, [specifically] addressing my adversaries (of whom, as I said, more than one took part in contradicting the said experiment), "and this, gentle adversaries, is that magnetic force with which the air . . ." etc., alluding to that attribute of magnetic force that had been proffered in the presence of their Highnesses.[13]

This metaphorical expression, Galileo wrote, should therefore not be taken as his own explanation, which had been set forth elsewhere in the same book. If, he said, he had felt any need to explain why the little ridges do not break down, he would not have appealed to "desires" or "self-preservation," or other such attributes in inanimate things, and still less to enmity between moisture and dryness, but would simply have attributed the cause to the ambient air and would have tried to establish this opinion more at length with reasons and experiments.

Galileo's explanation of the situation with regard to floating chips heavier than water was entirely in accord with the Archimedean principle and had been adequately set forth in *Bodies in Water*. He had observed that such floating bodies actually rest somewhat below the surface of the water, and that was what was meant when he said they were supported by ridges of water. He then reasoned that their floating was analogous to that of a boat or an empty kettle; one should consider that the floating object was made up partly of metal and partly of air, its overall density being precisely what was required by the Archimedean principle. Until the much later analysis of surface tension, this was the best available position, though it left unanswered the question why the water did not run over the metal surface, wetting it, with the result of its submerging and sinking. What held the ridges of water back[14] was astutely classified by Galileo with whatever it is that holds up a drop of water on a cabbage leaf. Its nature remained a mystery to him; he could only describe this as some natural emnity between moisture and dryness, for having said which he apologized after the above recital of the circumstances.

The other passage of special interest in Galileo's reply to Nozzolini concerned something closely related to the hydrostatic paradox:

Suppose there is a cylinder *AB*, immovably fixed and sustained at *A*; then suppose the vessel *CDE*, holding the volume *AB* and a little more, which vessel being separated and distant from cylinder *AB* is filled with water, of which it holds, say, 100 pounds. Putting this next under the fixed solid *AB*, slowly raise

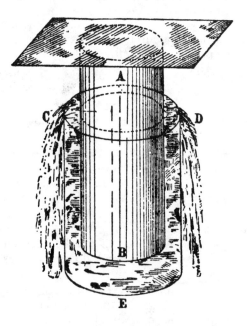

it toward this solid so that this enters it and slowly makes the water overflow as this vessel *CDE* is raised. Now, I say that whoever shall be raising the said vessel against the solid *AB* will always feel the same weight, although little by little the water is flowing out of it, nor will he feel any less weight when no more than two or three pounds of water remain in the vessel, which he will then feel to weigh down just as when it was quite full, though the solid *AB* does not touch the vessel and is, as we said, fixed and immovably sustained at *A*. This can be made evident to anyone by experiment, but beyond the experiment there is not lacking reason. For consider that the power which sustains the solid at *A* when that was outside the water must have felt greater weight than after the solid was immersed in the water, for there is no doubt that if I handle in air a stone tied to a rope, I feel greater weight than if someone placed under me a vessel of water in which the said stone submerged. The work being diminished, therefore, in the power that sustains the solid *AB* when it goes submerging in water in the vessel *CDE* that it meets, and the weight of this being unable to go nowhere,[15] it must be that it is sustained by the water, and consequently in the vessel *CDE* and in him who holds that up; and since we know that a solid submerged in water loses bit by bit as much weight as that of a volume of water equal to the volume of the solid submerged, we shall easily understand that the work of the power sustaining the solid *AB* at *A* is diminished as much as the weight of this solid is diminished by the water; therefore the solid *AB* weighs down on the force sustaining the vessel *CDE* as much as would the weight of a volume of water equal to the volume of the submerged solid.[16]

III

Late in 1612 Galileo had sufficiently perfected his methods of calculating the movements of the satellites of Jupiter to consider inclusion of tables, with instructions in Latin for their use, as an appendix to the *Sunspot Letters*. Instead of this he decided to prepare diagrams of predicted positions of the satellites for each night in February and March 1613, but because printing of the book went more slowly than he had been led to expect, he wrote to Cesi on 25 January to say he would prepare new tables, for March and April. To publish predictions may seem a rather daring project, but it worked out very well indeed. Galileo had reason to be confident, having apparently earlier sent predicted positions for January 1613 to Castelli, who wrote on 2 February:

I have with great pleasure observed the arrangements of the Medicean planets you sent me . . . and in a word everyone will have to confess one of two things—either that the [said] stars are most obedient to you and accommodate themselves to your thoughts and decisions, or else that you know their motions exactly and have marvelously arrived at ultimate precision about their positions, something I did not think would be granted to any one man, being suited to the force of many intellects and great diligence with the benefit of centuries, and not otherwise [to be expected].

Galileo's new diagrams reached Cesi on 15 February; they were engraved on five pages at the end of the book,[17] followed by this postscript:

The arrangements of the Medicean [stars] I send you are for for the two months of March and April and on to the 8th of May. I shall be able to send you others daily, perhaps more precise and surely more convenient for comparison with the observed positions by reason of the [coming] warmer weather and less inconvenient hours [of observation]. Meanwhile it still will be good to mention to you some considerations about these, as "Apelles" and others may wish to make the comparisons.

First it is to be noted that stars very close to the body of Jupiter, because of its brightness, are not easily seen without sharp vision and a good instrument; but upon their becoming more distant, getting away from his [Jupiter's] irradiation and accordingly revealing themselves better, they show that they shortly before were really close to Jupiter. For example, in the three positions [given] for the night of 1 March, the western star very near Jupiter will not be seeen at the first observation, three hours after sunset, being almost contiguous to Jupiter; but because it moves away it will be possible to see this at the fourth hour, and better at the fifth and for the rest of that night. The eastern star close to Jupiter on the night of 9 March will be seen only with difficulty at the hour noted, but since it moves away it will be seen well during later hours. The opposite will happen with the eastern star on the 15th of the same month, because at the hour noted it will be seen, using due diligence, though not much later, as moving toward Jupiter it will be [soon] hidden by his rays. It is true that one of these stars, being somewhat larger than the others (given that the air is clear, which is quite important in this matter), is distinguished even when it almost touches Jupiter, as you will be able to observe of the nearest westerly [satellite] on 22 March, which will be

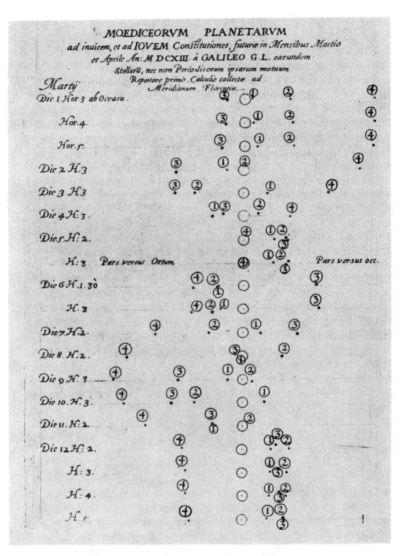

First page of Galileo's predicted satellite positions, from *Sun-spot Letters* (Rome, 1613). Numbers in circles are added to identify each satellite, centered at its correct position as calculated from modern tables. Satellites hidden by the body of Jupiter were omitted by Galileo. (Facsimile page courtesy of The Bancroft Library, University of California at Berkeley.)

nearing [Jupiter] and will be possible to see even when quite close to it.

But a more wonderful cause of the hiding of any of these is that which arises from various eclipses to which they are subject, thanks to the differing directions of the cone of shadow of Jupiter's body—which phenomenon, I confess to you, gave me no little trouble before its cause occurred to me. Such eclipses are sometimes of long and sometimes of short duration, and sometimes are invisible to us. These differences come about from the annual movement of the earth,[18] from differing latitudes of Jupiter, and from the eclipsed planet's being nearer to or farther from Jupiter, as you shall hear in more detail at the proper time. During this year and the next two we shall have no great eclipses [of satellites], but what you will see will be as follows. Of the two easterly stars on the night of 24 April, the one farther from Jupiter will be seen in the manner and at the time described; but the other, closer [to Jupiter], will not appear even though well separated from Jupiter, remaining immersed in its shadow. But around the fifth hour after sunset, leaving that shadow, it will be seen suddenly to appear at a distance from Jupiter of about two [Jovian] diameters.[19] Then, on 27 April, the eastern planet near Jupiter will not be seen until about the fourth hour after sunset, remaining in shadow until then; it will then suddenly emerge and will be seen at a distance of about 1½ diameters from Jupiter. Observed carefully on the evening of 1 May, the eastern star will be seen very close to Jupiter—but not until it has got about half a diameter of Jupiter away from it, remaining at the beginning in its shadow; and a like effect will be seen on 8 May. Other, more notable and greater, eclipses that will occur later will be sent by me with the other positions.

Finally I put to you for consideration by your discrete judgment that you should not wonder (but rather excuse me) if what I propound shall be not exactly comparable with the experiences and observations to be made by you and others, because there are many ways to err. One, almost inescapable, is some mistake in calculation; besides that, the smallness of these planets and their being observed with the telescope, which so greatly enlarges every object seen, means that an error of even one second in the meetings and separations of these stars is made more apparent and noticeable than one thousand times as great an error in the aspects of other [naked eye] stars. Most important of all, the newness of this and shortness of time [for its study to date], and the possibilities of other differences and anomalies in movements of these stars beyond those thus far observed by me, will excuse me among those who understand this art [of astronomical prediction]. That there are as yet no great number of men who, over thousands of years, have completely discovered and explained all the anomalies of the other planets, will indeed make excusable and tolerable the cause of one lone man's having in two or three years not explained with precision the little Jovian system—which, fabricated by the greatest Architect, may be believed not to lack artifices so great as to surpass the human mind.[20]

IV

About the time that Cesi received this remarkable appendix to the *Sunspot Letters*, he sent to Galileo a draft of the proposed preface for that book written at Rome by Angelo de Filiis, secretary of the Lincean Academy. It was contentious in tone, making much of Galileo's priority of discovery, and Galileo did not like it because he foresaw that it would excite more envy and malice toward him. Cesi urged on him the necessity of making known all his work not previously printed, lest absence of mention of anything be taken by his adversaries to mean it had not been done. Cigoli also wrote to dissuade Galileo from removing or censoring the preface, even though he himself considered its style turgid. He agreed that Galileo should not himself reply to innuendoes (particularly hints in the final letter of "Apelles" about Galileo's lack of priority even as to Venus and Saturn, in Cigoli's reading), but said that Galileo ought not to deny Cesi the right to have that done by someone else. The preface was printed, but Galileo's instincts had been sound; it aroused bitter protest from Jesuits. A few copies were bound without it, in order to dispatch them to Welser early in March. Printing was completed on 22 March, and copies reached various cities in Italy early in April.[21]

By an interesting coincidence it was just at this time that Sizzi, who had first brought religion into printed attacks on the *Starry Messenger*, sent from Paris a long letter to Orazio Morandi, a Dominican at Rome very friendly to Galileo. In France, where Sizzi had gone shortly after publishing his *Dianoia*, he had met Jacques Aleaume and other mathematicians interested in science. They had discussed Galileo's *Bodies in Water* and sided with it against the three attacks that had been published. More important, they had observed sunspots during the past months and had noted seasonal changes in the shape and direction of their paths, described sufficiently (if a bit obscurely) in Sizzi's letter.[22] Morandi sent this letter on to Galileo in July with the remark that Sizzi's good mind could not remain in the clouds of his former error: "All those born able to fit their minds to truth come sooner or later under the victorious banner of those who philosophize by contemplating the ample book of nature, and do not attach themselves to the sophistries of those who have tried not only to imprison this unhappy science but even to fetter it in the unworthy chains of Aristotelian opinion and the injurious manacles of capricious philosophasters who swear by the words of unsound masters."

What was contained in Sizzi's letter was destined later to give Galileo one of his strongest arguments for the Copernican system, so he had been right in refusing to attack Sizzi on the first occasion, just as he would have been better off without the contentious Roman preface to his *Sunspot Letters*. But by the time he received Sizzi's letter he was finished with sunspots for the time and failed to see at once its value to the Copernican case.

The first revelation of the identity of "Apelles," or rather an implication that this was Christopher Scheiner, is found in a letter written to G. A. Magini on 17 May 1613 by Giuseppe Biancani, the Jesuit who had previously been involved in the unpleasant matter of the Mantua dissertation against Galileo on the lunar mountains. "As to the work by Galileo," Biancani wrote, "I was glad to know it has been published. If in arrogating to himself that beautiful discovery of sunspots, he is not very cautious, he may be convicted [of falsehood] by Father Christopher Scheiner, because I have some of his [Scheiner's] manuscripts put out before he printed those letters in which may be seen the first origins [of the discovery]." In the same letter he referred to Scheiner "and his Apelles."

On 24 May Giovanni Bardi[23] wrote to Galileo from Rome, warning him that many would react by saying "Up to this time there has been no one who has contradicted a universal opinion held by all philosophers." He said that Father Grienberger thought well of the new book on sunspots, as he did of *Bodies in Water*. The other professors at Rome did not discuss it, while his fellow students jeered at it, having heard it called an extravagance and believing that with half a year of philosophy they should side against Galileo, who had labored over these things so long. But Bardi opined that it would be as with the *Starry Messenger*; those who first jested at its discoveries would come to have no doubt about them.

Early in June a fourth book was published against *Bodies in Water*, this one by Vincenzio di Grazia, who had been one of the principal participants in the original debate in August 1611.[24] Galileo's drafted reply to it was also turned over to Castelli for use in a book that eventually appeared in 1615.

On 9 June Agucchi told Galileo that many at Rome were contradicting his *Sunspot Letters*. He was pleased to see that everything he had noticed during observations in the past year was included in Galileo's book. The final sunspot letter particularly pleased him, presumably because of its contrast between science and philosophical speculation (for example, study of properties as against quest for essences). He went on to say that he had observed Jupiter's satellites frequently and had found Galileo's predicted positions to be in good agreement with those seen. Because Agucchi had shown by his previous letters that he fully understood the calculation of orbits and periods, his confirmation of Galileo's diagrams is especially significant. Galileo's reply is lost, but from Agucchi's next letter (dated 13 July) it appears that Galileo had complimented him on his observational work. Agucchi wrote:

> Meanwhile I thank you especially for what you say, and then for the information you gave me about Saturn—that as you predicted it began again to appear tricorporeal at the last solstice. I have seen it at various times, in oval form when I lacked a suitable instrument, and again with three distinct bodies; but I did not see it while it was solitary and perfectly circular in shape. I have just seen it clearly, in agreement with what you wrote, with its two little globes close by, and I have taken great pleasure that your message is becoming true, for the [sake of your] reputation which will be seen on this account also to increase.
>
> When I saw [in *Sunspot Letters*] the change in form it [Saturn] had had, I considered that this might have happened because it was in the upper part of its epicycle, for on account of its very great height it seemed to me reasonable that being so elevated, they [the companion globes] might by their smallness completely disappear [from sight]. Nor did I turn my thoughts to deducing from this the probability of motion of

the earth according to the system of Copernicus, because I had never got round to considering that diligently, not having put too much faith in its truth. Your authority alone, after I knew that you held a similar opinion, moved me to incline my mind to it, but not in such a way that I did not remain extremely dubious, or rather lean the other way, in the direction indicated by three principal reasons.

Agucchi went on to name these, the first being the authority of the Bible, second the authority of the greatest mathematicians after Copernicus, especially Tycho Brahe, and third the reason that vast useless voids were implied and that star magnitudes remain unaltered. Assuming a large epicycle for Saturn

. . . it may be judged that the hiding of its little globes comes simply from that [orbital] diameter, from which we shall be sure that in the sun's going to opposition, these will be revealed [again] as large and conspicuous as ever, Saturn having to descend from the mean distance of its deferent toward perigee and be easily seen at any time. Now, if none of this takes place, we shall expect to hear from you the true cause of their having been hidden; for I have only a general knowledge of the Copernican theory, so I did not understand why they must show themselves during the next years only at the summer and winter solstices. I write all this questioningly, not because I do not greatly esteem your judgment, being sure that you will not be publishing anything about the truth of this [Copernican] opinion unless you have in mind positive arguments to prove it; for if you do not render it demonstrable by necessary and mathematical proofs, people will be persuaded by only probable reasons that it is something not very well fitted to the human mind.

Evidently Galileo had hinted to Agucchi that deep reflection on the Copernican system and on what followed from the earth's motion around the sun would reveal to him how Galileo had predicted the return of Saturn's missing "ears." Clearly Galileo himself related that to Saturn's position with respect to its source of illumination and the observer.[25] Sagredo had also been advised of their reappearance at this time, mentioning it in a letter dated 13 July, but only to contrast this with Galileo's permanent disappearance from Padua. In this letter Sagredo repeated an earlier question of his about the date that would be ascribed to a given event by persons situated at various places on earth, Sagredo having already perceived the dateline paradox.

On 18 July Kepler received (at Linz) a copy of Galileo's *Sunspot Letters*. He had already expressed the opinion that sunspots were analogous to clouds and considered Galileo's reported discussions to be very accurate, though he had not previously had a chance to study the new book. Kepler's letter, addressed to Maelcote at Rome, was the first to call attention to a book by Johann Fabricius that had been published in June 1611[26] describing sunspots observed late in 1610 and drawing correct conclusions about them. (This made the impending priority dispute between Scheiner and Galileo rather ridiculous historically.) Kepler thought that the rotation of the sun implied by sunspots could be used to support the Copernican astronomy, having in mind a theory of a solar force that drove the planets around, rather than the seasonally changing paths of the spots already detected by Sizzi and others at Paris which were to lead Galileo to a more cogent Copernican argument in his *Dialogue*.

Aproino and Antonini had at this time been experimenting with a device to amplify hearing, inspired by observations made with certain seashells. Aproino wrote for Galileo's assistance in having a model made which would comfortably fit in the ear, with spiral turns opening out hyperbolically eight or ten degrees.[27] It is doubtful that Galileo had such an ear trumpet made, since he seems not to have employed an instrument maker at Florence as he had done at Padua, was in poor health, and remained much of the time at Le Selve where there were no craftsmen who could be instructed to do the work.

Sagredo also communicated the results of some of his experimental work. He had improved the thermoscope and introduced a numerical scale of degrees, which he applied in determining differences in temperature from one room to another. Wine was used in place of water, to enhance visibility, and larger channels reduced the effects of capillarity and meniscus. He was unsatisfied with Galileo's (lost) reply on the dateline paradox and was at work in optics, experimenting with a variety of lenses and considering the differences between glass reflectors and first-surface mirrors.[28]

TWELVE

1613

I

In The Autumn of 1613 Camillo Glorioso obtained Galileo's former chair at Padua and the chair at Pisa was given to Benedetto Castelli. When he took this position, Castelli was warned by d'Elci never to discuss the Copernican opinion that the earth moves. Replying that he would take care not to do so, he added that in more than twenty years of university teaching Galileo had always avoided the topic, and had already given him the same advice. He wrote to tell Galileo of the incident and remarked also that he was surprised to have heard nothing further about "our controversies." This was a reference to a book being prepared by Galileo in reply to his opponents in the matter of floating bodies, to be supplemented and edited by Castelli. The book was not printed until mid-1615, but since Galileo mentioned his work on it to Cesi late in 1613 it seems best to treat it as having been written mainly in that year.

As will be seen, Galileo found an opportunity to introduce into his replies to critics a variety of subjects that seem at first to have little to do with floating bodies. One such topic was the nature of the continuum, on which he had written a treatise (now lost) before he left Padua. This subject came up in the reply to Colombe concerning the question whether water offered any resistance to division as such. Colombe assumed that it did, while Galileo denied this except at the surface, or rather at the interface between water and air. Since even the finest particles of dust will settle to the bottom of still water if allowed sufficient time, its resistance to division must be vanishingly small, though its resistance to increased speed might be very great. In clarifying the distinction, he wrote:

What's this, Colombe? Is it possible that you still don't know that rest is remote from motion, however slow, by an infinite interval, whence the speed of lightning is no farther from rest than is a snail's pace? You believe that by increasing slowness you approach rest, and you are no less deceived than one who should hope to reach infinity by passing from large numbers to others successively larger and larger—not understanding that all the numerals that have been written up to now by all the calculators in the world, laid end to end, would yield a number that is no closer to infinity than is 3, or 7, or any other particular number. If I thought you knew what arithmetical and geometrical progressions are, and what a difference there is between them, I might expect that in order to make your error appear less you would go on to say that increase of slowness due to shape must take place in geometrical and not arithmetical progression, though your words indicate the contrary.[1]

When Galileo discussed the continuum in *Two New Sciences* he introduced the terms *parti quante* for parts having finite size and *parti non quante* for uncountable parts.[2] Among his surviving manuscripts those terms are first found in Galileo's reply to Colombe:

He says that continuous bodies are those of which one part cannot be moved without moving many, or all, parts, according to the hardness or fluidity of the body. . . . Now, from these words it is seen first that Sig. Colombe imagines that one part[3] alone can be taken in the continuum, and also many [parts], something not believed up to now by any mathematician, nor, I believe, even by any philosopher of moderate intelligence. Understanding how the continuum is divisible into ever-divisible parts [Aristotle's own position], they understand consequently that one part alone cannot be taken without taking innumerable parts along with it. But if that is true (as it is most true, and known to everyone having reason), Sig. Colombe's saying that one *part* of the continuum cannot be moved without moving many [parts] is the same as to say that one cannot move innumerable parts of the continuum without moving many, since there is no part whatever of the continuum that does not contain innumerable [parts]. It is to be hoped, then, that he will teach us how to go about taking just one single part in the continuum. Besides, [even] granting to Sig. Colombe that in the continuum one part alone may be taken, and that he means that on its motion, many besides those which it contains are necessarily moved, let us examine the rest of his consequences. He assumes that there are some continua [for instance, fluids] in which, upon the motion of one part, many parts are necessarily moved, and other [continua] in which upon the motion of one part, all parts are necessarily moved [that is, solids]. Now, I shall take one of the first [class of] continua, which shall

---

A   F:E:D:C: B

---

be *AB*, of which only one part (as for example *B*) being moved, many are necessarily moved (as for example *C*, *D*, and *E*), those from *A* to *F* remaining motionless. Since, therefore, at the motion of *B* there are necessarily moved *C*, *D*, and *E*, but no more, it is possible to move part *E* without the others *F-A* being moved. Therefore if parts *D*, *C*, *B* are cut away, then of the remainder *EFA* it will be possible to move part *E* without moving the remainder, *F-A*. But by Sig. Colombe's doctrine, that body of which one single part can be moved without moving any others is discontinuous; therefore body *AFE* is discontinuous and not continuous—which is against the assumption that the whole body *AB* was continuous. Therefore Sig. Colombe must find another property of the continuum by which to distinguish it from the contiguous.

But even given that the former as well as the latter are aggregated of *parti quante* [finite parts] that are determinate— as Sig. Colombe must have imagined, since he believed he could take from the continuum one part alone without taking many— and assuming also that the continuous differs from the contiguous only because the parts of the latter are detached, while those of the former are attached together, whence he deemed that in the aggregate of the contiguous, but not in the continuous, one part alone moved without moving others, still he cannot demonstrate anything against the discontinuity of water, and the experiments that he produces are beside the point, badly conceived and worse applied. For although of a heap of wheat, which is an aggregate of discontinuate parts, one *can* move a single grain without moving others, this will not be done recklessly by throwing in a stone [as in Colombe's example], or by stirring it with a rod. . . . Whoever wants to move a single grain must touch one alone with a little pick, and drive it to one side with great care—and so much the greater delicacy is required as the little component bodies are still smaller; hence I think it is going to take Sig. Colombe a lot of trouble to separate

one at a time his grains of cinnabar and lapis lazuli. So you
see how vain and irrelevant is Sig. Colombe's experience to
prove the continuity of water by throwing a stone into it and
observing that the motion of the first parts touched by the stone
then moves other parts. If he wants to make use of such a
proof, he must first teach us so to determine the parts of water
that we will know how to take only one part without [thereby]
taking many.[4]

In the continuation of the above passage we find the first mention of a phenomenon later described in *Two New Sciences*:

One can join two glass vessels, one above the other, by a
little tube; and if the lower is filled with red wine and that above
with water or white wine, the red will be seen to ascend and
the water or white wine above to descend, each liquid passing
through the other without mixing; and in a word we shall see
that contact alone does not suffice to make a mixture, but some
agitation is needed.[5]

In order to make clear the difference between resistance to
motion and resistance to speed of motion, Galileo wrote:

For your information, Sig. Colombe, you should notice that
resistance to motion simply is one thing, while [resistance]
to being moved with such-and-such speed is another, and
[resistance] to division is still another. Those moveables resist
simple motion that we wish to move against their natural
inclination, as when we would raise a 100-pound stone, which
absolutely will not move with a [force or] moment of 50 or 60
or 90, but a force is needed that surpasses the weight. And this
sort of resistance is quite different from resistance to speed
of motion; it is even so different that this latter [resistance, to]
speed, is found also in motion to which the moveable has a
natural inclination, as downward motion of a stone, in which,
if you want this to go faster than its natural speed, you will
feel its resistance, which is greater according as the moveable
is heavier. . . . In this regard a perfectly round sphere on a
smooth plane makes resistance to him who moves it, and will
resist the more according to the speed he wants to confer on it.
But to overcome this resistance does not require any determinate force; just as speed in itself has latitude and can be increased or decreased *in infinitum*, so there is no force so small
that it cannot impart some degree of speed to movements that
are not preternatural,[6] nor is there any force so great that it
is not resisted by some enormous speed [to be imparted].[7]

Galileo's realization that insistence on causes tends only to mislead the scientist, however precious it may be to philosophers, appeared in his answer to Colombe's complaint against Galileo's analysis of floating lamina. Colombe had objected: "For there is no necessity that gives a cause that the air does not set free the little board, since the water could run over the surface of the little board freely and occupy the place left by the air [contained within the little ridges of water] as being stronger than this air and capable of conquering the resistance it might make."[8]

In Galileo's hand, though published as Castelli's, is the following reply culminating with an example of the correlation of effects that served Galileo in place of alleged causes:

Sig. Colombe, do you mean to say that these things [I affirm] do not happen, or do you mean that they are bad? If you mean they do not exist, the falsity of your statement is manifest to our senses, for the air neither lets the little board free (it follows it), nor does the water run over its surface, nor does it occupy space left by the air, nor do any of those things occur that in your opinion ought to be done. But if you want to say that these things [that happen] are not good, and that on no condition ought they to happen so, I am on your side; I [too] say that the air *ought* to let the little board alone, and that the water *should* not be restrained within ridges or anything else, but indeed it *should* run over the chip, and not shamefully hold back from occupying the space of that air, than which water is stronger, and capable of defeating [air] in battle; and finally the air *should* abandon the field [to it]. All this is a very reasonable account, and things should happen that way, and I think that even Sig. Galileo understands matters so. But he could not do anything about it, so you should not lament for him but should rather quarrel with Nature which permits such injustices.

Then as to why those ridges do not break, and the water does not run over, and as to whether the air stays within and does not give way to a void because of magnetic force or something else, I do not want now to wear myself out further; it is enough, Sig. Colombe, that these actions exist, and are seen, and produce the effect; nor can that be denied. Indeed, I applaud your other accusation against those ridges which ought not (as you shrewdly observe) to hold back and bar the water so as not to cause a void, still less by magnetic force holding air attached to the chip; and I well understand (and am all yours on this) that magnetic force should rather pull together the water of the little ridges and make it unite [over the chip]. All these [other] actions are bad; but please do not make Sig. Galileo their creator, since he never wrote or thought such foolishness. Rather, blame him who did think them up.[9]

II

Elsewhere there is an interesting account, in Castelli's hand only, of Galileo's reasons for his not having replied to Colombe's manuscript treatise against the earth's motion.[10] Galileo had shown this to Castelli on request, because it had been mentioned in Colombe's *Apologetic Discourse*; he told Castelli that since the earlier treatise had not been published, and was no more directed against himself than against many others, Galileo had felt no obligation to reply to it personally. Instead, he showed to Castelli a book that he was writing against Aristotle and Ptolemy, giving all the necessary counterarguments and examples but without mentioning Colombe by name lest he aggrieve his fellow Florentine. From this it appears that Galileo had already commenced on the book that was to become his *Dialogue*, in which the ordinary anti-Copernican arguments indeed followed nearly the order in which Colombe had presented them in 1611.

Castelli went on to say that Copernicus had never said most of the things Colombe charged against him, and that if he had, neither Galileo nor anyone else would accept the Copernican doctrine. If Colombe wished to present a case against Copernicus, he must first understand him; and he might well begin by studying Euclid's *Elements*, starting from Book One, Definition One (the definition of a point); next he should understand Sacrobosco's *Sphere*, and Peurbach's *Theory of the Planets*. Only then should he read Ptolemy's *Almagest* and the *De revolutionibus* of Copernicus, at which time he would doubtless agree with the last named, it being impossible to understand Copernicus and not agree with his system.

Colombe's attack was answered in detail; the reply to Di Grazia was confined mainly to correcting his logical errors and pointing out his misstatements concerning what Galileo had published. A section near the beginning touched on definitions, principles, and methods in science that may be outlined to throw light on Galileo's approach. Di Grazia had rejected Galileo's definitions because they differed from those given by Greek philosophers. Galileo remarked that definitions are always mere impositions of names, and that just as the conic sections were originally defined by borrowing terms from rhetoric (ellipsis, hyperbole, and parable), so any mathematician might shorten ordinary language as he pleased, provided only that he used his defined terms consistently thereafter. Di Grazia declared that all Galileo's demonstrations were founded on false principles (as Descartes was to say later of Galileo's last book); Galileo replied that he had employed only two principles, both of which were omitted from his opponent's listing; these were (1) that equal weights moved with equal speed are of like power in their effects, and (2) that greater heaviness of one body could be offset by greater speed of another.

Di Grazia imputed to Galileo six principles, the first being that pure elements, and mixtures, had the same cause of motion and his proofs were therefore not general; Galileo asked in reply what logic made a proof necessarily less general by its being one instead of two. The second principle imputed to Galileo by Di Grazia is of particular interest because what he denounced as a false principle was precisely what most historians today regard (mistakenly) as Galileo's greatest glory; Di Grazia said that Galileo "wanted to demonstrate physical things with mathematical reasons." Castelli replied: "But in this Sig. Di Grazia is mistaken, since Sig. Galileo never makes use of such a principle in any demonstration of his, nor is it to be called a principle; nor has Sig. Galileo erred at all in demonstrating physical things by reasons other than physical, as was said above."[11] The last words refer to this earlier passage:

If you will consider the *Discourse* [*on Bodies in Water*] of Sig. Galileo, you will always find physical bodies conjoined with motion—up or down, slow or fast. Second, you will not find that he ever separates [physical bodies] from sensible matter, but always considers them to be of wood, or iron, or gold, or water, or air, and so on. Third, dealing with place, he never considers it as simple space, but always as filled with water, or air, or some other fluid body [which is] more or less dense, [and] more or less heavy, and from these he argues slowness or speed of motions. And finally he never considers lines or surfaces except as boundaries of physical bodies; that is, of water, air, ebony, lead, or the like.[12]

The third objectionable principle was that Galileo denied absolute lightness; Castelli admitted that indeed he did, but that he never used this denial as a principle in any demonstration. Fourth was his rejection of resistance to division on the part of water, which Castelli said Galileo had not taken as a principle but had proved in various ways. Fifth was the resistance of water to lifting, which Galileo admittedly had assumed without explicit mention; and sixth was his use of unconventional definitions, as discussed above.

Next Di Grazia asserted that when Galileo wanted to prove anything by universal induction, he was obliged to include all the particular cases. Thus, Di Grazia said, a demonstration involving shapes was incomplete if proved only for cones, cylinders, and pyramids. Galileo replied that, neglecting the fact that his opponent here showed himself ignorant of mathematics, his logic was also poor, "since he does not understand that if induction must go over all the particulars, it is either impossible or it is useless: impossible when the particulars are innumerable; and when they are countable, to consider them all would render induction useless, or better, the conclusion is not by induction. . . . And since for the most part the particulars are infinitely many, as is the case with shapes, the argument by induction is strengthened when the property to be demonstrated is concluded from particular [cases] which appear especially incapable of having [that property]."[13]

III

Because of an affront to Salviati's family at court in 1613 he embarked on a long journey from which he never returned, dying suddenly in Spain in 1614. At Venice Salviati met Cremonini, who "in conversation seemed to me very friendly and partial to you [Galileo] except as to matters of doctrine. I did not want to argue with him, as that seemed unsuitable, I seeing in him the most faithful portrait of a Peripatetic character." Salviati asked Galileo to send his two latest books to a young son of Guidobaldo's who had promised to show him a ruler capable of doing the same things as Galileo's sector.[14]

At the end of 1613 Salviati wrote from Genoa, where he had met G. B. Baliani, "a good geometer who laughs at Aristotle and all the Peripatetics." Baliani told him he had once gone to Venice to see Galileo, probably not having known of his move to Florence. He had made notes of something he objected to in *Bodies in Water*, would be interested to hear Galileo's thoughts on the weight of air, and had made experiments of heat by friction. Salviati suggested that Galileo open correspondence with Baliani, who had many interests similar to his.

As was its custom, the Tuscan court moved to Pisa in December. Castelli, who had just begun lecturing at the University of Pisa, was several times invited to dine with the Medici. Early in December it was rumored that Castelli followed Galileo's opinions, was against Aristotle, and rejected philosophy, which would turn his students and the university against him. When told of this, Castelli replied that perhaps the number of his students had made others envious. He was in the habit of strolling with them along the banks of the Arno in the evenings when his lectures were over, and though he had been told he could not expect many students of mathematics, he already had about thirty-five.

A letter from Castelli dated 14 December 1613 marked the resumption of events that had begun with Lorini at Florence a year before and were to lead in another year to more serious attacks:

Thursday morning I breakfasted with our Patrons, and when asked about the university by the Grand Duke I gave him a complete account of everything, with which he showed himself much pleased. He asked me if I had a telescope; saying yes, I began to tell about an observation of the Medicean planets I had made just the night before. Madame Christina wanted to know their position, whereupon the talk turned to the necessity of their being real objects and not illusions of the telescope. Their Highnesses asked Professor Boscaglia. He replied that indeed they could not be denied; and I took occasion to add what I knew and could say about your remarkable discovery and establishment of the motions of these satellites [that is, the success of Galileo's predictions]. Don Antonio de' Medici was at table with us; he beamed at me and showed himself well pleased by what I said. Finally, after many many things, all of which passed with decorum, breakfast was over. I left, but I had hardly come out of the palace when I was overtaken by the porter of Madame Christina, who had recalled me. But before I tell you what followed, you must first know that while we were at table Dr. Boscaglia had had Madame's ear for a while, and while conceding as real all the things you have discovered in the sky, he said that [in what you claimed] only the motion of the earth had in it something of the incredible, and could not occur, especially because the Holy Scripture was obviously contrary to that view.

Now, getting back to my story, I entered into the chambers of her Highness, and there I found the Grand Duke, Madame Christina and the Archduchess, Don Antonio, Don Paolo Giordano [Orsini], and Dr. Boscaglia. Madame began, after some questions about myself, to argue the Holy Scripture against me. Thereupon, after having made suitable disclaimers, I commenced to play the theologian with such assurance and dignity that it would have done you good to hear me. Don Antonio assisted me, giving me such heart that instead of being dismayed by the majesty of their Highnesses I carried things off like a paladin. I quite won over the Grand Duke and his Arch-duchess, while Don Paolo came to my assistance with a very apt quotation from the Scripture. Only Madame remained against me, but from her manner I judged that she did this only to hear my replies. Professor Boscaglia said never a word.

Everything that took place at this meeting during a good two hours will be recounted to you by Sig. Niccolò Arrighetti. Only this much I feel obliged to tell you—that being still in the chambers, I having begun to praise you, Sig. Antonio also took part in a way you can imagine, and when we left he made me many truly princely offers [of support]; and just yesterday he commanded me to recount all this to you, and what he had said, in these formal words: "Write to Sig. Galileo that I have made your acquaintance, and [tell him] what I said to you in his Highnesses's chambers." I replied that I would give an account of all of this good fortune of mine in becoming the dedicated servitor of his Excellency. Every favor was also done me by Sig. Paolo [Orsini] likewise, so that my affairs (praise be to God, who aids me) go along so happily that I could wish no more. And having no more time, I greet you and pray heaven for all good to you.

Professor Boscaglia, a philosopher and specialist in Plato, stood in high favor with the ruling family. From his role in this incident, and from Castelli's story of the rumor at the university in his previous letter, it is evident that official scholarship at Pisa was lining up against Galileo just as Colombe's "league" at Florence was determined to oppose him at every step. Galileo was aware of the latter group, remarking that it was as if some society had sworn an oath to oppose whatever Galileo wrote.

Galileo now composed a long letter to Castelli from which other details of the recent events at Pisa can be gathered. Its main purpose was to set forth clearly Galileo's view of the im-propriety of mixing religion and science. Since this letter was destined to play a large role in events a year later, it will here be set forth in full. Dated 21 December 1613 and addressed to Castelli, it read:[15]

Yesterday I went to meet Sig. Niccolò Arrighetti, who gave me an account of you from which I took great delight in hearing something I never doubted; that is, the great satisfaction you give to the whole University, to its superintendents as well as the professors and the students of all nations—which approval has not increased the number of the envious against you, as usually happens among people of that kind. Instead it has reduced them to but a few; and those few must fall silent if they do not want such rivalry, which ordinarily deserves also to be called strength, to generate and finally merge into blameworthy and injurious attitudes more toward them than anyone else. But the seal of my pleasure was to hear of the discussion that you had occasion, thanks to the benignity of their serene Highnesses, to carry on at their table and then continue in the chambers of Madame Christina in the presence of the Grand Duke and Duchess and the illustrious gentlemen Don Antonio and Don Paolo Giordano and some of those excellent philosophers. And what greater favor could you desire than to see their Highnesses taking pleasure in reasoning with you, raising questions, hearing their solutions, and finally resting satisfied with your replies?

What you said, as recounted to me by Sig. Arrighetti, has given me occasion to consider again some general things concerning the carrying of Holy Scripture into disputes about physical conclusions, and some other particular [things] about the passage in Joshua proposed to you by the Grand Duchess Mother and the most serene Archduchess as contradicting the mobility of the earth and stability of the sun.

As to the first general question of Madame Christina, it seems to me that it was most prudently propounded to you by her, and conceded and established by you, that Holy Scripture could never lie or err, but that its decrees are of absolute and inviolable truth. I should only have added that although Scripture can indeed not err, nevertheless some of its interpreters and expositors may sometimes err in various ways, one of which may be very serious and quite frequent, [that is,] when they would base themselves always on the literal meaning of words. For in that way there would appear to be [in the Bible] not only various contradictions, but even grave heresies and blasphemies, since [literally] it would be necessary to give to

God feet and hands and eyes, and no less corporeal and human feelings, like wrath, regret, and hatred, or sometimes even forgetfulness of things gone by and ignorance of the future. Hence, just as in the Scriptures are found many propositions which, as to the bare senses of the words, have an appearance different from truth, but were so put to accommodate the incapacity of the common people, so, for those few who deserve to be separated from the herd, it is necessary that wise expositors should produce the true senses and give particular reasons why they were offered in those words.

Scripture being therefore in many places not only accessible to, but necessarily requiring, expositions differing from the apparent meaning of the words, it seems to me that in physical disputes it should be reserved to the last place, [such questions] proceeding equally from the divine word of the Holy Scripture and from Nature, the former as dictated by the Holy Ghost and the latter as the observant executrix of God's orders. It was moreover necessary in Scripture, in order that it be accommodated to the general understanding, to say things quite diverse, in appearance and by the [literal] meaning of the words, from absolute truth; yet on the other hand, Nature being inexorable and immutable and caring nothing whether her hidden reasons and modes of operating are or are not revealed to the capacities of men, she never transgresses the bounds of the laws imposed on her. Hence it appears that physical effects placed before our eyes by sensible experience, or concluded by necessary demonstrations, should not in any circumstances be called in doubt by passages in Scripture that verbally have a different semblance, since not everything in Scripture is linked to such severe obligations as is every physical effect. Rather, if in this respect alone (in order to be accommodated to the capacity of rough and undisciplined people), Scripture has not abstained from adumbrating its principal doctrines by attributing to God himself attributes very far from and contrary to his essence, who is then going to sustain rigidly, ignoring the above consideration, that in speaking incidentally of the earth or the sun or some other created thing, Scripture must be contained rigorously within the limits and restraints of the meanings of words? Especially when it pronounces on such matters things that are far from the primary purpose of Holy Writ, and even such that when said and received as the bare and revealed truth, they would rather injure that primary purpose by rendering the common people contumacious to persuasion by [its] propositions concerning salvation.

That being the case, and it being moreover manifest that two truths can never contradict each other, it is the office of wise expositors to work to find the true senses of passages in the Bible that accord with those physical conclusions of which we have first become sure and certain by manifest sense or necessary demonstrations. Indeed, as I have said, granted that Scripture, though dictated by the Holy Ghost, admits for the above reasons expositions that are in many places far from the literal sound [of its words], and moreover as we are unable to assert with certainty that all interpreters speak with divine inspiration, I should think it would be prudent if no one were permitted to oblige Scripture and compel it in a certain way to sustain as true some physical conclusions of which sense and demonstrative and necessary reasons may show the contrary. And who wants to set bounds to the human mind? Who wants to assert that everything is known that can be known to the world? Hence, apart from articles concerning salvation and the establishment of the Faith, against the solidity of which there is no danger that anyone may ever raise a more valid and efficacious doctrine, it would be the best counsel never to add more [articles of faith] without necessity. And if that is so, how much greater disorder [it would be] to add things at the request of persons who, beside the fact that we do not know whether they speak inspired by divine power, are clearly seen to be completely devoid of the information that would be required—I will not say to disprove, but—to understand the demonstrations with which the most acute sciences proceed in confirming some of their conclusions?

I would believe that the authority of Holy Writ had only the aim of persuading men of those articles and propositions which, being necessary for our salvation and overriding all human reason, could not be made credible by any other science, or by other means than the mouth of the Holy Ghost itself. But I do not think it is necessary to believe that the same God who has given us our senses, reason, and intelligence wished us to abandon their use, giving us by some other means the information that we could gain through them—and especially in matters of which only a minimal part, and in partial conclusions, is to be read in Scripture, for such is astronomy, of which there is [in the Bible] so small a part that not even the planets are named. If the original sacred authors had intended to persuade people of the arrangements and movements of the heavenly bodies, they would not have dealt with this so sparingly that it is as nothing in comparison with the infinitely many lofty and admirable conclusions contained within that science.

So you see how disorderedly, if I am not mistaken, they would proceed in physical disputes not directly pertaining to faith, by taking at face value passages in Scripture often poorly understood by them. And if they really believe that they have the true sense of some particular scriptural passage, and are consequently certain they have in hand the absolute truth of the question they mean to argue, let them next tell me freely whether they appreciate the great advantage people have who sustain the truth in a physical dispute—I mean the advantage over others whose task it is to sustain the false? I know they will answer yes, that he who sustains the true position will be able to use a thousand experiences and a thousand necessary demonstrations on his side, while the other side will have nothing but sophisms, paralogisms, and fallacies. But if, confining ourselves to physics, they produce no other weapons but those of philosophy, and can know themselves so superior over the adversary, why, in doing battle, should they immediately take up an inexorable and tremendous weapon, such that the mere sight of it vanquishes even the expert and agile warrior? To tell the truth, I believe that those are the first to yield, feeling themselves unable to stand firm against the enemy assaults, and seek rather for means not to let themselves be accosted. But since, as I have already said, he who has truth on his side has a great, indeed the greatest, advantage over the adversary, and since it is impossible that two truths be contrary, we need not fear assaults made by anyone who pleases—provided that we also are given the right to speak and to be heard by understanding persons not excessively moved by their own passions and interests.

In confirmation of this I come now to consider that particular passage in Joshua concerning which you made three declarations to their Highnesses. I shall take up the third, which you adduced as mine (as it truly is), but I shall add another consideration which I do not believe I have told you before.

Therefore let it be assumed and conceded to the adversary for the present that the words of the sacred text must be taken in exactly the literal sense, that is, that God, at Joshua's prayer, made the sun stand still and prolonged the day so that he won the victory. But I insist on my part also that the same restriction must hold, so that the adversary shall not presume to bind me and leave himself free in his power to alter or change the meaning of the [scriptural] words. I [now] say that this passage

shows manifestly the falsity and impossibility of the Aristotelian
and Ptolemaic world systems and on the other hand accords
very well with the Copernican.

And first I ask the adversary if he knows by what motions
the sun is moved? If he does know, he must reply that it is
moved with two motions, that is, an annual motion from west
to east and an opposite diurnal motion from east to west.

Hence, in the second place, I ask if these two [Ptolemaic]
movements, so diverse and almost contrary to one another, both
belong to the sun and are equally its own? They are forced to
answer no; that one alone is its own and particular motion,
which is the annual, while other is not the sun's [motion] at all,
but that of the highest sky, called the Prime Mobile, which
sweeps along with itself the sun and the other planets and
also the starry sphere, constraining them [all] to make one
revolution around the earth in 24 hours, with a motion (as I
said) almost contrary to their natural and proper motions
[eastward].

So I come to the third question, and ask them by which of
these two motions the sun produces day and night, that is,
by its own [motion] or from the Prime Mobile? It is necessary
to respond that day and night are the effects of motion of the
Prime Mobile, while from the proper motion of the sun not
day and night, but the different seasons, and the year itself,
are produced.

Now, if day depends not on the sun's [own] motion, but on
that of the Prime Mobile, who can fail to see that in order to
prolong the day it is necessary to stop the Prime Mobile, and
not [just] the sun? Or rather, who will it be that understands
the first rudiments of [Ptolemaic] astronomy and does not
know that if God had stopped the [proper] motion of the sun,
then instead of lengthening the day he would have shortened it
and made it briefer? For the sun's [own] motion being contrary
to the diurnal rotation, the more the sun moves eastward, the
more its westward course will be retarded; and by diminishing
or annulling the sun's [proper] motion, in that much less time
it will reach the west. This effect is sensibly seen in the moon,
which makes its daily revolutions as much more slowly than
those of the sun as its own movement is faster than that of the
sun. It being therefore absolutely impossible, in the arrangement
of Ptolemy and of Aristotle, to stop the [proper] motion of
the sun and [thereby] lengthen the day, as the Scripture
affirms to have happened, either it is necessary that the [sun's]
movements are not arranged as Ptolemy wants, or else one

must alter the sense of the words and say that when the Scripture says that God stopped the sun, it means that he stopped the Prime Mobile, although to accommodate this to the capacity of those who have difficulty in understanding the rising and setting of the sun, it said the contrary of what it would have said if speaking [only] to judicious men.

Add to this that it is not credible that God stopped only the sun, letting the other spheres run on, because that would needlessly have altered and permuted all the orderings, aspects, and dispositions of the other stars with respect to the sun, and would greatly have perturbed the course of nature. But it is credible that He stopped the whole system of the celestial spheres, which, after that interposed time of rest, returned concordantly to their works without confusion or alteration of any kind.

But since we agreed *not* to alter the sense of the words of the text, it is necessary to have recourse to that other arrangement of the parts of the world, seeing whether that, in conformity with the bare sense of the [scriptural] words, runs along smoothly and without obstacle, as indeed will be seen to be the case. Therefore, I having revealed and necessarily demonstrated that the globe of the sun is turned on its [own] axis, making an entire revolution in about one lunar month in the same direction in which all the other celestial rotations take place; and it being moreover very probable and reasonable that the sun, instrument and chief minister of nature, as if the heart of the world, not only gives light (as it clearly does) but also motion to all the planets that revolve about it; then, if in conformity with the position of Copernicus we shall attribute the diurnal conversion principally to the earth, who does not see that in order to stop the whole system without altering in any way the rest of the changeable relations of the planets, but only prolonging the space and time of diurnal illumination, it sufficed that the sun be stopped [rotating], exactly as the words of the sacred text say? Behold, therefore, the second way, in which, without introducing any confusion among the parts of the world, and without alteration of the words of Scripture, it was possible by stopping the sun to lengthen the day on earth.[16]

I have written rather more than suits my illness, so I conclude, offering myself your servitor, and I salute you, praying for you from God a Merry Christmas and every joy.

It is of interest that the problem of Joshua had been first

brought up by the grand duke's mother and his wife; this gives us the probable reason for which Castelli had been called back as he was leaving the palace. Presumably the earlier conversation had been general before it turned to a particularly troublesome text for those who would move the earth. Castelli was called back to explain this, without having had a chance to prepare especially for it as he might otherwise have done. What three positions he advanced during the two-hour debate in Madame Christina's chambers is not known, except that the third was one he knew to be Galileo's, without knowing the *ad hominem* argument presented above to show that the Ptolemaic system could not be reconciled with the literal words of the Bible concerning Joshua's command. A clue is found in Galileo's later expansion of this letter, in which much was made of the advice of St. Augustine that Christians should avoid taking sides in astronomical questions; this was probably taken from Castelli's *ex tempore* arguments when he would naturally speak as a theologian. It was St. Augustine's view that since Christians should not give time to science that might be better spent in devotional exercises, they should not take sides in matters on which infidels might be better informed and thus able to discredit Christians. Castelli probably argued that in matters where Catholics had the good fortune to have the services of the best of astronomers, they should take advantage of this to get ahead of Protestants and infidels.

Early in 1614, further repercussions of this event were brought about by Christina's concern with advice from her confessor. Castelli naturally used Galileo's letter to counter this, so it is not surprising that the Joshua miracle, first brought up by her, was to become central in the public attack on Galileo at the end of 1614 with quite serious consequences, as will be seen in due course.

THIRTEEN

1614-15

I

IN JANUARY 1614 Salviati wrote again from Genoa to say that Baliani was much interested in what Galileo had written to him about the weight of air, from which it appears that experimental determinations of this had been made by Galileo no later than 1613. Galileo had also sent Baliani his *Sunspot Letters* and asked him for comments on *Bodies in Water*. Baliani replied at length, praising the work on sunspots but questioning Galileo's conclusion that the sun rotated and indicating his own preference for the Tychonic system over the Copernican. His main objection to the other book (mentioned to Salviati earlier) had since been withdrawn. Baliani had first considered ice to be condensed water, like Galileo's original opponents, but when Salviati had told him that ice occupied a greater volume than the water composing it, Baliani tried the experiment and was convinced. He also recounted experiments of his own in which he had found the heat generated by friction between iron wheels to be great enough for cooking. Baliani asked Galileo for experimental details of his weighing of air, to which Galileo responded on 12 March:

To weigh the air I take a glass flask *AB*, about the size of a man's head, which has in the neck the constriction *B* so that it may be tightly bound to the leather finger *CD*, in the middle of which is firmly fixed a football valve through which with a syringe I drive air into the flask *AB*, having first weighed it on a delicate balance. After having compressed much air by force, which remains imprisoned thanks to the valve, I weigh the

flask again and find it noticeably heavier, whence I note separately the weight that had to be added [for balance], which is
the weight of the alien air. And to assure myself that none is
leaking out, I first put water in the flask, holding this upside
down to make sure the air cannot escape, since it would drive

the water ahead of it and I should see drops of it. Then I take
another similar flask, *EFG*, with its neck constricted at *F* and
with a little hole at *G*, the mouth made very narrow as is seen at
E, where there is a very small hole. This I tie at the lower part
of the finger, that is toward *D*, so that the point *E* comes to
the hole of the valve; and after I have firmly tied it, I push
the point *E* against the little cover that seals the valve. This
opened, the air compressed in the vessel *AB* makes impetus and

drives out the water in the other flask through the hole *G*, or as much of it as the volume of air that leaves from the vessel *AB*, which is all that was compressed there beyond its natural contents. Therefore saving the water that comes through the hole *G*, I weigh this carefully and find what multiple it is of the weight of the air that was weighed in the flask before, which [water] as I recall it, weighed about 460 times as much, but I am not sure of this.[1] The operation could be repeated many times to arrive at certainty.

Galileo went on to answer Baliani's objection to the sun's rotation—that the medium must offer some resistance, though small, so that such a rotation could not continue uniformly. Galileo pointed out that in the *Sunspot Letters* he had postulated a like rotation of the medium, and hence had not there considered the question of a resisting stationary medium, which he agreed would slow the motion. He then asserted unequivocally his Copernican conviction, saying that Tycho's system left him with the same problems as Ptolemy's. Among the reasons for his support of Copernicus he listed the phases of Venus, Jupiter's satellites, and sunspots, and said he had further particulars of his own that seemed conclusive. The least of his worries, he said, were Tycho's objections to Copernicus, by which he meant those taken from the apparent straight fall of heavy bodies and the equality of cannon shots to east or west, supposed by Tycho to disprove the diurnal rotation of the earth.

Galileo's mention of other particular reasons of his own doubtless alluded to his tidal theory, but not to that alone. Among his important recent achievements had been the discovery and explanation of eclipses of Jupiter's satellites, in his predictions of which the annual motion of the earth played an important role. The same was true of his theory of Saturn's changing appearances. Satellite eclipses in turn had enabled him to determine rules for motions of the satellites in latitude as well as longitude.[2] Castelli told Antonio de' Medici of this new development, as he informed Galileo when acknowledging receipt of Galileo's final comments on Colombe's attack against his *Bodies in Water*.

II

By March the identity of "Apelles" became known to Cesi through a book on optics by another Jesuit, Franciscus Aguilonius, who claimed the discovery of sunspots for Christopher Scheiner and did not mention Galileo. Cesi told Galileo that this had surprised him in view of the contrary information in possession of the Jesuits at Rome (that is, Galileo had shown them sunspots months before Scheiner's book appeared, and no later than the earliest date mentioned in it). Cremonini's book *On the Heavens* had at last appeared; Cesi thought little of it "because I believe one should distinguish thoroughly the Peripatetic sky from the real one, or their reasoned one from the one we see."

Galileo was ill again in March 1614. Castelli had begged him weeks before to desist from writing more answers to critics and had undertaken to confirm the calculated positions of Jupiter's satellites for him so that Galileo would not have to expose himself to the night air. He now asked Galileo to forget about the stars and look to his health.

In April the brother of Cardinal Conti wrote from Parma concerning some studies of the biblical meaning of *firmament*. He asked Galileo to send his arrangement of the planets in order that Conti might write up his conclusions on the Copernican supposition. On 16 April Castelli recalled to Galileo the earlier argument at Pisa with Professor Boscaglia. Everything had gone well, he said, though the discomfiture of Boscaglia's party had induced Alessandro de' Medici to have Cosimo put a stop to the ensuing discussions. The bearer of this letter, Mario Guiducci, began a little later to study with Galileo.

Cesi asked Galileo to predict the positions of the satellites for October-November 1614, to replace the March-April 1613 diagrams in unsold copies of the *Sunspot Letters* to be sent to the autumn book fair. Galileo prepared to do this by sending interim predictions to friends for independent checking against observations.

About this time Sagredo, much concerned about Galileo's health, urged him to put aside study and ambition and pursue the kind of life Sagredo had described as his own in a letter to Welser, a copy of which he sent to Galileo. The letter is of interest not only with regard to Sagredo's character but also as it concerns worsening relations with the Jesuit group around Welser. At this time he had wanted to publish a series of letters between Sagredo and "a German Jesuit" concerning the dateline paradox. Sagredo replied that he was an amateur of science, a Venetian patrician who had no wish to embroil himself in public disputes but wished only to live quietly and pursue his inquiries in peace and among friends. The German Jesuit whom Welser had in mind was Franciscus Aguilonius, but for some reason Sagredo referred in his letter to the prospective adversary as "Apelles" and spoke strongly against his bad manners, foolish calculations and arguments, and plain errors. Welser doubtless took Sagredo's refusal as an Italian affront against Scheiner.

The replies by Galileo and Castelli to opponents of *Bodies in Water* had now been finished. Without name of author, but with a dedication by Castelli, this book was sent to a printer at the end of April. On 14 May it was returned by a messenger who told Galileo that the publisher would come to discuss it with him. Galileo's adversaries had apparently threatened to act against the printer if he published it, or made some move to suppress the book. The opening pages of the manuscript copy in Galileo's papers differ substantially from those of the eventually printed text.

III

On 31 May Francesco Stelluti informed Galileo of the publication at Nuremberg of Simon Mayr's *World of Jupiter*, the title page of which asserted his discovery of Jupiter's satellites in the year 1609.[3] Mayr's effrontery has gained him unwarranted celebrity in histories of astronomy. In 1611, a year after publication of the *Starry Messenger*, Mayr asserted that he had seen the satellites of Jupiter in December 1609. In his 1614 book he dated his first claimed observations back to the month of November, though the first date for which he described any position was 29 December 1609, equivalent to 8 January 1610 in the Gregorian calendar. The one position Mayr did describe conformed to Galileo's published diagram for that night, and Mayr neither published any other positions for early months in 1610 nor confirmed or challenged any of Galileo's diagrams on the basis of his own supposed observations during that time. Indeed, months passed after Galileo's first publication in March 1610 before anyone else was able to see the satellites, despite vigorous efforts, except by using Galileo's telescopes. Twice in 1612 Galileo had published data on the periods of the satellites, and early in 1613 he had forecast their positions in printed diagrams confirmed by others by observation. Eclipses of the satellites, also described and predicted by Galileo in print, still baffled Mayr in 1614.

At Galileo's suggestion Cesi sent to Stelluti Castelli's verifications of his continuing forecasts of satellite positions. Galileo forwarded to Stelluti a copy of his *Defense against Capra*, in which Mayr had been mentioned.[4] To Fabio Colonna at Naples, he sent new satellite forecasts for June 1614.

On 20 June Galileo received from Giovanni Bardi at Rome an account of his experiments supporting Galileo's *Bodies in Water* performed and described at the Collegio Romano at the request of Father Grienberger, successor to Christopher Clavius. Grienberger told Bardi that had not Aristotle been involved, the Jesuits would have agreed with everything, but that by order of the General of the Jesuits they could not oppose Aristotle in anything, "and he told me that it was no wonder that I was against Aristotle, since he was also clearly wrong about what you once told me about those two weights falling faster or slower." Thus Galileo's views on falling bodies[5] were already known to the Roman Jesuits, though he had as yet published nothing on this subject. Cesi and Stelluti had been present at the Bardi lecture, as were Valerio, Faber, and many prelates and literary men. Galileo wrote at once to commend Bardi and urge him to publish his discourse, as did others at Rome, especially because Galileo's book had been in Italian and did not reach many foreigners.

Galileo saw Mayr's *World of Jupiter* in July and wrote to Cesi that the fraudulent character of his priority claim was easily exposed. Cesi suggested that Galileo vindicate his own name in the form of a letter addressed to Kepler, which could then be published by the Linceans.[6] Welser's death after a long and painful affliction with gout occurred at this time, depriving the Academy of its principal foreign correspondent.

During the summer of 1614 Galileo continued to send predicted positions of Jupiter's satellites to others for independent verification. This was the result partly of Mayr's claims, and partly of Galileo's wish to be sure that his October-November forecasts, to be published by Cesi in place of the now obsolete 1613 predictions, should be entirely accurate. On 19 June Colonna wrote:

> You having favored me with the positions made by you of your Medicean planets, which reached me on the 18th, I found that you had exactly calculated and drawn the said positions in agreement with what I had observed on the 15th, 16th, and 17th, and yesterday evening I observed for the 18th; in my judgment, at the first hour after sunset, this differed only in that the two nearest Jupiter were not more than one diameter from Jupiter and from each other, while the two that were

conjoined—that is, the large one and the small one—were distant in my opinion five diameters from the edge of Jupiter, as they were drawn, though the second, closer to Jupiter, was drawn a little more distant, perhaps by a slip of the pen.

On 29 July he wrote again:

I wrote you that in observations of your Medicean [stars], very little on the first page sent to us differed, in one or two places, something that would perhaps not be noticed by everyone; and particularly on 10 July, for I had observed that carefully before your second page of positions reached me.

On 8 August Colonna wrote once more, having meanwhile received from Galileo another page of predictions and a correction previously sent for 10 July. It seems highly improbable that Galileo had received Colonna's letter of 29 July in time to include this correction; more likely he had himself made an observation on the 10th and noticed a discrepancy between it and his forecast. At any rate Colonna assumed that, and he was delighted to see that the correction conformed to what he had in fact observed that night; he congratulated Galileo on the detection and correction of a previous calculating error: "I am truly astonished that you have so exactly discovered the periods of such tiny planets."

Writing to Paolo Gualdo, Galileo said that his replies to adversaries on floating bodies were being printed, though in fact a license to print was not finally issued to the printer until 25 October and the book was not issued until May 1615. Evidently powerful pressures were applied to hold it back, but the story is not revealed by existing correspondence.

In mid-November Jean Tarde, a French canon, visited Galileo en route to Rome, discussing with him the sunspots and the manner of making powerful telescopes. On the latter subject Galileo was reticent. Though he had supplied scores of lenses to friends, the production of good astronomical telescopes abroad had lagged. Maestlin had still been unable in Germany to get one that showed Jupiter's satellites or even the phases of Venus. Kepler had had none at first, though his friend Simon Mayr had claimed one by November 1609. Antonini could find none in Holland, where even the supposed inventor, consulted by him, denied the possibility of a telescope so powerful. Galileo, then the target of foreign calumny and rival claims of priority, was disinclined to assist the stranger. He told Tarde that Kepler's *Dioptrics* might help him, though Galileo found it so hard to understand that he questioned the author's own comprehension; and it seems to be true that Kepler made no successful telescopes himself.

Tarde wrote from Rome on 6 December to say he would be in Florence again at the end of the month, and wanted a copy of the *Sunspot Letters* for Robert Balfour in France. He recorded in his diary his conversations with Galileo, but a few years later struck out the entries on sunspots and published two books, one in Latin and one in French, naming sunspots "the Bourbon Stars" and asserting (like Scheiner before him) that they were newly discovered stars that circled the sun.[7] Galileo's mistrust of his French visitor thus turned out to have been indeed well founded.

On 12 December 1614 Luigi Maraffi, who had recently been in Florence, wrote to Galileo from Rome.[8] He reported that Flaminio Figliucci was there to publish some poems by a Sienese poet, Lorenzo Salvi, concerning the new discoveries in the heavens. In fact "Salvi" was a pseudonym for the Jesuit Vincenzo Figliucci. Galileo promptly asked Cesi to get a copy for him. Cesi sent one on 7 March 1615, with the remark that the book scarcely mentioned Galileo and credited everything to others except the satellites of Jupiter. Along with it Cesi sent another book, to be mentioned later, that was of the greatest importance to Galileo's career.

Letters that were interchanged between Benedetto Castelli, Michelangelo Buonarrotti at Pisa (nephew of the famed Michelangelo), and Galileo at Florence on 19–20 December suggest that Castelli was in trouble over his activities at the University of Pisa. On 21 December, the fourth Sunday of Advent, a bombshell exploded at Florence; Tommaso Caccini, a young Dominican firebrand, denounced from the pulpit at Santa Maria Novella the Galileists, and all mathematicians along with them, as practitioners of diabolical arts and enemies of true religion. The biblical text assigned that day for exposition was the tenth chapter of the Book of Joshua, containing precisely the story that Castelli had been asked by Christina to reconcile with motion of the earth a year before, and which Galileo had singled out for special mention in the long "Letter to Castelli" a year earlier. Long afterward it was said that Caccini had taken as his text the passage from the Book of Acts, "Ye men of Galilee, why stand you gazing up into heaven?" *Se non è vero, è ben trovato.* Caccini's sermon marked the formal opening of the public onslought against Galileo and his followers at Florence, after two years of private intrigues.

Castelli wrote from Pisa on 31 December:

As to those thieves and waylayers of mathematicians I don't know what to tell you. From what I have heard, Father Lorini (who was here) felt badly that the good Father [Caccini] had let himself go so far. But be it as you wish; I beg you to make it known to their Highnesses at the first chance that the number of such thieves increases [against] me in such a way that I shall be unable to get away at all during Carnival, but will have to stay here, especially because I will have in addition to the usual students many cavaliers of St. Stephen and I hope to revive this study of mathematics, already nearly dead. And perhaps these adversary gentlemen that I have here at hand will remain reverent, even if incapable of understanding our reasonings. Meanwhile I am most displeased that the ignorance of some people has peaked so that, condemning sciences of which they are totally ignorant, they attribute [false] things to sciences they are incapable of understanding. Every ordinary student knows that no science is farther than mathematics from self-interest and cryptic language. But patience; for these impertinences are neither the first nor the last.

Maraffi wrote from Rome on 10 January 1615 expressing his regret at the incident, particularly because the offending priest was one of his own Dominican order. All wise men he had talked to at Rome felt as he did about it. Even though he knew Caccini's character and the conditions that had induced his action, Maraffi had found the attack hard to believe, particularly as he had had reason to think this would not happen—showing that while recently at Florence, Maraffi had become aware of what was going on there behind the scenes. He could only hope that it would not be taken as more than the anger of some other people and Caccini's own madness and ignorance.

Cesi wrote on 12 January from Acquasparta in reply to a lost letter from Galileo of 29 December: "These enemies of knowledge who take it on themselves to interfere with heroic and useful discoveries and labors are of those perfidious madmen who never keep quiet, nor is there any better way to fight them than to esteem them as nothing and attend to your health and the completion of your works, giving these to the world despite them; for if then they know [better] or pretend [to], let them come forward to show the learned their arguments—which they will not venture, or will do by mere vituperation. Meanwhile you shall hear more completely my views on checking their excesses and iniquities, and showing suitable and just resentment. I am sorry not to be at Rome . . . where I might deal with this matter you write to me with [diplomatic] dexterity. . . ." In some notes associated with this letter, Cesi mentioned that Cardinal Bellarmine had once told him he considered Copernicus heretical and the earth's motion against the Bible. Cesi himself wondered whether *De revolutionibus* could have been printed if the index of prohibited books had existed in 1543. He saw danger of censorship looming and thought that pressure should be put on the archbishop at Florence to reprimand Caccini. The strategy adopted should be that of preventing calumny against mathematicans, rather than supporting Copernicus as such, lest more be lost than gained. Mathematicians at the universities (presumably in Tuscany) should write to others, especially in Rome, while Galileo should remain in the background. Such was Cesi's suggested strategy.

IV

On 7 February Niccolò Lorini sent to Rome for study by the Inquisition a copy of Galileo's year-old Letter to Castelli along with a letter of his own saying that the document was circulating in the hands of many. His discussions of it with colleagues at the Dominican convent in Florence led him to believe it contained erroneous propositions adhered to by the Galileists in that city. The copy Lorini sent was not complete, lacking the preliminary matter of a personal nature. It was duly read by a delegated Church official, who reported that a few words in it were ill chosen but that otherwise it contained no offense to Catholic doctrine. Galileo seems to have heard of Lorini's action during the same week. Fearing that the text sent to Rome might have been tampered with, on 16 February he wrote to Piero Dini (at Rome) the first of two important letters relating to his planned strategy and his ideas of science:

Since I know that you were promptly advised of the repeated invectives that some weeks ago were pronounced from the pulpit against the doctrine of Copernicus and his followers, and further against the mathematicians and mathematics itself, I shall not repeat any of these particulars that you heard from others; but I do desire that you should know that although neither I nor others have made the slightest move, or shown resentment against the insults by which wc were uncharitably aggravated, the excesses of those men are yet not quieted. Rather, that same father [Lorini] who was heard from a year ago in private discussions, having returned from Pisa, newly raised his hand against me; and having come upon, I know not where, a copy of a letter that I wrote last year to the Father mathematician at Pisa [Castelli] regarding the propriety of bringing holy authority into physical disputes and into the explanation of that place in Joshua, he started exclaiming over this, and (from what they say) found in it many heresies; and in short, new fields have been opened up to injure me.

But since nobody else who has seen that letter has shown me the lightest sign of scruple, I wonder whether whoever copied it may perhaps have made some inadvertent changes of wording, which alteration, combined with some disposition toward censure, may make the thing appear very differently from my intention. And since some of these fathers, and in particular that same one [Caccini] who preached, may (as I hear) have come there to attempt something with his [Lorini's] copy of my letter, it appeared to me not inappropriate to send your reverence a copy exactly as I wrote it, asking that you favor me by reading it together with the Jesuit Father Grienberger, a distinguished mathematician and my good friend and patron, and also, if convenient, get this into the hands of the illustrious Cardinal Bellarmine. And these Dominican fathers have let it be understood that they will use it in the hope of at least having the book of Copernicus, and his opinion and teaching, condemned.

My letter was written casually (*currenti calamo*), but these recent agitations and the motives adduced by those fathers for showing the demerits of this doctrine, from which every merit is to be abolished, have made me look for anything further [I may have] written on the matter, and truly I have not only found that everything I wrote has been said by others, but much more besides, showing with what circumspection one must proceed to those physical conclusions that are not matters of faith, at which we arrive by experience and necessary demonstrations; and how pernicious a thing it would be to assert as a doctrine resolved in the Holy Scriptures some proposition of which one might some time have a demonstration to the contrary! On this subject I have composed a very copious writing, though I have not yet polished it in such a manner that I can send you a copy, but I shall do that as soon as possible, in which will be whatever there is of efficacy in my reasonings and discourses. Of this I am sure—that there will be found [therein] much more zeal for the Holy Church and the dignity of Holy Writ than there is in these persecutors of mine, since they are working to prohibit a book admitted by the Church for many years, without their even having seen, let alone having read and understood it. I merely demand that its doctrine be examined along with the reasonings of very Catholic and very understanding persons who compare their positions with sensible experience, and in a word who do not damn anything without first finding it false, if it be true that a proposition cannot be both true and erroneous [in faith] together. There are not lacking in Christendom men very well versed in their profession whose opinion about the truth or falsity of the doctrine should not be subjected to the judgment of someone uninformed of this, and only too clearly known to be moved by partiality, as many very well know who are here in fact and who see all the moves and are informed at least partly of the machinations and dealings.

Nicholas Copernicus was a man not only Catholic, but religious and a canon, and he was called to Rome under Pope Leo X when, in the Lateran Council, the emendation of the church calendar was dealt with, he being utilized as a very great astronomer. That reform remained nevertheless undecided for this reason alone: that the length of years and months, and the motions of the sun and the moon, were not well enough determined; hence he, by order of the Bishop of Fossombrone (who was then in charge of this matter), put himself to new observations and most accurate studies of those periods. Thence followed, in a word, such knowledge that he not only put in order all the motions of the celestial bodies, but acquired the title of greatest astronomer, whose teaching was later followed by all, and in conformance with this the calendar was finally adjusted. His labors on the courses and arrangements of the heavenly bodies he reduced to six books, which were published at the request of Nicholas Schönberg, Cardinal of Capua and dedicated to Pope Paul III; and from that time to this it has been seen publicly with no scruple at all. And now these good friars, solely out of ill-will toward me and knowing how I esteem that author, vaunt of rewarding his labor by having him declared a heretic.

242

But what is more deserving of consideration, at the first move against this opinion some of my enemies depicted it as my own work, without mentioning that it had been printed 70 years ago; and other persons keep up that same style, by which they seek to establish a sinister view of me, and they are succeeding in such a way that just a few days ago Monsignor Gherardini, Bishop of Fiesole, arrived here in full view of many people, where they were attacking some friends of mine, and he broke out with great vehemence against me, showing himself very angry, saying there had been a great dispute among their serene Highnesses because my extravagant and erroneous opinion caused much talk in Rome. But perhaps now he will do the right thing, if he has not already restrained himself, he having been tactfully advised that the author of this doctrine is not at all a living Florentine, but a dead German, who printed it 70 years ago and dedicated his book to the Supreme Pontiff.

I go on writing, forgetting that I speak to a person well informed on these matters, perhaps better than I am, since you are in that place where the loudest outcries were made. Excuse my prolixity, and if you discover any equity in my cause, lend me your favor for which I shall live forever obliged. With this I salute you reverently; remember me as your most devoted servitor, and from God I pray the summit of felicity for you.

Postscript: Although it is hard for me to believe that there is being precipitated a resolution to annul this author, yet knowing by other proofs the extent of my misfortune, and adding that to the malignity and ignorance of my adversaries, it seems to me reasonable not to be entirely reassured by the high prudence and holiness of those who must make the final decision, for even that may be partly tied in with this fraud that is going around under the mantle of zeal and charity. So in order to leave out nothing I can do for myself and for that writing of mine, you will soon see that this is true and pure zeal, I desiring that at least this may first be seen, after which that resolution may be taken which shall please God (for as to me, I am well edified and determined that before I would contravene my superiors, if I could do no other, so that what I now seem to believe and know would have to be only a mental prejudice—"If mine eye offend me, pluck it out"), I believe that the most present remedy is to knock at the door of the Jesuit Fathers as those who know best the common affairs of friars. Therefore you may give them the copy of the letter [to Castelli] and also read to them, if you like, this that I am writing to you; and then, with your usual courtesy, deign to notify me what you can infer. I do not know whether it would be convenient for you to meet with Sig. Luca Valerio and give him a copy of the said letter, as he is with the house of Cardinal Aldobrandini and might do some office with him. On this and all else I remit myself to your goodness and prudence, to which I entrust my reputation.[9]

Dini received this letter on 21 February and replied that he would not stop with Grienberger but would talk to others as well, especially Giovanni Ciampoli, who, in the presence of Alessandro Orsini, had recently supported Galileo against the orthodox views of Di Grazia. Galileo also wrote to Ciampoli, whom he had known since 1608, and was assured by him that few in Rome (and none in authority) were concerned about the Caccini incident. He had heard about it three weeks before (when Lorini's letter went to the Inquisition) and had gone at once to see Cardinal Barberini (later Pope Urban VIII), finding him most sympathetic to Galileo. On 27 February he visited Barberini again, this time being told to caution Galileo to limit his arguments to mathematics and physics without getting into the theology of the matter.

On 25 February Lorini's copy of Galileo's Letter to Castelli was read at the weekly meeting of the cardinals of the Inquisition. Because the copy was obviously incomplete, and the examiner had noted in it some objectionable words, it was ordered that the original be obtained. Letters were sent to officials at Pisa to that end, but Castelli happened to be in Florence at the time. When he returned, the archbishop of Pisa asked him for Galileo's letter. Castelli said he had returned it (Galileo having needed it to make a correct copy for Dini) but would get it back; this was duly reported to Rome on 7 March. Writing on 12 March to request the letter, Castelli described the interviews at Pisa and assured Galileo that he had meanwhile heard that there was no great excitement at Rome over Caccini's attack from the pulpit at Florence.

V

On 7 March Cesi sent Galileo the book of stanzas by "Salvi," mentioned previously, and with it "a book that has just come out; this is, a letter by a Carmelite father who defends the opinion of Copernicus while saving all the scriptural passages. This work could not have appeared at a better time—unless to increase the rage of the adversaries may do harm, which I doubt. The writer counts all Linceans as Copernicans, though that is not so; all we claim in common is freedom to philosophize in physical matters. He is now preaching here at Rome."

The Carmelite was Father P. A. Foscarini of Naples, whose little book[10] was perhaps the crucial factor in Galileo's decision to support Copernicus openly, against the advice he had received from Cesi, Ciampoli, and Barberini to keep the battle on more general grounds. He had already commenced the task of greatly expanding his letter to Castelli into a thorough discussion of all the issues, which was completed in mid-1615 and is known as the *Letter to the Grand Duchess Christina*.[11]

Dini had meanwhile discussed the matter with Cardinal Bellarmine, who assured him that he had not heard any talk of Galileo's Copernicanism since Galileo himself had talked to him about it, which can only have been during his visit to Rome in the spring of 1611. Bellarmine thought there was no danger that the *De revolutionibus* of Copernicus would be suppressed; the worst that might happen, he opined, was that some notes would be added to that book to make sure that it would be taken only as a mere hypothesis in astronomy. Bellarmine thought that for Galileo to argue that the Bible spoke as it did only for the common understanding would further enrage his adversaries, but said he would be glad to review any interpretations written out by Galileo.

Castelli wrote on 18 March repeating his request for the original letter, considerable pressure having now been put on him by the archibishop and by another prelate. On 21 March Ciampoli reassured Galileo that so long as he dealt with Copernicus apart from theology there would be no trouble; Cardinal del Monte, long Galileo's friend and patron, had offered advice very similar to Bellarmine's. Ciampoli also mentioned the Foscarini book; believing it likely to be suppressed soon, and not knowing that Cesi had already sent a copy, he undertook to find one for Galileo before it was banned. On 25 March Castelli wrote again, saying that he must have the original letter back, as it was now not just requested of him but formally demanded. Thinking that the appearance of Foscarini's book might calm the Pisan authorities, he asked for that also.

Galileo now wrote a second long letter to Dini,[12] who had told him that a passage in Psalm 18 stood in the way of Copernican doctrines and that Cardinal Bellarmine would welcome Galileo's comments. It was for that reason alone that Galileo ventured into a metaphysical dissertation on radiant heat and energy, often mentioned out of context as if Galileo had based his idea of science on it:

It appears to me that in nature there is found a very spiritual substance, most tenuous and swift, which diffusing itself through the universe penetrates through everything without resistance and heats, vivifies, and renders fruitful all living creatures. Of this spirit, as seems to be demonstrated to us by sense itself, the sun's body is the principal receiver, from which immense light expands through the universe accompanied by that calorific spirit, and penetrating through all vegetable bodies it renders them live and fruitful. This may be reasonably deemed to be something more than light, since it penetrates and diffuses through all corporeal substances, however dense, through many of which light does not penetrate, so that just as by our fire we see and feel the emitted light and heat, of which the latter penetrates through all bodies even though opaque and solid while the former is found to be resisted by solidity and opacity, so the emanation of the sun is lucid and calorific, and the calorific part is the more penetrating. Then that the solar body is the recipient of this spirit and this light, and so to speak a conserver that receives from without, rather than a primary beginning and source from which they are originally derived, seems to me to have positive evidence in Holy Writ, where we see that before the creation of the sun the spirit with its calorific and fecund power moved the waters, or [moved] on the face of the waters for the coming creations; and likewise we have the creation of light on the first day, whereas the sun was created on the fifth. Hence we may very probably affirm that this fertilizing spirit and this light diffused through all the world concurs and unites and fortifies itself in the solar body, located for this in the center of the universe, and thereafter made more splendid and more vigorous, being newly diffused.

Of this primogenital light, not very splendid before its union and concourse in the solar body, we have the attestation of the Prophet in Psalm 73,[13] v. 16: *The day is thine, the night is thine; thou hast prepared the dawn and the sun*, which passage comes to be interpreted that God made before the sun a light similar to that of the dawn; moreover, in the Hebrew text in place of "dawn" is read "light," to suggest to us that that light which was created before the sun, very much weaker than that received by it, was fortified and newly diffused by this solar body. To this opinion is shown to allude the view of some ancient philosophers who believed the splendor of the sun to be a concurrence at the center of the world of the splendors of the stars which, being spherically arranged around it, shed their rays, which, by concurring and intersecting in that center increased there and redoubled their light a thousand times. This light, thus fortified, was reflected and spread much more vigorously, full of masculine and lively heat, so to speak, diffused to vivify all the bodies that spin around this center. Thus, with a certain similarity, as in the heart of the animal there is made a continual regeneration of vital spirits that sustain and vivify all the members, while there come otherwise to this heart others administering food and nutriment, without which it would perish; so the sun, while its nutriment concurs from without, conserves that source, from which it continually derives and diffuses this light and prolific heat that give life to all the members that lie around it. Concerning the wonderful force and energy of this spirit and light of the sun, diffused through the universe, I might adduce many attestations of philosophers and grave writers, but a single place shall suffice me from the blessed Dionysius Areopagiticus in the book *Of Divine Names*, which is this: "His light gathers and converts to himself all things which are seen, moved, lighted, or heated; and in a word all things which are preserved by his splendor. For this reason the sun is called HELIOS, because he collects and gathers all dispersed things." And shortly thereafter he says: "This sun which we see remains one, and despite the variety of essences and qualities of things which fall under our senses, he bestows his light equally on them and renews, nourishes, defends, perfects, divides, conjoins, cherishes, makes fruitful, increases, changes, fixes, produces, moves, and fashions all living creatures. Everything in this universe partakes of one and the same sun by his will, and the causes of many things which are shared from him are equally anticipated in him. And for so much the more reason," and so on.

Now, taking this philosophical position, such being perhaps one of the principal doors by which one enters into the contemplation of nature, I believe, speaking always with that humility and reverence which I owe the Holy Church and all its learned Fathers, revered and obeyed by me and to whose judgment I subject myself and my every thought—I believe,

I say, that the passage in Psalm 18[14] may have this sense, that
is, that "God placed in the sun his tabernacle" as in the noblest
seat in the whole universe; and then where it says "The sun
proceedeth as a bridegroom from his chamber and exults as a
giant in running his course," I would understand this to be said
of the radiant sun, that is of the light and of the above-mentioned
calorific spirit fertilizing all corporeal substances, which,
leaving from the solar body, is swiftly diffused throughout the
entire world, to which meaning all the words are punctually
fitted. And first, in the word "bridegroom" we have the fertilizing
and prolific power; "exult" applies to that emanation of those
solar rays, made in a certain way by jumps, as the sense clearly
shows us; "as a giant" or "as a strong man" denotes the
efficacious activity and power of penetrating through all bodies,
and also the high speed of moving through immense spaces,
the emanation of this light being as if instantaneous. The words
"goeth forth from his chamber" confirm that this emanation
and movement must refer to that solar light, and not to the
body of the sun itself, since the body and globe of the sun is
the recipient, and is "as the chamber" of this light, and it
would not be good to say that a chamber proceeds from a
chamber. From what follows, "his going forth is from the high
heaven," we have the first derivation and departure of this
spirit and light from the highest part of the sky, that is, from
the stars of the firmament, or even from the most sublime seats
[of the blessed]. "And his circuit unto the highest of it," here,
is the reflection and so to speak the re-emanation of that same
light out to the same summit of the world. There follows:
"And there is nothing hid from the heat thereof," and here
behold the vivifying and fertilizing heat, distinguished from the
light and much more penetrating than it through all corporeal
substances, however dense, since from the penetration of light
many things are protected and covered, but from this other
power there is nothing that is hidden. Nor should I omit a
certain other consideration of mine not foreign to this purpose.
I have already discovered the continual parade of shadowy
materials in the solar body, where they show themselves to our
senses in the guise of very dark spots and are then consumed
and resolved there; and I have mentioned how these perhaps
may be deemed part of that food, or perhaps the excrements
thereof, which the sun was deemed by some ancient philosophers
to need for its sustenance. I have also demonstrated from
continued observations of those shadowy materials that the
solar body necessarily turns on itself, and have suggested

how reasonable it is to believe that upon such rotation the planets depend for their movements around the same sun. Moreover, we know that the intention of the Psalm is to praise the divine laws, the Prophet comparing those with the celestial body, than which, among corporeal things, there is none more beautiful, more useful, and more powerful. Therefore, having sung encomiums of the sun, and it not being hidden from him that that makes all the movable bodies of the world revolve around it, passing next to the greatest prerogative of divine law and wishing to place this before the sun, he adds: "The law of the Lord is perfect, restoring the soul," as if he means that this law is as much more excellent than the sun itself, as being spotless and having the faculty of turning souls around itself is a more excellent condition than being covered with spots, as the sun is, and making corporeal and mundane globes turn around it.[15]

This long letter, revealing in other passages much of Galileo's preparatory plan for protecting Copernicus against clerical censure, reached Rome by 28 March. Ciampoli read it and wrote to Galileo once again that only four or five people opposed to him were bothering with the Copernican matter in Rome, for which reason (as Cesi advised) it was not good to say too much. Caccini gave a deposition to the Inquisition at this time, but no action was taken against Galileo on the basis of it. Di Grazia was also in Rome to support Caccini from the philosophical side. Galileo had returned his original letter to Castelli, who read it to the archbishop and several minor churchmen at Pisa but did not surrender it to them. They were impressed by its moderate tone. Foscarini's book had also reached Castelli, and the fact that a theologian had supported Copernicus independently of Galileo impressed these men even more.

VI

Foscarini sent a copy of his book to Cardinal Bellarmine for comment, and in replying (on 12 April) Bellarmine included Galileo, saying that both men should confine themselves to dealing with the Copernican system as pure hypothesis. In sending a copy of Bellarmine's letter to Galileo, Dini said that Cardinal Barberini had also told him that if Galileo spoke only as a mathematician he would have nothing to worry about.

On a visit to Genoa toward the end of April Castelli met Baliani, who went to Florence about the beginning of June to visit Galileo, then bedridden. During their conversations Galileo told Baliani that the successive speeds of bodies falling from rest increased as the odd numbers from unity.[16] He did not offer a proof, but explained that only in that way could the ratios of successive speeds remain the same regardless of the unit of time adopted. They also discussed the forces required to draw bodies up various inclined planes, and Baliani asked Galileo if he had seen what François Vieta had written on this topic. Galileo had not, and Baliani undertook to send him a copy. Upon his return to Genoa after a visit to Castelli in Pisa, Baliani sent the section on inclined planes taken from Galileo's own old work on mechanics. Though it was in Italian this had somehow become attributed to Vieta, who wrote nothing in that language and never visited Italy. It is known from a much later letter of Baliani that Galileo wrote to tell him that the analysis was his own, not Vieta's.[17] Galileo's *Mechanics*, like his writings on fortification and cosmography, circulated widely in copies without name of author, and similar incidents occurred later.

The *Replies* of Castelli and Galileo to two opponents of the *Bodies in Water* of 1612 were finally printed in May 1615.[18] In that month Galileo forwarded to Cesi, for safe delivery to Foscarini at Naples, a set of notes and advice to be used in reply to Bellarmine's letter if Foscarini decided to answer it. Galileo would not accept the compromise suggested by Bellarmine, would not believe that the whole matter had been effectively dropped at Rome, and intended to go there to argue orally as soon as his health permitted. He was bedridden at the time of Baliani's visit in June and for several months afterward, spending his time on the *Letter to Christina*[19] and writing few letters to others. He received a number of letters from Sagredo, mainly concerning experiments with the thermometer and with lenses, but his replies have not survived.

At the end of November, his health restored, Galileo asked permission to visit Rome in order to clear his own name of any suspicion of heresy and to campaign against the suppression of Copernican theory. Piero Guicciardini, the Tuscan ambassador at Rome, advised the grand duke that this was no time for him to come to Rome and argue about the moon. He recalled that when he was first appointed ambassador, near the end of Galileo's visit in 1611, there had been animosity toward Galileo on the part of some cardinals of the Inquisition, and he knew that at present some Dominicans influential at the Holy Office were very much opposed to him. Nevertheless, on 11 December 1615 Galileo was once more lodged at the Trinità del Monte with Guicciardini.

FOURTEEN

1616-18

DURING JANUARY 1616 Galileo wrote out at Rome his theory of the tides much as it later appeared in the *Dialogue*.[1] He regarded this as a Copernican argument independent of astronomical technicalities that might appeal to potentially powerful supporters. Alessandro Orsini had recently been created a cardinal, and Galileo addressed the treatise to him after obtaining from the grand duke a formal letter of recommendation to Orsini.

On 23 February Orsini spoke to the pope on Galileo's behalf but was told instead to dissuade Galileo, since Paul V now felt he should have turned the matter over to the Inquisition. When Orsini left, the pope called in Bellarmine, on whose advice a papal commission was appointed to determine whether Copernicanism was erroneous and heretical. Guicciardini so advised the grand duke, saying he thought Galileo would not suffer personally because he would do as the Church wished. This pope, he said, abhorred men of letters so much that men of ingenuity pretended the opposite of their beliefs to stay out of trouble. It was dangerous to oppose him, so the ambassador hinted that Galileo should be recalled to Florence without delay.

This letter, probably written at Rome on 27 February, exists only in a Florentine copy marked *inserto de' 4 di Marzo 1616*, by which date all was over but the shouting. Even then Guicciardini must have known something about the fateful events of 25–26 February; since he did not mention them to the grand duke, he probably took Galileo's word for what had happened and only feared that if Galileo remained longer he might endanger himself, the young cardinal of the Medici, and that ruling house itself.

In view of all the documents I believe that though the pope probably wanted the Holy Office to proceed against Galileo personally, Cardinal Bellarmine counseled a less personal procedure. First a technically independent panel of theologians would find against the notions that the earth moved and the sun stood still, and then Galileo would be informed of this and asked to abandon those views. Bellarmine had no doubt that he would agree; a decree of general scope could then be published and the matter would be resolved without alienating either the Medici or the several cardinals who remained favorable to Galileo. The finding of the panel was handed in on 24 February; on the 25th, at the weekly meeting of the cardinals of the Inquisition, the pope instructed Bellarmine in their presence to inform Galileo of it and require him to abandon these opinions. If he resisted, then the commissary of the Inquisition was to instruct Galileo in the presence of a notary and witnesses that if he did not obey he would be jailed.

It is clear from the minutes of this meeting that two separate interviews with Galileo were intended, the second to occur only if the first was unsuccessful. A document in the files of the Inquisition shows, however, that only one meeting took place, at the home of Cardinal Bellarmine on 26 February. This document is a notarial statement, or rather the copy of one, naming the notary, witnesses, and principal persons present but bearing no indication that the document was ever signed by any of them. It states that on that day Bellarmine told Galileo of the official finding against the motion of the earth and stability of the sun and told him he must not hold or defend them any longer, and that immediately and without any intervening relevant event (*successive*), Bellarmine being still present, the commissary of the Inquisition admonished Galileo in the name of the pope that he must not hold, defend, or teach in any way, orally or in writing, the said propositions on pain of imprisonment. Galileo agreed.[2]

As I reconstruct the events, bearing in mind also some documents of later date, they were as follows. On 26 February Bellarmine sent two of his familiars (officers of arrest attached to a cardinal of the Inquisition) to fetch Galileo, intending to carry out his part of the instructions of the pope. Shortly after these officers departed, the commissary arrived with a notary and some other Dominican fathers. They had no business to be there, but (in my opinion) the Dominican commissary did not trust the Jesuit Bellarmine, who might cajole Galileo out of his objections and thus obviate a second meeting. Bellarmine at once divined the real purpose of this visit and resented it. When Galileo arrived Bellarmine went to meet him at the door, hat in hand, as was his custom with every guest of whatever station, and murmured to him that whatever happened he was not to question it. They then returned to Bellarmine's chair, where he advised Galileo of the finding as the pope had ordered.

The commissary had seen that something passed between the cardinal and Galileo and easily guessed that he could now expect no resistance on Galileo's part. Unless he thought of something, his purpose in coming would be defeated. Hence as soon as Bellarmine had finished, the commissary, without giving Galileo a chance to reply, delivered his further admonition in terms even stronger than the pope had authorized. Galileo was only then able to acquiesce.

Bellarmine, though doubtless astonished and indignant at this improper intervention, now rose from his chair and escorted Galileo from the room, saying that he had further business that morning but hoped that Galileo would call again before leaving Rome. Returning to the commissary, he then spoke privately with him. Probably he said that the pope's specific instructions, worked out in advance with Bellarmine, had been contravened, perhaps inadvertently; no notary should have been present, and to sign his memorandum of the meeting would only call this to the pope's attention. So far as he was concerned the only thing that had legally happened was that he had told Galileo of the impending decree and Galileo had agreed to be bound by it. That was all he would report back to the pope at the next meeting; the commissary would be present and could add more if he wished.

Guicciardini, with whom Galileo was residing, could hardly have been ignorant that Galileo had been taken to see Bellarmine by officers of the Inquisition on 26 February. Galileo probably told him only that he had been advised of a coming decree and had promised to obey it; thus Guicciardini was able to write as he did to Florence even before the decree was formally adopted.

That occurred on 5 March, when Bellarmine reported as I have said, and though the commissary was present he said nothing more, as shown by the minutes of this meeting. The cardinals then passed an edict which will be described presently.

Galileo returned to visit Bellarmine, and I believe he was told that the cardinal regretted the intervention of the visiting Dominican, no threat against him having been intended by the pope if Galileo accepted the instructions he himself had given him. He was asked to forget everything else but those instructions, lest rumors arise that might cause embarrassment. Galileo was experienced in dealing with authorities of church and state, and knew when to overlook things. But the notary's memorandum was not destroyed; it was copied into the Inquisition's records, whether through clerical ignorance or the commissary's design, and rumors did circulate before long, as will be seen.

On 6 March Galileo himself reported to Florence that the Church had prohibited books purporting to reconcile the Copernican system with the Bible, of which Foscarini's book alone was mentioned. Two other books were suspended until corrected, of which one was that of Copernicus, but only a few changes were to be made in that, mainly in the prefatory dedication.[3] Galileo's knowledge of the changes (not published until a year later) suggests that he had already been told of them by Bellarmine. His own books were not mentioned at all in the official decree.

Here it may be remarked that the edict of 1616 was worded with considerable care and did not prohibit Copernican books outright. It distinguished those which purported to reconcile the earth's motion with the Bible, like Foscarini's book, from those which alluded only incidentally to such matters. Books of the first type were to be absolutely prohibited and destroyed. Those of the second type, of which only *De revolutionibus* and a commentary on the Book of Job by Diego de Zuñiga were mentioned, were simply suspended "until corrected" by deletion of the offending passages. There followed a sentence repeating this distinction and the respective treatments with respect to future books. Hence it appears that the persons most concerned in 1616, including Galileo (who was not mentioned in the edict even though at the end of his *Sunspot Letters* he had unequivocally endorsed the Copernican astronomy), did not take the order to mean suppression of Copernican works as such, but only of those reconciling the new astronomy with the Bible, or of incidental passages in other books attempting such a reconciliation. This was not at all the later interpretation of the edict, after most of the principals in 1616 were dead, but was certainly Galileo's own understanding of its intention, concerning which he was well informed at the time.

On 11 March Galileo was granted a long audience with the pope. It is fairly safe to conclude that Bellarmine had meanwhile told Paul V what had actually happened at his palace on 26 February and had arranged this audience to put Galileo's mind completely at rest. At any rate when Galileo told him of his concern about false accusations made by his enemies, the pope assured him that he knew Galileo's integrity and sincerity, told him not to worry, said that not only he but the entire Congregation of the Holy Office knew about his unjust persecutions, and added the unusual remark that so long as he, Paul V, lived, Galileo remained secure. Considering Guicciardini's description of this pope and his previous attitude in this matter, it can hardly be doubted that his friendly remark reflected new information recently given to him.

But despite all evidence that Galileo personally was in good repute with the highest authorities at Rome, Sagredo wrote on this very day, 11 March, to tell him that word was spreading in Venice that Galileo had been called to Rome to account for his belief in the earth's motion and that he must bend his neck. In April Castelli wrote from Pisa that Galileo was said there to have abjured secretly in the hand of Bellarmine. Sagredo then wrote again; rumor at Venice now had it that Galileo had been severely admonished and forced to do penance. Hence before he left Rome Galileo spoke again to Bellarmine, showing him these letters (and perhaps others). It was all very well for the cardinal to ask Galileo to treat some things as if they had never happened, but such rumors would damage his credibility with the grand duke at Florence. Bellarmine at once recognized the danger and the injustice; he wrote out a signed statement that Galileo had neither abjured nor done penance, but had merely been informed of the general edict governing all Catholics.[4] With this affidavit in hand, Galileo returned to Florence and this stage of his relations with the Roman Inquisition was over. At Naples, however, the printer of Foscarini's book was arrested, and Foscarini himself died suddenly the next year.

II

Galileo was back at Florence in June and his first action was to revive negotiations with the Spanish government, which he had discussed with Gaspare Cardinal Borgia while in Rome.[5] Thus the immediate effect of the edict against Copernicanism on Galileo's scientific career was to turn his activities away from cosmology and focus them on practical applications of astronomy.

It has already been mentioned that there was nothing wrong in principle with Galileo's scheme for determination of longitudes at sea, though there were many practical difficulties about putting it into effect. The easiest way of using the satellites of Jupiter was to compare their observed positions with diagrams of their predicted positions at stated hours for a fixed place. This meant preparation of diagrams for long periods in advance, which required much calculation, since it was not to be expected that persons aboard ships would themselves be able to make the calculations. There was also the problem of making accurate observations with a telescope aboard a ship, especially when the sea was not perfectly calm. Galileo knew he could make accurate predictions, from experience of recent months with those made for the *Sunspot Letters* and afterward, and he had in mind ways to train persons who would make observations at sea and to facilitate their work. On the other hand it was not easy to convince ship captains and government officials that the scheme would benefit them enough to justify the expense of training and carrying observers. His approach to the whole matter is seen from a letter sent to Spain, I believe in June 1616, though Favaro associated this letter with Galileo's original proposal in 1613:

That great and marvelous problem of finding the longitude
of a given place on the earth's surface, so much desired in
all past centuries for the important relations of such a discovery
to the complete perfection of geography and of naval maps, has
induced various persons to work at solving it down to the
present time, not only for the glory such a discovery would
deserve, but also to gain royal prizes and rewards offered to the
discoverer. Up to this time, however, all this work has been
wasted and no advance has been made over the ancient
achievements, especially those of Ptolemy found through subtle
and noble inventions. And perhaps the solution of this problem
remained absolutely impossible until some other stupendous
problems were solved by human ingenuity which were at first

glance much harder to solve than this problem of finding the longitude. To explain myself better I shall say briefly what longitude and latitude are for a given place on earth, and how those were found by the ancients and up to now, and how difficult and involved this is.

Latitude, then, is simply the arc in the meridian taken between the zenith of a place and the equator, which is always equal to the arc of that same meridian taken between the earth's pole and the horizon, that is, the height of the pole [star] at that place. Longitude is nothing but an arc of the equator taken between the meridian of one place and meridian of another; and since the first meridian is generally taken by cosmographers to be established as the meridian passing through the Canary Islands, it will be said that the longitude of a place is the arc along the equator that lies between the meridian through the Canary Islands and the meridian of the place.

Now you should know that all ways of finding such longitude proposed up to now have deservedly been recognized as idle and fallacious except two. The first would be knowledge of the [length of] journey along the parallel of the place [between it] and the First Meridian. That way is quite useless if between the two meridians there are vast seas or other distances impracticable to travel [straight]. The second way, adopted by the best cosmographers up to now, is by means of eclipses of the moon, which is the most exact way ever practiced up to the present, though it also suffers from many and serious difficulties. To explain this briefly and as easily as possible, let there be sought (for example) the longitude of Rome by a lunar eclipse that would occur in Rome on 20 December 1638[6] at 13 hours 30 minutes after noon, while the same eclipse would be made at the Canary Islands at 11 hours after noon. Then the meridian of Rome is east of that of the Canary Islands by two hours and a half, and since one hour means 15 degrees at the equator, we shall therefore say that the longitude of Rome is 37° 30' [east].

Now, as was said, this way of finding the longitude is subject to various difficulties, of which the first is the rarity of eclipses of the moon, since there are not more than two visible lunar eclipses a year, sometimes only one, and sometimes none. Besides, it is very hard to observe precisely the beginning (or the middle, or the end) of an eclipse, inasmuch as when the moon begins to emerge from the earth's shadow that shadow is very tenuous and smoky, so that the observer is perplexed whether the moon has or has not begun to cut it. And since I do not think anyone of understanding will doubt that if a way were found to make eclipses more frequent, so that where now we have few per year, and for the most part there is only one, we might [instead] have 2 or 3 or 4 or 5 or even six [eclipses] in one night, this affair could be turned to great advantage, since there would be more than a thousand such eclipses per year; and even if they were not truly lunar eclipses, but things in the sky and appearances similar and equivalent to lunar eclipses, it is manifest that the gain would be great. Moreover it being the case, as was said, that lunar eclipses are not precisely observable at their beginnings, middles and ends, so that [in them] one may err by perhaps a quarter of an hour (which would be an error in longitude of about four degrees), it is evident that if this business were reduced to an accuracy that would not err by one minute of time, that would be a very considerable gain. Add to this that the tables of motions of the sun and moon on which calculations of lunar eclipses depend are not yet so accurate as not to be out by a quarter-hour or even more, so that when those tables must be used one could err in longitude by about eight degrees, and it becomes obvious that if the eclipses (or other appearances [used]) depended on and were governed by tables so accurate as not to err by one minute, then the whole affair would be reduced, so to speak, to complete perfection, so far as our knowledge may arrive.[7]

A shorter "General Relation" of this proposal was sent by Galileo himself to two Spanish grandees in November 1616, in which he stated that the use of his tables could be explained to any person of average intelligence, enabling them to be used at sea, and promised to show satellites to the king and his grandees in positions previously predicted, as well as ways in which the calculations could be made and the tables brought up to date over ages to come. A very long letter was also sent to the Tuscan ambassador in Madrid, in a postscript to which Galileo's discussions with Cardinal Borgia were mentioned.

III

It was probably in August 1616 that Galileo sent word to Cesi of a "new and strange phenomenon observed by me some days ago in Saturn, whose two companions are no longer two small perfectly round globes as they were before, but are at present much larger bodies and no longer round in shape, but as seen in the diagram here; that is, two half-ellipses with dark triangles in the middle and contiguous to the middle globe of Saturn, which is seen as it always has been, perfectly round." This passage was copied on 3 September by Johann Faber and sent to Cardinal Borromeo, writing the same day to Galileo to say that Cesi had just shown him his message. A drawing found by Favaro among Galileo's notes on Jupiter's satellites for June-October 1616 conforms better to the wording above than Faber's copy of the diagram sent to Cesi. Both Galileo's wording above and the diagram in his notes suggest that it was at this time that he first realized that the "companions" could not be simple spherical bodies.[8]

A letter from Cesi in October announced the death of Father Maraffi at Rome and receipt of a manuscript of Thomas Campanella's *Defense of Galileo*, which was published six years later in Germany.[9] Cesi sent a copy of this to Cardinal Cajetan, who was in charge of making the "corrections" to *De revolutionibus*. He mentioned to Galileo the displeasure expressed by Father Grienberger at the decision against Copernicus and the sympathy toward Galileo shown by Paul Guldin, a rising young Jesuit mathematician.

In November Galileo sent Sagredo a copy of the treatise on tides which he had written out while at Rome, and Sagredo highly approved of it. Virginio Cesarini, at whose house in Rome Galileo had debated against some adversaries of Copernicus, wrote to say that although at the time he had not been well versed in mathematics, he had since been studying this with assistance from Giovanni Ciampoli and was better able to understand what he had heard from Galileo.

IV

Early in 1617 a Spanish dignitary acknowledged receipt of Galileo's longitude proposal and promised to aid his cause, believing that the king would be won over by its importance. In the spring Galileo spent some time at Livorno to test the making of telescopic observations from shipboard, though he was able to use only a docked vessel while there. He had designed a kind of headgear (*celatone*) supporting a telescope, made for him at the Tuscan arsenal, to assist in observations made from a moving ship. Another plan of his to stabilize observations on shipboard was to place a platform for the observer in a large tank of water to be carried on deck. It is probable that he also designed at this period the brass "Jovilabe," a mechanical computing device for predicting positions of the satellites. Such an instrument is preserved at the Science Museum in Florence but the date of its making is not known. Galileo's design notes appear to belong to 1617.

The Tuscan ambassador reported that the king of Spain, having often expended large sums on promised inventions, had decided not to authorize work on Galileo's proposal for determining longitudes. Galileo replied, mentioning his new invention of the headgear fitted with a low-power field glass suitable for military as well as naval use. He spoke also of a new means for estimating the distance to a target, the basis for which had been outlined in a letter from Castelli not long before.[10] Galileo explained to the ambassador at Madrid why he had had to limit his proposal to things easily understood by persons not versed in mathematics. He assured him that to instruct others in the use of his tables for the satellites, if not in their construction, was quite practicable, as several distinguished men would vouch. Galileo wanted an annual fee of 2,000 florins for his services, less than the 2,600 florins discussed earlier at Rome with Cardinal Borgia.

In August the ambassador replied to the secretary of state in Florence that he could only wait in hope of help through the good offices of grandees already approached. In September he advised one of them that the grand duke would allow Galileo to travel to Spain and satisfy everyone there of his ability to make good on his proposal, if the king consented. At the end of 1617 Galileo wrote again at length in reply to a large number of questions and practical objections given to the ambassador by various Spaniards. Though he patiently answered all of these it had become evident that a stage had been reached at which there was little hope of a change of heart by the king of Spain.

V

Galileo fell ill again late in 1617. Giovanni de' Medici, a professional soldier who had long been antagonistic to Galileo, visited Pisa and was shown the *celatone* by Castelli; he was so struck by its military potential that he sent his greetings to Galileo and said this was a greater invention than the telescope itself. Soon afterward, in March 1618, the Archduke Leopold of Austria visited the Tuscan court, residing in Pisa as usual this time of year, and expressed regret that Galileo was confined to bed in

Florence, as he and the archduchess much wished to talk with him. In communicating this Castelli sent his greetings to Niccolò Arrighetti and Mario Guiducci, who were then studying with Galileo.

The archduke paid a visit to Galileo on his way back to Austria. In May, while Galileo was still bedridden, he wrote a long letter to Leopold accompanying the gift of two telescopes, one for astronomical use made with the lenses Galileo himself had been using for three years, and the other a short low-power glass for field observations. He also sent a copper *celatone* as a model from which local artisans could make a headgear fitting Leopold, asking that this device be kept secret. Along with these went Galileo's *Sunspot Letters* and a manuscript copy of his treatise on the tides. Explaining that soon after he had written that treatise the Copernican system had been forbidden, Galileo offered it to Leopold as "a pleasant fantasy" only, yet as containing things that persons outside the Catholic faith might develop without credit to Galileo, as he said had been happening with other things of his. Probably he hoped that the archduke would have his treatise on the tides published pseudonymously, as Welser had done with Scheiner's letters on sunspots, for a copy of Galileo's *Sunspot Letters* was sent at the same time. But Leopold did not take the hint.

Upon his recovery in May 1618 Galileo made a pilgrimage to Loreto, going on to Pesaro for a visit with the duke of Urbino which took place on 9 June. It was probably on his return to Florence, where in 1617 he had taken a house at Bellosguardo in the Florentine hills, that Galileo decided to arrange his long-neglected work on natural motion in systematic form for publication. In moving his effects to Bellosguardo, Galileo may have reread his long-neglected Paduan notes on motion, though because of other interests, occupations, and recurrent illness he did not resume work on them until this time.[11]

In order to have his earlier work in convenient form for systematic arrangement and to permit the interleaving of additional material Galileo now had copies made, one to a sheet, of those theorems which were in final or nearly final form but which had been crowded together on some fifteen sheets, written on both sides and sometimes mixed with material no longer of use. The copying was done by Mario Guiducci and Niccolò Arrighetti, on paper bearing a single watermark (spread eagle in circle with crown above) which is found also on letters and datable manuscripts written by Galileo at various times after his move to Florence, including letters of 1617 and 1618. Neither copyist duplicated work of the other, though they sometimes copied from the same sheet written at Padua. The work thus appears to have been done at Galileo's house, under his direction and within a short period of time. The first letter written to Galileo at Florence inquiring about his work on motion was sent from Rome in September 1618, which is probably about the time copying was finished.

Once again, however, he was confined to bed by illness and did little more than discuss with Arrighetti some questions raised by the latter. Few of Galileo's own notations on the copies appear to date before 1630–31. New events in the heavens once again distracted Galileo's attention from his projected treatise on motion.

VI

At the beginning of October 1618 Virginio Cesarini wrote a long letter to Galileo from Rome which was delivered by Giovanni Ciampoli, who had been residing with Cesarini for some time and was now returning for a while to Florence. Cesarini had met Galileo only during his visit to Rome nearly three years before, but their conversations had made a lasting impression on him:

Knowing you has marvelously inflamed in me a desire to know something, and with the guide of your discourses I chose a better road to philosophy and knew a certain logic more secure whose syllogisms, founded either on physical experiences or on mathematical demonstrations, open the mind to knowledge of truth no less than they stop the mouths of some vain and stubborn philosophers whose science is opinion, and what is worse, the opinion of other men and not their own, and of that one [Aristotle] who perhaps, if by chance he were now present to be able to enjoy the contemplation of things newly found, would be the first to forsake the opinion he formerly wrote.

I cannot deny that the discourses heard from you when you stayed at Rome were not to me the seeds of many reflections on my part at that time; what happened to me in listening to you was what happens to men bitten by little animals, who do not yet feel the pain in the act of being stung, and only after the puncture become aware of the damage received. So I, not perceiving that I was being taught, saw after your discourses that I had a somewhat philosophical mind. . . . Without having much frequented the springs of your science, I have nevertheless shared in the health-giving quality that those waters bring to intellects which often, like the sick bodies that sometimes need the waters of mineral baths, likewise require to be brought to earth and cured of stolidity or frenzy by washing in most limpid streams. Such is your eloquence and your science, through the latter of which, just as you know the most hidden demonstrations there are in nature, so by the former you make them available to the capacities of other people; for I have always admired in you no less what you understand than the way in which you explain it, not only illuminating the most obscure contemplations by the lamp of your intellect but also enlightening cloudy minds.

In return for Galileo's enlightenment of Cesarini and Ciampoli in science and in accord with his break with ancient authority, they wanted him now to set aside his preference for early Tuscan lyric poetry and listen to some compositions in a new strain, mixing novelties with ancient Greek beauties to advance beyond imperfections in what Italian poets had previously written. This was a movement in poetry curiously like the revolution in music which had been spearheaded by Galileo's father. Cesarini's appeal doubtless made a profound impression on his mentor, whose own principal venture into literary criticism (a comparison of Torquato Tasso and Ludovico Ariosto) was written not long afterward. Galileo's reply is lost, but on 1 December Cesarini wrote to thank him for his approval of the compositions taken to Florence by Ciampoli and to say that he valued Galileo's favorable opinion more highly than any public acclaim the poetry might receive.

A small comet had been sighted in October 1618 which was followed by another in mid-November and finally by a very conspicuous comet about 27 November. Cesarini wrote to Galileo that these comets had aroused great interest at Rome, calling forth the usual popular foolishness that attended such events. He had just talked with the mathematicians at the Collegio Romano, who had favored him with an opinion which he was forwarding to Galileo for comparison with his own observations and his views on the subject. What Cesarini sent was probably a manuscript copy of a public lecture that had been delivered by Orazio Grassi and was subsequently printed anonymously early in 1619 as "by one of the Fathers of the Collegio Romano."[12]

Galileo, still bedridden, also received inquiries during December from Stelluti and from Johann Remo, mathematician to Archduke Leopold of Austria. Remo suggested that comets were formed from sunspot material cast off by the sun and coagulated elsewhere in the sky. Stelluti noted that the comet showed little magnification by the telescope and opined from this fact that the comet must be very distant. That fallacy was also espoused by Grassi, who reasoned that since planets are noticeably magnified by the telescope and fixed stars are not, the comet must be farther away from the earth than the planets, and closer to the stars. Such complete misapprehension of the operation of telescopes was very disturbing to Galileo.

Moreover, though concrete evidence for this in the Galilean correspondence is found only a bit later (in a letter from G. B. Rinuccini in March 1619), observations of the 1618 comet were being taken at Rome as evidence against Copernicus, probably from the start:

> The Jesuits presented publicly a Problem [on the distance of the comet] which has been printed, and they hold firmly that it is in the sky [that is, beyond the moon], and some others besides the Jesuits have spread it around that this thing overthrows the Copernican system, against which there is no surer argument than this. So when I tell you I would give a thousand years [of life] to know your opinion, I believe you will forgive me.

A modern reader may reasonably be puzzled at this, since Copernicus did not discuss comets at all and they have no evident connection with planets. Rinuccini's statement about the Jesuit opinion had its basis in an idea of Tycho Brahe's, whose analysis of the comet of 1577 assigned to it a circular orbit around the sun very near the orbit of Venus; the comet was supposed to have originated and then been dissipated in this orbit, behaving like a sort of imitation planet. Kepler's teacher, Michael Maestlin, one of only two professors during the sixteenth century known to have lectured in recognized universities on the Copernican theory, had at first held back from Copernicanism precisely because of Tycho's discussion of the 1577 comet. Hence, however strange it may now seem, a contemporary basis existed for the Jesuits' contention that cometary orbits existed in the region of the planets. Just how this could damage Copernicanism is far from clear to me; perhaps it was believed that with new cometary evidence in support of Tycho, Copernicus would no longer be regarded as a serious competitor of his.

In fact comets do orbit around the sun, though not only not in circles, but in ellipses so enormously elongated as to be considered parabolas for all calculating purposes. The elliptical orbits of planets, which we owe to Kepler and which were the true origin of modern astronomy, are on the other hand very nearly circles. That Grassi had in mind circular cometary orbits is evident from the fact that in his attempt to determine the distance of the 1618 comet from the earth he had said nothing about any increase of distance during the time it was visible. Thus in effect Grassi had treated the comet as if it circled about the earth, so far as anything said in his original lecture is concerned. In this and other ways his lecture was burdened with hybrid astronomy and incompetent optics. It was what passed for scholarship at that time, ornamented with poetic thoughts, astrological lore, philosophical principles, and pretentious calculations while remaining almost devoid of constructive science in the sense that was to be clarified to the best of Galileo's ability during the ensuing controversy, which culminated in 1623 with a book that has been called "Galileo's scientific manifesto."

FIFTEEN

1619-23

IN JANUARY AND February 1619 Archduke Leopold wrote to Galileo urgently requesting his views on the comets. Though Galileo could not safely write on astronomy proper, nothing prevented his attacking the Jesuit book on comets, which for Aristotelians were not even celestial objects. He had two incentives for this; first, to correct the error about telescopic magnification, and second to separate comets entirely from planetary astronomy. Aristotelians considered comets to be fiery vapors below the moon, ignited by motion of the crystal sphere in which that luminary was embedded. Galileo saw how he could challenge both that and the Jesuit's arguments without affirming any definite theory of his own. A third incentive may have been the letter from Cesarini: to suggest a scientific method of analysis and illustrate it by examples might enable others to reach Galileo's own astronomical position without his having violated any Church order.

Guiducci had recently been made Consul of the Florentine Academy, so the form in which Galileo's arguments were first presented was that of Guiducci's consular lectures in the spring of 1619. Except for a few sections, mainly at the beginning, the printed *Discourse on Comets*[1] exists in manuscript in Galileo's hand together with papers written by Guiducci but reviewed and annotated by Galileo. Much of it was directed against Tycho, the anonymous Jesuit author being considered as his follower in most things. Near the beginning, however, there was a sarcastic allusion to "Apelles." Since that was now recognized as the

267

pseudonym of Scheiner, it implied an attack on the Jesuits. Both Grassi and Scheiner took offense at this publication and attributed it wholly to Galileo, whose thoughts Guiducci had said he included along with his own.

The controversy between Galileo and the Jesuits over the 1618 comets became of such importance to the remainder of his scientific career, and has been so superficially presented in most biographies, that it is advisable here to review the points at issue from the beginning in order to understand their proliferation. The lecture delivered publicly at Rome by Grassi (and subsequently published anonymously) was a calm and uncontentious work directed against common misapprehensions. Though riddled with solemn errors, it was not intended to offend Galileo or anyone else. The "Problem" to which Rinuccini had referred followed a general prefatory section; it was to determine approximately the distance of the comet from the earth. First the date of its appearance was established and its home was determined as near the middle of Scorpio. By comparing observations from different cities at a given time, the comet was shown to have exhibited no parallax much greater than 1°. Since that was about the parallax of the moon, Grassi next argued that the comet could not have been so near the earth, because if so it would have had a volume of 490,871,150 cubic miles; "Now if the comet was sublunar, it ought to have been fueled by exhalations from the earth; but good God! how great an amount of fuel would be consumed by such an immense fire over so long a time. Therefore it could not be located under the moon."[2]

Next Grassi argued that the path of the comet must have been a great circle and much resembled the motion of the planets, particularly Venus, using very defective reasoning clearly based on Tycho's analysis of the very different 1577 comet (though without mentioning Tycho's name). Again he called the comet a "fire," as before when speaking of its fuel.

Next came Grassi's argument from the telescope; the comet "suffered scarcely any enlargement. Nevertheless, it has been discovered by long experience and proved by optical reasons that all things observed with this instrument seem larger than they appear to the naked eye, yet according to the law that the enlargement appears less and less the farther away they are removed from the eye, it results that fixed stars, the most remote of all from us, receive no perceptible magnification from the telescope. Therefore, since the comet appeared to be enlarged very little, it will have to be said that it is more remote from us than the moon."[3]

The most charitable explanation of this absurd optical "law" is that Grassi had in mind not the ratio of magnification but the absolute size of any apparent increase observed through the telescope. The idea would then be that so large an object as the head of a comet would fail to show appreciable telescopic magnification only if it were more remote even than the planets. That was bad enough, but after Galileo destroyed Grassi's "law" by showing that if it were true we could also measure distances to remote terrestrial objects by telescopic sightings, Grassi chose to defend his "law" literally rather than by the above interpretation[4]—perhaps because he saw that that in turn would get him into trouble. In the original anonymous lecture he had added: "I know that this argument is of little significance to some, but perhaps they have given little consideration to the principles of optics." It is understandable that Galileo, to whom the argument was indeed of little significance, took this as a slur on his own knowledge of optics. On this matter we have a proper explanation later, by Grassi: he had had in mind originally only those persons who ignored all telescopic observations on the ground that they were merely illusions and proved nothing about the sky.

Grassi next calculated the approximate distance of the comet from the earth in the following way: "it can probably be placed between the sun and the moon. Since for those [celestial] lights which are excited by particular motions there is an established law according to which the more slowly they move the higher they are, and since the motion of our comet [3° per day] was midway between that of the sun and that of the moon, it will have to be placed between them. . . . [Its] distance from the center of the earth is established at 572,728 miles."[5] The length of the comet was figured as 600,000 miles, its bulk as 52,276,200,000 cubic miles, and the volume of the head alone, without the tail, as 19,361,555 cubic miles. A final postscript declared that Grassi opined the comet to be very near to the stars by virtue of its light, implying absurdly that Grassi thought the sun itself to be, if not beyond the stars, very close indeed to them.

Amid this welter of loose and incompatible arguments perhaps the most striking thing is that there was not a word to suggest that the comet might vary in its distance from the earth. In Tycho's cometary theory the circulation of the 1577 comet was around the sun, not the earth, so that even if the sun remained at a constant distance from the earth the comet would approach and retreat from us. Speaking as professor of mathematics for the Jesuit College, Grassi could in principle allow no heavenly motions but circular, and around no center but the earth, even though the satellites of Jupiter were accepted by the Jesuits and violated that dogma. All that can be said is that his theory of the comet was absurd in any astronomical system, and that Grassi only made it worse in his reply to Galileo later in 1619.

In considering the ensuing controversy, it is best to separate most of what is now known about comets from what it was that people saw in 1618. The tail of a comet does not begin to appear until the comet, which is itself a tenuous vapor, has come fairly close to the sun. Comets are now detected very far away, long before they become visible to the naked eye, but in those days the first appearance of a comet came when that vapor became distended by pressure of the sun's light, seldom before the comet was at least as close to the sun as is the earth. Consequently, during most of the time a comet was conspicuous it had already passed the sun and was proceeding very nearly in a straight line, the only sharply curved part of its orbit having occurred while it was necessarily too near the sun to be observed. The rest of the orbit being parabolic, it appears nearly straight. Since the tail of a comet always points away from the sun, it does not necessarily stream out behind the head of the comet but may go ahead of it or appear in any number of positions as seen from the earth. Stars are easily visible not only through the tail but through any part of a comet. Thus it was then a genuine question whether comets really were bodies or just clouds of vapor, or, as Galileo suggested, merely illuminated parts of much larger clouds of vapor high above.

The *Discourse on Comets*, published in June but drafted by Galileo in February, began conventionally with a summary of ancient theories about the origin and nature of comets in which a special attack was launched against Aristotle's idea that comets are fiery vapors below the moon. The view of later astronomers that they were bodies moving through the sky had seemed preferable to Guiducci until Galileo pointed out that this also was dubious. This remained the view of the Jesuit author, as it had been the "imitation planet" view of Tycho. The strongest argument in its favor was that no parallax, or at any rate less parallax than the moon's, could be detected in the position of the comet as observed from places far apart on earth.

Galileo questioned whether parallax determinations were significant except for true and solid bodies. Lights reflected from vapors, such as rainbows, moved with the observer, defeating the methods of measuring parallactic displacement. Hence until astronomers could first demonstrate that comets were true and real bodies, not just reflections in vapors, it would be rash for them to reason from parallax about cometary distances. For example, everyone has seen a lighted streak pointing toward the setting sun on a large body of water. Accordingly if, high above us, there were some huge cloud of vapor capable of reflecting sunlight as the sea does, might we not see a streak of light pointing toward the sun up there, where there might not be any tangible body present at all? Such was the core of Galileo's attack in the *Discourse*, intended not to assert a new theory of comets but rather to cast legitimate scientific doubt on the applicability to them of ordinary terrestrial parallax reasoning.

Grassi's argument of small magnification by the telescope was disposed of next. It implied the obviously false conclusion that we should be able to determine the distance to any terrestrial object by carefully measuring its telescopic magnification. Tycho's idea of a circular orbit for every comet was in turn demolished by consideration of the 1618 comet's observed elongation from the sun. The notion of straight motion away from the earth was introduced in its place as simpler and as more nearly borne out by observation. Yet a difficulty arose here, since straight motion away from the earth ought to make the comet tend ultimately toward the zenith, whereas this comet had never appeared directly overhead but remained somewhat northerly. "Hence we must be content with what little we may conjecture here among shadows, until there shall be given to us the true constitution of the parts of the universe, inasmuch as that which Tycho promised us still remains imperfect."[6] None of the foregoing was directed against Grassi, who was merely said to share Tycho's view in most things.

Next came the question of the apparent curvature of the tail of the comet, a completely different problem from the curvature of its path. Galileo considered Tycho right in saying that the

271

curvature of the tail was not real but merely apparent, though he rejected Tycho's reasoning on this matter. Galileo preferred to attribute the curvature of the tail to atmospheric refraction of sunlight reflected by the comet to us, since no observer on earth can be truly at the center of the earth's atmosphere. "And thus, worthy listeners, in my opinion the road to better philosophizing has been smoothed by what has here been discussed, as was not done by Tycho and his adherents."[7]

Guiducci had been very careful not to present any positive theory of comets either on Galileo's part or his own. The passages from the *Discourse* cited above show that its author pretended to no final knowledge on the subject, and in his old age Galileo remarked that even if he lived a thousand years he would never expect to understand such phenomena. In discussing the belief of some ancient authors, Guiducci remarked that in order to account for the supposed absence of comets between the tropics and farther to the south, those men had needed to adduce moist vapors to refract vision toward the sun:

You see, therefore, that they believed comets to be not real objects but mere images and appearances. . . . To have the comet appear as without parallax to all observers and still originate in the elemental sphere, it would [however] suffice for vapors (or other material of whatever sort) to be diffused on high and be capable of reflecting the sun's light. . . . I do not say positively that a comet is formed in this way, but I do say that just as there are doubts about this, so there are doubts about the other schemes employed by other authors; and if they claim to have established their opinions beyond doubt they will be obliged to show this and all other positions to be vain and fallacious.[8]

Grassi took this to mean that Galileo himself believed not only that comets are in fact mere reflections of sunlight in high vapors but that those vapors must originate on earth and rise into the skies. The aurora borealis had been mentioned in the *Discourse* as one of several illuminations in the sky not linked to true and real bodies there. It had been explained as a light in fumes and vapors arising from the earth at certain times of year, and in Italy the aurora was never seen except very low on the northern horizon. Grassi later seized on this explanation as if it had also been intended by Galileo as an explanation of comets. This was without justification. Since the aurora does not endure for weeks on end, does not move regularly through the heavens, and is seen only in a very restricted region of the skies, any analogy to comets beyond that of illumination in vapors is untenable. All Galileo had said in the *Discourse* was that he saw no reason why *celestial* vapors might not sometimes visit our lower regions, which is very different from asserting terrestrial origin of such vapors.

Thus, so far as the *Discourse* bore on any cometary theory, it served first to question whether comets were true and real bodies, and second to refute Tycho's orbital analysis. There were incidental comments on many other matters, particularly on heat and fire (because they were essential to Aristotle's theory and germane to Grassi's), on relative motions of smooth containers and their contained fluids, and on the nature of sensation. Later Grassi made an issue of each of these subsidiary topics and Galileo then explained his ideas on them further.

II

At the time Galileo had written out his tidal theory for Cardinal Orsini at Rome early in 1616, he had included a statement that was deleted from the text as revised, expanded, and finally published at the end of his *Dialogue* in 1632. This statement shows that he had been misinformed about a matter on which he was corrected at some time between 1616 and 1630, probably in 1619 by the Englishman Richard White who had studied mathematics with Castelli. Galileo had written in 1616:

The length of the Mediterranean gulf carries the reciprocations dependent on the secondary cause in about six hours to six hours, whereas at the beaches that bound the eastern part of the Atlantic Ocean, which extends all the way to the West Indies, the reciprocations are about 12 hours to 12 hours, as is daily observed at Lisbon on the outer shores of Spain; against these [shores] the ocean that reaches toward America to the Gulf of Mexico is twice as long as the stretch of the Mediterranean from the Straits of Gibraltar to the shores of Syria, the former being 120° and the latter about 56°. Therefore its having been believed that the periods of incoming and outgoing tides are [everywhere] six hours is a deceptive opinion, which has made writers prattle many vain fantasies.

In the mistaken belief that a twelve-hour period was actually observed at Lisbon, as might be expected from his tidal theory if the distance between shores of the Atlantic was double that of the Mediterranean, Galileo had gone on to say:

> From this . . . it will not be difficult to investigate the reasons for such inequalities of periods as are observed in lesser seas, as in the Sea of Marmara, the Hellespont, and others, in some of which the water currents reciprocate in three hours, or two, or four, and so on, with differences such as to have much troubled observers of Nature who, not knowing the true reasons, have taken up vain chimeras about motions of the moon and other fancies.

The elimination of this misinformation from Galileo's account of the tides probably occurred early in 1619, for on 14 April Toby Matthew at Brussels wrote to Sir Francis Bacon:

> It may please your Lordship, there was with me this day one Mr. Richard White, who hath spent some little time in Florence, and is now gone into England. He tells me that Galileo had answered your discourse concerning the flux and reflux of the sea, and was sending it unto me; but that Mr. White hindered him because his answer was grounded on a false assumption, namely that there was in the [Atlantic] Ocean a full sea but once in twenty-four hours. But now I will call upon Galileo again. This Mr. White . . . has his [Galileo's] discourse of the flux and reflux of the sea, which was never printed.

Thus it appears that White, who had sailed from England to Italy, was able to tell Galileo that his information about the tides at Lisbon was incorrect. It also appears that Galileo, at Matthews' request, had thought to base his reply to Bacon's theory on his mistaken information about tides at Lisbon rather than to send him a complete copy of his own explanation, in which that appeared only as an incidental remark.

III

Ciampoli, who had returned to Rome, read the *Discourse* that had been sent to Cesarini and was delighted with it, but he told Galileo that others thought Galileo should not have quarreled with the fathers at the Jesuit college where he had been publicly honored in the past. "The Jesuits consider themselves much offended and are preparing a reply; and though on this matter I know and recognize the soundness of your conclusions, still I am sorry that among them the benevolence and applause they used to have for your name have been so greatly diminished."

Remo, at Vienna, read the copy Galileo had sent to Archduke Leopold and wrote to Kepler that although it contained many paradoxes, it agreed more or less with his own ideas about comets. Remo provided Kepler with an accurate summary of the book and mentioned that Galileo wanted a copy of Kepler's recently published opening parts of the *Epitome of Copernican Astronomy*, a book prohibited in Florence (that is, in Italy, because of the 1616 edict).

Prohibition of Kepler's *Epitome* shows that the church edict was already being construed as banning all Copernican books, and not just those which attempted to reconcile the new astronomy with the Bible. Since Kepler had said little in the *Epitome* about scripture, that book should at most have been "suspended pending correction," like *De revolutionibus*, which it resembled in being principally a technical astronomical work. Perhaps it had been banned outright mainly because Kepler was a Protestant, but the precedent thus set was applied generally thereafter, to Galileo's disadvantage when it came to the *Dialogue*, in which the Bible was not mentioned at all.

Kepler had not only neglected to send a copy of the *Epitome* to Galileo, but included in it credit to Simon Mayr for having determined the periods of Jupiter's satellites. Yet the figures he gave were not Mayr's, but Galileo's as published in *Bodies in Water*, and Kepler did not mention the forecasts in the *Sunspot Letters*, of which Galileo had sent him a copy.

Kepler's book *De cometis* was also published at this time, independently setting forth the idea of rectilinear motion of comets. Thus both Galileo and Kepler, at the same time in 1619, espoused the introduction of straight motion in the heavens where in all past time only circular motions had been permitted by philosophers and astronomers. Kepler had indeed introduced elliptical motions in 1609, but nothing for or against this seems to have been published by other astronomers during the ensuing ten years.

Baliani wrote a long letter to Galileo relating to the *Discourse*, mostly dealing with matters omitted in the above summary as incidental to the principal argument. Approving Galileo's position that parallax offers a valid key to distance only when real bodies are differently sighted, he also liked the concept of straight motion for comets, except for Galileo's own qualification that in that case comets should verge toward the zenith. Baliani preferred to consider comets as of the same material as planets, endowed by God with regular motion but slowed down because their circles were very eccentric. Galileo, who considered the apparent slowing of a comet to be an optical effect linked to viewing long straight motion from a point outside the line of motion, noted on Baliani's letter: "In all these propositions [criticized] there is no trouble at all, and if what I said was inconsistent with this [that is, God's having slowed the motion of the comet], then it ought to be considered not only false but heretical. So I say that not only all these things [in the *Discourse*] can be said, but that this [straight motion] is the easiest, simplest, and most expeditious mode of resolving these and whatever other, more difficult, problems there may be."

A copy of the *Discourse* sent to the Archduke Leopold was forwarded by him to Scheiner, who after having read it vowed to repay Galileo in his own coin. This information was transmitted to Galileo by Johann Remo. Inasmuch as Scheiner did not publish anything about the comets of 1618 over his own name, it is probable that what he had written was sent to Grassi at Rome and that much of it was incorporated in the vigorous attack of "Lothario Sarsi"[9] aganst Galileo, discussed below.

Carlo Muti wrote to Galileo to thank him for his book and also for a treatise (now lost) on "perpetual and natural motion." Muti was awaiting the Jesuit reply to the *Discourse*, which had gone to Perugia for printing, and said he had been told that the book would deal with everything Galileo had ever done. On 18 October Ciampoli wrote that Grassi had returned from Perugia with the new book: "He told me he had put your reasoning the best he could, but had always treated you by honoring you." Considering the contents of the book, full of innuendo, reproach, scorn, and deliberate distortion of Galileo's arguments, this seems a queer statement unless we assume that Grassi was not the sole author and had been forced to include things he did not like, perhaps written by Scheiner. He might then have tried to hint to Galileo through Ciampoli that he had done the best he could and still respected him. Later events at Rome tend to support this hypothesis.

IV

The new book was called *Libra Astronomica* (The Astronomical Balance) because it purported to weigh Galileo's opinions as set forth by Guiducci. Cesi at once wanted to know whether Galileo would reply to it, and if so whether directly or through Guiducci. Stelluti deplored Galileo's wasting time on any reply when he could be writing better things. Sagredo remarked that he was not surprised to see the Jesuits replying so coldly to the *Discourse*, they having become melancholy through troubles in Germany brought on by their own misbehavior. At first Galileo would not believe that the *Libra* was actually written by Grassi, though Ciampoli assured him that the Jesuits wanted this work to be known as theirs and were so far from sharing Galileo's justly low opinion of it that they were glorying in its triumph; but "Father Grassi treats of you with much greater reserve than do many of the other fathers, among whom the word 'annihilate' is very common. The truth is that I have never heard Father Grassi use such a word; rather, he is so moderate in speech that I am the more astonished at his having made his book so glorious [*glorioso*, perhaps a slip of the pen for *orgoloso*, arrogant], and with so many biting asides."

The contents of the *Libra* are so unpleasantly personal, so replete with misrepresentations of the *Discourse*, and so feeble scientifically (except for descriptions of certain experiments not particularly germane to comets) that such parts of it as need to be mentioned will be deferred until discussion of Galileo's rejoinder four years later. Here it suffices to cite one passage that shows how the *Discourse* was viewed by others despite all the precautions that had been taken to avoid this:

Until the present no one has said that the comet ought to be counted entirely among vain apparitions . . . but because Galileo sought to give another, better, and wiser explanation of the comet [than ours], it is desirable that we pause for a careful consideration of this new discovery of his.[10] . . .

He says that smoky vapor from some part of the earth was carried upward above the moon and even the sun, and as soon as it had progressed beyond the shadowy cone of the earth it beheld the light of the sun, which the comet received and obeyed; and that the motion or ascent of this sort of vapor appears not to be wandering and uncertain but straight and deflected to neither side.[11]

No such theory can be found in the *Discourse*; yet at the end of the above section Grassi said: "He asserts repeatedly that comets are formed not otherwise than from these vapors when they pass beyond the shadow cone of the earth."[12] No cone of shadow was mentioned in the *Discourse* either, and the only reference there to smoky vapor applied to the aurora borealis, which is not carried upward. Since honest misunderstanding of Galileo's words cannot be credited to the author (or authors) of the *Libra*, deliberate distortion to discredit Galileo is evident; this is borne out by many other passages. The key to it may lie in the assertion: "I wish to say that here my whole desire is nothing less than to champion the conclusions of Aristotle."[13] Grassi had been far from doing, or saying, anything like that in his original lecture, in which his having located the comet far beyond the moon was in direct contradiction of Aristotle. Probably the intervention of high Jesuit authorities had compelled Grassi to pledge overt allegiance to Aristotle, since there is evidence later in this controversy that that policy was being ever more strictly enforced.

V

Early in January Galileo predicted to Fortunio Liceti, a professor of philosophy at the University of Padua, that the "companions" of Saturn would not again disappear from view as they had done late in 1612 until the year 1626. This long-range prediction is noteworthy because Saturn's ring did again become invisible about the time of the winter solstice of 1626. Galileo's forecast was sent in a private letter and not published by him, but Liceti published in a book printed in 1622.[14] It can hardly have been only a lucky guess, yet neither should Galileo be credited with having anticipated the discovery of Saturn's ring by Christiaan Huygens in 1655. Though Galileo clearly had some kind of theory about the changing appearances of Saturn, the only clue we have to it is found in the 1632 *Dialogue*. There he intimated casually that the appearance and disappearance of Saturn's "companions" resulted from rotation of the body of that planet during its revolution about the sun.[15] If he assigned to its rotation a period one-half that of Saturn's journey through the Zodiac, he may have expected the phenomenon to recur in 1627. Since he had no way of knowing how long the "companions" had been invisible before he noticed their absence in late 1612, it would not have been unreasonable for him to advance the prediction to the year 1626.

Although Cesi and other Linceans urged Galileo to reply to the *Libra*, he was reluctant to do so. Guiducci and Cesi joined him in dismissing the idea of a satirical answer. Lagalla, whose former intransigent Aristotelianism had considerably abated during his years of contact with Cesi, approved Galileo's preference not to reply at all. Stelluti suggested that Galileo write a reply in the form of a long letter to be addressed to some friend and include his philosophical opinions, in the manner of Galileo's rebuttal of Colombe on floating bodies—known to be his, though published over the name of Castelli.

In May 1620 Cardinal del Monte asked Galileo to make for him "a glass for seeing things close" in imitation of one taken from Rome to Florence by a painter. The painter's name was not mentioned, but he was probably a Venetian. In letters to Galileo from Sagredo shortly before his death in March 1620 he had made mention of his having such a device, with which he had enjoyed studying the details of paintings. This must have been equivalent to a modern reading glass, that is, a large, thick, doubly convex lens. It may seem surprising that such an invention had not been made much earlier; the probable reason is that sufficiently thick large glass blanks were normally made only for concave mirrors which did not require the same quality of glass. To grind a convex (let alone doubly convex) surface of large size also required new techniques and much time. However, Galileo made such a lens which he sent to the cardinal early in June. It was probably this event that led Galileo to investigate combinations of doubly convex lenses, from which in due course he made a number of compound microscopes. The year in which he perfected them is not certain, but he took one with him to Rome early in 1624. His description of a microscope he made for Cesi will be found in § VIII.

VI

In 1620 Guiducci protested the treatment he had received in the *Libra* by publishing a letter addressed to his former professor of rhetoric, Tarquinio Galluzzi of the Collegio Romano.[16] He had first considered replying directly to Grassi, but Cesi advised against that. Although Galileo probably participated in experiments described in Guiducci's letter countering those in the *Libra*, the letter was entirely Guiducci's. Following the advice of his fellow Linceans, Galileo decided to reply separately and asked their recommendations as to the third party to whom his letter should be addressed. Cesi first favored Father Grienberger, but other Linceans pointed out that this might only embarrass the one Roman Jesuit still friendly to Galileo. Ciampoli suggested Cesarini, who had been mentioned in the *Libra* and who was esteemed at the Collegio Romano. Galileo agreed to do this as soon as he had Cesarini's approval, and considered feigning ignorance in his reply that the *Libra* was truly the work of a professor at the Collegio. Cesi, however, assured him that the Jesuits were actually proud of Grassi's book. He advised Galileo at most to say that in replying he had been torn between the need to defend his reputation and his wish to retain the friendship of the fathers at the Collegio Romano. Two full years elapsed before Galileo finished his reply, which he did only under repeated prodding from other Linceans.

Probably one factor in Galileo's neglect of this project began with his receipt of a letter from Paris, dated 27 August 1620, in which Elia Diodati introduced himself. Diodati became Galileo's most important correspondent in France from that time on. He told Galileo that when Jacques Badovere was still living he had shown him letters from Galileo from which Diodati had known of the discovery of the satellites of Jupiter even before it was published (March 1610), as well as of Galileo's "singular speculations about the Pythagorean constitution of the universe" (that is, the Copernican system) and his work in mechanics. Since neither had yet been seen abroad, he asked Galileo what might be expected from him on these matters, inviting him to publish them in France if there were difficulties in Italy. Only a short extract from Galileo's reply survives; he explained that his proposed work on the system of the world had been restrained by a higher hand, while other controversies had retarded publication of his work on mechanics.

It is probable, however, that Diodati's suggestion started Galileo thinking again about the work, first promised in the *Starry Messenger*, which eventually emerged as the *Dialogue*. Another factor that probably distracted him from his scientific writings during the 1620s was the request by Cesarini that he turn his attention to modern Italian poetry. During this period he composed detailed notes for a comparison of Torquato Tasso with Ludovico Ariosto, strongly in favor of the latter, and late in life he ascribed whatever eminence he might have in literary style to his deep study of Ariosto. Though Galileo's Italian writings were always clear and good, there was a very marked trend of meticulous attention to words in his *Assayer* as compared with earlier writings, and still more in the *Dialogue*. In fact the manner in which Galileo accomplished the task of directing his readers' attention away from speculative philosophy to common observations of nature was fundamentally a linguistic device long used by poets but still novel at his time in the discussion of physics and astronomy.[17]

Early in 1621 several things happened which altered the circumstances of Galileo's life and work. Cosimo de' Medici died and was succeeded as grand duke by Ferdinando II, still a boy of eleven, under the regency of Christina and his mother. Pope Paul V also died, upon which event Rinuccini wrote that conditions at Rome were now much more favorable for men of letters and science, all the cardinals in line to succeed him as pope being men of a very different intellectual stamp. Gregory XV, the successor chosen in 1621, lived only two more years and was in turn succeeded by Maffeo Barberini, who in 1620 had composed a poem in "dangerous adulation" of Galileo.

Hardly any of Galileo's letters during 1621 have survived. By the middle of that year he had recovered from yet another illness. In December Cesi wrote to say that he rejoiced to hear that Galileo had finished his reply to Grassi's *Libra*, from which it appears that most of the *Assayer* was written, or at least drafted, during the second half of 1621. Ciampoli had been made papal secretary in charge of correspondence, a sign of the improving climate at Rome for intellectuals.

During these years Galileo supplied a large number of telescope lenses to various correspondents and there is little doubt that he ground these himself. There is no record of his employment at Florence of any craftsman assistant, as Mazzoleni had been employed at Padua, while an incidental remark in the *Assayer* concerned an observation made by Galileo when rounding a piece of glass by breaking its edges away. In 1621 he sent lenses to Tiberio Spinola at Antwerp on which the focal lengths and the initials GG were scratched. Spinola had told Galileo in May that on a visit to Holland he had visited the putative inventor of the telescope, who had shown him a six-foot instrument that was nevertheless incapable of revealing the things Galileo had seen in the heavens. This man said that his was the most powerful telescope possible, but Spinola replied that he had seen in France the far more powerful telescope made by

Galileo for Cardinal Joyeuse. Thus even after ten years, though scores of suitable telescopes had been made by Galileo at Florence and by Sagredo and a lens grinder at Venice, equivalent instruments were still rare elsewhere in Europe. Galileo told Spinola that the chief difficulty lay in obtaining glass of the necessary excellence.

VII

On 15 December Bonaventura Cavalieri wrote from Milan, where he had been transferred from Pisa by his order (Jesuate, not Jesuit) in June 1620. He had addressed several letters to Galileo earlier, discontented that his superiors at Milan had no appreciation of his mathematical studies and had expected him to employ himself mainly in rhetoric and preaching while studying with Castelli at Pisa. Previously he had asked Galileo to propose something he might work on; if Galileo did, its nature is uncertain (Galileo preserved Cavalieri's letters to him but his replies to Cavalieri are mostly lost). Now, late in 1621, there was a hint of what was to become Cavalieri's greatest work:

I attend continually to the study of mathematics and am demonstrating some propositions of Archimedes differently from him, and especially the quadrature of the parabola, different also from that [proof] of yours; and since a certain doubt assails me, which I shall explain, I desire your clarification of this.

The question is this, to which I put first this explanation: If in a plane figure any straight line be drawn, and then in that [figure] are drawn all possible lines parallel to it, I call these lines so drawn "all the lines of that figure"; and if in a solid there are drawn all possible planes parallel to a certain plane, I call these planes "all the planes of that solid." Now I want to know if *all* the lines of one plane [figure] have a ratio to *all* the lines of another; for it being possible to draw more and more of these forever, it appears that all the lines of a given figure are infinitely many and therefore lie outside the definition of magnitudes that have a ratio [to one another];[18] but then, since if the figure is enlarged, the lines are also made larger, [being] those of the first [figure] and also those additional that are in the excess of the enlarged figure over the given [figure], it appears that they do not fall outside that definition [Euclid Book Five, Definition Four]; hence I desire you to untie this

282

knot. If anything else occurs to me from time to time, I trust that you will favor me by enlightening me, content to waste a little time to show that you like this employment of mine, though of little moment.[19]

These definitions ("all the lines" and "all the planes") are two of the three used twelve years later in Cavalieri's book that opened one of the three paths that led to the infinitesimal calculus, except that he then made the parallels orthogonal to a chosen line or plane.[20] The infinitely many lines and planes (and later, points) constituted the "indivisibles" of plane figures and solids (and later, lines) used by Cavalieri, unlike the "actual infinitesimal" approach of Kepler, though the two were confused by Paul Guldin at the time, as by most modern historians of mathematics. Cavalieri never attempted to define "indivisibles" in general, by which he meant (in modern terminology) "designated elements of n dimensions within an entity having $n + 1$ dimensions."

Cavalieri had still not received an answer to his letter in February 1622 when he again wrote to say he supposed Galileo was too busy, but that he was going to send him some little geometric things that had passed through his imagination which he had not seen written elsewhere and which might seem very extravagant to anyone who did not consider them with due attention. It can hardly be doubted that these were some early fruits of his "method of indivisibles." He sent them on 22 March, having meanwhile satisfied himself as to the legitimacy of the ratios concerning which he had inquired before, appealing to Euclid Book Five, Defintion Four:

. . . for multiplying one of the said figures, "all the lines in the plane" (and "all the [plane] surfaces in the solid") are also multiplied, so that all the lines (or surfaces) [thus] increased can exceed [by multiplication] all the lines (or surfaces) of the others, and thus they will also be among the magnitudes that have a ratio. Then how I take these terms ("all the lines of a plane figure," or "all the [plane] surfaces of a solid"), I explain in this treatise. Please give me your opinion, which you may well believe I await with great desire, for then I shall send you also some other things about spirals.

In May, Galileo was urged by Cesarini to publish his reply to the *Libra*. Galileo had neglected this because of poor health. He had been elected Consul of the Florentine Academy in 1621, but at this time he asked to be relieved of duty by reason of repeated illnesses that had confined him to his home in Bellosguardo.

Toward the end of July Galileo thanked Fortunio Liceti for a book on new stars and comets written by that Paduan philosopher,[21] saying that his state of health had prevented his studying it but that he had glanced through it. Politely pretending that it deserved attention (which it did not, being an enormous volume of Peripatetic trivialities), he pretended that it had not arrived in time for him to mention this "atlantic labor" in his reply to the *Libra*, "forwarded several days ago to Rome." In fact Galileo's manuscript was not sent to Rome until October. He may have considered adding some replies to the intransigent Aristotelianism of Liceti, asking Guiducci to read through Liceti's book with that in mind, but in the end he confined his reply to Grassi's attack. Galileo's pretext for having omitted mention of Liceti was to come home to roost several years later.[22]

Late in October the completed reply to Grassi was received in manuscript by Cesarini, to whom the later printed book was to be addressed as a letter. Cesarini promptly sent it on to Cesi at Acquasparta in order that he might comment on any parts that might be too pungent or that might include doctrines not approved by Cesi, acting as head of the Lincean Academy by which it was to be published. Cesarini advised Galileo that the Jesuits at Rome had already got wind of it and would interfere with its licensing to be printed, if they could. At the end of 1622 Cesi returned the manuscript to Rome to be printed; it was called *Il Saggiatore*, meaning "the assayer," in allusion to the fine balance used for weighing gold as against the ordinary balance implied by Grassi's title, *Libra*.

The *Assayer* went well beyond the astronomical issues that had begun the controversy with Grassi. In order to counter his opponent's discussions of rotating solids and of fluids, brought in in connection with arguments about the structure of the heavens, Galileo introduced remarks about ships in water, river currents, stirred fluids, adhesion, and cohesion; in addition, he commented on the Aristotelian conception of motion as the cause of heat, examining instances in which heating is the result of friction. This led on to some discussion of the ways in which it is significant to postulate insensible particles by induction from observable particles, illustrating an approach Galileo considered proper in scientific investigations quite different from that of philosophical occult qualities. He regarded the physical entity heat as separable from the sensation of heat:

Many sensations which are deemed to be qualities residing in external objects have no real existence except in ourselves, and outside of us are nothing but names. I say that I am inclined to believe that heat is of this character. Those materials which produce heat in us and make us feel warmth, which [materials] we call by the general name of *fire*, would be a multitude of minute particles having certain shapes and moving with certain speeds. . . . I do not believe that in addition to [their] shape, number, motion, penetration, and touch, there is some *other* quality in fire which is "heat"; I believe that this belongs to us, and so intimately that when the animate and sensitive body is removed, "heat" remains nothing but a simple vocable.[23]

The distinction of our sensations from properties residing in external objects later became prominent in philosophy with John Locke's discussion of "primary" and "secondary" qualities. Galileo is often credited with its introduction and is sometimes said to have thereby alienated science from humanity. In fact the idea is much older, and Lucretius is probably the main source of its revival in the seventeenth century. What is striking about Galileo's discussion in the *Assayer* is its stress on the linguistic character of ordinary confusions about such concepts as that of "heat." Rather similar in this respect was his attack on the merely verbal aspect of the word *cause* as applied by his adversary:

Sarsi wants me to believe with Suidas that the Babylonians cooked their eggs by whirling them in slings. . . . I must say that the cause of this effect was very different from what he suggests. To discover the true cause I reason as follows: "If we do not achieve an effect which others formerly achieved, then it must be that in our operations we lack something that produced their success. And if there is just one single thing we lack, then that alone can be the true cause. Now, we do not lack eggs, or slings, or sturdy fellows to whirl them, yet our eggs do not cook but merely cool down faster if they happen to be hot. And since nothing is lacking to us except being Babylonians, then being Babylonians is the cause of the hardening of eggs, and not friction with the air."

VIII

Composition of the *Assayer* having been completed and arrangements having been made by the Lincean Academy for its publication at Rome, Galileo was able to turn his attention to other matters in 1623. It is probable that one of these was the perfection of the compound microscope, mentioned earlier as having awaited the grinding of doubly convex lenses, probably begun by Galileo only when he had been asked to make a reading glass for Cardinal del Monte in mid-1620. His description of an instrument made for Cesi indicates the degree of development probably reached by Galileo's compound microscopes during 1623, though the letter containing it is later. In 1625 the first printed illustrations of insects under the microscope appeared at Rome, made by using one of these instruments:

The object is attached to the rotating disc in the base, so that all [parts] can be seen, since that seen at each viewing is but a small part. The distance between the lens and the object must be precise, so in looking at objects that have relief one must be able to move the glass nearer or farther so as to see this or that part, whence the tube is made movable in its footing, or we may say its guide. It must be used when the air is clear and bright, and best in sunlight itself, getting the object well lighted. I have observed many tiny animals with great admiration, among which the flea is quite horrible, the gnat and the moth very beautiful; and with great satisfaction I have seen how flies and other little animals can walk attached to mirrors, upside down. . . . In short the greatness of nature can be infinitely contemplated, and [we may now see] how subtly and with what unspeakable care she works.[24]

At the beginning of 1623 Ciampoli wrote to Galileo with high praise for his treatise on the tides, having apparently received a copy of this from him with a letter indicating that it was being amplified. Cesarini notified Galileo that many Linceans had already read his reply to Grassi's *Libra* and were in agreement that some parts of it should be moderated or even omitted before it was printed. He asked Galileo for permission to make the necessary decisions about changes at Rome and proceed to print the book without further delay. The Jesuits there already knew what was in it through people to whom Cesarini had read the manuscript aloud, though they had not yet seen it. Cesarini intended also to have a fine Latin translation made, to be published later for the information of persons outside Italy.

About this time Campanella's *Defense of Galileo* had arrived at Rome from Frankfort in printed form; it had actually been written in 1616 at the height of the Copernican controversy. This now revived murmurings against Galileo at Rome. Jesuits at the Collegio Romano began to denounce publicly all the new discoveries, attempting to prove that there was no truth outside Aristotle. Cesarini had heard from Ciampoli that Galileo was expanding his treatise on the tides, which may be taken to mean that he was now seriously starting work on the book that was eventually to be published as the *Dialogue Concerning the Two Chief World Systems.*[25]

Early in February Father Niccolò Riccardi was appointed to examine the *Assayer* for the Holy Office before it could be printed. Riccardi not only approved it for printing, but wrote into the license special praise for it and for its author. Johann Faber, who had contributed a laudatory prefatory poem to the book, wrote on 3 March to say that printing would be assured the following week. Nevertheless, Cesarini advised Galileo that there were still a few changes in wording which were required to be made, though nothing substantial. Stelluti, who also contributed a prefatory poem, wrote in April to tell Galileo that his book would be out soon after Easter. Yet early in May, Ciampoli could tell Galileo no more than that printing had begun. Galileo thought that the license to print must have been held up, but on 27 May he received from Ciampoli the first two printed signatures to put his mind to rest on this.

On 24 June Maffeo Barberini wrote to thank Galileo for news about his nephew, Francesco Barberini, who had just received his doctorate at Pisa.[26] Then, in July, Pope Gregory XV died suddenly; Maffeo Barberini became Pope Urban VIII in August, to the intense joy of the Linceans. The engravings for the *Assayer* had not yet been made, so Galileo sent a design of his own for the title page. On 8 September, however, Stelluti notified him that this would not be used; it had been decided by the Lincean Academy that the book should be dedicated to Urban VIII and that the Barberini arms (three bees) should accordingly appear in the design of the title page. Galileo, ill again, sent his congratulations to the new pope on his election, forwarding this through Francesco Barberini, who was soon afterward made a cardinal and also elected to the Lincean Academy.[27]

Everything now suddenly appeared to be as auspicious as possible for Galileo, who notified Cesi that as soon as health permitted he would come to Rome to kiss the feet of the new pope and would then converse at length with the Linceans. Urban expressed delight on hearing that Galileo intended to visit Rome. A copy of the printed *Assayer* was sent to Galileo by Cesarini on 28 October 1623, saying that the pope was so charmed by it as to have it read aloud to him at table.

Grassi, when getting a copy of the *Assayer* from the bookseller at Rome on 1 November, remarked that though Galileo had consumed three years writing it, the Jesuits would remove it*s* sting in three months. This was an allusion to a sarcasm by Galileo, who had said that the *Libra* might more appropriately have borne the title *Scorpio*, its author having declared that the comet originated in that zodiacal sign and there being no lack of stings in his book for Galileo. At first, though Grassi complained of the *Assayer's* biting tone, he said that he would not reply in kind, and that indeed when Galileo came to Rome he wished to make friends with him. But then Grassi saw a letter from Florence in which it was said that the Jesuits would never be able to answer the arguments in the *Assayer*, whereupon his attitude changed. If the Jesuits could answer a hundred heretics every year, he said, they would know well enough how to deal with one Catholic.

Castelli told Galileo that it was being said in Pisa that had it not been for the protection of princes and cardinals in 1616, Galileo would have at once been put on trial by the Roman Inquisition. There may be some truth in this, for despite popular opinion about the antagonism of the church toward Galileo, he was never without support among cardinals and other churchmen of high rank, who merely happened in the end to be outvoted. The unanimity of hostility toward Galileo that existed among philosophers was not matched among church officials, though the former are often represented as friends of science and the latter as its enemies. In any event when Guiducci visited Rome in mid-December he found both the pope and Cardinal Barberini anxious to see him, as was also Father Grassi, with whom he held several conversations on scientific matters. The year ended with a letter to Galileo from Archduke Leopold of Austria, thanking him for the *Assayer*.

SIXTEEN

1624-26

I

On 16 JANUARY 1624 the Grand Duchess Christina informed Carlo Cardinal de' Medici that Galileo would soon come to Rome. Bad weather prevented his departure until the beginning of April. He paused to visit with Cesi at Acquasparta en route and talked at nearby Todi concerning the optics of spherical mirrors with G. B. Guazzarini, showing him that the focus of such a mirror was not a point but an interval along the axis. After fifteen days with Cesi, Galileo arrived at Rome on 23 April. The following day he was granted an hour's audience with Urban VIII, and on the 25th was received by Cardinal Barberini. These and like interviews made Galileo realize that he was getting old and was hardly up to the duties of a courtier.

To Cardinal Zollern, Galileo presented a microscope for the duke of Bavaria.[1] Faber, who wrote of this on 11 May to Cesi, observed a fly under this *occhialino* and was so astonished that he said Galileo was a kind of creator, having exhibited something no one before had known to have been created. Galileo held two long conversations with Zollern while at Rome and asked him to speak with the pope before returning to Bavaria. This request undoubtedly concerned Galileo's wish to publish his long-planned book on the system of the world.

By 8 June, when Galileo was preparing to return to Florence, he had had six audiences with Urban, who presented to him silver and gold medals and promised a pension to his son Vincenzio, to be administered by Ciampoli. Cardinals Zollern, Boncompagni, and Corbeluzzi had all spoken to the pope on behalf

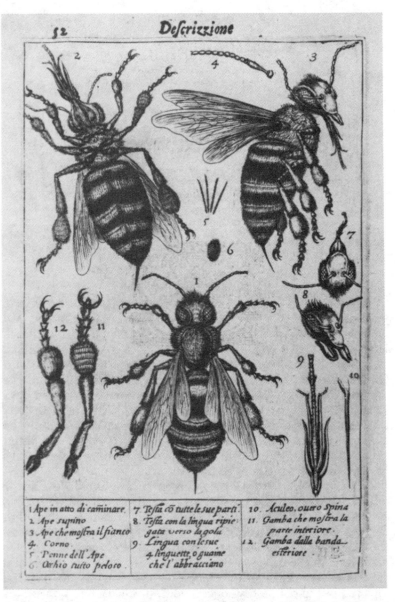

1 Ape in atto di caminare.	7. Teſta cō tutte le ſue parti.	10. Aculeo, ouero Spina
2 Ape ſupino	8. Teſta con la lingua ripie-	11. Gamba che moſtra la
3 Ape che moſtra il fianco	gata verſo la gola	parte interiore
4. Corno	9. Lingua con le ſue	12. Gamba dalla banda
5 Penne dell'Ape	4 linguette, o guaine	esteriore
6 Occhio tutto peloſo.	che l'abbracciano	

Studies of the bee made with a microscope taken by Galileo to Rome in 1624. First published as a broadside in Rome in 1625, this was reengraved for an Italian verse translation of the *Satire*s of Persius by Francesco Stelluti of the Lincean Academy, printed at Rome in 1630. (From the author's copy of that edition. Photo by University of Toronto Photographic Services.)

of Copernicus, though admitting that since his opinion was held by many Protestants any decision must be circumspect. The pope replied that the Holy Church had never condemned Copernicanism as heretical, and never would, holding it only to be rash, there being no fear that anyone would ever prove it true. Riccardi and the Jesuit Gaspar Schopp were convinced that Copernicanism was not a matter related to the faith. Riccardi's simple solution was that any system might be true because angels could guide the celestial bodies without difficulty however they moved.

On Galileo's departure the pope wrote to Grand Duke Ferdinand in praise of Galileo's science and his eloquence. Cardinal Barberini gave Galileo a letter to bear to Madame Christina and another to Ferdinand urging him to honor Galileo, who left Rome with assurances from Urban that he was free to write on the two systems of the world provided that he treated them impartially and did not go beyond the astronomical and mathematical aruguments on both sides. But because Bellarmine had instructed Galileo in 1616 to regard the admonition given him by the Commissary of the Inquisition as having no official existence, so long as Bellarmine's own words to him were heeded, Galileo never told Urban VIII what had actually taken place on that occasion. In the end that omission on his part turned out to have been a fatal error.

Guiducci did not return to Florence with Galileo but remained at Rome. Late in June he wrote to Galileo mentioning a treatise against the Copernican astronomy that had been written in 1616 by Francesco Ingoli, who was in charge of the recently created Propaganda Fidei.[2] Urban VIII appears to have mentioned this also, and perhaps to have suggested that Galileo reply to it, something he had been in no position to do in 1616. Galileo's instinct was to stay clear of controversies with men like Ingoli whose recognition, he said, had been earned through courtliness and piety. Guiducci, however, took the position that "it is necessary to review mercilessly their accounting; and if it is not presumptuous of me to advise you, I think that only those arguments which they call mathematical and philosophical should be answered, leaving out theology, at least for the present."

Guiducci was also hearing at Rome many rumors of a new battle threatened by Grassi, extending to the nonastronomical matters of which Galileo had written in his *Assayer*. It is not improbable that such a move was urged by Scheiner, who moved to Rome in 1624 and remained there until after Galileo's trial in 1633.

II

Shortly after Guiducci sent the unpublished treatise of Ingoli against Copernicus so that Galileo might reply to it, he fell ill at Rome. Grassi visited him during his convalescence and expressed a wish to be friendly. Among other things Grassi spoke of a work on the tides by Marcantonio de Dominis.[3] Guiducci told him that Galileo had written on the tides in terms of motions of the earth and was working to perfect this. "And here we fell to talking about the earth's motion, of which you write *ex hypothesi* and not as a principle established as true, whereupon the Father said that if a demonstration of that motion were found, it would be necessary to interpret Holy Scripture otherwise than had long been done . . . in the opinion of Cardinal Bellarmine. To that opinion I gave my complete assent." On a second visit they had spoken of Galileo's unpublished treatise on motion and his tables of the satellites of Jupiter. In this letter, dated 6 September, Guiducci mentioned that he had heard that Galileo had now finished his reply to Ingoli.[4]

A week later Guiducci wrote that Grassi had told him that a Greek Jesuit, Andrea Eudaemon-Ioannes, had informed him that while Galileo was still at Padua he had heard from him that a body dropped from a ship's mast fell to its foot whether the ship was moving or at rest.[5] Guiducci assured Grassi that this was true and had been confirmed by many experiments. Grassi at first would not believe this, and said that if it actually had been observed it must be due to the air moved by the ship. Guiducci replied that a moving person who drops a lead ball will be followed for some distance by the ball, which Grassi again wanted to attribute to air moved by the man's body, whereupon Guiducci said it would work even against a wind. Guiducci next brought up projectiles, saying that unless Galileo's proposition (of conserved motion) were true, the missile shot by a crossbow should fall immediately, since the bowstring moved very little air. They then went into a service that lasted an hour, at the end of which Grassi said he now understood what Guiducci had said, and was convinced. Thus, Guiducci told Galileo, he thought that Grassi would not abhor the earth's motion when good arguments were adduced and the contrary arguments refuted. He thought that

Grassi should be shown the reply to Ingoli if Galileo consented, though Grassi's praise of Galileo might be feigned.

III

Galileo's *Reply to Ingoli*[6] became a treatise of considerable size, in many ways a forerunner of the 1632 *Dialogue*, especially when we consider that Galileo was at the same time revising and expanding his treatise on the tides. The pretext for answering Ingoli eight years after he had written his arguments against Copernicus was that on a recent visit to Rome Galileo had come to realize that some people thought he had abandoned his Copernican views because he was convinced by Ingoli's arguments. Without asserting Copernicus to be correct, Galileo now wished to show that Ingoli's arguments were insufficient, considering only the astronomical and philosophical parts of Ingoli's treatise and leaving the theological part to the authorities. Galileo explained that it would not do for others to think that among Catholics nobody fully understood the force of Copernican considerations.

The first point cleared up was Ingoli's misapprehension of parallax. The second concerned his reasoning from constancy of magnitude of fixed stars that the earth must be fixed at their center. In this section Galileo cited his determination of the visual diameter of Jupiter as 40 seconds of arc, calculated in 1612 but not published, which implied that gross errors existed in all previous estimates of stellar diameters and sizes. Ingoli's third point involved the same mistake as that which had been made by Mazzoni in 1597.[7] It was similarly answered again, with the addition of a discussion of the supposedly disproportionate size of the stellar orb in relation to that of the solar system. Ingoli's fourth point was based on an error of Copernicus as to the eccentricity of Venus, which indeed needed correction but in no way disturbed the foundations of his theory.

Next came two arguments called by Ingoli "physical," of which the first was that since heavy bodies occupy lower places, the earth, as heaviest, is at the center. "You adduce the usual authority of philosophers," wrote Galileo, "to prove to me that the center ought to be called 'lowest' and the surface or circumference 'highest.' I reply that those are words and names, proving nothing and having nothing to do with calling anything into existence."[8] Ingoli's second physical argument adduced an analogy between planetary orbits and motions of grains of wheat in a winnowing sieve, irrelevant to motions around a single fixed center.

In arguing against the earth's diurnal motion Ingoli contradicted his own previous conclusions. Galileo took advantage of this discussion to mention his own experiment with objects dropped from the mast of a ship at rest and in motion and to explain the relativity and composition of motions.

I have been twice as good a philosopher as those others because they, in saying what is the opposite of the effect, have also added the lie of their having seen this by experiment; and I have made the experiment—before which, physical reasoning had persuaded me that the effect must turn out as it indeed does.[9]

Galileo also outlined briefly some arguments later repeated in his *Dialogue*, based on projectile motions, the flight of birds, and experiments made below deck on a resting and a moving ship.

In answering Ingoli's objections against the earth's annual motion, taken largely from Tycho, Galileo anticipated several arguments he was to use in his *Dialogue* and added this interesting comment concerning the irrelevance of the concept of "heaviness" to celestial physics:

Whence do you have it that the terrestrial globe is so heavy? For my part, either I do not know what heaviness is, or the terrestrial globe is neither heavy nor light, as likewise are all the other globes of the universe. Heaviness to me (and I believe to Nature) is that innate tendency by which a body resists being moved from its natural place and by which, when forcibly removed therefrom, it spontaneously returns there. Thus a bucketful of water raised on high and set free, returns to the sea; but who will say that this same water remains heavy *in* the sea, when being set free there it does not move?[10] . . . I tell you that if natural bodies have it from Nature to be moved by any movement, this can only be circular motion, nor is it possible that Nature has given to any of its integral bodies a propensity to be moved by straight motion. I have many confirmations of this proposition, but for the present one alone suffices, which is this. I suppose the parts of the universe to be in the best arrangement, so that none is out of its place, which is to say that Nature and God have perfectly arranged their structure. This being so, it is impossible for those parts to have it from Nature to be moved in straight, or in other than circular motion, because what moves straight changes place, and if it changes place naturally, then it was at first in a place preternatural to it, which goes against the supposition. Therefore, if the parts of the world are well ordered, straight motion is superfluous and not natural, and they can only have it when some body is forcibly removed from its natural place, to which it would then return by a straight line, for thus it appears to us that a part of the earth does [move] when separated from its whole. I said "it appears to us," because I am not against thinking that not even for such an effect does Nature make use of straight motion.[11]

Galileo adhered to this position in his *Dialogue*, at least as to the "integral bodies of the universe," by which he meant stars and planets, here called "parts of the universe." But he did not attempt to explain the planetary motions on any mechanical basis, nor does this argument from "best arrangement" have any bearing on inertial motion, which to Galileo was indifference to motion and rest and not a tendency to move, either circularly or straight.

IV

Galileo's reply to Ingoli was sent to Rome in October and enjoyed wide circulation in manuscript copies. Guiducci did not talk further with Grassi until the end of November, when he was asked if he might be named in Grassi's reply to the *Assayer*. Guiducci, who had thought there would be no reply, said that it did not matter to him and that he wished neither to consent nor refuse. Grassi told him that he was forced to write the reply; Guiducci did not ask him how he was forced, but asked if he had read Chiaramonti's *Antitycho* (which had no less refuted Grassi's original lecture), implying that if he had to reply to one book he should likewise reply to the other. He happened to have with him a letter of Galileo's in which "Sarsi" was defended against a feeble argument of Chiaramonti's, and read this to Grassi, who was pleased that Galileo had explained his point so clearly. Though he asked Guiducci to assure Galileo that he thought very highly of him, Guiducci decided not to show him the *Reply to Ingoli*.[12]

Meanwhile Chiaramonti had moved to the University of Bologna, where it was rumored that he was going to publish a book against the earth's motion and against Galileo's theory of the tides. Accordingly Galileo requested Marsili, who had sent this information, not to give Chiaramonti copies of some recently sent manuscripts including "my Dialogue on the tides."

The word *dialogue* here indicates that Galileo had by now recast his 1616 discourse on the tides into dialogue form, as it was published in 1632. The erroneous statement that a twelve-hour period characterized the tides at Lisbon was removed, presumably on the basis of information received from Richard White in 1619, and two phenomena not discussed in the earlier version were given attempted mechanical explanations. One of these is of particular interest as giving the moon a role in the tides, though neither directly nor in the manner of any previous tide theory. To be explained were the monthly variations from spring to neap tide and back, of which no previous mechanical account had ever been offered.

In Galileo's theory the existence of tides depended on changes in absolute speed occasioned by composition of the earth's diurnal and annual motions, in which case the sizes of tides would be affected by relative changes in those two components. On the assumption that the force driving the earth and its attendant moon around the sun remains constant, Galileo reasoned that the annual motion would be speeded when the moon is between the earth and the sun, and would be slowed when the moon moved behind the earth; in that way the moon would appear to be altering the sizes of tides though it would not be acting directly on the seas.

The other argument now added concerned differences in size of tides duing the year, for tides were said to be greater around the solstices by ancient writers such as Strabo and Posidonius. Galileo derived this supposed effect from seasonal changes of the angles at which annual and diurnal motions are compounded at any given latitude. Since in fact the greater tides occur around the equinoxes, this explanation was countered by the facts though it fitted the data on which Galileo relied. The actual effect is scarcely discernible in the Mediterranean, most of which is virtually a tideless sea.

Ciampoli wrote to Galileo at the end of 1624 to say that he was glad that the (tidal) Dialogue was nearly finished. He had read the *Reply to Ingoli*, much of which had also been read to the pope, who greatly enjoyed certain examples and experiments in it. Ciampoli also thanked Galileo for his promise to send a "treatise on the rudder." The contents of this are known only from fragments of uncertain date; they included discussions of the rudder, navigation against the wind, the potential increase in speed of a vessel by adding more pairs of oars, and the question how it was possible to sail against the wind. Possibly the lost treatise was organized from work done at Padua, where such questions were of more general interest than at Florence.

V

Early in 1625 Galileo was progressing well with composition of his future *Dialogue*. Guiducci suggested that he add to it something in answer to Richard White, who had objected to Galileo's treatment of the surface of water as level in *Bodies in Water*, whereas Archimedes had treated such surfaces as spherical, like that of the earth.[13]

A letter from Ciampoli in February indicates that Galileo was then writing something on "strength." This is a slender clue, though I think a valuable one, to the probable time of composition of a singularly interesting manuscript critique of some scheme offered to the Tuscan government by an inventor. The idea behind the scheme was to use a heavy counterweight to enable a man to accomplish tasks alone which would ordinarily require the strength of many men. A part of Galileo's discussion is translated below.

I cannot deny that I was admiring and confused when, in the presence of the Grand Duke and other princes and gentlemen, you exhibited the model of your machine, of truly subtle invention, conceived and built for use in overcoming with little force very great resistances, which was then applied to draw up with a pump, with little work, a quantity of water that without the help of your invention would require more work; and what caused my great admiration was my seeing you make use of a means which it seems to me anyone would judge should not facilitate the task, but make it much more difficult. For taking a force that lacks the power to raise 100 pounds of weight, who would think that by adding to this 100 [another] 1000, it [the force] would [then] lift the whole? And to increase my stupor, that the added 1000 [of load] should be that which strengthened the weak force of the mover? I saw it, and I myself tried with a simple light bent lever to raise a weight of (I think)

40 pounds with a limited force which was insufficient for the
the effect; then you weighted the said lever with more than 200
pounds of lead, and trying again to raise those first 40 pounds
with the same force, you were seen to lift these and [also]
the 200 [extra] with the same[bent part of the] lever, which
hanging perpendicularly made its motion upward, when driven,
so that (I repeat with the same admiration) the weight of
40 pounds which such a force could not raise with such a lever
weighing no more than two pounds, was freely raised by the
same force using the same lever made heavier by 200 pounds.

And since I long ago formed the idea, confirmed by many
experiments, that nature cannot be overcome and defrauded by
art, I remained admiring and confused to see such a marvel;
and being unable to put my mind at rest or stop it from thinking
about this case, I have made an accumulation of thoughts and
have decided to put them on paper and communicate them to
you in order that if the success of your truly acute invention
is seen in practice, and in very large machines, I may be excused
by you, and through you excused by others. For the difficulties
that I shall advance are not entirely unreasonable, and if inconclusive, they are in part at least probable; and if sometimes,
in the discourse I am about to make, there is something to raise
a doubt about your assumptions and foundations, you may by
the acuteness of your mind use appropriate remedies. For as
a man of honor I affirm to you, and I call God as my witness,
that I very much desire the success of this invention, [hoping]
that such an instrument may be advantageous above all others,
rather than the contrary, even though I have allowed myself
to understand in general that all machines are of equal value
as to the effect to be carried out by them, whenever those
impediments are removed that belong to matter; from which
it follows that the simpler the machines are, the less they are
subjected to impediments, and are consequently better in
operation. When I say that nature does not permit [herself] to
be overcome or defrauded by art, I mean (keeping to the matter
under discussion) that Nature having conceded to me for
example 10 degrees of force, which is to say the strength to
match 10 degrees of resistance, she denies to me and will not
permit me by any artifice to overcome more of this than 10
degrees; and I add moreover that she vetoes the application of
all my force of 10 degrees in overcoming or moving a resistance
that is of only 6 degrees, or in any way less than 10. And who
would say that when with all my force I break a cord, I would
or could use the same whole force in breaking a slender thread?

Or that if with all my force I raise a weight of 100 pounds,
I would use the same in raising one of 10?

This first statement of mine, that by no artifice is it possible
that any force should overcome or move any resistance greater
than it, seems to have against it a great many experiences in
which we see, not without marvel, very great weights moved
with very small force. Let us consider the steelyard, where
a counterweight weighing no more than 10 pounds is clearly
seen to balance and lift a bale that weighs more than a thousand.
Look at the winch; is it not seen that with the force of one man
a 3000-pound stone is raised on high? And is not that a conquering
by artifice of an immense resistance with a small force? Good;
but I, my dear sir, shall argue exactly the opposite from these
experiences, wondering how that 1000-pound bale *cannot* raise
the counterweight that resists only with 10 [pounds], and
why the 3000 [pounds] of the great stone does not push the man,
whose force is barely equal to the moment of 100 pounds.
From these two instruments, therefore, there cannot be drawn
more truly the consequence that artifice gains 100 or 300 to 1,
than that it misses and doubly loses 100 or 300. From these two
equally conclusive and contrary consequences, the true conclusion to be drawn is that artifice, in so far as making force is
concerned, gains nothing over natural resistance, and the esteem
we have for it [mechanics] comes from the convenience and
utility we obtain from it, since we make use of the counterweight
a thousand times daily to raise and weigh bales, or of men to
raise on high very heavy stones, but rarely or never do we
use bales to lift up counterweights, or stones to drive down
lifters. . . .[14]

Two other ways, seemingly different from the above, appear
to have been found by art to overcome great resistances with
very small force. One is the stroke or blow or percussion to
which it seems that there is no resistance that does not yield.
The other is to make, as I shall put it, a conservation and
accumulation of forces aggregated together; this is done when
I impress my force, say of 10 degrees, in a moveable that
conserves these for me, returning to impress as much again,
so that added with the first 10 degrees, 20 are found in that
which conserves this; and continuing to impress time after time
another and another 10, there are gathered in the conservation
100, 200, and 1000 degrees of power, capable of overcoming
very great resistances, against which my first strength of 10 is
of no effect. A suitable example of such conservation of force is
that very heavy pendulum, adapted to the lever by you yourself,

which, receiving impulses from the weak force, makes a conservation of them and an accumulation, or so to speak makes a capital of these so great that one can then go distributing and applying the excess to overcome resistances that the first force would be far from sufficing to move.[15]

Instancing olive presses as an example of accumulated impulses, Galileo went on to analyze the power that could be accumulated in the weighted bent lever, its dissipation in successive strokes against the pump or mill to be operated, and the incapability of the operator to do more work in this way than in any other. Of special interest is the notion of conservation introduced here, above and beyond the idea of equality of moments in connected machines in equilibrium used in Galileo's earlier *Mechanics*, and his striking illustration of the necessary connection between measures of force and of the resistance encountered by it. A similar commentary on a milling machine supposed to do more work by multiplication of moving parts revealed a similar illusion of inventors of the period, one of Galileo's duties having been to protect the grand duke from waste of public funds on worthless schemes.

It is not unlikely that Galileo further revised his treatise on mechanics about this time, amplifying its opening section about the real and fancied advantages gained from machines. At any rate the *Mechanics* again began to circulate, this time with Galileo's name on it, and copies reached both France and England in 1626. It was translated into English by Robert Payen in that year, but not printed.[16] Marin Mersenne published his French translation of it in 1634 together with commentaries of his own.

VI

Marsili and Guiducci were made members of the Lincean Academy in February 1625. In March Galileo fell ill and put aside his work on the *Dialogue*, on which he worked only sporadically during the next three years. In April he learned from Guiducci that some "pious person" had attempted to have his *Assayer* prohibited, or at least corrected, by the Holy Office. This person may well have been Scheiner, who had moved to Rome the year before. The complaint that Galileo had praised Copernicanism in the book was simply false. It was assigned for review to Giovanni di Guevara, whose opinion was that even if it had, the book ought not to be condemned. But Guevara had gone to

France in the company of Cardinal Barberini, and since no churchman then in Rome was likely to support Galileo, Guiducci thought it advisable for him to hush up his reply to Ingoli in which Copernican opinions were indeed defended. This information and advice persuaded Galileo to stop work on the *Dialogue* for some time. Guiducci also mentioned that though Cardinal Orsini remained affectionate toward Galileo, he had meanwhile become very friendly with Scheiner—a relationship that was destined to have unfortunate consequences for Galileo in later years.

In the *Assayer* Galileo had mentioned Chiaramonti with approval. Marsili now wrote, in March 1625, about an argument of Chiaramonti's against Copernicus. Galileo replied that he might find a place to answer this in his *Dialogue*, adding that he no longer thought that much was to be expected from Chiaramonti. Right at this time Kepler was predicting that Galileo would not long continue to praise Chiaramonti, whose attack against Tycho he was then refuting in a book called *Hyperaspistes*.[17]Later the same year Chiaramonti wrote to tell Galileo that he had received a copy of that book and that it contained an appendix commenting on the cometary controversy between Galileo and "Sarsi."

Castelli was called to Lodi in 1625 to give his expert opinion in a dispute between Bologna and Ferrara over hydraulic matters. While there he wrote to suggest that Cavalieri be given a chair of mathematics, and from later events it is probable that what he had in mind was his own chair at Pisa. In order to attain a professorship, Cavalieri realized that he must study astronomy and wrote for advice to Galileo. Since he did not mention the manuscript on indivisibles he had previously sent, it is probable that he had already received comments on it from Galileo.

Castelli went to Rome in October and soon afterward was appointed by Urban VIII to superintend water engineering and drainage works there. Back at Pisa in November, he announced to Galileo his discovery that the rate of flow in a river at different heads is given by the product of the ratios of speeds and heights. Galileo replied on 21 November, delighted to hear of his former pupil's advances in hydraulic theory: "I await with interest the last three propositions and their proofs; I say those three, because this first is clear." His reason for saying this was that the use of compound ratios to express continuous functions had become second nature to Galileo from his work in mechanics, strength of materials, and accelerated motion, so that it was evident to him that, as he wrote: "The height being the same, the water flowing is as the speed; the speeds being the same, the water flowing is as the height; hence when both height and speed vary, the water flowing has the ratio compounded from the two."

Castelli thanked Galileo for his reflections about the flow of rivers and asked him to consider the "key" to the principal phenomena involved. Galileo's only surviving papers on this subject date from 1630, when he was asked to decide between two rival schemes for flood control along the Bisenzio River. From those later papers it appears that the "key" meant was the fact that the flow of water differs fundamentally from the descent of a solid body along a slope, being affected not only by the incline but also by its own motion of leveling itself, as discussed in the next chapter. At the end of 1625 Galileo told Castelli he was considering the acceleration of water passing through a narrow channel when the bed of the river has uniform slope.

On 10 December Marsili forwarded a letter of Galileo's to Chiaramonti and asked him for a copy of Kepler's *Hyperaspistes*. Chiaramonti promised to send one to Marsili with some further writings of his own, and Marsili told Galileo he would forward it to him. Galileo received it early in 1626, having also heard of Kepler's book from Cesi and Stelluti.

VII

A letter from Cavalieri at the end of February 1626 is the first to mention that Galileo had decided to write a book on indivisibles. Cavalieri had recently visited Galileo on his way to Rome, telling him that he had begun to think about motion and planned next to write on this and on refraction, being still in search of something to show to university authorities in support of his candidacy as professor at Pisa. He wrote again on 21 March to say that Castelli had arrived in Rome to take up his position under the pope. Cavalieri had meanwhile found himself unable to prove that a body starting from rest and acquiring any speed must have first passed through all intermediate speeds, and asked Galileo to send him a proof if he had one.[18] Cavalieri wished to employ his time in rediscovering what "you have already found in those uncompleted materials to which you were not applying your mind," presumably Galileo's neglected notes on motion.

Meanwhile he hoped that Galileo would proceed at once with his work on indivisibles so that Cavalieri might then come out with his own, which he was continuing to polish. Thus it appears that on their meeting at Florence early in 1626, Galileo had asked Cavalieri to hold back his book on indivisibles until Galileo had published his own reflections on the nature of continuous magnitude, to which Cavalieri had agreed. Meanwhile he had heard that Aggiunti was to have the chair at Pisa vacated by Castelli.

Galileo replied to a suggestion from Bartolomeo Imperiali at Genoa, saying that he would not seek a reconciliation with Grassi at a time when that might inhibit the Jesuit from publishing his reply. Imperiali considered this a generous action and told Galileo that Baliani also had tried to dissuade Grassi from fighting a lost cause. A letter from Galileo to Cesi at the end of March shows that he had thought of replying to Kepler's critique of his dispute with Grassi, doing this in the form of a letter to Chiaramonti which the latter could add as an appendix to the defense he was writing against the *Hyperaspistes*; but since Galileo himself was strongly opposed to Chiaramonti's position he had decided instead to confute Chiaramonti in "another work of mine," meaning the *Dialogue*. If Cesi wished, Galileo could address his letter in reply to Kepler to him instead, which Cesi could then forward to Chiaramonti. Galileo also told Marsili he would write out his comments on the Kepler appendix and send them to him, to use as he wished with regard to Chiaramonti.

At this time an engineer at Bologna was exhibiting a certain ampule containing seawater which he claimed imitated the tides. Galileo replied to Marsili concerning this, saying that twenty years earlier he had, for fun, shown what he believed to be the same thing. It had nothing to do with the tides; seawater was unnecessary, as fresh water would do the same thing. The effect was only that of difference of air temperature by day and by night. It is evident that Galileo took the device to be a kind of thermoscope in which the water would rise in the neck at night when the contained air cooled and contracted, falling again during the heat of the day. Marsili wrote in June to say that the device had indeed proved to be a vanity so far as explaining the tides was concerned, but had since been applied to some different use that he had not yet been able to see.

In mid-1626 Galileo was once more engaged in magnetic experiments, surpassing William Gilbert's results from the armaturing of pieces of lodestone. It is highly probable that the part of the *Dialogue* relating to Gilbert[19] was written in 1626. Chiaramonti published his reply to Kepler, sent a copy to Galileo, and said that his next book would be on the new stars of 1572 and 1604 and on the comet of 1577. It was this book that Galileo chose for his devastating criticism of Chiaramonti in the *Dialogue*.[20]

On 29 August Galileo wrote to Marsili concerning a story that a large concave mirror made at Bologna had served as a telescope. Several letters on this had been exchanged previously; Galileo now said that he believed an additional lens or sighting device would be required, though not having such a mirror he had not tried the effect. In volume 83 of the Galilean manuscripts there is a large folding diagram and mathematical analysis labeled *Teorica speculi concavi sphaerici*, or theory of concave spherical mirrors.[21] Others have assigned to this the date of December 1610, for no clear reason. At that time Galileo was so busy day and night with the improvement and use of the refracting telescope that the elaborate calculations required for the *Teorica* are unlikely to have been carried out, nor would they have assisted him in any work he is known to have done at Padua. More probably it belongs to mid-1626.[22]

Giovanni di Guevara, who had defended the *Assayer* against suppression by the Holy Office, visited Galileo in the company of Cardinal Barberini on their return from France and in November 1626 wrote to him from Rome. This opened a correspondence concerning the so-called "wheel of Aristotle" that was to occupy an important place in Galileo's treatment of continuous magnitude in *Two New Sciences*.[23] Though it is probable that Galileo had arrived at his analysis of the wheel paradox a very long time before, and had certainly discussed it with Guevara at Florence, the event indicates something he had had in mind earlier in the year when he spoke to Cavalieri about writing a book on indivisibles.

Cavalieri was then investigating volumes of solids generated by the revolution of conic sections, ultimately incorporated into his *Geometry by Indivisibles of Continua*. Though not published until 1635, that work appears to have been substantially completed by the end of 1626, except for a final section (called "the seventh book") of which more will be said in later chapters.

At the end of 1626 Aggiunti complained to Galileo that his *Dialogue* had been neglected so long that it began to look as if he were never going to finish it. Galileo was told that Grassi had printed his reply to the *Assayer*, copies having reached Rome from Paris where it appears to have been sent for publication after some difficulties about having that done in Italy.

SEVENTEEN

1626-31

ON 20 FEBRUARY 1627 Baliani wrote to Castelli concerning a book he had written (not published until 1638) on motions of solids along inclined planes. He wished to add something to this about fluid motions, but had encountered difficulties. Consulting Castelli about these, he mentioned incidentally that he had found a proof for a proposition Galileo had given to him—that in natural motion bodies increase their speeds in the ratios of 1, 3, 5, 7, and so on forever. Galileo had not offered any proof, "but adduced a probable argument—that only in this proportion will more or fewer spaces keep always the same ratio."[1] What was meant was that in that arithmetical progression alone is it true that the ratio of the first term to the second is also the ratio of the first two terms to the second two, or the first three to the second three, and so on. It follows that whatever arbitrary unit of time is chosen in measuring successive distances from rest, the cumulative distances will always be related as the successive squared numbers from unity.

Galileo was again considering accelerated motion in 1626–27, his interest having perhaps been reawakened by Cavalieri's inquiry whether he had a proof that in reaching any speed from rest, a body must have passed through every possible smaller speed. Some of Galileo's notes on motion, especially those watermarked "pilgrim," appear to belong to this period. These relate to a preliminary solution of a difficult problem on which Galileo had begun work at Padua, which became Proposition Thirty-Four in *Two New Sciences*, and to the related Propositions

Fourteen, Fifteen, and Thirty-Three. The handwriting of these notes differs appreciably both from that of the earlier period and that of 1630–31, when Galileo seriously resumed work on his long-neglected treatise on motion.[2]

In April 1627 there was a dispute at Florence over the proper mathematical treatment of errors in estimation on which Galileo's opinion as referee was requested and given. He favored the use of ratio of discrepancy to correct value, rather than amount of discrepancy. This was not accepted by some parties to the dispute, which then spread to involve Nozzolini, Castelli, and Andrea Arrighetti.[3] It was about a year later that Galileo applied his theory of error in estimation to confute Chiaramonti in the matter of differences between skilled observers on an astronomical question, incorporating this in the *Dialogue*.[4]

Ciampoli wrote in July to implore Galileo not to neglect the writing of the *Dialogue*, as his friends at Rome were beginning to fear it would be lost to the world forever. The plea appears to have had its effect, for in September Cesi wrote of his pleasure at hearing good news from Galileo concerning both his health and his work. Soon after this Galileo learned that a prize of 30,000 florins had been deposited at The Hague for anyone who could establish a correct method of determining longitudes at sea. He wrote at once to learn more about the people concerned, especially as to their understanding of mathematics, having found out through long experience that it was a waste of time to deal with diplomats and naval officers alone in this matter.

In December Cavalieri complained of Galileo's varied occupations that were keeping him from replying to repeated inquiries. Cavalieri had sent to Ciampoli the book Galileo had seen in rough draft, now completed to the best of Cavalieri's ability: "not having changed my foundation in what I call 'all the lines of a figure' or 'all the planes of a solid,' since those appear to me sufficiently established by evident and sound reasons." He wished at least the approval of Castelli (if not Galileo) before publishing his method of indivisibles. Galileo had not replied earlier because of a serious illness late in 1627. He now pointed out an error in one proposition, acknowledged and corrected by Cavalieri in January 1628. Meanwhile Castelli had invited Cavalieri to come to Rome and publish his book there.

Guevara, who was writing a commentary on the *Questions of Mechanics*, wrote for Galileo's analysis of the "wheel of Aristotle," recalling their conversation about this at Florence a year before. Galileo assured him that ratios between infinite aggregates of points were legitimate, the question that had troubled Cavalieri in 1622. Galileo had employed such ratios repeatedly since 1604, but long after that remained hesitant to endorse them in pure mathematics. He was conscious of the paradoxes that arise without the most careful definitions relating to infinite aggregates. Cavalieri's continued adherence to his own definitions of 1622 and his wish for approval of them suggests that Galileo's conversation with him in 1626 had centered on the need for defining "indivisibles of continua," never done by Cavalieri.

In May 1628 Chiaramonti sent to Galileo his book *De tribus novis stellis* in which he attempted to show that new stars and comets must be beneath the moon. Though Chiaramonti knew about Galileo's earlier battle with Cremonini, he appeared to think that Galileo was going to agree with this Aristotelian position. As Kepler had predicted in the appendix to his *Hyperaspistes*, Galileo now ceased to speak well of Chiaramonti. In the *Dialogue* this book of Chiaramonti's was singled out for vigorous attack at the beginning of the Third Day, which was probably written in mid-1628. Not much else was done on the *Dialogue*, however, until a year later, despite the urging of friends.

Nearly all the surviving correspondence from 1628 consists of letters from Galileo's brother Michelangelo and from his daughter Virginia, known in her convent at Arcetri as Sister Maria Celeste, or else from Castelli relating to another family problem. Castelli was superintending the education of Galileo's son Vincenzio and also Michelangelo Galilei's son of the same name. Galileo's son resented his having been sent to Rome, which had been done chiefly because his cousin had been put in Castelli's charge by Galileo when he became responsible for his education at the request of his brother, who had recently visited Italy.

Galileo became the subject of a legal dispute in 1628, the University of Pisa having raised the issue whether they were obliged to pay him under the old contract of 1610, by which Cosimo de' Medici had freed Galileo of obligation to reside and teach at Pisa. This was resolved late in 1629 in favor of the grand duke and Galileo. Thus the correspondence of 1628 gives little clue to Galileo's scientific activities in that year. He considered replying to the second "Sarsi" book,[5] which he annotated sarcastically, but in the end he agreed with Cesi and others at Rome that it was unworthy of the dignity of an answer.

The chair of mathematics at Bologna vacated by Magini's death in 1617 had never been filled, so when P. A. Cataldi, holder of the other chair, died in 1626 it became necessary to fill one of these. Cavalieri was strongly recommended by Galileo in 1628. At the end of that year Castelli sent his book on the measure of running waters, which Galileo highly praised, but made one suggestion concerning it. In replying, Castelli mentioned that Scheiner's large new book on sunspots, begun in 1626, was expected to appear soon.[6] Three days later Castelli described a particularly large sunspot that had been observed until 9 January 1629, passing from view on that day and returning recognizably on the 24th.

These events probably had much to do with Galileo's resumption of work on the *Dialogue* and its completion in 1629, as will be seen. Printing of Scheiner's elaborate book had gone slowly at the Orsini family's press, and though Castelli thought it was nearing completion after three years, it was not in fact issued until mid-1630. Castelli's mention of it, however, probably stimulated Galileo to finish his own book and at the same time reawakened his interest in sunspot phenomena, with important consequences, mentioned later in this section and discussed further in chapter 18, § I.

A letter from Cavalieri to Cesare Marsili[7] at Bologna dated 27 February declared that Galileo had praised his book on geometry and encouraged him to publish it. This was evidently a recent development connected with Cavalieri's candidacy for the chair at Bologna, since three years earlier Galileo had asked Cavalieri to defer publication of his *Geometry by Indivisibles* until Galileo had disclosed his own work on the nature of continuous magnitudes.

In March 1629 Guevara sent Galileo his commentary on the *Questions of Mechanics*.[8] This book bears the date 1627, but was not published until 1629 because Guevara wanted further information from Galileo about ratios of infinite sets of points. In transmitting the book, Guevara said that he had awaited Galileo's reply for more than a year concerning the difficulty that troubled him in Galileo's remarks on the "wheel of Aristotle." Galileo praised Guevara's book in his later *Two New Sciences*,[9] though its treatment of that problem was quite different from his own.

Galileo's correspondence with Marsili had been interrupted for a time owing to a false rumor that the latter had died; in fact he had merely broken an arm and was unable to write for a while. On 7 April Galileo wrote to him again, and from his letter it is evident that the part of the *Dialogue* criticizing Chiaramonti (opening of the Third Day) had been completed. In another letter dated 21 April Galileo mentioned his having heard that Scheiner was publishing a long treatise on sunspots, remarking that it must be full of errors and irrelevancies because Galileo was sure that everything worth saying on that subject had already been put into his own book in 1613. This makes it certain that up to the end of April 1629 the important section of the *Dialogue* arguing for motion of the earth from the observed paths of sunspots had not yet been written. Except for minor additions, polishing, and recopying the whole manuscript for the printer, everything else in the book appears to have been done.

In August Cavalieri was appointed for three years to Magini's former chair at Bologna. About the same time Galileo suddenly took up the *Dialogue* again, writing to Diodati at the end of October:

And to give you some news about my studies, you must know that a month ago I took up again my *Dialogue* about the tides, put aside for three years on end, and by the grace of God have got on the right path, so that if I can keep on this winter I hope to bring the work to an end and immediately publish it. In this, besides the material on the tides, there will be inserted many other problems and a most ample confirmation of the Copernican system by showing the nullity of all that had been brought by Tycho and others to the contrary. The work will be quite large and full of many novelties, which by reason of the freedom of dialogue [form] I shall have scope to introduce without drudgery or affectation.

The principal novelties found in the *Dialogue* are the development of Galileo's conception of the physical relativity of motion, extended considerably beyond the discussion in his *Reply to Ingoli*, and his argument for motion of the earth from the annual variation in paths of the sunspots. This argument probably occurred to Galileo for the first time in mid-1629. Knowing that his rival Scheiner was again writing on sunspots, he went through his old papers on the subject and in that way came again upon the letter written in 1613 by Francesco Sizzi to Orazio Morandi, who had forwarded it to Galileo shortly after the printing of the *Sunspot Letters*. Preserved among Galileo's papers are both the original letter and a copy with corrections in Galileo's hand. Sizzi's letter reminded Galileo of the fact of annual variation in the apparent paths of sunspots, and now the strength of that fact as an argument for some motion of the earth, either around its axis or around the sun, or both, became suddenly clear to him. His remark to Marsili in April 1629 that there was nothing left to be said about sunspots shows that he had completely overlooked the possibility of this argument in the past. Recognition of its importance, I believe, was marked in the foregoing letter by the words "and a most ample confirmation of the Copernican system." Thus it was about September 1629 that Galileo suddenly decided to complete his *Dialogue* and get it to a printer as swiftly as possible.

On Christmas Eve 1629 Galileo wrote to Cesi that having taken up his pen again a couple of months before, he had now brought the *Dialogue* to virtual completion: "I lack the ceremonial introduction and the arrangement of the opening of the dialogue [to agree] with the things that follow; these are matters more rhetorical and poetic than scientific, though I do want it to have some spirit and charm." He wondered if he should move to Rome while the book was being printed, where Cesi intended to have it appear under the auspices of the Lincean Academy. In January 1630 the finished *Dialogue* in manuscript was being read at Pisa at the house of Canon Niccolò Cini "to the infinite applause and admiration of everyone," as reported by Aggiunti.

Difficulties began at Rome early in February 1630 when Castelli mentioned to Cardinal Barberini that Galileo assumed motions of the earth to explain the tides. Barberini objected that this would make the earth a star, against the theologians. Galileo's friends at Rome felt that all would go well, however, because Riccardi was in charge of the licensing of books and he was most favorable to Galileo. In March it was reported by Cesi that Campanella had told the pope about some Germans, who were about to be converted to Catholicism, having been scandalized to hear of the 1616 edict against Copernicus, upon which Urban had said: "That was never our intention, and if it had been up to me that decree would never have been issued."

Galileo arrived at Rome on 3 May 1630, where he lodged with Francesco Niccolini, the Tuscan ambassador to Rome. Niccolini advised the Tuscan court that though he was assisting Galileo and though Riccardi favored the new book, nevertheless he expected difficulties. Word spread soon that the *Dialogue* contradicted much that was held by the Jesuits. Correspondence during May and June shows that opposition to Galileo and his book remained constantly active but that Urban VIII and Cardinal Barberini counted themselves among his best friends. On 16 June Galileo was notified by Raffaelo Visconti, who had been assigned to review the manuscript, that Riccardi liked the book very much and would speak to the pope the following day about its title page; apart from the few little adjustments already agreed on, the book would then be returned to Galileo for printing. On 29 June the ambassador notified the grand duke's secretary that Galileo had left Rome entirely satisfied; the pope had been glad to see him, Cardinal Barberini had dined with him, and the whole papal court honored him.

A month after Galileo's return to Florence, Cesi died suddenly after a short illness during which he had refused to make a will. All the affairs of the Lincean Academy were thus thrown into confusion. It had always been Cesi's wish that the *Dialogue* would be published at Rome under the auspices of the Academy; hence Galileo had sought a Roman license and had left without any reason to think the matter was not settled. The sudden disorganization of the Linceans, however, revived the machinations of his opponents at Rome and precipitated a crisis.

II

Meanwhile Baliani had written to Galileo about a practical problem in physics. Genoa had installed a long two-inch pipe to bring water over the hills to the city, but found that when filled with water it behaved as if there were some leak of air at the top, the water running down on both sides of the summit. No leaks could be discovered. Galileo replied that he was sorry the work had been done without his having been consulted, as he had long before discovered the impossibility of operating a siphon higher than twenty braccia. (In *Two New Sciences* this figure was improved to eighteen, or about 34 feet.) Just as any rope or cable must break of its own weight if sufficiently long and suspended vertically, Galileo said, so also a "rope of water" must break; and water enclosed in a tube sealed at the top could be considered to be such a "rope." Neither the diameter of the pipe nor the total length mattered, but only the vertical height.[10]

At the end of this letter Galileo mentioned that he had been in Rome to license "the *Dialogues* that I write examining the two chief systems, Ptolemaic and Copernican, with regard to the tides, and having finally overcome some difficulties I have had it licensed and signed by [Riccardi] the Master of the Holy Palace. Had the season been different I would have stayed to have it printed, or else would have left it in the hands of Prince Cesi, who would take care of it as he has done other works of mine; but he was ill, and what is worse I now understand he is near death. So I sought a printer here, but there are neither the types nor compositors [suitable], and these times prevent my thinking of Venice. Please let me know how things stand there [in Genoa] in such matters, so that I may come to a decision."

A few days later Galileo learned that many arrests had been made at Rome in what was coming to be called the Great Case; this had to do with prosecution of astrological forecasters, including Galileo's good friend Orazio Morandi, the pope being much disturbed by some predictions inimical to his interests. Castelli had learned of Cesi's death and inquired of Visconti whether there was trouble about the *Dialogue*, but was assured there was none. About the first of September Galileo asked Castelli to speak to Riccardi, probably simply because he had not officially heard further about the license. Castelli's reply on 13 September mentioned his wish to consult Riccardi as soon as possible for some reason he could not put down on paper. At this time outbreaks of plague had alarmed Italy and commerce was suspended between many cities.

On 21 September Castelli reported that he had seen Riccardi and found him, as usual, well disposed toward Galileo. With regard to the book, however, Riccardi said that he had been awaiting Galileo's return to Rome for certain adjustments to the preface and text; now, in view of the plague, it would suffice to send a copy of the book to Rome where Riccardi could make the changes with Ciampoli, after which the *Dialogue* could be printed in Rome or elsewhere at Galileo's pleasure. Galileo negotiated permission to send Riccardi only the preface and the ending on condition that the whole book would be reviewed by the authorities at Florence, where Galileo had now decided that the book should be printed.

Baliani wrote a long letter concerning the siphon to Galileo in October. He said that ever since his first discussion with Galileo about the weight of air he had believed that a vacuum was not absolutely prevented by nature, though one could exist only by virtue of great force. He then gave a good account of various phenomena to be expected as a result of the weight of air, though in the end he doubted that his analysis could explain failure of a siphon even twice as high as the limit given by Galileo, let alone the failure at Genoa. Galileo did not pursue Baliani's correct approach in this letter; he adhered all his life to explanation in terms of the breaking strength of materials, likening water in a vertical pipe closed at the top to a rope or cable of solid material held from above.

III

Unworried about his *Dialogue*, though annoyed by its delays, Galileo now took up again his long-neglected treatise on motion. The short section on uniform motion was probably written in 1630, as well as a version of the prefatory material in the section on accelerated motion that in part is almost word for word the same as the text printed in *Two New Sciences*. A long and interesting part of this version, translated below, was omitted after Galileo hit upon the final form of Propositions One and Two, of which no text is found among his notes on motion. During 1630 and at the beginning of 1631 Galileo also reviewed all his previous notes, revised his treatment of one difficult problem, and added ten of the thirty-eight propositions that made up the final text.

About twenty of the final propositions have counterparts among Galileo's Paduan notes, counting among those some which survive only in copies made at Florence in 1618. As mentioned previously, he did nothing further on his projected treatise at that time. In 1626–27 he added notes on four propositions, starting from an unfinished problem among his latest Paduan notes. In 1630–31 he developed the following ten, as numbered in the final text.[11]

Propositions of *Two New Sciences*, Third Day, Book Two:
Eleven and Twelve (direct consequences of Proposition Ten)
Fourteen through Sixteen (diverted-motion problems and
  shorter-time theorem)
Twenty-One and Twenty-Two (related to Proposition Twenty-
  Three established at Padua)
Twenty-Seven through Twenty-Nine (from Proposition Twenty-
  Three, and a least-time theorem)

The manuscript version of the prefatory material to the treatment of accelerated motion in *Two New Sciences* differs from
the printed text by containing the material translated below; this
came between the part that was later printed and the formal
definition of uniform acceleration. A part of it was replaced by
a dialogue discussion immediately following that definition; the
rest was simply left out. It is of interest as providing clues to
the plan Galileo had in mind for presenting his new science of
accelerated motion. The manuscript has been variously dated by
editors, Favaro having assigned it to Padua. The ink and handwriting, however, show it to be Florentine, and other evidences
indicate late 1630 as the time of its composition.[12]

(And thus it is seen that we shall not depart far from the
correct rule if we assume the intension of speed to be made
according to the extension of time), unless something serious is
seen to disturb and weaken such an assumption. This, however,
being such that if, from the first beginning of motion from
rest, there is from then on an addition of perpetual new increments of swiftness according to the same rule and law [that]
according as the time run from the first instant, the same
perpetual new addition is taken on, it must be considered that
after the first instant there cannot be assigned any time so brief
that there does not intermediate [yet] another [and another],
still briefer and briefer, between this and the first instant. Just
so, after leaving rest, there cannot be assigned in motion any
degree of speed so tiny, or any [degree] of tardity so great,
that there is not another, still slower, in which the falling body
was previously constituted; so that tardity grows, or speed
diminishes, *ad infinitum*. And it will be necessary that any
moveable might possess such immense slowness of movement
that, with this motion, it would not traverse an inch in a whole
year. This seems miraculous or even absurd; yet what seems
remarkable is [in fact] neither false nor absurd, as experience
(powerful as any demonstration) can teach to everyone. Indeed,

we see that an iron or lead weight placed on top of a pointed
stake which we intend to drive into the ground will, by its mere
weight, push this to a certain measure and no farther; but if
the same weight, falling from on high, strikes on the stake, it
pushes it more and drives it deeper; and the more so, the
higher the place from which the blow is made. This new compression and impulse must be the effect of a new cause, that is,
of speed of the striking weight; and since we see the blows
become more powerful that come from the higher place—that
is, those which hit against this more swiftly—then from the
height, or rather from the speed of the striker, we may argue
the amount of penetration made by the stake; and, conversely,
the amount of penetration argues the speed of motion. Thus if
the blow of the striking device, driving the stake, has an effect
that is only minimally greater than that which originally
came from its simple weight, we may reasonably say that its
motion was minimal and very slow. And who does not see that
if a sledge resting on top of a stake is raised above it only an
inch, one thousand blows barely impel the stake; indeed, hardly
at all, or through any perceptible distance. And if it were lifted
only by the thickness of a sheet of paper, would not a thousand
blows hardly move the stake a nailsbreadth? Thus we know
that a moveable, even a very heavy one, will descend naturally
from rest, traversing every degree of slowness and pausing
in none; yet by the succession of instants of time it will always
acquire new degrees of swiftness. Many other experiences confirming the same thing could be set forth, which I establish
in my [treatise] *Of mechanical questions* [now lost] as a more
suitable place.

In this discussion it is necessary to note that to the same
degree of speed, others may be added in greater or lesser times,
for a variety of reasons, of which one will first be considered
by us, and this is the space over which the motion is made.
Indeed, a heavy body goes not only vertically toward the center
toward which all heavy bodies tend, but descends also over
planes inclined to the horizontal, more slowly on those of
greater tilt [from the vertical], and most slowly along planes
that are minimally above the horizontal. Finally [it is] infinite
in tardity, that is, at rest, on the said horizontal plane. Indeed,
so different are the various degrees of swiftness acquired in
motion that the degrees acquired by a heavy body falling
[vertically] in one minute will not be acquired over some inclined plane in a whole hour, or all day, or in an entire month,
or a year, though [it moves] with continual acceleration.
I can explain this by a suitable example.

316

Imagine to yourself the horizontal parallel *AB*, from the middle point *C* of which there descend two lines, *CD* and *CE*,

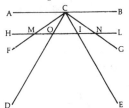

containing the acute angle *DCE*, and two others making at the same point *C* the obtuse [angle] *FCG*. Assume the line *HL*, at first coinciding with the horizontal line *AB* but then separated from that and descending in equable motion in such a way as always to remain parallel to *AB*. Now, since this descent is assumed uniform, its departure from the horizontal *AB* can represent the flow of time, which our minds cannot conceive except as uniform and equable. Next, note that the parts of this line *HL* that are intercepted under angle *C* within *DCE* and within *FCG*— that is, *OI* and *MN*—continually grow with the descent of *HL* from the horizontal *AB*. Finally, of the infinitely many lines less than *MN*, there is none to which some [line] intercepted by the same *FCG* would not [at some time] be equal as line *HL* recedes from *AB*; and [there is] none of the infinitely many [lines] less than *OI* to which there would not similarly be an equal part of the same *HL* intercepted between *DC* and *CE*. Further, no line contained under the very acute angle *DCE* is so short as not to have some other, equal to it, intercepted under the very obtuse angle *FCG* during the descent from *AB* to *HL*. Drawing perpendiculars to *AB* from points *O* and *I*, it is also manifestly deduced that *FC* and *GC* cut these [verticals] and intercept sections between them equal to *OI*. From this it appears that all the lines in triangle *OCI* that are parallel to *OI* (and they are infinitely many) can be assumed also to be comprehended within triangle *MCN* during the descent of line *HL*, though [there] in shorter times. Likewise, there is also no [line] parallel to *MN* in triangle *MCN* so long that another cannot be assigned to match it between *DC* and *CE*, if the descent proceeds by departure of line *HL* from *AB*, at any rate after some [sufficiently] long time.

Thus if we conceive mentally that the flowing of time corresponds to the equable departure of line *HL* from *BA*, then finally the first instant of time of separation would correspond to the ultimate conjunction of those lines. Again, [since] we assume that to the degrees of swiftness acquired [by moveables descending from rest at *C*] correspond the lines comprehended within triangles *MCN* and *OCI*, it will not be hard to understand how a rule can be made as to the degree to be attained by the moveable, now in a very short time and again in a very long time; and finally, as angle *FCG* is more and more widened, so that the lines *CF* and *CG* become closer to *CA* and *CB*, the more quickly line *HL* separates from *AB*. This is the same as to say that in a very brief time, or with the highest [degree of] swiftness, the motion of line *HL* will have designated all the lines (that is, infinitely many) and all magnitudes whatsoever that lie between point *C* and the maximum part of line *HL* intercepted under some very obtuse angle. This, I say, shows that there is not one of these [lines] to which the equal is not some one of the intercepts contained by the obtuse angle. Hence it comes about that the motion of points *M* and *N* may be very swift along lines *CF* and *CG*, even though the departure of line *HL* from *BA* may be minimal and most slow. Yet it may be finally that angle *C* is so obtuse and lines *CF* and *CG* so close to *AB* that lines *CM* and *CN*, or even *MN* itself, may surpass the distance between *AB* and *HL* by virtually an infinite excess. And at length, at the greatest and ultimate widening of angle *C* (that is, at the conjunction of lines *CF* and *CG* with lines *CA* and *CB*), motion similar to the motion already explained becomes instantaneous and infinite[ly swift] from terminus *C*. Is not this the expansion of light, which certainly is generated at one bounded place and [yet] is discovered at the same time at all places around this which are not screened [from it]?[13]

But back to our purpose. I think it is not hard, from the foregoing example, to understand and simultaneously to grant that moveables falling from rest acquire some degrees of speed in short times, others in longer, and still others [only] in a very long time; thus those [bodies] that fall along the vertical [fall] quickly [and] appear faster, and those that descend on a sloping plane are somewhat speeded up, but come in longer times to those moments of swiftness to which bodies falling vertically come more quickly.

From these things that have been explained, if I am not mistaken, all contradictions appear to be removed that prevented our defining uniformly or equally accelerated motion; this, then, is the definition: I call that motion uniformly or equably accelerated whose momenta or degrees of speed in descent from rest increase according to the same increments as the times from the first instant of motion.[14]

This definition, identical with that used in Galileo's final book, required that speeds change continuously in the mathematical sense, and not by successive jumps however tiny, just as time itself proceeds continuously. That requirement was the source of the principal and most intelligent resistance to Galileo's science of motion for several years after 1638, when it was published. Galileo was aware that it would be resisted, for both in the *Dialogue* and the later *Two New Sciences* he argued at length that in order to reach any given speed from rest a body must first pass through every possible smaller speed, using the principle of sufficient reason.

IV

In November 1630 Galileo had been advised by Caterina Niccolini, the ambassador's wife, that Riccardi had approved Father Hyacinth Stefani at Florence to review the *Dialogue*, for which the revised preface and ending were to be sent from Rome. After waiting months for this approval to be confirmed, Galileo asked the grand duke's secretary in March 1631 to take it up with the ambassador. Riccardi then said he had never approved Stefani as the Florentine reviewer, and insisted on a Father Nente instead. The grand duke suggested a compromise, and after many negotiations Riccardi wrote to the ambassador on 25 April 1631 acknowledging that Stefani had already reviewed the book, though without his having certain information concerning some particulars that would satisfy Riccardi and the pope. He insisted on a certain form of preface and ending, saying he would write about this to the Inquisitor at Florence, who could proceed when he saw that form to be observed. Riccardi's letter was forwarded to Galileo by the secretary "so that he might adopt whatever expedient he wished." Galileo replied to this attempted shift of responsibility with a long letter dated 3 May addressed to the secretary, outlining a procedure by which he could present his case to the grand duke. Finally, on 24 May, Riccardi wrote to the Florentine Inquisitor as follows:

Sig. Galileo thinks of printing a work of his that formerly had the title *De fluxu et refluxu maris*, which discusses this with probable reasons taken from the Copernican system according to mobility of the earth, and he claims to facilitate understanding of that great secret of nature [the tides] by this position, corroborating it vividly with this use [of the system]. He came here to Rome to show the work, which was signed by me, assuming accommodations that had to be made in it and his bringing it back to us to receive final approval to print. Being unable to do this because of closing of the roads and danger to the original [manuscript], and the author wishing to bring this business to an end, your Reverence may use your authority and approve or not approve the book independently of my revision, but keeping it in mind that it is his Holiness' view that the title and subject may not propose the tides, but absolutely [only] mathematical considerations of the Copernican positions about the motion of the earth, with the purpose of proving that, excluding divine revelation and holy doctrine, the appearances could be saved in this position, resolving all the contrary arguments that might be adduced from experience and the Peripatetic philosophy, so that this position is never conceded absolute but only hypothetical truth, and apart from the Scriptures. It must also be shown that this work was done only to show that all the arguments that this side can adduce are known, and that it was not from lack of their knowledge at Rome that this opinion was here abandoned, conformably with the beginning and the end of the book that will be sent from here corrected. With the above caution the book will have no obstacle here in Rome, and your Reverence may pacify the author and serve his Highness, who shows much pressure in this matter.

On 31 May the Inquisitor replied that he would carry out Riccardi's wishes punctually, that he had given the manuscript for review to Stefani, and that the preface and ending would be exactly as indicated by Riccardi. The preface, as later printed, was sent by Riccardi to the pope on 31 July, together with a statement that the ending of the book must include the pope's own arguments concerning divine omnipotence. By 5 July Galileo reported to Marsili that six signatures (forty-eight pages) had been printed, and that the edition was of one thousand copies, which made the work go slowly.

Such were the events affecting publication of the *Dialogue* up to the beginning of printing in June 1631. We may now turn back to consider Galileo's scientific activities of that year.

V

In the latter part of 1630 an engineer named Bartolotti had proposed to the Tuscan government a plan for straightening the river Bisenzio to correct troublesome flooding of lands. His plan had been turned over to Niccolò Arrighetti for comment and criticism. Early in December Niccolò was in correspondence with his cousin, Andrea, concerning the physics of flow of water in channels. He assumed the rules to be the same as for solid bodies, that is, that speeds acquired in dropping through the same vertical height are the same regardless of incline, which he said had been proved by Galileo in his writings on motion. The proof Arrighetti had in mind was doutbless that of 179–1, which he had copied for Galileo in 1618; at that time he had questioned Galileo's proof but Galileo had not abandoned it. Both cousins were then living outside Florence and appear not to have known of Galileo's current work on motion. Andrea questioned some of his cousin's assumptions.

Niccolò replied that some of Andrea's objections had formerly occurred to him and seemed correct, but subsequently he had perceived fallacies in them pointed out to him by Galileo and later by Castelli. On 17 December Andrea sent Galileo the correspondence, asking him to referee their dispute, which primarily concerned the applicability of rules for speeds along inclined planes to running water. The next day Niccolò independently wrote to Galileo, recalling that he had spoken in earlier years of a flooding problem on the Tiber. Galileo was engaged in considering these problems when on 20 December the grand duke requested that he visit the Bisenzio in the company of Bartolotti and his engineering opponent, Fantoni, considering their rival plans and rendering his judgment. The actual visit was deferred, but Galileo studied the two plans, and having decided in favor of Fantoni's he wrote out his criticisms of Bartolotti's reasoning. This analysis was sent to Rafaello Staccoli, a court official, on 16 January 1631. It represents Galileo's scientific work at the close of 1630. Since his analysis of water flow is little known and very interesting, it is translated in part below:

Having seen the opinions of the two engineers I shall say, as clearly and briefly as possible, what my own opinion is on this matter, which I have always held to be very difficult and obscure and in which many equivocations and errors have been committed, especially before professionals were cautioned by the findings of Abbot Benedetto Castelli in that truly golden book of his, written and published three years ago, about the measures of running waters.

It was the opinion of engineer Bartolotti, expounded in writing, that the parts of the river which are very winding should be reduced to a straight channel, he believing thus to avoid flooding. Engineer Fantoni examines that writing, which he very sharply opposes; engineer Bartolotti replies to the

objections in an attempt to sustain his advice as the best to take
in this dispute. Now since I incline to the other opinion, that
is, to leave the windings and to make other repairs proposed
by engineer Fantoni, I shall examine the last reply by Bartolotti,
showing to the best of my ability how easily one is misled in
these most puzzling movements of waters.

Engineer Bartolotti persists in reproaching as useless anything
done except the removal of tortuosities and straightening of
the river channel, saying that the cure proposed by engineer
Fantoni was done at another time, 44 years ago, and yet things
are now in the same state as before. But I should like to know
whether the repairs made at that time in the very tortuous
river were of some benefit, or were completely useless and fruitless. I do not believe it can be said that they were completely
in vain, because the other engineer would not [in that case]
propose them, nor would there be anyone in the country who
would not protest such a proposal. So if the [former] provisions
were successful and were made without removing the tortuosity,
then the [fact of the] same injuries having returned after
some time does not depend on the windings but on some other
cause, which is found to be that the riverbed is silted and restricted through the deposit of mud; and since it is impossible
to do away with mud [deposits] and silting, one must be content
to accommodate oneself to this and from time to time to remove
the deposits. Besides, if it was already seen that the provisions
made within the tortuosities succeeded—and of this we are sure
from experience—why attempt [instead] a dubious remedy
which, besides not succeeding better in carrying off the waters,
might introduce other damaging factors that we have not
anticipated in our foresight? . . .

From what engineer Bartolotti writes about this matter it
is gathered that he attributes two principal and great imperfections to the winding channel, both absent in his opinion
from the straight channel, assuming channels starting from
the same place and ending at the same terminal mouth. The first
is that when the same drop must be distributed over a long
channel (necessarily tortuous in comparison with the shorter),
its parts are less tilted, and consequently the motion made
in them is slower and the discharge of water [at the mouth] is
delayed. The second is that the water, striking at the turns of the
tortuous channel, is forced back and slows its course greatly.
Thus doubly retarded . . . the water more easily swells and
overflows between the banks, or breaks them and runs into
adjacent fields. Now, for a clear understanding in this matter of

what I must say, I shall separate these two [alleged] imperfections, considering first what is contributed to slowness of
motion by slope alone along a long channel, as compared with
the speed this same drop induces in a short channel, given that
both are straight. . . .

I shall produce three propositions which I do not doubt will
at first glance seem to be great paradoxes to anyone who hears
them; yet I shall strive to make them credible, as in fact they
are true.

First I say that in two channels of equal total drop the speeds
of motion will be equal, even though one channel is very long
and the other short.

I say second that in those same channels it can be said with
equal truth that the motion is faster in the less sloping one—
that is, in the longer—than in the shorter and more sloping.

Third I say that the different speeds do not follow the ratios
of the different drops, as engineer Bartolotti seems to think,
but may differ in infinitely many ways even over the same slope.

Coming to the first proposition . . . the speeds of two moveables may be called equal not only when they pass equal spaces
in equal times, but also when the spaces passed in unequal
times are in the ratio of the times of their passages. Thus, for
example, a man who goes from Florence to Pistoia in four
hours is not called slower than one who goes in two hours from
Florence to Prato, since Pistoia is 20 miles distant and Prato
only ten, whence each has made overall 5 miles per hour, which
is to have passed equal spaces in equal times. And whenever
two moveables descending through two unequal channels pass
them in times that have the same ratio as the lengths of the
channels, they can truly be called equally swift. . . . I say that
the time in which a moveable shall descend from A to B, to
the time in which it will descend from A to C, will have the same
ratio as the channels . . . and this is a proposition proved by me
in my books on natural motions and of projectiles. Hence it is
clear that the speeds through both channels are equal overall.
Since I understand the origin of the mistake people make in
considering false this which I affirm as true, I shall seek to
remove this [error].

Someone says: How is it that a ball
along the slope AC does not move more
swiftly than a similar one along AB if
the former, leaving from A, shall have
arrived at C when the latter has passed in AB only a space far
shorter than AC? I grant this [shorter distance along AB] as

most true, and consequently I also concede that if the speed in the rest of the line *AB* were [the same] as in the first part toward the beginning, *A*, the motion would definitely and with absolute truth have to be called slower through *AB* than through *AC*. But to take away this source of equivocation, I say that the fallacy of the reasoning depends on mistakenly figuring the movements made over these lines *AB* and *AC* as equable and uniform, not unequable and continually accelerated as they are in fact. What I affirm will be found true if we understand that these are two moveables which, leaving from rest at *A*, go successively acquiring greater and greater degrees of speed in the ratio truly observed. In explanation of this, one must know first that a heavy body, leaving from rest and descending through a straight channel tilted in any direction, or indeed descending vertically, goes accelerating in such a ratio that, dividing the time of descent into such-and-such arbitrary equal times, as for example into minutes, then if the space passed in the first minute shall be, say, one rod, that passed in the second minute will be 3 rods; in the third minute it will pass 5 rods, in the fourth 7, and successively the spaces passed in subsequent minutes will grow according to the odd numbers 9, 11, 13, 15, etc. And this also is among the propositions demonstrated by me.[15]

Next take again the same figure as above, in which *AB* shall for example be double the length of *AC*, and understand two balls descending freely through them; and let us assume that the ball in the steeper, *AC*, shall in one minute have descended one rod; it will in the second minute pass three rods . . . and thus in four minutes it will have passed the whole channel *AC*, assumed to be 16 rods long. But the other ball, in channel *AB*, twice as long and hence half as sloping, assumed to be moved half as fast—which conforms to the truth in the opinion of the engineer [Bartolotti]—so that in the first minute it has passed half a rod, and continuing to be accelerated by the rule assigned and demonstrated [by me], will pass in the second minute three half-rods . . . and *AB*, which is double *AC*, must be 32 rods or 64 half-rods, exactly as many as denoted 1,3,5,7,9,11,13,15, passed in 8 minutes of time; but the 16 contained in *AC* were passed in 4 minutes, from which it is clear that the overall speeds in the two entire channels are equal, since in one, 16 rods are passed in 4 minutes, and in the other, 32 [rods] in 8 [minutes]—though it is also true, for satisfaction of the other side, that the speed in *AC* is greater, since in the time that the moveable leaving from *A* along *AC* has passed 16 rods, the other has passed only 16 half-rods.

On the other hand it is also true that in the same time are passed the final 48 half-rods, or 24 rods, near *B*, so it can be said with equal truth that motion in *AB* is faster than in *AC*, which was the second proposition I proposed to prove.[16] So we conclude that taking the whole channels, the speeds in both are equal, but in the upper part of the long channel (which in this example is only one-quarter of it), the motion is slower, while in the remaining three-quarters it is correspondingly faster, passing in the same time a space 1½ times as great as the whole channel *AC*. And because for the discharge of a filled [channel] one must consider the course of the water along the whole length, it seems to me the engineer has no room left to doubt (so far as concerns greater or lesser length and lesser or greater slope of the two channels) that the long and less steep discharges as much as the shorter and less sloping, that is, the tortuous as much as the straight.

Here I do not want to omit from consideration by you how it might be that someone, erring in another direction, could persuade himself that it is not possible for a moveable passing the shorter and steeper channel with such greater speed not to have to discharge a greater quantity of the same material, and in shorter time, than through one longer and less sloping.

To this I reply by explaining a particular example, that if we must discharge for example 10,000 cannonballs by making them pass through this conduit, and it being the case that a ball runs the shorter in one minute but the longer in 2 minutes, it is true and obvious that if the discharge has to be made one ball at a time, so that the second is not released until the first has got to the end of the conduit, nor the third [released] until the second is discharged, and so for the rest, each with such an interval after the other, I repeat that it is true that the discharge through the shorter conduit would be made in half the time of that through the longer. But if the balls are released one after another without any space in between, so that they touch, things come out quite differently. For assume, for example, that the length of the shorter channel will hold a file of only 100 balls, and the long channel 200; it is true that the short one will have discharged its first 100 [balls] when the long one just commences to discharge its first [ball]; but then, the discharge continuing, and putting the remaining balls in both conduits with equal push, the short channel will be found to have no advantage in the entire discharge except for the first 100 balls of the 10,000, because only 100 will still remain in the long channel when the short one has finished its discharge. And so the advantage in time will not be by one-half, but one-hundredth, and it will be so much the less [in proportion] as the greater the number of balls to be deposited and discharged. Now, discharge of water is made in this second manner, that is, with its succeeding parts perpetually contiguous to the preceding, whence the discharge made by the short channel has no advantage, being half as long, beyond that of one filling with water, be it full as long as you like. Now see how many fillings pass in the time it stays full, and you will see the advantage to be very tenuous, or rather null and of no importance . . . because [flood] damage does not come from the first waters that commence to rise, nor the last that leave, but from those in the middle when the river is at its greatest height. . . .

[This is still more so] when I remove a certain assumption made thus far in favor of the other side:

It is granted as universally true, for the channel only half as long and twice as sloping, that motion is, at least in the first parts of the longer channel, twice as slow as in the short one. . . . But that is true only when the motion starts from rest; if the moveables enter the two channels when both have been impressed with a certain degree of speed, the acceleration that is added to them by the unequal slopes of the two channels will not at all differ as [much as] if they started from rest, and the space that will be passed in the long channel in the time the whole short channel is traversed will not remain half the length of the shorter, but [will be] more and more, according as the preceding impetus and speed common to both of them shall be greater, as follows.

Galileo refuted Bartolotti's assumption that the speed of water in a river depends only on the slope of its bed, and then continued:

I shall first explain what I find to happen with solids, in order then to see whether the same occurs in fluids. And first, by [our] "solid" let us mean a very hard metal ball, perfectly round and polished, and let us suppose the channel where motion is made to be also of solid material perfectly clean and smooth. If this channel is perfectly level and horizontal so that it lacks any tilt, there is no doubt that the ball will remain at rest, finding itself indifferent to being moved forward or back, or let us say because by its being moved it does not reach a better state, since it does not approach the center toward which its heavy nature draws it. But that does not happen with water, for if we imagine this ball to be a volume of water, it will collapse and run in all directions, flattening itself out; and if the mouth of the channel is open, it will all flow out—except for that minimum that remains, just wetting the bottom of the channel. Behold, then, that even in the channel lacking slope, where solid bodies stand firm and quiet, fluids are moved. Also the cause of their moving is evident, since water in levelling itself, by its parts approaching the center [of the earth], acquires and makes for itself some tilt, in a sense using its lower parts as a sloping bed for those above, or (as people say) its upper parts pressing upon the lower. And here it begins to be clear why it is not the tilt of the [river] bed or bottom of the channel that regulates the movement of the [flood] water. Let us now see what happens in channels of different slopes, and what may be the differences of speed in these.

Here Galileo gave the rule for speeds of solid bodies along planes differing in slope but having the same length, that is, the times inversely as the square roots of heights.

The proof of this proposition is also put by me in my treatise on motion, and it is found to happen punctually in the motions of solids, but not so in fluids, in which are seen greater variations of speed, not only because of small increases in slope of the bed of the channel, but also when that is not increased at all and the [slope of the] upper surface of the water is very little increased. For if we consider what increase of tilt there is in our river Arno when it rises 8 or 10 braccia [nearly 20 feet] here by us [at Florence], spread over 60 miles of length [to its mouth near Pisa], which is [equivalent to] the slope of its bed out to the end, doubtless there ought to be little increase in its speed over that which it has when its waters are low and perhaps do not reach the sea in 50 hours, whereas in high floods they may arrive there in less than 8 hours, though if governed according to the simple ratio of increased tilt, the difference in time should be very small. . . . So we must look elsewhere for the cause of the great increase in speed . . . and say that one of the powerful causes is that the tilt being increased in this manner, the volume and accumulation of water increases greatly, which, pressing and weighing on the forward parts by its trailing parts, drives them impetuously—something that does not happen in solid bodies, because that ball mentioned earlier is always the same at all slopes, and having no increase of matter coming against it, is only as much more easily moved in the more tilted channel than in the less tilted as the less tilted detracts more from its weight and consequently from the momentum that drives it downward.

Now because in the acceleration of the course of the highest waters little part is played by greater slope and much by the great quantity of supervening water, consider that in the short channel although there is greater tilt than in the longer, the lower waters of the long [channel] are more charged by the great abundance of higher waters pushing and driving, by which impulse is more than compensated the benefit that could be derived from greater slope. . . . But I think enough has been said on this first point. Let us get to the second, examining the inconveniences that many people think come from the tortuosity of the channel.

(Here there ensues a discussion of curves as opposed to right angles in the supposed resistances to flow.)

I know, Sir, that in this writing of mine there are some propositions which, presenting at first glance an appearance of paradoxes and impossibilities, make many people think I have an extravagant mind and enjoy contradicting opinions and doctrines commonly accepted even by professionals, hence they do not hide from me [the opinion] that it might be better to remain silent about truth that wears the face of a lie than to speak out and expose oneself to contradictions and impugnations, and sometimes even derision, by many. Yet in this, too, I have a different view from the ordinary, and I deem it more useful to propound new thoughts and expose them to contradiction than, to be safe against my adversaries, fill my pages with things already written in a thousand books. On this occasion, then, listen to me and consider me a censor—an office still permitted in republics, and perhaps among the most useful and necessary; take what I have said and am about to say not as born of my ambition, so that my counsel might be put ahead of the views of others more understanding than I am, but as originating from a desire to take part in great deliberations, if not positively at least negatively, that is, by my having given voice to inconveniences that should be avoided. I avail myself of the declaration that I am less knowlegeable than others in order to be able the more freely to bring in my imaginings.

Turning, then, to the tortuousity of the river, I shall say that another concept of mine which I think may be new, and also extravagant to the engineer (and maybe to others), is this: Given the same drop between two places to be passed through by a moveable, I affirm the quickest road and that passed in the shortest time to be not the straight, though that is shortest of all, but to be certain curves; and even some broken lines are traversed with greater speed and in less time [than the straight path]. And to explain this let us mark a horizontal plane along line *AB*, above which there is raised a part of a circle not greater than a quadrant, *CEFD*, so that the part of the diameter *DC* that ends by touching *C* is vertical.

Here Galileo outlined the argument given in the scholium to Proposition Thirty-Six, *Two New Sciences*, and offered reasons for increasing the slope of a riverbed as it goes downstream.

I am sure that in the horizontal plane, there being no external and accidental impediments, the speed received by a moveable is uniformly conserved and is such that in that plane it will pass double the space passed in the incline [to that plane] when its beginning was from the state of rest, as I demonstrate in my previously mentioned book on motion.[17]

It is interesting that Galileo here stated his belief in the uniformity of supported horizontal motion, not explicitly mentioned in his notes on motion though implied in many of his propositions, particularly those relating to projectiles. The remainder of his report may be neglected here.

On 3 December 1630, Cavalieri wrote to say he was delighted that Galileo had again taken up the theory of motion. He himself had put aside his book on geometry in favor of one on logarithmic trigonometry, largely because the university authorities were more interested in useful calculations than in theoretical mathematics. The university was closed because of plague.

EIGHTEEN

1631-33

I

On 16 February 1631 Cavalieri was asked by Galileo to solve a geometrical problem connected with a new proof of Proposition Thirty-Five, an attack Galileo had used in 1627 appearing to him unsatisfactory if not defective. Cavalieri received the request when he was suffering from a very painful attack of fever and gout, the second such seizure to be mentioned in his letters to Galileo. This was followed by a series of incapacitating illnesses and ultimately by Cavalieri's premature death in 1647. Because of his illness and discomfort, he said, he had thought of putting off the attempt to solve Galileo's problem, but then found it so challenging that he could not resist working on it, and after four days had dictated a solution that appeared satisfactory to him. The same letter shows that Galileo had told him he intended to write a discourse on the flooding conditions of rivers, probably expanding the report partly translated in chapter 17. This treatise, now lost, was sent to Marsili or Cavalieri early in April.

Cavalieri's solution of the problem sent by Galileo was in effect a kind of geometrical algorithm, if such an expression may be permitted. It did not satisfy Galileo, who however was at that time too much occupied with an architect in charge of work on the façade of the Florence cathedral to reply.

At the same time Galileo and Cavalieri learned from Marsili of his discovery the previous summer of an apparent alteration of the equinoctial line from that engraved on the floor of the church of San Petronio in Bologna. He wished Galileo to make similar observations using the meridian line at Santa Maria

Novella in Florence, sending him a little treatise on unreconciled observations relating to established longitudes and the earth's magnetic poles. Galileo inserted at the end of his *Dialogue* a brief mention of this communication and its possible implications for the earth's mobility, though in a different sense from that of Copernicus.[1]

Cavalieri, who had made some logarithmic calculations for Marsili in this matter, wrote to Galileo about it, adding that Marsili and others had seen a letter of Galileo's criticizing the solution he had sent for the geometrical problem mentioned above. He now sent a defense of this from which it can be seen that Galileo had considered Cavalieri's procedure as no more than a cut-and-try operation, not a straightforward deductive solution. Cavalieri maintained that since it was entirely systematic it should not be condemned any more than Euclid's solution of the problem of dropping a perpendicular to a plane from a point outside it. Cavalieri likened such procedures to the construction of the tangent to a given Archimedean spiral. The entire argument reveals a very interesting difference between Galileo and Cavalieri on methods allowable in geometry, not unrelated to their basic difference concerning valid applications of Cavalieri's "method of indivisibles." Having defended his previous procedure, Cavalieri then turned again to Galileo's problem, offering a different attack, though he feared this might also be rejected by Galileo as essentially an approximate rather than an exact and direct solution. Meanwhile Galileo had found his own second solution for Proposition Thirty-Five: "Given a line at an angle to the vertical, to find a part through which alone, from rest, motion is made in the same time as through it and that vertical together." What he had sent to Cavalieri was not this problem, but only a geometrical construction needed for its solution, with a diagram rotated 90° to conceal its relation to a motion problem. Galileo's new solution of the motion problem was derived from earlier work on Proposition Thirty-Four during the autumn of 1630.

In a long letter to Marsili on 5 April concerning observations of the meridian line, Galileo recounted his own attempts in past years to observe if possible any variation in the obliquity of the ecliptic by means of a method described in the *Dialogue*.[2] He opined that Marsili's observations at San Petronio might yield reliable results over a period of several years, but unevenness of the pavement at Santa Maria Novella precluded reliance on observations there. He stressed the difficulties of interpreting the findings, but said that Marsili's immediate adversaries

. . . were no less ridiculous than those who in great number opposed my first celestial discoveries, persuading themselves (as is usual in noisy altercations of idle words) that by texts, authorities, syllogisms and their foolishnesses they could force the course of nature to conform to their dreams. Malignity, envy, and ignorance are unconquerable beasts, and I see by daily experience that my contradictors, though overthrown by a hundred confrontations and past experiments, and made certain that new opinions introduced by me and at first denied by them are true, do not cease to oppose themselves to other things day by day propounded by me, still hoping some day to have me on the hip and that some one small error of mine will cancel all the other true teachings I have introduced. Now, you must let the vulgar shout, and just continue in conversation with the Muses, enemies of the tumultuous rabble.

Sent with this was Galileo's treatise on river flooding, which was appreciatively read by both Marsili and Cavalieri. In transmitting it Galileo appears to have said that he had lost much of his memory and power to theorize; Cavalieri replied that he doubted that, "since you have discovered something not even easy to understand" about the flow of water. Galileo had asked Cavalieri about his work with logarithms, to which he replied not by outlining their basis but by offering a striking illustration of their utility.

It was on 26 April 1631 that Galileo first heard (from Campanella) that Scheiner's *Rosa Ursina* was finally published, this book having been on the presses of the Orsini family since 1626. Galileo mentioned to Paolo Giordano Orsini his desire for a copy, but because Orsini was away from Rome none was sent until late in the year. During July it appears that Galileo reopened his negotiations with Spain on the longitude proposal, dormant for a decade though there had been sporadic letters mentioning it during the invervening years.

On 16 August Galileo wrote to Diodati explaining why the title of his *Dialogue* had been altered to omit any reference to the tides. At this time he said the book was one-third printed, and he expected it to be finished in three months. Letters written to

Nicole Fabri de Peiresc in September confirm this progress. Castelli wrote from Pesaro on 26 September, saying that he had glanced at Scheiner's *Rosa Ursina* and was shocked at its author's poisonous rage.[3] He thought that a printed reply should be addressed by some friend of Galileo's to the General of the Jesuit order in protest. Fulgenzio Micanzio wrote from Venice at the same time, sarcastically remarking that Scheiner should be highly commended, since the Jesuits made their reputation by speaking ill and could not have picked a loftier and more conspicuous target than Galileo. Micanzio said in this letter that he recalled Galileo's having shown sunspots to him and Paolo Sarpi, thinking at first they must be deceptions of the telescope but then deciding they must be true, shortly before Galileo departed for Florence in mid-1610. No other evidence supports so early an observation by Galileo, though he, thus prompted, added a similar assertion in the *Dialogue* by having Salviati say "He discovered them in 1610 while he was still professor of mathematics at the University of Padua. He spoke about them to many people here in Venice, some of whom are yet living, and a year later he showed them to many gentlemen at Rome. . . ." There is no doubt that Galileo exhibited sunspots at Rome in April 1611, but if he had first observed them at Padua or Venice in 1610 it is extremely probable that he would have mentioned that fact in his *Letters* printed in 1613, when the priority issue was first hotly debated.

Galileo mentioned the *Rosa Ursina* to Marsili early in October, seemingly only on the strength of information he had received from Castelli and Micanzio since as yet he showed no concern. Cavalieri, who had not seen the *Rosa* at the end of October, saw the book at Bologna soon afterward and wrote to Galileo on 18 November, saying that he was first astounded by its expense, and next by the author's manner of writing. Cavalieri suggested that Galileo add a few pages to his *Dialogue* refuting what Scheiner said against him. What Cavalieri had in mind was a supplement or appendix to the *Dialogue*, with a separate title page entitled *Apologia* against Scheiner's attack, a procedure not uncommon in those days. But there are several pages in the Third Day of the *Dialogue* concerning sunspots, arguing from their annual variation of paths for motion of the earth, and many historians have supposed this section to have been hastily added by Galileo during the actual printing. Scheiner himself later believed that Galileo had stolen the idea for the *Dialogue* argument from his *Rosa Ursina*; hence the question is an important one.

The first positive evidence that Galileo had actually seen the *Rosa Ursina* is in a letter dated 30 December, written by Paolo Giordano Orsini in embarrassed apology to Galileo for the excesses of Scheiner. Had he known of these, he said, he would never have permitted his ministers at Bracciano to accept the book. He did not give the date of Galileo's letter of protest, but since there was no mention of any delay in replying to his offended friend of many years it seems likely that Galileo had not written to Orsini before early December. It is also probable that he did write immediately on seeing the first page of Scheiner's book, where offensive language toward Galileo is prominently apparent. Now, on 29 November Galileo had written to Marsili concerning some argument against Copernicus based on the motions of the moon, "and what most displeases me is that this did not come to me in time to permit my inserting them [Marsili's arguments] in my book, which is already reduced [to print] near the end, where only the tides are dealt with and there is no appropriate place to insert your objection." Hence for Galileo to have belatedly written and inserted the material about sunspots, which came about seventy pages before his discussion of the tidal theory, he would have had to have read Scheiner's book considerably earlier, before October, against weighty evidence set forth above.

Assuming, however, that Galileo did have Scheiner's book in time to insert in the *Dialogue* his argument from the paths of sunspots, it is very improbable that he would, or could, have added it then for the first time. The printer could not safely accept so substantial a change without permission from the Inquisitor at Florence, who already knew how sensitive the whole matter of this book was at Rome and would certainly not have approved it. In the turmoil that followed publication, the printer could not have escaped arrest if he had made the addition without permission. Nor is that all. Riccardi's two specific demands related to the preface and the ending of the book, in which the slightest deviation from what had been approved would be swiftly detected. Yet in the ending, the argument from sunspots was named as second among three strong and five possible arguments for Copernicus, being given precedence there even over

Galileo's argument from the tides. Hence Galileo cannot have introduced the entire argument at the last moment while the book was in press, though it is probable that he did add the two or three sentences in which he asserted firmly his own priority and dated it back to Padua,[4] relying for this not on his own memory but on the letter from Micanzio mentioned earlier.

The same conclusion is supported by the fact that Galileo indicated in the *Dialogue* neither the degree of tilt of the sun's axis nor the annual dates of maximum and minimum curvature of sunspot paths. It is true that for the purposes of Galileo's argument neither of these was necessary, yet it is also true that Scheiner had published both with creditable accuracy, and had Galileo known the tilt and dates before writing his argument, or in time to include these in it, it seems unlikely that he would have left it in a form revealing his knowledge to be less complete than his old rival's. Indeed, if Scheiner's book had been the source of Galileo's argument, one would hardly expect him to have written it in so general and abstract a form.[5]

The fact is that in order to know the annual dates of maximum and minimum curvature of the paths, observations for every day around those times are necessary, and since sunspots are not always to be seen this would normally mean the accumulation of observations from several different years. Galileo had had no time for that if, as I believe, the argument first occurred to him in 1629. A few observations in that year combined with those he had recorded in 1612 would have sufficed to assure him that the hints in Sizzi's old letter were reliable, but not to supply him with the specific information in question, which is in fact lacking from his account.[6]

II

In Galileo's letter to Marsili about the latter's belated argument from the moon's motions, he said: "I am thinking of publishing the first book on motion right after the *Dialogue*." This supports other evidence from Galileo's correspondence with Cavalieri and from his manuscript notes on motion, that virtually all the material for the Third Day of *Two New Sciences* was completed in 1630–31. The phrase "first book" suggests that Galileo intended to deal separately with the motion of projectiles, later made the subject of the Fourth Day of the same book. Although the fundamental theorems of that subject had been derived at Padua in

1609, the tables of trajectories and some theorems relating to them are in Galileo's writing characteristic of his last years and had not yet been done in 1631.

Printing of the *Dialogue* was completed on 21 February 1632 and the presentation copy to the grand duke was delivered the next day. Cavalieri is the first person known to have written to Galileo describing his reaction to the book; he said that his experience reminded him of reading Ariosto's *Orlando Furioso*— "wherever I begin, I can't put it down." Niccolini wrote from Rome advising that copies for that city be held until May, when it was hoped that the quarantine for plague would be lifted, since until that time books would continue to be taken apart and fumigated. As will be seen, a few copies were nevertheless taken to Rome by a friend of Galileo's. Just at this time Galileo suffered a severe eye affliction that made it difficult for him to read or write.

Baliani wrote to inquire how Galileo had found that a heavy body falls 100 braccia in five seconds, saying that at Genoa there was no tower that high for experiments and that the implied fall of 4 braccia in the first second of time was very difficult to verify. Baliani, like Newton and others later, had taken as an assertion of fact something that Galileo had put into the *Dialogue* merely as an illustrative example for which he had arbitrarily taken figures adapted to easy calculation that the general reader could follow without trouble.[7] He did not reply to this inquiry until Baliani repeated it some years later, in another connection which will be discussed in chapter 21, § II. Baliani also mentioned his attempts to construct a pendulum that would beat exact seconds, "but up to now I have not succeeded in discovering the exact length of the string." Galileo's comments on the way to determine this and on the utility of any such device in scientific experiments were also delayed and will be found in chapter 21.

On 29 May Castelli wrote from Rome that some copies of the *Dialogue* had arrived there, referring probably to those brought from Florence by Filippo Magalotti which will be mentioned presently. Cardinal Barberini had allowed Castelli to read one, "and I still have it by me, having read it from cover to cover to my infinite amazement and delight; and I read parts of it to friends of good taste to their marvel and always more to my delight, more to my amazement, and with always more profit to myself." The argument from sunspot paths seemed to Castelli compelling, though he called it "false witness" either in jest or because it was not prudent for an abbot to acknowledge his Copernican sympathies in writing. That this argument was new to Castelli confirms the conclusion drawn earlier that it occurred to Galileo only in 1629, after Castelli had moved to Rome.

On 19 June Castelli wrote again, this time mentioning an incident in a Roman bookshop. Scheiner, he said, on hearing a priest praising the *Dialogue* as the greatest book ever printed, turned livid and shook so badly that the bookseller who told Castelli about the event had been astonished. Scheiner had said that he would give ten gold ducats for a copy in order to be able to compose an answer to it immediately. (When he did, it was so violent that his fellow Jesuits prevented its publication until after his death in 1650.) Castelli went on to say he was entirely satisfied with Galileo's tide theory and admired the "appendixes" to it, that is, the explanations of monthly and annual variations in tidal heights mentioned in chapter 16, § IV. It was in this letter that Galileo first heard of Evangelista Torricelli, mentioned by Castelli as the most brilliant student of geometry he had ever had excepting Cavalieri.

Early in August Campanella wrote to Galileo praising the *Dialogue*; he also mentioned that Scheiner was hostile "because he would at all costs be the discoverer of the [sun]spots." The first sign of serious trouble came in a long letter dated from Rome on 7 August, written by Filippo Magalotti to Mario Guiducci. Magalotti had paid little attention to grumblings against the book at Rome until the first of August, when Riccardi had asked him to gather up and turn over to him all the copies Magalotti had brought from Florence, promising to return them in ten days. There were eight of these, sent by Galileo, of which copies had been given to Cardinal Barberini, Riccardi, Niccolini, Ciampoli, Campanella, Father Serristori of the Holy Office, and the Jesuit Leon Santi. Magalotti could not graciously request these back. Riccardi implied that what he wanted with them was for Galileo's good, but when pressed to explain would only say he could not reveal secrets of the Holy Office.

Riccardi had then raised a point that Magalotti blushed to repeat: questions had been raised about a vignette on the title page showing three fish. Magalotti assured Riccardi this was the printer's emblem and not some secret device of Galileo's to hint at holy mysteries. Magalotti suspected that the problem was not merely, as Riccardi hinted, that some arguments of the pope's were omitted from the ending and that this might offend him if he saw the book, but rather that the Jesuits were hard at work to have the *Dialogue* prohibited. His advice was to make sure that everything done at Florence with regard to the printing had been carried out as previously agreed in writing. If so, there was no reason for concern; if not, a simple offer to permit any deletion, change, or addition required should suffice.

Galileo must have heard of the trouble at the same time, because a letter from Micanzio refers to one from Galileo dated 7 August mentioning a move to suppress his book. On 15 August Niccolini reported that he had been unable to see Riccardi but had heard that a hostile delegation which had met with Cardinal Barberini would approach Niccolini personally. Meanwhile Chiaramonti had been summoned as an expert astronomer hostile to Galileo. On 21 August Campanella wrote that a congregation of irate theologians ignorant of mathematics had been convened to prohibit the *Dialogue*. He knew that the pope was still not informed, though Riccardi professed to speak for him. Campanella's advice was to have the grand duke insist that he and Castelli be included in any panel appointed to discuss the book. A letter drafted by Galileo was sent by the secretary of state to Niccolini expressing dissatisfaction that a book properly licensed should be challenged and that any charges made had not been sent in writing to Florence, but this letter arrived in Rome too late to be used. Supposedly sent on 24 August, it appears rather to have been dated 30 August.

On 31 August Magalotti again saw Riccardi, who complained this time that the preface had been set in different type from the text, so that it appeared not to be connected with it; that the pope's argument at the end[8] was only one (instead of three); and that this had been placed in Simplicio's mouth, making it appear to be derided. Magalotti pointed out that there was nowhere else to put this argument, and that Salviati's final speech gave full credit to divine omnipotence. The 1616 decree being mentioned, Magalotti cited Galileo's earlier *Letter to Christina*, which Riccardi had not seen. After consulting with Castelli, Magalotti made a copy of this and gave it to Riccardi on 4 September. Meanwhile the ambassador Niccolini had talked with Riccardi, who had told him he was merely carrying out orders

and that if Galileo strictly obeyed these all would go well. Magalotti counseled above all that the pope not be brought into the
matter. Writing to Galileo on 4 September, he opined that at
worst some small modifications in the *Dialogue* might be required out of respect for the old decree.

On that very day, however, things had taken a different turn.
Niccolini had brought the subject up with the pope himself and
was angrily interrupted with the statement that Galileo had entered on the most dangerous ground there was. The pope said
he had been imposed on by Riccardi and Ciampoli. He rejected
Niccolini's request that Galileo be informed and allowed to defend himself, saying that the Holy Office never gave out information in advance and that Galileo knew well enough where the
difficulties lay, adding that the grand duke should not intervene,
as he could not then emerge with honor. Prohibition of the *Dialogue* was the least Galileo could expect, and he had better be
careful or he would be called by the Holy Office. The pope imposed secrecy on Niccolini and the grand duke, adding that he
had used Galileo kindly, "because he had penetrated what he
[Galileo] knows" and yet did not turn the case over to the
Inquisition as he ought to have done. He had only created a
special commission, thus treating Galileo better than the latter
had treated him.

Niccolini went on to say that in talking to Riccardi on 30
August he had been told that Riccardi did not believe there
would be any prohibition of the book. Niccolini, like Magalotti,
counseled caution, advising dealings thereafter only with Cardinal Barberini and officials other than the pope.

This angry intervention of Urban VIII, so contrary to what
was expected, strongly implies that some particular matter had
been brought to his attention that turned him irrevocably against
Galileo. His remark that Galileo knew where the difficulties lay
and that Urban had found out "what Galileo knows," together
with his assertion that he had used Galileo better than Galileo
had treated him, shows that Urban now knew of the notary's
unsigned statement in 1616 stating that Galileo had been personally ordered not to deal with Copernicanism in any way. No
other explanation of the pope's sudden and implacable anger
seems adequate. Galileo, when asking for permission to publish
a book on the system of the world in 1624, had not told Urban
about the incident in 1616; hence the pope, whose only informa-

tion about the events of that year came from the unsigned notarial memorandum, believed himself to have been deliberately
deceived by a trusted friend. There was no way he could have
known what Cardinal Bellarmine had told Galileo about the
commisary's intervention and precept.

On 9 September the secretary, Bali Cioli, wrote to Niccolini
that Grand Duke Ferdinando was so angry about his last report
from Rome that he did not know what would happen. Meanwhile other matters occupied Galileo's attention.

Cavalieri had written to Galileo on 31 August that he was
putting into his book on parabolic mirrors[9] (which he had previously mentioned on 18 May) a proposition about the parabolic
trajectory of projectiles, assuming Galileo's law of free fall and
crediting him with much of what was said on this matter. Again
he urged Galileo to publish his promised book on motion. This
letter came to Galileo's hands just as he was in the midst of all
the bad news from Rome. On 11 September he wrote to Marsili
his great displeasure that "a study of mine of more than forty
years, imparted largely in confidence to the said Father [Cava-
lieri], should now be wrenched from my priority. . . . Truly what
first moved me to speculate about motion was my intention of
finding this path which, although once found it is not very hard
to demonstrate, still I, who discovered it, know how much labor
I spent in finding that conclusion." Ordinary courtesy, he felt,
demanded that Cavalieri should have told him of his intention
sooner, in which case he would have begged Cavalieri to allow
him to bring out his own book first, adding whatever he liked
thereafter.

On the same day Torricelli introduced himself by letter to
Galileo, saying that he had studied mathematics for six years with
Castelli and two years with the Jesuit fathers. He was the first
in Rome to have thoroughly studied Galileo's new book, being
thus finally forced to adhere to Copernicus and counting himself
professionally a Galileist. Father Grienberger, he said, had taken
great pleasure in the *Dialogue* even though the (Copernican)
opinion should not be praised or held true. Scheiner commended
the book grudgingly and found the digressions boring; moreover,
he said, Galileo had ill-treated him in it and he did not wish to
talk about it.

On 11 September Niccolini conferred again with Riccardi, who
now knew that the pope was taking the position that the *Dia-*

logue dealt with matters of faith and not just mathematics, that it had been printed without the proper authorizations, and so on. "But above all, he [the pope] said with the usual confidentiality and secrecy that it had been found in the records of the Holy Office that about 12 (*sic*) years ago, it having been heard that Galileo held this [Copernican] opinion and was sowing it at Florence, and he having been called to Rome for this, he was prohibited in the name of the Pope and the Holy Office by Cardinal Bellarmine to hold this opinion; and that this alone was sufficient to ruin him now." Riccardi asked Niccolini to warn the grand duke that the only service he could render Galileo was to leave things alone.

On 18 September Niccolini notified Cioli that on the 15th a secretary to the pope visited him to say that as a result of the findings of the special commission, His Holiness was obliged to turn the matter of the *Dialogue* over to the Inquisition. Niccolini had delayed writing until he could speak with the pope himself, but without effect.

On 21 September Cavalieri wrote to Galileo much distressed by his complaint to Marsili. He sent some pages of his new book to show that he had credited Galileo and Castelli. Cavalieri had never been told to keep Galileo's work on motion confidential; indeed, he said, it had been his impression that Galileo had dealt with the projectile trajectory in some book, though he did not have a copy. He had heard it talked about for a long time, and ten years earlier Muzio Oddi had told him that Galileo had made some experiments of this effect with Guidobaldo del Monte (who had died in 1607).[10] He offered to put a further acknowledgment in the remaining copies of his book, of which only a few had been given out, or to destroy them if Galileo wished.

Marsili wrote at the same time to assure Galileo of Cavalieri's innocent intentions and full loyalty. Because of the rapid series of events that were much more serious for him, Galileo did not reply until 16 October. He then recounted the events to Marsili and said that he had not questioned Cavalieri's good faith, but that his misfortune (in losing priority of publication) had resulted in resentment toward the person causing it. Far from wishing anything to be changed in Cavalieri's book, he thanked its author for mentioning him there with honor.

On 25 September the Inquisitor at Florence forwarded to Antonio Barberini at Rome the original manuscript of the *Dia-*

logue. Francesco Barberini simultaneously instructed Florentine authorities to stop sales of the book and order Galileo to present himself before the Roman Inquisition in October. This order was given to Galileo on 2 October. A letter of Galileo's dated 6 October shows that he intended to leave for Siena, where the grand duke and his secretary Bali Cioli had gone, on Sunday, 10 October. He remained, however, at Florence, where on 13 October he appealed by letter to Francesco Barberini that he be spared the journey to Rome in ill health and old age, and instead be permitted to respond in writing. A copy of this letter was sent to Cioli in Siena and was forwarded on 16 October by Cioli to Niccolini, who wrote to Galileo that in his opinion the more he offered to defend his book the more likely it was to be prohibited outright and not merely altered. Though Castelli wrote that he thought the trip might be postponed, on 13 November Niccolini advised Galileo that the pope insisted that he come, and all that could be done was to ease the conditions of travel and waive some quarantine regulations along the road. The pope, still blaming Riccardi and Ciampoli, discharged the latter as papal secretary and sent him to a distant city.

On 20 November the Florentine Inquisitor granted Galileo a month's delay because he was bedridden and in care of a doctor. The pope was displeased to hear this, as Niccolini advised Galileo on 12 December. On 17 December the Florentine Inquisitor sent to Rome a statement that he had visited Galileo in bed, where three doctors had certified in writing that Galileo could not be moved without peril to his life.

The year ended appropriately with a further letter from Galileo to Marsili praising Cavalieri's recent book to the skies and recommending that authorities at the University of Bologna leave the brilliant mathematician free to follow his mathematical genius, rather than expect him to calculate ephemerides. The Roman Inquisition decreed at year end that Galileo's subterfuge of illness was not to be tolerated, and that if he did not proceed to Rome at once, or as soon as his life was not thereby endangered, he would be carried there in chains and charged for the expense of all doctors and transportation. On 11 January 1633 Cioli expressed to Galileo his indignation at this and told him the grand duke had put at his disposition a litter and an attendant to make his journey as easy as possible. On 20 January

Galileo departed for Rome, where he was lodged with Niccolini at the Trinità del Monte, seat of the Tuscan embassy, arriving on 13 February after about two weeks quarantine at Acquapendente.

On 25 February Galileo wrote that so far as he could learn, all the imputations against him came down to one thing that he would have no trouble in meeting. This was doubtless the charge, mentioned by Niccolini in a letter three days later, that in 1616 Galileo had been ordered "not to dispute or discuss this [Copernican] opinion; nevertheless he says that the command was not given in this form, but rather that he should not hold or defend it, he believing that he has a way of justifying himself . . . [and] that all other things seem to be of less importance or easier to get out of." The pope made it clear to Niccolini that he allowed Galileo to reside at the embassy only as a favor to the grand duke, rather than having him imprisoned as was customary, with which the grand duke expressed his satisfaction in due course.

On 7 March Luke Holste[11] wrote to Peiresc concerning Galileo, his "divine book," and his persecution by being brought to Rome in the middle of winter to answer to the Inquisition. "All these storms are believed to be born of the hatred of one monk whom Galileo will not admit to be the greatest mathematician in the world." Had Holste stopped with those words, it would seem evident that he meant Scheiner, for Gabriel Naudé, then librarian to Cardinal Barberini (as Holste was to be later), wrote to Pierre Gassendi in April that "Galileo has been cited by the Roman Curia through manipulations of Father Scheiner and other Jesuits who want him destroyed." Holste, however, went on to say that the envious monk he meant was "Commissary of the Holy Office," whom Favaro identified in a footnote to this letter as Vincenzo Maculano of Firenzuola. Now, Maculano was indeed Commissary General of the Inquisition at Galileo's trial in 1633, but there is no evidence that Galileo had previously met him or that Maculano had had anything to do with Galileo's having been ordered to Rome. Maculano was hardly a mathematician, let alone one who laid claim to great distinction, and throughout the trial he behaved toward Galileo in the most upright way. There is some evidence, though at present tenuous, that Ippolito Lanci may have been the person intended by Holste.[12]

III

On 12 April Galileo was transferred to the offices of the Inquisition, where he was received in a friendly way by the commissary and housed in a comfortable apartment there, with his own attendant lodged with him. The hearings opened on 13 April, as follows:

Called, there appeared personally at Rome in the Palace of the Holy Office, in the usual quarters of the Reverend Fathers Commissaries, in the presence of the Reverend Father Vincenzo Maculano, Commissary General, and the Reverend Doctor Carlo Sinceri, Fiscal Procurator of the Holy Office, etc., Galileo, son of the late Vincenzio Galilei, Florentine, seventy years of age, who, sworn to testify the truth, was asked by the Doctor:

Q: By what means and at what time did you arrive in Rome?

A: I arrived at Rome the first Sunday of Lent, and I came in a litter.

Q: Were you called to come, and by whom?

A: At Florence the Father Inquisitor ordered me to come to Rome and present myself to the Holy Office.

Q: Do you know or can you guess the cause that this order was given to you?

A: I imagine that the cause of my having been ordered to come before the Holy Office is to give an account of my recently printed book; and I suppose this because of the order given to the printer and to me, a few days before I was ordered to come to Rome, not to issue any more of those books, and similarly because the printer was ordered by the Father Inquisitor that he send the original manuscript of my book to the Holy Office at Rome.

Q: Explicitly what is in the book you imagine was the reason for the order that you come to the City?

A: It is a book written in dialogue, and it treats of the system of the world, or rather, the two chief systems, that is, the arrangements of the heavens and of the elements.

Q: If you were shown your said book, would you recognize it as yours?

A: I think that if it is shown to me, I shall recognize it.

And there was shown to him a book printed at Florence in the year 1632, with the title *Dialogue of Galileo Galilei* etc.; and when he had looked at it and inspected it, he said: "I know this book very well, and it is one of those printed at Florence, and I recognize it as mine and composed by me."[13]

Q: And do you recognize each and every word contained in said book as yours?

A: I know this book shown to me, printed at Florence, and everything contained in it I recognize as composed by me.

Q: Why and at what time did you write the said book, and where?

A: As to the place, I composed it at Florence, [starting] about ten or twelve years ago, and I was occupied on it about six or eight years, though not continuously.

Q: Tell whether you were at Rome another time, particularly in 1616, and for what occasion.

A: I was in Rome in 1616, and afterward I was here in [1624] the second year of the pontificate of His Holiness Urban VIII, and last I was here three years ago, on the occasion of my wish to have my book printed. The occasion for which I was at Rome in the year 1616 was that, hearing questions raised about the opinion of Nicholas Copernicus concerning the motion of the earth and stability of the sun and the order of the celestial spheres, in order to assure myself against holding any but holy and Catholic opinions, I came to hear what must be held concerning this matter.

Q: Did you come because you were called, and if so, for what reason were you called, and where and with whom did you treat of the said matter?

A: In 1616 I came to Rome of my own accord, without being called, and for the reason I told you; and in Rome I treated of this business with some Cardinals who governed the Holy Office at that time, in particular with Cardinals Bellarmine, Araceli, San Eusebio, Bonzi, and d'Ascoli.

Q: Tell in detail what you treated of with the said cardinals.

A: The occasion of dealing with the said cardinals was that they wished to be informed of the doctrine of Copernicus, his being a very difficult book to understand for those not of the mathematical and astronomical profession; and in particular they wanted to know the arrangement of the celestial orbs under the Copernican hypothesis, etc.

Q: You say you came to Rome to be able to have the truth about the said matter; say also what was the outcome of this business.

A: Concerning the controversy that went on about the said opinion of the stability of the sun and motion of the earth it was determined by the Holy Congregation of the Index that such an opinion, taken absolutely, is repugnant to Holy Scripture, and it is only to be admitted hypothetically, the way in which Copernicus took it.

Q: Were you then notified of the said decision, and by whom?
A: I was notified of the said decision of the Congregation of the Index, and I was notified by Cardinal Bellarmine.
Q: What were you told of the said decision by his Eminence Bellarmine, and did anyone else speak to you about it, and what?
A: Cardinal Bellarmine informed me that the said opinion of Copernicus could be held hypothetically, as Copernicus held it; and his Eminence knew that I held it hypothetically, that is, in the way Copernicus held it, as may be seen from the same cardinal's reply to a letter of Father Paolo Antonio Foscarini, of which I have a copy and in which are these words: "It appears to me that your Reverence and Signor Galileo did wisely to content yourselves to speak hypothetically and not absolutely," and this letter of the said cardinal is under date of 12 April 1615.
Q: What decision was made and then notified to you in the month of February, 1616?
A: In the month of February, 1616, Cardinal Bellarmine told me that since the opinion of Copernicus absolutely taken contradicted the Holy Scriptures it could not be held or defended, but that it might be taken hypothetically and made use of. In conformity with this I have an affidavit of the same Cardinal Bellarmine, made in the month of May, on the 26th, 1616, in which he says that the opinion of Copernicus cannot be held or defended, because of its being against the Holy Scriptures, of which affidavit I present a copy, and here it is.

And he exhibited a sheet of paper written on one side, about twelve lines, beginning "We Robert Cardinal Bellarmine, having" and ending "This 26th day of May, 1616," which was accepted as evidence and marked with the letter *B*.[14] He then added: "The original of this affidavit I have with me in Rome, and it is entirely written in the hand of Cardinal Bellarmine."
Q: When the aforesaid was notified to you, were others present, and who?
A: When Cardinal Bellarmine told me what I have said about the opinion of Copernicus there were some Dominican fathers present; but I did not know them, and did not see them again.
Q: Did the said fathers then being present, or anyone else, give you a precept of any kind about the same subject, and what?
A: As I recall it, the affair came about in this manner: One morning Cardinal Bellarmine sent for me, and he told me a certain particular[15] which I should like to speak to the ear of his

Holiness before that of anyone else; but in the end he told me
that the opinion of Copernicus could not be held or defended,
as contrary to the Holy Scriptures. As to those Dominican
fathers, I do not remember whether they were there first, or
came afterward; nor do I recall whether they were present
when the Cardinal told me that the said opinion could not be
held. And it may be that some precept was made to me that
I might not hold or defend the said opinion, but I have no
memory of it, because this was many years ago.

Q: If I were to read to you what was then said and intimated
to you as a precept, would you recall this?

A: I do not remember that I was told anything else, nor can
I know whether I should recall what was then said to me even
if it were read to me; and I say freely what I do recall, because
I claim not to have contravened in any way the precept, that is,
not to have held or defended the said opinion of the motion
of the earth and stability of the sun on any account.

And I told him what was contained in the said precept, given
in the presence of witnesses, namely that Galileo might not
in any way hold, defend or *teach* the said opinion.

Q: Now say whether you remember how and by whom this was
intimated to you.

A: I do not recall that this precept was intimated to me otherwise than by the voice of Cardinal Bellarmine, and I remember
that the precept was that I might not hold or defend; and
there may have been also *nor teach.* Nor do I remember that
there was this phrase "in any way," but there may have been,
I having not given any thought to it or called it to mind because
of my having, a few months later, that affidavit of the said
Cardinal Bellarmine of the 26th of May which I have presented,
in which is told the order to me not to hold or defend the said
opinion. And the other two phrases now notified to me of
the said precept, that is "nor teach" and "in any way," I have
not kept in my memory, I think because they are not set forth
in the said affidavit on which I relied, and which I have kept
as a reminder.[16]

* * * *

The affidavit (Exhibit B) read as follows:

We, Robert Cardinal Bellarmine, having heard that Sig.
Galileo Galilei is being slandered or imputed to have abjured
in our hand, and also to have been given salutary penance here,
and the truth of this matter being sought, say that the said
Sig. Galileo has not abjured in our hand nor in that of anyone

347

else here at Rome, or anywhere else so far as we know, concerning any doctrine or opinion of his, and still less has he received salutary or any other sort of penance, but he was only told of the declaration made by his Holiness and published by the Congregation of the Index, that [to say] the earth moves around the sun and that the sun stands still in the center of the universe without motion from east to west is contrary to Sacred Scripture and therefore may not be defended or held. In witness whereof we have subscribed and signed this with our own hand this 26th day of May 1616.[17]

The unsigned notary's memorandum from which the prosecutor had taken the things alleged to have been said, on the other hand, read as follows:

In the palace and residence of Cardinal Bellarmine, Galileo being called by him and being in the presence of the Cardinal and of the reverend Father Michelangelo Seghizzi of Lodi, Commissary General of the Holy Office, the Cardinal admonished the said Galileo of the error of the above-mentioned opinion and warned him to abandon it; and immediately and without delay, the said Cardinal being still present, the said Commissary gave Galileo a precept and ordered him in the name of his Holiness the Pope and the whole body of the Holy Office to the effect that the said opinion that the sun is the center of the universe and the earth moves must be entirely abandoned, nor might he from then on in any way hold, teach, or defend it by word or in writing; otherwise the Holy Office would proceed against him. This took place in Rome, there being present the reverend Badino Nores and Augustino Mongardo, witnesses, and familiars of the said Cardinal.[18]

In the balance of the first hearing Galileo admitted that he had said nothing of this even when obtaining the license to print the *Dialogue*, and he outlined the steps that had been taken in approving it for printing. He was then returned to his quarters.

The prosecutor did not press Galileo to reveal what Bellarmine had said to him on his arrival, nor did the pope ever allow Galileo to speak to him again personally. Galileo was not asked to explain anything contained in his book; as he had foreseen, the only real issue was whether or not he had received and disobeyed a specific personal order. On this matter, the paramount question was which of the two foregoing documents could be believed. Galileo had stated that he had with him at Rome the original affidavit in Bellarmine's own hand. Doubtless a search was then undertaken for the signed original of the notarial document on which the Inquisition had relied in bringing charges, but no such thing was ever found. Under the rule of best evidence, Galileo had therefore won his case on the only issue actually brought.

The Inquisition, however, could not let Galileo off scot-free; to bring a false charge of heresy was as serious a crime as heresy itself, and this charge had been brought by the highest authorities. Accordingly something more had to be done, but the Inquisition neither badgered Galileo in his quarters nor confronted him with the objections to his book that had been compiled by the special panel appointed by the pope. The suggestion they did follow originated with Cardinal Barberini, who had throughout all these months acted in Galileo's best interests. He and the pope were residing at Castel Gandolfo, and a letter sent to him there by Maculano, dated 28 April, tells the next event:

Yesterday, in accordance with orders from his Holiness, their Eminences of the Holy Congregation took up the case of Galileo, reviewing its state briefly. And having approved what has been done thus far, they next considered various difficulties as to the manner of prosecuting the case and getting it speedily under way again. In particular, because Galileo denied at his hearing what is evident in the book he wrote, there would have to be greater rigor in the proceedings and less regard for niceties in this affair. Finally I proposed a means: that the Holy Congregation grant me power to deal extra-judicially with Galileo to the end of convincing him of his error and bringing him to the point of confessing it when he understood. At first this appeared too daring a proposal, for there seemed little hope of succeeding by means of reasonable persuasion, but when I mentioned my basis for putting forth the idea[19] they gave me this power. And not to lose time I went to reason with Galileo yesterday after luncheon, and after many exchanges between us I gained my point, by the grace of God; for I made him see that he was clearly wrong and that in his book he had gone too far. He agreed to confess this judicially, but asked me for a little time to honestize his confession, which I hope will in substance follow the line suggested [by you?]. I felt obliged to let you know at once, having told no one else, so that you and his Holiness will be satisfied that in this way the case can be brought to a point where it can proceed without difficulty.

The tribunal will retain its reputation and be able to use benignity with the accused. However things turn out, Galileo will recognize the grace accorded to him, and all the other satisfactory consequences that are wished for will follow. Today I plan to examine him to obtain the confession; with that in hand, as I hope, nothing will remain but to interrogate him on intention and permit him his defenses, which done, it will be possible to return him to his house for imprisonment as you mentioned to me.[20]

Thus Galileo was offered a promise of leniency in return for some admission of wrongdoing. On Saturday 30 April he appeared for the brief second hearing, at which he was merely asked to say what occurred to him and replied by saying that in the past several days he had thought over the earlier questions and had asked to see his book again; having reread it he realized that in many places a reader ignorant of his intention might think the arguments carried the day for the position he meant to confute, especially the arguments from sunspots and from the tides. He could only excuse himself on grounds of vanity and ambition, every man liking to show himself cleverer than others in his own subtleties. He had not meant any disobedience but confessed vain ambition, ignorance, and inadvertence.

Having signed this confession Galileo left the room, but he returned immediately and offered to refute satisfactorily the offending parts of the *Dialogue* in a book he was now writing, with the same interlocutors, on various physical problems separate from the subject of the *Dialogue*. Maculano then, in the presence of witnesses, released Galileo to the custody of the Florentine ambassador, subject to recall and under orders of secrecy as to the proceedings. The next day, 1 May, Niccolini wrote to Cioli:

Galileo was sent back home here, unexpectedly since his examination is not finished, and this through the offices of the Father Commissary and [Francesco] Cardinal Barberini, who freed him of his own accord without the Congregation [being present], to recover from his discomforts and usual indispositions.

It is known from a letter of Niccolini's that Galileo's case was expected to be closed at the end of May, probably by prohibition of the *Dialogue* and imposition of some salutary penances on Galileo for his having violated personal instructions which had been given him by Bellarmine in 1616. Niccolini's expectation was based on conversations with Francesco Barberini, whose views at this time (late May) it may be taken to represent. But there was to be disagreement among the other cardinals on the sentence. Some wished to impose a merely nominal penalty in accord with the extrajudicial bargain with Galileo, while others feared that if set free he would boast of their defeat on the only charge that had been formally pressed in the hearings, thus weakening the authority of the Inquisition. The final decision was made by Urban VIII, who on 16 June ordered Galileo's examination on intention,[21] to be followed (if he sustained this) by imprisonment for an indefinite term at the pleasure of the Holy Office, confiscation of the *Dialogue*, and mandatory public reading of the sentence to professors of mathematics throughout Italy and elsewhere.

On 19 June Niccolini, not knowing of this, requested that the pope expedite the case. He learned that the decision had already been made and that Galileo was to be imprisoned at Rome (subject to further negotiations) after formal sentencing. In order not to afflict Galileo unnecessarily, Niccolini told him only that he should expect prohibition of the *Dialogue*. On 21 June Galileo was examined as to intention; he stated that until the 1616 decree he had considered the two world systems to be freely debatable, but that thereafter he had adhered to the fixed earth and movable sun; in his book he had considered no argument as conclusive and the decision of "sublime authority" as binding. Asked whether he spoke truly, on pain of torture, he replied: "I am here to obey, and have not held this opinion after the determination made, as I said." Galileo was not put to torture, Francesco Barberini having forbidden that.[22]

On 22 June the sentence of life imprisonment was read to Galileo at a formal ceremony in the presence of the cardinals of the Inquisition and witnesses, after which he had to abjure on his knees before them. Significantly, three cardinals of the ten refused to sign the sentence: Francesco Barberini, who throughout the whole affair had acted in Galileo's interests with great skill and judgment; Gaspare Borgia, who realized the importance of Galileo's scientific proposals to the Spanish government even though he had been unable to assist Galileo in gaining their adoption; and Laudivio Zacchia.

On 26 June Niccolini reported that Francesco Barberini had immediately commuted the place of Galileo's imprisonment at

Rome to the Florentine embassy there. Niccolini then undertook to secure a pardon for Galileo from the pope, who refused but permitted Galileo to be moved to the custody of Archbishop Ascanio Piccolomini, of Siena, who had written during the trial to invite Galileo there after it was concluded. On 6 July Galileo left Rome, and on 9 July he was in Siena.

NINETEEN

1633-35

I

Ascanio Piccolomini Belonged to a family long distinguished in Italian scholarship and the humanities; he had studied mathematics with Cavalieri and greatly admired Galileo. In the company of this cultured and gracious host it was not long before Galileo regained his composure. He was very badly shaken, not by the prohibition of his book, but by a sentence which he regarded all the rest of his life as a deliberate breach of the agreement under which he had confessed to any wrongdoing at all. A letter dated from Siena on 21 July by a sympathetic resident says that at first "there were many nights that he did not sleep, but went through the night crying out and rambling so crazily that it was seriously considered whether his arms should be bound" lest he injure himself. Nevertheless, Piccolomini managed soon to turn Galileo's thoughts back to science and enable him to put behind him his months of anxiety and suffering.

It is known from later letters that Galileo began work at Siena on *Two New Sciences*, and since the section of that book on local motion is its most celebrated part it has always been assumed that formal writing of that section started at Siena. That, however, is incorrect. Whether or not the Third Day had been essentially completed at Florence early in 1631, as I believe, the writing Galileo began at Siena had to do not with motion but with the structure of matter and the strength of materials. It will be seen in due course that the First Day was not finalized until early in 1635, much of what it contains having been suggested by events that belong to 1634. What Galileo began writing at Siena was the Second Day, consisting mainly of formal propositions about the strength of materials, for that was the subject of the only scientific correspondence conducted by Galileo during his five months at Siena. In connection with this, parts of the First Day were composed in dialogue form.

During his residence with the archbishop Galileo took part in many discussions that enraptured his host and the guests who were invited to dine with Galileo during Piccolomini's campaign to restore his equanimity and compensate for his recent ordeal. These affairs scandalized some priests and resulted in reports to Rome, of which one at least survives, saying that Galileo was being treated as an honored guest rather than as a condemned heretic. Probably such reports had something to do with Galileo's release to Arcetri, near Florence, at the end of 1633.

Soon after Galileo's arrival at Siena there occurred an event of a practical nature, recognizable in some of the correspondence, of which we have Piccolomini's own account written two decades later. It was probably to Vincenzio Viviani, who came to live with Galileo during his final years, that Piccolomini wrote in 1657 when Viviani was collecting materials for a biography of his teacher:

I can hardly satisfy your wish and command in the matter of dialogue fragments of Sig. Galileo, because although it is true that most of it [*Two New Sciences*] was written out here in my house, he left no copy whatever concerning the particulars you mention, with me or anyone else. I can indeed tell you briefly what happened and was said about the casting of bells [known to Viviani only from oblique allusions in Galileo's letters], and consequently about the quicksilver experiment. The great bell for this tower had to be recast, and the mold being made, things went badly when the molten metal was running in, this [metal] spreading out under the base of the mold. People speculated about the cause, and Sig. Galileo said positively that this could be no other than the weight of the [molten] metal that had lifted up the said mold. To demonstrate this by experiment he had brought into the house an exact wooden model, and turning it upside down he filled it with shot. Then he took a glass urinal with which he covered it, leaving between the glass and wood a space the thickness of a *piastra*.[1] This done, he began to pour in quicksilver [entering the model] through a hole that the glass had on top, and he said that as soon as the quicksilver had risen to the height demonstrated by him in his *Floating Bodies*,[2] with this little weight [of mercury] the mold full of shot would be lifted up, which weighed twenty times as much as the quicksilver. And the event succeeded precisely; hence it was concluded that to insure the casting of the bell it was necessary to tie and fix firmly the mold to the pavement on the ground where it was placed. And thus, the second time, the casting went very well.

More than this little bit is not to be hoped for from here, since no one else took part in the conversation except Dr. [Alessandro] Marsili, with whom I am certain nothing whatever will be found.

Alessandro (not Cesare) Marsili was a professor of philosophy at Siena with whom Galileo corresponded intermittently in later years. There is a considerable difference between the Simplicio of the *Dialogue*, a stubborn Peripatetic patterned on Cesare Cremonini and Ludovico delle Colombe, and the Simplicio of *Two New Sciences*, much more reasonable and willing to learn; the contrast indeed occasioned comment from Cavalieri when he read the later book. Perhaps the new Simplicio drew on arguments raised by Marsili at Siena, especially those concerning the nature and properties of fluids dealt with in the First Day.

Discussion of fluids at Siena revived Galileo's interest in questions of the structure of matter and thereby in the strength of materials. The first six propositions on that subject, as set forth in *Two New Sciences*, had been known to Galileo by 1609, but only now did it occur to him that there could exist no two geometrically similar bodies of the same material that could have identical breaking strengths. This became Proposition Seven of the Second Day, and its fascinating implications for physics were used to excite general interest early in the First Day. In September 1633 Galileo sent this proposition to Niccolò Aggiunti, who saw how it implied that there must be a definite limit to the size of any structure with given materials. Galileo then sent Proposition Eight to Mario Guiducci and Proposition [Nine][3] to Aggiunti, inviting him to seek a proof. Guiducci advised Galileo that Andrea Arrighetti had independently found a proof of Proposition Eight, different from Galileo's, and mentioned that he was going to discuss the bell-casting problem with Pietro Tacca, presumably a Tuscan foundryman or engineer whose opinion or information Galileo had sought.

Aggiunti replied with an attempted proof of Proposition [Nine], while Galileo sent this proposition also to Guiducci for Arrighetti's attention. On 25 September Arrighetti wrote directly to Galileo, sending his previous proof of Proposition Eight and a further comment on the proof of Proposition [Nine] along similar lines. Galileo was so pleased with Arrighetti's approach as to ask permission to include his proof of Proposition Eight in the treatise he was writing, that is, the Second Day of *Two New Sciences*. In slightly modified form it is there, appended to Galileo's proof, Arrighetti having expressed delight to Guiducci at having earned Galileo's approval, saying he hoped Galileo would treat the proof as his own, since Arrighetti had learned from him what he knew of this science.

This correspondence, together with the testimony of Piccolomini, makes it safe to conclude that the Second Day of *Two New Sciences* was put into dialogue form and part of the First Day was written at Siena during the latter part of 1633.

On 13 November Niccolini asked the pope to permit Galileo to return to Florence, or at least to his villa at Arcetri. He found Urban displeased that others were defending Galileo's views. These men were being watched by the Holy Office. That is probably the reason why few of Galileo's letters survive from this period, when there was reason to fear that their possession might lead to trouble.[4] On 1 December, the pope recommended to the Holy Office that Galileo be permitted to return to his villa at Arcetri, in the hills some distance from Florence, provided he receive few visitors and refrain from teaching. On 17 December Galileo wrote from Arcetri to Cardinal Barberini, thanking him for his many favors and especially for aiding in his return.

Best known of all stories about Galileo is the one which tells how he is supposed to have muttered a defiant "yet it does move" as he rose from his knees after abjuring before the cardinals of the Roman Inquisition. That popular version is preposterous, since no sympathetic ear could have been there to hear him, nor could Galileo have escaped the most dire consequences for any such foolish defiant act. The story was long believed to have made its first appearance in the mid-eighteenth century in a book of anecdotes by a French abbé,[5] and was accordingly considered apocryphal by serious historians. Yet there is a sound basis for believing that Galileo uttered this famous phrase, though at a different time and place.

The story in fact first appeared in print in English, in *The Italian Library* published by an Italian man of letters, Giuseppe Baretti, at London in 1757. Baretti wrote: "The moment he was set at liberty, he looked up at the sky and down to the ground, and, stamping with his foot, in a contemplative mood, said *Eppur si m[u]ove*; that is, 'still it moves,' meaning the earth."[6] Properly speaking Galileo was never "set at liberty," least of all by the Inquisition at Rome in June 1633. The nearest thing to Galileo's having been set free was when in December of that year he was allowed to leave the custody of the archbishop of Siena and return to his own villa at Arcetri.

Now, in 1911 a Belgian family which owned a painting supposed to represent Galileo in the dungeons of the Inquisition, dated 1643 (1645?) and attributed to Murillo or some painter of his school at Madrid, sent this painting to be cleaned. When it was removed from the frame it was found to be larger than supposed, having been deliberately folded back when originally framed. As previously seen, the gaunt figure representing the prisoner seemed to be pointing with a finger at a dungeon wall precisely at the edge of the painting as framed. Unfolded, it revealed the words *Eppur si muove* written on that wall. There was no question of the authenticity of the painting or of its Spanish origin, though the date was partly illegible.[7]

Nothing would have been more in character for Galileo, at the moment of leaving the hospitality of his good friend and host Ascanio Piccolomini, than—just before his entering the waiting carriage—to stamp a foot on the ground, perhaps wink, and utter the famous words. Ascanio's brother Ottavio was then stationed in Madrid as a professional soldier. Quite possibly the story, which could not be circulated widely with safety to Galileo, was passed on within the family and the picture was commissioned by Ottavio at Madrid at the time of Galileo's death. Thereafter it lived on in oral tradition. Printed a century later, it became widely popular in the incorrect form for which Baretti was in no way responsible. In any case there is no doubt now that the famous words were already attributed to Galileo before his death, not invented a century later merely to fit his character.

It is to Archbishop Piccolomini that the world owes restoration of Galileo's peace of mind after his long and terrible ordeal. Without his solicitude at a critical time, Galileo might never have turned back to scientific studies. Piccolomini remained

Galileo's friend thereafter, sending him wine each year with comments on the vintage, accompanied by game from the autumn hunts and cheering letters.

II

Awaiting Galileo on his return was a letter from Mathias Bernegger promising to translate the *Dialogue* into Latin for him. The first letter of scientific interest that Galileo received at Arcetri came from Cavalieri, who told him he was going to publish his *Geometry* and had it half done in fair copy. He wanted to include a proportionality proposition for which Galileo had once asked him, but would not do so if Galileo needed this for his own book.[8]

About the time Galileo arrived at Arcetri, François de Noailles passed through Florence en route to Rome as French ambassador. They did not meet at this time, but the presence of Noailles in Rome and his later return to France were of importance to Galileo's last book. He had been a pupil of Galileo's at Padua in 1603, was personally friendly to him, and was aware of the strong sentiment in France against his condemnation, concerning which Nicole Fabri de Peiresc, Pierre Gassendi, Marin Mersenne, René Descartes, Elia Didodati, Pierre Fermat, Pierre Carcavy, and others were outspoken. Some correspondence between Galileo and Noailles took place while the latter was at Rome, where the ambassador made several efforts to secure a pardon for Galileo. The significance of this will appear presently.

During Galileo's absence from Florence, Niccolò Aggiunti and Geri Bocchineri had obtained the key to his villa for the purpose of removing or hiding any books or manuscripts that might tend to damage his case if seized by officers of the Inquisition. This is known partly from a letter written by Galileo's eldest daughter, who had the keys, and partly from a letter to Galileo from Aggiunti on 27 December, very soon after his return. Some things removed by Bocchineri had been returned, but Galileo did not find among them certain documents of great concern to him. There is little doubt that the missing manuscripts were those relating to his work on motion, needed for the new book. Aggiunti assured Galileo that he himself had sequestered only some printed books, not manuscripts, but was sure that Galileo would find everything safe. That this turned out to be the case is known from another letter, dated 4 January 1634.

A letter from Cavalieri on 10 January 1634, rejoicing to hear that Galileo was at last putting his book on natural motion in shape for publication, begged him to include something in it on the theory of indivisibles "for the benefit of my *Geometry*," since the dialogue form of Galileo's book would allow scope for such material. Galileo complied by bringing a discussion of indivisibles into the exposition of a theory of matter in the First Day, which served him also for his discussion of accelerated motion in the Third Day. When Cavalieri published his *Geometry by Indivisibles* in 1635[9] he did not mention Galileo by name, but that did not mean that their relations were in any way strained; it was simply because after the public reading of Galileo's sentence in all university cities it would have been dangerous for a professor of mathematics to honor Galileo in a published book so soon, even if Cavalieri had not been a member of a religious order.

III

It was probably in the course of reviewing his discussion of the definition of uniform acceleration in the form already translated in chapter 17 that Galileo began once more to think about problems of the force of percussion. On 1 February Aggiunti wrote to him that "your proposition about percussion is truly wonderful, and if demonstrated it carries along some consequences no less wonderful, among which one seems to me to be this—that any impact, however light, will have infinite force; for taking any weight, however great, we shall be able to find a resistance such that a light percussion on it will act no less than the pressing of the assumed great weight." No other correspondence of this period bears on percussion.

Early in 1634 a philosopher named Antonio Rocco published a book against Galileo's *Dialogue*.[10] This was seen by Fulgenzio Micanzio, who later held several conversations with Rocco, finding him to be a reasonable man but absolutely committed to defend everything Aristotle had ever said. Micanzio suggested that Galileo consider Rocco's book while writing his new treatise on motion. About the end of February Galileo sent to Micanzio seventy-five marginal notes on Rocco's book, to which he later added some longer comments on separate sheets. These are of importance as containing material incorporated into the First Day of *Two New Sciences* later the same year; some extracts from them will be given below.

At this time Galileo suffered a painful hernia and applied to the Holy Office at Rome for permission to see doctors in Florence. The request was not only refused, but the Florentine Inquisitor was instructed to tell Galileo that any more such petitions from him would result in imprisonment. The Inquisitor was at Galileo's villa to give him this bad news when Galileo returned from a visit to the nearby convent in Arcetri (on 1 April) where his daughter Virginia lay mortally ill. Galileo had just been told that she would probably not live through that night when he arrived home to learn the additional bad news from Rome. Because this is a scientific biography, already far too long to include discussion of Galileo's personal life, the many beautiful letters from Sister Maria Celeste (as Virginia was called in her religious order) have been omitted. She was deservedly by far the most cherished person in the world to Galileo. She died on 2 April after a brief and sudden illness.

Galileo was completely inconsolable. For the next three months there is no evidence of his having done any further work. An indication of his frame of mind is found in a letter from Cavalieri in June, telling him that he had been unable to find a copy of certain religious poems Galileo had asked him for and was able only to forward a "dialogue between Christ and the Soul" published by the same author. A letter of Galileo's in this period says: "My hernia has come back, larger than at first; my pulse is irregular, with palpitations of the heart; I feel immense sadness and melancholy, together with extreme inappetite; I am hateful to myself, and continually hear my beloved daughter calling to me."

Cavalieri's letter indicated that his *Geometry* was now ready for the press, though he hoped that Galileo would first publish his own work on motion and include in it something on the topic of indivisibles. It was probably this plea that succeeded in getting Galileo's mind back to his work, adding to the Rocco postils a lucid exposition of his views on the topic which so much occupied Cavalieri (concerning which Galileo's opinion differed somewhat from that of his young disciple). In August Cavalieri sent him the first printed sheets of his *Geometry*, apparently the first "book" (of an introductory character and not concerned with indivisibles) and a part of the second, in which the basic definitions and an important scholium to Cavalieri's fundamental theorem were included.[11] In the accompanying letter Cavalieri explained his reasons for having composed a seventh (and last) book, in which certain of the results obtained earlier were again derived but without the use of infinite aggregates. About the time he received this, Galileo wrote to Elia Diodati in Paris of his resolve to publish his long-awaited book and also to reply separately to various critics.

IV

In mid-1634 Marin Mersenne translated Galileo's *Mechanics* into French and published it with additions and commentaries of his own. Carcavy had been given a copy of the *Dialogue* by Pierre Fermat and was so enchanted that he intended to publish Galileo's entire argument in French. Descartes first saw the *Dialogue* in August 1634, a copy having just been lent to him by Isaac Beeckman.

A second set of postils to Rocco's book was sent to Micanzio; in acknowledging this he told Galileo that the first set had been seen by Rocco and a friend of his, both of whom were impressed but remained convinced that Aristotle could not be wrong.

Galileo now returned to active work, examining the part of Cavalieri's *Geometry* that had been sent to him. A letter from Cavalieri dated 2 October shows that Galileo had generally approved his method of indivisibles but warned him about some paradoxes of the infinite. To illustrate these, Galileo had composed the "soupdish paradox" that was later printed in *Two New Sciences*,[12] based on a proposition of Luca Valerio's and so presented as to show that two surfaces could remain always equal in a certain plane, moved until suddenly, at a limiting position, one surface degenerated into a line and the other into a point. It followed that under a certain way of speaking about "equality" we should be obliged to call the circumferences of concentric circles "equal" and even to say that all of them were equal to a single point. Cavalieri's first retort was no less clever than Galileo's paradox; in the ultimate extinction of a magnitude, he said, nothing remains of the entity whose existence was required in order to create the paradox.

In a comment on Rocco's book at this time Galileo revived the *parti quante* and *parti non quante* of his 1613 reply to Colombe, adding now a third category of elements that he called "neither denumerable nor continuous, but answerable to any number," much as we now think of a variable in an equation.[13] The section in the First Day of *Two New Sciences* introducing this concept was accordingly most probably written in the autumn of 1634.

Micanzio wrote to Galileo (14 October): "I took to the villa your *Dialogue* and Rocco's book; nothing else. I have read both with pleasure, my mind being in that state in which the eye is when watching the clown imitating the acrobat. The point is that your works so satisfy my taste that I can no longer read anything of speculative physics, and it seems to me that in reexamining the Peripatetic principles as you have done, everything [of theirs] goes up in smoke for me." That seems to have been precisely Galileo's objective in all his published works.

On 19 November Galileo replied to Micanzio concerning a lost treatise of Paolo Sarpi's on the subject of condensation and rarefaction. In this letter he recounted his own early perplexities on that problem and his sudden insight into the possibility of a "stupendous operation of Nature." The idea first came to Galileo while talking to Salviati at Le Selve (as he told Dini in 1615), probably in 1613 while writing the replies to Colombe cited in chapter 12, § 1. His inspiration was the concept that in some ultimate sudivision of matter it might exist as *parti non quante*. In his *Assayer*, light had been suggested as a possible example. The idea was further extended in *Two New Sciences*, placed where discussion of the "wheel of Aristotle" afforded a pretext for this, probably in November 1634. He now said: "the treatise on motion, all new, is in order, but my unquiet mind will not rest from mulling it over with great expenditure of time, because the latest thought to occur to me about some novelty [repeatedly] makes me throw out much already found there." Micanzio was not alone in protesting to Galileo against those perpetual revisions.

The postil to Rocco concerning indivisibles was sent to Micanzio early in December, evcking from him the comment that it quite transported him: "I seem to be in another world; body is to me completely different from what it ever was before; this makes a new universe for me. I had heard the ancient opinion [of the atomists] in [reading] Aristotle and others, but being [there] introduced without reason or explanation it seemed to me strange. Now your reasons seem marvelous to me, nor do I know what opposition Sig. Rocco can avail himself of." Galileo's conception had nothing to do with ancient atomism as such, a fact that was instantly perceived by Micanzio through Galileo's mathematical analogy to certain puzzling physical phenomena. The enormous difference between the finest conceivable powder and any fluid, in which ultimate particles are somehow suddenly reached, illustrated his point.

Galileo's postil had been written in reply to Rocco's disapproval of a discussion in Galileo's *Dialogue* concerning the proposition that a sphere touches a plane at only a single point.[14] In introducing this as a pretext for developing his view of the nature of continuous magnitude, Galileo wrote:

You believe this to be manifestly absurd and most false because philosophers and mathematicians deem that it would follow that a line must be composed of points, whereas they both will have it that on the contrary every continuous magnitude consists of parts always divisible. I reply by conceding that the composition of a line from points and the continuum from indivisibles is difficult, and has been up to now almost unintelligible, but not at all false.[15] And you show little study of mathematical authors when you put them in the same group as philosophers,[16] the former having never dealt with this question, except perhaps some second-rate mathematicians, or worse.

I, Sig. Rocco, differing from others, deem both propositions true. Being certain that the continuum consists of parts always divisible, I say that it is most true and necessary that the line be composed of points and the continuum of indivisibles, that is, that since truth is one, we must admit that it is the same thing to say that the continuum consists of *parts* always divisible, and [to say] that it consists *of* indivisibles. Please open your eyes to the light that has perhaps been concealed till now, and perceive clearly that the continuous is divisible into parts always divisible solely *because* it consists of indivisibles, inasmuch as if division and subdivision must go on forever, the multitude of parts must be such that it can never be exceeded, whence the parts must therefore be infinitely many, otherwise the division would come to an end. And being infinite, it is impossible that they are quantified, since infinitely many quanta compose an infinite quantity, and we are speaking of bounded quantities; hence the highest, ultimate, or rather first components of the continuum are infinitely many indivisibles. Do you not see that to say that the continuum consists of parts always divisible implies that by dividing and subdividing, one *never* arrives at its prime components? The prime components, therefore, are those which are no longer divisible, and the no-longer-divisibles are the indivisibles.

Here the philosophasters customarily resort to act[uality] and potentiality,[17] saying the divisibles in the continuum are potentially infinite but always actually finite—an escape that they may understand and that satisfies them, but on which I can put no construction whatever; perhaps Sig. Rocco will instruct me. Hence I ask in what manner, in a line four palms long, there are contained four parts, that is four lines of one palm each; I mean, whether these are actually contained, or only potentially? If you tell me they are contained only potentially when they are not marked or divided, but actually when they are cut, I will then prove to you that neither in act nor in potency can quantified parts be infinite in the line. For I ask whether in newly actuating, by dividing, the four parts, this line of four palms increases, diminishes, or does not change in magnitude? I believe you will reply that it remains exactly the same magnitude. Therefore I conclude that if a line always remains of the same magnitude, whether it has its quantified parts in act or has them only in potency, then, being unable to contain infinitely many of these in actuality, no more can it contain them in potency; and thus neither in act nor in potency can there be infinitely many quantified parts in a bounded line.

After remarking that to bend a strip of paper into a circle accomplishes at one stroke what could never be attained by forming with the same strip polygons of more and more sides, Galileo went on:

Other remarkable consequences you will hear at another time, when I hope to show you that the path commonly supposed to serve in understanding Nature's steps is about as effective in leading philosophers toward their desired goal—by their banishing from mind infinities, indivisibles, and voids as vain and pernicious concepts detestable to Nature—as a painter's or a smith's pupil would be led who was told as a first step to throw away colors, brushes, anvils, hammers and files as useless materials and instruments only hurtful to their pursuits.[18]

Even better than the more measured language of *Two New Sciences*, this passage expresses Galileo's instrumentalist view of mathematics in physical science in opposition to Platonist fancies about the "real" universe. Purely mathematical concepts, like a painter's tools, are essential to a finished product but need not be part of it.

On 19 December Cavalieri, having learned that some things he had sent to Galileo had never arrived at Arcetri, offered a new reply to the "soupdish" paradox in this even better form:

> In the concept of "all the lines of a plane figure" or of "all the planes of a body" according to my definitions, the extremes are not included, though they appear to be of the same kind; for I call "all the lines of a plane figure" the common sections by the plane cutting the figure in the motion made by this *from* one extreme *to* the other, or *from* one tangent all the way *to* the opposite tangent. Now, since the beginning (and the end) of motion is not motion, one should not compute the extreme tangents as among "all the lines," and thus there is no wonder (understanding the same for the planes in solids) that these extremes should remain unequal as in the example of the "soupdish."

That is, a point considered as the extreme limit of a set of lines was not properly identifiable also as the extreme member of such a set.

Micanzio, unable to obtain Galileo's earlier work on bodies in water from booksellers, obtained from Galileo copies of that and other works of his. He was so impressed with them that he wished to have them reprinted. From a sentence copied from a lost letter of Galileo's to Diodati on 21 December 1634, it appears that Galileo now asked Micanzio to arrange for printing of *Two New Sciences*: "In short, I shall commence to send to Venice what remains of my labors, that is, what is considered by me to be entirely new and all mine, and there to arrange that it be printed."

Galileo's second group of comments on Rocco's book gives a good picture of the work he was doing in the latter part of 1634, much of which was to be reflected in the First Day of *Two New Sciences*. The fallacies of Aristotle's rule of speed in fall proportional to weight were explained to Rocco in more detail and in a more elementary way:

> I have already exposed above the indirect consequence you draw from the premises when you say: "The effect of heaviness is to tend downward; therefore, where more heaviness is found, there the motion of the falling body must be more accelerated."

That consequence cannot be drawn from the premises, in which no mention is made of speed but only of "downward," whence this argument should go thus: "The effect of heaviness is to tend downward; therefore, where there is greater heaviness, there it should more greatly tend downward," and that is indeed true. And if perhaps by changing the assumption you think you can conclude directly, saying: "The effect of heaviness is to induce speed; therefore, where there is greater heaviness there will be greater speed," I question whether you do not run into another kind of mistake, of proving *idem per idem*, because if you wish to be able with Aristotle to infer that speed grows proportionately to heaviness, it does not suffice to assume indeterminately that heaviness induces speed, but one must suppose that the speed grows according to the increase of heaviness, which is then the same conclusion you intended to prove, so this new error is worse than the first.[19]

Finally, to meet the other part of my self-imposed obligation, I must produce also the reasons which, over and above experience, confirm my proposition—although to assure the mind, no reason is necessary where experience reaches—which I shall nevertheless produce, for your benefit and also because I was persuaded by reason before sense assured me.[20]

Galileo then explained the process by which he had come to doubt Aristotle's rule because of his experience in a hailstorm, set forth above in chapter 1. He was thus led, he said, to an axiom that every falling body has some determinate speed limited by nature, to increase or diminish which required the use of force,[21] for which no source could be found in the tying together of two equal weights, while the tying together of two unequal weights led to a direct contradiction of Aristotle's rule. He then passed on to the effect of resistance of the medium, discussing first the question of resistance to separation by parts of a fluid. This must be very small, and incapable of entirely preventing the descent of any heavy body having the slightest excess of heaviness over that of the medium. This resistance, however, becomes greater as the *speed* of separation is increased, and must finally result in uniform descent. (The effect of viscosity, as distinguished from buoyancy, was separately noted in this discussion.) As to separation of parts, "a small boy might draw with a slender thread through still water, though very slowly, a boat that the force of a hundred galley-slaves would not suffice to move against the opposition of water that had to be opened with great speed to give way to the boat."

V

Early in 1635 Galileo heard from a Florentine engineer, Giovanni Pieroni, then in the service of the Holy Roman Emperor. Pieroni urged Galileo to publish his book on motion and was later to try unsuccessfully to find a publisher abroad for it. Micanzio also wrote to tell Galileo that there was a great desire at Venice to see the new book and that he believed there would be no difficulty about printing it there, despite the timorous nature of the local Inquisitor. On 27 January he received from Galileo the first three "folios" of the manuscript of *Two New Sciences.* Three more went to him early in February, dealing with the "wheel of Aristotle." Since Galileo was accustomed to writing on sheets gathered into groups of five and folded together, the six gatherings Micanzio had received indicate that he now had sixty pages of manuscript. Ensuing discussions show that the text being sent to him was that of the First Day as later printed. On 10 February he wrote that the Inquisitor had told him that he could not reprint Galileo's book on bodies in water because it was forbidden to print anything whatever edited by Galileo. Micanzio asked the Inquisitor what would happen if Galileo wanted to edit the Credo, or the Lord's Prayer? He requested a copy of the exact wording of the order and assured Galileo that if it did include future works, he would somehow get around it. During February he showed Galileo's manuscript to Antoine De La Ville, a French engineer stationed at Venice, and to Paolo Aproino, who had studied with Galileo at Padua. Both sent Galileo questions and objections.

Having seen the official order against the printing of Galileo's writings, Micanzio next thought of depositing a manuscript copy in the Marciana library at Venice, since printing it would invite persecution. Aproino suggested that a copy be deposited in each of several libraries abroad, he also fearing for Galileo's well-being if the book were printed. He remarked that De La Ville was an engineer, little fond of theory, "and without very careful observations he cannot well cope with you, who are the father of experiments and of all their exactness." Aproino remembered personally Galileo's experiments at Padua around 1608.

De La Ville had mistakenly supposed Galileo to believe that machines could be made as large as one wished, provided only that the same proportions were maintained and that the material were perfect. Galileo replied in March:

I confess that I was unable to explain my conception with that clarity required in good explanation, especially when the opinion is remote from common beliefs. So I say that my intention was very different and even the exact opposite of the sense you have drawn from it, inasmuch as it is false that I believed that machines which work in small size must also succeed enlarged, provided that the same proportions are kept, etc. Rather, I meant that they cannot in any way succeed. You next add that I said that imperfection of matter is not a good argument to prove the contrary, that is, to prove that [some] large machines cannot work though they would if made smaller. On the contrary I affirm that the cause of their not succeeding cannot lie in the material, subject to a thousand imperfections, changes, and all those other things you enumerate with great particularity, of which I never claimed, nor (I believe) gave any indication of claiming, that a science could be formed. The cause I refer to and repose in matter is very different from all these and is not subject to any variation whatever, but is eternal, immutable, and for that very reason appropriate to be comprehended under necessary demonstrations; but I think it has not been alluded to by others.

Galileo went on to explain that for any given material, the strength of a particular piece against fracture being assigned by experiment, his rules gave the strength of any other piece. Other information developed in the Second Day, which had not yet been seen at Venice, was added in this letter.

During March Galileo received encouragement from France for the printing of his book there. Diodati sent Galileo a copy of Mersenne's French translation of his *Mechanics*, published the previous year from a manuscript which he said had been brought to France about 1616. Bernegger's Latin translation of Galileo's *Dialogue* also appeared about this time. It was Diodati's initial idea to have Galileo's new book printed at Lyons, where Roberto Galilei (a distant relative) was receiving and forwarding mail from and to Galileo for France. Roberto wrote to Galileo late in May to say he had heard that a copy of the manuscript was being taken to Germany by Prince Mathia de' Medici, to be printed there. This matter requires separate discussion.

In April 1635 the grand duke, knowing of Galileo's proposed book, suggested that Prince Mathia take a copy of the manuscript to Germany when he went there on a military mission. This concerned the Holy Roman Emperor, who was the employer of Giovanni Pieroni, the Florentine engineer who had already written to Galileo urging publication of his book on motion. Up to this time Galileo appears to have regarded the work on motion as separate from his treatise on strength of materials, but he now considered combining the two into a single volume about the size of the ill-fated *Dialogue*. Certain confusions arise in the terminology used by various correspondents in the ensuing period as a result of this. Micanzio, writing late in May, referred to Galileo's "two Dialogues," having received only a part of what later came to be called the First Day and apparently expecting a dialogue on motion to be added to this. In fact Galileo's time during May was taken up in completing the First Day and polishing the Second Day, neither of which concerned motion except incidentally. The manuscript carried to Germany by Prince Mathia, who left Florence on 9 June, included only those two "days," of which even the last two propositions had not yet been written. Writing to Diodati at that time, Galileo spoke of *four* dialogues to be printed, and when Pieroni received the manuscript at Vienna he already knew that this was but a part of the entire book. Except for the two propositions mentioned above, however, no more was ever sent to him. The manuscript without those two propositions will hereafter be called the Pieroni manuscript; it is the only known copy of any part of Galileo's final book.

Micanzio was notified by Galileo of the new plan to print his book abroad and for several months everything was left to Pieroni, who acknowledged receipt of the manuscript early in August. It is reasonable to suppose that during the latter part of 1635 Galileo set to work to polish the Third Day for printing. Since he had spoken to Diodati of four proposed dialogues, the general form and content of the book had been determined; now it was important to be able to supply the remainder if Pieroni succeeded in finding a publisher. Meanwhile Diodati had spoken to the Dutch publisher Louis Elzevir, who on a visit to Lyons in June told Roberto Galilei that he intended to speak to Galileo. About that time, however, Prince Mathia left for Germany with the Pieroni manuscript. This new turn of events resulted in Diodati's writing to Galileo on 17 July, tactfully congratulating him on the intervention of the grand duke while suggesting that if difficulties were encountered he might have his book printed promptly by the Elzevirs in Holland. A year was to pass before that suggestion was adopted.

Only two letters of scientific interest written by Galileo in the latter part of 1635 survive. One dealt with the purely mathematical question of the angle of contact (or tangency), addressed to Glorioso who had quit Padua and returned to Naples. The other concerned a challenge to Copernican astronomical views by J. B. Morin,[22] concerning which Galileo wrote to Jean de Beaugrand who had recently visited him at Arcetri. Another visitor at this time was Thomas Hobbes, who told Galileo that an English translation had been made of his *Dialogue*.[23]

VI

It was only in rewriting and polishing the Third Day late in 1635 that Galileo finally found the rigorous logical basis for his theorems on accelerated motion that had so long eluded him. In retrospect, the problem had been to avoid either of the two assumptions relating accelerated motion to uniform motion which, though plausible, lacked full conviction. One of these, used in the *Dialogue* as late as 1632, was duly acknowledged by Galileo there to be merely probable reasoning; this was that the overall speed in uniformly accelerated motion from rest was a kind of sum of all the individual speeds, however briefly each endured, and that by representing these as parallel lines in a triangle, overall speed might be represented by the area of the triangle. Since taken literally, the "sum" of an infinite number of *magnitudes* ought not to be finite, this assumption was not quite satisfactory. The other available approach was the medieval mean-degree postulate, which it seems Galileo must have heard of though no trace of it is found in any of his notes on motion or his books. In this it was assumed that one member of an infinite set can be taken that somehow represents the entire set, and in particular that the middle speed, taken as the speed existing at the middle instant of time, represents the overall speed. In its earliest (English) form this required the existence of a determinate speed at the middle instant, which was all right if the number of instants was odd but not if that number was even. In the later (French) form given to this assumption by Nicole Oresme, that difficulty vanished because the approach was geometrical rather than arithmetical; but then there was a different difficulty in that the existence of a single "instantaneous speed" had to be postulated without an associated motion, interval of time, and distance traversed. Whether Galileo ever considered this alternative approach remains questionable, but there is little doubt how he would have regarded it. The mean speed to be assumed was inherently incapable of ever being actually measured, and as such it was unsuitable as a foundation in Galileo's view of mathematical physics.

The *terminal* speed of a body in accelerated motion, on the other hand, could be actually measured at the end of any given time from rest by utilizing its continuation in uniform horizontal motion as in the experiment of f. 116v carried out by Galileo long before. One-half the terminal speed was the measure of uniform motion equivalent to uniformly accelerated motion from rest to that speed, and Galileo used this to establish Proposition One on accelerated motion, from which the law of free fall was easily deduced as Proposition Two. Proposition One is perhaps the only theorem capable of rigorous proof relating the law of fall to the definition of uniform acceleration. Neither the "summing" of lines into an area (which Galileo called only a "probable argument" in his *Dialogue* and there excluded from mathematical proofs), nor the medieval technique of selecting one value as representing an infinite set of which it is a member (which differs fundamentally from our present conception of "average speed"), is free from objection. By the use of one-to-one correspondence established uniquely between all parallels to the bases of a rectangle and of a right triangle, neither areas nor selected speeds need be considered, but only congruence of triangles as in Proposition One.

Galileo's modest-looking Proposition One was the fruit of many years of reflection about mathematical rigor in physics. No trace of that proposition is found in his notes; it made its first appearance in his final printed book. When he hit on it there was no need for him to draft the proof, for that was immediately evident to him. What had stood in its place before he polished the Third Day late in 1635 was a proposition much like the "probable argument" he had used in the *Dialogue*, as evidenced by a reference in the scholium to Proposition Twenty-Three to the presence of similar reasoning in Proposition One, where in fact there is no trace of it. Galileo's recent correspondence with Cavalieri and his 1634 postil to Rocco's book concerning *parti non quante* probably led him to Proposition One as it now stands. Had he published his treatise on accelerated motion in 1609, or 1618, or even in 1632, it would have lacked its present elegant logical foundation.

The only postulate Galileo now required for the balance of his theorems was a physical one—that the speed acquired in fall through a vertical height is the same as that acquired in motion along any inclined plane of that same vertical height. This had been assumed long before in order to establish 179–1. Proposition Three, which was to replace 179–1, was supported by the single unproved postulate adopted on the basis of physical illustrations. Galileo's later thoughts about proving his single postulate dynamically will be discussed in chapter 21.

In December 1635 Galileo had heard nothing more from Pieroni, who had met with a succession of disappointments. Scheiner was in Germany and the Jesuits were strongly against Galileo, so that any hope of getting a license to publish from a foreign censor not aware of the general prohibition against Galileo's books was rapidly vanishing. Just when Galileo wrote to Micanzio to say that Pieroni had reported nothing, Pieroni was writing an account of his difficulties to Galileo. His letter was still in transit when Galileo wrote to Diodati early in 1636 to say that he felt enough time had now been wasted and to reopen the door he had closed in the spring of 1635.

TWENTY

1636-38

DURING THE EARLY months of 1636 Pieroni continued to explore the possibility of having Galileo's book printed abroad. On 15 March Galileo told Micanzio he had asked Pieroni to return the manuscript, though it is doubtful that this letter was ever received. Pieroni had had diagrams engraved for the part of the book he had, and in April he found in Moravia a patron willing to proceed with the publication. This was Cardinal Dietrichstein, who had a press of his own but who died suddenly before the work began. Pieroni, dissatisfied with conditions in Germany, asked for permission to return to Italy; Galileo took up his request with the grand duke and diplomatic negotiations were conducted for Pieroni's release, though in fact he decided to remain when these were concluded. Grateful to Galileo for his assistance, he asked what was to be done with the manuscript. Ultimately it was returned to Galileo and survives among his papers.

During the spring of 1636 Galileo was at work on tables of projectile motions to be included in the Fourth Day. Many sheets of his calculations survive, one of which is the blank side of a letter received by Galileo in March 1636. Since all are in a fairly distinctive handwriting it is safe to ascribe all this work to the period mentioned.

Meanwhile at Toulouse Pierre Carcavy, who a year before had offered to seek a publisher in France, suggested the printing of Galileo's earlier works in Latin translations. On 15 April Carcavy asked for the new work on motion and Galileo's (now lost) commentary on the *Questions of Mechanics*. Having already corresponded with Diodati about a Latin collected edition of his works, Galileo did not take up Carcavy's proposal. Eventually the correspondence with Diodati resulted in a visit to Galileo at Arcetri by Louis Elzevir in May 1636; having agreed to publish *Two New Sciences*, he stayed for a time in Venice and remained in touch with Galileo through Micanzio. Within two weeks Galileo had copied the text of the First and Second Days, advising Micanzio on 28 June that this was done and the diagrams were being drawn. Micanzio received this part of the text in July, seeing the Second Day then for the first time. The Third Day was forwarded in August, completing the material that Elzevir took with him to Germany, where he remained the rest of the year. Thus the printers in Leiden could not begin their work until 1637.

Because the terminology of letters referring to parts of the book is sometimes confusing, and our knowledge of the dates of finished work depends on those letters, some comments are in order. On 16 August Galileo wrote that he was sending "the book on motion," meaning the Third Day. A week later Micanzio acknowledged receipt of "two books on motion," which might seem to mean the Third and Fourth Days, though the Fourth Day was then hardly started, let alone completed. What Micanzio meant was that he had received the Third Day, which was divided into two "books," one on uniform motion and the other on accelerated motion. Early in December Elzevir arrived in Leiden with the first three "days," but a letter then speaks of "the third part" as remaining in Galileo's hands and as being augmented by him. This meant the third "book" on motion, namely that on projectile motion, which when printed was called the Fourth Day.

In mid-1636, shortly after sending the uncompleted manuscript to Venice for Elzevir, Galileo again took up his scheme for determining longitudes, this time with the Dutch government. He wrote long explanatory letters in August, and negotiations continued to occupy a good deal of Galileo's time during the next two years. Since nothing of a scientific nature that had not previously been involved in his negotiations with Spain came into them, they will not be discussed here. As before, objections were raised by naval officers and Galileo offered detailed answers, emphasizing also the value of accurate longitudes to a colonial power quite apart from their utility at sea.

On 18 October Castelli advised Galileo that Noailles was on his way to Siena, returning from Rome to France. While at Rome he had attempted to secure Galileo's pardon from the pope, working mainly through Antonio Cardinal Barberini. This was an unfortunate choice; unlike Francesco, Antonio seems at all times to have been hostile to Galileo's cause.[1] Noailles was anxious to see Galileo en route and various negotiations had been carried on to make this possible, since Galileo was not permitted to leave Arcetri even to visit nearby Florence. It is fairly certain, from a letter of Ascanio Piccolomini's after the event, that they nevertheless met at Poggibonsi about 25 October and that Noailles was pleased by the "compliment" made to him there by Galileo. Some think that Galileo delivered to him at this meeting a manuscript copy of the text of *Two New Sciences*, as was certainly implied in the later dedication to Noailles. There is, however, ground for doubt that any such copy existed, and the "compliment" was perhaps no more than a promise to dedicate the book to Noailles, Galileo having confided in him that it was already in the hands of Louis Elzevir.[2] The only evidence that a manuscript copy reached France is that Mersenne saw the Third Day early in 1637. Since Diodati was able to describe exactly what Elzevir had brought back from Italy, writing from Paris at that time, it is probable that the manuscript used for printing was at least briefly in Paris, where it could have been seen by Mersenne.

It was now urgent that Galileo complete the Fourth Day, as actual printing was about to begin. On 6 December 1636, he had written to Diodati:

I am [working] on the treatise of projectiles, a truly admirable subject in which the more I go theorizing, the more I find new things never observed by anyone before, let alone proved. And though in this part also I open the way for speculative minds to go much deeper, I should myself like to amplify it a bit more. But I find how greatly old age takes away the vividness and speed of my thoughts, when it is hard work for me to understand not a few of the things I found and demonstrated at a younger age. I shall send as soon as possible this treatise on projectiles, with an appendix of some demonstrations of certain conclusions about the centers of gravity of solids, found by me at the age of 22 after two years of study of geometry, for it is good that these not be lost.

This was Galileo's first mention of his decision to include the early theorems on centers of gravity of paraboloids. That Galileo was at work on the Fourth Day is again attested in a letter to Alessandro Marsili, dated 10 January 1637: "I am about the third part of my speculations concerning motion, which is that of projectiles." Dino Peri, successor of Aggiunti in the chair at Pisa, was pleased to have heard in late January "that you are working on projectiles." But on 11 February Galileo mentioned difficulty in seeing because of a cataract that had formed on his right eye, and on 7 March he wrote to Diodati that he had decided to finish the section on projectiles with a table of artillery and mortar shots, though much more had occurred to him.

Galileo's statement that he was having trouble understanding work he had done long ago on the parabolic trajectory is corroborated by the fact that on some pages of notes written at Padua there are new diagrams pasted over old ones and new approaches to demonstrations written in Galileo's distinctively aged handwriting. The first eight propositions of the Fourth Day all have counterparts among the Paduan notes; the rest, including the tables of elevation, range, and height, was new. Also new at this time were passages in the Fourth Day explaining Galileo's mature view of the necessarily approximate and progressive character of physical science: theorems and calculations generally neglect things not necessary to consider in ordinary applications, he said, and accordingly often need modification when extended beyond the range of ordinary observation and experience, and sometimes even within it.

II

A clear exposition of the mature scientific position just mentioned is found in a letter to Carcavy on 5 June 1637. He had earlier sent to Galileo a demonstration (by Pierre Fermat) that the path of a body falling to the center of a rotating earth would be a kind of spiral, and not semicircular as Galileo was believed to have said in his *Dialogue*. He had in fact spoken only of fall from a high tower to its base, but his printed diagram had led Mersenne and others to extend the fall to the earth's center.[3] Carcavy included another demonstration of Fermat's (against Galileo's law of free fall, to be discussed later). Galileo replied:

I come now to the oppositions that your friend [Fermat] makes to some of my propositions, which with one exception [the second, to be discussed later] I admit as true and conclusive, but not as unforeseen or unexpected by me, since it is a long time since I, having studied with great admiration the Archimedean spiral composed of two equable motions, one straight and one circular, thought [also] of a spiral composed from uniform circular and straight accelerated motion in the ratio of acceleration of naturally falling bodies, which [ratio] I am persuaded I have proved to be as the squares of the times; and this [composition] is your friend's spiral.[4] And though it was said in the *Dialogue* that it might be that, mixing the straight motion of fall with the uniform diurnal circular motion, there would be composed a semicircle that would go to end at the center of the earth, this was said in jest, as quite manifestly appears, since it was there called *bizzaria*,[5] that is, a rather daring jocularity. So for this part I wish to be forgiven, and especially having drawn from this poetic fiction, as I shall call it, those three unexpected consequences that the motion would be always circular, and second, always uniform [along this path], and third, that in this apparent motion downward nothing would be moved more than it would have been had it remained at rest [on the rotating tower].

I now add that although from the composition of uniform horizontal motion and straight vertical fall with the acceleration assigned by me, there would be described a spiral line that would go to end[6] at the center, nevertheless if we do not get [far] away from the earth's surface I do not hesitate to assign to that combination a parabolic line, asserting this to be the line described by projectiles—which assertion could be used as material for impugning me much more than [can] that semicircular motion, which at least would go to end at the center, where I am also sure that projectiles would go to end, though the parabolic line gets always farther and farther away from the axis vertical to the center. Now, here your friend may be still more surprised at me who, knowing and confessing my error, yet go persevering in it. Yet I hope to gain pardon from his generosity, and ask this even more when I understand that his criticisms derive from the desire to caution me so that I shall not run into those errors that are made and have been made by all the most intelligent mechanicians, and by Archimedes himself, the greatest and superhuman intellect, who assuming mechanically in his *Plane Equilibrium* and *Quadrature of the Parabola*, as do all engineers and architects, that heavy bodies descend along parallel lines, gives occasion for doubt that they know that such lines are not parallel at all, but go to meet at the common center of gravity. From this really false assumption, if I am not in error, derive your friend's oppositions against me, which acquire such force and energy as we approach the center of the earth, and vary so greatly from what we assume at its surface with error, but [only] slight error, that [indeed] the things we call up here "horizontal planes" finally become at the center vertical lines, while lines without slope [that is, vertical] degenerate [there] into totally sloped [that is, horizontal] lines.

I add moreover, as you and your friend may soon see in my book now in press, that I argue *ex suppositione*, picturing to myself motion with respect to a point from which [a thing] leaving from rest goes accelerating, increasing its speed in the same proportion with which time increases, and in this way I conclusively demonstrate many events; then I add that if experience shows that such events are found verified in the motion of naturally descending heavy things, we can without error affirm this [natural motion] to be the same motion that I defined and assumed; if [they are] not, my demonstrations founded on my assumption lose nothing of their force and conclusiveness, just as it in no way prejudices the conclusions proved by Archimedes about the spiral that no naturally moving body moves spirally in that manner. But in the motion I defined it is found that all the properties that I demonstrate are verified in the motion of naturally descending heavy bodies—these are verified, I say, in that when we make experiments upon the earth and at heights and distances practicable to us, no sensible difference is discovered, though a sensible, great, and immense difference would be made by approaching to and closely nearing the center. And although your friend should declare that in making experiments of this they might come out without error, but that nevertheless he wants to place reason before sense, which [latter] may deceive, I shall show him an experiment that ought to be sensible and without sensory deception. Hang from two equally long threads two heavy bodies, such as bullets; attach one thread from the highest place you can, and the other from the lowest; take their lengths to be [each] of four or five braccia. There being two observers, one in the higher place and the other in the lower, remove these balls from the vertical and set them free [through equal arcs] at the same moment of time, counting their vibrations continuing the number into the hundreds; you will find that they both count the same number and do not vary by one in many hundreds, or even thousands, an argument that shows each of these to go in equal times. And because what happens in these movements in arcs of circles happens also in the chords that they subtend [that is, equal times to the vertical], all that your friend says collapses about what should happen along parallel inclined planes of which one is closer to the earth than another[7]—I mean, this collapses entirely when they are both situated above the surface of the terrestrial globe. As to what should happen when one [pendulum] is above the earth's surface and the other is so far inside that it would even terminate at the very center, I do not wish now to tell you what I think about this, but up to now I have no reason that necessarily persuades me to assume that the moveable which goes to end at the center would pass its distance in a shorter time than that other moveable would pass its distance. But I may say that for my part it is not clear and proven that a heavy moveable leaving from a distance therefrom of only one braccio must arrive sooner at the center of the earth than another going a thousand miles. I do not affirm this, but offer it as a paradox, to destroy which perhaps your friend will have, or will find, a necessarily conclusive demonstration.

In order to understand what came next, it must be explained that Fermat had earlier written out a mathematical demonstration that Galileo's law of free fall, or indeed any law of mathematically continuous acceleration from rest, must contain an internal contradiction.[8] This mistaken argument circulated widely and was also criticized by Descartes, on grounds quite similar to those given below by Galileo but with an entirely different conclusion.[9] Galileo's reply was as follows, and it is interesting to see how he presents the argument against a basic assumption that had so long kept him, years before at Padua, from accepting the idea of mathematically continuous change:

As to what he produces to destroy my assertion that the heavy thing leaving from rest necessarily passes through all [possible] degrees of speed, I really do not know how to apply his postulate. He demands it to be conceded that there is no motion without speed, which seems to me to mean the same as to say "There is no line without length." Just as in starting from a point that lacks any length, one cannot enter into a line without passing through all the infinite lines, shorter and shorter, included between any assigned line and the point, so the moveable that leaves from rest, which has no speed at all, in order to acquire any degree of speed whatever, must pass through the infinite degrees of slowness included between any speed whatever and the highest and infinite slowness. Let there be the angle between the lines *AB* and *AC*, and through *A* draw the line *DE* which is understood to descend to *FG*, remaining always parallel to itself. It is manifest that at the apex *A* there is no part of the line *DE* which has any length at all; but in

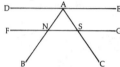

descending and going to *FG* there are intercepted between *AB* and *AC* greater and greater parts according as the length of descent is greater; in this example the intercepted part is *NS*. Now it is manifest that no line can be assigned of such small length that infinitely many [lines], shorter and shorter, are not included between *AN* and *AS* toward the angle *A*; hence to assert that in the motion of the traversal *FG* it has passed through all the imaginable lengths between *NS* and the corner *A*, so that none is left out, seems to be a proposition beyond any doubt. And thus when I establish an instant of time in which the moveable, leaving from its state of rest at the assigned instant, and entering into motion which must be accelerated in that proportion in which the amount of time increases, which is nothing at the said instant, then just as no tiny space of time can be assigned that does not have smaller amounts [of time] consumed after the first assigned instant, so, in leaving from rest, the moveable does not exceed any quantity whatever of speed assigned for which a still smaller [speed] is not found. I should like you to ask your friend if he admits with me that a moveable that continually loses speed, as does a heavy projectile sent vertically upward, reaches a slightly smaller degree of speed before it reaches one still smaller; as for example a lead ball, which thrown upward goes continually losing speed, must pass from 10 degrees to 9 before it passes [from 10] to 6, or 4. I believe he will concede this, there being no reason at all to pass immediately from 10 to 6, jumping over and skipping degrees, 9, 8, 7, as I believe he also will grant. Next, consider that ball continually and successively going [up] and losing force and speed until it is finally reduced to rest, between which and any assigned degree of slowness there are still others. When, therefore, it shall have got to 100 degrees of slowness for instance, what reason can he adduce that it should pass from 100 degrees of slowness [immediately] to rest (that is, to infinite slowness), skipping over 120, 200, and 1,000 degrees of slowness, which are always closer to 100 than [they are] to infinity? And so, turning now to its movement from the highest point downward, it would be more arbitrary than reasonable, in my opinion, to argue that it should be denied that [all] these same degrees are passed in reverse.[10]

In his reply to the argument that had been mistakenly directed against his restricted "semicircular fall" by extending it to cases remote from the possibility of observation, Galileo showed his mistrust of purely mathematical arguments incapable of physical corroboration. He was equally opposed to purely verbal arguments based on principles of supposed universal validity, as offered by philosophers. Judicious mixture of the two, trusting neither to the exclusion of the other, might alienate both Aristotelians and Platonists but was the only means of obtaining trustworthy physics. The price was deliberately narrowed scope of physical science.

III

About the first of March Galileo had written to Micanzio that he would send the Fourth Day, and Micanzio replied that arrangements had been made for its safe delivery to Elzevir. Meanwhile Elzevir wrote to Micanzio (on 16 March) asking for "the rest of the book and the title page." Engraving of the diagrams had already begun, and proofs of four of these were included. I believe that what Galileo forwarded at this time ended abruptly with the artillery tables, without the final fourteen speeches of the printed text. From later correspondence it is evident that Elzevir expected a Fifth Day, on the force of percussion, probably on the basis of his 1636 conversations with Galileo at Arcetri but possibly from a lost letter of Galileo's accompanying the incomplete Fourth Day. In any case that material included a definite promise to the reader about such a discussion to come immediately after the section on projectiles.

On 24 April Galileo wrote to Diodati concerning Carcavy's wish to reprint his old works and said that "I am at present polishing up my works not published before, which will be a book on the centers of gravity of solids, or a collection of problems, partly physical and partly mathematical, or a book of postils to books by my opponents." No work on projectiles was mentioned; as has been said, that appears to have been sent in March, but the appendix on centers of gravity seems not to have been with it. On 2 May Galileo sent to Micanzio something the latter forwarded to Elzevir on 8 May and described in a letter to Galileo as "the two folios of your speculations, which I sent yesterday to Sig. Elzevir, they having come to me opportunely and in time to be able to do this. . . . I expect today also the first printed folio of your work, which he wrote me he would send, and if I get it you shall have it with this."

Assuming that the word *folio* has the same meaning in both cases, what Galileo had sent were two *quinternetti* of manuscript, each of ten leaves about letter size, or twenty pages, making forty written pages. The appendix on centers of gravity as printed is titled *Appendix in qua continentur Theoremata . . .* and occupies twenty-five printed pages. Hence it is reasonable to assume that what Micanzio had received and sent in May was the appendix; the word *speculation* commonly meant "theory" in Italian, and *speculations* for *theorems* was not unreasonable, nor would Micanzio have bothered to study this technical appendix and comment on it. In the same letter he said "I see that you took the trouble to transcribe these in your own hand, and I don't see how you can stand it, for to me it would be absolutely impossible." What was sent was therefore something transcribed that might equally well have been done by a copyist, probably Galileo's work on centers of gravity.

Now, on 20 June Micanzio wrote: "I received by courtesy of Sig. Resident [Francesco] Rinuccini [the Tuscan agent at Venice] your letter with the completion of your Dialogues, which I sent yesterday to Sig. Elzevir. . . . I do not see in these two last folios the dedication that you intended to send." Here I think that the word *folios* should be taken in its literal sense, that is, two large pages folded together forming eight ordinary pages of writing, properly described as "the completion of your Dialogues." These became the five printed pages containing the last fourteen speeches which followed the artillery tables and brought the Fourth Day to a close. The situation as I view it was this.

At the time Galileo sent the Fourth Day, with its abrupt conclusion, he had finished with his treatment of projectiles but had not decided to end the book there. There was still his promise, earlier in the Fourth Day (just before Proposition Five), to follow the discussion of projectiles with one on the force of percussion. Hence an abrupt ending of the Fourth Day did not matter; but if there was no more to come (except the appendix, which was not part of the dialogues), some kind of ceremonial ending of the whole book was needed. This, I believe, is what Micanzio received late in June. Near its end, the earlier promise to discuss the force of percussion was much modified; Sagredo said only that Salviati's convenience would have to be observed, and Salviati's reply called attention to the theorems on centers of gravity, upon which Sagredo spoke of the meetings now concluded and "those in the future," rather than of another to follow immediately.

Probably when Galileo supplied to the printers the final pages of the Fourth Day he had still not abandoned the idea of including a section on the force of percussion in *Two New Sciences*. The work he had done on that subject probably included most of the text we have in a posthumously printed dialogue of about twenty-five printed pages, without the passages in which impact was considered as made on a body of constant resistance, as when two equal weights are suspended by a rope passing over a pulley, and one weight is dropped while the other is resting on a table. These passages appear to have been added only after *Two New Sciences* had been printed. Meanwhile Galileo's much older reasoning (1602; see end of chapter 4) that impact had an infinite—or rather, incommensurable—effect as compared with that of dead weight involved a kind of paradox which he preferred not to put in print without some further resolution of it, which he went on hoping to find. His consequent vacillation over including a discussion of percussion and its effects resulted in some delay in the completion and printing of *Two New Sciences*.

In September, when printing of the Third Day was commenced, the printers sent a memorandum for Galileo's attention in which it was asked "if there are more days than four, and how they should be divided. We have divided off the Third Day [to begin] with *De motu locali*. We do not find any Fifth Day if it should be before the Appendix. Ask that he tell us if we have all the copy. He should let us know at once, otherwise we will wait; and he should not use so many abbreviations in his copy." Here the use by the printers of the specific expression "Fifth Day" suggests that Galileo had mentioned to Elzevir, in sending the closing passages of the Fourth Day on 20 June, that more was planned. The form of the dialogue on percussion as we have it begins by reference to lapse of a fortnight since the Fourth Day and adverts to the appendix. Probably when Galileo sent the closing on 20 June he remarked that its wording would permit addition of a Fifth Day on the force of percussion after the appendix, if he could complete it satisfactorily, and if not it would not matter. Loss of use of his right eye in July 1637 probably influenced his decision to abandon the task.

On 17 October Micanzio saw a reply Galileo had written to Elzevir but did not say what was in it; probably it was a statement that no more was to come and the book was complete. On 1 November Elzevir wrote to say he had long been in Denmark and Poland, accounting for his silence. "Today I have received your letter via Sig. Justus Wiffeldich,[11] with the included folio of the Fourth Day, through which [letter] I hear with displeasure of your illness. Meanwhile I shall not hold up continuation of printing, awaiting, if it shall be possible, the Fifth Day."

It would be natural to take this letter as a reply to Galileo's letter sent from Venice on 16 October, in which case the prospect of a final dialogue on the force of percussion was still open then. I am inclined to believe, however, that the memorandum sent in late September was not from Elzevir himself, who had gone to Denmark, but from his printers, and that Elzevir had just seen the 20 June communication when he wrote on 1 November. He understood it completely, and shortly afterward saw Galileo's mid-October letter explaining it to the printers, who had not understood.

IV

In the autumn of 1637 Galileo composed a brief treatise called "Astronomical Operations."[12] This first explained the use of a suitable pendulum for very accurate determinations of time by counting its oscillations through the entire period between culminations of a selected star on two successive nights. Next it explained how a sextant could be made accurate to very small arcs by use of a tightly wound fine wire, as on the hydrostatic balance described in 1586. The First Operation provided a way of determining precisely the diameter of the pupil of the eye, applied in Operation Two to the estimation of visual stellar diameters by means of a tightly stretched cord of known diameter and distance from the eye. (Galileo had already pointed out in the *Dialogue* that enormous errors existed in common estimates of stellar diameters, amounting to thirty times the true values.) The third operation described use of an upright beam erected on a distant mountain and of telescopic observation to improve still further determinations made by stretched cords. The fourth operation explained the use of similar means for computing relative changes in distances between the earth and moon, sun, and planets (except Mercury). The fifth operation gave methods of improving estimates of the effect of atmospheric refraction on star positions, while the sixth proposed new star maps made with the above improvements. A supplemental note by Niccolò Arrighetti recounted a conversation with Galileo on 10 October 1638 concerning a method of precisely timing star movements and obtaining still greater accuracy for their visual diameters, using measured rectangular obstacles to vision.

On 7 November Galileo announced to Micanzio his new discovery of a libration of the moon different from the optical libration he had already described in the 1632 *Dialogue*. This discovery was later explained in great detail, though for our purposes it suffices to cite Galileo's letter to Micanzio:

I have discovered a very marvelous observation in the face of the moon, in which body, though it has been looked at infinitely many times, I do not find that any change was ever noticed, but that the same face was always seen the same to our eyes. This I find not to be true; rather, it changes its aspect with all three possible variations, making for us those changes that are made by one who shows to our eyes his full face, head on so to speak, and then goes changing this in all possible ways, that is, turning now a bit to the right and then a bit to the left, or else raising and lowering [his face], or finally, tilting his left shoulder to right and left. All these variations are seen in the face of the moon, and the large and ancient spots perceived in it make manifest and sensible what I say. Add, moreover, another marvel, which is that these three different variations have three different periods; for one of them changes from day to day, and thus comes to have the diurnal period; the second goes changing from month to month, and has its period monthly; the third has the annual period in which it finishes its variations. Now, what will you say on confronting these three lunar periods with the three periods, daily, monthly, and annual, of the movements of the sea, of which by common agreement of everyone the moon is arbiter and superintendent?[13]

Elzevir sent proofs of the final pages on 26 January 1638, together with a request for the index and list of errata. He also thought there should be some explanation of the absence of material on force of percussion, if none was to come, which could be printed after the appendix. Also the title page and dedication had still not been received.[14] Galileo doubtless considered that the final speeches sufficiently explained absence of a section on percussion; as to the dedication, he had had to await formal acceptance from Noailles. Diodati probably sent the dedication to Elzevir late in February, as it was dated 6 March in the printed book. But he failed to send Galileo's title page, so Elzevir designed one which Galileo much disliked when he finally saw (or more likely only heard) it, calling it undistinguished and common. There is a slender clue to the wording Galileo himself had intended, contained in a fragment of his letter to Diodati. Using that clue and the style of Galileo's titles for the *Starry Messenger* and the *Dialogue*, I reconstruct his wording as follows; italicized words are found in the letter of 4 July 1637 to Diodati:

> *Dialogues* of Galileo Galilei . . . *Containing Two Entire Sciences, All New and Demonstrated from their First Principles and Elements, so that, in the Manner of other Mathematical Elements, Roads are Opened to Vast Fields*, with Reasonings and Mathematical Demonstrations *Filled with Infinite Admirable Conclusions*, from which far *More Remains to be Seen in the World than has been Seen up to the Present Time*.[15]

Accustomed as we now are to brief and modest title pages, this may appear flamboyant, but it was then customary to set forth both subject and purpose in them. Galileo's letter conveys the idea that what was important to him was that his book contained the *elements* of sciences leading to vast fields yet to be explored. The same thing was emphasized in the printed preamble to Galileo's discussion of accelerated motion in the Third Day.

The printed *Two New Sciences* appears not to have been offered for sale before June 1638, despite its March dedication. On 7 May Micanzio reported his surprise that the book was not even mentioned in a list of titles sent by Elzevir to his Venetian agent. Noailles did not acknowledge receipt of the dedication copy until 20 July. No copies were sent in advance to the author, as will be seen below.

At this time Galileo was sent a valuable gold chain by the Dutch government in recognition of his contribution to the de-

termination of longitudes at sea. On the grounds that his proposals had not been actually put in practice, partly because he
had not been able to supply updated tables of the positions of
Jupiter's satellites, Galileo refused the gift. The real reason for
his refusal, however, was that he had been advised that Rome
would look unfavorably on his acceptance of anything from a
Protestant government, and when Francesco Barberini was told
of the refusal he commended Galileo's action.

From a letter to Diodati supposed to have been written by
Galileo on 7 August it appears that only a single copy of his book
had been received, and only after he was totally blind and could
not see it. It was in this letter that he expressed his displeasure
at the title page and at the publisher's failure to send him either
a supply of this book or of their edition of his *Letter to Christina*
printed in 1636.[16] Since he was still negotiating with Elzevir for
a collected edition of his earlier works translated into Latin,
however, he did not complain directly. I believe that Diodati was
really responsible for the changed title, he not having sent Galileo's wording on to the publishers along with the dedication.

V

On 11 October 1638 Descartes addressed to Mersenne a long letter reviewing the new book. This letter throws light on the re-
ception of Galileo's science outside the circle of his friends and
former pupils, illustrating the conception of science most opposed by Galileo and the ineffectiveness of his own work in altering traditional goals. It is accordingly translated here, the indicated paginations in *Two New Sciences* being those of Favaro's
edition rather than of the 1638 edition (as in Descartes' original
letter).

I shall commence this letter by my observations about
Galileo's book. I find generally that he philosophizes much
better than ordinary, in that he avoids as best he can the errors
of the scholastics and undertakes to examine physical matters
by mathematical reasonings. In this I accord with him entirely,
and I hold that there is no better way to find the truth. But
he seems to me very faulty in continually making digressions
and never stopping to explain completely any matter, which
shows that he has not examined things in order, and that without having considered the first causes of nature he has only
sought the reasons of some particular effects, and thus he has

built without foundation. Now, in so far as his fashion of philosophizing is closer to the truth, one can the more easily know his faults; or rather, one can better say when those who sometimes follow the right road go astray, than when those go astray who never enter on it.

Pp. 50–53. He proposes what he will treat, that is, why large machines, of the same shape and material as smaller ones, are weaker than the latter, and why a child is less hurt by falling than a grown man, or a cat than a horse, etc. In which, in my opinion, there is no difficulty, or any subject for creating a new science; for it is evident that in order for the force or resistance of a large machine to be exactly proportional to that of a small one of the same shape, they must not be of the same material, but the large one must be of material harder and less easy to break, since its shape and weight are greater. And there is as much difference between a large [thing] and a small one of the same material as [there is] between two [things] of the same size, one of which is of much less heavy material and [is] thereby harder than the other.

P. 56. He is right to say that the fibers of a rope are held together because they press on one another, but he does not add why the pressure is the cause that they hold together, which is because of little unevennesses in their shape which prevent any of them from gliding between those that press it.

The invention for descending (p. 58) goes back to the same thing, and there is nothing in all this that is not common [knowledge]. But his fashion of writing in dialogues, where he introduces three persons who do nothing but exalt each of his inventions in turn, greatly assists in [over]pricing his merchandise.

P. 59. He gives two causes why the parts of a continuous rope hold together: one is horror of the void, the other a certain glue or linkage that holds them, which he explains also afterward by the void, and I think both to be false. What he attributes to the void (p. 60) should be ascribed only to the weight of air, and it is certain that if it were horror of the void that prevented two bodies from separating, no force would be capable of separating them.

The way he gives for distinguishing the effects of those two causes (pp. 62–63) is worthless, and what he makes Simplicio say (p. 63) is truer, and (p. 63) the observation that pumps draw water no higher than 18 braccia should not be related to the void, but either to the material of the pumps or to that of water itself, which escapes between the piston and the tube rather than be raised higher.

Pp. 65–66. He examines the glue that he adds to the void for the linkage of the parts of bodies, and attributes this to other little voids which are not even imaginable. And what he says (p. 68) to prove these little voids is a sophism, because the hexagon he proposes leaves no void in the space through which it passes, but each of its parts is moved with continuous movements which describe curved lines that fill all the space; one should not, as he does, consider one single straight line. Nor does it matter that in his diagram the parts of the straight line *IO*, *PY*, etc. are not touched by the perimeter *HIKL*, since in compensation they are [touched] by other parts of the surface *ABC*, and thus they are no more voids than [are] the parts *OP*, *YZ*, etc.

Pp. 74–75. Also a sophism is his argument to prove that a point is equal to a line or a surface. For formally all that can be concluded is that the line or surface is no larger a solid than is the point;[17] not that it is not absolutely larger.

Pp. 76–85. He is faulty in all this he says about the infinite, in that notwithstanding his confessing that the human mind, being finite, is incapable of understanding it, he does not abstain from reasoning just as if he understood it.

P. 85. He says that hard bodies on becoming fluid are divided into an infinity of points, which is an imagining easy to refute, and of which he gives no proof.

P. 86. He shows himself little knowledgeable in catoptrics, he believing in the burning mirrors of Archimedes, which I demonstrated to be impossible in my *Dioptrics*, p. 119.

P. 88. His experiment to know if light is transmitted in an instant is useless, since eclipses of the moon, related so closely to calculations made of them, prove this incomparably better than anything that could be tested on earth.

Pp. 91–92. He considers a straight line described by the movement of a circle to prove that this [line] is composed of an infinity of actual points, which is pure imagination.

Pp. 93–96. All that he says about rarefaction and condensation is a sophism, since the circle leaves no void points among its points, but is only moved more slowly. And for my part, I conceive on this only that when a body is condensed its pores are narrowed, pushing out a part of the subtle matter that filled them, as happens when a sponge is pressed and water comes out. And contrarily when a body is dilated its pores enlarge and more subtle matter enters it, as I have explained in several places in my *Meteors*.

Pp. 97–98. What he says about drawn gold is not relevant to explain rarefaction, since [by drawing] gold is not rarefied at all, but only changes shape.

Pp. 105–12. He is eloquent to refute Aristotle, but that is not hard.

P. 113. He says rightly that bodies descend more unequally fast in water than in air, but he says nothing at all about the cause, and he is wrong (p. 114) in saying that water does not at all resist being divided.

P. 115. He says he does not know what holds up drops of water on cabbage leaves, which I sufficiently explained in my *Meteors*.

Pp. 116–17. Everything he says about the speeds of bodies descending in the void, etc., is built without foundation, for first he should have determined what weight is, and if he had known the truth, he would have known that it [weight] is nothing in the void.

P. 123. His way of weighing air is not bad, if its weight were such as to be noticeable by this means; but I doubt this.

Pp. 127–29. All that he says here cannot be determined without knowing what weight is. And everything he puts near the end of the dialogue concerning music is common [knowledge] for you and me.

Pp. 146. He says that the pitch of gold strings is lower than those of copper because gold is heavier; but this is rather because it is softer. And he is wrong to say that the weight of a string resists its speed of movement more than [does] is thickness.

P. 156. He compares the force needed to break a beam across with that needed to pull it apart lengthwise, and says that crosswise it is like a lever whose support is in the middle of its thickness, which is not true at all, and he gives no proof of it.

Pp. 170–71. His consideration why fish can be larger than land animals is not bad.

Pp. 180–81. What he says about wood having to be cut semi-parabolically to resist everywhere equally is approximately true, but all the rest [of the Second Day] is common [knowledge].

Pp. 185–86. His two ways of describing parabolas are entirely mechanical and are false in good geometry.

Pp. 197–98. He supposes that the speeds of falling weights always increase equally, which I formerly believed like him, but I now believe I can prove that it is not true.

P. 205. He supposes also that the degrees of speed of the same body over different planes[18] are equal when the elevations of the planes are equal, which he does not prove and is not exactly true, and since everything that ensues depends on those two assumptions, one can say it is entirely built in the air. For the rest, he seems not to have written his third dialogue except to give a reason why all descents [*tours*] and returns of the same cord [of a pendulum, through different arcs of a circle] are equal to one another, and yet he does not do this, but concludes only that weights descend faster along the arc of a circle than along the chord of the same arc, which also he has been unable to deduce exactly from his assumptions.[19]

P. 268. He adds another assumption to the preceding [two], which is no more true; namely, that bodies thrown in air go uniformly fast following the horizontal,[20] but that in falling their speeds increase in the squared [(*sic*); square-root] ratio of the distance. Now, given this, it is very easy to conclude that the movement of bodies thrown ought to follow a parabolic line; but his [sup]positions being false, his conclusion can well be very far from the truth.

P. 296. It is to be noted that he takes the converse of his proposition without proving or explaining it, that is, if the shot fired horizontally from B toward E follows the parabola BD, the shot fired obliquely following the line DE must follow the same parabola DB, which indeed follows from his assumptions. But he seems not to have dared to explain these from fear that their falsity would appear too evident. Yet he makes use only of this converse in all the rest of his fourth discourse, which he seems to have written only to explain the force of cannon shots fired at different elevations. Moreover it is to be noted that in setting forth his assumptions he excludes artillery in order to make them more easily accepted, and yet toward the end it is mainly to artillery that he applies his conclusion. This is to say, in a word, that all is built in the air.

I say nothing of the demonstrations in geometry with which most of his book is filled, and I hope they are all true. I remark only, in seeing his propositions, that he did not need to be a great geometer to discover them; in glancing through some of them I have perceived he much needed to follow in them the shortest paths.

For the rest, this must not be seen, please, by anyone but you who wanted me to write you, and to whom I am so obliged I believe I should refuse you nothing in my power. Otherwise I would not be amused to reprehend the faults of another, for nothing is more contrary to my disposition. At least, if I had done that, I should have added my reasons for speaking more carefully than I have done, so that those who do not know me as you do could not imagine that I had judged without reason.

I skip to the articles in your letter which violent drowsiness prevented my answering before. And first, concerning Galileo, I tell you that I have never seen him nor had any communication with him, and consequently could not have borrowed anything from him. Also I see nothing in his books to make me envious, and hardly anything I should wish to avow mine. The best is about music, but those who know me may rather believe he had it from me, than I from him, for I had written almost the same 19 years ago, at which time I had never been in Italy, and I gave my writing to M. Beeckman who, as you know, paraded it around in writing here and there as a thing that was his. . . .

For the force of percussion, it is not at all hard to explain by my Principles, as Galileo represents it at the end of his book; but I cannot say anything without explaining my Principles; that is to say, my *Monde*[21] . . .

What Galileo says that falling bodies pass through all degrees of speed, I do not at all think that happens ordinarily, though it is not impossible that it sometimes happens. And there is error in the argument used by M. F[ermat][22] to refute this, in that he says that "speed is to be acquired either in the first instant or in some determined time"; for neither the one nor the other is true, and in scholastic terms one can say that "[speed] is to be acquired in time inadequately taken." In sum everything that he [Fermat] says about degrees of speed of movement can be said in the same way about degrees of length of triangle *ABC*, and yet I do not believe that he wants to deny that between point *A* and line *BC* there are not all the lengths that are less than *BC*.

You note very aptly in your letter some of Galileo's paralogisms, but I have said at the beginning of this [letter] what I thought of his whole book. Thank you for your experiment of the oak cylinder. I attribute nothing at all to the void, or to horror of the void, yet I tell you that the explanation of all the things Galileo deals with is very easy by my Principles. . . .

And for refutation of Galileo's opinion touching movements on inclined planes, M. F[ermat] is mistaken in that he founds his argument on tendency of weights toward the center of the earth,[23] which he imagines as a point, and Galileo assumes that they descend along parallel lines.

It is evident that Descartes, like all his contemporaries outside Italy and most of them there, considered the discovery of causes to be the whole point of science, in which everything (and not just some things) must be causally explained. Neglect of causes and lack of universality were seen as irremediable and fatal faults of Galileo's books by those who demanded an impossible certainty and applicability of science without restriction. That claim was to become the keynote of the "mechanical philosophy" which swiftly supplanted Galileo's program for science as restricted to the domain in which no appeal need be made beyond sensate experiences and necessary demonstrations.

TWENTY-ONE

1639-40

I

PUBLICATION OF *Two New Sciences* marked the climax of Galileo's scientific career in one sense, but even blindness and old age did not entirely end it. In October 1638, stimulated by questions from the young Viviani who had come to live at Arcetri as his pupil and amanuensis, Galileo began to think again about the possibility of demonstrating, rather than simply assuming, his postulate that the speed of a descending body is the same at the end of all straight paths having equal vertical heights. In his earliest discussion of motion along inclined planes, in 1591, he had shown that a body could be moved in the horizontal plane by a vanishingly small force, while in the vertical it could be moved only by a force exceeding its natural heaviness. Having subsequently established the law of free fall independently of those propositions, dynamical in character, and also without using the postulate mentioned above, he now sought to derive that postulate logically from his old dynamical propositions and the definition of uniform acceleration. Later on he somewhat modified this proof and expressed his wish that it should be included in future editions of *Two New Sciences*, where since 1655 it has been placed immediately before Proposition Three on accelerated motion.

In the next (and last) chapter it will be seen that in several curious ways, as in this return to very early thoughts for a foundation of his work on motion, Galileo's latest days resembled his earliest. What one thinks of his dynamic foundation for the science of kinematics will depend on individual taste. To me

it seems that a science founded on one definition and one postulate, the latter having been made plausible by experimental evidence, is better grounded than the same science founded on
postulates using the undefined notions of "force" and "impetus."
Perhaps Galileo himself had lingering doubts about changing his
published basis, since he did not remove his old postulate when
he asked to have the new derivation added.

On 6 November Famiano Michelini wrote from Siena to say
that Prince Leopold de' Medici regarded the postulate as not
sufficiently evident, and that he had heard of Galileo's having
found a way to demonstrate it which he wished to see. Later on,
when Galileo took steps to establish his priority in finding
means to prove the former postulate, he appears to have forgotten that a copy had been sent to Siena at this time.

In mid-December Galileo received from Baliani the book on
motions of heavy bodies begun a decade earlier.[1] He had not yet
seen Galileo's book, published at almost the same time. The
great difference between the two books in method, despite their
close agreement on many important conclusions, now became
the occasion of letters in which Galileo explained more clearly
than anywhere else his mature conception of physical science.
The first of these was dated 7 January 1639:

> Your welcome letter, together with your book *De motu*, was
> brought to me today by . . . [Clemente Settimi], colleague of . . .
> [Famiano Michelini], and since my unfortunate blindness of
> the last two years does not permit me to see even sunlight, to
> say nothing of objects so much smaller and devoid of light
> as writings and geometrical diagrams, I have managed today
> to get Father Clemente to come and talk with me for several
> hours, during which we have, with others, perused your book,
> truly to my great pleasure although I have been unable to
> understand the demonstrations distinctly, not being able to
> compare them with the diagrams; but from my experience with
> the subject, and hearing most of your propositions to agree
> with mine already written, I have penetrated your meanings
> and concepts.
>
> I have dealt with the same material, but somewhat more at
> length and with a different attack; for I assume nothing except
> the definition of the motion I wish to treat of and whose
> properties [events, *accidenti*] I wish to demonstrate, imitating
> in this Archimedes in his *Spiral Lines*, where he, having ex-
> plained what he means by motion made in the spiral that is

compounded from two uniform motions, one straight and the other circular, goes on immediately to demonstrate its properties [*passioni*]. I declare that I want to examine what symptoms [*sintoni*] occur in the motion of a moveable which, leaving from the state of rest, goes moving with speed growing always in the same way, that is, that the acquisitions of this speed grow not by jumps [the medieval impetus conception], but equably according to the increase of time, so that for example the speed acquired in two minutes of time is double that acquired in one minute, and that acquired in three minutes, and four, is triple, and quadruple, that same which was acquired in the first minute. And putting in nothing more, I come to the first [actually his second] demonstration, in which I prove the distance passed by such a moveable to be in the squared ratio of the times, and then I go on to demonstrate a large number of other properties. Of those you touch on some, but I add many more, and perhaps more wonderful ones, as you will be able to see in my Dialogues on this matter, already printed two [actually one] years ago in Amsterdam [actually Leiden], of which none have come to me except page by page, sent to me for the corrections and to make an index of the most notable things. Since then only one copy has come to me, though I know they are distributed throughout the southern provinces, and what is more I hear that in Rome they arrived and are sold at three florins each; perhaps these are the ones that [first] went to Prague and were immediately collected by the Jesuit fathers so that not even the Emperor himself could get a copy, he having sent to his chamberlain Sig. Francesco Piccolomini to have it, as that gentleman told me when he returned here about two months ago. If any ever come to me I shall not fail to send you one. Meanwhile I eagerly await to hear your thoughts about [motion of] liquids, a subject to my mind very obsure and filled with difficulties.

But getting back to my treatise on motion, I argue *ex suppositione* concerning the motion defined in the above way, so that even if the consequences [deduced] did not correspond to the events of natural motion of descending heavy things, it would matter little to me, just as it in no way derogates from the demonstrations of Archimedes that there is found in nature no moveable that is moved through spiral lines. But in this I have been, as I shall put it, lucky [*avventurato*], since the motion of heavy things and their events correspond punctually to the events demonstrated by me of the motion defined by me. I treat also of the motion of projectiles, demonstrating various properties [thereof], among which the principal is the proof that the projectile thrown by the projector, as would be the ball shot by firing artillery, makes its maximum flight and falls at the greatest distance when the piece is elevated at half a right angle, that is at 45°; and moreover, that other shots made at greater or less elevation come out equal when the piece is elevated an equal number of degrees above and below the said 45°.

You will see also in my same Dialogue[s] a treatise on the resistance of solid bodies to breakage, a subject very useful in the mechanical arts. I have in mind a great many miscellaneous problems and questions, partly quite new and partly different from or contrary to those commonly received, of which I could make a book more curious than the others written by me; but my condition, besides blindness on top of other serious indispositions and a decrepit age of 75 years, will not permit me to occupy myself in any study. I shall therefore remain silent, and so pass what remains to me of my laborious life, satisfying myself in the pleasure I shall feel from the discoveries of other pilgrim minds, and especially yours.

It should be mentioned that Baliani's book assumed the law that the period of a pendulum varies as the square root of its length as a means of deriving the law of free fall. Both Castelli and Cavalieri found Baliani's basic assumptions somewhat difficult to accept. His conception of the conservation of acquired momentum was quite different from Galileo's and contradicted the inertial principle as we see it, as a result of which Baliani's derivation of the parabolic trajectory was not that of Cavalieri or of Galileo. In the 1646 edition of his book he introduced an ingenious causal speculation about the law of free fall that shows how different his physical conceptions were from Galileo's.

II

On 30 April 1639 Micanzio announced to Galileo the arrival at Venice of a shipment of copies of *Two New Sciences,* of which fifty copies were reported earlier to have been sold at Rome. It was not until 4 June, however, that Micanzio wrote that copies had been sent to Galileo. Cavalieri acknowledged Galileo's gift of a copy on 28 June; one comment of his is important:

I owe you no little debt because the indivisibles of my *Geometry* will be indivisibly brightened by the nobility and clarity of your indivisibles. I did not dare to say that the continuum was composed of those,[2] though indeed I showed that between continua there was no other ratio than that of the aggregates [*congerie*] of indivisibles (taken parallel, however, if we speak of straight lines and plane surfaces, [which are] the particular indivisibles considered by me), which truly made me suspect that what you have finally pronounced might be true. If I had had such courage I should have prayed you not to omit confirmation of this, if not for the truth of the above conclusion, at least so that others would have attentively reflected on this new way of mine to measure continua.[3]

On the first of July Baliani acknowledged Galileo's book and a (lost) letter of 20 June accompanying it. Probably Galileo had again stressed the difference in their approaches, for Baliani said:

I thank you likewise for your patience in reading my things and for the considerations of them you made. I in truth have judged that experiments ought to be placed as principles of the sciences, when they are certain, and that from the things known by sense it is the role of science to lead us to knowledge of the unknown. But I do not reject by this what you promise to deal with on this particular at another time, as I also think of reasoning about it thoroughly in a treatise I intend to publish on logic, and [there] show that science does nothing except this for us, and that to seek causes belongs to a different habit [of mind] called wisdom, as I suggested in the preface of my book on motions; and just as the principles of the sciences are customarily definitions, axioms, and postulates, [I say] that in physical things these [principles] are for the most part experiences, on which are founded astronomy, music, mechanics, optics, and all the rest.

Baliani had cited in his book a proposition from Galileo's *Mechanics* that he would take as proved, so Galileo had asked what proposition he had had in mind. Baliani reminded him of an incident in 1615, when he thought the *Mechanics* to be a work by François Vieta, it having been given to him with that attribution, but on sending to Galileo its analysis of weights on inclined planes he had learned it was Galileo's own. Baliani asked again about the example in the earlier *Dialogue* of a body falling 100 braccia in five seconds, his first request in 1632 having elicited no response. Certain other questions and comments by Baliani are also reflected in Galileo's reply on the first of August:

I shall defer it to another time to satisfy that part [of your letter], full of generosity, and shall say now only, and briefly, something about the scientific particulars you touch on.

You tell me you would like to know the device by which I was able to assure myself that the vertically falling body leaving from rest passed 100 braccia of height in five seconds. Here two things are sought: the first is the time of descent through 100 braccia, and the second is to find what part that time is of 24 hours in the stars [*del primo mobile*]. As to the first operation, the descent of that ball that I make descend through a channel, arbitrarily sloped, will give us all the times—not only of 100 braccia, but of any other quantity of vertical fall— inasmuch as (as you yourself have demonstrated) the length of the said channel, or let us call it inclined plane, is a mean proportional between the vertical height of the said plane and the length of the whole vertical distance that would be passed in the same time by the falling moveable. Thus, for example, assuming that the said channel is 12 braccia long and its vertical height is one-half braccio, one braccio, or two, the distance passed in the vertical will be 288, 144, or 72 braccia, as is evident. It now remains that we find the amount of time of descent through the channel. This we shall obtain from the marvelous property of the pendulum, which is that it makes all its vibrations, large or small, in equal times. This requires, once and for all, that two or three or four patient and curious friends, having noted a fixed star that stands against some fixed marker, taking a pendulum of any length, shall go counting its vibrations during the whole time of the return of the fixed star to the original point, and this will be the number of vibrations in 24 hours. From the number of these we can find the number of vibrations of any other pendulums, longer or shorter, at will, so that if for example those counted by us in 24 hours were 234,567, then taking another shorter pendulum with which one [friend] counts 800 vibrations while another counts 150 of the longer pendulum, we already have, by the golden rule, the number of vibrations for the whole time of 24 hours; and if we want to know by these vibrations the time of descent through the channel, we can as easily find not only the minutes, seconds, and sixtieths of seconds, but beyond that as we please. It is true that we can pass to a more exact measure by having observed the flow of water through a thin passage, for by collecting this and having weighed what passes in one minute, for example, then by weighing what passes in the time of descent through the channel we can find the most exact

measure and quantity of this time, especially by making use
of a balance so precise as to weigh one-sixtieth of a grain. So
much for the device, which I think you will deem very exact,
though if you then want to experiment whether what I wrote
about the 100 braccia in five seconds be true, and you should
find it false, [remember that] to exhibit the extreme foolishness
of him who wrote [Scheiner] and assigned the time of a cannonball from the lunar orb [to the earth], it mattered little
whether the five seconds for 100 braccia was true or not.

You, though approving those subtleties I brought up, of
those distributed vacuities [in matter], for my explanation of
condensation and rarefaction without the necessity of introducing interpenetration of bodies or finite vacuous spaces, next
add that you are not entirely satisfied. I am not surprised, our
intellects having to mix together infinites and indivisibles, of
which the former are too great and the latter too small, [those]
being excessively disproportionate to our minds, which are
bounded and finite; and indeed it would be most pleasing to
me to hear some reflection of yours concerning these two
effects, for I am sure I should hear concepts much more reasonable than those introduced in the past by other philosophers.

As to your wish to be assured that in my first proposition
of the second Dialogue [Second Day], the force of resistance
has the same ratio as CB to $\frac{1}{2}BA$, that seemed to me quite
clear when the subject was prisms or cylinders around the
the center of which are distributed resistances of equal moments, in which operation the same thing happens as occurs
in the lever $A[C]B$, whose fulcrum is at C, where any equal
weights being put at the [ends of the] shorter distance CB,
hanging at equal distances, they make the same resistance to
the force applied at A as if both the said weights, reduced to
one, hung from the middle of BC. And if some doubt remains
about this (as I do not believe), I shall try to remove it with a
more detailed demonstration. . . .

Then that the principle I assume on p. 166 [the postulate,
mentioned earlier] does not, as you note, appear with that
[self-]evidence that is required of principles to be postulated
as known, I concede this to you now—though you make the
same assumption yourself, that is, that the degrees of speed
acquired by moveables descending by different planes through
the same height are equal. Know, then, that after my having lost
my sight, and consequently my faculty of going more deeply
into propositions and demonstrations more profound than those
last discovered and written by me, I [instead] spent the

nocturnal hours ruminating on the first and simplest propositions, reordering these and arranging them in better form and
evidence. Among these it occurred to me to demonstrate the
said postulate in the manner you will in time see, if I shall have
sufficient strength to improve and amplify what was written
and published by me up to now about motion by adding some
little speculations, and in particular those relating to the force of
percussion, in the investigation of which I have consumed
hundreds and thousands of hours, and have finally reduced
this to very easy explanation, so that people can understand it
in less than half an hour of time.

And here I want to tell you again that I have no memory
of those writings you say were sent to you as ideas of Vieta and
were affirmed by me to be mine, whence I desire you to refresh
my memory about this, and in particular what was written
about percussion, which must have been imperfect, I being
satisfied that this was not discovered by me until a few years
ago, nor do I know of having given out full notice of it.

What Baliani had meant was the brief appendix on the force
of percussion in Galileo's *Mechanics*, forgotten along with the
mistaken attribution to Vieta. Galileo's recent reflections on percussion had meanwhile led him to consider the case of constant
resistance, unlike the driving of a stake, in which one of two
weights connected over a pulley is dropped. He then saw that
the troublesome "infinite" force had a certain symmetry to it.
Impact imparted to a constant resistance had a limited effect in
that the speed imparted could not exceed the speed of the body
giving the impact, but an unlimited effect in the distance that
would be traversed by the body receiving the impact, all friction
and other impediments being removed. On the other hand impact against a changing resistance, as in the case of the pile
driver, was limited in the distance that the body receiving the
impact could be driven, but unlimited in the resistance that
could be overcome by any percussion, however small, at least
in theory. This resolution of the paradoxical aspect of "infinite"
force of percussion was explained in dialogue form, first published in 1718 from a manuscript no longer extant.[4]

III

Galileo probably never wrote the dialogue on force of percussion
in his own hand, but dictated it during 1638, putting Aproino in
place of Simplicio and including all the material he had drafted

before June 1637 (when he abandoned the idea of including that in *Two New Sciences*). The opening sentence shows that this dialogue was supposed to take place a fortnight after the Fourth Day, and it should be called the Fifth Day. Unfortunately, Viviani appropriated that phrase for an entirely different composition, intended to open still another book, dictated by Galileo to Torricelli shortly before his death. The dialogue on percussion was probably dictated before Viviani came to live with Galileo in the latter part of 1638; being in the hand not of Galileo but of some scribe, it may not have been regarded by Viviani as unquestionably authentic. In any event it was omitted from the first collected edition of Galileo's works, in 1655–56, which was supervised by Viviani.

Baliani replied to Galileo's previous letter on 19 August. Concerning the time of fall from a tower, he said that meanwhile the Jesuit Niccolò Cabeo, at Ferrara, had found the length of a pendulum that would beat seconds, which he gave at 223 mm from suspension to center of weight.[5] Baliani believed this would be very useful for measuring short times, as well as time of fall from a tower. He suggested that Galileo might well have put as a postulate his statement (in the scholium to Proposition Twenty-Three) that any degree of speed in a moving body is indelibly impressed in it; yet (as remarked above) Baliani's own use of this idea was far from our inertial principle. He duly copied and sent the short discussion of percussion that since 1594 had been appended to Galileo's *Mechanics*. Galileo's reply on 1 September illustrates his experimental acuity:

In reply to your welcome letter of 19 August, I say that to measure time with a pendulum adjusted to make its vibrations in one second precludes the labor of making the calculation by simple use of the golden rule after having once counted the number of vibrations of any pendulum made in 24 hours—which observation Father Cabeo must have made with a pendulum of some length and then, using the discovery of the mean [proportional], have drawn from it the length of the seconds pendulum, which invention is subject to some error that, though small, can give rise to a notable error when multiplied by the many vibrations [during any experiment]. This does not happen with vibrations unrestricted by length of the thread, which, repeated many hundreds of times, must give the measure of the time. Thus any little error in the length of the [seconds] pendulum becomes multiplied many hundreds of times, whereas in my other operation no error can arise except in the [original] number of vibrations [in twenty-four hours], which can be greater or less than correct by only a part of one vibration. Hence (to explain by an example) the same thing comes about that would happen to a person who wanted to assign the length of the year from two entries of the sun into the equator, taken at the interval of just one year between entry and departure. There an error of a half or quarter of an hour would come into the determination of the length of the year, and retaining that as correct, with such an error, in assigning the amount of time in 100, 200, or more years, there would arise errors of 100 or 200 times as great as that which entered into the determination of just one year. But if we take the entry of the sun into the equator that occurred 1,000 or 1,500 years ago, assuming that the ancients erred by half an hour and that we no less run into a similar error, then that quantity divided over 1,000 or 1,500 years is the most I can be wrong in assigning the length of one year, nor can there arise a greater error than the thousandth or 1,500th part of the whole error introduced.

That the use of the pendulum as a measurer of time is very exact I have said many times, and I have even gathered together various astronomical operations in which, thanks to this measurer, I attain precision infinitely better than do those who, using astronomical instruments (quadrants, sextants, armillaries or the like), should have their sides or diameters not just 2 or 3 braccia long like Tycho's, but even 20, or 30, or 50, and divided not just into degrees and minutes, but into parts of minutes. To have found a way to measure very exactly the diameter of a star, besides being in itself a beautiful operation, is the more to be esteemed when I find that astronomers who have tried to determine such magnitudes have been wrong not by 20% or 30%, but I say by 2,000 or 3,000 percent.[6]

As to what you tell me of your opinion about condensation and rarefaction—that is, that you assume the penetration of one body by another, I already wrote (as you may see) that I concede that, or whatever he pleases, to anyone who wishes to admit such things, I having had in mind, in writing what I wrote about this, only [to write] for the benefit of those who deny that interpenetrations or void spaces can exist in nature.

As to the first proposition of my second Dialogue—whether it should be taken as a principle or demonstrated—I allowed it as a thing known of itself and very clear, because . . . [the

law of the lever] . . . can be taken as known; then, bending
the lever at right angles to form its longer and shorter arms,
the force [still] encounters the same opposition from the
resistance. . . .

That which I put as a postulate—that is, that the degrees
of speed acquired by falling bodies over any planes having the
same elevation are equal when they reach the horizontal—I have
since demonstrated clearly, and if you like I shall send you
the demonstration.

The writing about percussion [sent by you] is absolutely
mine, done more than 40 years ago, but I have amplified it very
much and explained it much more in detail.

IV

Baliani replied on 9 September, saying that he believed Cabeo
had indeed proceeded in the way Galileo assumed, except that
he had counted for only an hour or so and not twenty-four
hours, deriving his seconds pendulum then by the golden rule.
Since I do not know of any accurate way then available for determining an exact hour, or indeed any time shorter than an
astronomical day, I do not understand what Baliani could have
had in mind. Satisfaction with it shows how far Baliani was
from understanding what Galileo was talking about in the matter of experimental precision.

A week later Baliani wrote again to say that he had overlooked Galileo's offer to send a proof of his earlier postulate. He
said that he had also found a proof, using the law of free fall,
which he intended to add to his book on the occasion of printing
a correction leaf; he would have sent his proof to Galileo, but
then remembered he was unable to see diagrams. He went on to
mention an experiment he had just made by dropping a weight
from a ship's mast more than 40 braccia high; although the ship
traveled at least 16 braccia during the fall of the body, this
alighted at the foot of the mast. Baliani's test was made at
Genoa some three years before the more famous experiments of
Gassendi made at Marseilles.[7] Baliani's appears to have been the
first to be reported with numerical data, though Galileo had seen
satisfactory tests at Venice many years before.

It was doubtless Baliani's announcement that he was going to
publish a proof of Galileo's postulate that induced Galileo to
establish his priority of proof, toward the end of 1639. The first
of several letters relating to this was sent to Castelli on 3 De-

cember, more than a year after the proof had been formulated. First sent to Michelini for Prince Leopold, it had been worked out as the result of a visit and discussion with Viviani, who had subsequently come to live with Galileo:

It is only too manifest, your Reverence, that in philosophizing doubt is the father of invention, opening a road to the discovery of truth. Objections made to me many months ago by this young man [Viviani] who is now my guest and disciple, against that principle postulated by me in my treatise on accelerated motion, which he was then [1638] studying with much application, made me think about this again in such a way as to persuade him that that principle might be conceded as true. Finally, to his and my great delight, I succeeded in finding a conclusive demonstration, if I am not mistaken, which I have by now shown to many. This he has now put down for me, since being deprived of my eyes I would be confused about the diagrams and lettering needed. It is written in dialogue [form] as occurring to Salviati, so that when my *Discourses and Demonstrations* are reprinted it can be inserted right after the scholium to the second proposition . . . as a theorem essential to the establishment of the science of motion advanced by me. I communicate this to you by letter, before anyone else,[8] principally out of regard for your opinion, and after that [will give it] to our friends here, with the thought of sending copies later to other friends in Italy and France if you encourage me.

V

Meanwhile the groundwork had been laid for a correspondence of great interest during Galileo's last years. Fortunio Liceti, professor of philosophy at the University of Padua, had sent him a book in which Galileo was mentioned, promising another soon on the Bolognese stone. In September 1639 Galileo wrote to him in part:

I particularly liked your naming me with praise where you disputed at length about the size of the universe and whether it should be believed finite or infinite. The reasons on both sides are very clever, but to my mind neither one is necessarily conclusive, so that it always remains ambiguous which assertion is true. Yet one argument alone of mine inclines me more to the infinite [universe] than the finite, this being that I cannot imagine it either as bounded *or* as unbounded and infinite;

and since the infinite, by its nature, cannot be comprehended by our finite intellect, which is not the case for the finite, circumscribed by bounds, I should refer my incomprehension to the incomprehensible infinite [rather] than to the finite, in which there is no necessary reason of incomprehensibility.

Any kind of "actual infinite" was repellent to orthodox Aristotelians. On 14 February 1640 Cavalieri wrote to Galileo, displeased by Liceti's book but not wishing to reply to his trivial objections against indivisibles. In this letter Cavalieri mentioned the problem of quadrature of the cycloid, sent to him by Parisian mathematicians, and the volume of a cycloid of revolution "which I remember you once asked me about, and I worked on it fruitlessly. Please tell me if these two things have been demonstrated by anybody, because they look to me very difficult." Galileo replied, on 24 February, "I do not know that those questions sent to you from France have been demonstrated by anyone. I hold with you that they are very difficult to solve. That arched line occurred to me to describe more than fifty years ago, and I admired it as a very gracious curve to be adapted to the arches of a bridge.[9] I made various attempts to demonstrate some of its properties, and concerning the space included by it and its chord it seemed to me from the beginning that that space might be triple the circle which described the curve, but it was not so, though the difference [by weighing] was not great. It needs the mind of Cavalieri and no other to find the whole thing or else to make all theorists despair of bringing this contemplation to a head." It has been mentioned earlier that Galileo's attempt to show the area of the cycloid to be three times that of the generating circle was empirical only.

Liceti's book on the Bolognese stone[10] attacked Galileo's explanation (in the *Starry Messenger* and the *Dialogue*) of the secondary light of the moon seen in thin crescent as a reflection of sunlight from the earth. These attacks became the subject of several letters to Galileo early in 1640. On 11 March, Prince Leopold wrote from Pisa that although to him Liceti's arguments seemed too frivolous to deserve reply, nevertheless he would like to have Galileo's opinion. Galileo then composed a lengthy treatise in the form of a letter to Prince Leopold, copies of which circulated for several months before Liceti asked to have one in order that he might formally reply. Galileo's Letter to Prince Leopold was several times revised and expanded, the final version occupying about fifty printed pages.

When asking Galileo for a copy of this letter, Liceti complained that he had been injured without any cause after a long and friendly relationship. He remarked on the earlier occasion when his book on new stars and comets was ignored in Galileo's *Assayer*. Galileo pretended not to have received that book in time to include it, but Liceti was able to cite to him his own letter in 1622 acknowledging receipt of it. Nevertheless, Liceti assured Galileo that their friendship continued on his side despite all differences of philosophical opinion. This was in July, and Galileo then sent Liceti a copy of the letter.

Liceti replied on 3 August, taking umbrage especially at "that final puncture in which you say that your defenses are undertaken against him who has 'sinisterly used the Peripatetic philosophy,' for I should not want a few pungent words to lay waste the treasure of an old friendship founded on a basis of virtuosity." He went on to express regret that Galileo had written his letter in Italian, rather than in the Latin that Liceti intended to use in his reply. Also, since Galileo had not published his letter, Liceti suggested that a copy be formally forwarded to him by Leopold or by some mutual friend in order that he might properly publish it along with his answer.

Galileo wrote on 25 August, saying that he would prefer to readdress his letter directly to Liceti, leaving Prince Leopold out of the affair and allowing Galileo to polish his composition and add more arguments, though without altering or omitting anything he had already written:

And indeed it is fitting that one who has written a simple letter without thought of publishing it should be conceded the right to review and if necessary polish it, not placing it at the disposition of someone who intends to put under a million eyes that which its author revealed only to four or six. That is my view; I await your opinion. . . .

As to the other, that you call a puncture, of my having written about responding only to him who clumsily (*sinistramente*) used the Peripatetic doctrine: I said that because against all reason I am impugned as an impugner of the Peripatetic doctrine, whereas I claim (and surely believe) that I observe more religiously the Peripatetic or I should rather say

Aristotelian teachings than do many who wrongfully put me down as averse from good Peripatetic philosophy; and since one of the teachings given to us admirably by Aristotle in his *Dialectics* is that of reasoning well, arguing well, and deducing necessary conclusions from the premises, when I then see conclusions deduced that have no connection with the premises, which therefore deviate from the Aristotelian doctrine, I think I may rightfully deem myself a better Peripatetic, and [consider] that I more dextrously [*destramente*] use that doctrine than anyone who makes use of it clumsily [*sinistramente*].

Before Liceti received this letter he wrote again on 31 August, having had more time to study Galileo's little treatise. He now praised it and said he had learned from it, though he remained in his original opinion and was therefore even more anxious to have it published so that he could reply. A week later Liceti replied also to the above letter, including this amusing remark: "That you profess not to contradict the Aristotelian doctrine is most welcome to me, just as (to speak frankly) it is news to me, I seeming to have gathered the contrary from your writings; but it may be that on this particular I was mistaken, along with many others of the same opinion." On 15 September Galileo wrote:

I am glad to hear that you, and as you say many others, hold me averse from the Peripatetic philosophy, for this gives me occasion to free myself from such blame (for so I deem it) and to show how beneath the surface I admire such a man as Aristotle. I shall content myself now to hint briefly what I think, to be able when I have more time to explain and confirm this in more detail.

I consider (and believe you do, too) that to be truly Peripatetic—that is, an Aristotelian philosopher—consists principally in philosophizing conformably with the Aristotelian teachings, proceeding by those methods and with those true assumptions and principles on which scientific reasoning is founded, assuming those general informations from which to diverge would be a very great defect. Among these assumptions is everything that Aristotle teaches us in his *Dialectics* relating to our taking care to avoid fallacies in reasoning, directing the latter well and using it adroitly to syllogize and to deduce from the conceded premises the necessary conclusion; and this teaching relates to the form of rightly arguing. As to this part,

I believe I have learned sureness of demonstration from the innumerable advances made by pure mathematicians, never fallacious, for if not never, then at least very rarely, have I fallen into mistakes in my argumentation. Thus far, therefore, I am Peripatetic.

Among the safe ways to pursue truth is the putting of experience before any reasoning, we being sure that any fallacy will be contained in the latter, at least covertly, it not being possible that a sensible experience is contrary to truth. And this also is a precept much esteemed by Aristotle and placed [by him] far in front of the value and force of the authority of everybody in the world. You yourself assume this, for not only should we not yield to the authority of another, but we should deny authority to ourselves whenever we find that sense shows us the contrary.

Now here, good sir (let it be said in peace to you), I seem to be judged as [going] contrary to Peripatetic philosophizing by those who clumsily make use of the above pure and most safe precept—that is, they would have it to be good philosophizing to accept and sustain any dictum and proposition written by Aristotle, to whose absolute authority they subject themselves. To maintain these they induce themselves to deny sensible experience and give strange interpretations to the texts of Aristotle; for in explanation and limitation of these they would often make that same philosopher say things no less extravagant [than their opinions] and surely far from his imagining. There is no contradiction in a great craftsman's having sure and complete precepts of his art, and yet sometimes making mistakes in some particular. Thus, for example, a musician or a painter possessed of the true precepts of the art may in practice make some discord or some inadvertent error in perspective. Knowing such craftsmen to be not only possessed of true precepts, but themselves the inventors thereof, must I then, when I see some defect in a work of theirs, accept that work as well done and worthy of being defended and imitated by virtue of the authority of those men? Certainly I shall never give my assent to that. I want to add only this: that I am sure that if Aristotle should return to earth he would accept me among his followers on account of my few but conclusive contradictions [of him], much rather than [he would accept] a great many other people who, in order to sustain his every saying as true, go filching from his texts conceptions that never entered his head. And if Aristotle should see the things newly discovered in the sky, though he affirmed it to be unalterable and immutable because no change had then been seen there, doubtless he, changing his opinion, would now say the contrary. For indeed it is gathered that when he says the sky is unalterable *because* no alteration has been seen there, he would now say it is alterable because alterations *are* perceived there. It is getting late, and I should embark in a great sea if I wished to adduce all that has passed through my mind from time to time on such things, so I reserve this to another occasion.

As to your having attributed to me opinions not mine, that may have happened by your taking some [things] attributed to me by other people though never written by me. For example, according to the philosopher Lagalla I hold light to be corporeal, while the same author in the same place writes that I have always ingenuously confessed my not knowing what light is. Similarly [you] take as positively and primarily mine some thoughts set forth by Sig. Mario Guiducci; it might be that I had no part in those, though I regard it as an honor to have those concepts believed mine, deeming them true and noble.

At Galileo's advanced age, especially in private letters, he had no reason to dissemble. It may seem strange that he should speak favorably of Aristotle, but that is largely the effect of our habit of crediting the self-styled Aristotelians with having faithfully represented the thought of the ancient Greek sage, rather than considering whether they had not badly distorted it by superficial verbal gambits remote from the study of nature he had inaugurated. In any event Galileo's correspondence with Liceti remains his last will and testament on the relation of science as he saw it with philosophy as it was practiced, and is as deserving of study as anything else he ever wrote.

VI

On 27 October Galileo wrote again concerning still another book by Liceti, *On Center and Circumference, in which are Diligently Treated Physico-Mathematically the Names, Varieties, Species, Properties, and Uses Thereof. . . .*[11] Having had this book read to him, Galileo told Liceti:

Your so many definitions of center and circumference have made me lament the sterility of my mind—never, beyond some information given by simple geometers and mechanics, able to think up the least new knowledge [about centers]. And if, as the said mathematicians deduce from their definitions a very large number of theorems and problems, with their very subtle proofs, it shall be that you or others deduce likewise new consequences [from your definitions], there will be born a new and admirable science; and you, as first and principal innovator, will come to open by example the gate to the long new road that remains.

Of yet another book by the prolific Liceti, Galileo said:

But truly to find a way to adapt physical, metaphysical, and theological senses to words that may have been but a simple fantasy, not to say a chimera of your spokesman [Simmia Rhodio], redoubles in me my marvel at minds so acute and speculative.

Three more books by Liceti were sent to Galileo in January 1641. One of these, on the earth as unique center of the universe,[12] brought forth from Galileo some comments later that month which may at first seem surprising, so seldom had he in past years met philosophers on their own grounds, having long preferred to stick to sober science in which very careful measeurement and observation play an essential role:

The problem or question of the center of the universe, and whether the earth is situated there, is among the least worthy of consideration in all astronomy, inasmuch as it has sufficed for the greatest astronomers to assume that the terrestrial globe is of insensible size in comparison with the starry orb, and as to its location that it is either at the center of the diurnal revolution of that [starry] orb or removed therefrom by an insignificant distance. There is no reason to tire oneself out in trying to prove this, nor that the fixed stars are situated in a space determined by a spherical surface, beyond [the fact] that they are located at an immense distance from us. Likewise to want to assign a center to that space, whose shape is neither known nor can be known, or even whether it has a shape, is in my opinion a superfluous and idle task; hence to believe that the earth can be located at a center not known to exist in the universe is a frustrating enterprise.

But if we wish to consider the lower celestial bodies, whose motions we can assert to be circular and [which] therefore must have a center for their turnings, then to put the earth as their common center is not only a vain idea but is absolutely false, it being manifest that each [orbit] of those movable bodies [the planets] has its own particular center, different from every other, in none of which can the earth be placed.

Rather, this earth is not only not the center of any of their circular movements but is located far outside [some of] their circles and orbs, as is evident in [the case of] Mercury and Venus; and for the others, this earth is so far from their [orbital] centers that Mars, for example, in traveling around its circle, has parts of that [travel] so near to, and those opposite so far from the earth that the latter are eight times as far [from the earth] as the former. Now you see what a task they undertake who want to place it [the earth] in the center of such revolutions; and what I say of Mars is also true of Jupiter and Saturn, though with not so great a difference. One place that could almost be put as the center for all planets but the moon would be the sun, better than any other; not that all the centers of the [orbits of] the planets agree perfectly with that center, but rather that they are more or less located around the sun with infinitely less deviation therefrom than they have with respect to the earth.

Hence as to this matter, my good sir, in my opinion you may give up trying, either with the texts or the authority of Aristotle, to persuade people of a doctrine too obviously false. And to understand and get hold of astronomical science you need to study others than Aristotle, from whose writings all that is gathered is that he possessed no more of that science than every simple man comprehends. . . .

I shall conclude only that having as your aim the maintaining as true every saying of Aristotle's, and sustaining that experiences show nothing that was unknown to Aristotle, you are doing what many other Peripatetics combined would perhaps be unable to do; and if philosophy were what is contained in Aristotle's books, you would in my opinion be the greatest philosopher in the world, so well does it seem to me that you have ready at hand every passage he wrote. But I truly believe the book of philosophy to be that which stands perpetually open before our eyes, though since it is written in characters different from those of our alphabet it cannot be read by everyone; and the characters of such a book are triangles, squares, circles, spheres, cones, pyramids, and other mathematical figures, most apt for such reading.

It was not until January 1641 that Galileo finally sent off his polished and amplified text of the Letter to Leopold. Liceti acknowledged receipt of a copy on 5 February, and in due course he did publish his reply to it, in 183 sections.[13] But for our purposes the importance of this debate ends with the year 1640.

TWENTY-TWO

1641-42

I

ONE HARDLY EXPECTS new contributions to scientific thought from a blind man of seventy-seven in his last year on earth, when return to memories of events long past is more usual. In this, Galileo was no exception; yet even his last year was no less a phase of his scientific career than any other. Partly this was the result of communications from others, and partly it was the product of that incredible tenacity that induced him, in the last weeks before his terminal illness, to venture on the composition of still another book. Because the brief unfinished beginning of that book marked the end of Galileo's scientific career, and because it is not without interest to the logical foundations of mathematical physics and even of mathematics itself, much of this final chapter will be occupied with a translation of a little dialogue on certain Euclidean definitions that reflects Galileo's earliest and latest thoughts on the theory of ratio and proportionality.

The first letter sent to Galileo after the conclusion of his debate with Liceti came from Vincenzio Renieri, newly installed in Galileo's old chair of mathematics at the University of Pisa. To the disappointment of Galileo, Cavalieri, and the grand duke, Castelli had been prevented from reassuming that previous position of his upon the death of Dino Peri in 1640. Renieri had been working with Galileo for many months in the preparation of revised tables for prediction of the positions of the satellites of Jupiter. On 5 February 1641 he wrote from Pisa (where the annual residence of the Tuscan court kept him from visiting his mentor at Arcetri) a letter that will recall some events of Galileo's early days as professor at Pisa:

"Not infrequently I am in some battle with the Peripatetic gentlemen, particularly when I note that those fattest with ignorance least appreciate your worth, and I have just given the head of one of those a good scrubbing." Two weeks later he wrote Galileo that the university auditor had reinstated the regulation requiring traditional doctoral togas, "hence now none are seen ungowned, and the *capitolo* you once wrote would be most appropriate." This referred to a jocular poem written by Galileo in his first days as professor.[1] Called "Against Wearing the Toga," it had evidently not been forgotten at Pisa, especially among young and poor lecturers who could not afford costly robes and a few others who, like Renieri, were averse to pomp. On 6 March Renieri regaled Galileo with the story of an Inquisitor who had compelled the author of a book recently printed at Florence to change the words "most distinguished Galileo" to "Galileo, man of noted name." Then, on 13 March, Renieri sent a most surprising letter containing this significant paragraph:

We have had occasion here to make an experiment of two heavy bodies falling from on high, of different material, that is, one of wood and one of lead, but of the same size; for a certain Jesuit[2] wrote that these fall in the same time and arrive at the earth with equal speed, and an Englishman affirmed that Liceti had made a problem here [of this] and offered the reason. But finally we found the fact contrary, because from the top of the campanile of the cathedral[3] there were at least three braccia of difference between the lead ball and the wooden one. Experiments were also made of two lead balls, one the size of an ordinary cannonball and the other that of a musket bullet, and it was seen that between the larger and the smaller, from the height of the campanile, there was a good *palmo*[4] of difference by which the larger anticipated the smaller. What I noted in these experiments was that it seemed to me that the motion of the wooden ball, having accelerated to a certain point, then began to fall not vertically but transversely, in the same way as we see drops of water that fall slantingly, which, coming near the earth, turn sideways, whence their motion begins to be less rapid.

The surprising thing about this is that though Renieri had been working with Galileo for some time and was now professor of mathematics, he had obviously not read *Two New Sciences*, for in that book the lag of a musket ball behind a cannonball from a great height had been described as the same *palmo*, and Sagredo had asserted that he had made the test.[5] It is noteworthy that though Galileo's jocular poem against gowns was still remembered at the University of Pisa, his demonstration from the Leaning Tower with bodies of the same material more than fifty years earlier was quite forgotten. Indeed, most historians believe that there was nothing to be remembered and that no such test as described in Viviani's biography of Galileo was ever made. I am now inclined to believe that if Galileo's answer to the above letter had been preserved, it would long ago have provided definite evidence to the contrary.

It will be recalled that Viviani's account specified different weights of the same material, as in the second experiment described by Renieri. That was indeed the only result of which Galileo could have been confident under his early theory of speeds in fall, and Viviani's accuracy on this point had always inclined me to believe that whether or not the Leaning Tower demonstration was historical, Viviani had heard of it from Galileo's own lips. Nevertheless I found it hard to understand why in his old age Galileo should suddenly recall for Viviani an incident never mentioned before. What had not struck me was that Viviani, to whom Renieri sent regards in his letter of 20 February, was at this very time Galileo's amanuensis. It was Viviani who wrote the letters to Liceti dictated by Galileo, as well as all other surviving letters by Galileo in this period. Hence he doubtless read the foregoing letter to the blind Galileo and wrote the lost reply to Renieri, of which the contents can be guessed from Renieri's answer on 20 March. Galileo had evidently referred him to *Two New Sciences* concerning the second experiment and had asked him to repeat the first experiment, since deflection of the wooden ball was not a phenomenon Galileo had observed, nor could it result from or account for reduced speed. Renieri replied:

Your last Dialogue [*Two New Sciences*] has been read by me only here and there because last summer, when I might have been able to attend to this with due diligence, you know how I was; and later I did not have time to look at it with that application required by its demonstrations. I know it is true that two bodies of different specific weight, though equal in

volume, follow no ratio of weights in [their] descending, and
indeed that for example, in water, wood will move opposite to
lead; hence from the outset I laughed at the Jesuit's [account
of his] experiment, who affirmed that lead and a loaf of bread
(to speak as he wrote) would be moved with equal speed to
the center. But that two bodies unequal in weight, of the same
material, falling vertically from the same height, can arrive
at the center with different speeds and at different times seemed
to me impossible, as I had heard said by you, or had read, for
indeed I do not recall which. Therefore I shall read in these
few days of [Easter] vacation your last Dialogue, though I
reserve complete reading to next summer with more leisure.
Meanwhile we shall return to making the experiment of the
[wood] balls and see if we were mistaken in the observation
that when they near the ground they turn and do not go vertically, and will give you notice of this.

Thus Galileo had replied along the line one would expect, at a
time when Viviani was writing his letters for him and was fully informed about the events. The entire account of Galileo's Pisan
demonstration written out by Viviani may not have been included in Galileo's reply to Renieri, but nothing would have been
more natural than for Galileo to tell the story to his young
amanuensis. The amusing coincidence of Renieri's having repeated the same observation from the same place, except for
varying the materials used, would not only remind Galileo of
his long-forgotten demonstration but would also induce him to
emphasize that he had used weights of the same material, a fact
that Viviani would hardly have had reason to specify had he not
heard it from Galileo himself. Nothing had changed at the University of Pisa; the lone mathematician still had to battle against
all the philosophers, and it must have greatly amused Galileo to
learn that not even his own protegé had troubled to read his
book on the science of motion.

II

At this time Castelli visited Galileo at Arcetri, having first spent
months in obtaining permission to do so. It is interesting that
the church appears not to have forbidden Protestants like
Hobbes and Milton to visit Galileo, but made it very difficult for
his own former pupil, now a Benedictine abbot, to do so. Castelli
brought along a letter from his most promising pupil, Evangelista Torricelli, together with a manuscript work on falling

bodies and projectiles described to Galileo by the brilliant young mathematician and physicist as "paraphrases of your sciences." Galileo was much impressed by it, and in April he requested Torricelli to come to Arcetri as his assistant. Previous commitments prevented his arrival before October, just before Galileo's final illness.

On 23 March Rinuccini wrote from Venice concerning some telescopic observations made by Pieroni in Germany nearly a year before. Pieroni declared that he had detected motions of fixed stars amounting to some seconds of arc, with as much certainty as he would have in noting one degree of arc in naked eye observations of the skies. In these observations Pieroni believed he had found conclusive evidence for the Copernican system. Remarkable as it is, it can hardly be doubted that what Pieroni had observed was what James Bradley a century later at first mistook for parallactic displacement due to the earth's annual motion, subsequently realizing it to be far too great for that and correctly ascribing the apparent stellar motions to aberration of light. Galileo's reply to Rinuccini on 29 March may at first astonish the reader:

The falsity of the Copernican system must not on any account be doubted, expecially by us Catholics, who have the irrefragable authority of Holy Scripture interpreted by the greatest masters in theology, whose agreement renders us certain of the stability of the earth and the mobility of the sun around it. The conjectures of Copernicus and his followers offered to the contrary are all removed by that most sound argument, taken from the omnipotence of God. He being able to do in many, or rather in infinite ways, that which to our view and observation seems to be done in one particular way, we must not pretend to hamper God's hand and tenaciously maintain that in which we may be mistaken. And just as I deem inadequate the Copernican observations and conjectures, so I judge equally, and more, fallacious and erroneous those of Ptolemy, Aristotle, and their followers, when [even] without going beyond the bounds of human reasoning their inconclusiveness can be very easily discovered.

And since you say you are perplexed and disturbed by [that is, in answering] the argument taken from our always seeing one-half the sky above the horizon from which it can be concluded with Ptolemy that the earth is in the center of the stellar sphere,[6] and not distant therefrom as much as the radius

417

of the Great Orbit [of the earth, or sun]—then [you should]
reply to that author that truly one-half the sky is *not* seen,
and deny this to him until he makes you certain that exactly
half *is* seen—which he will never do. For whoever has said
positively that half the sky is seen, and that therefore the earth
is established at the center, has it in his head to begin with
that the earth *is* established at the center, which is why he says
that half the sky is seen—because that is what would have to
happen if the earth were at the center. So it is not from seeing
half the sky that the earth's being in the center is inferred
[by these men], but it is deduced from the assumption that the
earth is at the center that half the sky is seen. And Ptolemy
and those other authors would be obliged to teach us how to
know in the sky the [exact] first points of Aries and Libra,
because for my part I cannot even discern these.

Now let us add that if the observations of Captain Pieroni
be true about the motions of some fixed stars, made through a
few seconds of arc, [then] small as these are, [this] implies to
human reasoning changes by the earth different from any that
can be attributed to it [while] retained at the center. And if
there is such a change, and it is observed to be less than one
minute of arc, who wants to guarantee to me that when the
first point of Aries rises, the first point of Libra sets so precisely
that there is not even a difference to us of one minute of arc?
Those points are indivisibles; horizons are not that precise on
land, or sometimes even at sea; ordinary astronomical instruments cannot be so exact in such observations as to guarantee
against an error of one minute; and finally, refractions [of star
light] near the horizon can cause alterations that involve not
just one minute, but many minutes, as observers themselves
admit. Hence what should we want to deduce, in a very delicate
and subtle observation, from experiences that are crass and
even impossible to make? I might add other things on this
subject, but what was already said in my unfortunate *Dialogue*
may suffice.

Among all Galileo's surviving letters, it is only this one on
which his name at the end was scratched out heavily in ink. I
presume that Rinuccini valued and preserved Galileo's letters
no matter what they said, but did not want others to see this
declaration by Galileo that the Copernican system was false, lest
he be thought a hypocrite. Yet there was nothing hypocritical in
Galileo's saying that all science, including astronomy, is a fiction
to the extent that it lies beyond the range of practicable obser-

vations; indeed, astronomy as Copernicus left it could not be reconciled with many actually observed facts known to Galileo. More important yet is Galileo's flat statement that the traditional geocentric astronomy was even more erroneous than the heliocentric. Thanks to Galileo's own telescopic discoveries that was certainly true, while that astronomical instruments could not establish stellar parallax was not only true in his time but remained so for two centuries afterward.

It was probably in mid-1641 that Galileo, reflecting on the use of the pendulum as a precise measurer of time, dictated to his son the design of a mechanism by which it could be applied to ordinary clocks. Previously he had described only a mechanical counter of beats of a solid metal pendulum, having it drive a gear that was advanced one tooth per beat by means of an attached bristle. The new mechanism was described by Viviani in 1659 as follows:

One day in 1641, while I was living with him at his villa in Arcetri, I remember that the idea occurred to him that the pendulum could be adapted to clocks with weights or springs, serving in place of the usual *tempo* [verge and foliot], he hoping that the very even and natural motions of the pendulum would correct all the defects in the art of clocks. But because his being deprived of sight prevented his making drawings and models to the end of determining what device would be best fitted to the desired effect, and his son Vincenzio coming one day from Florence to Arcetri, Galileo told him his idea and several discussions followed. Finally they decided on the scheme shown in the accompanying drawing, to be put in practice to learn the fact of those difficulties in machines which are usually not foreseen in simple theorizing.[7]

This letter was part of a very unpleasant quarrel started by Viviani after Christiaan Huygens published his invention of the pendulum clock, Viviani then insisting on priority of the idea for Galileo. A model had been begun by Galileo's son but had not been finished at the time of his death in 1649. This model was described and depicted by Viviani; its existence was attested to ten years later by Prince Leopold, and the model was listed in the inventory of possessions of Vincenzio Galilei's widow when she died in 1669. The device was limited, however, to an escapement, ingenious in conception but not fitted with either a drive or a clock face; nor is there any reason to think that Huygens

Vincenzio Viviani's drawing of Galileo's design for use of pendulum to measure time, dictated by the blind Galileo to his son in 1641. (*Opere di Galileo*, 19:656. Photo by University of Toronto Photographic Services.)

owed anything whatever to Galileo's work in designing his own justly famed pendulum clock. Viviani's letter is of value in showing Galileo's intimate familiarity with actual mechanisms, so that even when blind he could design an original regulator applicable to a clock. Galileo indeed understood the clocks of his time very well; his daughter Virginia, despairing of getting anyone else to adjust the convent clock to keep time and to strike properly, sent it to Galileo after several unsuccessful attempts on the part of her brother Vincenzio to regulate it. Galileo soon returned it working very well; this was in 1630.[8]

III

In September Galileo wrote to Torricelli: "I hope to enjoy your company for some few days before my life, now near an end, is finished . . . as also to discuss with you some relics of my thoughts on mathematics and physics and to have your aid in polishing them, that they may be left less messy to be seen with other things of mine." In fact when that letter was written Torricelli was already on his way to Arcetri, and the end was truly near. He arrived in October, and in November Galileo was confined to bed by low fever and severe kidney pains. It was the beginning of his terminal illness, about which his greatest grief was that he was no longer permitted to drink wine—what he had long called "light held together by moisture."

The work that Torricelli was able to do for Galileo was accordingly very limited. It consisted chiefly in writing out from dictation, in dialogue form, Galileo's reflections on two definitions found in Euclid's *Elements*, that of "same ratio" in Book Five, and that of "compound ratio" in Book Six. These were the two most important keys taken from antiquity in creating Galileo's mathematical physics, so that his exposition of them as the last act of his scientific career reflected his earliest scientific steps at Pisa and Padua. Like the Leaning Tower affair, this dialogue linked his last days with his first; Galileo had come full circle.

From the strictly human viewpoint the most striking thing about the dialogue translated below is that Galileo on his death-bed had it in mind to begin still another book, assembling once more his three old interlocutors to discuss things brought up by *Two New Sciences*. What other topics the book would have contained is not known, but very probably they also would have been expositions of elementary fundamentals necessary to be understood thoroughly before progress could be made in physical science as Galileo envisioned it. Thinking over during his years of blindness what he had already published, he realized that mastery of the theory of proportion was essential to lay readers if they were to know "that sharpness of true proof by which the taste may be awakened to know how insipid is the ordinary fare" of natural philosophy.[9] That accordingly became the opening of the final book he did not live to complete.

From the mathematical standpoint Galileo's critique of these definitions is by no means trivial. His discussion of Book Five, Definition Five shows how a rigorous theory of irrational magnitudes can be built on the natural numbers by means of equimultiples, a term left undefined in Euclid's presentation. That is a large step in formulating a rigorous analysis of the continuum. His discussion of the spurious Book Six, Definition Five illuminates the nature of mathematical definitions in general, essential to foundational analysis. The work thus started, on both counts, was taken up again only a century ago; it is only the conspicuous advances made since then that make Galileo's beginnings appear trivial.

On Euclid's Definitions of [Sameness of] Ratios[10] [and on Compounding of Ratios]

SALVIATI. I feel great consolation today in seeing our customary meetings renewed after the lapse of some years. Since I know that your keen mind, Sagredo, is such as to be unable to rest in idleness, I am sure that you will not have failed during our time of separation to make some reflections concerning the theory of motion expounded in the last day of our former colloquies. Having always harvested the fruit of uncommon erudition from your learned conversation, as from that of our Simplicio, I beg you to suggest some new consideration regarding those things of our Author's that we have previously learned. Thus we may have a beginning for our usual discussions, and spend this day in pursuit of scientific entertainment.

SAGREDO. I won't deny that during these past years various thoughts have passed through my mind concerning the novelties demonstrated by that venerable man about the science of motion, which he subjected and reduced to geometrical demonstrations. And since you request it, I shall now try to

recall some matter that will give you occasion to improve my
mind with your learned reasonings.

To start in an orderly way, from the beginning of the treatise
on motion, I shall propose a very old question of mine that
comes back to me when I consider the demonstration put forth
by our Author in his first proposition on uniform motion.[11]
That proceeds (as do many other propositions of ancient and
modern writers) by the use of equal multiples. Now there is
a certain ambiguity which I have always had in mind relating
to the fifth (or, as some call it, the sixth[12]) definition of the
fifth book of Euclid. I am glad to have occasion to impart this
question to you, hoping to be entirely freed from doubt.

SIMPLICIO. I, also, shall regard this renewed conversation
with both of you as a special favor of fortune if it turns out
that I manage to receive some illumination on the topic suggested by Sagredo. Since I never encountered a more serious
obstacle than this, in that little of geometry which I studied
in school as a youth, you may imagine how pleased I shall be
if, after so long a time, I am to hear anything that will give
me satisfaction on this matter.

SAGR. I say next that when I [first] heard the Author, in his first
proposition on uniform motion, make use of equal multiples
in accordance with that fifth (or sixth) definition of the fifth
book of Euclid, I, having long entertained doubts about that
definition, did not reach the clarity that I might have wished
from the said proposition. It would be gratifying to me if I
could thoroughly understand that first beginning, so as to be
able with that much more certainty to understand all that
follows concerning the theory of motion.

SALV. I shall try to satisfy your wish by making that definition
of Euclid's familiar in another way and by clearing the way
as far as possible to the introduction of proportionalities.
Meanwhile I want you to know that in your hesitancy you have
for company some very able men who have long felt the same
small satisfaction you tell me that you have felt up to the
present time.[13]

Indeed, I confess that for some years after I studied the fifth
book of Euclid, my mind remained shrouded in the same fogs.
I finally overcame the difficulty when, studying the admirable
book of Archimedes *On Spirals*, I found in the elegant opening
of that work a demonstration[14] similar to that of our own
Author. That occasion started me wondering whether there
might perhaps be another, easier road, by which one might
reach the same end, that would yield to me and to others precise

knowledge in the matter of proportions. I then applied my
mind with attention to this purpose, and I shall now expound
my speculations on that occasion, subjecting each of my steps to
your most strict judgment.

First let us suppose (as Euclid also assumes when he defines
these) that proportional magnitudes exist, that is, that three
magnitudes being given in any manner, that same proportion,
or ratio, or relation of quantity, which the first has to the
second,[15] may be had by the third to a fourth. Next I say that,
in order to give a definition of the assumed proportional
magnitudes suitable to produce in the mind of a reader some
concept of the nature of these proportional magnitudes, we
must select one of their properties. Now, the simplest [prop-
erty] of all is precisely that which is deemed most intelligible
even by the average man who has not been introduced to
mathematics; Euclid himself has proceeded thus in many
places. Remember that he does not say [for example] that the
circle is a plane figure within which two intersecting straight
lines will produce rectangles such that that which is made of the
parts of one line will equal that which is made with the parts
of the other, or [that it is a plane figure] within which all
quadrilaterals have their opposite angles equal to two right
angles. These would have been good definitions, had he spoken
thus; but since he knew another property of the circle more
intelligible than the preceding, and easier to form a concept of,
he did much better to set forth that clearer and more evident
property [equidistance from a point] as a definition, and later
to draw from this those other, more hidden, properties, demonstrating them as conclusions.

SAGR. So he did, certainly; yet I believe that very few indeed
are the minds that would be completely satisfied by this definition, when I say with Euclid:

> Four magnitudes are proportional when equal multiples
> of the first and third, taken according to any multiplica-
> tion, always alike exceed, fall short of, or equal, equal mul-
> tiples of the second and fourth.

Who is there so fortunate of mind as to be able to be certain
that when four magnitudes are proportional, these equal multiples will always [thus] agree? Indeed, who knows that such
equal multiples will not *always* agree, even when the magnitudes are *not* proportional?

Euclid has already said, in the preceding definitions, that a
ratio between two magnitudes is a respect or relation between
them which pertains to quantity.[16] Now the reader, having

already conceived intellectually what "ratio" is between two magnitudes, will find it difficult to understand that this "respect or relation" which exists between the first and the second magnitude is [indeed] similar to that respect or relation which is found between the third magnitude and the fourth, when [and only when] equal multiples of the first and third agree always in the said manner with equal multiples of the second and fourth, [that is], in being always [both] greater, or less, or equal.

SALV. Be that as it may, it appears to me that [in any event] this [statement] of Euclid's is more a theorem to be demonstrated than a definition to be set forth. And having encountered many minds that have run aground at this place, I shall do my best to reinforce, by a definition of proportionality, the conception of men unlearned in geometry.[17] I shall proceed as follows.

We shall say that four magnitudes are proportional among themselves—that is, that the first will have the same ratio to the second as the third has to the fourth—[either] when the first is equal to the second, and the third is likewise equal to the fourth, or when the first shall be as many [integral] times a multiple of the second as the third is of the fourth.

Will Simplicio have any doubt about understanding this?

SIMP. Certainly not.

SALV. But since it will not always happen that among four magnitudes, the said equality of exact [integral] multiplicity will be found, we shall go further. I ask Simplicio: Do you understand that four magnitudes are proportional when the first contains (for example) three and one-half times the second, while the third also contains three and one-half times the fourth?

SIMP. I understand very well, up to this point. I grant that four magnitudes are proportional not only in the example which you have given, but also for any other designation of multiple, superpartient, or superparticular [ratio].[18]

SALV. Now, to summarize briefly and with greater generality everything that has been said and exemplified up to this point, let us say:

We understand four magnitudes to be proportional when the excess [by multiplication] of the first over the second, whatever this may be, is similar to the excess [if any] of the third over the fourth.

SIMP. I have no difficulty thus far, though it appears to me that in this manner you have a definition of proportional magnitudes only when the antecedent quantities are greater than their consequents, since you assume that the first exceeds the second and likewise that the third similarly exceeds the fourth. But I ask how I am to be guided when the antecedents are less than their consequents?

SALV. I reply that whenever you have four magnitudes such that the first is less than the second and the third is less than the fourth, then the second will be greater than the first and the fourth will be greater than the third. Hence you must consider these [terms] in reverse order, and imagine the "second" to be first and the "fourth" to be third. In this way you will [again] have the antecedents greater than the consequents, and you will not have to seek a different definition from that which we have already given.

SAGR. Precisely. But please go on with the assumption just made, considering the antecedents always to be greater than the consequents, which I think greatly facilitates both your arguments and our understanding of it.

SALV. This established as the definition, I shall add this other mode in which four magnitudes are to be understood as proportional:

When, in order to have the same ratio to the second that the third has to the fourth, the first is neither greater nor less than it need be, then the first is understood to have to the second the same ratio as the third [has] to the fourth.

At this point I shall also define "greater ratio," saying:

When the first magnitude is greater than it need be in order to have to the second the same ratio which the third has to the fourth, then we must agree to say that the first has "a greater ratio" to the second than that which the third has to the fourth.

SIMP. Good. And if the first is less than it need be, in order to have to the second the same ratio that the third has to the fourth?

SALV. When the first is less than required for it to have to the second the same ratio that the third has to the fourth, this will be an evident indication that the third is greater than it need be in order to have to the fourth that ratio which the first has to the second. So in this case, also, you must be content to conceive the *order* in another way, imagining those magnitudes that were "third" and "fourth" to become first and second, and those which were "first" and "second" to be put in the places of the third and fourth.

SAGR. Thus far, I understand quite well your conception and this introduction with which you commence the theory of proportions. It seems to me that you have placed yourself under obligation to add one of two things, that is, either to demonstrate from these principles of yours the entire fifth book of Euclid, or else to deduce, from the two definitions you have set forth, the two other [definitions] that Euclid puts for the fifth and seventh[19] among his definitions, on which he bases the whole structure of his fifth book. If you will demonstrate his two [definitions] as conclusions [from yours], nothing more will remain to be desired in these matters.

SALV. That is precisely my intention. For when it is understood clearly that given four proportional magnitudes according to the above definition, equal multiples of the first and third eternally and necessarily agree in equaling, or falling short of, or exceeding, equal multiples of the second and fourth, then without any other guide one may enter the fifth book of Euclid, and one will be able to understand clearly its theorems on proportional magnitudes. Likewise, if, assuming my definition of "greater ratio," I demonstrate that in such cases, taking equal multiples of the first and third, and also of the second and fourth, that of the first shall exceed that of the second, while that of the third does not exceed that of the fourth, then one may with this demonstration run through the other theorems of disproportional magnitudes, since this conclusion of ours will be precisely the [seventh] definition that Euclid makes use of as a first principle.

SIMP. If I were persuaded of these two properties of equal multiples—that is, that when four magnitudes are proportional, they eternally agree in equality, or in excess, or in defect, and that when four magnitudes are not proportional, they disagree in that respect—then for my part, I would not require any other light for the clear understanding of all the fifth book of the *Elements of Geometry*.

SALV. Now tell me, Simplicio: Supposing that the four magnitudes A, B, and C, D are proportional [in that order]—that is,

$$A.B.C.D.$$

that the first, A, has to the second, B, the same ratio that the third, C, has to the fourth, D, do you also understand [as well] that twice the first has to the second the same ratio that twice the third has to the fourth?

SIMP. I understand this quite well. If once the first has to the second the ratio of once the third to the fourth, I cannot imagine for what reason twice the first to the second should have a different ratio from that which twice the third has to the fourth.

SALV. Then, since you understand this, you will understand that four, or ten, or one hundred of the first will have the same ratio to the second, as four, or ten, or one hundred of the third will have to the fourth.

SIMP. Yes indeed; and provided that the multiples are numerically equal, I easily comprehend that the first, taken twice, or ten times, or one hundred, will have to the second the same ratio that the third, taken also twice, or ten times, or one hundred, has to the fourth. It would be hard indeed to persuade me otherwise.

SALV. Then it will not be hard to understand that the multiple of the first has the same ratio to the second as the equal multiple of the third has to the fourth, that is, the first [magnitude], multiplied as many times as you like, has to the second, that same ratio which the third, multiplied the same number of times, has to the fourth.

Now, all that I have exemplified thus far by multiplying the [two] antecedent magnitudes, but not the consequents, must be supposed to be said also of multiplying the consequents only, without altering the antecedents in the least. So tell me; do you believe that given four proportional magnitudes, the first has a different ratio to twice the second from that which the third has to twice the fourth?

SIMP. Absolutely not; rather, given that once the first has to once the second, the same ratio which once the third has to once the fourth, I understand perfectly well that that same first has to two, or four, or ten of the second, the same ratio which the third has to two, or four, or ten of the fourth.

SALV. Admitting this, then, you confess yourself satisfied, and you easily understand that given four proportional magnitudes, *A*, *B*, *C*, and *D*, and the first and third [*A* and *C*] being equally

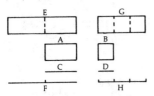

multiplied, the ratio which *E*, the multiple of the first, has to the second, *B*, is observed precisely by *F*, the [equal] multiple of the third, *C*, with respect to the fourth, *D*.[20] Imagine, therefore, that these are [now] our proportional magnitudes; *E*, *B*, *F*, and *D*; that is, the multiple *E* of the first [*A*] shall [now] be first; the second, *B* itself, shall be second; then the multiple *F* of the third [*C*] shall be third, and the fourth, *D*, shall be fourth. You have also told me that you understand that the consequents, *B* and *D* (that is, the second and fourth), being equally multiplied without in any way altering the antecedents, the first will have the same ratio to the multiple of the second as the third [has] to the multiple of the fourth. But these four magnitudes will be precisely *E* and *F* (equal multiples of the first and third) and *G* and *H* (equal multiples of the second and fourth).

SAGR. I confess myself entirely satisfied with this, and I now understand quite well the necessity by which equal multiples of four proportional magnitudes agree eternally in being greater, or less, or equal, etc.[21] For when equal multiples of the first and third are taken, and equal multiples of the second and fourth, you prove to me that the multiple of the first has the same ratio to the [different] multiple of the second that the multiple of the third [has] to the multiple of the fourth. I see clearly that when the multiple of the first is greater than the multiple of the second, then, to preserve the proportionality, the multiple of the third must necessarily be greater than the multiple of the fourth. For if it were less, or equal, the multiple of the third would also have to be less, or equal, with respect to the multiple of the fourth.

SIMP. I also feel in this no repugnance whatever. But I still wish to understand how it is true, supposing the four magnitudes to be disproportional, that the equal multiples do not [likewise] always observe this same agreement as to being [both] greater, or [both] less, or equal.

SALV. I shall see to it that you have also entire satisfaction as to this.

Let there be the four magnitudes *AB*, *C*, *D*, and *E*, and let the first, *AB*, be somewhat greater than it need be in order to have to the second, *C*, the same ratio which the third, *D*, has to the fourth, *E*. I shall show that equal multiples of the first and third [*AB* and *D*] being taken in a particular manner, and other equal multiples of the second and fourth [*C* and *E*] being taken, the multiple of the first [*AB*] will be found to be greater than that of the second [*C*], while that of the third [*D*] will in no way be greater than that of the fourth, and indeed I shall prove it to be less [than the like multiple of *E*].[22]

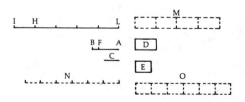

Therefore it is assumed that from the first magnitude *AB* there shall be removed that excess which makes it greater than it should be for precise proportionality. Let that excess be *FB*. The four magnitudes will now be proportional, that is, the remainder *AF* will have to *C* the same ratio that *D* has to *E*.

Let *FB* be multiplied sufficiently to become greater than *C*, and let this product be designated *HI*. Then take *HL* as many times a multiple of *AF*, and *M* likewise of *D*, as *HI* is a multiple of *FB*. This done, no doubt the composite *LI* will be as many times a multiple of the composite *AB* as *HI* is of *FB*, or *M* of *D*.

Now take *N* to be that [integral] multiple of *C* that will [first] make *N* greater than *LH*; finally, make *O* a multiple of *E* as many times as *N* is a multiple of *C*.

Now, *N* being the first multiple [of *C*] that is larger than *LH*, if we suppose removed from *N* one of the magnitudes composing it, which we made equal to *C*, then the remainder will not be greater than *LH*. Therefore when we restore to *N* the magnitude equal to *C* that we supposed removed, if to *LH* (which is not less than the said remainder) we add *HI*, which is greater than the restoration to *N*, *LI* will be greater than *N*. So this is one case in which the multiple of the first [*AB*] exceeds the multiple [*N*] of the second. But the four magnitudes *AF*, *C*, *D*, and *E* were made proportional by us; and taking the equal multiples *LH* and *M* (of the first and third) and *N* and *O* (of the second and fourth), the latter will, by what we said before, always agree as to being greater, or less, or equal; hence the multiple *LH* of the first magnitude being less than the multiple *N* of the second, by construction the multiple *M* of the third will necessarily be less than the multiple *O* of the fourth.

Thus it is proved that whenever the first magnitude is somewhat larger than it need be in order to have the same ratio to the second that the third has to the fourth, there is a way of taking equal multiples of first and third, and other [equal multiples] of second and fourth, and showing that this multiple of the first exceeds the multiple of the second, while the [equivalent] multiple of the third does not exceed that of the fourth.

SAGR. I have understood well enough what you have thus far shown. It now remains for you to deduce as necessary conclusions from these demonstrated premises those two controversial definitions of Euclid. I expect that this will be easy, with the two theorems (that are their converses) already demonstrated.

SALV. Indeed, it turns out to be easy. To demonstrate the fifth definition, I proceed as follows.

If of the four magnitudes *A, B, C, D,* equal multiples of the first and third, taken according to any multiplier, shall always agree in equaling, or falling short of, or exceeding, equal multiples of the second and fourth, jointly, I say the four magnitudes are proportional.[23]

For if possible, let them be not proportional; then one of the antecedents will be greater than it need be in order to have to its consequent the same ratio that the other antecedent has to its consequent. Let this be, for instance, the one designated *A.* Then by what was already shown, taking in such a way multiples equally of *A* and *C,* and multiples equally of *B* and *D* in the manner already shown, the multiple of *A* will be shown to be greater than the multiple of *B,* while the multiple of *C* will not be greater (but rather, less) than the multiple of *D;* which is counter to our assumption [of their agreement].

To demonstrate the seventh definition, I say this:

Let the four magnitudes be *A,B,C,* and *D,* and suppose that taking equal multiples of the two antecedents, first and third, in some particular way, as [likewise some] equal multiples of the two consequents, second and fourth, a case is found in which the multiple of *A* is greater than the multiple of *B,* while the multiple of *C* is not greater than the multiple of *D.* Then I say that *A* will have a greater ratio to *B* than *C* has to *D,* that is, *A* will be somewhat greater than it must be in order to have to *B* the same ratio that *C* has to *D.*

If possible, let *A* be not greater than the said just amount. Then it will either be exactly proportional, or less than it should be to be proportional. As to the first, if it were precisely fitted and proportional, then (by the things previously proved) equal multiples of the first and third, taken in any manner, would always agree in equaling, or falling short of, or exceeding the equal multiples of the second and fourth; which is contrary to the supposition [of one greater, one less]. And if the first is less than the exact amount to make it proportional, this is a sign that the third must be greater than it should be in order to have to the fourth the ratio that the first has to the second. Then, I say, subtract from the third this excess which makes it greater than just, so that the remainder will then be precisely proportional. Now, considering those certain multiples assumed at the outset, it is manifest that the multiple of the first being greater than the multiple of the second, the multiple of the third (that is, of this remainder) will also be greater than the multiple of the fourth. Hence if, instead of taking the multiple of this remainder, we take the equal multiple of the entire third, this will be greater than the multiple of that remainder; and therefore this will be much greater than the multiple of the fourth; which goes against our supposition.

SAGR. I am quite satisfied by the explanation you have made to me, in a matter in which I have long needed this; nor can I tell you which is greater—my pleasure in this knowledge, newly acquired, or my regret that I did not obtain this by asking you [for it] at the outset of our previous conversations.[24] This regret is the greater since I know that you had imparted it [that knowledge] to various friends who were close to your villa and able to frequent it. But let us proceed with our discourses, if you please—if Simplicio has nothing to add concerning the matter discussed up to this point.

SIMP. I cannot add anything. I am quite satisfied with the reasoning, and understand the demonstrations I have heard.

SALV. These foundations laid, it would be possible to expand and partly rearrange the fifth book of Euclid;[25] but that would constitute too long a digression, and would be too far from our principal purpose. Besides, I know that you both have seen such additions [to Euclid] printed by other authors.

Now, the fifth and seventh definitions of the fifth book having been considered at your request, I hope you will be willing to concede to me the right to propose next a very old observation of mine, one that occurred to me in connection with another of Euclid's definitions. The subject will not be entirely diverse from this beginning, and will not seem alien to our purpose, since it concerns compound proportion, used by our Author[26] many times in his books.

Among the definitions of the sixth book of Euclid, the fifth [and last] is found to deal with compound ratio, and reads thus:

"A ratio is said to be composed of several ratios when the quantities of the said ratios multiplied together shall have produced that ratio."[27]

I note that neither in Euclid nor in any other ancient writer is this definition made use of in the form in which it is put in this book. From that fact, two difficulties follow—a difficulty to the reader's understanding, and a redundancy on the part of this writer.

SAGR. That is most true. But it seems to me improbable that Euclid's supreme precision allowed him to place this definition in his books inconsiderately and in vain. Hence it is not beyond suspicion that it was added by another, or at least that it has been altered in such a way that today it is no longer recognizable when [the thing defined is] put to use by authors demonstrating theorems.[28]

SIMP. I am willing to believe you, gentlemen, that other authors did not make use of it [the above definition], since I have made no great study of them; yet it makes me unhappy that Euclid himself, whom you deem so precise in his writings, should have included this in vain. Here I confess that my mind, which has never been above average in its penetration into mathematics, meets with a difficulty about this definition that is not less, perhaps, than the ones already remarked by Salviati. Long ago I sought help by reading very long commentaries written on this subject, but to tell you the truth, I don't know that I ever shook off those clouds that kept my mind in shadows. Therefore if you have some particular consideration that will aid me in this, I assure you that you will be doing me a great favor.

SALV. Perhaps you believe that this will be a matter of profound speculation; yet you will find that it consists in no more than one very simple [thing to] notice.

Imagine two magnitudes *A* and *B* of the same kind. Magnitude *A* will have some ratio to *B*; hence conceive of another magnitude, *C*, also of the same kind, put between them. It is then said that the ratio of magnitude *A* to [magnitude] *B* comes to be "compounded" from the two intermediate ratios [created]; that of *A* to *C*, and that of *C* to *B*. This is precisely the sense according to which Euclid does make use of the aforesaid definition.[29]

SIMP. It is true that Euclid means "compound ratio" in this way, but I still do not see how magnitude *A* has to *B* the "compound ratio" of the two ratios, that of *A* to *C* and of *C* to *D*.

SALV. Tell me, Simplicio: Do you understand that *A* has some ratio to *B*, whatever this [ratio] may be?

SIMP. Yes, since they are [magnitudes] of the same kind.

SALV. And that ratio is immutable, and can never become any other, or different from what it is?

SIMP. I understand this also.

SALV. I now add for you, that (in just the same way) *A* has to *C* an immutable ratio, and so also *C* has to *B*.

The ratio, then, that exists between the two extremes, *A* and *B*, is said to be "compounded from" the two ratios intermediating between these two extremes, that is, from the ratio that *A* has to *C*, and from that which *C* has to *B*.[30]

A.C.B.[31]

Moreover, I add that if you imagine not just one magnitude interposed between the two magnitudes A and B, but more than one, as you see in these marks A, C, D, B, you will also understand the ratio of A to B to be compounded from all the ratios

A.C.D.B.

intermediary between them, that is, [here] from the ratios of A to C, C to D, and D to B. And if there were more magnitudes, the first would always have to the last a ratio compounded from all these ratios intermediary between them.

On this occasion, I point out that if the component ratios are equal among themselves (or, to speak better, if the ratios are the same), then (as wc said above) the first [magnitude] will have to the last a ratio such as is compounded from all the intermediate ratios; and since those intermediate ratios are [in this case] all equal, we can express the same meaning by saying that the ratio of the first to the last is a ratio "just as many times" a multiple of the ratio which the first has to the second, as there are ratios interposed between the first and the last. For example, if there are three terms, and the ratio between the first and second is the same as that between the second and third, then it is true that the first has to the last a ratio compounded from the two ratios that exist between the first and second, and the second and third. But since these two ratios are supposed equal (that is, to be the same), it may be said that the ratio of the first to the third is the "duplicated" [or "doubled"] ratio of the first to the second. And thus if there were four, it could be said that the ratio of the first to the fourth is compounded from those three intermediate ratios, and also is the "triplicated" [or "tripled"] ratio of the first to the second, the ratio of the first to the fourth being compounded from the ratio of the first to the second taken three times.[32] And so on.

But here, to conclude, there are no theories or demonstrations, because this is a mere imposition of names.[33] If the word "compounded" does not please you, let us call this [ratio] "decomposed," or "stuck together," or "confused," or anything else that you like better. Grant me only this, that when we shall have three magnitudes of the same kind, and I call the ratio "decomposed" or "stuck together" or "confused" [from or into other ratios], I shall mean the ratio of the extreme magnitudes, and not some other.

SAGR. I understand all this very well, and I have noticed more than once the stratagem of Euclid in the proposition [VI, 23] where he proves that equiangular parallelograms have the ratio compounded from the ratios of the sides. In that case, he finds that the two component ratios have four terms, which are the four [unequal] sides of the [two] parallelograms, whence he demands that those two ratios be put into three terms only, so that one of those ratios exists between the first term and the second, and the other between the second and the third. Hence, in the proof, all he does is to prove that one parallelogram is to the other as the first term is to the third, that is, this ratio is compounded from two ratios—that which the first term has to the second, and that which the second has to the third—which are the two ratios that he had disjoined before, in the four sides of the [two] parallelograms.

SALV. You reason very well. Now, the definition of compound ratio being understood and established in this way (which consists only in agreeing on what is meant to be clothed under that name), one may demonstrate the twenty-third proposition of the sixth book of Euclid as he himself demonstrates it; for there he assumes the definition not in the way in which he [is reported to have] phrased it, but in the way just related by us. [Only] *after* the twenty-third proposition would I add, as a corollary thereof, the fifth definition as given in the sixth book (that of compound ratio), transforming this into a theorem:[34]

Let there be two ratios, one between the terms A and B, and the other between C and D. The common definition says that the ratio compounded from these two ratios will be obtained if we "multiply together" the "quantities" of these two ratios. I concur with Simplicio in believing that this is a hard proposal to understand, and one that needs proof; hence with a little trouble, we shall demonstrate it thus:[35]

If the four terms of the two ratios are not lines, but other magnitudes, let us imagine them to be represented by straight lines. Then make a rectangle of the two antecedents, A and C, and another rectangle of the two consequents, B and D. It is

clear by Euclid VI, 23, that the rectangle made of A and C has to the rectangle [made] of B and D, the ratio that is compounded from the two ratios of A to B and C to D, which two ratios we took from start to finish in order to discover the ratio that resulted from their composition. The ratio compounded from the ratios A to B and C to D being therefore that of the rectangle AC to the rectangle BD, by Euclid VI, 23, I ask Simplicio what we have done to find these two terms, in which the ratio sought consists?

SIMP. I believe that we have done no more than to form two rectangles with those four lines [which were] proposed at the outset, that is, one [rectangle] with the antecedents, *A* and *C*, and the other with the consequents, *B* and *D*.

SALV. But the formation of rectangles corresponds exactly, in the lines of geometry, with multiplication of numbers in arithmetic, as every beginner in mathematics knows; and the things we "multiplied" were the lines *A* and *C*, and the lines *B* and *D*, that is, homologous terms of the assumed ratios. You see, then, how, by "multiplying together" the "quantities or values" of the given simple ratios, the "quantity or value" of that ratio is produced which is then said to be compounded from them.

IV

By 17 December 1641 Cavalieri had learned from Torricelli that this time there was little hope of Galileo's recovery. On New Year's Day 1642, Castelli wrote to Cavalieri that news from Florence about the venerable scientist was all bad. On Thursday, 9 January, Galileo died. His body was privately deposited in Santa Croce, though the grand duke wished to erect for it a sumptuous tomb across from that of Michelangelo. There Galileo now rests, thanks to Viviani's later efforts; but at the time of Galileo's death the Church forbade any honors to a man who had died under vehement suspicion of heresy. On 18 January, Luke Holste wrote from Rome to G. B. Doni at Florence:

Today news has also come of the loss of Signor Galilei, which touches not just Florence, but the whole world and our whole century that from this divine man has received more splendor than from almost all the other ordinary philosophers. Now, envy ceasing, the sublimity of that intellect will begin to be known which will serve all posterity as guide in the search for truth.

APPENDIX
BIOGRAPHIES

THE PURPOSE OF this appendix is to identify persons mentioned in the text whose biographies are otherwise not easily accessible and of whom something more is known than is evident from the context of their mention. Information about them deemed relevant to their relations to Galileo or his work is given preference to events of greater significance in their own lives when the entry would otherwise run beyond a few lines. Bibliographical information is minimized in the interests of brevity.

ACQUAPENDENTE, GIROLAMO FABRICIO OF. Born at Acquapendente in 1533, he became professor of surgery at the University of Padua in 1565 and of anatomy in 1589. He designed the famed anatomical theater at Padua, was the teacher of William Harvey, and personal physician to Galileo. His description of the valves in the veins, said to have been inspired by Paolo Sarpi, was important to Harvey's work on circulation of the blood. He died in 1619.

AGGIUNTI, NICCOLÒ. Born at Borgo San Sepolcro 6 December 1600, he studied first at Perugia and later at Pisa where he was a pupil of Benedetto Castelli. After receiving his degree in 1621, he was employed to tutor Ferdinand II de' Medici. In 1626 he obtained the chair of mathematics at Pisa as successor to Castelli. He died at Pisa on his thirty-fifth birthday.

AGUCCHI, GIOVANNI BATTISTA. Born at Bologna 24 November 1570. Educated at Faenza, he entered the service of Pietro Cardinal Aldobrandini and in 1604 joined the court of Pope Paul V at Rome, where he was introduced to Galileo by Luca Valerio in 1611. For a time secretary to Pope Gregory XV, he became archbishop of Amasia at Venice, where he died early in 1632.

AGUILONIUS, FRANCISCUS. Born at Brussels in 1566, he entered the Jesuit order in 1586, taught philosophy at Douay, and then moved to Antwerp where he gained recognition as an architect. His very large book on optics contained little that was novel; he died at Antwerp in 1617.

ALTOBELLI, ILARIO. Born near Macerata in 1560, he joined the Minorites and became doctor of theology in 1591. After being in charge of parochial schools at Rimini and Fermo, he settled in Verona from 1601 to 1605. About 1618 he was a candidate for the chair of mathematics at Bologna left vacant by the death of Magini. Known as a preacher and a poet, he applied himself mainly to the study of mathematics and astronomy and the construction of instruments, dying about 1630.

AMADORI, GIOVANNI BATTISTA. Born at Florence in 1567, he may have been a schoolmate of Galileo's at Pisa. He was a physician at Florence, where he died 30 May 1621.

AMMANNATI, GIULIA. Mother of Galileo, she was the daughter of Cosimo, of Pescia, who before 1536 moved to Pisa where she was born in 1538. Married to Vincenzio Galilei at Pisa 5 July 1562, she died at Florence in August 1620.

ANTONINI, DANIELLO. Born at Udine 16 July 1588, he studied mathematics first at Bologna under Pietro Cataldi and then under Galileo at Padua in 1608. After military service in Flanders, 1611–12, he returned to Udine. In 1615 he entered the Venetian campaigns against Austria, in which he was killed 10 March 1616.

APROINO, PAOLO. Born at Treviso about 1584, he studied with Galileo at Padua, was graduated in 1608, and was entered in the "college of philosophers" at Treviso later that year. In 1613 he became canon of the cathedral at Treviso, where he died 13 March 1638. His role as interlocutor in Galileo's unpublished dialogue on the force of percussion was to describe experiments of Galileo's at which Sagredo had not been present, having left Venice to serve as consul at Soria.

ARRIGHETTI, ANDREA. Born (at Florence?) 24 August 1592, he studied mathematics at Pisa under Benedetto Castelli, was made a member of the Crusca Academy in 1613, and was later superintendent of fortifications in Tuscany. About 1618 he heard either Galileo or Castelli discuss the cycloid as a curve first studied by Galileo, according to his sworn testimony in 1663. He died 13 February 1672.

ARRIGHETTI, NICCOLÒ (cousin of Andrea). Born (at Florence?) 11 November 1586, he studied with Galileo at Florence and assisted in the copying of his notes on motion in 1618. In 1623 he became Consul of the Florentine Academy on Galileo's resignation due to illness. He died at Florence 29 May 1639.

BADOVERE, JACQUES. Born (at Paris?) about 1575, of a branch of the Badoer family at Venice which migrated to France on becoming Protestant, he studied with Galileo at Padua 1597–99. Converted by a French Jesuit, he maintained correspondence with Paolo Sarpi after revisiting Venice and Padua 1607–8. Early in 1609 he assured Sarpi of the value of the newly invented Dutch telescope. Sent on various missions by the king of France, he incurred the enmity of Sully and fell into disgrace, dying probably about 1620.

BALFOUR, ROBERT. Born near Dundee about 1550, he studied at St. Andrews and Paris. In 1582 he was professor of Greek at Bordeaux, and in 1591 went to teach mathematics at a new college founded in Guienne, summoned by a celebrated editor of Euclid, François de Foix (Candalle). He died in September 1621.

BALIANI, GIOVANNI BATTISTA. Born at Genoa in 1582, he was superintendent of the fortress in Savona in 1611 and there performed experiments on the fall of heavy bodies. Galileo began correspondence with him in 1614, at Salviati's suggestion, and in 1615 he visited Galileo in Florence. He was first to explain the siphon in terms of the weight of air. His book on motion in 1638 discussed free fall, the pendulum, and motion on inclined planes; the second edition in 1646 included fluid motions, on which he had consulted Castelli, and offered an impetus-theory explanation of acceleration in fall. In 1647 he published on the plague with comments anticipating Malthusianism. He died in 1666.

BARBERINI, ANTONIO. Born at Florence in 1569, he was younger brother of Maffeo, later Pope Urban VIII, who made him cardinal in October 1624. Antonio acted as papal secretary of state in the absence of Francesco (see below). He died 11 September 1646.

BARBERINI, FRANCESCO. Born at Florence 23 September 1597, he studied at the Jesuit college in Rome and then with Castelli at Pisa under Galileo's guidance. His uncle, Maffeo, made him cardinal in 1623; he was papal legate to France in 1624, visiting Peiresc on his return from Paris in 1625. In 1627 as Vatican librarian he founded the celebrated Barberini Library. Made papal secretary of state, he was Galileo's most highly placed protector during the 1633 trial, minimizing the time he had to remain in custody, forbidding his torture, devising means of his pleading guilty to a lesser fault than charged, and refusing to sign the sentence against him. He died 10 December 1679.

BARBERINI, MAFFEO. Born at Florence in 1568, he was educated by Jesuits there before studying philosophy at the Collegio Romano in 1586 and law at Pisa, graduating in 1588. Pope Clement VII assigned him to regulate the waters of Lake Trasimeno. He was nuncio to

France under Paul V, who made him cardinal in 1606. In 1611 he sided with Galileo in the dispute at Florence over bodies in water. In 1623 he was elected pope and took the name Urban VIII. In 1631, following an attempt on his life, he acted strongly against the astrologers. He died 29 July 1644.

BARDI, GIOVANNI. Probably born at Florence about 1590, he studied at the Collegio Romano in 1613. There he publicly supported Galileo's work on bodies in water by lectures and experiments, published in 1614 at Rome in a book sometimes mistakenly ascribed to Giovanni Maria (see below).

BARDI, GIOVANNI MARIA (Count of Vernio). Born (at Florence?) about 1533, he pursued a military career; when not on active duty he led the Florentine Camerata in the vanguard of musical reform. Under Pope Clement VII he was general of the papal guard, returning to Florence on the succession of Paul V in 1604 and dying there 11 September 1612.

BARONIO, CESARE. Born at Sora 31 October 1538, he became cardinal in 1596. A celebrated church historian, he met Galileo at the home of G. V. Pinelli in 1598 on a visit to Padua in the company of Cardinal Bellarmine. In the *Letter to Christina*, Galileo cited Baronio as having said that the Bible tells us how to go to heaven, not how the heavens go; Galileo had probably heard this *viva voce* in the jovial company around Pinelli. Baronio died at Rome in 1607.

BEAUGRAND, JEAN DE. A French mathematician whose principal work, called *Geostaticae*, published at Paris in 1636, became the center of controversy for a time. His visit to Italy in 1635 marked the beginning of rivalry between Italian and French mathematicians for many years. In 1640 he printed a letter concerning Desargues' projective geometry, but by September 1641 he had died.

BELLARMINE, ROBERT (English style for Roberto Bellarmino). Born at Montepulciano 4 October 1542, he entered the Jesuit order in 1560, taught rhetoric and astronomy at Florence, and went to Belgium 1570–76. He then was professor at the Collegio Romano and was created cardinal (unwillingly) in 1598. He was a cardinal of the Inquisition at Giordano Bruno's condemnation in 1600. In 1605 he would probably have been elected pope had he not declined consideration. He was official theologian to Paul V during the papal dispute against Venice, 1606, in which Paolo Sarpi was theological adviser to that state. Bellarmine's polemics against King James II made his name a synonym for papism in England. He died at Rome 17 September 1621.

BENEDETTI, GIOVANNI BATTISTA. Born at Venice 14 August 1530, he studied mathematics briefly under Tartaglia about 1550. In 1553 he published an argument for equal speed of fall by bodies differing in weight but of the same material, amplifying this in 1554 "against Aristotle and all the philosophers." In 1558 he went to Parma as mathematician to the duke, moving in 1567 to Turin as mathematician to the court of Savoy. In 1585 he published a collection of treatises and letters which show him to have been the leading Italian physicist of his time. He died at Turin 20 January 1590.

BERNEGGER, MATHIAS. Born at Hallstatt (Austria) 8 February 1582, he studied at Strassburg and Vienna. In 1603 he was appointed professor of history at Strassburg; on his journey back from Vienna he described Galileo's sector to Johann Faulhaber, who was first in Germany (1610) to publish on that instrument. In 1613 Bernegger published a Latin translation of Galileo's *Compasso*, with valuable additions, and in 1635 he translated Galileo's *Dialogue* into Latin. He died 3 February 1640.

BIANCANI, GIUSEPPE. Born at Bologna in 1566, he entered the Jesuit order in 1592 and studied with Clavius at Rome, after which he taught mathematics at Parma. In 1610 he was involved in an unpleasant attack against Galileo on lunar mountains, and in 1613 supported Scheiner against him on the discovery of sunspots. In 1615 he published a book on the mathematical passages in Aristotle that is still of value. He died at Parma 7 June 1624.

BOCCHINERI, GERI. Born at Florence probably about 1590, he was the brother of Galileo's daughter-in-law, Sestilia. He was private secretary to Ferdinand II for many years, held other high offices at Florence and Prato, and died in May 1650.

BORGIA, GASPARE. Born in Spain in 1589, he was created cardinal by Paul V in 1611 and served long in Rome as the Spanish ambassador. In 1620 he was viceroy of Naples. As a cardinal of the Inquisition in 1633 he refused to sign the sentence against Galileo, whom he had assisted in the longitude negotiations with Spain. He died at Madrid in November 1645.

BORRI, GIROLAMO. Born at Arezzo in 1512, he taught medicine and philosophy in several universities, with terms at Pisa in 1553–59 and 1575–87. His books on the tides and on motion were read by Galileo. Borri quarreled with Francesco Buonamici and left Pisa for the University of Perugia in 1587, where he died 26 August 1592.

BOSCAGLIA, COSIMO. Born probably about 1550, he was professor first of logic and then of philosophy at Pisa from 1600 to 1621. He was also a poet, a specialist in Greek literature, and was known as an expert in Plato's philosophy. Much favored by Ferdinando I and Cosimo II de' Medici, he died in 1621.

BRAHE, TYCHO. Born at Knudstrup (Denmark) 14 December 1546, he studied at Copenhagen, Wittenberg, and Basel. His first notable studies concerned the new star of 1572, demonstrating its location by its lack of parallax. Observations of the comet of 1577 enabled him to overthrow the supposed solid celestial spheres. With royal aid he equipped his observatory on the island of Hveen with superb instruments of his own design. Brahe was an outstanding observer; in 1598 he entered the service of the Holy Roman Emperor Rudolf II, and Kepler soon joined him as an assistant at Prague. Tycho's name is given to a system in which the earth is motionless at the center but the planets are arranged around the sun as by Copernicus, being carried with it around the earth. His careful observations of Mars enabled Kepler to determine the three basic laws of planetary motion in 1609 and 1619. Tycho died 14 October 1601.

BRENGGER, JOHANN. A medical doctor of Augsburg who had studied at the University of Padua 1584–85, he was married at Augsburg in 1589, challenged Galileo's *Starry Messenger* in 1610, and became dean of the medical college at Augsburg in 1629, the last year he is known to have been living.

BRUCE, EDMUND. Described by Paolo Gualdo as an English gentleman well versed in mathematics, military matters, and botany, he appears to have known Kepler at Graz before moving to Padua in 1597. After his departure from Padua around 1605, probably for England, nothing is known of him.

BUONAMICI, FRANCESCO. Born at Florence probably about 1535, he was professor of philosophy at Pisa from 1565 to 1603. He was a highly orthodox Aristotelian, author of an enormous volume *De motu* (Florence, 1591) in which the medieval mathematics of motion was slighted. Galileo was almost certainly one of his pupils. He was a member of the Florentine Academy, much esteemed by the Medici, and died at Pisa 29 September 1603. His power at the University of Pisa is evident from the fact that two of his colleagues there, Borri and Libri, left in the wake of disputes with him.

BUONAMICI, GIOVANFRANCESCO. Born at Prato in 1592, he studied law and followed a diplomatic career, serving first as secretary to the Tuscan ambassador at Rome and then in Germany and Spain. After the marriage of his sister-in-law Sestilia Bocchineri to Galileo's son Vincenzio in 1629 he corresponded with Galileo and took part in the longitude negotiations at Madrid. In 1630 he went to Rome and was there during the trial of Galileo, of which he left an account. He died 10 January 1669.

CABEO, NICCOLÒ. Born at Ferrara in 1585, he entered the Jesuit order in 1602 and taught for many years at Parma and Ferrara. He is remembered mainly for a large book on magnetic phenomena, and published also a two-volume commentary on Aristotle's *Meteorologica* that shows bitter hostility toward Galileo. He was a friend of Baliani, whose interest in pendulums and falling bodies he shared, and late in life went to teach at Genoa where he died 30 June 1650.

CACCINI, TOMMASO. Born at Florence 26 April 1574, he entered the Dominican order in 1589. In December 1614 he publicly denounced from the pulpit in Florence all mathematicians and Galileists, leading to Galileo's first encounter with the Roman Inquisition, Caccini testifying secretly against him at Rome in 1615. He died 12 January 1648.

CAMPANELLA, TOMMASO (usually called Thomas in English). Born in Calabria 5 September 1568, he entered the Dominican order about 1582. In 1590, at Naples, he became an adherent of the philosophy of Bernardino Telesio, which emphasized the importance of observation. In 1594, after visits to Rome and Florence, he met Galileo at Padua but was soon ordered back to Rome to defend certain philosophical views. Returning to Calabria in 1597, he was imprisoned by the Spanish government in 1599 and condemned to life imprisonment in 1603. In 1626 Urban VIII removed him from Naples to Rome under the pretext of reviewing his case, but in fact allowing him virtual freedom and in 1629 liberating him from the Inquisition. Befriended by François de Noailles, he went to France in 1634 and died there 27 May 1639.

CARCAVY, PIERRE. Born at Lyons about 1600, he lived mainly at Toulouse where as a parliamentary counsellor he was a colleague of Pierre Fermat. He was later placed in charge of the royal library at Paris and in 1666 became one of the first members of the Academy of Sciences at Paris, where he died in 1684.

CASTELLI, BENEDETTO. Born at Brescia in 1578, he joined the Benedictine order in 1595. By 1604 he was at Padua, where he studied with Galileo. There he probably wrote his commentary on the *Bilancetta* and participated in Galileo's work with the thermoscope. He was transferred to La Cava in 1607, but soon after publication of the *Starry Messenger* he applied for transfer to Florence to assist Galileo. In 1613 he obtained the chair of mathematics at Pisa, his most brilliant pupil there being Bonaventura Cavalieri. His specialty in physics was hydraulics, and Urban VIII (who in early life had had a similar assignment) called him to Rome to superintend water and drainage projects. There he taught at the Sapienza and in 1628 published his pioneering book on the measure of running water. His outstanding student at Rome was Evangelista Torricelli. Castelli also performed valuable experiments in optics, radiant heat, and color. He died at Rome 9 April 1643.

CASTELLI, ONOFRIO. Born at Terni in 1570, he studied at Padua with Galileo in 1597. Unrelated to Benedetto Castelli, he too was a hydraulic engineer, working mainly in Germany and Italy. In 1631 he published a book on river management, dying soon afterward.

CAVALIERI, BONAVENTURA. Born at Milan about 1598, he joined the Jesuate (not Jesuit) order in 1615 and was sent to Pisa to study theology. Castelli interested him in mathematics, recognizing his unusual talent. At Milan in 1622 he had already begun work on his "method of indivisibles," and in 1629 secured a chair of mathematics at Bologna. He introduced logarithms into Italy, investigated lenses and mirrors, and envisioned a reflecting telescope. His most celebrated work was *Geometry Advanced by Indivisibles of Continua*, published in 1635. He died 27 November 1647.

CESARINI, VIRGINIO. Born at Rome 20 October 1596, he met Galileo there in 1615 and was elected to the Lincean Academy in 1618. His literary talents led to his appointment as secretary to Gregory XV and chamberlain to Urban VIII. Galileo addressed to him the *Assayer*, published in 1623. Cesarini died at Rome 1 April 1624, not having reached even thirty years of age.

CESI, FEDERICO. Born at Rome in March 1585, he inherited the title of marquis of Monticelli, was made prince of certain papal lands in 1613, and became duke of Acquasparta on the death of his father. In 1603 he founded the Lincean Academy for scientific studies, against his father's wishes; Cesi financed and directed this until his death. His second marriage in 1616 linked him with the Salviati and Medici families at Florence, while his mother was of the Roman Orsinis; these connections assisted the survival of the academy which under his able leadership became the first international scientific society but swiftly disintegrated after Cesi's premature death 1 August 1630.

CHIARAMONTI, SCIPIONE. Born at Cesena 21 June 1565, he studied at Ferrara and for a time taught mathematics at Perugia, becoming then professor of philosophy at Pisa from 1627 to 1636. He wrote against Tycho, Kepler, and Galileo, who, after having mentioned him favorably in the *Assayer*, criticized him sharply in the *Dialogue*. His valuable library is preserved at Cesena, where he died 3 October 1652.

CHRISTINA OF LORRAINE. Daughter of Charles, duke of Lorraine, she married Ferdinando I of Tuscany in 1589 and was the mother of Cosimo II de' Medici. After Ferdinando's death in 1609, she retained the title of grand duchess, contrary to custom, Cosimo's wife (Maria Madeleine of Austria) being called archduchess. Christina was at all times favorable to Galileo, and it was to her that he addressed his celebrated letter advocating freedom of scientific inquiry from religious interference. She survived her son Cosimo II and was regent jointly with his widow on the accession of Ferdinando II at the age of eleven in 1621. She died 20 December 1637.

CIAMPOLI, GIOVANNI. Born at Florence about 1590, he early exhibited remarkable poetic talents and became a protegé of the poet G. B. Strozzi (called "the Blind"). Galileo met Ciampoli at Florence in the summer of 1608. He studied philosophy and theology at Pisa, entering the priesthood at Rome in 1614, where he served as Latin secretary to a cardinal and then became confidential secretary to Urban VIII. In that capacity he maneuvered Niccolò Riccardi into granting a license for printing of Galileo's *Dialogue.* For this he was later punished by the pope, who transferred him to minor posts outside Rome. He died at Iesi 8 September 1643.

CIGOLI, LUDOVICO CARDI DI. Born at Cigoli in 1559, he was first active as an architect at Florence and then as a painter in various European cities. At Rome in 1611 he decorated the Pauline Chapel in Santa Maria Maggiore, depicting lunar mountains and the phases of Venus, newly discovered by Galileo. Cigoli credited Galileo for his knowledge of perspective, though he was already a successful painter before Galileo left school. Having in mind Galileo's maltreatment by jealous rivals, and not just his own, he painted a metaphorical portrait called *Calumny.* He died at Rome 8 June 1613.

CLAVIUS, CHRISTOPHER (Christoff Clau). Born at Bamberg in 1537, he joined the Jesuit order in 1555 and studied at Coimbra. As the leading astronomer at Rome he played an important role in the adoption of the Gregorian calendar in 1582. His commentaries on Euclid and on the *Sphere* of Sacrobosco were for many decades standard university texts throughout Europe. He published also on arithmetic, algebra, and the construction of sundials. He was professor of mathematics at the Collegio Romano until his death 6 February 1612.

COIGNET, MICHAEL. Born at Antwerp in 1544, he became a teacher of French and mathematics in 1568. In the 1580s he devised the pantometric rule, a set of scales engraved on brass which, with the aid of a pair of dividers, served many of the purposes of Galileo's later sector; in 1610 he transferred these scales to a pair of sectors, there being too many for a single instrument. He wrote mainly on mathematical instruments and navigation, becoming mathematician to Archduke Albert of Austria in 1608. He died at Antwerp 4 December 1623.

COLOMBE, LUDOVICO DELLE. Born at Florence 20 January 1565, he was elected to the Florentine Academy about 1598. His contemporary reputation as a philosopher, astronomer, mathematician, and poet is hardly justified by his publications except as to the first-named. From 1610 to 1614 he led the opposition against Galileo at Florence. Since no more is known of him after his attack on Galileo's *Bodies in Water*, to which Galileo and Castelli replied in 1615, he probably died soon after that year.

COMMANDINO, FEDERICO. Born at Urbino in 1509, he studied classics in his youth, was a secretary at Rome in 1530, and from 1534 to 1544 he appears to have been at Padua. Commandino received a medical degree at Ferrara in 1546 but did not long practice medicine "because of its uncertainty." He edited many Greek mathematical works of which he made Latin translations and commentaries of superlative quality, notably the books of Euclid and Archimedes. His own work on centers of gravity of solids was published at Bologna in 1565; from 1569 on he lived at Urbino where he was the teacher of Guidobaldo del Monte and of Bernardino Baldi. He died at Urbino in 1575.

CORESIO, GIORGIO. A native of the island of Chios, he taught Greek at Pisa from 1609 to 1615. He was one of three professors there to publish against Galileo's *Bodies in Water*; Galileo drafted a reply jointly with Castelli, but withheld it from publication when Coresio was expelled from his chair, perhaps as a Greek schismatic but more probably because of mental instability that began to afflict him in 1614.

CORNARO, GIACOMO ALVISE. Born at Venice 13 September 1539, of a very distinguished family, he settled at Padua where Galileo became his near neighbor and friend about 1598. His age and probity lent weight to his testimony relating to the Capra incident in 1607. He died at Padua 29 August 1608.

CREMONINI, CESARE. Born at Cento in December 1550, he studied at Ferrara where he was a friend of Torquato Tasso and Francesco Patrizzi. Upon graduation he was appointed professor of philosophy, remaining at Ferrara until in 1590 he was called to the second chair of philosophy at Padua, succeeding Giacomo Zabarella. His indifference to religion and defiance of censorship kept him under the eye of the Inquisition but did not damage the enormous respect in which he was held as the leading Aristotelian in Italy, and perhaps in Europe. He died 29 July 1631.

CRESPI: See Passignano

DIETRICHSTEIN, FRANCISCO. Born at Madrid in 1570, where his father was ambassador, he studied at Rome and was made cardinal in 1599, later becoming bishop of Olmütz. He died at Brünn 19 September 1636.

DINI, PIERO. Born probably about 1570, he studied at Parma, Perugia, and Bologna. He was elected to the Crusca Academy in 1595 and in

1605 was Consul of the Florentine Academy. As nephew of Cardinal Bandini he settled at Rome, holding office at the Vatican until in 1621 he became archbishop of Fermo, where he died 14 August 1625.

DIODATI, ELIA. Born at Geneva shortly before 11 May 1576, he became a parliamentary lawyer at Paris where he remained all his life, in contact with the leading scientific and literary men of his time. He probably met Galileo during a visit to Italy in 1620, and was the most helpful of all persons in the difficult task of securing publication of Galileo's last book in 1638. He died at Paris 21 December 1661.

ELCI, ARTURO PANNOCCHIESCHI COUNT D'. Born at Siena about 1564, he studied there and at Rome, gaining note in philosophy and theology and for oratory. Disappointed in his plans to attain a high place at Rome, he returned to Siena and in 1609 was made overseer of the University of Pisa and prior of a church in that city. He died 20 September 1614.

ELZEVIR, LOUIS. Born at Utrecht in 1604, he was made foreign representative of the distinguished Leiden publishing house founded by his family. In 1637 he became a citizen of Amsterdam, where he founded a rival printing house of his own. He died at Leiden in June 1670.

EUDAEMON-IOANNES, ANDREA. Born at Caneas (Greece), he went to Italy as a youth and entered the Jesuit order in 1581. He met Galileo at Padua probably around 1600, and certainly before the expulsion of Jesuits from Venetian territory in 1606. He taught philosophy at Rome and was made rector of the Collegio Greco by Urban VIII. He accompanied Cardinal Barberini on the legation to France in 1624, dying at Rome 24 December 1625.

FABER, JOHANN. Born at Bamberg in 1574, he moved to Italy in 1598, teaching medical botany at the Sapienza in 1600. He was elected to the Lincean Academy in 1611, becoming its chancellor the next year, with the principal task of editing its great projected work on the botany of Mexico. He died at Rome 17 September 1629.

FABRICIUS, JOHANN. Born in Frisia 8 January 1587, he was the son of a noted astronomer, David Fabricius. He studied at Helmstedt in 1604, transferred to Wittenberg in 1606, and to Leiden in 1609. He was the first to publish on sunspot observations, giving an essentially correct interpretation of them in a book dedicated 13 June 1611 and printed in the autumn of that year. He died about the end of 1616.

FERMAT, PIERRE. Born near Montauban in August 1601, he studied law and in 1631 was made counsellor to the parliament at Toulouse, where he resided all his life. An outstanding mathematician, famed

447

especially for his work in theory of numbers, he is hardly less important in the history of analytic goemetry and the infinitesimal calculus. He engaged in disputes with Descartes over the determination of tangents to curves and the principles of optics; with Blaise Pascal he founded the theory of probability; his admiration for Galileo was not diminished by the criticisms he made of parts of the *Dialogue*. He died at Toulouse in January 1665.

FIGLIUCCI, VINCENZO. Born at Siena in 1584, he joined the Jesuit order and taught mathematics and philosophy before giving those up for theology. After a term as rector of the Jesuit college at Siena, he went to Rome and taught moral theology at the Collegio Romano, dying there 5 April 1622.

FOSCARINI, PAOLO ANTONIO. Born about 1580 at Montalto in Calabria, his family name was in fact Scarini. He entered the Carmelite order, served twice as provincial, governing the order first at Naples and then at Messina where he also taught philosophy. His visit to Rome in 1615 to debate in favor of Copernicus ended before Galileo's arrival there for the same purpose at the end of the year, but it appears from some documents that a joint strategy was planned and that Galileo intended to go on to visit him at Naples, a plan abandoned after the edict of 1616. Foscarini died 10 June 1616 at a Carmelite convent he had founded in Montalto.

GALILEI, GALILEO I. This name appears on a tombstone in the floor of the nave of Santa Croce (Florence)—*Galileis de Galileis olim Bonaiutis*. The implication is that he was christened Bonaiuti. He was a celebrated doctor, professor of medicine, official of the University of Florence, Prior of the Florentine Republic, and Gonfaloniere of Justice. Born in 1370, he died after 1445. His father, Giovanni, and his grandfather, Tommaso, had also been Priors (members of the governing council) of Florence; his great-grandfather, Giovanni Bonaiuti, who flourished in the latter half of the thirteenth century, is the earliest member of the family recorded. Some believe the surname Galilei to have been adopted earlier because in the will of a younger brother of this Galileo the testator was called "Michael olim Iohannis Tommasi Iohannes Galilei." But no matter how this is interpreted there are problems. If taken to mean that Michael was christened Giovanni, then his own father was not mentioned, which is hardly possible. Nor can it be read as ". . . olim . . . Galilei," all his descendants (including our Galileo) having been called Galilei. Accordingly it appears that the name "Bonaiuti" should have appeared after *olim*, just as on the tombstone of the brother. In that case it was Michele, born about 1387, who worded the tombstone and who at that time changed his own surname to Galilei, regarding this illustrious Galileo as the founder of a new Florentine family.

GALILEI, LIVIA I. Born at Florence 6 October 1578, she was Galileo's youngest sister (except perhaps for a Lena, mentioned in only one letter). In January 1601 she married Taddeo Galletti; no more is known of her after the birth of her fourth child in 1610.

GALILEI, LIVIA II. Born at Padua 18 August 1601, second daughter of Galileo, she took the name Sister Arcangela in 1617 upon entering the convent of San Matteo in Arcetri, where she died 14 June 1659.

GALILEI, MICHELANGELO. Born at Florence 18 December 1575, he was Galileo's only brother to survive infancy. A professional musician, he traveled abroad in 1605 and in 1608 he was settled in Munich. He married Anna Bandinelli in 1607 (?); his eldest son Vincenzio was born in 1608 and lived with Galileo for a time, probably from 1619 to 1622. In 1626 this nephew was again in Italy and was sent by Galileo with his own son Vincenzio to study at Rome under the charge of Castelli. In 1627 Michelangelo appears to have again visited Italy; he died at Munich 3 January 1631.

GALILEI, ROBERTO. Born at Florence 30 November 1595 of a collateral branch of Galileo's family, he moved to Lyons as a youth to enter business there with an uncle. In 1621 he became a citizen of Lyons. He acted as intermediary for Galileo's foreign correspondence after his permanent house arrest at Arcetri.

GALILEI, VINCENZIO I. Born at Florence in 1520, he was a great-grandson of the Michele Galilei who adopted the surname about 1450 (cf. Galileo Galilei I, above.) Vincenzio studied music theory under Gioseffo Zarlino at Venice, probably about 1573, and subsequently became engaged in polemics against him when Zarlino attacked his *Dialogue on Ancient and Modern Music* published at Florence in 1581. In 1562 he married Giulia Ammannati at Pisa; much of her dowry was paid in cloth goods, and Vincenzio was the partner of Muzio Tedaldi, husband of Bartolommea Ammannati at Pisa, in some merchandizing of wool. When mentioned in contemporary documents, however, Vincenzio was described not as a wool merchant but as a lutenist and teacher of music. (One document seems to imply that he had once been a monk.) A leader in the move from contrapuntal embellishment to harmonic modulation and in the birth of modern opera, he died at Florence in 1591.

GALILEI, VINCENZIO II. Born at Padua 21 August 1606, he was the only son of Galileo, legitimized at Florence in 1619. In 1629 he married Sestilia Bocchineri, sister of Geri. He left some poetry said by Favaro to be of extremely ingenious organization. In 1641 Galileo dictated to him the design of a pendulum escapement to replace the traditional verge and foliot in clocks. He died at Florence 15 May 1649.

GALILEI, VINCENZIO III. Galileo's nephew, born at Munich in 1608; see Michelangelo Galilei, above.

GALILEI, VIRGINIA I. Born at Florence 8 May 1573, Galileo's eldest sister married Benedetto Landucci in 1591. His father's death the same year placed on Galileo the burden of paying the balance of her dowry, resulting in lawsuits by Landucci that made it difficult for Galileo to revisit Florence after his move to Padua in 1592. In 1608 Galileo obtained a minor court position for Landucci at Florence. Virginia died in May 1623.

GALILEI, VIRGINIA II. Born at Padua 12 August 1600, Galileo's eldest daughter took the name Sister Maria Celeste on entering the convent of San Matteo in Arcetri in 1616. Her letters show her to have been a sensitive and intelligent woman whose loyalties to her religion and her father were exquisitely balanced. She died 2 April 1634.

GALLUZZI, TARQUINIO. Born at Montebuono in 1574, he entered the Jesuit order in 1590 and taught rhetoric and ethics at the Collegio Romano. One of his pupils was Mario Guiducci, who in 1620 published a letter of protest addressed to him against the *Libra Astronomica* of Orazio Grassi. Galluzzi was for eighteen years rector of the Collegio dei Greci at Rome; he published a volume of poetry in 1616, and died 28 July 1649.

GHERARDINI, NICCOLÒ. Born probably about 1600, he obtained a degree in law and lived at Rome until October 1633, when he moved to Montici and then to Florence. During Galileo's enforced residence at Rome in 1633, Gherardini obtained in conversations with him biographical material which he later wrote out for Viviani's use in compiling a life of Galileo. He died in 1678.

GHETALDI, MARINO. Born at Ragusa (now Dubrovnik) in 1566, he met Galileo at Pinelli's home in Padua before 1600. His treatise on hydrostatics, published at Rome in 1603, is distinguished for its experimental data. Ghetaldi's principal contributions were to mathematics, especially to algebra. He died at Ragusa 11 April 1626.

GIUGNI, NICCOLÒ. Born at Florence in 1585, son of Vincenzio (see below), he studied with Galileo at Padua in 1605–6 and later held various positions in the Tuscan government. He died at Florence in February 1648.

GIUGNI, VINCENZIO. Born at Florence about November 1556, he served in the court of Ferdinand I and acted as Tuscan ambassador to France in 1601. He was also director of the Opere of the Florence cathedral. He died 19 January 1622.

GLORIOSO, G. CAMILLO. Born near Salerno in 1572, he earned degrees in philosophy and theology but became interested principally in astronomy and mathematics. In 1606 he went to Padua, aspiring to lecture concurrently with Galileo there. In 1610 he spread rumors that Galileo's sector was really invented by Michael Coignet, who in that year transferred his "pantometric scale" to a pair of sectors; nevertheless, when Galileo left Padua Glorioso wrote asking for his endorsement to succeed him. He obtained the vacated chair in 1613 and held it until 1624, when he refused to lecture unless granted additional privileges, whereupon the chair was again declared vacant. Glorioso returned to Naples, where he died 8 January 1643.

GONZAGA, FERDINANDO. Born at Mantua 26 April 1587, son of Vincenzo (see below). He was made cardinal in 1605, but in 1612 on becoming duke of Mantua he surrendered his cardinalate and married. He died 29 October 1626.

GONZAGA, VINCENZO. Born 21 September 1562, he became duke of Mantua in 1587. In 1584 he married a daughter of Francesco I de' Medici. His lavish expenditures wasted much of the family fortune; he was in particular a great patron of the theater, and it was probably to see the performance of a play written by Girolamo Magagnati that Galileo visited the Mantuan court in the winter of 1603–4. Vincenzo died 18 February 1612.

GRASSI, ORAZIO. Born at Savona about 1590, he joined the Jesuit order in 1608 and later became professor of mathematics at the Collegio Romano. In his lectures there in 1617 he supported Galileo's astronomical discoveries, but the ensuing controversy over comets alienated the two men. He wrote on many topics but published only anonymously and pseudonymously. He was the architect of the church of St. Ignatius at Rome and inventor of an unsinkable boat. He died at Rome 23 July 1654.

GREGORY XV. Born at Bologna in 1554, he became archbishop of Bologna in 1612 and a cardinal in 1616, was elected pope in February 1621, and died 8 July 1623.

GRIENBERGER, CHRISTOPHER. Born in the Tyrol in 1561, he entered the Jesuit order in 1580, studied mathematics under Clavius at Rome, and succeeded him as professor of mathematics at the Collegio Romano at various periods between 1613 and 1636, the year of his death.

GUALDO, PAOLO. Born at Vicenza 25 July 1553, he earned the doctorate in civil and canon law at Padua in 1581 after entering the priesthood in 1579. After some time at Rome he settled in Padua in 1591, where in 1609 he was made archpriest of the Cathedral (of San Antonio). He died at Padua 16 October 1621.

GUALTERROTTI, RAFFAELLO. Born at Florence 2 June 1548, he knew Galileo as a young man and showed him how stars could be seen in daytime through a long hole in a castle wall. In 1605 he published books about the new star of 1604 and about an eclipse, describing his observation of a sunspot in September 1604 but without recognizing its nature. He also mentioned observations of stars through a dark tube, and from a letter written shortly after Galileo's telescopic discoveries it appears that he, like Porta, had employed a lens or lenses in a tube without developing the potentialities of the device. He was interested in alchemy and composed much poetry. He died at Florence in May 1639.

GUEVARA, GIOVANNI DI. Born of a Spanish family at Naples in 1561, he became General of the Minor Regular Clerics, and in 1627 was made bishop of Teano. Accompanying Francesco Cardinal Barberini to France in 1624, he conversed at Florence with Galileo, after which he published a commentary on the pseudo-Aristotelian *Questions of Mechanics* that was mentioned with praise by Galileo in *Two New Sciences*. He died at Teano 23 August 1641.

GUICCIARDINI, PIERO. Born at Florence in 1560, he was sent by Cosimo II to the French court in 1609 and was made ambassador to Rome in 1611, serving in that capacity until 1621. He died at Florence 13 September 1626.

GUIDUCCI, MARIO. Born at Florence in 1585, he studied at the Collegio Romano and then at Pisa, taking a degree in law and intending a diplomatic career. His studies with Castelli, however, inclined him to science, and he pursued these with Galileo, becoming his assistant in 1618; in the same year he was elected Consul of the Florentine Academy. In 1625 he became a member of the Lincean Academy, and during the plague of 1630–31 he was in charge of preventive measures at Florence. He died at Florence 2 November 1646.

GULDIN, PAUL. Born near San Gallo of a Protestant family 12 June 1577, he was converted to Catholicism and joined the Jesuit order in 1597. His talent for mathematics resulted in his being sent to Rome for study, after which he taught in Austria at Graz and Vienna. He is remembered for a theorem anticipated by Pappus of Alexandria and for his published attack against Cavalieri's "method of indivisibles" based on a total misapprehension of its nature. Cavalieri replied in 1647, but Guldin had meanwhile died at Graz 3 November 1643.

HASDALE, MARTIN. Born in Germany about 1570, he spent much time at Padua and Venice where he became a friend of Paolo Sarpi and of Galileo. On his return he went to Prague, enjoyed the favor of Rudolf II, and informed Galileo of pressures on Kepler as imperial astronomer at the time of the *Starry Messenger*. On Rudolf's death in 1612 Hasdale was imprisoned, and thereafter retired to private life.

HERWART (OF HOHENBURG), JOHANN GEORG. Born at Augsburg 11 February 1553, a nephew of Mark Welser, he studied at Ingolstadt 1574–77. Though he followed an administrative career he remained in correspondence with principal scientists including Tycho, Bernegger, Grienberger, and above all Kepler. He died at Munich 15 January 1622.

HOLSTE, LUKE. Born at Hamburg in 1596 and educated there, he lived for a time at Leiden and then visited Italy in 1618. Soon afterward he traveled in England and France, where Peiresc recommended him to Francesco Cardinal Barberini in 1625. Invited to Rome, he was attached in 1627 to the cardinal's court and in 1636 was made his librarian. He died at Rome 2 February 1661.

HORKY, MARTIN. Born in Bohemia about 1590, he joined Magini at Bologna shortly before publication of the *Starry Messenger* and promptly became Galileo's bitter foe. Though Magini seems at first to have encouraged him, his excesses resulted in his being ordered from Magini's house, and his attempt to alienate Kepler from Galileo met with a like response. Long after his attack on Galileo he published a minor astronomical book from which it appears that he was still living in 1650.

INGOLI, FRANCESCO. Born at Ravenna 21 November 1578, he earned in 1601 the degree in civil and canon law at Padua where he may have met Galileo. He joined the clergy, studied oriental languages, and in 1616 was made the first secretary of the Propaganda Fidei, superintending the establishment of its famed printing press. He died at Rome 29 April 1649.

JOYEUSE, FRANÇOIS DE. Born in Piedmont 24 June 1559 of a noble French family, he became an ecclesiastic and was made cardinal in 1583. He was much interested in astronomy, seeking enlightenment from Galileo and acquiring from him a telescope capable of confirming his discoveries in the heavens. He died 23 August 1615.

KEPLER, JOHANN. Born at Weil der Stadt 27 December 1571, he studied at Tübingen under Michael Maestlin and began teaching at Graz. His fundamental discoveries in planetary theory were made possible by the accurate observations of Tycho Brahe, with whom he worked from 1599 to 1601. That Kepler and Galileo differently conceived the goals and proper methods of science in no way marred their mutual respect and admiration. Each criticized the other in published works, but on valid grounds and without animosity. Galileo ignored Kepler's most important discoveries in astronomy; Kepler remained ignorant of Galileo's most important discoveries in physics, dying at Regensburg 15 November 1630.

LAGALLA, GIULIO CESARE. Born near Naples in 1576, he studied philosophy and medicine and became chief of the pontifical medical establishment at Rome, where for twenty-one years he taught logic at the Sapienza. His attack on the conclusions Galileo drew from telescopic observations of the moon illustrates the academic tradition with regard to scientific method then sponsored by logicians. He died at Rome 15 March 1624.

LANCI, IPPOLITO. Born at Acqua Nigra, this Dominican became Commissary General of the Inquisition in 1621. Vincenzo Maculano of Firenzuola had that title during Galileo's trial in 1633. Maculano's deportment toward Galileo and his conduct of the trial were above reproach. Hence the charge that professional jealousy of a commissary of the Inquisition aggravated Galileo's case, if it has any foundation, presumably referred to Lanci.

LEOPOLD OF AUSTRIA, ARCHDUKE. Born at Graz in 1586, he married in 1625 Claudia de' Medici, daughter of Ferdinando I of Tuscany. His sister, Marie Madeleine, married Cosimo de' Medici in 1608. Leopold died near Innsbruck in 1632.

LIBRI, GIULIO. Born at Florence about 1550, he became professor of philosophy at the University of Pisa; as the result of disputes with Francesco Buonamici he moved to the University of Padua as professor of logic from 1595 to 1600. He then returned to teach philosophy at Pisa, where he died in December 1610.

LICETI, FORTUNIO. Born at Rapallo 3 October 1577, he studied at Bologna. In 1600 he was teaching dialectics at Pisa, rising to special professor of philosophy and then to professor of medicine. In 1609 he was called to the University of Padua as special professor of philosophy, where Galileo met him a year before leaving Padua for Florence. Liceti rose to the second chair of philosophy at Padua, left in 1637 to teach at Bologna, and returned to Padua where he became professor of medical theory in 1645. He died at Padua 17 May 1657.

LORENZINI, ANTONIO. Born at Montepulciano probably about 1540, he appears to have resided mainly at Padua. No record exists of his having taught at either Pisa or Padua, nor did he claim any academic title in his published books. His *Discourse* on the new star, published at Padua in 1605, was the target of scornful remarks by Kepler and was refuted by Baldessar Capra and (under a pseudonym) by Galileo. Another of his books on astronomy was printed at Paris in 1605, on which Kepler left critical comments.

LORINI, NICCOLÒ. Born at Florence in 1544, he joined the Dominican order and in 1580 became prior of a church in Fiesole. He was much favored by Grand Duke Ferdinand I, who gave him the chair of church history at the University of Florence. Lorini appears to have taken no further part in the Galileo affair after transmitting to Rome the Letter to Castelli early in 1614, though he was still living in 1617.

MACULANO, VINCENZO. Born in Firenzuola 11 September 1578, he joined the Dominican order at Pavia in 1594. After service as Commissary General of the Inquisition during Galileo's trial in 1633, he was made a cardinal and then archbishop of Benevento, where he remained until 1643. The pope sent him to Malta to superintend its fortification against the Turks; he was also put in charge of fortifications at Bologna and was consulted as a military architect by Urban VIII in connection with a plan to build a wall around Rome. He died at Rome 15 February 1667.

MAELCOTE, ODO VAN. Born at Brussels 28 July 1572, he entered the Jesuit order in 1590. He taught mathematics and Hebrew at the Collegio Romano, dying at Rome 14 March 1615.

MAESTLIN, MICHAEL. Born at Göppingen in 1550, he studied theology and mathematics at Tübingen, where he later taught astronomy and mathematics. Kepler was his pupil, and he was one of the first professors in Europe to explain fairly the Copernican system, extending much aid and advice to his famous pupil during the writing of the *Mysterium Cosmographicum* in 1595–96. He died 20 December 1631.

MAGAGNATI, GIROLAMO. Born at Lendinara (south of Padua) probably about 1560, he was a glass manufacturer at Murano who was also celebrated as a poet, writing pastoral plays and facetious verses. He shared Galileo's fondness for rustic Paduan dialect, and from at least 1604 on the two men were very close friends. Both were gourmets and habitually exchanged delicacies characteristic of their places of residence. A good practical chemist, Magagnati enjoyed a monopoly on certain colored glasses. In 1610 he was made a member of the Crusca Academy and Galileo tried to induce him to move to Florence to expand its important glass industry. He remained at Venice, however, where he became blind in 1617 and died probably in 1621.

MAGINI, GIOVANNI ANTONIO. Born at Padua 14 June 1555, he began his studies there and completed them at Bologna in 1579 in astronomy and mathematics. In 1588 he became professor of mathematics at Bologna and remained there until his death, spending his summers frequently in Padua. In addition to astronomical and mathematical works he published a famed geography of Italy and translated into Italian the *Geography* of Ptolemy. He was also devoted to astrology and alchemy. Though Magini certainly supported Galileo's adversaries on numerous occasions and never endorsed Galileo's opinions publicly, his letters to Galileo denied encouragement of his opponents. He died at Bologna 11 February 1617.

MAGIOTTI, RAFFAELLO. Born near Montevarchi in September 1597, he became a priest and spent his early years at Florence. About 1630 he moved to Rome, where he was a scribe at the Vatican Library and became a friend of Castelli, Torricelli, and others having scientific interests. His experiments in support of the Torricellian vacuum were of particular importance in his time. He died of plague at Rome in 1658.

MARSILI, ALESSANDRO. Born at Siena 26 December 1601, he studied law and philosophy there and took his degrees in 1622–23. In 1627 he became professor of logic at the University of Siena, rising to professor of philosophy. In 1638 he went to Pisa as professor of philosophy and became overseer of the university in 1662. He died at Siena 17 January 1670.

MARSILI, CESARE. Born at Bologna 31 January 1592, he quickly rose to responsible municipal posts there. He met Galileo at Rome in 1624 and became a member of the Lincean Academy the next year. He was instrumental in obtaining for Cavalieri the chair of mathematics at Bologna long left vacant after the death of Magini. A talented amateur of science, he died at Bologna 22 March 1633.

MARZIMEDICI, ALESSANDRO. Born at Florence in 1563, he made his career in the church, becoming bishop of Fiesole in 1596 and archbishop of Florence in 1605. He interested himself in all intellectual activities, showing intelligence and objectivity as a judge of disputed points. He died 13 August 1630.

MAYR, SIMON. Born at Guntzenhausen in 1570, he studied at Heilsbronn and then went to Prague, intending to pursue astronomy under Tycho Brahe; arriving there only shortly before Tycho's death in 1601, he proceeded to Padua where he enrolled in the medical curriculum. In 1602 he began tutoring Baldessar Capra in mathematics and astronomy and was made head of the German "nation" at the university in 1604–5. He was probably the author of a Latin appendix to Capra's book on the new star, and of parts of the Latin translation of Galileo's manuscript instructions for use of his "military compass" incorporated in Capra's book on that instrument. In mid-1605 he returned to Germany as mathematician to the margrave of Brandenburg, whose name he conferred in 1614 on Jupiter's satellites, claiming to have observed them before Galileo. He died at Ansbach 26 December 1624.

MEDICI, ANTONIO DE'. Born at Florence 28 August 1576, he was presented by Bianca Cappello to Francesco I as their son and was handsomely treated by him. On Francesco's death in 1587 all Antonio's titles were revoked by Ferdinand I, to be immediately restored on his taking the vows of the Jerusalemite order. Antonio took great interest in Galileo's scientific work and experimented with the fusion of metals and other alchemical arts. He died 2 May 1621.

MEDICI, CHRISTINA DE': See Christina of Lorraine

MEDICI, COSIMO II DE'. Born 12 May 1590, heir to Ferdinando I, he succeeded as grand duke in 1609, the year after his marriage to Marie Madeleine of Austria. He was Galileo's pupil in the summer of 1605 and became his employer in 1610, allowing him freedom as to residence and activities. He died 21 February 1621.

MEDICI, FERDINANDO I DE'. Born at Florence 30 July 1549, he was the son of Cosimo I, first of the Medici to hold the title of grand duke. (The earlier and more celebrated Cosimo de' Medici had been simply duke of Tuscany.) He was made cardinal in his youth but abandoned that status when his brother Francesco I died without male heir in 1587. He then assumed the throne and married Christina of Lorraine. After a reign distinguished by good judgment and patronage of arts and sciences, he died 3 February 1609.

MEDICI, FERDINANDO II DE.' Born at Florence 14 July 1610, son of Cosimo II, he succeeded to the throne in 1621 under the regency of Christina and Marie Madeleine. His own reign began at the age of seventeen in 1627. He has been said to have given little support to Galileo following publication of the *Dialogue* (dedicated to him), but considering his youth and other relevant circumstances there is little in him to blame. During his long reign Florence remained of first rank in science and became the seat of the first experimental academy of science, called the Cimento. He died 23 May 1670.

MEDICI, FRANCESCO I DE'. Born at Florence 25 March 1541, he succeeded his father Cosimo I as grand duke of Tuscany. In 1565 he married Johanna of Austria, after whose death he married Bianca Cappello in 1578. He died in 1587.

MEDICI, GIOVANNI DE'. Born at Florence 13 May 1567, he was the illegitimate son of Cosimo I and Leonora degli Albizzi. After a military apprenticeship he went to Flanders in 1586, where Tuscany supported the Spaniards. Ferdinando I recalled him in 1589 to supervise fortifications in Tuscany. From 1594 to 1600 he campaigned in Hungary against the Turks for Emperor Rudolf II, his half-brother Antonio de' Medici serving under him. In 1601, after a year in Florence and Rome, he was sent again to Flanders for four years, serving then as a Tuscan diplomat in Paris until 1608, when he returned to Florence. Late that year he contracted to serve the Venetian Republic, but on the death of Ferdinando I early in 1609, Cosimo II obtained his release to resume charge of Tuscan fortifications and to improve the harbor at Livorno. In 1615 he entered the Venetian military service, and died at Murano 19 July 1621.

MEDICI, GIULIANO DE'. Born at Florence in 1574, he entered the clergy and from 1608 to 1618 served as Tuscan ambassador to two successive Holy Roman Emperors at Prague. From 1618 to 1626 he was sent on diplomatic missions to Spain, Hungary, and Poland; then, returning to Italy, he was made archbishop of Pisa, where he died 6 January 1636.

MEDICI, LEOPOLD DE'. Born at Florence 6 November 1617, younger son of Cosimo II, he was governor of Siena from 1636 to 1641. Throughout his life he was an enthusiastic amateur and patron of science. He founded the Academy of the Cimento in 1657 and asked Viviani to put together a biography of Galileo. In 1667 the Cimento published a famed collection of experiments, known as the *Saggi*; in the same year Leopold was made a cardinal and the academy began to decline. He died at Florence 10 November 1675.

MEDICI, MATHIA DE'. Born at Florence 9 May 1613, son of Cosimo II, he served as governor of Siena from 1629 to 1636. He then went to Austria for military service, carrying to Giovanni Pieroni the manuscript of the first half of *Two New Sciences*. In 1641 he returned to the governorship of Siena, where (after other tours of military duty) he died 14 October 1667.

MERCURIALE, GIROLAMO. Born at Forlì 30 September 1530, he studied philosophy and medicine at the University of Padua and served seven years at Rome in the court of Cardinal Farnese. In 1569 he obtained the first chair of practical medicine at Padua, moving in 1587 to Bologna and in 1591 to Pisa, where he died in 1606.

MERSENNE, MARIN. Born at La Soultière 8 September 1588, he studied philosophy at Mans and entered the Jesuit college of La Flèche in 1604; from there he went to the Sorbonne, and in 1611 he entered the Minim order. The rest of his life was spent mainly at Paris. Mersenne corresponded with the principal scientists of his time, published numerous works of his own and of others, performed careful experiments with penduluins and falling bodies, and wrote extensively on the theory, practice, and instruments of music. More than any other man of his time he drew together the scientists of Europe and encouraged the growth of experimental science. He died at Paris 1 September 1647.

MICANZIO, FULGENZIO. Born near Brescia 8 June 1570, he entered the Servite order in 1590, studied at Venice, and graduated from Bologna in 1600. In 1606 he joined Fra Paolo Sarpi in the Venetian defiance of the interdict imposed by Paul V, remaining as aide to Sarpi and succeeding him as theologian to the Venetian Republic in 1623. His biography of Sarpi was first published anonymously in 1646. He died at Venice 7 February 1654.

MICHELINI, FAMIANO. Born at Rome about 1600, he joined the order of the Scuole Pie and enjoyed the patronage of Leopold de' Medici from the beginning of his governorship of Siena. He succeeded Vincenzio Renieri as professor of mathematics at Pisa in 1647, remaining ten years and then withdrawing from his religious order to become a secular priest. One of the principal early promoters of hydraulic science, he died at Rome 20 January 1666.

MOLETTI, GIUSEPPE. Born at Messina, probably about 1520, he became professor of mathematics at Padua in 1577 after tutoring Vincenzo Gonzaga at Mantua. His published works included books on geography and astronomical tables needed for the Gregorian calendar. He died at Padua 25 March 1588.

MONTE, FRANCESCO MARIA DEL. Born at Venice 5 July 1549, he entered the church and in 1563 began preaching at Pesaro. Refusing the bishopric offered to him, he served at the Tuscan court, and when Ferdinand I surrendered the cardinalate to become grand duke he arranged to have del Monte made cardinal in his stead. Francesco died 17 August 1626.

MONTE, GUIDOBALDO DEL. Born at Pesaro 11 January 1545, he was the elder brother of Francesco. He studied mathematics first at Padua and later as the private pupil of Commandino at Urbino, 1572–75. In 1577 he published his *Mechanics* and in 1588 his commentary of the work of Archimedes on centers of gravity, just when Galileo sent to him his own theorems on that subject. Guidobaldo was made inspector of Tuscan fortifications in 1588 but continued to reside mainly at Monte Baroccio, near Urbino, pursuing his studies and experiments and publishing several more books on mathematical topics. He remained in intermittent correspondence with Galileo until his death 1 January 1607.

MORANDI, ORAZIO. Born at Rome about 1570, he joined the Vallombrosan order in 1590, studied literature, and enjoyed the friendship of both Antonio and Giovanni de' Medici. He became general of his order but in 1630 was imprisoned by the Inquisition on charges of necromancy and of having forecast the death of Urban VIII. He died in prison 9 October 1630.

NAUDÉ, GABRIEL. Born at Paris 2 February 1600, he studied philosophy and the humanities. In 1626 he went to Padua and in 1631 to Rome, to be librarian to a cardinal, returning to Padua for a degree in medicine. In 1641–42 he was librarian to Francesco Cardinal Barberini but was then called back to Paris as librarian to Cardinal Richelieu and his successor, Cardinal Mazarin. Queen Christina of Sweden called him to Stockholm, but he soon returned to France and died at Abbeville 29 July 1653.

NICCOLINI, FRANCESCO. Born in Tuscany 29 November 1584, he was a page at the court of Francesco I until his father took him to Rome, destined for a career in the church. At his father's death he relinquished the cloth and married Caterina Riccardi in 1618. He was sent as Tuscan ambassador to Rome in 1621, succeeding Guicciardini, and retained that post until 1643. The rest of his life was spent at the court of Ferdinando II; he died at Florence 25 July 1650.

NOAILLES, FRANÇOIS DE. Born in France 19 June 1584, he was a pupil of Galileo's at Padua in 1603. He served in the French army, becoming lieutenant in 1614. In 1633 he was made a counsellor of state and in 1634 was sent as ambassador to Rome. While there he befriended Campanella and sought a pardon for Galileo. On his return he met Galileo by special arrangement at Poggibonsi, the only time Galileo is known to have been permitted to leave Arcetri. Noailles may have carried back to France a manuscript of *Two New Sciences*, but this is doubtful. After his return in 1636 he served in the religious wars, dying at the end of 1645.

NORI, FRANCESCO. Born at Florence probably about 1575, he became a canon in 1603 and in 1620 was appointed doctor of theology at the University of Florence. Twice Consul of the Florentine Academy (1598 and 1613), he was made a bishop in 1624 and died 31 January 1632.

NOZZOLINI, TOLOMEO. Born at Florence (?) in 1569, he taught logic at the University of Pisa in 1589–90, and afterward physics. In 1606 he was assigned by Alessandro Marzimedici to supervise country churches, holding that post until 1640. In one of his poems he praised Galileo's *Dialogue*. He died 1 May 1643.

ORSINI, ALESSANDRO. Born at Rome in 1593, he was a nephew of Ferdinando I and spent most of his youth at the Tuscan court. In December 1615 he was created cardinal and it was to him that Galileo addressed his first known written account of the ocean tides (January 1616). He died at Bracciano 22 August 1626.

ORSINI, PAOLO GIORDANO. Born at Rome in 1591, elder brother of Alessandro, he likewise spent his youth at the Tuscan court. He traveled extensively, was an accomplished poet and deeply interested in music and drama. He died 24 May 1656.

ORTELIUS, ABRAHAM. Born at Antwerp 4 April 1527, he was a renowned geographer. His first studies were in pure mathematics, his *Theater of the World* not being published until 1571. As a geographer he traveled extensively and was in Italy three times to collect material for his *Geographical Treasure*. He died at Antwerp 28 January 1598.

PAPAZZONI, FLAMINIO. Born at Bologna about 1550, he gained degrees in medicine (1572) and philosophy (1573), entering the faculty at Bologna as professor of philosophy in 1576. From 1580 to 1587 he was professor at Pavia, returning to Bologna until 1611, when with Galileo's recommendation he was called to Pisa to fill the chair of philosophy vacated by the death of Libri in 1610. He died at Pisa in 1614.

PASSIGNANO, DOMENICO. Born Domenico Crespi at Passignano in 1560, he studied painting with Battista Naldini and Federico Zuccheri. He also studied anatomy at the University of Pisa, moving then to Venice to carry out public commissions. He later painted for several years at Rome, where he was knighted, returning to Florence and dying there in 1638.

PAUL V. Born Camillo Borghese on 17 September 1552, he studied law at Perugia and Padua, became cardinal in 1596, and was elected pope 16 May 1605. The next year he placed Venice under the interdict in a dispute over the temporal power of popes extending outside Rome. Venice, guided by Paolo Sarpi, successfully resisted, and Paul V remained hostile to intellectuals thereafter. He died 16 January 1621.

PEIRESC, NICOLE FABRI DE. Born in Provence (of a family originally of Pisa) 1 December 1580, he studied at Avignon and then under the Jesuits at Aix, going to Padua about 1603 where he was a pupil of Galileo's. He became a parliamentary counsellor at Aix, where he formed a famous library, corresponded with the principal men of letters and of science of his time, and pursued astronomical observations with skill and intelligence. His friendship with Francesco Cardinal Barberini, whom he had entertained at Aix, induced him to intervene strongly against Galileo's imprisonment. He died at Aix 24 June 1637.

PERI, DINO. Born at Florence in 1604, he took his degree at Pisa in law and later studied mathematics as a private pupil of Galileo. When the death of Niccolò Aggiunti vacated the chair of mathematics at Pisa, he received Galileo's endorsement and was chosen in 1636. He died prematurely in July 1640.

PICCHENA, CURZIO. Born at San Gimignano 11 January 1553, he became a protegé of Belissario Vinta. As a youth he was sent as ambassador to France, and thereafter to Spain. About 1590 Ferdinand I gave him a special mission to Switzerland, after which he was secretary to Ferdinand from 1601 to 1609 and then to Cosimo II until 1613. On Vinta's death in that year he became Tuscan secretary of state. As a result of quarrels with Bali Cioli, another grand-ducal secretary, he was dismissed from the court during the regency of Ferdinando II. He died 14 June 1626.

PICCOLOMINI, ASCANIO. Born at Florence around 1590, he joined the court of Francesco Cardinal Barberini in 1623. In 1628 he was made archbishop of Siena, remaining in that office until his death at Rome 14 September 1671.

PICCOLOMINI, ENEA. An older brother (or half-brother) of Ascanio, Enea appears to have been born in Spain. He frequented the court of Ferdinando I de' Medici and became private secretary to Cosimo II. In the 1615 dedication to him of published replies to Galileo's opponents in the controversy over floating bodies, Castelli addressed him as "captain of cavalry." Enea went to Germany in the service of the Holy Roman Emperor and was killed during a campaign in Bohemia.

PICCOLOMINI, FRANCESCO. Born at Siena in 1522, he studied philosophy and taught logic there before going to teach philosophy at Macerata and then at Perugia. In 1560 he went to Padua, rising in 1565 to the first chair in philosophy. In 1601 he retired to Siena, where he died in 1604. (A younger man of the same name, captain of the guards under Ferdinando II de' Medici, was of a Florentine branch of the Piccolomini family.)

PIERONI, GIOVANNI. Born at San Miniato 4 March 1586, he taught civil and military architecture at Florence before entering the service of the Holy Roman Emperor in 1622. Despite repeated applications to the emperor in later years, he was not permitted to return to Tuscany. He made diligent efforts to find a publisher for *Two New Sciences* in Germany, Poland, or Austria. About 1639–40 he believed he had detected annual parallax in the fixed stars, having probably misinterpreted the effect of aberration of light through observations remarkably precise for the time, though quite possible to be carried out by a patient engineer familiar with techniques of surveying.

PIGNORIA, LORENZO. Born at Padua 12 October 1571, he studied literature and philosophy under the Jesuits. Having become a priest he was taken by a Venetian bishop to Rome and there pursued archeological investigations for two years. Returning to Padua he published a number of books on archeology and some poetry. He died of plague at Padua 13 June 1631.

PINELLI, COSIMO. Born at Naples in 1569, he was a nephew of Giovanni Vincenzio (see below) and hereditory duke of Aceranza. It was probably to him that Galileo sent the revised instructions for his sector that were the first to include all the scales, about March 1599. On his uncle's death he went to Padua to assemble the library and other collections; about to return to Naples he fell ill at Venice, was taken to Padua by Paolo Gualdo, and died there 3 November 1602.

PINELLI, GIOVANNI VINCENZIO. Born at Naples in 1535, he settled at Padua in 1558 and became there the leader of a literary and cultural group of great importance to Galileo's development. His library and collections of maps, instruments, objects of art and archeological relics attracted visitors from all over Italy and from abroad, whom he delighted to entertain and to introduce to scholars at Padua and Venice. Galileo is said to have lived with Pinelli at Padua in 1592–93 until he found suitable quarters of his own, and they remained in close touch until Pinelli's death 4 August 1601.

PORTA, GIOVANNI BATTISTA DELLA. Born at Naples in 1535, he won fame in his youth for a book on natural magic, published in 1558 and reprinted innumerable times, with translations into many languages. Soon afterward he inaugurated at Naples an academy "of the curious," but this became suspected of sorcery and was discontinued after Porta was interrogated at Rome by the Inquisition. In 1580 he visited Venice and met Paolo Sarpi. In 1589 he greatly expanded his first book, adding passages later interpreted as foreshadowing the telescope. Cesi visited him at Naples during the persecution of the Lincean Academy by his father, in 1604, and in 1610 Porta was made a member of the Academy. He was the author of books ranging from cryptography through agriculture to mathematics. He died at Naples in February 1615.

QUERENGO, ANTONIO. Born at Padua in 1546, he became a priest and served at Rome as secretary to several cardinals. In 1600 he returned to Padua as penitentiary canon of the city. His home became the center of intellectual activity there after Pinelli's death in 1601. Galileo dedicated to him his pseudonymous rustic dialogue written against Lorenzini in 1605. Querengo was a distinguished Latin poet as well as a diplomat. He died at Rome 1 September 1633, and on his deathbed he praised Galileo despite the fact of his recent trial and condemnation in that city.

REMO QUIETANO, GIOVANNI. Born Johann Ruderhauf, probably about 1590, he studied at Padua in 1608, presumably under Galileo, and was head of the German "nation" there in 1608–9. In 1617 he applied unsuccessfully for the chair of mathematics vacated by the death of Magini. In the 1620s he was attached to the court of Leopold of Austria and was frequently at Ingolstadt. Also a friend of both Kepler and Scheiner, Remo provided Galileo with useful information about friends and foes in Germany. He died after 1640.

RENIERI, VINCENZIO. Born at Genoa 30 March 1606, he joined the Olivetan order which sent him to Rome in 1623. In 1633 he was at Siena, where he met Galileo, who later entrusted to him the task of updating and improving his tables of the motions of Jupiter's satellites. This work brought Renieri often to Arcetri, where he became a friend of Viviani. On the death of Dino Peri, Renieri obtained the chair of mathematics at Pisa with the additional duty of teaching Greek. He added many observations of Jupiter's satellites to Galileo's and somewhat improved his tables of their motions, but these remained unpublished when he died prematurely at Pisa 5 November 1647.

RICCARDI, NICCOLÒ. Born at Genoa in 1585, he was sent to Spain and there joined the Dominican order. Phillip III of Spain nicknamed him "Father Monster" for his enormous body, incredible eloquence, and phenomenal memory. In 1629 he was made Master of the Sacred Palace at Rome, an office which included the responsibility of licensing books to be printed. His predecessor had assigned him in 1623 to review the *Assayer*, which he not only approved but highly praised in the imprimatur itself. In 1630, however, he made many difficulties about licensing the *Dialogue*, and when other circumstances required its printing at Florence (rather than Rome) he agreed only after adding further conditions. He died 30 May 1639.

RICCI, OSTILIO. Born at Fermo (near Naples) in 1540, he is said to have studied mathematics under Niccolò Tartaglia. He had become attached to the Tuscan court before 1583, when his lessons on Euclid attracted Galileo to the study of mathematics. From 1593 on, Ricci was active in the Academy of Design at Florence. In 1597 he was supervisor of fortifications (succeeding Guidobaldo del Monte) and served also as state hydraulic engineer. The "archimetro," a surveying instrument concerning whose use he composed a treatise about 1590, may have been of his invention, though that was not claimed in the treatise. He died at Florence in 1603 holding the title of mathematician to the grand duke, acquired by Galileo in 1610.

ROBERVAL, GILLES PERSONNE DE. Born near Beauvais 8 August 1602, he settled in Paris in 1628 and was professor of mathematics at the College de France from 1634 to the end of his life. His posthumously published *Traité des Indivisibles* opened one of the principal roads to the infinitesimal calculus, quite different from that followed by Cavalieri despite the seeming similarity of titles to their books. As a device for supporting Copernicus without risk, Roberval published a pretended lost work of Aristarchus in Latin translation (1643). His pioneer mathematical analysis of the cycloid remaining unpublished, he accused Torricelli of having plagiarized it from oral information, a charge that became a source of great bitterness between French and Italian mathematicians during the latter half of the seventeenth century. He died at Paris 27 October 1675.

ROCCO, ANTONIO. Born in 1586 at a town in Aquila, he studied philosophy first at the Collegio Romano, then at Perugia, and finally at Padua under Cremonini. After teaching privately at Venice he was appointed public lecturer on rhetoric there, where he died in March 1652.

ROFFENI, GIOVANNI ANTONIO. Born at Bologna about 1580, he there received degrees in philosophy (1607) and medicine (1622). He taught both subjects privately at Bologna and was probably also a lecturer in philosophy at the University of Bologna from time to time. He died 7 December 1643.

RUDOLF II (Holy Roman Emperor). Born 18 July 1552, at Vienna, he was a grandson of Charles V and was educated by the Jesuits at Madrid. He succeeded to the throne on the death of his father, Maximilian II, in October 1576, establishing his capital at Prague. Tycho Brahe and Johann Kepler both served him as imperial astronomers. He died 20 January 1612.

SAGREDO, GIOVANFRANCESCO. Born at Venice 19 June 1571, he studied under Galileo at Padua privately about 1597–1600. From 1605 to 1607 he was treasurer at Palma (Minorca) and from 1608 to 1611 was Venetian consul at Soria. Despite those long absences he remained a close friend of Galileo's, and on his return to Venice in 1611 resumed a lifelong correspondence with him. He was very active as an amateur of science, experimenting in magnetism, optics, mechanics, and thermometry. He died at Venice 5 March 1620.

SALVIATI, FILIPPO. Born at Florence 19 January 1582, of a very prominent patrician family, he planned a military career but was excluded from that by frail health. From 1606 to 1609 he turned to wide-ranging private studies, chiefly literary, at the end of whch he was elected to the Crusca Academy. About the time of Galileo's move to Florence, Salviati became interested in mathematics, astronomy, and experimental philosophy. His palace in Florence soon became a kind of Lyceum. Galileo was frequently invited to live at Salviati's Villa delle

Selve in the hills of Signa, some fifteen miles west of Florence, where *Bodies in Water* and the *Sunspot Letters* were largely written. Offended in a matter of court precedence at Florence late in 1613, Salviati traveled abroad and died at Barcelona 22 March 1614.

SANTORIO, SANTORRE. Born at Capodistria (now in Yugoslavia) 29 May 1561, he received his doctorate in medicine at Padua in 1582, practiced for several years in Croatia, and in 1599 returned to Venice, where he soon formed friendships with Sarpi, Sagredo, and Galileo. His adaptation of the pendulum to medical practice by invention of the *pulsilogium* was probably inspired by discussions with Galileo of the latter's experiments with pendulums in 1602; the instrument was described in a book published by Santorio late in that year or early in 1603. He was a pioneer of the utilization of physical measurements in medicine, his most famous device being a large balance used in studying metabolic changes in experimental subjects, among whom was Galileo. In 1611 he was appointed professor of medical theory at Padua. While there he published descriptions of thermometric devices which had probably evolved from Galileo's thermoscope of 1606. He died at Venice 25 February 1636.

SANTUCCI, ANTONIO. Born in Pomerania, probably about 1560, he gained the chair of mathematics at Pisa in 1598 jointly with Francesco Sanleoni and occupied it alone after his colleague's death. Cosmographer to the grand duke of Tuscany, he is celebrated for design and manufacture of superb astronomical spheres and other scientific instruments. He long ridiculed the Copernican astronomy, but moved by Galileo's telescopic discoveries he restudied it and became a convert. Nevertheless he continued to oppose Galileo's physics, writing against *Bodies in Water*. He died at Pisa in 1613 and was succeeded in the chair of mathematics by Castelli.

SARPI, PAOLO. Born at Venice (?) 14 August 1552 as Pietro Sarpi, he took the name Fra Paolo on entering the Servite order in 1565. In 1579 he was graduated from the University of Padua and thereafter lived mainly at Venice, with frequent visits to Rome on business of his order. He maintained voluminous correspondence with foreigners, many of them Protestants, seeking always to be fully informed of every kind of development, including those in science. He noted and explained in part the valves in the veins, important in the later discovery of circulation of the blood; was first in Italy to hear of the Dutch invention of the telescope; and kept a notebook of scientific and philosophical speculations, many of them on motion. He met Galileo at the home of Pinelli, probably late in 1592, and from then until 1606, when the interdict required all his attention, participated in his principal scientific investigations. Sarpi was a key figure in

Galileo's dealings with the Venetian government in 1609 relating to the telescope. He died at Venice 7 January 1623.

SCHEINER, CHRISTOPHER. Born in Swabia 25 July 1573, he joined the Jesuit order in 1595 and was sent to Ingolstadt in 1601, where he first studied and then taught mathematics (1610–16). There he published on sunspots and on atmospheric refraction. In 1616 he went to Innsbruck, where he published on optics, and in 1620 to Freiburg. In 1624 he was transferred to Rome, where he taught mathematics and astronomy and published his *Rosa Ursina* (Bracciano, 1626–30), bitterly attacking Galileo. He remained at Rome through the trial of Galileo, which he was instrumental in bringing about. In the autumn of 1633 he moved to Vienna, where he composed a book against Galileo's *Dialogue* that was withheld from publication during his lifetime, probably by order of his superiors (*Prodromus pro Sole Mobile* . . . 1651). In 1639 he went to Niesse, where he died 18 June 1650.

SEGHIZZI (OR SEGIZZI), MICHELANGELO. Born at Lodi in 1585, he joined the Dominican order in 1599. After service as Inquisitioner at Cremona and Milan he was ordered to Rome by Paul V and made Commissary General of the Holy Office. In 1616, after the edict against Copernicanism and the silencing of Galileo, Seghizzi was made bishop of Lodi, where he died in 1625.

SINCERI, CARLO. Concerning the prosecutor who questioned Galileo in the trial of 1633, it is known only that in 1606 he was made a counsellor of the Inquisition and in 1609 became its *procurator fiscale* (prosecuting attorney), remaining in that office until October 1641.

SIZZI, FRANCESCO. Born at Florence probably about 1585, he initially opposed Galileo's telescopic discoveries on astrological and theological grounds. Sizzi was not a priest, as is often said, but a young patrician of such intellectual promise that Galileo refused to attack his book when urged by others. Soon afterward Sizzi moved to Paris and became friendly with French mathematicians whose sunspot observations were later to be of great value to Galileo. In the wave of anti-Italian sentiment at Paris following the accession of Louis XIII, Sizzi was accused of sorcery because of horoscopes he had provided to Elena Galigai, and after her execution he was barbarously tortured and put to death for having taken part in a publication supporting Catherine de' Medici against the new king. He died at Paris 19 July 1618.

SPINELLI, GIROLAMO. Born at Padua about 1580, he entered the Benedictine order in 1600 and became the friend of Benedetto Castelli, studying with him under Galileo in 1604. He wrote a reply to Baldessar Capra's unfair criticisms of Galileo in connection with the new star of that year, which Galileo forbade him to publish, and assisted Galileo in writing his rustic dialect booklet against Lorenzini and Cremonini in 1605. Spinelli was abbot of monasteries at Venice, Padua, and Parma in later years, dying after a rather stormy career in 1647.

STEVIN, SIMON. Born at Bruges in 1548, he had moved to Leiden and was teaching mathematics there in 1583. In 1585 he published his important *L'Arithmetique*, which among other things introduced decimal fractions and considerably advanced algebra. This was followed in 1586 by a book of fundamental importance to mechanics and to hydrostatics, but which received limited recognition until it was translated from Dutch into Latin in 1605. Stevin confirmed by experiment in 1586 the reasoning of Benedetti that speed of fall is not dependent on weight. Engineer to Prince Maurice of Nassau, Stevin published also on dikes and fortification, favored the Copernican astronomy, contributed to the theory of musical tuning and temperament (though this remained unpublished), and in every way displayed outstanding scientific talent. He died at Leiden in 1620.

TARDE, JEAN. Born in Perigord about 1562, he joined the clergy and studied at the Sorbonne, becoming canon of Sarlat. In 1593 he met Clavius at Rome. In 1614 he twice conversed with Galileo at Florence, but ignored him entirely a decade later when he published on sunspots and christened them the "Bourbon stars." He died in 1636.

TARTAGLIA, NICCOLÒ. Born at Brescia about 1500 and self-educated, he developed an unusual talent for mathematics and taught the subject privately, first at Verona and then at Venice. He discovered a method of solving cubic equations which he imparted to Girolamo Cardano under vows of secrecy; Cardano extended this and published it with the excuse that it had previously been found about 1515 by Scipio del Ferro at Bologna, who however appears to have solved only certain special forms of cubics. In 1537 Tartaglia pioneered artillery science; in 1543 he published an Italian Euclid that first restored Eudoxian proportion theory. In 1551 he published on the raising of sunken vessels, expounding in Italian translation the principle of Archimedes, and at the end of his life he was publishing a comprehensive survey of pure and applied mathematics. He died at Venice in 1557.

TEDALDI, MUZIO. Born at Florence probably about 1540, he moved to Pisa and there married Bartolomea Ammannati, a sister or cousin of Galileo's mother Giulia. Tedaldi, a customs official, was also partner with Galileo's father in some ventures in the wool market. Galileo resided with Tedaldi in 1572–74 and again while he was studying at the University of Pisa in 1581–85. Tedaldi was also the godfather of Galileo's younger brother, Michelangelo.

TEDESCHI, LEONARDO. Born at Verona about 1571, he studied philosophy and medicine at Bologna and Padua. In 1599 he was made a member of the college of medicine at Verona, but in 1606 withdrew to become a cleric. He died at Verona 23 January 1634.

TENGNAGEL, FRANCIS. Born in Bohemia, probably about 1570, he studied astronomy under Tycho Brahe, whose daughter he married. After the death of Tycho in 1601, Tengnagel left Kepler in charge of the analysis of Tycho's astronomical observations and turned to politics, becoming counsellor and librarian to Rudolph II, who sent him on diplomatic missions to Holland and England.

TORRICELLI, EVANGELISTA. Born at (or near) Faenza 15 October 1608, he was first taught by an uncle who was a Camaldolese monk, then studied mathematics under the Jesuits, and finally with Castelli at Rome. His most celebrated achievement was the invention of the barometer and its correct explanation in terms of atmospheric pressure. Appointed to succeed Galileo as mathematician to the grand duke of Tuscany, he carried on Galileo's work on motion, projectile trajectories, and the force of percussion. He became extraordinarily proficient at the grinding of lenses for more powerful telescopes. Torricelli's work in pure mathematics was also important, but those papers were not published; he died suddenly 24 October 1647, having requested in his will that they be edited by Cavalieri, who perished a month later.

VALERIO, LUCA. Born at Ferrara about 1552, he studied mathematics and devoted his energies to the simplification of Archimedean methods of proof. In 1590 he visited Pisa and there met Galileo, settling soon afterward at Rome where he taught mathematics at the Sapienza most of his life. He was elected to the Lincean Academy in 1612 but later opposed its tolerance of Galileo's support for Copernicus. On this he was voted down and reprimanded by the other members. He died at Rome in 1618.

VALORI, BACCIO. Born at Florence 30 October 1535, he was made senator in 1580. He was Consul of the Florentine Academy in 1588 and later was representative of Ferdinando I in the Academy of Design. He died 4 April 1606.

VIETA (OR VIÈTE), FRANÇOIS. Born at Fontenay-le-Comte in 1540, he was by profession a lawyer but through his mathematical genius became the father of modern algebra. His unpublished writings on astronomy show him also to have been of outstanding attainments in that field. During the Wars of the League he penetrated the cipher used by the Spanish and was accused of necromancy as a result. He died at Paris 13 December 1603.

VILLE, ANTOINE DE LA. Born in France, probably about 1600, he entered the service of the Venetian Republic as military engineer about 1630. In 1633–34 he was placed in charge of fortifications at Mantua and Vicenza; during this time, on his frequent returns to Venice to report, he became acquainted with Fulgenzio Micanzio. He published an exhaustive treatise on fortification, reprinted at Amsterdam in 1662, which was probably the year of his death.

VINTA, BELISARIO. Born at Volterra 13 October 1542, he was made a citizen of Florence in 1579 and entered the secretariat of the grand duke, rising after various other duties to secretary of state under Ferdinando I. He became senator in 1610 and died at Florence 14 October 1613.

VIVIANI, VINCENZIO. Born at Florence 2 April 1622, he was instructed in mathematics by Clemente Settimi of the Scuole Pie. Viviani soon attracted the attention of Ferdinando II, who recommended him to Galileo. Viviani resided with Galileo at Arectri from October 1639 as his pupil, amanuensis, and assistant. On the death of Torricelli in 1647 Viviani became mathematician to the grand duke. In 1657 he was appointed to the Academy of the Cimento by Prince Leopold and began a biography of Galileo. Made one of the eight foreign members of the Academy of Sciences founded at Paris in 1666, he was given a generous pension by Louis XIV though he remained at Florence. He published many mathematical books and edited the first collected edition of Galileo's works (1655–56). Viviani died at Florence 22 September 1703, leaving in his will funds for the construction of Galileo's sepulchral monument in Santa Croce.

WEDDERBURN, JOHN. Of Scottish birth, he studied medicine at Padua, leaving in 1611; in 1614 he was physician to the prince of Lichtenstein and a friend of Kepler's. In 1628 he was established as a physician in Moravia, where he had settled permanently.

WELSER, MARK. Born at Augsburg 20 June 1558, he studied at Padua, Paris, and Rome. A banker and man of affairs, he also held municipal posts in Augsburg from 1583 on, wrote on civic history and archeology, and was made a member of the Crusca Academy in 1613 and of the Lincean Academy in 1614. Welser was very favorable to the Jesuits but remained open-minded in the Scheiner-Galileo dispute. Afflicted with gout and distressed by financial difficulties brought on by a default on the part of Rudolf II, he took his own life 23 June 1614.

WHITE, RICHARD. Born in Essex in 1590, brother of the prolific anti-Jesuit English Catholic Thomas White, he settled at Rome after studying mathematics at Pisa under Castelli in 1616. He was critical of various writings of Galileo's but took as many of them as he could find to England and left them with Sir Francis Bacon. In 1648 he published at Rome a book on the volumes of sections of the hemisphere; he made experiments of specific gravities of alloys, observed the comet of 1653, and was still living when Robert Southwell visited Italy in 1660.

WURSTEISEN, CHRISTIAN. Born at Basel in 1544, he obtained his degree in philosophy there in 1562. In 1568 he published a commentary on the *Sphere* of Sacrobosco (often reprinted) in which Copernicus was mentioned but not favored. His main work was a history of the city of Basel, where he died 29 March 1588.

WURSTEISEN, CHRISTOPHER. Born about 1570, perhaps a son of Christian, he was enrolled in law at the University of Padua in 1595 and may there have offered some lectures on the Copernican astronomy.

ZABARELLA, GIACOMO. Born at Padua 5 September 1533, he was graduated in philosophy at Padua in 1553. In 1564 he was made professor of logic, rising steadily in rank from 1569 to 1585, when he took second chair in philosophy, Francesco Piccolomini holding the first chair. Zabarella was the leading contemporary exponent of Aristotelian method in science, unsympathetic to mathematical reasoning in physics and strongly advocating appeal to experience in the study of natural phenomena. He died 25 October 1589.

ZIECKMESSER, JAN EUTEL. Born at Spira, probably about 1575, he was enrolled at Padua in October 1600. His name was spelled as above in his own hand on enrollment; yet a letter in 1610 apparently referring to the same man calls him Zugmesser, mathematician to the archbishop of Cologne. In 1603 he brought to Padua an instrument resembling Galileo's sector; he had apparently not heard of Galileo's instrument when studying earlier at Padua but had encountered something similar abroad.

ZUÑIGA, DIEGO DE. Born at Salamanca, he published there a commentary on Job, reprinted at Rome in 1590, which contained a passage asserting the Copernican system to be better in agreement with that book than was the traditional geocentric system.

NOTES

1564–89

1. See appendix under Galilei, Galileo I.

2. In the Julian calendar, replaced in Italy by the Gregorian calendar in 1582. All other dates herein have been made to conform to the new style.

3. This very ancient monastery was in no way connected with the Jesuits, to whom Galileo's education is often mistakenly attributed.

4. 7:731. See further in chapter 19, § V.

5. Vincenzio Viviani and Niccolò Gherardini; see 19:603–5, 636–37.

6. Euclid Book Five, Definition Four, numbered fifth among the definitions in most early editions. Euclid Book Five, Definition Five (then called Six) became the chief topic of Galileo's last composition, translated in chapter 22, § III.

7. Called analytic geometry, it first appeared in print as an appendix to the *Discourse on Method* of René Descartes in 1637.

8. *Opera Archimedis . . . per Nicolaum Tartaleum . . . in luce posita . . .* (Venice, 1543); the Latin translations therein had been made by William of Moerbecke in the thirteenth century.

9. *Archimedis opera . . .* (Basel, 1544), with Greek texts and the Latin translations made by James of Cremona in the fifteenth century. Galileo later owned a copy of this edition in which he made notes.

10. 19:35.

11. 1:15–177.

12. 1:27, 36.

13. W. A. Wallace, *Galileo's Early Notebooks: The Physical Questions* (Notre Dame, Indiana, 1978). I could not consult this work, but am indebted to Father Wallace for information communicated during its preparation.

14. Christopher Clavius, *Commentarium in Sphaeram Ioannis de Sacro Bosco* (Rome, 1581, often reprinted and revised). (The *Sphere* of Sacrobosco (John Holywood, thirteenth century) remained a university textbook for four centuries.) Benedict Pereira, *De communibus omnium rerum naturalium principiis* . . . (Rome, 1562, often reprinted).

15. For a brief excerpt see 9: 291–92; the whole work was not published.

16. 1: 215–20. Thomas Salusbury, tr., *Mathematical Collections and Translations*, tome 2 (London, 1665, repr. 1967); modern translation in L. Fermi and G. Bernardini, *Galileo and the Scientific Revolution* (New York, 1961).

17. Best known was that in Vitruvius, *Architecture,* introduction to Book Nine.

18. 1: 367–408. For translation see S. Drake and I. E. Drabkin, *Mechanics in Sixteenth-Century Italy* (Madison, 1969), pp. 331–77. © 1969 by the Regents of the University of Wisconsin. All rights reserved. Hereinafter cited as *Sixteenth Century.*

19. 1: 251–340. For translation see I. E. Drabkin and S. Drake, *Galileo Galilei on Motion and on Mechanics* (Madison, 1960), pp. 13–114. © 1960 by the Regents of the University of Wisconsin. Hereinafter cited as *Motion and Mechanics.*

20. Girolamo Borri, *De motu gravium et levium* (Florence, 1576), pp. 214–17.

21. The chief factor is the yielding of the plane under weight. For an attempt by Galileo to dismiss weight as a factor, see chapter 6, § I.

22. G. B. Benedetti, *Resolutio omnium Euclidis problematum* . . . (Venice, 1553), dedicatory letter.

23. G. B. Benedetti, *Demonstratio proportionum motuum* . . . (Turin, 1554); *Sixteenth Century*, pp. 154–65.

24. G. B. Benedetti, *Diversarum speculationum mathematicarum* . . . (Turin, 1585); partial translation in *Sixteenth Century*, pp. 166–237.

25. See S. Drake, "Impetus Theory Reappraised," *Journal of the History of Ideas* 26 (1975): 27–46.

26. At any rate that was the prevailing opinion concerning Aristotle's teaching held by Peripatetics of Galileo's time; cf. chapter 11, n. 2.

27. Cf. Aristotle, *Physica* 232a, 25 ff.

28. 2: 211–55; see also S. Drake, "An Unrecorded Manuscript Copy of Galileo's *Cosmography*," *Physis* 1 (1959): 294–306.

29. 1: 187–200; cf. S. Drake's translation of Galileo Galilei, *Two New Sciences* (Madison, 1974), pp. 261–80. © 1974 by the Regents of the University of Wisconsin System. All rights reserved. Hereinafter

cited as *TNS*. Only the first and last sections can definitely be dated to 1587.

30. Two chairs of mathematics were maintained at Bologna, one of astronomy and one of geometry; Galileo's specialty at this time was the latter. Magini was an astronomer and geographer.

31. Coignet was in correspondence with Guidobaldo, who may also have told him of Galileo's abilities.

32. 9: 31–57. The first mention of Galileo in print concerned his lectures on Dante; cf. [Filippo Valori], *Termini di mezzo relievo . . . tra gl'archi di Casa Valori . . .* (Florence, 1604).

33. 1: 344–66; for a summary of the contents see S. Drake, "The Evolution of *De motu*," *Isis* 67 (1976): 239–50.

34. *Supplementi Musicali del Rev. M. Gioseffo Zarlino . . .* (Venice, 1588, repr. Ridgewood, N.J., 1966). Attack on Vincenzio Galilei in Book Three, especially pp. 83–93.

35. Cf. S. Drake, "Renaissance Music and Experimental Science," *Journal of the History of Ideas* 31 (1970): 483–500.

36. Vincenzio Galilei, *Discorso . . . intorno alle opere di messer Gioseffo Zarlino . . .* (Florence, 1589; repr. Milan, 1933), pp. 127–28.

37. 1: 412; *Sixteenth Century*, p. 283 (memorandum 20*a*).

38. See chapter 5, § V.

1589–92

1. [Jacopo Mazzoni], *Difesa della Commedia di Dante* (Cesena, 1587).

2. Girolamo Mercuriale, *De arte gymnastica*, first published as *Artis gymnasticae* (Venice, 1569).

3. 18: 153–54.

4. 1: 314

5. 19: 606; cf. chapter 22, § I.

6. Simon Stevin, *De Beghinselen der Weegconst* (Leyden, 1586), p. 65; C. Dijkshoorn, tr., *Principal Works of Simon Stevin* (Amsterdam, 1955), 1: 507, 509.

7. 19: 603.

8. Antonio Favaro, *Sulla veridicità . . . della "Vita di Galileo" dettato da Vincenzio Viviani* (Florence, 1916), p. 17. The lamp installed in 1587 (and since electrified) was originally designed to be extenguished by motion, hence it would not have been seen swinging in Galileo's day.

9. *TNS*, pp. 98–99.

10. Santorre Santorio, *Methodi vitandum errorum . . . in arte medica . . .* (Venice, 1603), p. 109. There is said to be an edition of 1602.

11. *De caelo* 277*b*, 1.

12. Cf. E. J. Dijksterhuis, *Mechanization of the World Picture*, trans. C. Dijkshoorn (Oxford, 1961), p. 334.

13. See S. Drake, "A Further Reappraisal of Impetus Theory," *Studies in History and Philosophy of Science* 7 (1976): 319–36.

14. 7: 182 (20–30); cf. S. Drake's translation of Galileo Galilei, *Dialogue Concerning the Two Chief World Systems* . . . (Berkeley and Los Angeles, 1967), p. 156. © 1953, 1962, and 1967 by the Regents of the University of California. Hereinafter cited as *Dialogue*. "What is it that stays with the ball, except that motion received from your arm?"

15. B. Pereira, *De communibus* . . . (Venice, 1586), p. 475.

16. 1: 412 (19–22). The wording of this memorandum shows that Galileo wrote *De motu* with the intention of publishing it.

17. N. Tartaglia, *Nova Scientia* (Venice, 1537), bk. 2, supposition 2; *Sixteenth Century*, pp. 84–85.

18. Cf. chapter 18, § II. For convenience in distinguishing Galileo's Pisan from his Paduan writings, the year 1591 will hereinafter be assigned to *De Motu*.

19. 5: 95(12–13); cf. S. Drake, *Discoveries and Opinions of Galileo* (New York, 1957), p. 90. © 1957 by Stillman Drake. Hereinafter cited as *Discoveries*.

1592–99

1. See S. Drake, "The Earliest Version of Galileo's *Mechanics*," *Osiris* 13 (1958): 262–309.

2. A Favaro, *Delle Meccaniche* . . . *da Galileo* . . . (Venice, 1899), p. 11. The 1594 version, published separately because it was discovered at Regensburg too late to be printed in its proper place in the *Opere* directed by Favaro.

3. Cf. *Sixteenth Century*, pp. 241–328 for abridged translation.

4. Drake, "The Earliest Version of Galileo's *Mechanics*," p. 277, ll. 190–91.

5. Guidobaldo del Monte, *Perspectivae libri sex* (Pesaro, 1600).

6. Guidobaldo del Monte, *De cochlea libri quatuor* (Venice, 1615).

7. 19: 128–29.

8. 19: 119–20. In 1598 Galileo lectured on the pseudo-Aristotelian *Questions of Mechanics* instead of on astronomy.

9. 7: 154–55; *Dialogue*, pp. 128–29.

10. The first known Copernican professor, Duncan Liddel, taught at Rostock.

11. A. Favaro, *Galileo e lo Studio di Padova* (Florence, 1883), 1: 178, n. 2.

12. See S. Drake, *Galileo Studies: Personality, Tradition, and Revolution* (Ann Arbor, 1970), chapter 10. © 1970 by the University of Michigan. All rights reserved. Hereinafter cited as *Galileo Studies*.

13. [Fulgenzio Micanzio], *Vita del Padre Paolo* (Leyden, 1646; often reprinted); *The Life of the Most Learned Father Paul* (London, 1651).

14. 2: 414–23, including additions made in 1599 and further alterations made in 1606.

15. 2: 93, where it was called by Galileo *squadra*.

16. Added after Galileo wrote his syllabus on military architecture and another on fortification, where only the less adaptable *quarto buono* was described; 2: 60, 142.

17. A primitive sector, first published in G. P. Gallucci, *Della Fabrica et Uso di Diversi Stromenti . . .* (Venice, 1598). A more useful form of sector, devised independently of Galileo's, was published by Thomas Hood, *The Making and Use of the Geometricall Instrument, called a SECTOR . . .* (London, 1598).

18. 2: 345–61. For the relation of this to the later versions see S. Drake, "Tartaglia's *Squadra* and Galileo's *Compasso*," *Annali dell' Istituto e Museo di Storia della Scienza di Firenze* 2 (1977); 35–54.

19. Jacopo Mazzoni, *In universam Platonis et Aristotelis philosophiam . . .* (Venice, 1597).

20. 2: 198

21. 10: 68

22. See chapter 16, § III.

23. See chapter 6, § II.

24. Virginia (b. 13 August 1600), Livia (b. 18 August 1601), and Vincenzio (b. 21 August 1606).

25. Angelo Ingegneri, *Contro l'Alchimia . . .* (Naples, 1606).

26. 2: 519

27. 7: 136; *Dialogue*, p. 110.

28. *Dialogue*, p. 113: ". . . our discourses must relate to the sensible world and not to one on paper."

1600–1602

1. For details see *Galileo Studies*, p. 126 ff.

2. 10: 104–5.

3. 19: 147 ff.

4. 2: 211–12

5. See Thomas Heath, *Aristarchus of Samos* (Oxford, 1913), pp. 275–76.

6. 2: 223.

7. Question 24; cf. 8: 68–72. Translation in *TNS*.

8. 2: 155–90; translated in *Motion and Mechanics*, pp. 147–82.

9. See J. L. Berggren, "Spurious Theorems in Archimedes' Equilibrium of Planes, Book 1," *Archives of the History of Exact Science* 16 (1976): 87–103. An additional reason for dating the proof before Archimedes is its separate treatment of commensurable and incommensurable distances.

10. Galileo used this term sometimes for static moment (plural, moments) and sometimes for momentum (plural, momenta). It quickly became the source to him of fruitful investigations of natural motion.

11. 2: 189; *Motion and Mechanics*, p. 180.

12. 2: 164; *Motion and Mechanics*, p. 156.

13. *Dialogue*, p. 400.

14. Detailed analysis in S. Drake, "Galileo's 'Platonic' Cosmogony and Kepler's *Prodromus*," *Journal of the History of Astronomy* 4 (1973): 174–91.

15. 16: 163; this was in 1634.

16. As bound now in volume 72, Galilean mss., National Central Library, Florence. This volume is sometimes still referred to as *Codex A*, following Favaro. All manuscript references herein not otherwise identified refer to volume 72.

17. This was equally true for Aristotelians, who held that the celestial substance was neither heavy nor light, and for Galileo, who used *weight* to mean the measure of downward tendency (*gravità*, heaviness) of a resting heavy body.

18. 7: 44–45, 53; *Dialogue*, pp. 20–21, 29.

19. *Four Letters from Sir Isaac Newton to Doctor Bentley* (London, 1756), p. 29.

20. 7: 50–52; *Dialogue*, pp. 26–28.

21. 8: 227; *TNS*, p. 184 (Proposition Nine).

22. 8: 386(1–11), which was followed by 8: 379(7–26).

23. 8: 376(1)–377(2).

24. See 8: 221–22 and notes.

25. At this time Galileo regarded the speeds as constant but as different for the different slopes. The rule, however, applies to "overall speeds" whether or not they are constant; see S. Drake, "Velocity and Eudoxian Proportion Theory," *Physis* 15 (1973): 50–64.

26. 8: 222(1–17); *TNS*, p. 179.

27. See chapter 2, n. 10.

28. Such arcs are passed in equal times only when very small, so that the general proof Galileo sought was not possible.

29. 2: 190–91.

1603–4

1. 19: 595.

2. 19: 624–25.

3. A. Favaro, *Galileo e lo Studio di Padova* (Florence, 1883), 2: 49–51.

4. Wustrou commenced private lessons with Galileo on 21 January 1602 (fortification), soon afterward taking the course on use of the sector; see 19:150–51.

5. 2: 545.

6. On f. 128 is the demonstration to which Galileo referred in a letter to Paolo Sarpi dated 16 October 1604; the same watermark is found on it, on the cover sheet of that letter, and on some notes about the supernova which appeared in that month.

7. Spread eagle in circle with crown above; this appears on sixteen of the copies, the other twenty bearing no watermark but having chain lines and texture similar to those watermarked. Full sheets, usually cut into four parts by Galileo, sometimes bore a watermark centered in one part and a countermark at the corner of another part; this was usual for the paper used at Padua, while I have found no countermarks among Galileo's notes on motion at Florence. The mark referred to in note 6 is a countermark in this sense.

8. In chapter 14, § V, reasons will be given for assigning 1618 as the year of copying.

9. 8: 221; *TNS*, p. 178.

10. This was done in S. Drake, "Mathematics and Discovery in Galileo's Physics," *Historia Mathematica* 1 (1974):136–37.

11. 8: 405(22)–406(14).

12. 8: 407(23)–408(19).

13. 8: 394(1–14).

14. A long dash here, unique among Galileo's notes on motion, suggests that what ensues was added as an afterthought, the ink and handwriting being similar to what had preceded.

15. 8: 378 (12) – 379(6). An error in punctuation and capitalization in Favaro's transcription of the part following the long dash makes the *Opere* text puzzling or misleading.

16. 8: 386(12–19). Favaro considered the first line here to be an addition by the copyist; I do not. On the other side of the same sheet (f. 177) the copyist transcribed f. 180*r*, having probably first copied the above from f. 180*v* in the mistaken belief that it was the demonstration Galileo wished copied. Coming to the end he recognized his error and broke off in the middle of a word, canceling what had been written and going on to copy a short demonstration which Galileo had subsequently written as a better way to establish the theorem on f. 180*r*. Then, turning the sheet over, he copied f. 180*r*.

17. 8: 383(24) – 384(13). Lines 14–24 on 8: 384 were added much later (1607) and in different handwriting.

18. Earlier I assumed the other ordering, mainly because the double-distance rule was not mentioned in Galileo's letter to Sarpi dated 16 October 1604. That letter did, however, include a blanket

reference to properties of natural motion previously communicated to Sarpi.

19. 8: 620–21. Galileo's later entries on f. 130r, based on calculations from the law of free fall, were not published in Favaro's *Opere*.

20. The entry embodying this attempt, which remains unpublished, must have been related to the diagram on f. 130v; it cannot be reconciled with the diagram now seen immediately above it, which therefore was most probably drawn afterward. A column of figures related to the odd-number rule (see § V, below) was also entered later on f. 187r, for had that rule been known to Galileo when he began writing on that page he would surely have used it rather than the unsuccessful approach he did try.

21. Cf. 8: 114; *TNS*, p. 73; also S. Drake, "An Unpublished Letter of Galileo to Peiresc," *Isis* 53 (1962): 201–11. This letter was subsequently acquired by Bern Dibner, who has placed it in the Smithsonian Institution Library.

22. 6: 545.

23. 7: 171; *Dialogue*, p. 145.

24. 8: 128; *TNS*, p. 87.

25. This document was first published and discussed in S. Drake, "The Role of Music in Galileo's Experiments," *Scientific American* 232 (June 1975): 98–104. On f. 107r there is a drawing probably representing a hanging fine chain and related to investigations undertaken by Galileo with Guidobaldo del Monte during the summer of 1602; cf. chapter 18, § II and n. 10. The drawing bears an additional curve and some numerical indications, added later in a small hand, showing this catenary to be not quite a parabola.

26. It is assumed that musical beats were used, in which optimal precision can be obtained at approximately half-second intervals. The experiment was separately carried out by me in Toronto and by Ben Rose in New York. Each of us began by using a metronome and independently learned by trial that coincidence of two external sounds is far harder to judge than coincidence of one such sound with a strong internal rhythm, obtained by singing crisply "Onward Christian Soldiers."

27. From S. Drake, "The Role of Music in Galileo's Experiments." © 1975 by Scientific American, Inc. All rights reserved.

28. Rubber bands were used in place of gut frets for convenience in the actual trials at Toronto and New York.

1604–6

1. This document was first published and discussed in S. Drake, "Galileo's Discovery of the Law of Free Fall," *Scientific American* 228 (May 1973): 84–92. I then thought the blank space in the second

line to contain the numeral 5 followed by a question mark, but (as may be seen in the last line on f. 152r) that strongly resembles Galileo's way of writing the word *in*. Galileo's quest here for *times* of descent through *distances* related as 4 and 9 shows the first two lines to have been written before he knew the times-squared law, though some contend that f. 152r belongs as late as 1608; see Wisan, *New Science of Motion*, pp. 210–15.

2. Figures implying similar conjectures are found also on f. 121v, jotted over part of the diagram discussed in chapter 4, § IV.

3. The assignment of integral values to "degrees of speed" had long been in use; thus a speed of 4 was considered to be twice as fast as a speed of 2, and so on. Actual measurement was another matter, for *speed* had not yet been given any unequivocal meaning except in comparisons. Thus "greater speed" meant that more distance was covered in the same time, or that less time was consumed in traveling a given distance, by one of two moving bodies.

4. 8: 380(1–12).

5. An error with respect to accelerated motions, though to Galileo, accustomed as he then was to thinking of uniform speeds that differed only from one slope to another, it seemed simply another way of saying the same thing as before.

6. By "the law of free fall" I mean always the statement that distances traversed from rest are proportional to the squares of the elapsed times. That is the ordinary meaning, to which Galileo's statement here is equivalent, putting the square roots of distances proportional to the times from rest. Winifred Wisan, in her *New Science of Motion*, p. 207 ("Galileo's Erroneous Law of Fall"), regards "the law of fall" as the statement that speeds are proportional to times, a proposition not found in Galileo's notes before early 1609. But Galileo took that as a definition of *uniform acceleration* for use in deriving the law of free fall, which was already implicit in 147–2 and was made explicit in October 1604, as will be seen. His difficulties during the next few years did not lie in finding the law, but in finding a correct definition of *speed* on which to base a rigorous proof.

7. 8: 371(7) – 372(2).

8. 8: 381(16–20), which gives only the words on f. 174r and a misreading of *rg* for *ra*. Not published from this page was an important diagram that put into Galileo's hands the way of dealing with a single descent along a steeper and then a less steep slope, the problem he had attacked without success on f. 187r.

9. Except for the part mentioned next, neither side of f. 189 was published. On f. 189v, before his discovery of the law of free fall, Galileo had first attempted to solve a problem relating length of a pendulum to time in free fall; he later corrected this solution using

that discovery. His original data on f. 189v were apparently experimental.

10. 8: 391(24)–392(7), with unexplained editorial additions of the words *longitudine* and *tempora*.

11. 8: 392(16)–393(9).

12. 8: 393(10–17).

13. Implied, that is, to us; Galileo was slow in perceiving the need to make this distinction, without neglecting which it is perhaps impossible for us to understand the difficulties he encountered and his attempts to overcome them before 1607.

14. 8: 383(1–23).

15. 8: 426(26–31), with an incorrect diagram.

16. It is again necessary to repeat (see n. 3) that the word *velocità* had never been given a quantitative definition except in terms of certain comparisons or the arbitrary assignment of integers to represent speeds. This explicit assumption did define Galileo's use of the word in terms of a specific natural phenomenon—incorrectly as we now view things, but unambiguously.

17. This does not mean that Galileo thought of velocità as the square of something else; it is just that in order for us to understand the physics of what he was doing it is convenient to employ modern equivalents. At this stage he did think of overall speeds as the squares of acquired speeds, but the latter appeared to him as simple physical entities; we have no name for them, but they correspond to our v^2 in writing $\frac{1}{2}mv^2$. For a given mass, we might say that after a given free fall it has a tendency to continue horizontally at a certain *speed*, and also a different tendency to continue vertically downward with a certain *punch*, the former being measured by v and the latter by $\frac{1}{2}v^2$. In regarding the latter as an elementary physical entity and calling it "speed," Galileo applied an arbitrary definition which he later abandoned; but he did not violate customary usage of the word *velocità* at the time, since when $v_1 = v_2$, $v_1^2 = v_2^2$, and when $v_1 > v_2$, $v_1^2 > v_2^2$—except for fractional values less than unity, and it had always been the practice to assign integral values to speeds. The exception first struck Galileo about the beginning of 1606, in connection with f. 179–3; see § III, below.

18. The identity of these drawings is striking; it can hardly be doubted that Galileo's inspiration for the ensuing demonstration came when he was looking at f. 180 before his old query on it was cut off.

19. 8: 373(1)–374(8).

20. 10: 134–35; the intended recipient was Girolamo Mercuriale and not Onofrio Castelli as conjectured by Favaro.

21. 2: 277–78, 281.

22. Detailed bibliography in S. Drake, *Galileo Against the Philosophers* (Los Angeles, 1976), pp. xv–xvi. The principal books considered here are Antonio Lorenzini (and Cesare Cremonini?), *Discorso Intorno alla Nuova Stella* (Padua, 1605) and Galileo's pseudonymous *Dialogo de Cecco di Ronchitti in Perpuosito de la Stella Nuova* (Padua, 1605; repr. Verona, 1605).

23. Lorenzini, *Discorso* (see n. 21), beginning of chapter 5.

24. 7: 62; *Dialogue*, pp. 37–38.

25. 2: 309–34; translated in S. Drake, *Galileo Against the Philosophers*.

26. From 1605 through 1609 there are no surviving letters by or to Galileo that mention Copernicus, or even astronomy except as to the new star. Nothing of Galileo's but his tide theory would be affected by doubts about the Copernican system, and he is not known to have written that in detail until 1616.

27. 8: 416(10)–417(7); respectively ff. 186*v* and 185*r*. Most of f. 148*r*, for which see 8: 419(1–9), also belongs to 1605; cf. chapter 7, § III.

28. 8: 419(16)–422(22). These documents and some associated working papers (ff. 184, 192) bear watermarks found also in dated letters and notes that confirm their origin in late 1605.

29. This theorem had probably been written out earlier and was not copied onto f. 138*r* (judging from handwriting) until Galileo again resumed work on motion late in 1607.

30. 8: 372.

31. 8: 387(16)–388(28).

32. 8: 389(1–14).

33. 8: 376(1)–377(2).

34. See Pierre Costabel, *Leibniz and Dynamics*, trans. R. E. W. Maddison (Paris, London, and Ithaca, 1973), p. 114, n. 2.

35. 8: 380(15–24), with incompletely lettered diagram.

36. Cf. n. 16

37. 8: 205; *TNS*, p. 162. Galileo cautioned against extending the postulate to curved descent, remarking that acceleration in such cases proceeded differently.

1606–8

1. 20: 597–98.

2. Ludovico delle Colombe, *Discorso . . . nel quale si dimostra che la nuova stella . . . non è cometa . . .* (Florence, 1606).

3. Translated in S. Drake, *Galileo Against the Philosophers*, pp. 76–130.

4. Ibid., p. 102.

5. Ibid., pp. 128–29.

6. 2: 365–424; see S. Drake's translation of Galileo Galilei, *Operations of the Geometric and Military Compass* (Smithsonian Institution Press, 1978).

7. 19: 144(455).

8. Baldessar Capra, *Usus et Fabrica Circini . . . Proportionis . . .* (Padua, 1607); 2: 427–511.

9. Although the year 1602 is here implied, the incident more probably took place after Galileo's confrontation with Zieckmesser in 1603.

10: 2: 515–601; *Difesa . . . Contro alle Calunnie . . . di Baldessare Capra* (Venice, 1607).

11. As numbered in Second Day of *TNS*. Not all propositions were numbered in the original edition; cf. chapter 19, § III.

12. 8: 260–61, notes below the line.

13. 8: 406(15) – 407(3) and 8: 380(25) – 381(15), in order of writing.

14. 8: 381(21) – 382(6).

15. 8: 235 *n.*, 407(9–22).

16. 8: 375(14–22); cf. 7: 48–50; *Dialogue*, pp. 24–26.

17. 8: 380(13–14). This seemingly routine note redefined *velocità* (cf. chapter 6, n. 6 and n. 15) to mean what we call instantaneous speed during accelerated motion, ending Galileo's ambiguities in use of that word.

18. 8: 323–25; *TNS*, pp. 283–85.

19. This document, not published by Favaro, was first discussed in S. Drake, "Galileo's Experimental Confirmation of Horizontal Inertia," *Isis* 64 (1973): 291–305.

20. 1: 299–300; *Motion and Mechanics*, pp. 66–67.

21. 8: 384(14–24).

22. Aristotle(?), *Questions of Mechanics*, 848*b* 15 ff. The ancient author, perhaps Strato of Lampsacus, also foreshadowed an inertial notion; 858*a* 14–23.

23. 8: 268; *TNS*, p. 217.

24. We use what is called the gravitational constant, a measure in conventional units applicable to single determinations. Galileo made only relative determinations, in pairs.

25. This slope is made probable by certain agreements between terminal speeds, and selected ratios of speeds, on f. 116*v* and f. 114*v*; these are reflected in a tabulation given below.

26. Galileo never tried to measure distances and times in vertical descent for reasons he explained in 1639 to G. B. Baliani; see chapter 20, § II. Marin Mersenne, who did, noted discrepancies between vertical and inclined-plane descents as Galileo related them, but did not attribute the relative slowing on planes to rolling as such.

27. Discussion of experimental corroboration of Galileo's data will be found in S. Drake and J. MacLachlan, "Galileo's Discovery of the Parabolic Trajectory," *Scientific American* 232 (March 1975): 102–10. © 1975 by Scientific American, Inc. All rights reserved.

28. 4: 32 n. 3.

1609–10

1. Cf. 4: 182–84, and see chapters 10, § I, 11, § II, and 20, § I.

2. 8: 368(19) – 369(29).

3. 8: 280(1–14), 281(12) – 282(13); *TNS*, pp. 229–31, except the parts in dialogue form and the final paragraph.

4. 8: 226; *TNS*, p. 183. This would give a rule for equal times along different slopes, while the postulate gave a rule for equal speeds acquired from rest along different slopes, these two rules sufficing for derivation of the other theorems. In the reconstruction offered by Wisan (*New Science of Motion*, pp. 222–25), Galileo would appear to have asked for Valerio's approval of two extensive arguments, not two basic principles. Also, it seems to me, the phrase "double ratio" must have appeared in the first statement in some way that could plausibly have been misinterpreted by Valerio; cf. chapter 22, n. 32.

5. See *Galileo Studies*, chapter 7, for a full chronology of events.

6. 6: 257–58; *Discoveries*, p. 244.

7. A facsimile of this accompanies S. Drake, *The Unsung Journalist and the Origin of the Telescope* (Los Angeles, 1976).

8. *Atti del Reale Istituto Veneto* . . . 87 (1927, pt. 2): 1160.

9. 3 (pt. 1): 60–61; *Discoveries*, pp. 28–29. The instruments were about three-power and eight-power; Galileo indicated power in terms of area.

10. 6: 259; *Discoveries*, pp. 245–46.

11. This is particularly true of pioneer discoveries, becoming less so with increase of variety and number of established results.

12. 10: 253–54. Galileo had recently obtained a minor court post for Landucci and could count on him to circulate the news, thus sparing Galileo the embarrassment of explaining his actions directly to the grand duke.

13. Florence had long been the best source of optical glass in Italy, though Venice was more celebrated for glassmaking because of its decorative and colored glass artifacts. See Vincent Ilardi, "Eyeglasses and Concave Lenses in Fifteenth-Century Florence and Milan," *Renaissance Quarterly* 29 (1976):341–60. Working at Florence from 1610 on, Galileo kept well ahead of other telescope makers, whose main problem he ascribed to the difficulty of obtaining suitable glass (which must be hard as well as clear and homogeneous).

14. Translated in S. Drake, "Galileo's First Telescopic Observations," *Journal of the History of Astronomy* 1 (1976): 153–68.

15. See *Reason, Experiment, and Mysticism in the Scientific Revolution*, ed. M. L. Bonelli-Righini and W. R. Shea (New York, 1975), pp. 59–76.

16. 10: 277–78.

17. 6: 357; S. Drake and C. D. O'Malley, *The Controversy on the Comets of 1618* (Philadelphia, 1960), p. 319. © 1960 by the Trustees of the University of Pennsylvania. Hereinafter cited as *Controversy*.

18. 3 (pt. 2): 427–28.

19. The clause placed here in brackets was included with the entry for 11 January when published in Galileo's *Starry Messenger* at Venice in March 1610.

20. Entered on a sheet previously used by Galileo to draft his letter to the Doge of Venice, presenting his telescope in August 1610.

21. Jean Meeus, "Galileo's First Records of Jupiter's Satellites," *Sky and Telescope* 24 (1962): 137–39; reprinted in the special Galileo issue of February 1964. Tables of satellite positions calculated by Meeus permit corroboration of multitudinous observations made by Galileo in connection with his longitude project (chapter 10) and provide valuable evidence concerning the relative merits of claims that have been made by, or on behalf of, Simon Mayr and Galileo.

22. The lunar crater now called Albategnius.

23. 7: 53–54; *Dialogue*, p. 29.

1610–11

1. Translated in Edward Rosen, *Kepler's Conversation with Galileo's Sidereal Messenger* (New York, 1965).

2. April 24th and 25th were particularly good nights for observation of satellites well separated from Jupiter, as shown by Dr. G. D. Parker, University of Arizona, in an unpublished paper dated 17 August 1976 "On the Discovery of the Galilean Satellites of Jupiter" (private communication). Galileo saw two of them on 24 April and all four on 25 April (3 [pt. 2]: 436), so that failure of others at Bologna to detect them was the fault neither of their configurations, the weather, nor Galileo's telescope.

3. See § IV for Papazzoni's subsequent activities.

4. Kepler's *Dissertatio* was sent to Galileo in manuscript before it was printed.

5. Later expanded and published as the *Dialogue*. Since no notes survive from Galileo's Paduan period relating to such a work, it is probable that the description he gave here was based mainly on his tidal theory and Platonic cosmogony.

6. Later organized as the Third and Fourth Days of *TNS*, on uniform, accelerated, and projectile motions.

7. The *Mechanics*, left unpublished, and theorems on strength of materials expanded in the Second Day of *TNS*.

8. A lost commentary on the pseudo-Aristotelian *Questions of Mechanics*, probably begun in 1598 when Galileo lectured at Padua on the ancient text.

9. All now lost except for the tidal theory as expanded in 1616 and finalized in the *Dialogue*, and discussions of the continuum in replies to critics (chapters 12 and 15), marginal notes (chapter 19), and the First Day of *TNS*. Galileo's interest originated partly from the "wheel of Aristotle" in *Questions of Mechanics* (cf. n. 8) and partly from the search for rigorous mathematical foundations for the law of free fall leading to his recognition of continuous change in speed in 1607 and its proportionality to time in 1609. An early drawing relating to Galileo's treatment of the wheel of Aristotle (vol. 81, f. 32, mss. Gal.) is among his astrological papers, watermarked the same as his horoscope for his daughter Livia dated 18 August 1601.

10. The entire letter is translated in *Discoveries*, pp. 60–65.

11. Martin Horky, *Brevissima Peregrinatio Contra Nuncium Sidereum* . . . (Mutina, 1610); 3 (pt. 1): 129–45. Replies were published by John Wedderburn, *Quatuor Problematum* . . . (Padua, 1610) and G. A. Roffeni, *Epistola Apologetica* . . . (Bologna, 1611); 3 (pt. 1): 147–78, 193–200.

12. Francesco Sizzi, *Dianoia Astronomica* . . . (Venice, 1611); 3 (pt. 1): 202–50. The license to print was given at Florence in 1610, suggesting that printers in that city refused it.

13. This confirms other reasons to doubt claims made by Kepler's friend Simon Mayr, concerning which see chapter 13.

14. Welser was a pro-Spanish, anti-Venetian banker to the Jesuits; though he became friendly toward Galileo, he fanned the flames of early Jesuit opposition to his discoveries.

15. Johann Kepler, *Narratio de observatis a se quatuor Jovis satellitibus* . . . (Frankfort, 1611; repr. Florence, 1611); 3 (pt. 1): 183–99.

16. 3 (pt. 1): 163–64.

17. 11: 12.

18. 3 (pt. 2): 442.

19. Clavius died in 1612. In his final revision of his *Sphera*, though he did not moderate his rejection of Copernicus, he noted Galileo's telescopic discoveries and the necessity for astronomers to account for them; C. Clavius, *Commentarium in Sphaeram* . . . (Mainz, 1611), p. 75 in volume 3 of the collected works of Clavius, published 1611–12.

20. Communicated to Galileo by Piero Dini in 1615; see chapter 13, § IV. Before Galileo left Rome, Bellarmine asked the Venetian Inquisition whether Galileo was implicated in proceedings against Cremonini; 19: 275.

21. See, for example, *Dialogue*, p. 113.

22. Author of a celebrated work on natural magic containing remarks on combinations of lenses for seeing both near and far.

23. See *Galileo Studies*, chapter 4.

24. The fact that the proposition was cited in Latin, in a letter written to him in Italian, suggests that Galileo had written it at Padua before 1610. His proof of the proposition as published later (8:203; *TNS*, p. 160) was widely challenged because of its being misunderstood by all who wrote on it except J. A. Le Tenneur; see *Galileo Studies*, pp. 230–36.

25. Colombe also composed a manuscript treatise against Copernican astronomy and defied Galileo to reply; 3 (pt. 1): 253–90. Galileo ignored it for reasons given in chapter 12, § II, but in writing the *Dialogue* he placed in the mouth of Simplicio most of Colombe's arguments, in much the order of his treatise.

26. J. C. Lagalla, *De phoenomenis in Orbe Lunae* ... (Venice, 1612); 3 (pt. 1): 311–93. Galileo wrote notes in his copy, some of which will be mentioned below.

27. 4: 30–32.

28. Ludovico Ariosto, *Orlando Furioso*, canto xi, stanzas 45 ff.

29. 4: 49–51.

30. Probably Giovanni de' Medici.

31. These results show how nearly the periods of the satellites could be obtained simply from study of the diagrams published by Galileo in March 1610, without actual observations. The data published in 1614 by Simon Mayr were slightly better, but they should be compared with the still better determinations Galileo had made meanwhile, left unpublished but set forth at length in his working papers for the longitude project (3 [pt. 2]), rather than with his earliest published figures (as has been ordinarily done by historians partial to Mayr).

32. 3 (pt. 2): 859(10–21).

33. 3 (pt. 2): 859(1–9); cf. pp. 446 and 539.

1612

1. 4: 57–141; translation in Thomas Salusbury, *Mathematical Collections and Translations* (London, 1661–65; repr. 1967), tome 2. Separately printed in S. Drake, ed., Galileo Galilei, *Discourse on Bodies in Water* (Urbana, 1960). © 1960 by the Board of Trustees of the University of Illinois. Hereinafter cited as *Bodies in Water*.

2. Because Archimedes was concerned principally with ships, he dealt with floating in bodies of water immeasurably larger than the floating object. The hydrostatic paradox was discussed by G. B. Benedetti in 1585 (hydraulic lift) and by Simon Stevin in 1596 (pressure).

3. An example of argument *ad hominem*, used often by Galileo to destroy an opponent's position without committing himself to any particular alternative. Cf. chapter 12, n. 16.

4. "Apelles latens post tabulam," *Tres Epistolas de Maculis Solaribus* . . . (Augsburg, 1612); 5: 23–33. In using the pseudonym "Apelles," the author (Christopher Scheiner, S.J.) meant that he would await comments before disclosing his identity. His superior, Theodore Busaeus, had ordered him not to publish in his own name a book that might bring discredit on the Jesuit order. Because his identity remained unknown in Italy for more than a year, he will here be called "Apelles" over that period to remind the reader of this.

5. 5: 71–249; hereinafter cited as *Sunspot Letters*. Abridged translation in *Discoveries*, pp. 87–144.

6. The "proper motion" attributed to all planets when the fixed stars were still regarded as revolving around the earth.

7. This was done in 1613, 700 copies of Galileo's *Sunspot Letters*, including the "Apelles" letters for the information of Italians, and 700 being issued without them, for sale abroad where Scheiner's letters were protected by copyright.

8. 5: 133–35; cf. *Discoveries*, pp. 112–14.

9. 11: 327 (16 June 1612).

10. Cf. *Dialogue*, p. 112.

11. 4: 145–82.

12. Didacus à Stunica, *In Iob commentaria* . . . (Rome, 1591, after an earlier printing at Salamanca). In 1616 this book was suspended "until corrected" together with the *De revolutionibus* of Copernicus; see chapter 14, § I.

13. 3 (pt. 2): 338.

14. 4: 68.

15. 4: 77–78.

16. J. F. Montucla, *Histoire des Mathématiques* (Paris, 1799; repr. 1968), 2: 565, 579–82.

17. Though with modern techniques in mathematics this assumption is not technically required, Galileo actually calculated by using it; cf. chapter 11, n. 18. It is certainly the simplest way to explain the timing of satellite eclipses, that is, as involving change of the observer's position. Long-range eclipse predictions were not possible until long after Galileo's death, because of the finite speed of light, the slightly elliptic shape of orbits taken by Galileo to be circular, and small perturbations by mutual gravitational attraction among the satellites. Short-range predictions were practicable, however, especially for the satellite most distant from Jupiter, and part of Galileo's program was frequent revision of the epochs used as bases for his tables of the satellites.

1612–13

1. *De Maculis Solaribus et Stellis circa Iovem Errantibus Accuratior Disquisitio* (Augsburg, 1612); 5:38–70.

2. Giorgio Coresio, *Operetta intorno al Gallegiare* . . . (Florence, 1612); 4: 199–244. In passing, the writer asserted that bodies dropped from the Leaning Tower of Pisa showed Aristotle to be correct, the whole of a body falling faster than a part of it (4: 242). Another professor at Pisa likewise interpreted Aristotle's position as did Galileo For a contrary modern interpretation, see Lane Cooper, *Aristotle, Galileo, and the Leaning Tower of Pisa* (Ithaca, 1935).

3. The customary abbreviation of "Co" resembled the letter "I".

4. In 1620 Galileo predicted their disappearance in 1626; see chapter 15, § IV.

5. 5: 238.

6. 5: 186–88; *Discoveries*, pp. 122–24.

7. 5: 190–91; *Discoveries*, pp. 126–27.

8. 5: 231–34; *Discoveries*, pp. 140–42.

9. Probably with additions to his theorems of 1587, completing the text published in 1638 as an appendix to *TNS*; cf. chapter 1, n. 29.

10. Ludovico delle Colombe, *Discorso Apologetico d'intorno al Discorso di Galileo* . . . (Florence, 1612); 4: 313–69.

11. Johann Kepler, *Dioptrice* . . . (Augsburg, 1611). Though Galileo was cited in the preface, he seems not to have been sent a copy. This book first described the combination of two convex lenses, applied to telescopes by Scheiner about 1615.

12. Giovanni de' Medici.

13. 4: 298–99.

14. Described by Galileo as an incompatibility between air and water; cf. *TNS*, pp. 74–75. See also chapter 12, end of § I.

15. The kernel of a conservation principle used by Galileo appears here, as also in his *Mechanics* (ratios of power, weight, speed, distance, and time); in his restricted inertial rule for uniform horizontal speed; and in his criticism of an engineer's scheme discussed in chapter 16, § V.

16. 4: 307–8. An earlier version (4: 182–84) is found in notes for a reply to the Unknown Academician, not published by reason of Papazzoni's death early in 1614.

17. 5: 241–45.

18. Cf. chapter 10, n. 17. Galileo clearly considered it essential to take into account a motion of the observer through space.

19. Galileo's eclipse predictions for Jupiter's satellites have been corroborated by computations from the modern tables published by Jean Meeus in *Journal of the British Astronomical Association* (72 [1962]: 80–88). This work was done by William Peters of the

McLaughlin Planetarium, Toronto, who found Galileo's predictions correct on the whole, though not as to the time given for ending of the eclipse on 24 April 1613.

20. 5: 247–49.

21. This delay rendered obsolete Galileo's predictions of the satellite positions for March. Several of his predictions for April and May, however, were confirmed to him in letters from Italian observers.

22. See *Galileo Studies*, pp. 183–84, and cf. chapter 17, § I.

23. Giovanni was a young Florentine, not the patron of Galileo's father. Based on experimental demonstrations he exhibited at the Jesuit college in Rome, Bardi published *Eorum quae vehuntur in aquis experimentis* . . . (Rome, 1614), a book in support of Galileo sometimes mistakenly attributed to Bardi's deceased namesake.

24. Vincenzio di Grazia, *Considerazioni . . . sopra il Discorso di Galileo* . . . (Florence, 1613); 4: 373–439. Like Coresio, he rejected Galileo's known anti-Aristotelian position that bodies of the same "earth" but of different size fall with equal speed (4: 432).

25. Nevertheless Galileo's basis for his correct prediction is puzzling, since he continued to speak of Saturn as accompanied by two smaller *spheres*.

26. Johann Fabricius, *De Maculis in Sole observatis* . . . (Wittenberg, 1611).

27. 11: 518.

28. 11: 506, 545, 549, 553–56. Sagredo later ground a large doubly convex lens, with interesting implications relating to Galileo's construction of compound microscopes; see chapter 16, § IV.

1613

1. 4: 510. That infinity is more nearly related to unity than to some very large number was amusingly argued later by Galileo; see 8: 82–83; *TNS*, pp. 44–45.

2. 8: 71–72; *TNS*, pp. 32–33.

3. A point is not *part* of a line, since it lacks magnitude.

4. 4: 526–27.

5. 4: 531–32; cf. 8: 115–16; *TNS*, pp. 74–75. The effect is quite striking; see James MacLachlan, "A Test of an 'Imaginary' Experiment of Galileo's," *Isis* 64 (1973):374–79.

6. A technical term applied by Galileo to any speed in a given medium that could not be reached in free fall through any distance whatever in that same medium; cf. 8: 136–37, 277–79; *TNS*, pp. 94–95, 226–29.

7. 4: 553.

8. 4: 338(30–34).

9. 4: 583.

10. 4: 587; see chapter 9, n. 25.

11. 4: 699(12).

12. 4: 697.

13. 4: 701.

14. Probably the "pantometric rule" devised by Michael Coignet in the 1580s and consisting of various scales engraved on a brass plate to be used by taking values with a pair of dividers. In 1610 Coignet had transferred the scales to two sectors.

15. 5: 281–88. Often called the Letter to Castelli, this was the forerunner of Galileo's famed *Letter to the Grand Duchess Christina*, for which see *Discoveries*, pp. 175–216.

16. The concept here adduced in the form of an *ad hominem* argument was to be more fully developed in the second of two letters to Piero Dini in 1615 and is partly translated in chapter 13 § V. Kepler believed that rotation of the sun actually caused the planetary revolutions through the agency of magnetic chains of some kind. Galileo's argument here, on the contrary, was purely logical. It was meant to show his adversaries that even on their own grounds they would be obliged to abandon literal interpretation of the biblical "Sun, stand thou still" if they wished to support the accepted pre-Copernican cosmology.

1614–15

1. Cf. 8: 123–26; *TNS*, pp. 82–86. The actual weight of air with respect to water is about double Galileo's finding.

2. Their exact motions are more complex; nevertheless, Galileo's observations and conclusions enabled him to detect a serious error, and to account for its probable origin, in Simon Mayr's description of satellite latitudes published soon afterward; cf. 6: 214–17; *Controversy*, pp. 165–67.

3. Simon Mayr, *Mundus Jovialis anno M.DC.IX detectus* . . . (Nuremberg, 1614); translation by A. O. Prickard, *Observatory* 39 (September 1916): 367–81; 39 (October 1916): 403–12; 39 (November 1916): 443–52; 39 (December 1916): 489–503. The title shows clearly Mayr's intent to claim priority over Galileo.

4. Galileo's allusions to Mayr in 1607 had not been hostile, in contrast with those later in the *Assayer*; cf. *Discoveries*, p. 233.

5. Though Galileo had not yet published his views on this, they were already known to Coresio and Di Grazia, who rejected them in their attacks against him. Cf. chapter 11, n. 2.

6. Galileo did not reply until 1623, in the *Assayer*; cf. *Discoveries*, p. 233.

7. Jean Tarde, *Borbonia sydera* . . . (Paris, 1620) and *Les astres de Borbon* . . . (Paris, 1623).

8. Published in the *Opere* as if dated 12 December 1615.

9. 5: 291–95.

10. P. A. Foscarini, *Lettera . . . sopra l'opinione . . . del Copernico . . .* (Naples, 1615); translated in Thomas Salusbury, *Mathematical Collections . . .* (see chapter 10, n. 1), tome 1, pp. 471–503.

11. 5: 309–48; translations in Thomas Salusbury, *Mathematical Collections*, and in *Discoveries*, pp. 175–216.

12. Often called the "Letter to Dini." The part here translated was written in response to Bellarmine's specific suggestion and was intended exegetically, not scientifically.

13. Psalm 74 in the King James Bible.

14. Psalm 19 in the King James Bible.

15. 5: 297–305.

16. Baliani mentioned this a decade later without dating the event. It probably took place during this visit, no other meeting between the two men being known. See chapter 17, § I.

17. 18: 68–69.

18. *Risposta alle opposizioni del . . . Colombe, e del . . . di Grazia . . .* (Florence, 1615); no name of author, but with dedication to Enea Piccolomini signed by Castelli; 4: 451–787. Cited hereinafter as *Replies to Oppositions.*

19. See chapter 20, n. 16. Though not printed until 1636, this amplified version of the Letter to Castelli circulated in manuscript copies from 1615 on.

1616–18

1. 5: 377–95; cf. 7: 442–86; *Dialogue*, pp. 416–63. See chapter 15, § II concerning the 1616 version.

2. 19: 321–22; for translation see chapter 18, § III.

3. 19: 322–23.

4. 19: 348; for translation see chapter 18, § III.

5. In 1633 Borgia was one of the three cardinals inquisitors who withheld their signatures from the sentence against Galileo.

6. Probably this date was inserted in place of some earlier eclipse date when the document was rewritten for use in negotiations with the Dutch government in 1636 (chapter 20, § I).

7. 5: 419–25. Such accuracy had to await discovery of the speed of light half a century later.

8. See chapter 11, § IV, for Galileo's previous prediction about Saturn.

9. Thomas Campanella, *Apologia pro Galileo . . .* (Frankfort, 1622); translation by Grant McColley, *The Defense of Galileo . . .* (Northampton, Mass., 1937).

10. 12: 319. Holding two telescopes parallel in a frame, of which one was movable, Castelli found that the distance to an object could be measured by superposing the images.

11. Between the time of Galileo's move to Florence in 1610 and late 1618, no letters exist related to Galileo's studies of motion except for Antonini's mention in 1611 of a proposition written at Padua (cf. chapter 9, § II).

12. 6: 23–35; [Orazio Grassi], *De Tribus Cometis . . . Disputatio Astronomica . . .* (Rome, 1619); *Controversy*, pp. 3–19. Grassi was professor of mathematics at the Collegio Romano.

1619–23

1. 6: 39 ff; Mario Guiducci [and Galileo], *Discorso delle comete . . .* (Florence, 1619); *Controversy*, pp. 21–65. In the text, this short work will be referred to as *Discourse*.

2. 6: 32; *Controversy*, p. 15. This argument seems to reject Aristotle's theory of the fiery nature of comets, though later Grassi asserted that his sole purpose was to support Aristotle. This and other inconsistencies may have arisen from intervention of his Jesuit superiors, instigated by Scheiner, in the ensuing controversy with Galileo.

3. 6: 33; *Controversy*, p. 17.

4. Later, and under an assumed name (see n. 9, below): Lothario Sarsi, *Libra Astronomica . . .* (Perugia, 1619); cf. 6: 126–30; *Controversy*, pp. 80–84. Hereinafter cited as *Libra*.

5. 6: 33–34; *Controversy*, pp. 17–18.

6. 6: 99; *Controversy*, p. 57.

7. 6: 102; *Controversy*, pp. 61–62.

8. 6: 72–73; *Controversy*, p. 40.

9. "Lothario Sarsio Sigensano" was a slightly defective anagram for Oratio Grasio Savonensis. The presence in it of an "l" and absence of a "v" induced Galileo's friends to joke that the author was not from Savona, as Grassi was, but from Salona, celebrated for its fat oxen. A very different appraisal of Grassi from that presented here, and a totally different view of the controversy on comets, is set forth in W. R. Shea, *Galileo's Intellectual Revolution*, chapter 4.

10. 6: 134; *Controversy*, p. 86.

11. 6: 136; *Controversy*, p. 87.

12. 6: 150; *Controversy*, p. 104.

13. 6: 151; *Controversy*, p. 105; cf. n. 2.

14. Fortunio Liceti, *De novis astris et cometis . . .* (Venice, 1622), p. 194.

15. 7: 287; *Dialogue*, p. 263.

16. Mario Guiducci, *Lettera al M. R. P. Tarquinio Galluzzi . . .* (Florence, 1620); 6: 183–96; *Controversy*, pp. 133–50.

17. See S. Drake, "Galileo's Language: Mathematics and Poetry in a New Science," *Yale French Studies* 49(1973):13–27.

18. Both zero and infinity were excluded as legitimate terms of ratios by Euclid Book Five, Definition Four.

19. 13: 81.

20. Without altering the concept, this facilitated establishment of one-to-one correspondences by means of which Cavalieri could define "all the points on a line" after having first defined "all the lines in a plane." Similarly, Galileo had first reasoned about "all the lines in a triangle" to reach the double-speed rule, the proof for Sarpi, and f. 179-1, before treating speeds as literally continuous like the points in a line.

21. See n. 14.

22. See chapter 21, § IV.

23. 6: 350–51; *Controversy*, p. 312; cf. *Discoveries*, pp. 277–78. As in the case of the *Dialogue* and *Two New Sciences*, the *Assayer* contains much of interest with regard to Galileo's view of science and its philosophical imitation which, for reasons of space, has been omitted in this book. An abridged translation of the *Assayer* is included in *Discoveries*, and a complete translation in *Controversy*.

24. 13: 208 (23 September 1624).

25. Galileo wanted to call this book *Dialogue on the Tides*, but in obtaining license to publish it he had to change that, since Urban VIII frowned on his adducing physical arguments in favor of the earth's motion not countered by others for the traditional view.

26. Francesco Barberini, who studied under Castelli but also with Galileo's guidance, was later Galileo's ablest and most highly placed protector at Rome under very difficult circumstances.

27. Hereinafter the phrase "Cardinal Barberini" will mean Francesco unless otherwise qualified.

1624–26

1. This fact makes it highly probable that by this time Galileo had made a number of the instruments.

2. Francesco Ingoli, *De situ et quiete Terrae* . . . This remained unpublished but may be found in 5: 397–412.

3. Marcantonio de Dominis, *Euripus sive sententia de fluxu et refluxu maris* (Rome, 1624).

4. A letter from Galileo to Cesi dated 23 September shows the reply to have been still unfinished but promised in another week.

5. See chapter 5, § IV and chapter 21, § IV.

6. 6: 509–61.

7. Chapter 3, § IV. A very brief and extremely effective reply to this perennial objection will be found in chapter 22, § II.

8. 6: 535.

9. 6: 545; cf. 7: 171; *Dialogue*, p. 145, where a very similar statement has been widely misinterpreted as meaning that Galileo never made the test—simply because he there stressed his having known the outcome in advance, as indeed was true.

10. 6: 556–57.

11. 6: 558–59.

12. Galileo had already advised against that on 9 December, as known from Guiducci's reply on 21 December.

13. In the diagrams of Archimedes the water was shown as extending to the center of the earth, his main concern being with ships. Galileo's book had dealt with water in containers.

14. 8: 571–73.

15. 8: 574.

16. Preserved at the British Museum in Harleian ms. 6796.

17. Johann Kepler, *Tychonis Brahei dani Hyperaspistes* . . . (Frankfort, 1625), to which an appendix dealt with the Galileo-Grassi dispute. Translation in *Controversy*, pp. 339–55.

18. It is odd that Cavalieri did not realize that no proof is possible, but that such a postulate can be based on the negative principle of sufficient reason, as indeed Galileo based it. The request for a proof shows how strongly the Aristotelian and medieval notion of quantum changes in speed was entrenched. Descartes rejected Galileo's argument, while Honoré Fabri published a book in 1646 interpreting Galileo's experimental results in terms of medieval impetus theory, and in the same year Baliani opined that quantum changes really underlay the appearance of continuous change of speed in fall.

19. That is, the closing section of the Third Day.

20. Opening section of the Third Day, criticizing Chiaramonti's *De tribus novis stellis* . . . (Cesena, 1628).

21. See 3 (pt. 2): 869.

22. Galileo's interest in spherical mirrors in 1624 was evidenced at the beginning of this chapter.

23. 8: 68–72; *TNS*, pp. 29–33.

1626–31

1. Cf. chapter 13, § VI. Whether Galileo had told Baliani the odd-number rule in 1615, as seems to me most probable, or at some later time, it is not surprising that he did not also offer to Baliani a proof of it. What he did offer as a "probable argument" was essentially different from the reasoning Galileo later put into his *Dialogue*, though that in turn was characterized by the same phrase and was considered by Galileo inconclusive (7: 254–56; *Dialogue*, pp. 227–30). Part of the justification given in the *Dialogue* much resembles the argument used by the fourteenth-century English writers who originated

the mean-speed or Merton rule, though that rule was not applied specifically to free fall until the mid-sixteenth century (by Domingo de Soto) and Galileo never deduced, or applied, such a rule. His interest, unlike that of medieval writers, was in actual fall of heavy bodies, for which an instantaneous speed at the middle time of any given descent was inherently incapable of direct measurement. The argument he gave to Baliani reflected his original reasoning at the time of his first experimental measurement of speeds in free descent as recorded on f. 107*v*. There, in the margin, he wrote the successive odd numbers from unity; a little lower down and to the right we see the numbers 3 and 1 with a mark rather like an 8 on its side. I take this to have been a notation of the unique and curious property of that arithmetic progression, namely, that the ratio 3:1 holds between the first two members, and between the sum of the first two and the sum of the second two, the sum of the first three and that of the second three, and so on. It follows that the successive distances (and speeds) in consecutive equal times will grow in that same manner regardless of the unit distance (or speed) chosen.

2. An idea of the work done at this time may be formed from 8: 398–404, 411–12. The corresponding notes occupy, in approximately the following order, ff. 62, 96, 144, 72, 77, 71, 69, 76, and 61, though some notes on those sheets were entered at other times. Thus, for example, work on f. 144 had begun at Padua.

3. See 6: 565 ff.

4. Beginning of Third Day, written in mid-1628 as will be shown.

5. 6: 375–500; *Ratio Ponderum Librae et Simbellae* . . . (Paris, 1626; repr. Naples, 1627). Though published under the same pseudonym as was the *Libra* of 1619, this new book may have been written by Grassi in collaboration with Scheiner.

6. Christopher Scheiner, *Rosa Ursina* . . . (Bracciano, 1630).

7. Galileo and Marsili had met at Rome in 1624.

8. Giovanni di Guevara, *In Aristotelis Mechanicas commentarii* . . . (Rome, 1627 [*sic*]).

9. 8: 68, 165; *TNS*, pp. 29, 123.

10. Cf. *TNS*, pp. 25–26.

11. The handwriting is that of notes written by Galileo on a letter received in January 1631. Those notes were related to a problem of flood control, which explains why Galileo was dealing at so late a time with some matters concerning inclined planes that had been known to him since his Paduan days. See chapter 17, § III.

12. Concerning this dating, which long remained the subject of controversy among specialists, I am in complete accord with Wisan, *New Science of Motion*, p. 277.

13. Cf. *Discoveries*, p. 278, but see *TNS*, pp. 49–51.

14. 2: 263–66.

15. It is to this section that the material mentioned in n. 11 pertained.

16. Here Galileo presents in another way the seeming paradox in speaking of "speed" in accelerated motions, noted by him on 164–5 and presented early in his *Dialogue*. Cf. *TNS*, Proposition Thirty-Seven (Problem Fifteen), which was also written at this time.

17. 6: 627–45; the date 16 January 1630 was Florentine style for 16 January 1631.

1631–33

1. 7: 487; *Dialogue*, p. 463.

2. 7: 414–15; *Dialogue*, pp. 388–89.

3. On the first page of Scheiner's book he fulminated against his "Censor," transparently meaning Galileo, in very offensive language.

4. 7: 372; *Dialogue*, p. 345.

5. It is perhaps unnecessary to remark that Scheiner's book contained no statement of any kind that resembled Galileo's argument, since Scheiner did not admit any motion of the earth. In a posthumously published attack on Galileo's *Dialogue* he argued at length against this passage; in trying to account for changes in sunspot paths in his own way, however, he encountered difficulty with the diurnal motion, which has made some historians believe him to have been a crypto-Copernican.

6. Galileo's argument for motions of the earth based on cyclical changes in sunspot paths is more cogent than generally acknowledged. The rule of parsimony in adoption of scientific hypotheses compels it, and that is how Galileo presented it when Simplicio invoked the concept of geometric equivalence. Galileo's list of motions thus required in the sun shows him to have been aware of complications now ignored by his adverse critics; see *Galileo Studies*, chapter 9.

7. Unlike Galileo, who concerned himself only with ratios, not only Baliani but other scientists of his time and after (Mersenne, Cabeo, G. B. Riccioli, and the young Newton) sought the number of feet or other arbitrary units traversed in fall from rest during a given number of astronomical seconds. Some figures given in the *Dialogue* as an example for purposes of calculation (7: 250; *Dialogue*, p. 223) were accordingly misunderstood as assertions of experimental determination. Baliani's misapprehension was corrected by Galileo in a private letter; see chapter 21, § II.

8. That God could produce the observed appearances in myriads of ways, so that nothing certain could be concluded from them. The nature of the pope's other two arguments remains unknown.

9. Bonaventura Cavalieri, *Specchio Ustorio* . . . (Bologna, 1632; repr. 1650).

10. In notebooks left by Guidobaldo he conjectured that projectiles moved in paths like the parabola or the hyperbola, and also mentioned two ways of quickly drawing parabolas, both described also in *TNS*, pp. 142–43. A drawing on f. 107*r*, probably made before 1604, appears to have been made from a hanging slender chain; the figures first written on it differ markedly from others in which the approximately parabolic form was tested. It is likely that Galileo and Guidobaldo had made various experiments together shortly before the correspondence of late 1602, but none that could conclusively establish the parabolic path in the manner of f. 116*v*.

11. Attached to the court of Cardinal Barberini, Holste probably reflected informed opinion shared by the cardinal.

12. See S. Drake, "An Unpublished Letter, Possibly by Galileo," *Physis* 7 (1966): 247–52, written before this possibility was taken into account.

13. This book was then entered as Exhibit "A."

14. There was no way in which the prosecution could have known of the existence of this document which, if authentic (as was made certain by Galileo's later producing the original on request, now filed with the other documents), effectively destroyed the principal charge against him.

15. See chapter 14, § I; I take this to mean that Bellarmine told Galileo *sotto voce*, before delivering his instruction, that he must comply.

16. 19: 336–40. The balance of the first hearing is summarized below.

17. 19: 342.

18. 19: 321–22.

19. The idea was almost certainly suggested by Cardinal Barberini before he left for Castel Gandolfo. He knew the extent of the pope's anger, and he alone of all the high officials really wanted Galileo to have every opportunity to escape its consequences.

20. 15: 106–7. This letter remained unknown to freethinkers and to defenders of the church in hot nineteenth-century debates following the return of the trial documents to Rome after their theft by Napoleon. It was eventually discovered by Sante Pieralisi, librarian of the Barberini archive, who published it in 1875.

21. A procedure in which the accused, if he did not admit improper motives, was shown instruments of torture. If he still refused, he was put to torture.

22. The evidence of Barberini's intervention is indirect; the official report said only that after having been shown the instruments of

torture he was returned to his rooms "because nothing further could be done." Some say his age exempted him from torture, though no such regulation of the Roman Inquisition at that time has been identified. On the contrary, as recently as 1942 a Dominican authority on canon law, Orio Giacchi, wrote that the only legal error in the proceedings was *failure* to put Galileo to torture; *Nel terzo centenario della morte di Galileo Galilei* (Università Cattolica del S. Cuore, Milan, 1942), pp. 400, 406.

1633–35

1. A large, rather thin gold coin. This small distance was left between the side of the mold and the side of the glass container, so that the shot-filled mold would be free to rise when the mercury poured into the top passed the shot, and on reaching the glass below, this exerted an upward thrust on the hollow part of the mold.

2. 4: 76–77; *Bodies in Water*, p. 16. Since in the case under discussion it is mercury, and not water, that lifts the mold, while the mold, though of greater specific gravity than water, is of less specific gravity than mercury, the proposition referred to (hydrostatic paradox) is applicable but is to be read with "mercury" in place of "water." A very interesting theorem concerning upward thrust of molten metal in bellcasting will be found in the eleventh edition of the *Encyclopaedia Britannica*, 14: 118, col. 2, where the diagram strikingly resembles that of Galileo's soupdish paradox, his "cylindrical razor" (8: 74; *TNS*, p. 36) corresponding to the volume of revolution of the curved wedge *APQ* in the *Encyclopaedia* article. To visualize the demonstration at Siena, consider the glass urinal to be represented in cross section by the rectangle enclosing the mold, but extending the width of a *piaster* beyond *A* on either side. The shaded part of the mold would then represent mercury poured through the funnel *HB* into the shot-filled space between the two semicircles. Since Galileo's soupdish paradox was first discussed (with Cavalieri) soon after this time, it is possible that its origin was connected with the Siena incident.

3. In the original edition, propositions were not numbered beyond 8; bracketed numbers were supplied in *TNS*.

4. It was at this time that Descartes decided, because of the banning of Galileo's *Dialogue*, to hold back from publishing his completed *Le Monde*.

5. [Abbé Irailh], *Querelles littéraires . . .* (Paris, 1761), p. 49.

6. *Italian Library*, p. 52.

7. A. Favaro, "Eppur si muove," *Il Giornale d'Italia* (Rome, 12 July 1911), p. 3. For a reproduction of the painting see J. J. Fahie, *Memorials of Galileo* (London, 1929), pl. 16.

8. Probably the proportionality stated on f. 61 without proof; 8: 411(26–30), written about 1627.

9. Bonaventura Cavalieri, *Geometria indivisibilibus continuorum nova quadam ratione promota* (Bologna, 1635; repr. 1650). Often incorrectly translated *Geometry of Indivisibles*, as if some special geometry applied to these magnitudes of less than three dimensions. The same word was applied by Roberval to infinitesimal magnitudes which he regarded as capable of being neglected, causing Newton to say that the "hypothesis of indivisibles seemeth a trifle harsh." Cavalieri's approach was entirely different; his book should be called *Geometry by Indivisibles*, those being in no way infinitesimals and the geometry meant being classical Euclidean and Archimedean geometry, advanced by a new method.

10. Antonio Rocco, *Esercitationi Filosofiche* . . . (Venice, 1633); 7: 571–712.

11. The 1635 edition was made up of parts printed at various unspecified times.

12. 8: 74–76; *TNS*, pp. 35–38.

13. Rigorous treatment of continuous variables was not achieved before 1872, requiring as it did a redefinition of the concept of number. Cf. E. V. Huntington, *The Continuum* (Cambridge, Mass., 1917), pp. 1–4. The use of one-to-one correspondence between elements of infinite aggregates by Galileo and Cavalieri remained unnoticed until publication of Bernard Bolzano, *Paradoxes of the Infinite* (Leipzig, 1851); F. Prihonsky, tr. (London, 1950), pp. 141–42 (concerning Galileo's soupdish paradox).

14. 7: 234–35; *Dialogue*, p. 278.

15. Prior to Galileo, *indivisibles* meant tiny parts having the same dimensionality as the continuum comprising them. It was simply the Latin word for the Greek *atom*. The pseudo-Aristotelian treatise *On Atomic Lines* was translated into Latin by Robert Grosseteste in the thirteenth century. Soon afterward a treatise *De continuo* by Thomas Bradwardine gave currency to the use of *indivisible* as a noun. The same word was applied by Galileo and Cavalieri to elements of the next lower dimensionality than that of the continuum analyzed.

16. Earlier, Galileo had been scandalized when Sagredo distinguished mathematicians from philosophers (see chapter 10, § IV), and in 1611 he himself had repudiated any such distinction as made by an opponent in the original controversy over floating bodies (chapter 9, § III). Yet experience had shown him that physical science as he envisioned it was universally rejected by philosophers, who in his day appealed to mathematics, if at all, in a way utterly different from his. Mathematicians did not reject his science; on the contrary, some encouraged him. Bradwardine's *De continuo* (n. 15)

concluded, among other things, that propositions were true so long as they did not assume indivisibles and that any such assumption would destroy music and philosophy. That alone would have induced Galileo to dismiss Bradwardine as "a second-rate mathematician, or worse" in alluding to past investigations of the continuum.

17. This was Aristotle's main strategem in the avoidance of any "actual infinite"; Galileo dismissed it as mere verbiage. Cf. 8: 80–81; *TNS*, pp. 42–44.

18. 7: 745–48.

19. 7: 725(25) – 726(4).

20. 7: 731.

21. Galileo has been said never to have properly associated force with acceleration, and so far as his published books are concerned that is true. Those may, however, inadequately represent his thought. He did avoid the concept of force as cause; yet he was aware of the fact that speed is changed only by natural tendency or by application of force, as is apparent in the 1611 debate over bodies in water.

22. J. B. Morin, *Famosi et Antiqui Problematis de Telluris Motu* ... (Paris, 1631); cf. 7: 549–61.

23. Probably by Joseph Webbe, who was graduated in medicine at Padua in 1612 and may have been there before Galileo left for Florence in 1610. The manuscript is preserved in the British Museum as Harleian ms. 6320. It remains unpublished, most likely because Bernegger's Latin translation of the *Dialogue* appeared in 1635, about the time the English translation was finished. The English translation by Thomas Salusbury (*Mathematical Collections*, tome 1), published at London in 1661, was made independently of this.

1636–38

1. Antonio was the cardinal who had ordered that Galileo's sentence and abjuration be read to all mathematicians in every university city throughout Catholic Europe.

2. The only conflicting evidence is in a letter copied, probably inaccurately, by Viviani, of which the original is lost.

3. See *Galileo Studies*, pp. 257–60.

4. Cf. *Dialogue*, p. 164.

5. *Dialogue*, p. 166, where the translation is "curiosity."

6. This phrase in its technical usage never implied actual arrival; cf. *Controversy*, p. 262: "... otherwise he would have to suppose that saying to 'sail toward the pole' or 'throw a rock toward the sky' meant that a ship arrived at the pole and a rock at the sky."

7. This alludes to an issue in the "geostatics" controversy then current among French mathematicians. It had been started by Jean Beaugrand, who had met Cavalieri and Galileo on a recent visit to Italy, whence Galileo's familiarity with it.

8. P. Tannery and C. De Waard, eds., *Oeuvres de Pierre Fermat* (Paris, 1891–1922) 5: 36 ff. Fermat probably sent this argument to Mersenne in 1635 or 1636.

9. See end of this chapter. After Fermat saw Galileo's *Two New Sciences*, he not only accepted the law of free fall but wrote out for Pierre Gassendi in 1645 a long proof, of the Archimedean type, to show that speeds in fall could not be proportional to distances from rest; see *Oeuvres* 3: 302 ff.

10. 17: 89–93.

11. Agent of the Elzevirs, stationed at Venice.

12. 8: 453–66.

13. W. R. Shea (*Galileo's Intellectual Revolution*, p. 186) suggests that Galileo in his old age abandoned his tidal theory in favor of "lunar influence" on the basis of this discovery. If so, Galileo was rather casual in giving up his lifelong convictions about the nature of scientific explanation. Since a part of his tidal theory was that motions of the moon introduce variations in speed of the earth's annual motion (chapter 16, § IV), he may merely have wished to point out an unexplained coincidence of periodicities.

14. These had been sent to Diodati with instructions to obtain Noailles' acceptance of the dedicatory letter before transmitting this final material to Elzevir.

15. The concluding words here, coupled with what was said in chapter 19, n. 16, remind me of a definition given in Aldous Huxley's *Brave New World* by the Savage who had read nothing but Shakespeare: A philosopher is a man who dreams of less things than there are in heaven and earth.

16. Galileo Galilei, *Nov-antiqua sanctissimum patrum . . . doctrina, de sacrae scripturae testimoniis in conclusionibus mere naturalibus . . . in gratiam sereniss. Christinae . . . scripta . . .* (Strassburg, 1636). The Italian text accompanied this Latin translation of Galileo's *Letter to Christina*.

17. The passage referred to contains the soudish paradox, on which the comment of Descartes much resembles the second defense offered by Cavalieri in response to Galileo's critique; cf. chapter 19, § IV. Galileo's purpose, however, eluded Descartes. It did not escape Bolzano (*Paradoxes*, p. 141); Galileo introduced it to exhibit the caution required when using the word *equal* in such instances.

18. Galileo's assumption related to speeds not over planes, but at the ends of descents along them.

19. Descartes' conjecture about Galileo's motivation has no support from the working papers or from anything Galileo published. Two notations on f. 166r (1605), never pursued, alone relate to circular descent. Wisan (*New Science of Motion*, chapter 4) suggests that Galileo embarked on his investigations of motion along inclined

planes in a search for the brachistochrone, by which is meant the curve of descent from a higher to a lower point in the shortest time of any. But Galileo was interested in motion along inclined planes when writing *De motu*, in which there was no mention of a shortest time, nor of any curve except the circle. Euclid's geometry, like Aristotle's physical science, was restricted to straight lines and circles. It is probable that when Galileo used the phrase "swiftest movement of all" for motion along a circular arc (scholium to Proposition Thirty-Six, *TNS*, pp. 212–13), even late in life, he meant only that no descent along straight chords could be faster. Analysis of all possible curves belongs to calculus of variations, a branch of mathematics invented considerably later. On the other hand there is good evidence that Galileo began his long train of fruitful studies of motion by seeking and finding the shortest *straight* path from a higher to a lower point; see chapter 5, § III.

20. Here Descartes denies conservation of horizontal motion by an unsupported body, though he is famed for having been first to state the inertial principle.

21. Cf. chapter 19, n. 4.

22. The reference is to the argument dealt with second by Galileo in the letter to Carcavy translated in chapter 19. Its fallacy lay in the assumption of a "first" instant of motion, intimately connected with the medieval impetus theory of acceleration in fall, and meaningless in mathematically continuous change. The simultaneous existence in the fourteenth century of acute analyses of uniform acceleration from the mathematical standpoint and of the impetus theory of fall from a physical standpoint, without any attribution of uniform acceleration to free fall, reflects a keen medieval appreciation of both mathematics and physics coupled with an Aristotelian determination not to confuse the two. Only the intervention of experiment and careful measurement, with full appreciation of the character of approximations, broke the deadlock, and for this it is to Galileo that credit is due. The resistance of men like Descartes and Honoré Fabri shows how little Galileo's procedures were already "in the air." Fermat's change of position was that of an intelligent mathematician and able physicist, not of a philosopher.

23. This refers to the "geostatics" controversy; see n. 7, above.

1639–40

1. G. G. Baliani, *De motu naturali gravium solidorum* (Genoa, 1638); cf. beginning of chapter 17.

2. That is precisely what Cavalieri has been accused of doing, however, from his day to our own, despite his having denied any such gratuitous assumption at the earliest opportunity in his *Geometry*

(scholium to Book Two, Proposition One). On this matter Galileo was more radical than his disciple, for which Cavalieri thanked him (see n. 3), though in the matter of the soupdish paradox Galileo remained more conservative than Cavalieri.

3. This constitutes the thanks mentioned in n. 2. The scholium named there made clear Cavalieri's refusal to consider the continuum as *made up* of its indivisibles. Either it is or it is not, he said; if it is not, then whatever else enters into its constitution may be regarded as uniformly distributed and therefore incapable of affecting the ratios he employed.

4. 8: 321–46; *TNS*, pp. 281–306.

5. The length is shown by a line drawn in the letter.

6. Galileo's method was set forth in his unpublished "Astronomical Operations." In his *Dialogue*, pp. 337–38, he had already exposed the great errors in the estimates of stellar diameters accepted by pretelescopic astronomers.

7. Reported in Pierre Gassendi, *De motu impresso a motore traslato* . . . (Paris, 1642).

8. Galileo appears to have forgotten that this had already been communicated to Famiano Michelini for Prince Leopold; see § I.

9. The cycloid; see chapter 2, § I.

10. Fortunio Liceti, *Litheosphorus, sive de lapide bononiensi* . . . (Udine, 1640). Bolognese stone was a mineral capable of absorbing sunlight and then glowing in the dark which had attracted the attention of the Linceans in 1611, soon after its discovery.

11. Fortunio Liceti, *De centro & circumferentia* . . . (Udine, 1640).

12. Fortunio Liceti, *De Terra unico centro motus* . . . (Udine, 1640).

13. Fortunio Liceti, *De lucidis in sublimi* . . . (Padua, 1641).

1641–42

1. *Contro il Portar La Toga*, 9: 213–23.

2. Perhaps Niccolò Cabeo, whose experiments with falling bodies were mentioned by Baliani, though they appear not to have been published until after Galileo's death.

3. The Leaning Tower of Pisa.

4. About 6 inches, in agreement with the test mentioned by Sagredo.

5. 8: 107; *TNS*, p. 66.

6. The argument concerning which Galileo had replied at great length to Mazzoni in 1597 and again to Ingoli in 1624. This time the burden of proof is simply shifted to the people who asserted that we do always see exactly half the sky, none of whom had any idea of the actual problems in making such precise observations. As Galileo's spokesman had said in the Cecco dialogue of 1605, "What has philosophy got to do with measuring anything?"

7. 19: 655. A detailed account is given in S. A. Bedini, *Galileo and the Measure of Time* (Florence, 1967). The French book mentioned by Bedini on p. 11, however, is incorrectly ascribed to Galileo; it was a work of Mersenne's.

8. 14: 68, 81.

9. 6: 237; *Controversay*, p. 189.

10. 8: 349–62.

11. 8: 192–93; *TNS*, pp. 149–50.

12. So numbered in the medieval Latin Euclid of Campanus which was still followed in many sixteenth-century editions.

13. Many mathematicians felt that Euclid, Book Five, Definition Five, like the more famous "parallel postulate" of Book One, ought to be a theorem with proof rather than an unproved foundation. Early in the eighteenth century Girolamo Saccheri, famed for his critique of the parallel postulate, devoted an extensive section of the same book to this definition as an imputed blemish on the *Elements*; see *Euclides ab omni naevo vindicatus . . .* (Milan, 1728).

14. Of the proposition concerning uniform motion in which distances are shown to be proportional to times; see 8: 192; *TNS*, p. 149.

15. These being magnitudes of the same kind, as required by Euclid.

16. Cf. Euclid, Book Five, Definition Three. Galileo's word *quantity* is the most usual translation of a Greek term used here by Euclid but in only one other place, of doubtful authenticity. The idea is that of excess, and though we say that one man's age exceeds that of another man, we would hardly speak of the "quantity" of his age. The Greek word, found elsewhere in the *Elements* only in the spurious definition added to Book Six discussed by Galileo at the end of this treatise, was perhaps responsible for the medieval concept of "denomination" of a ratio by numbers, as it is found also in arithmetical writings in the tradition of Nicomachus. But numbers, as defined by Euclid in Book Seven, play but a limited role in Book Five, ratios expressible in numbers being adequately treated in Book Seven. The universal properties of all magnitudes (except numbers, if indeed they may properly be called magnitudes) are *kind* and *size*; by Definition Three, Euclid meant to establish comparative *size* as the essential relation in ratios. Cf. n. 27 and n. 35.

17. That is, by using ordinary words and phrases as much as possible, as throughout Galileo's science.

18. These were traditional classifications of *numerical* ratios. Superparticular ratios are of the form $(n + 1)/n$, an example being the ratio 9:8 assigned to the semitone in music. Ratios of this class could not be "equally divided" because they cannot have rational square roots; cf. chapter 1, § V.

19. Book Five, Definition Seven defines "greater ratio."

20. Postil: Proposition One, which is Euclid V, 4.

21. Postil: Corollary, which is the converse of Euclid V, Definition 5.

22. Postil: Proposition Two, which is the converse of Euclid V, Definition 7.

23. Postil: Proposition Three, which is Euclid V, Definition 5.

24. That is, before entering on the study of strength of materials and of natural motion in *Two New Sciences*.

25. Benedetti had previously offered such an arrangement, though not along the lines Galileo had in mind, and another was proposed later by G. A. Borelli. Both used propositions of Book Five as axioms so that they could then prove Euclid's fifth definition as a theorem, they considering the propositions selected to be more nearly self-evident than Euclid's definition. Viviani pursued the line suggested by Galileo; he also published an Italian Euclid for use in schools that included this treatise of Galileo's. It went through several editions in the seventeenth and eighteenth centuries.

26. That is, Galileo.

27. Postil: Euclid VI, Definition 5.
This spurious definition, probably due to Theon, is absent from many Greek manuscripts and appears only as a marginal addition in the best extant text. The *quantity of a ratio* (cf. n. 16) is nowhere defined and is essentially gibberish, a ratio being not a magnitude but a relation. We now tend to overlook this, largely because of the introduction of decimal fractions by Stevin in 1585, and we commonly confuse ratios with fractions. Neither did "multiplication of ratios" have any clear meaning, as Galileo pointed out; cf. n. 34.

28. Compound ratios had been used by Archimedes and Ptolemy; they were also ingeniously employed by Galileo in theorems on strength of materials and on motion in a way that perhaps adumbrated the later concept of "function" in mathematics. Cf. also chapter 16, § VI, for Galileo's comment on a hydraulic theorem of Castelli's.

29. Here Galileo should have said "term" rather than "definition," because in the twenty-third proposition of Euclid, Book Six, the only place where composition of ratios was used in Euclid, there was no "multiplication of ratios" in the modern sense, nor was there any arithmetical concept whatever. Note that in Galileo's diagram, the magnitudes are all of the same *kind* (areas) but not of the same size; cf. n. 16.

30. Postil: Definition to be put in place of Euclid VI, Definition 5.

31. The two ensuing paragraphs are found in only one manuscript, in which the next diagram was clearly in error and has here been corrected.

32. This constitutes an explanation of Euclid Book Five, Definitions Nine and Ten, employing Euclid's terminology for what we call "squared" and "cubed" ratios. It was quite natural to speak of

doubling a ratio when the same ratio was taken twice, though numerically this way of compounding two equal ratios yields the square of (either) one of them. Euclid's terminology of "doubling" and "tripling" ratios induced medieval writers to refer to what we now call multiplication of two ratios as *addition of ratios*.

33. Cf. 8: 74; *TNS*, p. 36: "Note here what sort of things mathematical definitions are, that is, the mere imposition of names, or we might say abbreviations of speech, arranged and introduced to remove tedious drudgery. . . ." Galileo's proposed definition said only what something whose existence was undoubted was thereafter to be *called*. In contrast, the spurious fifth definition of Euclid, Book Six, imposed a name on something which was supposed to be constructed by an operation not defined.

34. Postil: Proposition Five, which is Euclid VI, Definition 5. (Cf. n. 33; the operation having been actually performed, its result can then be demonstrated to fall under the definition that until then remained the "mere imposition of a name.").

35. Postil: Here it is assumed that we know what the "quantities" of ratios are, and what it means to "multiply them together." But the whole affair goes better by writing and proving the proposition here set forth.

INDEX

Italic number denotes biography of person named.
Number in parentheses () indicates particular note on designated page.
Topics starred thus * were discussed in Galileo's Dialogue.

509

Index

513

Index

Index

Index

Index

Index

Index

Index